MW01195299

NATIVE AMERICANS
IN THE MOVIES

NATIVE AMERICANS IN THE MOVIES

Portrayals from Silent Films to the Present

MICHAEL HILGER

ROWMAN & LITTLEFIELD
Lanham • Boulder • New York • London

Published by Rowman & Littlefield
A wholly owned subsidary of The Rowman & Littlefield Publishing Group, Inc.
4501 Forbes Boulevard, Suite 200, Lanham, Maryland 20706
www.rowman.com

Unit A, Whitacre Mews, 26-34 Stannary Street, London SE11 4AB

Copyright © 2016 by Rowman & Littlefield

All rights reserved. No part of this book may be reproduced in any form or by any electronic or mechanical means, including information storage and retrieval systems, without written permission from the publisher, except by a reviewer who may quote passages in a review.

British Library Cataloguing in Publication Information Available

Library of Congress Cataloging-in-Publication Data

Hilger, Michael, 1940–
  [From savage to nobleman]
  Native Americans in the movies : portrayals from silent films to the present / Michael Hilger.
      pages cm
  Revision of the author's From savage to nobleman
  Includes bibliographical references and index.
    ISBN 978-1-4422-4001-8 (hardback : alk. paper) — ISBN 978-1-4422-4002-5 (ebook) 1.
Indians in motion pictures—Catalogs. 2. Silent films—United States—Catalogs. I. Title.
  PN1995.9.I48H55 2016
  791.43'6520397—dc23

                                                                      2015016282

♾️™ The paper used in this publication meets the minimum requirements of American National Standard for Information Sciences—Permanence of Paper for Printed Library Materials, ANSI/NISO Z39.48-1992.

Printed in the United States of America

To my daughters,

Lisa and Amy

CONTENTS

Acknowledgments

Thanks to my colleagues in the English Department and the American Indian Studies Committee, and to my students in Eng/AIS 242 (The American Indian in Literature and Film) at the University of Wisconsin–Eau Claire for their insights on individual films dealing with Native Americans. Thanks also to Theresa DeRusha, a network administrator (for a major Wisconsin law firm); Kaya N. Sims and Wesley Franson of the UW-EC Computer Training Center for helping me with formatting and indexing and Marl Scheppke, technology coordinator of the Altoona (WI) School District for helping me format this book; and to Melinda Smith, who edited the manuscript. Thanks to Katelyn Powers at Rowman & Littlefield, for her assistance with the appendixes. Finally thanks to Stephen Ryan, senior editor at Rowman & Littlefield, who guided me through the process of preparing the manuscript for publication.

Traditional Images of Native Americans

AN INCIDENT FROM John Ford's *Cheyenne Autumn* (1964) dramatizes the two prevailing images of fictional Native Americans in narrative movies. A newspaper editor repeats the typical headlines about the Cheyenne in all the major papers, "Bloodthirsty Savages on the Loose, Burning, Killing, Violating Beautiful White Women" and concludes, "It's not news anymore." He then says, "We're going to take a different tack. We're going to 'Grieve of the Noble Red Man.' We'll sell more newspapers that way." With a disregard for historical accuracy similar to that of the editor, directors of westerns have used the images of the Savage or the Noble Red Man to show the superiority of their heroes, or to comment on political, social, and moral issues of their day. These images force the Native American characters into a circle where they are ultimately too bad or too good to be believable fictional characters. They become only vehicles for contrast to the white heroes of westerns and the values of white culture.

Behind this portrayal of Native American characters is also a movement of racial attitudes. At one extreme is the unconscious or overt racism of the Savage image; at the other extreme is liberal sympathy or pity for the mistreated, and often doomed, Noble Red Man. Somewhere between the extremes is empathy, a sense of understanding and respect for the uniqueness of Native American cultures drawn from characters with a mixture of bad and good traits. As such, they are more believable representations of human beings. This empathy is reflected primarily in recent films dealing with contemporary Native American life and is noticeably lacking in most westerns. As this study traces the stereotypical images of the Savage and Noble Red Man through the historical periods of the cinema, it will reveal little about Native American people, but a lot about the evolution of white American attitudes and values.

The image of the Savage, along with the racism it reflects and promotes, has been part of the western from the beginning. In D. W. Griffith's *The Battle of Elderbush Gulch* (1913) a Native American tribe attacks a group of settlers who have killed the son of their chief. After the warriors sack a town; kill men, women, and a baby; and are about to massacre some people in a ranch house, the Cavalry routs them. In Griffith's later movie, *America* (1924), savage Mohawks fight with the British against the colonists and attack a fort, only to be driven off by the hero and his men. With seemingly endless minor variations, this plot formula, in which the Native Americans are wild, unpredictable savages, motivated by vengeance and bent on raping and killing, became a staple of the westerns.

For many in the white movie audiences, and some Native Americans who lived away from their people, this was how they got to "know" Native Americans. Richard Wagamese, now a well-known Ojibwa writer, comments on this child-hood view of Native Americans: "The most popular way of learning about Indi-ans was television. Man, I remember Saturday mornings watching them Western [movies] and cheering like crazy for the cowboys like everyone else and getting all squirmy inside when the savages were threatening and feelin' the dread we were all supposed to feel when their drums would sound late at night. Injuns. Scary devils. Heathens. All of a sudden popping up at the top of a hill, taking scalps, stealin' horses, talking stupid English and always riding right into the guns of the pioneers. We tumbled off horses better'n anybody and that was about all you could say" (Wagamese 2006, 14).

This negative image of the Savage persists through most of the history of the western, and even though more recent movies such as *Little Big Man* (1970), *The Outlaw Josey Wales* (1976), and *Dances with Wolves* (1990) seem to reject this image, they really just transfer it to evil white soldiers or politicians.

The opposing image of the Noble Red Man, and the associated guilt and pity for the vanishing Native American, also has been part of the western from the beginning. In D. W. Griffith's *The Redman's View* (1909), white settlers displace a band of Kiowa from their land and finally allow the noble young Minnewanna, the chief's daughter, and her lover, Silver Eagle, to rejoin their banished tribe and visit the grave of her father. The *Biograph Bulletin* notes that the film beautifully depicts the suffering of Native Americans who were made "to trek from place to place by the march of progress which was ever forging its way into the West" (Bowser 1973, 149). Another Griffith film, *Iola's Promise* (1912), subtitled "*How the Little Indian Maiden Paid Her Debt of Gratitude,*" also follows the pattern of the Noble Red Man. After a white miner helps Iola, she repays him by rescuing his beloved just as she is about to be burned at the stake. Though Iola is fatally wounded in the rescue, she also shows her gratitude by locating gold for the man before she dies. Such stories of tribes being pushed out of existence by the settlers and soldiers, or of Native Americans good enough to be friendly to whites whatever the sacrifice, also became formulas. That the image of the Noble Red Man exists side by side with the image of the Savage in *Iola's Promise* and in other Griffith westerns is not unusual. In fact, they are often juxtaposed to emphasize the nobleness of positive Native American characters like Iola. Throughout the history of the western, these images continue to be unpredictably mixed until the Noble Red Man becomes the predominant image, as in the more recent films mentioned above and in *Geronimo, an American Legend* (1993).

The western always measures the goodness of the Noble Red Man and the badness of the Savage by the way these character types react to the superior white characters, never by their intrinsic nature as Native Americans or as members of different nations, tribes, and bands. The noble characters are good because they are friends to the whites and realize they must adapt to white culture or face extinction. On the other side of this equation, the savage characters are bad because they are enemies to the whites and obstacles to westward expansion. The profiles of typical female and male characters reveal this bias.

The noble female characters are usually darkly beautiful and sensual "princesses" who show a special willingness to love and be loyal to white men, even though they must often suffer for their devotion. Some of the most extreme examples of this type appear in the silent films. For instance, in *The Indian Squaw's Sacrifice* (1910), the title character, Noweeta, nurses a wounded white man back to health and then marries him. After they have a child, her husband meets a white woman he had loved before. When Noweeta realizes that her husband still loves the woman, she goes off to the woods and kills herself so that her husband can be free to marry the white woman. This same pattern, with minor variations, occurs in *The Kentuckian* (1908) and De Mille's *The Squaw Man* (1914), a movie so popular that it was remade several times.

A similar character type is the noble young woman who decides to leave her beloved white man even though she still loves him deeply. For example, in *The Far Horizons* (1955) Sacajawea leaves Captain Clark at the end because she doesn't fit into his civilized life, and in *Captain John Smith and Pocahontas* (1953), the title character stays behind to keep the peace (and marry another white man) when John Smith returns to England. Like Pocahontas, the typical noble young women will almost always choose to marry a white man rather than a man of their race.

However, the romances and marriages between Native American women and white men usually have a sad ending. For example, in *Broken Arrow* (1950), the beautiful Sonseeahray rejects the Apache she is promised to and marries the white hero, only to be gunned down at the end. In *A Man Called Horse* (1970), the lovely Running Deer refuses the offer of Black Eagle and weds the white hero, only to be killed during a battle with the Shoshone. This taboo against mixed romances and marriages in the plots of westerns persists even to *Dances with Wolves* (1990), in which the "Lakota" woman who falls in love with the hero is really a white woman. When the characters involved in a mixed marriage or romance do survive in films like *The Red Woman* (1917), *The Big Sky* (1952), or *Black Robe* (1991), they do so only in the wilderness, far away from white society. So, even though the good and beautiful Native American woman of the westerns has a special ability to recognize the superiority of the white heroes, she is punished if her love or loyalty goes too far.

The opposing image is the savage female or "squaw," who is frequently hostile to whites and often a physically unattractive character. For example, in *The Last of the Mohicans* (1936) a crowd of ugly and mean-looking Huron women harass two white female captives and then, with diabolical looks on their faces, torture the hero by jabbing him with sharp sticks. In *A Man Called Horse* (1970), an old woman, Buffalo Cow Head, treats the hero very harshly at first, hitting him with a heavy stick. Though they adopt each other at the end, at one point the hero refers to her as "a horrible old hag." Even more sympathetic female characters become objects of derision if they are not beautiful. In *The Searchers* (1956), the young friend of the hero unwittingly acquires a plump Cheyenne "wife" whom he calls "Look." Immediately, she becomes the butt of humor when the snide hero ridicules their "marriage," and later when the young man kicks her away from his bedroll and she rolls down a hill. After she leaves their camp, they later find her body in a tepee of a village raided by soldiers. Even in this unrequited "romance," the female character dies. Ultimately, then, Native American female characters, whether they are beautiful or not, can seldom survive a companionship with a white man.

The companionship between the white hero and his Native American friend, on the other hand, is always positive and a key to the noble male. Some notable examples are Hawkeye and Chingachgook (*The Last of the Mohicans*, 1936), Tom Jeffords and Cochise (*Broken Arrow*, 1950), Josey Wales and Lone Watie (*The Outlaw Josey Wales*, 1976), John Dunbar and Kicking Bird (*Dances with Wolves*, 1990) and, of course, the Lone Ranger and Tonto. Because he is the hero, the white man is dominant in these companionships. However, especially in the more recent movies, the directors portray the hero and Native American characters as more equal in knowledge and intelligence.

The most typical and well-known example of such a relationship is the story of the Lone Ranger and Tonto as portrayed on TV during the late 1940s and early 1950s. That legendary duo comes together when Tonto (Jay Silverheels), a member of a tribe that had been massacred, finds the Lone Ranger (a member of the Texas Rangers), who had been left for dead by the villains. Tonto recognizes the wounded man as "Kimosabe" (the bright scout) who had saved his life when they were boys. With typical gratitude, the noble Tonto uses traditional medicines to nurse the Ranger back to health. Then Tonto helps the Lone Ranger find and heal the white stallion, Silver, who had been wounded by a buffalo. Finally, Tonto gives the masked man the idea of using silver bullets to represent a new kind of justice not based on killing, and the two loners become friends who devote their lives to the cause of law and order in the old West. Because Tonto and his friend are caught up in a noble cause, especially given the concern for law and order and social responsibility in the 1950s, he is an admirable character, though one decidedly inferior to his white companion in his ability to speak English and think out problems. Not surprisingly, in a newer version of the story, *The Legend of the Lone Ranger* (1981), Tonto (Michael Horse) is less inferior to his white friend and not only speaks well, but is outspoken on Native American rights.

An episode from the 1950s *Lone Ranger* TV series, in which the masked man and Tonto help a starving tribe, epitomizes the basis for the images of the typical noble and savage male Native American characters. The Noble Red Men of this episode are a chief named White Hawk, his son, Little Hawk, and a boy called Arrow Foot. The Savage is White Hawk's other son, Fleet Horse, the pawn of white villains who are after silver on the tribe's land. The story begins as the Lone Ranger and Tonto rescue a stage coach from an attack by the villains and find that one of the passengers is Little Hawk, a young man they know who is on his way back to his tribe after graduating from college. The heroes take Little Hawk, dressed in a suit and wearing a narrow headband over his short-cropped hair, to his village. As he greets his father, his brother, Fleet Horse, appears, wearing an Apache tunic and sash and a headband over his long hair, and spouting anti-white rhetoric. In quick succession, the Lone Ranger defeats the evil brother in a traditional fight, and Little Hawk persuades his people to work to cultivate fields rather than follow his rebellious brother in a war with the whites. When the tribe agrees to work, the Lone Ranger promises to bring supplies, which have been donated by the white settlers. Then he and Tonto capture the villains who have been inciting Fleet Horse to violence. At the end, with the tribe working diligently in nearby fields, White Hawk kills his son Fleet Horse. He then says to his noble son, "The bad part of me died with your brother; the good part will be reborn tomorrow when you become chief." Before the heroes leave, Tonto says to the Lone Ranger, "Them happy now, Kimosabe." Then, as they ride away, Little Hawk says to young Arrow Foot, who has learned his lesson about being a good Native American, "We should all give thanks to the men who made it possible to hold our heads up and walk with pride."

By contemporary standards, the messages of this episode are, of course, too extreme and obvious. However, the paternalism of the hero and the sneering exploitation of the tribe by the white villains, are typical, in varying degrees of subtlety, in most westerns. This Lone Ranger episode also reveals one other typical kind of noble Native American character, the wise older chief. The basis of White Hawk's wisdom (and his rejection of his rebellious son) is his belief that his tribe must adopt the new ways of the more educated whites if they are to survive. Other peace-loving chiefs, like Old Lodge Skins in *Little Big Man* (1970), have a similar belief that their tribes cannot escape the domination of the whites and thus must face extinction or learn to accommodate their way of life to that of the whites. Once again a typical noble character is portrayed according to his acceptance of white superiority.

In the recent feature-length *The Lone Ranger* (2013), a very old Tonto (Johnny Depp), who appears in a carnival side show as an example of the Noble Red Man completely revises the images of the TV series as he narrates his part in the story of the man who becomes the Lone Ranger. In his story, which becomes the film, he is a proud member of the Comanche nation, which is led by Chief Big Bear (Saginaw Grant) who knows exactly what the white man is doing with the building of the new railroad. With droll humor, Tonto establishes himself as a warrior who saves the life of the character who will become the Lone Ranger and transforms him into a worthy companion in his quest to avenge the massacre of his village. The actor who portrays Tonto, Johnny Depp, comments on the character, "Since cinema has been around, Native Americans have been treated very poorly by Hollywood. . . . What I wanted to do was play Tonto as a warrior with integrity and dignity. It's my small sliver of a contribution to try to right the wrongs of the past." (*Indian Country Today Media Network* Staff 2013, 8–13). This revisionist 2013 film bears testimony to the traditional images by the vigor of its attempt to overturn them.

Another measure of the traditional noble or savage Native American male of the westerns is his attitude toward white women. Just as the noble female characters are drawn to white males, so also are the noble males attracted to white women. And their romances often come to the same sad endings as those of the females, again because of a taboo against miscegenation. For example, in *A Red Man's Love* (1910) the Native American abandons the woman from his tribe he has promised to marry after he falls in love with a white woman whom his tribe has captured. Motivated by his love, he rejects his tribe, rescues the woman, and brings her to the home of her father. However, when he asks the white woman to marry him, she and her family cruelly reject him. Another classic example is the romance between Nophaie and Marion, the white schoolteacher, in *The Vanishing American* (1925). The noble Nophaie's love, which can never be truly requited, pushes him to numerous grand and selfless actions, including his death as he tries to restore peace between his tribe and the whites.

On the other hand, the savage characters, driven by their hostility, capture and rape white women. For instance, in *The Stalking Moon* (1968), a renegade Apache kills many whites as he tries to recapture his white wife and son. The woman deeply fears the savage warrior who had captured her and given her only the choice of death or marriage. She is safe and happy only when the hero finally kills her savage husband. Another example of the way savage characters treat captured white females occurs in *The Searchers* (1956). The Comanche first rape and kill a mother and then kidnap her daughters, one of whom they also rape and kill later. As the heroes search for the other daughter, they observe at an army post the bodies of captured women and the survivors who have been driven to pathetic states of insanity by their Comanche captors. Near the end of the film, when the hate-filled hero finds the surviving daughter, he tries to kill her because she has lived with the chief of the Comanche, Scar. Later he rescues her only after achieving a catharsis of his hate by scalping the dead body of Scar. *The Searchers*, one of the great westerns, is sadly also a prime example of the racism behind the portrayal of the savage Native American as defiler of white women.

The savage, hostile characters, like the Comanche, Scar, or Fleet Horse of the *Lone Ranger* episode, are the fierce, unscrupulous adversaries of the white hero and thus the antagonists in typical plots of westerns. Often they are rebellious young braves like Fleet Horse who reject their peace-loving old chiefs and join the white villains to accomplish their evil ends. Or they are hostile bands who ambush stage-coaches and attack everything from remote farms to pony express riders. In the older films, the stock savage characters are often neither identified by tribe, nor given adequate motivation for their vengeance; they are simply the melodramatic villains who complicate the plot and allow the heroes to triumph over them. In the later films, especially those of the 1950s and 1960s, the hostile characters have clearer motivation. Even in *The Searchers* (1959), the Comanche chief, Scar, attacks the farm of the hero's relatives and kidnaps the two girls because whites have killed two of his sons. In fact, the sympathy toward Native Americans in movies like *Apache* (1954) or *Geronimo* (1962) can often be measured by the degree of motivation given to the main characters. Whatever the motivation, however, the savage Native Americans of the western must be vanquished by the hero and the degree of ignominy or honor in their inevitable defeat is another measure of sympathy.

Generally, then, whether the Native American characters are friendly or hostile, they have a poor survival rate in the plots of westerns. These stereotyped film characters are victims of their primitive emotions: if treated well, they are capable of love, loyalty, or gratitude so powerful that it can become destructive. If treated badly, they are capable of vengeance so mindless and fierce that it surely will lead to their destruction. And, of course, such characters emphasize the superiority of white society and the male hero, which is the primary wish fulfillment that drives the genre of the western. With only minor variations, from the beginnings of the western genre to *Dances with Wolves*, all Native American characters have been reduced to the extremes of the Noble Red Man or the Savage. The repetition of these images encodes or programs audiences, depending on their individual backgrounds, to believe they really know Native Americans as mistreated noblemen or dangerous enemies. As Fredric Jameson notes, "movies are a physical experience, and are remembered as such, stored up in bodily synapses that evade the thinking mind" (1992, 1). Audiences of westerns "remember" Native Americans according to the repeated content of the images. They feel they own these characters that exist as pictures in their memories, pictures that never talk back and that behave in wonderfully predictable ways. However, if audiences can learn to recognize the content of the images and see that they have been a consistent and fairly obvious part of westerns, they can begin to reduce this level of encoding rather quickly.

A more complicated encoding, however, involves the form of the movies, the movie or film techniques used to color attitudes toward the Native American characters in individual movies. From the beginning, the directors of westerns have played upon certain basic film techniques in their portrayal of Native Americans. Long, medium, and close-up shots; camera angles; composition; editing; and acting are key to what the movie "language" says about Native American characters. The repetition of these techniques throughout the history of the western deeply encodes attitudes toward Native Americans in audiences. A discussion of the portrayal of Native Americans in narrative movies, therefore, must not only consider the content of the images but also how attitudes toward Native American characters are expressed by film techniques.

The distance and angle from which audiences see characters and settings are basic techniques filmmakers use to shape responses. The long shot, which gives a view of the whole scene, emphasizes the setting or environment. In the western, the landscape is central and thus long shots are common and often the first perspective from which the audience sees hostile tribes about to attack. A classic example occurs in John Ford's *Stagecoach* (1939), a movie in which the threat of an attack by Apaches is a major source of tension. Just before the attack, Ford cuts to a long shot of the stagecoach from a bluff high above (a high-angle shot), to a long shot of the Apaches on the bluff from the perspective of the stagecoach (a low-angle shot), and then to a medium shot of the Apaches, and finally to a close-up shot of their leader, Geronimo (both low-angle shots). The long shot starts this scene; then the camera angles, medium and close-up shots, and editing all work together to manipulate the reaction of the audience to the attack. As we shall see when we look at the other techniques Ford uses in this scene (camera angles and editing), the form of the shots emphasizes the basic image of the savage Apaches. The long shot also can be used to portray the noble but doomed Red Man. For example, at the end of *The Vanishing American* (1925), in an extreme long shot of considerable duration, a funeral procession for the dead warrior, Nophaie, starts to fade away into the landscape (and sunset). This long shot gives the audience the illusion that the hero and his tribe are literally vanishing.

The medium shot, which focuses on the body of the character, often from the knees to the head, is a more neutral perspective than the long shot, and often is as close as the audience gets to Native American characters in the western. The close-up shot, however, focuses attention on a character's face or a significant object in the setting. A pattern of such shots of the hero, for example, will cause the audience to identify with and respect the character. On the other hand, a close-up of a character that the audience has seen only in long shots or not at all, such as Geronimo in *Stagecoach* (1939), will cause fear or a sense of threat. Another good example is the first view of Scar, the savage Comanche chief, in John Ford's *The Searchers* (1956). Ford's camera follows a little girl who runs from her home, which is about to be attacked by the Comanche, and tries to hide. Then he cuts to a close high-angle shot of the girl as she cowers to the ground while a shadow moves over her. Finally, he cuts to a close-up of Scar's face from the low-angle perspective of the girl. The shot, angle, and lighting (Scar's face is lit from below) make the savage character deeply threatening and memorable.

In the above examples from the two John Ford westerns, camera angles are also a key part of the shot's effect. In the low-angle shot, the camera looks up at the subject and makes it appear imposing, strong, or threatening, as in the above-mentioned close-ups of Geronimo and Scar. In the high-angle shot, the camera looks down on the subject and makes it appear dominated, powerless, or threatened, as in the long shot of the stagecoach. These camera angles have characteristic patterns in westerns: the white hero is often "looked up to" in a series of low-angle shots, whereas victims of hostile tribes or warriors defeated by the heroes frequently are seen from a high angle. In some of the newer westerns like *Broken Arrow* (1950) or *Little Big Man* (1970), the low-angle shot is used to portray noble Native American characters like Cochise, who is usually seen in medium and close-up low-angle shots, or Old Lodge Skins, who is frequently seen in warmly lit low-angle close-ups.

In westerns, techniques of composition, especially placement of characters in the frame, often favor the white hero by placing him more in the foreground and higher in the frame than the other characters. Such placement is typical in movies with Native Americans who are companions of the hero. For instance, in the *Lone Ranger* series, the hero is often placed in a more emphatic position than his friend, Tonto. In *The Last of the Mohicans* (1936), Chingachgook and Uncas usually appear on either side of and slightly behind Hawkeye. A more recent film, *The Outlaw Josey Wales* (1976), breaks from this pattern when Wales and Ten Bears, the Comanche chief who is very much his equal, are placed in close to the same plane in the frame. In each of these examples, the way the placement directs the attention of audiences has a subtle, and maybe unconscious, effect on whether they remember the Native Americans as positive or negative characters.

Editing also controls the attention and feelings of the audience. In westerns some of the most powerful examples occur in the depiction of attacks by hostile tribes. In the above example from *Stagecoach* (1939), Ford's slow pace of cutting between the shots leading up to the attack of the Apaches (for the purpose of suspense) changes to a more rapid crosscutting between the two lines of action, the attacking warriors and the whites defending themselves in the stagecoach. The crosscutting, with the camera moving at the speed of the Apache horses (tracking shot) to the reactions of those riding inside the coach to the Apaches lets the audience identify with the terror of the passengers. This crosscutting builds to the point where the pregnant woman in the stagecoach is about to shoot herself to avoid being captured. Then the sound of the bugle signals a cut to the cavalry routing the Apaches. In *The Searchers* (1956) Ford intensifies the horror of an impending attack by crosscutting between the men who learn they have been tricked by the Comanche into leaving the farm and the helpless people on the farm as they realize the Comanche are about to attack. In each line of action, Ford focuses on the reactions of anxiety and terror among the white characters. In fact, he never shows the attack itself, but only the reactions of the men who return to find the bodies. This classic example of manipulation, in which what is not shown is more frightening and involving than what is shown, leaves the audience with an intense feeling that the whites have been terribly victimized by the savage Comanche.

In more recent films, editing, especially crosscutting and rapid cutting, also has been used to influence the audience's attitude toward sympathetic, noble Native American characters who are attacked by evil soldiers. In *Little Big Man* (1970) the editing of Custer's attack on the Cheyenne camped at the Washita River is a striking example. The crosscutting between the hero's somewhat humorous rescue of Old Lodge Skins, who thinks he's invisible, and rapid successions of shots of Cheyenne women and children being brutally murdered by the soldiers emphasizes the horrible victimization of the tribe. This feeling is punctuated at the end of the sequence by a cut from a slow-motion shot of the hero's Cheyenne wife and their baby being killed to a shot of the hero watching helplessly, during which the harsh sounds of the attack drop out, and the silence lets the horror of the massacre impact on the audience.

Another example of such editing occurs in *Windwalker* (1980), in which a Cheyenne family are the good characters and a group of Crow warriors pursuing them are the villains. Because this movie has only a small amount of dialogue, the action sequences become crucial for engaging the audience. In one scene, the director depicts the movement of the hero and his family through the woods in a tracking shot (the camera and audience move with the characters) from a slightly high-angle perspective that suggests their vulnerability. Then he crosscuts to low-angle close shots of the Crow in their war paint, positioning themselves for the attack on snow-covered ridges above the family. The contrast of their war paint with the snow seen in close-up shots makes them appear especially threatening. Thus crosscutting not only builds suspense but also draws the sympathy of the audience to the noble Cheyenne.

As the above example from *Little Big Man* indicates, the use of sound complements the impressions of Native American characters. For the savage characters, especially during war dances and attacks on whites, their almost other-worldly whooping and yelping is the most common sign of their terrible fury. In addition, music, whether in the background or as part of the synchronous sound, sends somewhat more subtle messages about such characters. The rhythmic sound of war drums, with its descending parallel tones, signals the presence of hostile tribes and builds suspense about when they will attack. Also, of course, the sound of the bugle signifies the rescue of the white victims by the cavalry and the impending defeat of the hostiles. Such synchronous music also can create sympathy for noble Native American characters. In *Little Big Man*, the drum rolls and the melody of "Gerry Owen," played by Custer's band, strengthen the feeling of pity for the Cheyenne in the Washita massacre sequence discussed above. Finally, in addition to synchronous sound and the musical score, another technique, the voice-over (the use of narration in which the words are not spoken by anyone on the screen), conditions the response of the audience to the Native American characters. In such films as *Broken Arrow* (1950), *Dances with Wolves* (1990), and *Geronimo, an American Legend* (1993), voice-overs by the hero or heroine reinforce the already positive images of the noble characters and tribes.

All of the above film or movie techniques help to encode the images of the Savage and Noble Red Man. Another key element in this process is acting, especially in the sense of the actor as a presence on the screen. The non–Native American actors who played most of the major Native American characters in the westerns often acted their parts well, but they were not believable as screen presences, especially when Native American actors played minor characters in the film. Long after the powers of Hollywood decided that white actors could no longer play Black or Asian characters, they still chose them for Native Americans in westerns. This practice began to change, though very slowly, when actors like Chief Dan George in *Little Big Man* (1970) and *The Outlaw Josey Wales* (1976), and Jay Silverheels as Tonto before him, illustrated the importance of having Native American actors play Native characters. The screen presence of Jay Silverheels gave the character of Tonto a dignity that could not be destroyed by all its other negative elements, and the presence of Chief Dan George as Old Lodge Skins and Lone Watie dramatized conclusively the believability that a Native American actor could infuse into a major character. The recognition of what Native Americans could bring to the screen led to the selection of actors like Will Sampson, Graham Greene, and Rodney Grant to play major characters in Hollywood movies. The use of Native American actors, which is becoming more and more a given in significant independent and Hollywood films, is a major step toward a more empathetic portrayal of Native American characters. This, in turn, will encode more positive and more realistic images of Native Americans.

Like acting, all of the above film or movie techniques are part of a film "language" that repeats itself and changes throughout and beyond the history of the western. This book will trace the images of the Savage and Noble Red Man, and the film language used to express them, throughout the history of film. A better understanding of "film language" will help the reader "read," or interpret, the evolution of the traditional images.

Each of the following discussions of the historical decades will focus on representative movies, with attention to both the content of their images of Native Americans and the filmmaker's use of film technique to manipulate the perception of the images.

Representative Movies from
Silent Films to the Present

The Silent Movies

ESPECIALLY IN THE EARLY PART of the silent era, which began less than twenty years after the Wounded Knee Massacre (1890), Native Americans were a very popular subject for narrative films. Among the movies of the first star of the westerns, Bronco Billy, are *The Cowboy and the Squaw, The Dumb Half-Breed's Defense, An Indian Girl's Love, The Faithful Indian,* and *The Tribe's Penalty* (Weaver 1971, 30–31). Also among the movies of the first movie studios in New Jersey are *His Indian Bride, How the Boys Fought the Indians, The Indian Land Grab, The Redman and the Child, An Up-to-Date Squaw,* and *The True Heart of the Indian* (from the listings in Spehr 1977). Although many of the early films are no longer extant, the ones that remain and contemporary film reviews suggest that a considerable number of films had a sympathetic view of Native American characters as Noble Red Men. However, the image of the Savage also found its way into many films, especially toward the end of the silent period when the western became a more defined genre. Two early films by D. W. Griffith, *Iola's Promise* (1912) and *The Battle at Elderbush Gulch* (1913), represent well these opposing images in the first part of this era. Later in the period, *The Vanishing American* (1925) not only develops a more complicated image of the Noble but doomed Red Man, but also depicts the central Native American character as a victim of white prejudice. And, finally, *The Silent Enemy* (1930) uses native actors to portray the culture of Native Americans before contact with whites. These films mark continuing patterns in the history of the western.

Contemporary film reviews reveal the controversy over the portrayal of Native American characters. In a 1912 review of the Bison 101 Headliners, Louis R. Harrison rejects the portrayal of Native Americans as victims and argues that it was historically appropriate for whites, "the representatives of progress," to overcome "the representatives of degeneration." Harrison sees the Native American as a person who uses only "that part of his brain which enabled him to be crafty in the hunt for food." On the other hand, the white man "cultivated brain along with brawn," and was able to conquer the inferior native tribes because the settler was "a man, every inch of him, and the iron in his blood has descended to those who promulgated the Monroe doctrine" (*Moving Picture World*, Apr. 27, 1912, 320–22). Harrison's view of Native Americans in this and other reviews represents the attitudes of white supremacy, social Darwinism, and racism that demanded the image of the Savage or Victim.

Harrison's need to write such reviews, however, suggests that the opposing image of the Noble Red Man, and the associated liberal belief that Native Americans were being terribly mistreated by whites, is prominent in the early westerns. Another unidentified writer for *Moving Picture World* represents this view. In a 1911 review, he argues that the public is aware that Native Americans have been "misjudged and slandered in the past" because the new movies are "helping to set the Red Man right in history and in his position before the American people." He points out that the best western films hold up the nobility of the Indian way of life to "the belated admiration" of the white audience, and concludes that "this tendency to do the Indian justice runs through all the pictures" and accounts "for the continued popularity of Indian films" (Aug. 5, 1911, 271). Films such as *Lo, the Poor Indian* (1910), in which the character is punished by laws he doesn't understand, or Griffith's *Ramona* (1910), based on a popular Helen Hunt Jackson novel about the plight of Native Americans, are examples of early attempts to raise social consciousness.

D. W. Griffith's *Iola's Promise* (1912) highlights the image of the Noble Red Man, but also uses the opposing Savage image. At the beginning, Iola (Mary Pickford), a maiden who has been captured by cutthroat villains, is rescued by a Yankee prospector, who takes her to his cabin, treats her wounds, and feeds her. The note between the scenes describes her reaction: "And the simple savage touched by the goodness of her benefactor gave him her heart in a sudden ecstasy of gratitude." This beautiful woman, draped in a blanket and wearing her dark hair in a headband, promises to help the miner find gold. When he asks her to cross her heart on the promise, she calls the whites "cross-heart people" and devotes herself to them. Because the prospector she loves has told her to do so, she reluctantly returns to her village, described as "The camp of Iola's savage and turbulent tribe." Though Griffith paints Iola as a noble character, he depicts the other members of her tribe, especially the warriors, as typical Savages.

When a wagon train comes near their camp, the warriors ride out and stage a fierce attack, during which they are seen from a high angle as they ride around the wagons in "the circle of death." During the attack, the warriors drag away the prospector's sweetheart and her father, roughly tie them to a tree, and pile up branches for "the terrible death at the stake." At this point, Iola tells them not to hurt the cross-heart people, but they push her away. Iola, however, rescues the whites by taking the woman's hat and cloak so that the braves chase and shoot her while the others escape. After the miners drive off the hostile warriors, the prospector's girl tells him that Iola "let them shoot her to save us." He rushes to find her, and, fatally wounded, she staggers toward him and shows the gold she has found for him. He reaches to shake her hand and says, "Put her there. Girl, you sure done noble!" She tells him that she kept her promise and that he shouldn't feel bad because she won't suffer anymore. Then she dies in his arms to end the story of "the Indian maid's supreme sacrifice." Iola is a prime example of the grateful, loyal, and noble character who is willing to give even her life for the white man. As such, she is a perfect foil to the savagery of her tribe.

Similar noble Native American characters, many of whom are in love with a white person even though they are from tribes hostile to whites, persist throughout the silent period. A notable example of this type of character is Nophaie in *The Vanishing American* (1925). Although this film is sympathetic to the Native American, it uses the image of the doomed Noble Red Man to stress the superiority of white society in general and the Christian religion in particular. At the beginning, the filmmakers use a note between the scenes, the parallel of the voice-over for silent films, to quote Herbert Spenser's idea that in history, as in nature, the fittest survive. As the film progresses, the story of a Noble Red Man, Nophaie, the warrior, shows how the Native Americans lose the Darwinian battle for survival to the whites.

In a long prologue depicting the history of native people in North America, Nophaie first appears as the "Indian" conqueror of the Cliff Dwellers, one of whom prophesies that a stronger race will eventually conquer the Native Americans. In the next episode, the Spaniards appear and challenge the warrior. Nophaie, seen in an extreme long shot from the low-angle perspective of the Spaniards, rides his white horse back and forth on the high bluff and seems invincible. However, one shot from a Spanish gun kills him, and his death moves large numbers of Native Americans, already weakened by Spanish wine, to bow in homage to a few Spanish soldiers. In the final episode of the prologue, set in the early days of the United States, Kit Carson and the cavalry challenge Nophaie and his tribe. Again Nophaie rides his white horse on a high bluff, and this time he is killed by a shot from a cannon positioned far below him. The members of his tribe end up, contrary to the promises of Kit Carson, dominated by an evil Indian agent on a reservation. In this setting, Nophaie appears as the main character of the film.

On the reservation, Nophaie meets the forces that will ultimately destroy him as the symbolic leader of his tribe. His first mistake is falling in love with Marion, the white schoolteacher on the reservation, and accepting her Christian religion. In one scene, Marion reads her Bible to Nophaie, who is seen from a slight high angle sitting on the floor at her feet, as she teaches him about self-denial and martyrdom. This perspective suggests the Warrior is less powerful than the white woman and is already being controlled by her religion. This control becomes apparent later in a scene during World War I when a little Bible given to him by Marion prompts Nophaie to save the life of his white rival for her affections. After the war, as Nophaie tries to worship the gods of his tribe, he looks at the Bible and decides to invoke instead the Christian god. Finally, near the end of the film, as he tries to stop the attack of his people on the whites, he is fatally shot in the chest through the little Bible.

The attack of his tribe on the evil Indian agent, Booker, is fully justified. While the men of the tribe were away fighting for their country, Booker (who dies from an arrow through his throat) had taken their land and caused the death of a young woman from the tribe. In spite of this, Nophaie, motivated by the Christian spirit, tries to stop the fighting, only to be fatally wounded by one of his own people. While lying on the ground with Marion holding him in her arms and a member of his tribe on either side, he says, in his last words, that he finally understands the idea that losing one's life means gaining everlasting life. The Warrior has literally become a saint, a martyr whose death brings peace between his people and the whites. However, this act marks the ultimate end of the Navajo warrior spirit because it has been transformed into a Christian spirit.

The film ends with an extreme long shot of a lengthy procession of the tribe vanishing into the horizon as they carry the body of Nophaie away for burial. This procession makes a striking image of the doomed Noble Red Man slowly but steadily being moved out of the picture by the stronger society and religion of the whites. Such an image fills the audience with sympathy, but the film as a whole frees them from any direct sense of responsibility because it suggests that the destruction of Native American culture is just the natural result of social evolution.

Another notable film of the late part of the era, *The Silent Enemy* (1930) (the title refers to hunger or starvation), also uses the Noble but doomed Red Man image, but counteracts it with the outcome of its plot. The film deals exclusively with Native American life before contact with the white man, as did a considerable number of silent films with titles such as *The Squaw's Love* (1911), *The Legend of Scarface* (1910), *A Sioux Spy* (1911), *An Indian Idyll* (1912), and, of course, *Hiawatha* (1913). The *Silent Enemy* also has an all-Native cast, with a Sioux actor (Chief Yellow Robe) playing Chief Chetoga; a Blackfeet (Chief Long Lance) as the hero, Bulak; a Penobscot (Spotted Elk), as Newa, the woman who loves him; and an Ojibwa (Chief Akawanush) as Dagwan. After noting the tribal heritage of the actors, the filmmakers explain that the film was "produced with a full awareness that the Indian and the wilderness were both rapidly vanishing." The opening monologue of Chetoga, seen in a full shot from a low angle that underscores his power as a spokesman, reinforces this attitude: "How! This picture is the story of my people. I speak for them because I know your language. Soon we will be gone. Your civilization will have destroyed us, but by your magic we will live forever. We thank the white man who helped us make this picture."

The plot of *The Silent Enemy*, said to be based on the journals of the Jesuit missionaries, is, however, clearly fictitious. The opening shots establish the Ojibwa as children of nature, happily working together in their camp. However, the tribe faces a problem: the game in their area has disappeared and the hero, Bulak, the great hunter, and the villain, Dagwan, the medicine man, are in conflict over the best solution. They also both want to marry the beautiful Newa, who has been promised to Dagwan but loves Bulak. After Bulak leads a hunting party down river, winter arrives and Dagwan misuses his magic to find food for the tribe who are becoming victims of the "silent enemy," hunger. When Bulak returns empty-handed, the chief calls a council and finally decides to reject the plan of Dagwan and take Bulak's advice to travel north and find the caribou herds. After much suffering, and other devious activities of Dagwan, the tribe arrives at the land of the caribou. However, the herd is nowhere to be seen, and Dagwan convinces the tribe that Bulak, who was named the new chief by the dying Chetoga, must die. Just as Bulak is about to be killed, the caribou appear and he is vindicated. At the end, the treacherous Dagwan walks into the wilderness to face a death from hunger, and Chief Bulak, with his wife, Newa, looks forward to sharing years of abundance with his tribe. Although this melodramatic plot shows the Native Americans' ability to survive before the arrival of white men, the movie as a whole accepts the image of the doomed Noble Red Man.

The opposing image of the Savage also appears in the silent melodramas. Iron Eyes Cody, an Italian actor whose career spanned many years, explains the need for this kind of film: "There had been bloody wars fought out on the plains, at this time just 40 years ago. The people wanted blood and sentiment and nobody in the movie business was about to deprive them of it" (Cody 1982, 33–34). One of the earliest silent movies on record, *The Pioneers* (1903) portrays the image of the bloodthirsty Savage by showing warriors attacking a family of settlers living in a remote cabin, killing the parents, and kidnapping a young daughter.

Even D. W. Griffith, who made numerous films sympathetic to Native Americans, emphasizes the Savage image in his *The Battle at Elderbush Gulch* (1913). The tribe in this movie are Savages, who first appear during a ritual described as "The Dog Feast—Sunka Alawan—May you eat dog and live long." In the next scene, members of the tribe, some with war bonnets, dance wildly and then are seen asleep when the chief's son returns. Because this young man and his friend have missed the feast and still have a hunger for dog meat, they move out and find two little dogs that belong to the young heroine. Just as they are about to kill the dogs, a rancher shoots the chief's son. This provokes a fierce response, as a note between the scenes indicates: "The death of the chieftain's son fans the ever ready spark of hatred and revenge [in the tribe]." The warriors ride out of camp, to start "The Attack," which involves the entire second reel.

They first attack and overrun the town. Griffith emphasizes the savagery of the attack in several distinctive shots. In one of them, at the edge of the frame, a warrior scalps a woman, and, though the actual scalping occurs outside the frame, the audience sees the movement of his arm and the woman's feet twitching. Then he grabs her baby and starts the movement of dashing it to the ground as Griffith cuts to the next shot. In another shot, a brave reaches down and grabs the hair of a wounded settler and then is seen rising up with his knife after the scalping. Though Griffith couldn't show these acts of violence because of the movie codes of his time, his editing and attention to detail make them seem more grim than a graphic depiction.

In the last part of the attack on the ranch house, Griffith uses crosscutting between the actions of the tribe, the people in the house, and an approaching cavalry troop to build suspense about the outcome. After rapid cuts from the warriors, who move ever closer to the house and burn one of the out-buildings, to the beleaguered people in the house, several of whom are women, Griffith cuts to an extreme high-angle shot of the warriors circling the house, a perspective that emphasizes the hopelessness of the settlers. However, just as the men in the house are running out of ammunition and the warriors are ready to break in, the cavalry comes to the rescue and routs the savage tribe.

This pattern of savages as a threat to white settlers repeats itself in numerous films, a few examples of which are *Riders of Vengeance* (1919), with marauding Apaches, *In The Days of Buffalo Bill* (1922), a serial with chapters such as "Prisoners of the Sioux" and "The Scarlet Doom"; and *The Pony Express* (1925), with hostile Sioux attacking a town. This image of the Savage complements that of the doomed Noble Red Man. Just as audiences could accept destruction of noble Native American tribes as inevitable social evolution, so they could also feel good about the killing of bloodthirsty savages. Both scenarios allowed them to walk out of the theatre feeling that justice had been served in the settling of North America.

These movies represent some of the perspectives from which one can look at the images of the Savage and Noble Red Man in the silent period. Obviously, a significant number of films could fit under several categories. The reader could also note that a connection, or subtext exists in the opinions of contemporary film reviewers on the portrayal of the Native American characters. Though most of the critics probably knew relatively little about the history and cultures of the Native American tribes (and indeed sometimes had very stereotypical views), they evaluate the characters as if they really know Native American peoples. In all likelihood, much of what they knew was drawn from the movies and the print media, especially popular dime-novel fiction, newspapers, and advertising (though this must remain speculation). To the degree that this is true, the early reviewers are good examples of how audiences reacted to the Native American characters in westerns throughout much of the history of American film. To illustrate this point, the alphabetical entries on individual films will quote some appropriate selections from contemporary film critics.

The above representative films and other examples of the Savage and Noble Red Man images, are by no means exhaustive. From 1910 to 1913 alone, one hundred or more films with Native American themes and characters appeared each year. Throughout the silent period, Native Americans remained popular subjects for film. Also, the 1930 cut-off date for the silent films is arbitrary because some films before this date have music, sound effects, and recorded dialogue.

For those who want a more complete listing of silent movie titles, please see Ralph and Natasha Friar's book, which gives extensive lists of silent films in the early chapters and on pp. 287–323. The best primary source for plot summaries is *Moving Picture World* (*MPW*), the first movie magazine. Published from 1907 to 1927, this periodical, most of which is now online, describes many of the movies dealing with Native Americans. Finally, *The Biograph Bulletin* (Bowser 1908–1912) provides detailed plot summaries of the early D. W. Griffith films.

The Early Sound Movies (1931–1949)

During this period, as the western grows into a distinct genre, the image of the Noble Red Man becomes less dominant than that of the Savage. Native American characters more often are hidden enemies in a hostile landscape or savage adversaries of the white hero. Frequently, a fierce and sudden attack on vulnerable whites, or scenes of captives about to be tortured, are characteristic of the Savage. Some good examples of these portrayals appear in the western serials, which emerged and peaked during this era. Produced by the major studios and starring well-known actors, these shorts added up to feature movies over time, and were a sort of precursor to TV series. Usually every week the plot of the serial ended with the hero or heroine in a dire situation such as the one in *Heroes of the West* (1932) entitled "Captured by Indians." In the next episode, a miraculous rescue occurs and then the plot would quickly lead to the next threat by the villainous Native Americans. Another classic example of an attack occurs in a sequence from a John Ford film, *Stagecoach* (1939), which we have looked at before in more detail. Apaches come out of nowhere and chase the stagecoach on horseback. After the fast-paced editing builds to the point where the people on the stage are about to be killed, the sound of the bugle signals the arrival of the cavalry, and the attack is over as fast as it began. The main function of the savage Apaches is to be an absent threat to the whites early in the movie and then a vehicle for cinematic excitement near the end.

In varying degrees, notable historical romances of this period, *The Last of the Mohicans* (1936), *Drums along the Mohawk* (1939), *Northwest Passage* (1940), and *They Died with Their Boots On* (1942), also diminish the stature of the Native American characters. Though the Savage image is often repeated in this era of the western, another type emerges in this decade, the domestic drama, such as *Duel in the Sun* (1946). Such films expose racial prejudice, and portray individual Native American characters struggling to survive in white society.

The first of the representative historical romances, *The Last of the Mohicans* (1936), differs from Cooper's novel by changing the nature of the companionship between Hawkeye and Chingachgook. At the end of the novel, as Chingachgook is mourning the loss of Uncas, Hawkeye says, "Sagamore, you are not alone" (Cooper 1892, 212). Then Cooper describes their expression of feeling for each other: "Chingachgook grasped the hand that, in the warmth of feeling, the scout had stretched across the warm earth, and in that attitude of friendship these two sturdy and intrepid woodsmen bowed their heads together, while scalding tears fell to their feet, watering the grave of Uncas like drops of falling rain" (Cooper 1892, 212). At the end of the novel, then, Hawkeye and Chingachgook affirm the depth of their friendship as lonely heroes. The contrast between the novel and the film offers a useful perspective for understanding how the film portrays the Native American characters. The film diminishes this relationship between Hawkeye and Chingachgook so that Hawkeye can become the central hero and fall in love with the heroine. In the Hollywood fashion, the romance of Hawkeye and Cora Monro dominates the plot, and the noble Mohicans become sidekicks.

As friends of the hero, Chingachgook (Robert Barrat) and Uncas (Phillip Reed) are Noble Red Men in the novel; however, the film's composition and dialogue reduce their stature in the novel. The placement of Hawkeye and his two friends in the frame depicts Chingachgook and Uncas as subservient to the hero. In their first appearance, they are walking together behind Hawkeye. This pattern continues in many other shots where the two Mohicans are on either side of the hero, who is slightly more in the foreground. Only at the end of the film, after the death of Uncas and Hawkeye's commitment to his beloved Cora, do Hawkeye and Chingachgook walk together, with the British hero on his horse between them. In addition, Chingachgook's dialogue is typically clipped and gruff. For example, when Uncas offers food to his beloved Alice, his father says, "Mohican chief no wait on squaw." Later, when Hawkeye asks about the condition of the wounded Uncas (who had just been visited by Alice), Chingachgook answers, "Bad, got squaw fever." Chingachgook's son speaks a little more poetically when he refers to his beloved Alice as "the one with the moon in her hair," but generally his dialogue, and that of his father, is less eloquent than that of their counterparts in the novel. The dialogue of the evil antagonist of Chingachgook and Uncas, Magua (Bruce Cabot), also is reduced to typical Native American movie talk. This savage character, who in the novel incites the hostile Hurons to violence with powerful orations, has lines in the film like "You take em trail, me follow."

Though the film takes away Magua's eloquence, it gives him an evil presence, typical of the Savage. Driven by vengeance, he captures the daughters of Colonel Monro and demands Alice as his "squaw" because Monro had once ordered him to be whipped. Near the end, he also shoots Uncas, whom he has trapped on the edge of a cliff with Alice. After Uncas falls, Magua, seen in a menacing close-up, approaches Alice and she jumps to her death (where her beloved Uncas crawls to her and holds her hand before he dies). Then Magua and Chingachgook have a fierce hand-to-hand battle before the noble Mohican gains his revenge and drowns his evil adversary.

Just as the savage antagonist is punished at the end, so also is the savage tribe, the Hurons, who resort to ambushes, a savage attack on a surrendered fort, and torture of the hero. These enemies of the Mohicans and allies of the French are portrayed in the classic image of the Savage. Led by the treacherous Magua and sporting the typical "Mohawk" haircuts of villainous characters, they ambush the party of Heywood, Alice, and Cora, only to be driven off by the hero and his Mohican companions. When they continue their pursuit of the hero and his party in canoes, Hawkeye leads them away from the others and eludes them by pulling into a backwater while they continue to paddle feverishly down the river, apparently oblivious to the fact that the hero's canoe is no longer in front of them. As is often the case with Savages, they are not only fierce, but also rather stupid. Later, they attack the British fort, a sequence described by a *New York Times* film critic: "The massacre of Fort Henry is by far the bloodiest, scalpingest morsel of cinematic imagery ever produced" (Sept. 3, 1936). This intensely edited sequence begins with a shot of the Hurons breaking down the gate and then cuts from a close-up shot of a brave scalping a colonist, to shots of the Hurons burning the houses, and to Magua shooting Monro and capturing his daughters. The Hurons' final act of violence is their torturing and burning at the stake of the hero, who is rescued at the last moment by a troop of British soldiers and American colonists, who then rout the Hurons decisively.

Such Savages are also the fierce antagonists in another historical romance of this period, *Drums along the Mohawk* (1939). The hero of this film is Gil Martin, a newly married colonist whose attempt to build a successful farm is thwarted by the Savages who are allies of a wicked royalist. Martin's Native American friend, Blue Back (Chief John Big Tree), is the only Noble Red Man in the film. A convert to the Christian faith, he first appears in the hero's cabin, where he terrifies Gil's new wife. Seen from a low angle, he is a striking presence, wrapped in a long red blanket and holding a flintlock. After the woman recovers, Blue Back returns and gives Gil a stick to discipline his wife. Like Chingachgook, Blue Back is not only a male chauvinist but also a man of few words; when the hero is fussing over his wife as she is about to give birth, Blue Black says, "Having babies, that woman's business. She better go far off by herself, leave husband alone." Despite his terse language, throughout the film his noble stature is emphasized by low-angle close-ups, the most notable of which is the final shot, which shows him putting on the eye patch of the villain, whom he has caught and killed.

The hostile Iroquois, on the other hand, are depicted as almost naked, painted warriors (again with "Mohawk" haircuts) who burn the crops and cabins of the settlers. In one scene, two drunken savages, who come into the home of a feisty old woman, are so weakened by drink that they let her browbeat them into carrying her out of the house on her bed before they burn it down. In another scene, a man who has tried to run for help is captured by the tribe and pulled into the view of the fort in a cart filled with straw so the whites can see him suffer. As they start the fire, a preacher from the fort shoots the man to stop his agony. While the people in the fort, who call them "greasy devils" and "filthy pagan heathens," prepare for the final attack, the hero outruns three stocky hostiles and brings soldiers, who rescue the people in the fort and quickly drive off the vicious but inept warriors.

In another historical drama, also set on the east coast, *Northwest Passage* (1940), virtually all the Native American characters are diminished to the image of the Savage. Based on Book I of the Kenneth Roberts novel, the film makes heroes out of Major Rogers and his Rangers. Unlike Gil Martin, Rogers has only disdain for Native Americans and even looks down on his devoted but drunken Stockbridge guide, Konkapot. Other Native Americans, like the Mohawks who accompany him on part of his trek are viewed as treacherous "snakes." However, for the Abenaki, allies of the French and the tribe who attacked his people, Rogers has the deepest hatred. He says of them, "Those red hellions hacked and murdered us, burned our homes, stole women, burned babies, scalped stragglers, roasted officers over slow fires." Though he has this reason for his feelings, his hatred really over-reaches the motivation. In fact, Rogers is one of the more notable "Indian hater" characters, a type that reappears throughout the history of the westerns. And his hatred is based on a thorough knowledge of his adversaries: as one of his Rangers says, "The smartest Indian alive can't think like an Indian like Rogers." Implicit in heroes like Rogers is the idea that to know Native Americans is to hate them. In fact, hatred and revenge are the primary motivation for the heroic trek of the Rangers to the land of the Abenaki and their French allies.

When the Rangers get close to the Abenaki town, they hear the tribe celebrating and Rogers, with his characteristic attitude, says, "They're probably all drunk, but we can't count on it." In the early morning, the Rangers attack, and the still dazed Abenaki run in different directions as waves of Rangers shoot and bayonet them. Shots from the perspective of the Rangers show the Abenaki being picked off like targets, hacked with hatchets and bayoneted. The rapid pace of the editing and the variety of close shots give the audience an exciting sense of being part of the killing of the hated tribe. The whole short attack sequence also reduces the fierce Abenaki tribe to cowardly sheep being slaughtered by the superior Rangers. After several high-angle shots of the town burning and the ground strewn with Abenaki bodies, Rogers looks through a pile of moccasins left on the outskirts of the town and says, "Don't any of the redskins have man-sized feet," and then concludes with "there's nothing but roast Indian left in the town." Such vicious comments by the hero about a massacre, which the movie depicts as a heroic action, are typical of the racist tone in *Northwest Passage*.

Though a much less hateful movie than *Northwest Passage*, the later historical drama, *They Died with Their Boots On* (1942), diminishes the Native American characters in a somewhat different way, by making them a very insignificant part of the plot. This movie follows the career of George Armstrong Custer from his days at West Point through the Civil War to his final battle. The major part of the movie, which focuses on his life before he comes to the plains to fight the hostile tribes, portrays him as a jaunty, courageous leader who wins battles during the Civil War with the flair of all-out cavalry charges. Seen throughout the film in low-angle shots, he grows in heroic stature right up to the final battle. In this process of turning Custer into a mythic hero, the filmmakers, of course, play havoc with history, as a contemporary *Variety* critic noted: "In westerns . . . major errors in history and persons mean little to producers or audiences. The test of a yarn is not its accuracy but its speed and excitement" (Nov. 19, 1941). One of the ways this film distorts history is by making one Sioux warrior, Crazy Horse (Anthony Quinn), the antagonist to Custer. The movie disposes of Custer's other fights with hostile tribes in a montage of battle scenes, after noting that the Seventh Cavalry "Cleared the Plains for a Ruthlessly Spreading Civilization That Spelled Doom for the Red Race." After dismissing all that history, the movie focuses on Crazy Horse. In the first confrontation between Custer and Crazy Horse, they charge each other on horseback and Custer cuts his rival's lance and reins with his saber, and then knocks him off his horse and takes him prisoner. This meeting establishes their rivalry and shows that the best of the Sioux horsemen is no match for Custer in a one-to-one fight.

Later, after Crazy Horse escapes, he will only trust Custer when he is ready to make a treaty. When the treaty is broken by the action of greedy businessmen, Custer shows his respect for the Sioux warrior when he says, "If I were Indian, I would fight with Crazy Horse until my last drop of blood." The director of the film, Raoul Walsh, explained the reason for such a portrayal of Custer and Crazy Horse: "Most westerns had depicted the Indian as a painted, vicious savage. In *They Died . . .* , I tried to show him as an individual who turned violent when his rights as defined by treaty were violated by white men" (*Motion Picture Guide*, Vol. 7, 3355). Though Walsh may have had such a general purpose, his portrayal of Custer totally defies historical accuracy, as does his depiction of the Battle of Little Big Horn.

While Custer and his cavalry move toward the battle, the hostiles hide behind rocks, or in trees or the high grass. The camera looks from the perspective of the hostiles in the hills down on Custer and his men in the valley and thus emphasizes their vulnerability. The only close-up view of the Native American characters is in a brief scene from their camp in which each chief identifies his tribe, a scene that basically emphasizes how greatly the Native Americans outnumber Custer's men. In the actual Battle of Little Big Horn, the moving camera shows Custer making one of his characteristic cavalry charges, only to find that warriors, who attack in waves, surround him. As Custer and his men make their stand, they kill many of their rivals before they are overwhelmed, and Crazy Horse, the worthy rival, shoots Custer, who is standing above his fallen comrades. The sense of movement and the crosscutting between Custer and the hostile tribes makes for a quick, exciting climax in which the audience sees Custer as the outnumbered but mythic hero, who was depicted in the many paintings of his last stand.

At the end of the movie, Custer comes across as a man who had the courage to sacrifice himself to save the other soldiers and settlers in the area, who, according to Custer, would have been killed by the united hostile plains tribes if he had not engaged them at Little Big Horn. At the very end, Custer's wife, Libby, reads a letter of her husband, which identifies the villains who broke the treaty and forced him to fight Crazy Horse. After hearing it, General Sheridan promises that Crazy Horse will get his treaty rights and tells Libby, "Your soldier won his last fight after all." Though the ending has no historical basis, it does nicely complete the glorification of Custer at a time when Americans needed military heroes.

Each of the above films has such a patriotic ending, though only in *They Died with Their Boots On* are the hostile tribes treated with any respect. In *The Last of the Mohicans*, the heroes march off to conquer the French in Canada only after they have defeated the savage Huron, the allies of the French in the American colonies. At the end of *Drums along the Mohawk*, the colonists cannot defeat the British and become Americans until they have routed the savage Iroquois, who have been incited to violence by the British royalists. And at the end of *Northwest Passage*, Rogers promises his men that the savage allies of the French are nothing compared to the great tribes of the plains that they will meet and conquer on their quest for the Northwest Passage. In each of these three films, the tribes portrayed in the image of the Savage are connected to and manipulated by the royalist or French antagonists of the heroic future Americans. As such, they are obstacles to progress that must be eliminated before the British colonists or Americans can achieve their patriotic destinies in North America.

In contrast to these historical movies, *Ramona* (1936) and *Duel in the Sun* (1946) focus on the domestic life of Native Americans who are victims of white society and their own natures. In each, the central characters are mixed-blood females who are living with rich families and eventually become involved in tragic love affairs. The story of Pearl Chavez (Jennifer Jones) is different from that of Ramona because she falls in love with a white man rather than a Native American. However, like Ramona, Pearl, the doomed mixed-blood lover in *Duel in the Sun* is typical of characters in such films which both play on the stereotypes and attempt to expose the prejudice of white society.

A voice-over narrator describes the setting of the beginning and end of the film, Squaw's Head Rock, as the place where, according to Comanche legend, Pearl died and then grew into a desert flower. Within this frame, the movie tells the story of Pearl Chavez, the daughter of a Native American mother and a Creole father. The primitive and deadly sensuality of Pearl's mother is established early in the film. Wearing a long skirt and beaded headband and standing on a circular bar in the saloon, she does a wild dance, which drives the male crowd wild. Seen from a high angle, she shoots a pistol at the height of her dance before she throws herself at her white lover and leaves with him. Shortly thereafter, Pearl's father shoots his wife and her lover, for which he is condemned to be hanged. Pearl's mother is the typical dark, passionate Native American femme fatale, and this heritage is what her daughter must struggle with when she goes to live with the McCanles family on the huge Spanish Bit Ranch. The two McCanles sons, Jesse, an educated, kind man like his genteel Southern mother, and Lewt, a wild, uncontrollable man like his dominating rancher father, represent the forces that will play on Pearl in this setting.

Pearl, whose dark hair is long and curly, dresses like her Native American mother in a long dark skirt and exudes the same "native" sensuality. She responds to the respect and kindness shown to her by Jesse and his mother by promising them to be a "good girl." On the other hand, Lewt sees Pearl as a "bob-tailed little half-breed" he can possess, and his father, the senator, looks down on her Native

American heritage. Commenting on Pearl's outfit, the old man says "Is that what they're wearing this season in wigwams?" And later, referring to her sarcastically as "Pocahontas" or "Minnehaha," he makes Lewt promise not to marry her because he doesn't want the ranch turned "into no Indian reservation." Lewt, who is used to making conquests of women, gives her his Pinto and then on a stormy night comes to her room and embraces her until she gives in and makes love with him. Thus she becomes Lewt's girl and she finally has to tell Jesse, who finds Lewt in her room. In a close-up, with tears in her eyes, she says to Jesse, "I couldn't help it. You must think I'm trash like my Ma." Jesse, who like his mother treats Pearl with respect, rejects her at this point and leaves her alone to face her destiny.

Pearl decides, however, to regain respectability by persuading Lewt to marry her. She comes to a dance at the ranch in a white dress and, after Lewt teaches her the ballroom dances, she begs him to marry her, but he refuses. After this rejection, she tries for respect (and revenge on Lewt) by agreeing to marry Sam, the foreman of the ranch. Lewt, however, shoots Sam, claiming that he has his "brand" on Pearl. In one last desperate attempt, Pearl hides Lewt from the sheriff, but he refuses to take her with him to Mexico even though she clings to his leg as he leaves. At this low point, Jesse returns and promises to let Pearl live with him and his betrothed so that they can care for and educate her. However, when Lewt hears of this, he comes and shoots Jesse, an act that finally drives Pearl to vengeance.

When Pearl learns that Lewt is at Squaw's Head Rock, she puts on a dark blouse, pulls her hair back into a ponytail, takes a rifle and rides her Pinto to carry out her revenge. Her wild look and horse (the Pinto being the "Indian" horse) emphasize her change to the avenging Savage, a role she pursues with an animal-like intensity, shown in a scene where she lowers herself to the ground to drink out of the same water hole as her horse. When she finds Lewt, she shoots him twice before he shoots her. After Lewt tells her he loves her, she crawls to him, tells of her love, and they kiss and die. Ultimately, Pearl seems to be doomed just like her mother, and dies a similar violent death with her white lover. Though the film reveals the prejudice that Pearl suffered because of her heritage, it also fosters the stereotype of the mixed-blood femme fatale and reduces her character to a variation of the doomed Noble Red Man.

This movie and the versions of *Ramona* develop the morality of the domestic tragedy, but the historical dramas remained the dominant vehicle for the portrayal of Native Americans. In the late 1930s and early 1940s, the patriotism of the historical romances resonated with public sentiment before and during World War II. A *Variety* critic alludes to this phenomenon when he describes *They Died with Their Boots On* as a "surefire western, an escape from bombers, tanks and Gestapo . . . American to the last man" (Nov. 19, 1941). Characters like General Custer (Errol Flynn) in this film, Gil Martin (Henry Fonda) in *Drums along the Mohawk*, and Major Rogers (Spencer Tracy) in *Northwest Passage* provided Americans with patriotic heroes who fought the savage tribes, just as the allies were fighting the savage Germans and Japanese.

After the end of World War II, the image of the Savage begins to yield to that of the noble, peace-loving chief. For example, in *Apache Chief* (1949), Young Eagle, a peaceful chief, overcomes the hostile Black Wolf, and establishes peace with the whites. Another example is Chief Yellowstone (Iron Eyes Cody) in *Massacre River* (1949). Chief Yellowstone wants peace but must first control the hostile young braves of his tribe. After these braves attack some settlers and kill a white woman, Chief Yellowstone expresses sorrow for her death and not only promises peace, but gives his land to the settlers. This peace-loving and wise chief character type becomes a dominant one in the movies of the 1950s.

The Movies of the 1950s

In this decade, not only do westerns reach the height of their popularity, but they also show more sensitivity toward the history and social problems of their Native American characters. In 1950, *Broken Arrow* starts this trend with its characterization of the Apache chief, Cochise, as a peace-loving friend to a white man. Since the Apache were usually portrayed as one of the most hostile tribes, this movie marks a significant change in Hollywood's depiction of Native Americans, one that continues in *Battle at Apache Pass* (1951), *Conquest of Cochise* (1953), and *Taza, Son of Cochise* (1954). This new version of the Noble Red Man, a historical chief as a central positive character, becomes well established in the first half of the 1950s with the above movies about Cochise, plus *Seminole* (1953), *Sitting Bull* (1954), and *Chief Crazy Horse* (1955). Though notable films of the period such as *The Searchers* (1956) and *Run of the Arrow* (1957) still depict Native American tribes as savage and cruel, westerns like *Devil's Doorway* (1950) focus on the other side of the issue, the cruelty and prejudice of white society.

Broken Arrow (1950), based on Elliot Arnold's *Blood Brother*, a 1947 historical novel about Tom Jeffords and Cochise, is the first of the major westerns to portray a historical Native American leader as a heroic central character. Employing a technique common to sympathetic portrayals, the movie begins with voice-over by Jeffords in which he acknowledges the Apache language and by implication their culture as he tells the audience, "When the Apaches speak, they will be speaking in our language." Another such voice-over occurs a little later after Jeffords has nursed a wounded Apache boy back to health and, for this good deed, has been spared by Apache warriors, who shortly thereafter kill and torture miners for invading their land. He says, "I learned something that day. Apache women cried over their sons and Apache men had a sense of fair play." Throughout the film, as Jeffords learns more about the Apaches through his friendship with Cochise (Jeff Chandler) and his marriage to Sonseeahray (Deborah Paget), his voice-overs about what he has learned become a commentary aimed at building respect for Apache culture and Cochise.

The friendship of Jeffords and Cochise grows because they are both men of courage, intelligence, and honor. When Jeffords first meets Cochise, the camera favors the chief with low-angle and close-up shots, which emphasize his authority.

As the movie continues, such perspectives become a pattern, establishing him as a central character equal to Jeffords. From the beginning, Cochise is imbued with an intelligence that shows through in his dialogue with Jeffords and his interactions with his people. For example, when he tries to persuade the assembled bands of the Apache to accept his peace plan, he uses a pithy analogy: "If a big wind comes, a tree must bend or be lifted out by its roots." He also has a sense of humor, one example of which occurs when he sees Jeffords trying to impress Sonseeahray by what turns out to be a feeble shot of an arrow; he says to her, "Never mind, by the time he's a grown man, he'll know how." In addition to the cleverness of his dialogue, his intelligence comes out in the way he leads his warriors.

A good example of his military shrewdness occurs when a large wagon train, with soldiers hiding in the wagons, enters his land. Seen from a vantage point above the wagons, he directs his carefully planned and orchestrated attack by having lookouts in key locations shoot arrows to signal each group of his braves to attack at the appropriate times. With almost no casualties, his warriors rout the soldiers and take over the wagons and all the supplies in them. In the entire attack sequence, the camera angles show the confusion and vulnerability of the soldiers with high-angle, long-shot perspectives, and the superiority of Cochise and his men with low-angle medium and close-up views. This sequence, which marks a complete reversal in the portrayal and outcome of attacks on U.S. soldiers, is a significant instance of how this movie attempts to alter the stereotypes of Native Americans in westerns.

However, despite such good intentions on the part of the filmmakers, the characterization of Cochise as the heroic, peace-loving chief ultimately conforms to the Noble Red Man image. Just as Cochise's friend, Tom Jeffords, is contrasted to the crass townspeople and treacherous ranchers who kill his wife, so Cochise is set off against the savage Apache Geronimo (Jay Silverheels) and the other Apache rebels. Ultimately, Cochise is a heroic character because he learns the way of peace from his white friend and has the wisdom to accept the inevitability of white dominance in the West. Geronimo, on the other hand, is the hostile, rebellious Savage because he refuses to give in to the whites and honor a peace treaty. Near the end of the movie, after Cochise stops an attack by Geronimo's warriors, he says, "Let this peace hold. If it is broken, it must not be by Indians, not even bad Indians." As is true of characters drawn to the image of the Noble Red Man, Cochise is so good in all the ways that will make him pleasing to the white audience that he is diminished as a believable fictional character. As a character drawn to the reverse Savage image, the same is true of Geronimo. *New York Times* film critic Bosley Crowther picks up on this excess: "No, we cannot accept this picture as either an exciting or reasonable account of the attitudes and ways of American Indians. They merit justice, but not such patronage" (July 24, 1950).

Another way to appreciate how the movie falls back on the image of the Noble Red Man is to compare it to the novel. The film focuses on just a small part of Cochise's biography and never touches on the novel's depiction of Cochise's continuing depression over his brutal killing of a Mexican or his drinking and disillusion in later life, all "negative" but humanizing characteristics. In addition to sanitizing the character of Cochise, the movie adds a subplot that doesn't exist in the novel, the romance between Tom Jeffords and Sonseeahray. On one level, the marriage of the hero and an Apache woman heightens the theme of friendship between whites and Native Americans. However, as with the characterization of Cochise, the film ultimately conforms to a formula, namely the killing off of the Native American woman involved in such a mixed marriage. At the end of the film, after evil whites shoot Sonseeahray, she becomes not a believable character but only a symbol, a vehicle for concluding the theme of peace. When Tom Jeffords vows revenge for the killing of his wife, Cochise tells him, "You will bear this. Your loss has brought us together." Jeffords accepts the advice of his friend, and, as he rides off alone, says in a voice-over, "The death of Sonseeahray put a seal on the peace. . . . I always remembered my wife was with me." Like Nophaie in *The Vanishing American*, the Native American character who loves a white can ultimately only exist in the mind of his beloved, as a memory and as a martyr for the greater peace.

The theme of the peace-loving Noble Red Man continues with the depiction of Cochise in *Battle at Apache Pass* (1951). This movie is a sequel to *Broken Arrow* in that the two central characters of Cochise (Jeff Chandler) and Geronimo (Jay Silverheels) are played by the same actors and are again the contrasting friendly Noble Red Man and hostile Savage. However, unlike Tom Jeffords, the white friend of Cochise is a marginal character displaced by a power-hungry government agent who hates Cochise and his band because their attempt to keep the peace prohibits him from taking their land. To force Cochise to make war and thus break the treaty that protects his land, the evil agent aligns himself with Geronimo. The fierceness of Geronimo is established at the beginning of the film when he is seen from a low-angle rallying his rebellious band, and reinforced when he attacks a wagon train. As his men kill and mutilate men, women, and children, he grabs a terrified little girl and one of his braves carries off a woman.

While Geronimo is killing the families of the settlers, Cochise is first seen in a warm domestic setting with his beautiful wife, Nona (Susan Cabot), who is expecting a child. Though treated badly by the evil agent, he still insists on peace at a council meeting, during which Geronimo asks the warriors of Cochise to fight with him against the whites. However, Cochise persuades his people to keep the peace and enhances his status as leader by killing in hand-to-hand combat the hostile brave of Geronimo's band who had captured the woman from the wagon train. In an attempt to restore the peace, he takes the white woman to the fort, where a military doctor shows his gratitude by treating the wound Cochise received in the fight to save her.

This peaceful gesture only heightens the efforts of the villain, who gives guns to Geronimo and incites him to attack a ranch. After this attack, the arrogant young lieutenant who has replaced the friend of Cochise as commander of the fort tries to capture the chief and takes his wife as a hostage. When the lieutenant has some Apache prisoners hanged, Cochise must finally wage war. As he prepares for the battle, he tells his wife he is reluctant to leave her but now must go out and fight because "the soldiers like snakes have turned against the Apache." Cochise shrewdly traps the soldiers in a valley but cannot compete with their firepower. When the soldiers start killing and wounding not only the warriors but also women and children with their cannon fire, Cochise is forced to stop his attack. During this time of truce, the military doctor and the woman rescued by Cochise treat the wounds of his wife, Nona, and his friend takes control of the soldiers after the death of the villains.

Cochise, however, has only a moment of peace before Geronimo, who wants to continue the fighting, challenges him to a hand-to-hand battle. After a violent fight, he subdues Geronimo but refuses to kill him, so "he will live in shame, an outcast." Then he goes to his wife, who, with the help of the white woman, has just given birth to a son. After his friend tells him that the evil agent and Geronimo have been responsible for all the troubles between his tribe and the whites, Cochise says to him, "When the wounds heal, we will again speak of peace." At the end of this movie, Cochise is a sadder and more skeptical character than in *Broken Arrow* because he has seen more hostility from the whites and his own people and found that he lives in a world he can no longer control. This ending has a more realistic feeling than that of *Broken Arrow* and may be part of what prompted a contemporary *Variety* critic to write: "*Apache Pass* rates a large 'A' for its handling of Indian character and customs. The redmen emerge as human beings instead of in the characteristic rigging to which they are usually fated" (Apr. 2, 1952).

In *Conquest of Cochise* (1953), Cochise (John Hodiak) again is committed to peace even though he faces hostility from white villains, his own tribe, and his former allies, the Comanche. This version of the story, which a contemporary *Variety* film reviewer sees as a "sympathetic treatment of the problems of Indians" (Aug. 26, 1953), begins with scenes of warriors attacking a Mexican settlement and a voice-over that tells of the earlier alliance of the dreaded Apache and Comanche. Against this historical background emerges Cochise, who has decided to keep the peace with whites because he knows great numbers of them will keep coming to the West. After meeting with the hero, who will become his friend, Cochise promises to advise his Apache warriors to keep the peace with the whites. Seen from a low angle, which reinforces his stature as a hero and a perspective that becomes a pattern, he tells a council of his tribe that he wants peace, but if war becomes necessary the tribe should fight the Comanche rather than the Americans. One of his rebellious warriors, Tukiwah (Steven Ritch), opposes him and warns of the danger of fighting the Comanche. The contrast between a peace-loving character and a bellicose one occurs again when Cochise meets with the Comanche at their camp. The hostile chief of the Comanche, Running Cougar (Joseph Waring) is for war with the Mexicans, and Red Knife (Rodd Redwing) is for peace.

When Chief Running Cougar and his hostile braves decide to attack the Mexicans, Cochise and his loyal warriors intervene and not only rescue the Mexicans but also kill some of the Comanche. This turns Red Knife and Tukiwah against

Cochise and both the Comanche and hostile Apaches threaten war against the whites. Cochise, however, still holds out for peace, even after the henchman of the villain kills his beloved Terua (Carol Thurston) with a shot meant for him. After this, his white friend tries to find the killer of Terua and thwart the efforts of the villain who, like the one in *Battle at Apache Pass*, foments war to get land from the Apaches. In the meantime, Cochise attacks the Mexicans and takes one of their women as a hostage.

Though Cochise does this to bring the hero to his camp, the beautiful female allows the filmmakers to expand his character to a romantic lead and spokesman for his culture. Even though the woman interrupts Cochise during the ceremonial funeral of Terua, he seems happy to teach her about Apache culture. He tells her that because "survival is our religion," the boys and girls are taught in the same way and one of their early lessons is to run four miles holding water in their mouths. As he goes on to describe their cosmology and courting and marriage customs, the woman is clearly falling for him. When she finally kisses him, he allows that "it is a superior custom." The noble Cochise has won the heart of the woman to whom his white friend is also attracted. At this point, however, a potential war with the Americans, not love, is his main concern. He must once again deal with hostile warriors in his tribe and with the warlike Comanche. After the hero brings in the man who killed Terua, Cochise is able to stop the war dance of his warriors.

When Cochise goes to the Comanche camp to ask for peace, the hostile warriors take control and torture him with boiling water, knife cuts from warriors on horses, and burning at the stake. Just as he is about to be killed, his friend and the soldiers come to the rescue. Then, just as the Comanche are about to overwhelm the outnumbered soldiers, Tukiwah and the Apache warriors arrive and drive off the hostiles. Finally, Cochise has not only gained the support of his former rival, Tukiwah, but also has achieved a lasting peace. At the end, the peace-loving chief makes one last noble gesture: he gives up, for complicated reasons, the beautiful Mexican woman, who sadly rides off with the hero.

Such peace-loving Cochise characters, which contrast with hostile warriors in and outside their tribe, also appear in *Fort Apache* (1948), *I Killed Geronimo* (1950), *Indian Uprising* (1952), and *Taza, Son of Cochise* (1954). In this latter movie, the story of Cochise (Jeff Chandler) comes to a close after his death. Shortly thereafter, Taza (Rock Hudson), his noble son, wins the peace by fighting his hostile brother, Naiche (Bart Roberts), and the warriors of Geronimo (Ian MacDonald) who have been supplied with guns by the villain. The image of the noble, peace-loving historical chief, again contrasted with hostile warriors, continues with the depiction of Tecumseh in *Brave Warrior* (1952) and the title character in *Chief Crazy Horse* (1955) (for further discussion, see Biskind 1983, 230–45).

Two other representative examples of this character type are Chief Osceola in *Seminole* (1953) and the title character in *Sitting Bull* (1954). Described in the beginning as "Taken from the pages of History," *Seminole* (1953) tells the story of Osceola (Anthony Quinn), the peaceful mixed-blood chief, the white woman he loves, Revere Muldoon (Barbara Hale), and his white friend, a young officer who has known him from childhood. In contrast to these positive characters are an ambitious, hateful military leader who thinks the Seminoles stand in the way of progress and a hostile Seminole warrior, Kayjeck (Hugh O'Brian). In a flashback, which comprises much of the film, the hero, who had been sent to the fort as junior officer, tells of the events leading to the death of his friend. The sad story begins when the evil commander sends him to the camp of Osceola to persuade his friend to come to the fort for a peace parley. During their meeting, Osceola, seen in low-angle and close-up shots that emphasize his authority, is portrayed as an educated man who acknowledges that his tribe cannot prevail over the ever-growing number of whites. He is a man torn between his responsibilities to his tribe, his appreciation of white culture, derived from his education at white schools, and his love for a white woman. With the help of his wise old friend, Kulak (Ralph Moody), he finally convinces Kayjeck and his warriors that they should not attack the soldiers, until he goes to the fort to negotiate a peace treaty. However, unknown to the hero, the commander's offer of a peace talk is only a trick. When Osceola and his friend return to the fort, the commander has him seized and imprisoned in an underground cage. Though Revere Muldoon tries to bring help, his own tribesman, Kayjeck, kills Osceola, who has become the victim of treachery and his own divided loyalties. As the story continues, however, his death will ultimately be an occasion for a peaceful resolution of the hostilities between his tribe and the whites.

Meanwhile, the evil commander, who desperately wants to make a name for himself, forces the hero and his troops to make a deadly trek through the swamps to attack the stronghold of the Seminoles. Many of the soldiers die, either from the rigors of the march, or during the attacks by the Seminole warriors. When the hero finally rebels against his leader, he is framed and sentenced to death by a firing squad. At the last moment, the white woman rescues him by bringing Kayjeck and the Seminole warriors, who surround the fort and stop the execution. Kayjeck exonerates the hero and reveals his own treachery and collaboration with the evil commander, who will be punished by an honorable general who has come to the fort. As the Seminoles, described as "a proud people," leave the fort in a procession carrying the body of Osceola, the general says, "Perhaps we see the beginning of a new way of life," and the hero replies, "I know these people well and really believe that they would like to live with us in peace."

This ending, with its optimistic promise of a new era of peace between the Native Americans and whites, is typical of the peace-loving chief films. Like Sonseeahray in *Broken Arrow*, Osceola becomes a martyr who helps to establish new opportunities for peace. Though this film leans toward the other extreme of the Noble Red Man, it does continue a positive new direction. However, the upbeat ending of the film also blatantly distorts history to provide the kind of orderly closure standard in 1950s westerns.

A final representative movie, *Sitting Bull* (1954), follows the same patterns of characters and plot as in the other examples. Sitting Bull (J. Carrol Naish) must face Crazy Horse (Iron Eyes Cody), his hostile adversary in the tribe, and must deal with the military hero sympathetic to the tribe, who gets into trouble for his attitudes. He also must confront an ambitious, disobedient military leader, General Custer, a villainous Indian agent, and President Grant, who promises peace at the end. The film begins (and ends) with a chorus singing a rather jaunty hymn, "Great Spirit," and then the voice-over of Sitting Bull telling of the hostility of the seven Lakota warrior tribes because the whites have come in great numbers to the sacred Black Hills. Sitting Bull immediately shows his desire for peace after hostile warriors from his tribe led by Crazy Horse attack a wagon train. Seen in a close-up, Sitting Bull stops the attack and has his men take only the supplies of miners who are illegally in the land of his tribe. Unlike Crazy Horse and the chiefs of the other hostile tribes, Sitting Bull has the wisdom typical in such peace-loving characters. He understands that, because of the vast number of whites, the only way his people will survive is to make peace with them. However, like the Cochise characters, he will be pushed to the extreme to keep the peace.

Sitting Bull's first test comes when the evil agent at Red Rock kills his son, Young Buffalo (Felix Gonzalez), after the young man helped captured members of his tribe escape from the horrible stockade at the agency. Even after this terrible provocation, Sitting Bull prays to the Great Spirit and decides to make one last attempt for peace by negotiating with President Grant. However, he is tested again when Custer and his soldiers come to the Black Hills during the gold rush and kill some Sioux warriors. After gathering all the tribes, Sitting Bull again argues for peace and gets his way after his white friend not only defeats the warlike Crazy Horse in a traditional hand-to-hand fight, but also promises to bring President Grant to the West for peace talks with the tribe. Finally, however, when Custer disobeys orders and decides to attack the united tribes, Sitting Bull and the other chiefs must declare war and meet Custer in the battle of Little Big Horn.

After the battle and the victory, which Sitting Bull never wanted, the hero helps the chief and his tribe escape and then is sentenced to death for his actions. In a scene like the one at the end of Seminole, the hero is about to be executed when his woman brings Sitting Bull to the rescue. The chief speaks to President Grant: "For many years I have tried to keep the peace. This man understood and risked his life for peace. For all time the Indians will respect this man. The Great White Chief will let this man live and the Indians and whites can again sit in peace council." President Grant agrees and the film ends with a low-angle close-up of Sitting Bull and the hymn "Great Spirit" playing in the background. Such an optimistic ending, like that of Broken Arrow and the other films with peace-loving chiefs, is, of course, far removed from the brutal history of the Plains Indian wars.

Though the portrayal of historical chiefs as Noble Red Men reflects a growing sympathy for Native American characters, the opposing image of the Savage still appears in some of the best westerns of this period. The saddest example, which will be treated briefly here, is John Ford's The Searchers (1956), possibly the best western of any period. The hero, Ethan Edwards, knows the culture and language of the Comanche well and hates the tribe so intensely that he shoots the eyes out of a dead brave to condemn him to wander blindly in the spirit world. Later he keeps firing at a herd of buffalo just so the tribe will have less to eat in the winter. Though he has some reason for his feelings, his hatred overreaches the motivation, much like that of Major Rogers in *Northwest Passage*. Also like Rogers, he is clearly the hero, who is literally looked up to in low-angle shots throughout the film, and his attitude is that to know the Comanche is to hate them. Another film of this kind, though not as overtly racist as *The Searchers*, is *Run of the Arrow*, which portrays the Sioux tribe in the image of the Savage.

Though *Run of the Arrow* also takes a harsh view of white culture after the Civil War, it focuses on the savagery of the Sioux warriors. The hero, who hates the Yankees, escapes from the south to the far west and meets a drunken old Sioux scout, Walking Coyote (J. C. Flippen), who tells him that the word *Sioux* means "fierce enemy." Though the hero responds, "I'd like to be one, I'm a cutthroat too," he eventually finds out that even he cannot live the code of the warrior. Shortly thereafter, the two men come upon Sioux warriors of Blue Buffalo (Charles Bronson) who have attacked and burned a wagon and are drinking whiskey they found on one of the wagons. While they watch, Crazy Wolf (H. M. Wynant), the most hostile of the warriors, captures them and they agree to the run of the arrow, a ritual in which a barefoot captive starts at the distance of an arrow shot from the bow of the pursuer and then tries to outrun him. Crazy Wolf easily kills Walking Coyote and then is closing in on the hero when a woman from the tribe, Yellow Moccasin (Sarita Montiel), rescues him. After she nurses him back to health they fall in love, and he decides to join the tribe and live with her.

Soon his adopted tribe comes in contact with the cavalry, led by a cocky young officer who looks down on the Sioux. Despite an attempt at a peace talk, hostility breaks out when Crazy Wolf kills a soldier. After several skirmishes, the Sioux finally attack and burn the camp of the soldiers, a scene that ends in a high-angle shot that emphasizes the devastation. This fierce attack and the torturing of the evil soldier by skinning him alive are too much for the hero, who puts the man, his mortal enemy during the Civil War, out of his misery by shooting him. Yellow Moccasin comments on his reaction, "You could not watch the man be skinned. You are an American (not a Sioux)." Convinced that he can't live by the code of the Sioux warrior, he leaves with Yellow Moccasin and a mute boy for an uncertain future. Though the film offers a cynical view of both white and Native American behavior, it clearly suggests that the uniqueness or "otherness" of Sioux culture is defined by its harshness and cruelty. *Run of the Arrow*, then, despite its complex and grim view of life on the plains after the Civil War, certainly plays upon the racist image of the Savage in its depiction of the Sioux.

On the other hand, the last of the representative movies, *Devil's Doorway* (1950), takes a dark look at a white society defined by its greed, cruelty, and prejudice. Portraying the Shoshone tribe as noble victims, this film tells the sad story of (Broken) Lance Poole (Robert Taylor), a Shoshone who fought with the whites in the Civil

War and won the Congressional Medal of Honor. However, when he returns to his ranch in Wyoming, he soon finds out from his friend, Red Rock (James Mitchell), and his father that he will not be treated as a hero at home. His father, referring to the whites, who have taken much of the Shoshone land and are now after their ranch, tells him, "Our people are doomed. An Indian without land loses his heart and soul with it." Soon Lance finds out that the local whites and sheepherders new to the area, many of them spurred on by a hateful old lawyer, are deeply prejudiced toward him and want his land. He also finds a female lawyer sympathetic to his plight, who not only works to secure his rights, but also falls in love with him. However, after he loses an appeal to homestead his land because, ironically, he is not considered an American citizen according to Wyoming law, he decides to fight for his land.

Joined by a starving band of Shoshone led by the old Chief Thundercloud (Chief John Big Tree), Lance makes his last stand on his land, which is known as Sweet Meadows. When the lawyer he loves asks him to make concessions to those who are coming, he tells her, "It's hard to understand how an Indian feels about the land. I know I belong. If we lose it now we might as well be dead." After a big fight with the townspeople and sheepherders, the U.S. Cavalry arrives for the final confrontation. Again his beloved lawyer begs him to surrender, but he refuses, telling her not to cry because "a hundred years from now it might have worked." After putting on his Civil War uniform, he walks out of his house and is shot as he offers to give up if the Shoshone women and children are allowed to go to the reservation. As he is about to die, he tells a boy from the tribe that he is the "man" who will take them back to the reservation. Then, seen in a low-angle shot, he salutes and falls to the ground, a noble character who would have been a hero in a world not filled with greed and prejudice.

Like *Broken Arrow* and the other movies with peace-loving chiefs, *Devil's Doorway* attempts to tell the story of the westward expansion from a perspective sympathetic to the tribes involved. *New York Times* critic Bosley Crowther writes, "Perhaps it is too late now to change the course of fiction which has established the American Indian as a ruthless savage, but our movie makers appear to be endeavoring to right some of the wrongs they themselves have done the red man over the years" (Nov. 10, 1950). Though movies like *The Searchers* and *Run of the Arrow* keep the racism of the Savage image alive, a significant number of the filmmakers do attempt to "right the wrongs" of this image. In spite of their good intentions, however, their films usually move to the opposite extreme of the Noble Red Men. Though such characters appeal to the sense of law and order in this period, they are finally too good to be believed and too divorced from history to be taken seriously.

In the tradition of the classic Hollywood cinema, the western plots of this decade regularly take a page out of melodrama and place rebellious and peace-loving characters in violent opposition. And the resolutions always reward peace-loving Native Americans and punish the rebellious savages. As would be expected in the Eisenhower years (1953–1961) when devotion to law and order and peace between nations was at a high point, the plots of the very popular westerns, with a few notable exceptions, establish a view of the frontier as a place where Native Americans and whites can live in peace. This view continues in the early movies of the 1960s until America become seriously involved in the Vietnam War.

Movies of the 1960s

The sympathetic portrayal of Native American characters continues in this decade during which the popularity of the western begins to decline. The degree to which the positive images of the 1950s had become ingrained is echoed in an early 1960s review of *Geronimo* (1962). The *Variety* critic begins with an exclamation: "They sure don't make Injun pictures the way they used to." Then, bemoaning the loss of the "uninhibited action ingredients that characterized the early indifferent-to-racial-stereotypes westerns," he concludes: "In some ways the modern Indian picture may be better, but something haunting and stirring has been lost in the metamorphosis" (Apr. 25, 1962). Though "the uninhibited action" of attacks by hostile tribes still occurs in the westerns of this period, some notable films, like their predecessors in the 1950s, depict Native Americans as positive, heroic central characters who must struggle with life on reservations.

In *Geronimo* (1962), the perennial, rebellious, hostile leader becomes an honorable, peace-loving chief who wins new rights for his people. *Cheyenne Autumn* (1964) depicts Dull Knife and Little Wolf as heroes who lead their people from a bleak Oklahoma reservation on an epic journey back to their homeland. In *Hombre* (1967) and *Tell Them Willie Boy Is Here* (1969) the heroes fight for their identity and survival in a West where their tribes suffer the indignities of reservation life. Even *The Stalking Moon* (1968), in which the central Apache character is an avenging Savage, expresses hostility in the context of a defeated and driven tribe. Finally, in *Flaming Star* (1960), a heroic mixed-blood and his noble Kiowa mother suffer the prejudice of both white and Native American society. Though the characters of these movies are still drawn to the extremes of the Noble Red Man and Savage images, they do reveal a continuing change of attitude in the western.

The early positive attitude reveals itself in the plot of *Geronimo* (1962), in which this fierce, proud warrior, driven to rebellion by a crooked Indian agent, finally becomes a family man who is willing to make peace with friendly, honest whites. Geronimo's adversaries are the Bible-spouting Indian agent who sees Apaches as "children of the devil" and the captain who feels Geronimo's band is "nothing but a pack of dirty wild animals." On the other hand, two good whites, a lieutenant who respects the rights of the tribe, Lt. John Delany (Adam West), and an honorable Senator Conrad (Denver Pyle), eventually enable Geronimo (Chuck Connors) to choose a peaceful resolution. The other character that helps Geronimo evolve into a peace-loving chief is Teela (Kamala Devi), the educated woman from his tribe who bears his son and thus gives him a reason for making peace.

Seen in a pattern of close-ups and low-angle shots from the beginning, Geronimo is established as a powerful central character in contrast to the other Apaches. His friend Mangas (Ross Martin) has capitulated and is trying to grow crops in the barren land to support his wife and baby son. And Teela, Geronimo's wife, teaches the Apache children to read the white man's books. When Geronimo shoots an arrow into her book to show his disdain, she tells him he should learn to read and he responds, "I want them to respect me for what I am, not what they want me to be." However, when the Indian agent sells Apache land to a cattleman, even Mangas joins his friend in declaring war against the evil whites. Though Teela still resists the decision to start a war, she clearly will follow the lead of her beloved Geronimo.

After Geronimo and his warriors steal horses and escape from the reservation, he tells them the strategy behind his declaration of war, "We can win because we don't have a chance. We will fight long enough so Americans will wonder why such a people must fight and will make a treaty that will recognize the honor and dignity of the Apaches." As he and his warriors continue their war, Geronimo shows his skill by silently overcoming a patrol of soldiers and, later, by an efficient attack on a wagon train in which his warriors take over the food wagons with tactics as clever as those of Cochise in *Broken Arrow*. Even during this attack, Geronimo thinks of Teela and takes a book (ironically, the U.S. Army Regulations) for her. After overcoming her resistance and taking her from the reservation, Geronimo starts to change when they declare their love and Teela tells him she is pregnant. Geronimo responds, "He will be a fine warrior, but maybe he should read." Despite this domestic interlude and signs that his strategy is affecting public opinion, however, hunger and a growing number of soldiers drive Geronimo's band to the point where surrender seems their only answer, especially as the evil captain sets up cannons, which can hit their location. Even when his warrior Natchez (Armando Silvestre) calls for surrender, Geronimo holds out and fights back by shooting a flaming arrow to blow up the soldiers' powder. However, when Teela has their son, he finally changes his mind.

As Geronimo approaches the baby, Teela begs him to surrender so his son will not be killed, and he replies, "I wondered if I am right [to surrender]; when I look at you and the child I stop wondering." And on cue, the honorable senator and good lieutenant walk up the hill and offer Geronimo a fair treaty. Smiling at Teela, Geronimo accepts and he and his people walk down the hill to join the whites in a life of peace. Hence the great hostile warrior of the 1950 films also becomes a peaceful-loving chief. From *Broken Arrow* to this film, such orderly, happy endings are typical of the plots, which depict historical chiefs as central heroic characters. Making a statement that could apply to any of these films, a *Variety* critic comments on the ending of *Geronimo*: "The picture has an uplift ending that may fool youngsters into concluding that the Indians ultimately got a decent shake-a false note of resolution contradicted to this day" (Apr. 25, 1962). Such fantasy resolutions, however, become rarer later in the period, though the next representative film, *Cheyenne Autumn* (1964), follows a similar pattern.

Based on the historical novel of the same name by Mari Sandoz, *Cheyenne Autumn* portrays historical chiefs Dull Knife (Gilbert Roland) and Little Wolf (Ricardo Montalban) as heroic central characters who survive against great odds until they, as was the case in Geronimo, are offered a treaty by a good government official. John Ford saw this epic story of the Cheyenne as his chance to make amends for the way he and other directors of westerns had depicted Native American characters: "There are two sides to every story, but I wanted to show their [Native Americans] point of view for a change. Let's face it, we've treated them very badly—it's a blot on our shield; we've cheated and robbed, killed, murdered, massacred and everything else, but they kill one white man and, God, out come the troops" (Bogdanovich 1968, 104). To accomplish his purpose, Ford not only uses honorable chiefs as central characters, but also establishes a white hero, Tom Archer, who respects the Cheyenne and is a sympathetic voice-over narrator, much like Tom Jeffords in *Broken Arrow*.

John Ford also acknowledges the Cheyenne language by using it for the dialogue between members of the tribe. He further builds respect for the uniqueness of the tribe through the attitudes of Tom Archer and his friend, the Polish sergeant. Archer shows his appreciation when he says to the Quaker woman. "All you've seen are reservation Indians. The Cheyenne are the greatest fighters in the world, fierce, smart and meaner than sin." The Polish sergeant shows empathy for the Cheyenne by pointing out the parallel between the Cossacks attempt to exterminate his people and the U.S. Army's attempt to kill off the Cheyenne. Throughout the film, Tom Archer's voice-overs emphasize the suffering and heroism of the Cheyenne as they escape from the Oklahoma reservation and make the dangerous trek to their homeland in the north.

In addition to using this technique, Ford and the screenwriter also imbue the characters of Dull Knife and Little Wolf with the intelligence to speak with simple eloquence and fight with shrewd tactics. For example, Little Wolf responds to an officer, "We are asked to remember much; the white man remembers nothing." And later he says, "Even a dog can go where he likes, but not a Cheyenne." The cleverness of the Cheyenne leaders, however, goes beyond their words. When superior numbers of the cavalry draw close, Little Wolf and Dull Knife direct their warriors to start grass fires, which not only put the cavalry into disarray but also give the warriors a cover from which to shoot. The shrewdness and tenacity of these chiefs, who are emphasized as heroes by patterns of close low-angle shots, enable their people to hold out until Tom Archer and the good secretary of the interior can come to their rescue.

As in *Geronimo*, just as the Cheyenne are trapped by the cavalry and have artillery trained on them, the hero and honorable government official praise the heroism of the tribe and offer them a treaty. The official tells them, "You have made one of the most heroic marches in history." Then when Dull Knife asks him who will tell about Fort Robinson, the place where many of his people were killed, he promises to inform those in government. After the two chiefs accept the treaty, Little Wolf kills the rebellious young son of Dull Knife and Spanish Woman (Dolores Del Rio), Red Shirt (Sal Mineo), because the young warrior had stolen one of his wives. Then Little Wolf gives Dull Knife the medicine bundle, which had earlier been given to him by the old Chief Tall Tree (Victor Jory) and, seen from a low angle, he rides off into the horizon. As is typical in the peace-loving chief films, the rebellious warrior must be punished while the noble characters that accept peaceful coexistence with the whites are rewarded with new land and opportunities.

To tell the Cheyenne's side of the story, Ford relies on the image of the Noble Red Man and thereby distorts the historical novel from which the film was adapted. He depicts Little Wolf as a noble character to the end, even though he kills the son of Dull Knife. On the other hand, in Mari Sandoz's historical novel a drunken Little Wolf kills, for no immediate good reason, a member of his tribe who had earlier flirted with his wives. For this shameful act, he spends the rest of his life in exile. In a much more obvious way than in the novel, Ford contrasts his noble chiefs to cruel, unfeeling whites like the cowboy who kills a starving Cheyenne for his scalp, or the fanatical German commander of Fort Robinson who shows the Cheyenne no mercy. Such a depiction of the two chiefs as Noble Red Men who are badly treated by whites does build a kind of sympathy for the Cheyenne. *New York Times* critic Bosley Crowther believed that the film "is a stark and eye-opening symbolization of a shameful tendency that has prevailed in our national life—the tendency to be unjust and heartless to weaker people who get in the way of manifest destiny" (Dec. 24, 1964). Ford's *Cheyenne Autumn* does tell an important side of American history, but the noble Native American characters are more symbols of white exploitation than believable characters in themselves, as they are in the novel of Mari Sandoz.

Later in the decade, *Hombre* (1967) also treats the theme of Native Americans reduced to living on reservations and exploited by greedy whites, though with a much less positive ending than *Cheyenne Autumn*. The hero, John Russell, is a white man raised by the Apache who rejects the greed and prejudice of white society and chooses the harsh, but honorably self-contained, life of the Apache. First seen dressed as an Apache with his two friends from the tribe, Russell finds out he has inherited a boarding house from the man who gave him his white name. His Mexican friend encourages him to take the inheritance with a statement that turns out to be sadly ironic: "It pays to be a white man now. Put yourself on the winning side for once." After selling the house, Russell joins a group of people on a stagecoach and encounters the kind of prejudice he knows well as an adopted Apache. One young wife says that she knows what Apaches do to white women, and the other woman, the wife of the crooked Indian agent from the San Carlos Reservation, says she can't imagine eating a dog like the Apache. Russell asks her if she has ever been hungry and then tells her that, as an Apache, he has eaten dog and "lived like one." After hearing this, the wife insists Russell not ride in the stage.

When villains hold up the stage, take the agent's wife hostage and later pin down the rest of the group at an abandoned mine, Russell is the only one who can save them. Accepting this role with quiet resignation, he decides to call the bluff of the villains only after he finds out that the agent has stolen a large amount of money from the Apache at San Carlos. As the wife of the agent, whom the robbers have staked out in the sun, begs for help, Russell at first shows his anger toward the woman's prejudice and refuses to help her. When the one woman in the party who admires him asks why, he responds, "Up there in the mountains, there's a whole people who have lost everything. They don't have a place to spread their blessings. They've been insulted, diseased, made drunk and foolish. I know the men who did this as white men and I don't respect them." Finally, Russell decides to go down and take on the villains because he knows he's the only one who can ensure that the money stolen from his people at San Carlos by the Indian agent will be returned to them.

In the ensuing shootout, Russell is fatally wounded, but he dies knowing that he has paid his debt to his adopted tribe. The last shot of this man who dies for his people is a high-angle close-up of his face followed by a cut to a grainy picture of him as a boy with the Apache. Commenting on this last scene, Bosley Crowther in the *New York Times* notes that his death is "mindful of the selfless sacrifices made by the Indian hero in *Broken Arrow*" (Mar. 22, 1967). Though Cochise doesn't lose his life at the end of that movie, the comparison is apt because John Russell's devotion to his adopted tribe does transform him into a version of the doomed Noble Red Man.

Another later movie that deals with Apaches after they have been conquered and put on reservations is *The Stalking Moon* (1968). In this movie, however, the Apache character, Salvaje (Nathaniel Narcisco), is a renegade bent on vengeance and a notable example of the Savage image in this period. The beginning of the movie emphasizes the sad state of the Apache as the hero and some soldiers round up a small starving band, which includes a white woman, Sarah Carver, and her mixed-blood son (Noland Clay), fathered by Salvaje. The soldiers reveal their attitude toward the Apache when they look at the woman, and one says, "I wonder what she went through all those years?" Another comments, "God only knows what's going on in that woman's head." Because she knows her Apache husband, Salvaje, is close behind, she asks the hero, the leader of the troop, Sam Varner, to take her and the boy with him. Finally he agrees and they head toward his ranch in New Mexico, though that place will offer no escape from the fierce Salvaje.

As Salvaje searches for his son he leaves a bloody trail of destruction, killing three men in a wagon, all the men and women (and even the hero's horse) at two stage stations, and a group of Mexicans. When the hero realizes Salvaje has arrived at his ranch and the woman, whom he now loves, offers to leave, he says, "Dead people all the way across Arizona. If I can, I have to stop it." Thus starts his deadly confrontation with Salvaje, during which the savage warrior beats up the white woman, kills the hero's Mexican farm hand and his dog, and murders his mixed-blood friend, Nick Tana (Robert Forster). Through all this Salvaje, whose name means "ghost," remains a hidden enemy who is always there but is seen only in flashes until the final fight, during which he charges and jumps on the hero even after being shot several times. The portrayal of this savage character prompted a

Variety critic, who apparently had read the Theodore Olsen novel of the same name, to comment: "Salvaje never is developed so as to project the terror force he is supposed to be. Instead he is little more than a savage Indian" (Dec. 18, 1968). Indeed, this character, though he has reasons for his vengeance, overreaches so violently in his revenge that he becomes the typical Savage.

The next representative movie, *Tell Them Willie Boy Is Here* (1969), is also a dark portrayal of the hero, Willie (Robert Blake), who is a renegade like Salvaje, but also a sympathetic character victimized by white prejudice. The first high-angle shots of Willie as he leaves a freight train and runs through the rocky desert terrain establish him as a pursued man, an image that persists until his death near the end. When Willie arrives in the town near the reservation he immediately encounters the old prejudice: as he buys a yellow scarf for his girlfriend, Lola (Katherine Ross), the store keeper says (in a statement that turns out to be ironic), "You're going to make some squaw happy tonight." And when he tries to get in a game at the pool hall, a man tells him, "Why don't you get back to the reservation where you belong?" Willie's real trouble, however, starts when he kills Lola's father. As they start their escape, Willie says to Lola, "One way or the other you die at the end. Nobody gives a damn what Indians do, nobody!" Though on one level what he says is true, his words are also ironic because the murder draws in not only the local sheriff and the female Indian agent who feels she owns Lola and her tribe, but also the press, who make a big story out of the fugitives' attempt to escape the sheriff and his posse.

When Willie eludes the posse by shooting their horses, Lola says to him, "You can't beat them." And he replies, "Maybe, but they'll know I was here." He also dismisses the possibility of surrendering and going back to prison: "Indians don't last in prison. They weren't born for it like whites." Finally, they arrive at the old village and Willie puts on the Ghost Dance shirt of his father (such shirts were originally believed to stop the bullets of the soldiers). The scene ends with Lola vowing to never leave him. Shortly thereafter, the sheriff finds Lola lying on her back, wearing the white dress she originally wore to please the female Indian agent, with the yellow scarf Willie gave her covering the gunshot wound from which she died. Two members of Lola's tribe who are with the sheriff have different opinions about the mystery of her death; one feels that Willie followed the warrior tradition of killing one's wife to save her from the enemy, and the other thinks she killed herself so she wouldn't hold him back.

Whatever the truth of her death, Willie continues to run, as the camera cuts between tracking shots of him moving through the rough terrain with his rifle on his shoulder and low-angle shots of the sheriff pursuing on his horse. As he promised he would, he finally catches up with Willie, who is sitting on a high rock. Clearly Willie has let him come close, and, when Willie stands up and turns, he shoots him, only to find out that Willie's rifle is empty. Thus the inexorable pursuit by the sheriff, who is the son of an Indian fighter, ends with the death of a Native American who never really had a chance. A *Variety* critic comments on this ending:

"(in a sense, repeating the whole white-Indian history in America) is what the film is about" (Oct. 22, 1969). This film from the end of the decade reflects the kind of heavy and ironic social criticism typical of the Vietnam War era.

The last representative movie (from the beginning of this period), *Flaming Star* (1960) is a less political but even more overt and heavy-handed critique of racial prejudice than *Tell Them Willie Boy Is Here*. Like *Broken Lance* (1954), this movie deals with prejudice toward a Native American wife of a white man, Neddy Burton (Dolores Del Rio), and her mixed-blood son, Pacer (Elvis Presley). These two characters, who are often seen together, first appear at a large dinner at the Burton ranch. As they sit together at the table, their conversation about their friends reveals the first hints of prejudice toward them, a prejudice that grows deadly after warriors from Neddy's Kiowa tribe attack and kill their neighbors. When the other ranchers come to the Burton ranch and question their loyalty because "a Kiowa squaw" lives with them, the deadly battle between their white friends and the Burtons begins with the killing of the Burton's cattle. Another striking example of prejudice occurs while Neddy and Pacer are alone at the ranch. Two men ride up and ask for food, and Neddy, with her characteristic warmth and hospitality, starts to prepare a meal. However, after they make a comment about "Injuns living in a house like this" and one of them tries to kiss Neddy, she deftly defends herself and kicks them out of the house. Then Pacer takes over and avenges this affront to his mother by severely beating the two men. Pacer and his mother hug at the end of the scene, but this will be their only triumph over the forces of prejudice.

In addition to the prejudice of the whites, Pacer and Neddy must deal with the anger of the Kiowa led by Buffalo Horn (Rudolfo Acosta), who tries to persuade Pacer to fight with him against the whites. Referring to the ranchers' unending encroachment on their traditional lands, he tells Pacer, "We have no place to go. We have to fight or die. This is the great fight of our dreams. If I have a one-half white leave his father's people and fight for his mother's people, I will have great medicine." Pacer resists turning against his father and brother, who truly love him and his mother, but he reluctantly agrees to accompany Neddy to the Kiowa camp and then says, "They ain't my people. To tell you the truth, I don't know who's my people. Maybe I ain't got any." At the camp, Pacer sits in the circle of warriors, exchanges jokes with them and smokes the pipe, while his mother sits with her family. Though this scene establishes the Kiowa as honorable people who have been pushed into fighting the whites, it also shows that Neddy and Pacer no longer fit into the ways of the tribe.

On their way back to the ranch, one of their former friends who had been wounded by the Kiowa shoots Neddie and Two Moons (Perry Lopez), an event that finally forces Pacer to choose sides in the fighting. After a cowardly doctor resists helping Neddy and she dies, Pacer's pent-up feelings about the prejudice come out: "All Ma and me ever got was dirty looks." Now he will go to war against the whites, though he tells Buffalo Horn he will never fight his father and brother. During the fighting, however, the Kiowa wounds his white brother, and

Pacer goes against the tribe by rescuing him. At this point, Pacer takes off his shirt and uses his brother's blood as war paint and kills some of the warriors in hand-to-hand combat. When his brother tells him that he is hopelessly outnumbered, Pacer responds, "If it's going to be like this for the rest of my life, to hell with it." Pacer's situation is indeed hopeless, and the next day, when he returns (with his shirt on) to the town where his brother was taken, he is fatally wounded. As he rides away into the horizon to face his flaming star of death, he says, "Maybe someday, somewhere, people will understand people like us."

New York Times critic A. H. Weiler wrote that this unhappy ending "seems to underline the sadness of the period when the Indian began to vanish" (Dec. 17, 1960). Pacer's final cry for understanding and the reviewer's interpretation of the ending offer an appropriate perspective for a conclusion. During this period, overt sympathy for Native American characters becomes more the rule than the exception. However, the motivation of the sympathy is often a sentimental attitude like that of the above reviewer, one that sees the characters as Noble but doomed Red Men, victims of the inevitable march of white civilization. Though such an attitude is well intentioned, it falls short of any real empathy for the Native American characters.

In numerous 1960s films depicting the plight of the Noble Red Man, guilt often mixes with excessive sympathy. Later in the 1960s when the Vietnam War becomes a painful experience for everyone, such sympathy gives way to political and moral indignation that leads to grim westerns such as *The Stalking Moon* and *Tell Them Willie Boy Is Here* (1969). This moral indignation grows even stronger in the anti-westerns of the 1970s.

Movies of the 1970s

This decade of the anti-western with its dark, cynical views of American values, occasioned in part by the Vietnam War, is exemplified in *Little Big Man* (1970). In the words of its director, Arthur Penn, this film "challenges the notion that the heroes of America are the ones you read about in history books. It challenges the glorification of the gunfighter and the simple proposition that the cavalry was the good guys and the Indians the bad guys" (Calder 1977, 213). Such a purpose leads Penn to make the Cheyenne the "good guys," and a similar revisionist purpose informs the portrayal of Native American characters in other anti-westerns of this era. In *A Man Called Horse* (1970), a movie that claims to be an authentic depiction of a Sioux band's spirituality and rituals, a band of warriors captures the hero, John Morgan, and ultimately transforms him into the warrior, Man Called Horse. *Ulzana's Raid* (1972) gives a harsh view of Apache warriors whose guerrilla culture cannot survive in a changing West. And in *The Outlaw Josey Wales* (1976), a movie that plays against many of the western formulas, three Native American characters are the only equals to the hero in a grim post–Civil War western landscape. While such revisionist westerns are playing against the background of Vietnam, two other representative movies, *Spirit of the Wind* (1979) and *When the Legends Die* (1972) mark the beginning of a new trend, the portrayal of contemporary Native American characters who find new identities in the traditional ways of their tribes.

Little Big Man (1970) depicts the Cheyenne and their chief, Old Lodge Skins (Chief Dan George), as the moral center against which the corrupt values of the major white characters can be measured. In Old Lodge Skin's worldview everything is alive and connected. When Little Big Man (Dustin Hoffman) asks him why the soldiers killed women and children, he replies, "Because they are strange; they don't know where the center is." Later, after another massacre by the soldiers, Old Lodge Skins elaborates on the difference between the Cheyenne and whites, "The Human Beings believe that everything is alive . . . the white man believes everything is dead. If the Human Beings try to keep living, the white man will rub them out. That is the difference." And indeed each of the main white characters has no respect for human dignity or life. The hypocritical Pendrakes care only for their own sensual desires; the deeply cynical Merriwether rejects any moral order and lives only to exploit others; the paranoid Wild Bill Hickok kills with complete detachment; and the megalomaniac General Custer exterminates women and children at Washita. Each of these characters represents part of the mentality that Penn connects to the victimization of the Vietnam War.

The character of Old Lodge Skins, however, is not just a contrast for emphasis of this political theme; it is also a vehicle for the first Native American to play a major role in a big-budget western. Chief Dan George brings to his part a film presence and sense of humor that make Old Lodge Skins one of the most human and memorable Native Americans in the westerns. Often seen in warmly lit low-angle close-ups that emphasize his dignity, he delivers his lines with droll understatement and a unique twinkle in his eye. For example, when he is talking to Little Big Man, he asks him about his white wife: "Does she show a pleasant enthusiasm when you mount her? I've never noticed it in a white woman." At the end of the movie, he again shows his humor after he lies down to die and then blinks when raindrops hit his face. He asks Little Big Man, "Am I still in this world?" Then, after a groan of recognition, he says, "I was afraid of that—sometimes the magic works; sometimes it doesn't." Such lines, and the fact that he represents the privileged morality of the film, make him a charming and significant character. Unfortunately, however, the director ultimately reduces his characterization to the Noble Red Man image.

Because Penn is so committed to making Old Lodge Skins and his Cheyenne the good guys, he takes away what made them more believable and rounded characters in the Thomas Berger novel on which the movie is based. For example, in the novel, the tribe of Old Lodge Skins kills Jack Crabb's family after they make the mistake of giving the warriors whiskey rather than coffee. In the movie, the Cheyenne are kept pure by having the Pawnee massacre the family. And, in the novel, during the battle at Washita, Cheyenne braves kill a unit of soldiers, Little Big Man's wife escapes, and Old Lodge Skins leaves the camp with a show of bravery and strength. Whereas, in the movie, the soldiers not only kill everyone, including Little Big Man's wife, Sunshine (Amy Eccles), and her baby, but Old Lodge Skins, who thinks he's invisible, must be helped out of camp by Little Big Man. This diminishing of his character continues at the end of the movie when Old Lodge Skins fails to die, as he had wanted. At the end of the novel, however, in a crass world where he no longer fits, his death is appropriate and honorable. These changes allow Penn to make his political point about Vietnam and maintain the quirkiness of Old Lodge Skin's character to the end, but they also transform the Cheyenne and their leader into the doomed Noble Red Man image.

Similar intentions also turn the Sioux tribe in *A Man Called Horse* into Noble Red Men. Although the filmmakers note at the beginning that the film uses new research on the Sun Dance and depicts authentic Lakota rituals, they ultimately fall back on a pattern noted by Dan Georgakas: "Stripped of its pretensions, Horse parades the standard myth that the white man can do everything better than the Indian. Give him a little time and he will marry the best looking girl (a princess of course) and will end up the chief of the tribe" (Georgakas, 1972, 28). The Sioux, led by Yellow Hand (Manu Tupou), capture the hero, John Morgan, an Englishman on a hunting trip, and treat him cruelly from the beginning, making him get on his hands and knees and wear a horse blanket and then dragging him behind a horse. The harshness of the Sioux way of life is also exemplified in a mother who cuts off a finger to grieve the death of her son and then gives away all his possessions as other women from the tribe tear apart her teepee and drive her from the camp. After more insults, torture, and a failed escape, the hero finally cries out in a sort of Shakespearean anguish, "I am not an animal; I am a man." This impresses some of the women and marks the beginning of the hero's evolution into a Sioux Warrior called Horse.

After Morgan lives through a winter with the tribe and learns the Lakota language, he falls in love with Running Deer (Corinna Tsopei), a beautiful young woman who has rejected an offer of marriage from Black Eagle (Eddie Little Sky). She is quick to recognize Morgan's superiority and reciprocate his love. However, before they can marry, Morgan must have gifts for her family and must prove himself as a warrior. An attack by the Shoshone, during which he kills several warriors and reluctantly scalps one of them, allows him to become a warrior and capture horses that can be given to the parents. However, he still must be initiated into the tribe by participating in the Sun Dance ritual. After doing a sweat ceremony, he goes to the lodge to make his Sun Vow, during which bones are inserted in his chest by a medicine man (Iron Eyes Cody) and he is suspended in the air by ropes attached to the bones. In his agony, he has a vision of sacred animals as he takes on the Lakota identity. After this test, he not only changes from an Englishman to a super leader in the tribe, but also finally gains the right to make love with Running Deer.

His bliss, however, is short-lived because the Shoshone soon make a revenge attack on the tribe, during which Running Deer, Yellow Hand, and Horse's friend, Batise, are mortally wounded. Just when defeat seems inevitable, Horse rallies his tribe by killing in hand-to-hand combat Striking Bear (Terry Leonard), the chief of the Shoshone. Then he has his warriors use long bows (in the medieval English tradition) to drive off the remaining Shoshone. After this battle and the funeral of his wife and Yellow Hand, he becomes the chief, but he soon leaves the tribe to return to England when his adopted mother, Buffalo Cow Head (Judith Anderson), dies. This ending depicts the tribe as doomed Noble Red Men left without a leader.

In a sequel, *The Return of a Man Called Horse* (1976) the hero returns to the West to again rescue the tribe. Despite what might be good intentions, that movie, like the original, clearly diminishes the Native American characters, as Penelope Gilliatt notes: "The attitude of the film towards Indians is patronizing in the extreme. It feeds the notions about the Western white male as omniscient savior which are already too current" (Gilliatt, 1976, 87).

A Man Called Horse attempts to portray the Sioux as a distinctive culture with its own unique rituals but ultimately fails because it lets the hero preempt the culture. *Ulzana's Raid* (1972), on the other hand, succeeds in portraying the Apache warriors of Ulzana (Joaquin Martinez) as members of a unique culture, though it defines their "otherness" in terms of their fierce (and again doomed) way of life as guerrilla warriors. In this anti-western, the West is a gritty and grim place in which Ulzana dies at the end. After Ulzana and his men escape from the San Carlos reservation, the cynical old scout tells a young Christian soldier that "their probable intention is to rape, pillage and maim." As guerrilla fighters in a hopeless cause, Ulzana's warriors do terrorize soldiers and settlers in ways reminiscent of Salvaje in *The Stalking Moon*. With harsh efficiency, the Apache attack a woman and her son, and the soldier protecting them shoots the woman and himself. Though the Apache shoot the horses and cut the heart out of the soldier, they do not harm the boy because of their tribal respect for young males. Then, using binoculars taken from the soldiers, they stalk the father of this family who has stayed behind to guard the farm. After shooting his dog and burning his outbuildings, they trick him out of his hiding place by playing a bugle taken from the soldiers, and then torture him to death. Later they attack a homestead, torture a family, and rape the mother.

The Christian soldier, stunned by these acts of violence, asks his Apache scout, Ke-Ni-Kay (Jorge Luke), why his Apache people are so cruel. Ke-Ni-Kay, explaining that in his culture the killer takes the power of his victims, says, "Here in this land a man must have power. Ulzana will want to kill many." Then the soldier asks the old scout if he hates the Apache, and he replies that hating the Apache would be "like hating the desert because it has no water." Later, after the soldier sees another soldier brutally stabbing the body of an Apache warrior, the old scout comments on his angry reaction, "I see you don't like seeing white men acting like Indians—kind of confuses the issue." As the conflict between the soldiers and the warriors of Ulzana moves toward its grim ending, the line between them does blur, especially when the soldiers use the woman raped by the Apache as bait to lure them into a fight. This showing of atrocities on both sides is one of several parallels between the plot of this film and the story of the Vietnam War, in which the line between the cynicism and ferocity of the American soldiers and the enemy also is blurred.

In the final fight, the hero is fatally wounded after he kills several of the remaining warriors, and Ke-Ni-Kay kills Ulzana after he has acknowledged his defeat with a death song. At the end, the disillusioned Christian soldier and Ke-Ni-Kay, the Apache who has decided to survive by working for the whites, are the only witnesses in the conclusion to the bitter war with Ulzana. This ending is a sharp contrast to the upbeat conclusion of *Apache* (1954), also directed by Robert Aldrich and starring Burt Lancaster as the Apache warrior. In that film, the soldiers hunt down the hostile warrior but finally allow him to live the rest of his life in peace; in the harsh West of *Ulzana's Raid* no such happy ending is possible for the aging scout (Burt Lancaster) or for Ulzana. The movie at least suggests the same could be said for the Vietnam War.

The last of the representative anti-westerns, *The Outlaw Josey Wales* (1976), also depicts the post–Civil War West as a harsh place, corrupted by politicians, evil soldiers, bounty hunters and vicious Comancheros. In this world, Wales, whose wife and son were killed by soldiers, is one of few truly moral characters, though ironically he is known as an outlaw. His only equals, in the sense of their being outsiders and good warriors, are three Native American characters, Lone Watie (Chief Dan George), Little Moonlight (Geraldine Keams), and Ten Bears (Will Sampson). Just as Clint Eastwood plays against the formula of the lonely hero, so also do these characters (all played by Native American actors) play against the images of the Savage and Noble Red Man.

After Wales has escaped to the Indian Nation, he sneaks up on Lone Watie, the old Cherokee who becomes his friend, and tells him that he thought this wasn't supposed "to happen with Indians." Lone Watie replies, "I'm an Indian all right, but here in the nation they call us a civilized tribe because we're so easy to sneak up on. The white man have been sneaking up on us for years." He then tells how he lost his wife and children on the Trail of Tears and how the government gave him medals for being so civilized and dressed him like Abraham Lincoln. In fact, he talks so long that Wales falls asleep. Like Wales, Lone Watie lost his family but never gave up the fight, and this establishes a bond between them. While Wales goes to find a horse for his new friend, he comes upon Little Moonlight, who is being mistreated by a trader and two vile buffalo hunters. After rescuing her and taking the horses of the recently deceased hunters, the lonely hero now has two companions and a dog.

Little Moonlight, a Navajo who had been captured by Cheyenne and raped by the Arapahoe, is just as talkative as Lone Watie, though she speaks in her native tongue. Thus both the characters play against the image of taciturn Native American. Little Moonlight is also a skilled warrior. When she and Wales return, Lone Watie sneaks up on Wales, only to have Little Moonlight sneak up on him. Later, when Wales and Lone Watie have a shootout with soldiers in a town, she stops the pursuers just long enough so that the two can escape. When she catches up with them and Lone Watie, thinking she is one of the posse, jumps from a rock and knocks her off her horse, she quickly recovers and is about to stab him when Wales intervenes. With typical wry humor, Lone Watie says to him, "Lucky you stopped me when you did. I might have killed her." As in *Little Big Man*, Chief Dan George brings an endearing humor to his character. Another example occurs when Lone Watie and Wales are talking about the shootout and Wales, assuming that Little Moonlight has been killed by the soldiers, says, "Whenever I get to liking someone, they aren't around long." Lone Watie responds, "I noticed that when you get to disliking someone, they aren't around long either."

Just as the humorous character of Lone Watie plays against the image of the stoical Noble Red Man, so the character of the Comanche chief, Ten Bears, plays against the image of the Savage. A minor character in the movie describes Ten Bears: "He is the greatest Comanche war chief. Each year he is pushed farther across the plains. But Ten Bears will move no more." Like Wales, he is a warrior who has been mistreated by corrupt politicians and soldiers, and when the two men meet they become blood brothers. Seen in close shots that emphasize their equality, Ten Bears eloquently accepts the offer of Wales to live in peace: "It is good that warriors such as we meet in the struggle of life or death. It shall be life." Though he is a fierce adversary to evil whites who are after his land, Ten Bears responds with honor to an equally honorable character.

Ten Bears, Little Moonlight, and Lone Watie are among the most rounded, least stereotypical Native American characters in the western genre. The same is true for the character of Wales, who doesn't ride off into the sunset like the typical lonely hero but returns to live with his extended, multi-racial family after he and the man pursuing him make their peace. As in his recent *Unforgiven* (1993), Eastwood questions the formulas of the western in *The Outlaw Josey Wales* and portrays outsiders like Lone Watie with a new sense of empathy. As such, the movie is an appropriate transition to *Spirit of the Wind* and *When the Legends Die*, both of which depict contemporary Native American characters who transcend the images of westerns.

Though a less intense movie than *The Outlaw Josey Wales*, *Spirit of the Wind* (1979) also focuses on a Native American who feels like an outsider. Based on the life of George Attla, an Athabascan who overcame tuberculosis to become a champion dog sled racer, this movie portrays the dynamics of a Native American family living in the backcountry of Alaska. Unlike Abel, George Attla Jr. (Pius Savage) is surrounded by a loving family. His father, George Attla, Sr. (George Clutesi) has the patience to let his son make his own decisions. When George Jr. leaves his family because of his identity crisis, he eventually has the help of an extended family in the person of Moses Paul (Chief Dan George), who becomes a kind of grandfather for the young man. Without the traditional wisdom of these two elders, George would never have found the strength and identity to become a champion.

When George is a young man, his father teaches him by example the skills of trapping and negotiating for the best possible prices for the finished pelts. A calm and dignified man, he shows his wisdom even when he has a trapping accident.

After he catches his hand in a trap and George looks at the deep cut across his fingers, he says to his son, "I've been catching animals all my life; it's only fair that I catch myself once." Another example of his father's concern and humor occurs later, after George has spent years in the city recuperating from the tuberculosis that permanently crippled his leg. When George is about to make a deal for a lead sled dog with crafty old Moses Paul, his father says to the old man, "You've got to go easy on George; he's been around white men too long." George, however, has learned to deal from his father, and makes a clever bargain to get Jarvy, the dog that will lead his championship teams. A last example of his father's wisdom is some advice he gives George. Referring to the fighting and drinking the young men of the tribe do in the cities, he tells George, "If a man wants to prove himself, the land is the place for it." This, however, is a lesson George will not learn until he decides to leave his family.

Despite the patient support of his family, beautifully portrayed in a summer fishing camp sequence with the chanting of Buffy St. Marie in the background, George finally decides he doesn't fit with them. After he injures one of his father's dogs in a race and his father reacts with typical patience, George yells, "I'm not you! . . . I feel like two different people and I don't know what to do." George leaves for the city and ends up washing dishes at an Asian restaurant where he sees Moses Paul one evening. Moses insists that George come with him for the winter trapping season (he thinks George can cook Chinese food), and during this time, acting as a grandfather in an extended family, convinces George that if he wants to be a dog sled racer he must learn from his father. George heeds the advice of Moses and returns to his home, where he can find the traditional knowledge he needs.

After his return to his family, George and his father train Jarvy and the rest of the team in the old ways, and he wins his first big race in Anchorage. When George celebrates his victory by hugging Jarvy and the announcer praises the dog, the film cuts to his father and Moses listening on the radio, and Moses, with a twinkle in his eye, says, "I knew I should have kept that dog." Only Chief Dan George could say that line so perfectly, just as only George Clutesi, a noted Canadian Native actor, could respond with just the right sly smile. Their acting, along with that of the rest of the Native cast, and the singing of Buffy St. Marie in the background, provide the audience with a picture of a very different culture, one that is worthy of respect.

The knowledge, wisdom, and good humor of these two elders give George Attla the chance to appreciate the strength of his Athabascan tribe and find in himself the strength to overcome his disabilities and become a champion dog-sled racer. This movie leaves the audience with a respect for George Attla's tribe, a feeling that is the first step toward empathy for their way of life.

The last of the representative movies, *When the Legends Die* (1972) also tries for such empathy in its portrayal of a contemporary Native American, but finally provokes more sympathy than empathy. Based on the Hal Borland novel of the same name, the film highlights the exploitation of Thomas Black Bull (Frederick

Forrest) by white society. In its attempt to expose the effects of prejudice on the main character, the script of the film leaves out major parts of the novel that detail Thomas Black Bull's family life, his education in the old ways of the Ute tribe, and his final catharsis of hatred in a hunt for a bear. These details from the novel give the reader a sense of empathy for Ute culture and are part of the reason it became a classic of adolescent literature. The film focuses on the rodeo career of Thomas Black Bull and thus fails to depict a very complete picture of the traditions he loses in the white world.

At the beginning of the movie an old Ute, Blue Elk (John War Eagle), comes for young Thomas (Tillman Box), who, after the death of his parents, is living the traditional life of the Utes in a wilderness lodge. Blue Elk forces Thomas and his pet bear to accompany him to a school for young Native Americans. Like George Attla, who finds life in the city stifling, Thomas cannot stand the civilized life at the school and tries to escape with his bear. However, Blue Elk tricks him and forces him to go back to the school, saying to him, "I have done this for your own good. You must learn the new ways." Thomas Black Bull's years at the school introduce him to the new ways and also start the destruction of his identity.

This process continues when he leaves the school and becomes the ward of a white man, who, like Blue Elk, sees a way to exploit the young man. Just as Blue Elk had taken Thomas to the institution for money, Red Dillon becomes his guardian because he recognizes that Thomas's skills with horses will allow him to use Thomas to make money on the rodeo circuit. Thomas arrives at Red's ranch house and undergoes grueling training for the saddle-bronco event. In the training sequences, Red is seen on the top of the corral from low angles, dominating his student, and Thomas is seen from a high angle as a victim even in this early stage of his rodeo career. When Meo, the old Mexican companion of Red who had been a great bronco rider (and also exploited by Red) tells Thomas that he is a good rider, the young man just says, "I like horses." At the rodeos, however, when Red starts to make him cheat so they can con more money out of local bettors and white cowboys sneer and refer to him as "chief," "Geronimo," and "Crazy Horse," Thomas finally confronts Red and says, "The old days are gone. I feel like a thief; I'm sick and ashamed." Red responds by telling Thomas he owns him and then beats him up. After this incident, Thomas can only express his frustration and anger by hurting the horses he once loved, so badly that he becomes known as (horse) Killer Tom Black.

After Thomas leaves Red, he joins the major rodeo circuit, makes a great deal of money, and becomes an empty, depressed man. After a serious injury and an attempt to live with a white nurse, he finally decides to go back to Red's ranch. In their final scene together, Thomas stands above Red who is dying of alcoholism in a hotel bed, and the high-angle and low-angle perspectives of their early scenes together are reversed. Figuratively, Thomas is finally free from the one who gave him such a bitter lesson in the new ways of greed and exploitation. Thomas completes his separation by burning Red's ranch house before returning to his reservation. Entering a room with black and white posters of famous chiefs like Dull Knife, Thomas tells members of the tribal council gathered there the types who had forced him as a young man to give up his old ways—"Listen to me. I have learned the new ways." After he tells them he will work with the horses on the reservation, a closeup of his face freezes to black and white, making him look like the other traditional leaders in the posters.

The implication at the end of *When the Legends Die* is that Thomas Black Bull will renew his identity on the reservation by living a new version of the traditional ways, though the film never makes the nature of these ways very clear. This change of emphasis from the novel and the choice of a white actor to play the central character diminish the empathy of the movie, at least in comparison to *Spirit of the Wind*. However, like George Attla in that movie, Thomas Black Bull finds new strength in a return to his homeland and ancient tribal traditions. This theme of finding a new identity within traditional tribal values appears in a growing number of films about contemporary Native Americans during the next decade.

So a great change occurs between the anti-westerns of the first part of this decade and the later part with films like *When the Legends Die*. Early on, the depiction of the Sand Creek massacre in *Soldier Blue* (1970) and the Washita massacre in *Little Big Man* (1970) reveal the excesses of the politically motivated films. In each case, the filmmakers suggest a parallel between the Cheyenne, especially the women and children, and the civilian victims of the Vietnam War. Both groups are victims of evil U.S. soldiers. Thus they make the point that the U.S. soldiers in the Vietnam War are recapitulating the victimization of native peoples in the westward expansion. Later in the period, several years after the Vietnam War, *Three Warriors* (1977) and *Spirit of the Wind* (1979) herald a new type of film, like *When the Legends Die*, in which central Native American characters become significant in and of themselves. Such films dealing with the lives of contemporary characters also become more common in the next decade.

Movies of the 1980s

In this decade, variations of the Savage and Noble Red Man images persist in the western, even though the genre itself is near extinction. In *Windwalker* (1980), a movie that portrays Native American life before contact with Europeans, a noble Cheyenne family struggles to survive the attacks of savage Crow enemies. A more traditional western, *The Mountain Men* (1980), while focusing on a typical romance between the white hero, Bill Tyler, and a Native American woman, Running Moon (Victoria Racimo), portrays the Crow as Noble Red Men and the Blackfeet as the Savages led by a villainous chief. The four other representative films continue the trend of depicting Native American characters in contemporary settings. In *Emerald Forest* (1985), Noble Red Men from the Amazonian jungles adopt a white boy who then leads them in a fight against an enemy tribe and whites, who are exploiting their rain forest. In *War Party* (1989), three young Native Americans get caught up in a vicious battle with their white neighbors in which the whites become the savages and the young men noble warriors. On the other hand, in a much less intense family film, *Journey to Spirit Island* (1988), young members of a Canadian tribe save a sacred island from a developer. And, finally, *Running Brave* (1983) tells the story of Billy Mills, the mixed-blood Lakota runner who must overcome the prejudice of white society and his own identity problems before he can become an Olympic champion runner.

The first of the representative westerns is *Windwalker* (1980), a film based on a novel by Blaine Yorgason, a Mormon writer known for his children's stories, and produced by Mormon filmmakers for the family market. Through a series of flashbacks, it follows two generations of a Cheyenne family and uses the motif of the lost son reunited with his family. This complicated narrative structure gives the movie the feeling of a folk tale. Beginning in the present with an ailing, old Windwalker (Trevor Howard), surrounded by the family of his son, Smiling Wolf (Nick Ramus), the film flashes back as Windwalker tells his story to the children. In this extended flashback, the young Windwalker (James Remar) falls in love with the beautiful Tashina (Serene Hedin). After stealing horses from the Crow to give to her parents, he marries her and they have twin boys. With occasional cuts back to old Windwalker, the story continues with the idyllic life of young Windwalker until it is destroyed when a disgruntled suitor of Tashina and the evil Crow Eyes (Rudy Diaz) kill the young mother and kidnap one of their sons. After telling his story, old Windwalker is ready to die, and his son, Smiling Wolf, puts him on a platform grave. Then, riding a white stallion, the warrior leads his family into the wilderness.

At this point, Crow warriors, Crow Hair (Harold Goss-Coyote), Wounded Crow (Roy Cohoe), and Crow Eyes, whose face is covered with eerie black and white war paint, begin to stalk Smiling Wolf and the Cheyenne women and children. In a sequence that makes effective use of camera angles and crosscutting, the savage Crow finally attack and seriously injure Smiling Wolf before the family manages to hide from them. While the audience is in suspense about when the Crow will find the family, the film cuts back to the platform grave where Windwalker, in a scene similar to the one at the end of Little Big Man, realizes that he is not dead and says in a voice-over, "My feet are cold. Grandfather [the Great spirit], this is a good joke. Free my spirit or free my limbs, but do not leave me in this cold." Apparently the Great Spirit has more work for Windwalker to do because he lets him escape from a wolf attack and kill a giant bear, after which the old warrior says, with characteristic humor, "Grandfather, such a long life is not healthy for an old man." After these adventures, he finds his son's family and realizes he has been sent back to save them from the Crow warriors.

In this last part of the movie, the Cheyenne children, though a key part of the family structure from the beginning, are central to its survival. The two boys (both played by Native American actors) save one of the women during the first Crow attack, and then, tutored by Windwalker, they set traps that sabotage the final assault by the Crow and allow for the capture of a warrior (the Lost One, Nick Ramus) who turns out to be the other son of Windwalker. The little girl in the family also shows her spunk and kindness in a scene where she chews a piece of meat and then puts it in the mouth of the captured Lost One. Throughout the film, these children have an honored place in the family and their actions at the end prove their worth. The Crow, on the other hand, are portrayed as lone warriors who kidnap children and, in the case of the Lost One, treat them very harshly.

In fact, throughout the movie, the Crow are the savage enemies who must be defeated by the noble Cheyenne, with their strong family and religious values. At the end, before Windwalker rejoins Tashina in the cloud spirit world, his lost son defeats Crow Eyes in hand-to-hand combat and makes him leave in shame. Though the movie follows the formula of Savage versus Noble Red Man, it does offer a unique perspective on Native American cultures. A *Variety* critic, noting the use of the Cheyenne and Crow languages and subtitles, comments: "Coupled with the absence of non-Indian characters in the film, which takes place in the 18th Century, this gives the Indians on the screen a dignity they have been denied previously, even in the most sympathetic westerns" (Dec. 10, 1980). This movie, which deals exclusively with Native American life, a type very popular in the silent movies, does portray the culture of "Indians" positively, unless, of course, the viewer happens to be of Crow heritage.

Given the vagaries of the traditional images, in *The Mountain Men* (1980) the Crow are the roguish but Noble Red Men who are friendly to the hero and the Blackfeet woman he loves, Running Moon. At the beginning, Cross Otter (Cal Bellini), whose Crow band takes turns with the hero, Bill Tyler, in stealing each other's horses, helps the hero rebuff an attack by the Blackfeet, during which the warriors from each side moon each other. Later, at the rendezvous of the trappers, Bill Tyler meets Iron Belly (Victor Jory), the chief of another Crow band, known for his Spanish breastplate. Iron Belly shows his friendship by telling him of a valley in Blackfeet country where he can find many beaver to trap. Another Crow at the rendezvous is Medicine Wolf (David Ackroyd), a trick rider and old friend of the hero. Both of these characters suffer for their friendship: when Heavy Eagle (Stephen Macht) and his warriors seek vengeance on the hero, they kill everyone in Iron Belly's camp and torture Medicine Wolf.

These Blackfeet characters, and especially their chief, Heavy Eagle, are depicted as deadly Savages. From the beginning, Heavy Eagle, seen in a close-up with black war paint on his face and flames flickering in front of him, is portrayed as a vengeful, diabolical character. Heavy Eagle lives up to his image, not only by his vicious treatment of the Crow mentioned above, but also by scalping Bill Tyler's friend, torturing Tyler, and raping the beautiful and devoted Running Moon. As if that's not enough, he also cuts off the head of a man who comes to parley with him. In the climactic scene when the hero comes to rescue his beloved Running Moon, Heavy Eagle, whose face is then completely painted black, engages him in hand-to-hand combat, and, after gaining an advantage by biting, is about to kill him when

Running Moon shoots the evil warrior. Thus ends the career of a Savage character so extreme that his presence in a 1980s film is quite surprising.

Played against the background of the savage Blackfeet and the noble Crow is the romance between Bill Tyler and Running Moon. Their first two meetings are something less than romantic: in the first, he knocks her out with a musket, and in the second, she pushes him into a river after finding him with a woman at the rendezvous. After that, she stays with him because, as she says, "I could never go back to Heavy Eagle" (not surprisingly) and "it is the custom that I go with you." After the hero is separated from his trapper friend, Running Moon comforts him. Then, in a softly focused sequence with equally soft music in the background, they hunt and work together, make love, and exchange gifts that reveal their devotion to each other. Their peaceful time together is short-lived, however, because Heavy Eagle captures them and they are separated until the end when Running Moon saves her lover's life. At the very end, seen from a high angle that emphasizes their vulnerability, they ride off to the high country, the only sort of remote place where, in westerns, a happy romance between a white and a Native American can be lived out.

A similar remote setting occurs in *The Emerald Forest* (1985) where a noble tribe of Native South Americans is threatened by whites building a dam in the Amazon wilderness. This tribe, known as the Invisible People, captures and raises a white boy whose father is one of the builders, whom the tribe calls Termite People because they are "eating up" the forest. The chief, Wanadi (Rui Polonah), a wise and good-natured man, becomes the surrogate father of the boy, whom he calls Tomme. This character stands out because the native actor who plays him has a strong screen presence, similar to that of Chief Dan George. For example, when Tomme aims his arrow at a sloth, Wanadi, seen in a close-up, tells him not to shoot the animal and then, with a sly smile, says, "he is old and slow like me." As with Chief Dan George in *Little Big Man*, Wanadi's charming character enhances the noble image of his tribe.

On the other hand, the antagonists of Wanadi's tribe, the Fierce People, are Savages, displaced from their traditional land by whites building a dam. Supplied with guns by evil whites, the Fierce People prey on the peaceful tribes to capture young women to sell as prostitutes to the whites. These Savage characters, led by a vicious, evil-looking chief, move through the forest looking for the women of the Invisible People.

The most beautiful young woman in Tomme's adopted tribe is Kachiri (Dira Pass), and when Tomme becomes a young man he falls in love with her. When Wanadi sees this happen, he knows the time has come for Tomme's initiation into manhood. In a harsh ritual, reminiscent of *A Man Called Horse* (1970), Tomme is covered with large ants and must survive the agony of their bites. At the end of his ordeal, Wanadi pulls him out of the water and says, "The boy is dead and the man is born." In the second stage of his initiation, the chief blows a powder through a long pipe into Tomme's nose and this powerful hallucinogen transports his consciousness to his spirit being and he sees through the eyes of an eagle. After gaining this vision and knowledge about himself, he becomes a warrior and is free to marry Kachiri after he gives gifts to her parents.

Tomme's marriage to Kachiri marks the end of tranquility for his adopted tribe. Shortly thereafter, when Tomme and Wanadi are away from the tribe, the Fierce People attack, burn their village, and kidnap Kachiri and the other young women. In the last part of the film, Tomme, Wanadi, and his warriors attempt to rescue them, the lifeblood of the tribe, from these evil characters. Because the compound where the captured women are being forced to be prostitutes is surrounded by a high fence and guarded by men with automatic weapons, Tomme and the warriors not only fail in their first rescue attempt but Wanadi is fatally wounded. After giving the old man the traditional funeral of burning his bones and consuming part of the ashes in a liquid, Tomme becomes the leader of the tribe.

Like the hero of *A Man Called Horse*, Tomme becomes the savior of his adopted people. To do this, Tomme calls upon his spirit eagle, travels to the city where his family lives, and elicits the help of his father, who had earlier found his son in the jungle and finally decided he belonged with Kachiri and the Invisible People. With the help of his father, Tomme and his warriors rescue the women and return to the jungle. However, to save his people, Tomme must also destroy the dam so that the land of the Invisible People will not be inundated. Again taking the form of his eagle spirit, Tomme makes the frogs sing, which in turn brings torrential rains that cause a flood that becomes "the great anaconda" that breaks up the dam. With a shot of Tomme, Kachiri, and other young men and women who will be the new life of the tribe, the movie ends with statistics about the destruction of native peoples and a note about the few tribes who have never had contact with the outside world and who "still know what we have forgotten." Though this sympathy for the people and the land of the Amazon region is laudable, the movie's subtext about the white savior isn't much different from that of *A Man Called Horse*, and the contemporary Native South Americans become a version of the Noble Red Man.

A similar concern for the exploitation of contemporary Native Americans appears in *War Party* (1989), a movie with the message that as long as racism exists the massacres of the past will be replayed in the present. Though such a message is also laudable, if rather obvious, the tone of the film is irresponsible. Stephen Holden in the *New York Times* notes, *War Party* is a movie that "pretends to be high-minded in its concern for the plight of Indians while exploiting existing tensions in order to portray a bloodbath" (Sept. 29, 1989). What leads to the bloodbath is a decision by Mr. Crowkiller (Dennis Banks), the head of the tribal council, and the mayor to draw tourists by reenacting a historic battle between the U.S. Cavalry and the Blackfeet during the town's "Bonanza Days." When the simulated battle turns into a real one, the whites take on the traditional characteristics of the Savage, and the three young heroes, Sonny Crowkiller (Billy Wirth), Skitty Harris (Kevin Dillon), and Warren Cutfoot (Tim Sampson) become doomed Noble Red Men.

From the beginning the white men are driven by hatred and vengeance. The violence begins when a hateful young white man starts a fight with a young Black-feet after a pool game and gets cut on the face. The next day, in the reenactment of the battle, the young thug from the pool game, using real bullets, kills the Blackfeet man who cut him, and Sonny, in turn, kills him with a war axe from the original battle, which he had stolen from the local museum. After more killing on each side, the three heroes escape and the savagery of the townspeople starts to reveal itself as the rest of the film becomes a pursuit drama. The first instance of this savagery occurs when they surround one of the companions of the heroes with their pickups and finally shoot and then scalp him. As the three young men continue to elude their pursuers, the governor brings in the troops, a move resisted by Sonny's father, the usually conciliatory Mr. Crowkiller. When he realizes that the whites are out for total revenge, he exclaims, "All my life I've tried to understand the white man and I've never learned a goddamned thing." At this point, however, he is powerless to stop the deadly pursuit of his son.

As the troops and a professional tracker and his Crow companion (Rodney Grant), close in on the three young men, Skitty, exhibiting the same frustration as Mr. Crowkiller, says, "Same old shit! Nothing has changed in 100 years." When he and Sonny are finally trapped, however, they ask to see not Mr. Crowkiller but Freddy Man Wolf (Saginaw Grant), the rebellious and drunken old medicine man. After singing the proper songs, this traditional member of the tribe tells the young men that those negotiating with them are telling lies. He finally advises them to die like warriors. Shortly thereafter, baring their chests and putting on war paint, they ride their horses into the deadly fire of automatic weapons. As the camera looks at their bodies from a high angle, it focuses in on the war axe Sonny had been carrying, the same axe seen in close-up at the beginning of the film, which depicts the aftermath of the original battle. The recurring use of this symbolic object is typical of the heavy-handed way this movie reinforces its message about racism, certainly a good message but one expressed in a quite sad and maybe hateful way.

The next representative movie, *Journey to Spirit Island* (1988) is a family film, and thus much less violent than *War Party*, with a more upbeat message about the struggles of young Native Americans. It tells the story of a healing relationship between a young Nahkut woman, Maria (Bettina Bush), and her Grandmother, Jimmy Jim (Marie Antoinette Rodgers). At the beginning of this film, in which the beauty of the Northwest coast is brilliantly photographed by Vilmos Zsigmond, Maria sits on the top of a jutting cliff by the sea, where she is seen first from a low-angle long shot and then in close-ups (a pattern of such shots throughout the film establishes her as a strong central character). As she writes in her journal, she asks herself in a voice-over, "Why is it so hard to be an Indian?" and "Did Raven really make the trees and paint the birds?" This setting and the journal are frames the film returns to at the end when she has found her strength and pride. Maria is not only struggling with her identity but also with recurring dreams about Spirit Island, where the spirit of her great grandfather, Tupshin, a shaman, still is trying to free the soul of his son who died on the island. Her Grandmother, who has had the same dreams, understands what Maria is going through and becomes her teacher and protector.

Her Grandmother takes Marie to a tribal council meeting where a member of the tribe, Hawk (Tony Acierto), and his friend, a white businessman, are trying to persuade the council to develop and build on Spirit Island. Grandmother tells the council that protecting the island is not a matter of profit "but our spiritual life" and, as she concludes with "Respect the sacred place," a wind comes through the room. Later Maria writes in her journal that "something is going on," and then has a dream about Tupshin and herself on the island. When she tells her Grandmother about the dream, the old woman gives her an amulet to protect her and then blesses the cedar canoe that Maria and her brother, Klim (Tarek McCarthy), will use on a trip to the islands. Two white boys who are visiting from Chicago, the youngest of whom adds humor to the film with his wild misconceptions about Native Americans, join Maria and her brother on their trip. At this point, Maria must become a leader, determine the meaning of her dreams, and prove herself without any direct help from her grandmother.

After an accident with one of the boats, all the kids get in the cedar canoe, which is then drawn by a powerful force to Spirit Island. That night Maria tells the story of Tupshin to her white friends and then dreams of things that will happen to her on the island. The next day they search for the canoe, which has disappeared, and Maria tell her teenage friend, Michael, "I don't know what's going on. You think because I'm Indian I should know all the great mystical secrets. Those are two completely different worlds. I know just enough about the old ways to scare me." Shortly thereafter, they find the bones of Tupshin's son and an amulet that matches the one given her by Grandmother. Then Maria puts the bones in a cloth, buries them in the bow of his boat, and does a ceremonial dance she learned from her Grandmother.

Meanwhile, the evil Hawk (Tony Acierto), a greedy member of the tribal council, and his tough-guy sidekick arrive at the island to get rid of the eagles there, the last legal obstacle to the planned development. After they chase the young people into a cave and seal them in with a boulder, Maria comes to the rescue. Strengthened by a vision of her Grandmother and using the knowledge gained from her dreams, Maria finds a way out by swimming through a tunnel to the shore of the island. Then they find the canoe and return to the mainland just in time to foil Hawk. As they rush into the tribal council meeting, the contract has just been signed despite the opposition of Grandmother. However, when Hawk's white friend who is a developer, hears about his machinations from the kids, he tears up the contract—a rather unbelievable part of the plot. As with *Three Warriors*, this last part of the film is standard family show adventure fare, but it also offers an ending with a strong image of a young Native American woman who understands the power of dreams in her culture and her own new identity. The camera zooms in on Maria as she again sits on the cliff seen at the beginning. She writes in her journal and says in a voice-over, "I feel so different since we buried the bones. Tupshin can rest now. I'm not afraid of my dreams anymore. Grandmother says we have Great Grandfather to thank for all this. Thank you!" Maria is now a proud member of her tribe and has a new sense of its history. Though the last scene is a rather obvious family movie ending, it does call attention to the history and tradition of Maria's tribe.

The last of the representative movies, *Running Brave* (1983), is also rather obvious in its attempt to reveal the prejudice of white society toward Native Americans. Produced by the Canadian Ermineskin tribe, this movie is based on the life of Billy Mills, the Olympic champion and potential role model for young Native Americans. The title character is played by Robbie Benson, a white actor who looks the part of a runner and somewhat resembles Mills. Some Native Americans objected to the choice of a white actor and to the fact that Native American actors only play the minor characters of Billy's reservation family. In fact, a *Variety* critic finds the portrayal of the family to be a problem: "Billy's Indian relatives come and go throughout the movie as stereotypical Indians. One is bitter and hateful of white men [Eddie], the other is a crushed alcoholic with unrealized talent [Frank]" (Oct. 5, 1983). Billy's father (August Schellenberg) and traditional grandfather (George Clutesi) are seen rather briefly in flashbacks, and his half-brother, Frank (Denis Lacrois), sister, Catherine (Margo Kane), and friend, Eddie (Graham Greene), appear in only a few parts of the film.

The real center of the film is the story of Billy's struggle to prove himself as a runner. His coach at the University of Kansas reveals the stereotypes Billy must overcome in a comment to a colleague: "You know as well as I do what happens to these Indian boys. They are gifted natural runners, but they have no discipline. They can't take orders and they're quitters. Sooner or later they all end up back on the reservation pumping gas or dead drunk on skid row." Billy, however, feels confident that he will be different: in a letter/voice-over to his sister (a recurring device), Billy says, "I want to prove that this is one Indian who can make it in the white world." At first he has great success and does whatever his coach wants, including leading the races from the beginning and crushing his opponents, both of which feel unnatural to him. However, as time goes on he lets the coach use him up to the degree that he tells his sister, "I've lost my love for running. I'm just a running machine." Despite the love and encouragement of a white woman and the friendship of his roommate, Billy finally feels he must quit school and return to the reservation.

While at the reservation, Billy rekindles his relationship with Frank and his friendship with Eddie, whose anger and distaste for whites had earlier disrupted a party at the home of Billy's fiancée. During this happy time in his homeland he also rediscovers his love of running. Then Frank commits suicide and Billy decides to leave the reservation, marry his beloved Pat, and join the armed forces so he can train for running in his own way. As he trains for the Olympics, he says that he "feels his family running with him" and that his competing is "his chance to give something back to his people." However, the rest of the film focuses on the big race at the Olympics and the only other allusion to his "people" occurs at the end of the film while the crowds are cheering him. Billy sees an old Native American man in the crowd and they exchange a mysteriously knowing glance.

This ending makes the audience feel as though they have missed something. And in a way they have, because this film is more about a sports hero than about contemporary Native American life. In fact, the director insisted on a pseudonym because he was so unhappy with this emphasis. Though the movie suggests that Billy's triumph is connected with his return to the reservation and tribal values, it doesn't illustrate this theme with the detail or empathy of a movie like *Powwow Highway* (1989).

Movies of the 1990s

A testimony to what goes around comes around in westerns, *Dances with Wolves* (1990), the most notable movie of this decade, is very similar to *Broken Arrow*, the movie that established Native Americans as viable central characters in westerns forty years earlier. In each, a hero, who speaks to the audience in voice-overs, becomes friends with noble leaders of hostile tribes and falls in love with a woman from the tribe. In addition, not only are the Noble Red Man characters set against hostile members of their own tribe (Geronimo) or other more savage tribes (the Pawnee), but also the languages of the Native American characters are either ac-knowledged by the narrator or used in the film with subtitles. And, finally both movies were so popular that they took on a social status among liberal critics that belied their ultimate portrayal of the Native Americans as typical Noble Red Men.

Such echoes of earlier movies are common in the self-conscious westerns of this decade. *The Last of the Mohicans* (1992), a western set in the East, follows the script of the 1936 early sound film. Even though it portrays Chingachgook, Uncas, and Magua as more believable screen presences, it finally gives in to the doomed Noble Red Man image. However, the revisionist history of *Black Robe* (1991) avoids the images of Cooper and the 1992 *Last of the Mohicans* and depicts life among the Eastern tribes with a detached and somewhat more historical view of Algonquin, Iroquois, and Huron cultures. Another Canadian movie, *Clearcut* (1992), takes an equally detached and harsh look at a contemporary tribe struggling for its rights with a lumber company. The next representative movie, *Thunderheart* (1992), deals with a similar, and equally violent, struggle on a contemporary Sioux reservation in South Dakota. And finally, *Smoke Signals* (1998), basically a Native American production, rejects and satirizes the traditional images and depicts contemporary Native American characters with empathy.

The first representative film is *Dances with Wolves* (1990), the winner of the Academy Award for Best Picture and a surprisingly popular western that reestab-lished national interest in the western genre and in the history of Native Americans. A *Variety* critic comments on the film's characterizations: "The script by Michael

Blake portrays the Sioux culture with appreciation, establishing within it characters of winning individuality and humor" (Nov. 12, 1990). Often seen in medium and close-up shots and given a significant amount of dialogue in their native language, the major Lakota characters do become memorable presences. The handsome and well-dressed Kicking Bird (Graham Greene) is a spiritual leader and philosopher who tries to learn about the hero, John Dunbar, so he can figure out the best course for his tribe in a world he knows is changing. And yet he is also a man who can be startled by the antics of Dunbar and is chided by his wife, Black Shawl (Tantoo Cardinal), when he is slow to tell Stands-with-a-Fist (Mary McDonnell) that her mourning period is over. The brash warrior, Wind-in-His-Hair (Rodney Grant) can unwittingly reveal fear or affection for Dunbar by speaking a little too loudly, and yet later calmly stand up for him in a conflict with another warrior. Chief Ten Bears (Floyd Red Crow Westerman) shows his quiet leadership as he cleverly handles conflicts between members of his tribe. And Stands-with-a-Fist, the white woman rescued from the Pawnee, is devoted to the ways of her adopted tribe and must struggle to translate Dunbar's English words into her now native Lakota tongue. Despite such distinguishing touches to the characters, the film as a whole portrays their tribe as Noble Red Men, especially as they are described in Dunbar's journal/voice-over.

The voice-over narration of the hero highlights the nobility of the Sioux tribe (just in case the audience didn't get the point). For example, as he begins his journal, he tells that in his first contact with "wild Indians," the man he encountered (Kicking Bird) was "a magnificent looking fellow." Later, after the tribe accepts him, he notes that "the Indians" are not like what he had heard, but noble and courteous. After the buffalo hunt while he lives with the tribe, he observes how dedicated the "Indians" are to each other. He says "the only word that came to me was *harmony*." Finally, after the battle with the Pawnee, he praises the warriors of the tribe because they fight only to protect their families, not for motives of greed or conquest like the whites. This running commentary on the wonderful characteristics of the tribe, as the white hero sees it, tends to reduce the tribe to Noble Red Men, and finally, even the individualized main characters blend into this image.

The Pawnee antagonists of Dunbar's adopted tribe, on the other hand, have few distinguishing traits, other than their bloodthirsty ways, which establish them as stock Savages. Their nameless leader (Wes Studi), a bare-chested warrior with Mohawk-type hair and a sinister, fierce visage, leads his warriors against the mule-skinner, whom they riddle with arrows, scalp, and mutilate. Seen from low-angle and close-up shots that emphasize their fierceness, these warriors appear later as they prepare to attack the Lakota camp. Before that attack, suspense builds with shots of the Pawnee warriors stalking toward the camp, killing a dog, and going for the Lakota horses. However, the Lakota warriors, warned and armed by Dunbar, are ready for their savage enemies and quickly rout the main force. Then, in the climactic scene of the battle, they surround the leader of the Pawnee in a river and, though he resists with the fury of a wild animal, they close the circle, shoot him,

and smash his body with rifle butts. After the defeat of the savage Pawnee, their
new antagonists are the soldiers who eventually capture the hero. As is typical in
recent revisionist westerns, these soldiers have the same evil traits as the traditional
Savages, and, like the Pawnee, are routed when Dunbar's noble adopted tribe
rescues him.

Though this rescue now means the soldiers will relentlessly hunt the tribe, it
is a typical gesture of gratitude and friendship that Noble Red Men make toward
heroes such as Dunbar. Like John Morgan in *A Man Called Horse* (1970), Dunbar
is both the savior of his adopted tribe and the reason for its vulnerability at the end.
Also like Morgan and Tom Jeffords in *Broken Arrow* (1950), he and Stands-with-a-
Fist must ride off alone. Jeffords and Morgan, however, because of the traditional
depiction of Native American women and white men, must see the death of their
wives. On the other hand, Dunbar can leave with his white wife, who was only
an adopted Native American. Though *Dances with Wolves* never really transcends
the images of the Savage and Noble Red Man, it does depart from earlier westerns
in the degree of its respect for the native languages. All of the dialogue of the native characters is in Lakota (with subtitles) and Dunbar learns the language of the
people he grows to respect and love. The amount of time that the cast of whites
and Native Americans of various tribes spent learning Lakota from Doris Leader
Charge and Albert White Hat of Sinte Gleska College imbued them with a feeling
for Lakota life, a feeling most clearly expressed in the warmly lit teepee scenes. Like
Broken Arrow forty years earlier, *Dances with Wolves* certainly does mark a step forward in the portrayal of Native American characters, unless, of course, the viewer
happens to be of Pawnee heritage.

The hectic pace of the second representative film, the new *The Last of the Mohicans* (1992) gives little chance for the development of even its major characters,
Chingachgook (Russell Means), Uncas (Eric Schweig), and Magua (Wes Studi). Our
first view of the hero, Nathaniel/Hawkeye, Chingachgook, and Uncas, is of them
running wildly through the forest as they hunt down an elk. When the hero shoots
the animal, they converge on it and Chingachgook says in his native tongue (with
subtitles), "We are sorry to kill you brother. We do honor to your courage, speed
and strength." This statement gives the audience a sense of the Mohicans' tribal beliefs, and the use of the native languages throughout the film highlights that part of
the culture in a positive way similar to that of *Dances with Wolves*. By contrast, in the
1936 *The Last of the Mohicans*, from which this movie is adapted, the primary Native
American characters, played by white actors, speak in the clipped "Movie Indian"
version of English. In the new version, the two Mohicans and Magua, played by Native American actors, not only converse in their native tongues, but also in English
and French. Despite this significant change, and other revisions in pace and historical
setting, the Native Americans are ultimately only somewhat more believable variations of the Noble Red Man and Savage images as the movie progresses.

Chingachgook, played by former AIM activist Russell Means, is the most developed character in the new version in that he has some dialogue and is often seen

in close-up shots. Dressed in a fine outfit and wearing nice long hair (the hero and his Mohican friends all have fine hairdos), he is a noble father figure and a skillful warrior, whose weapon is a large blade, which can cut, chop, or be thrown. In the first Huron ambush, he throws the blade with deadly accuracy, and at the end of the film he again uses it to hack apart Magua after the evil warrior kills Uncas. Though his character has some new trappings of historical accuracy and a vivid screen presence, it is basically as flat as the one in the 1936 version of the film because his deep friendship has been diminished to emphasize the romance of Hawkeye and Cora. At the end of the film, he stands next to Hawkeye and Cora and gives his speech about being the last of the Mohicans, "The frontier moves with the sun and pushes the Red Man of these wilderness forests in front of it until one day there will be nowhere left. Then our race will be no more, or be not us." Unfortunately, the audience doesn't have much reason to care about his words because they are probably thinking about the happy couple.

The character of Uncas is even more undeveloped, given that he has almost no dialogue and little importance in the plot. In the novel and the 1936 film version, Uncas falls in love with Alice Munro and their relationship is a significant subplot. In the new version, either to keep the focus on the romance of Hawkeye and Cora or to avoid the issue of miscegenation, this love relationship is just hinted at. Uncas becomes just an attractive part of the setting, often seen in lingering close-up shots. Like his father, Chingachgook, he is a powerful screen presence, but little is ever revealed about his past or about the unique culture of his tribe. When he dies at the hand of Magua, the audience has little reason for grief or sense of what is lost in his passing.

Magua, on the other hand, is more developed and sympathetic than the evil character of the 1936 version. The first view of Magua is a long shot in the shadows at the back of a room, followed by a close-up as he speaks in his native tongue and then in English. Though he looks the part of a fierce warrior with his mostly bare chest and Mohawk type hair, he also proves to be an intelligent and skilled manipulator of his enemies. Portrayed as a character eloquent in his native language as well as in those of his white enemies and allies, he is considerably more eloquent than the Magua character in the 1936 version. The new version also builds more sympathy for his character by giving him a stronger motive for his vengeance on Colonel Munro, whose allies, the Mohawk, destroyed Magua's village, killed his children, and took him as a slave. Though this motivation makes his desire for vengeance more believable, his overreaching revenge itself is that of a Savage: he cuts out Colonel Munro's heart, forces Alice to jump off a cliff, and finally slits the throat of Uncas. When Chingachgook takes revenge on him, the audience knows that another Savage character has received his just deserts.

Because both *The Last of the Mohicans* and *Dances with Wolves* follow the Hollywood pattern of the historical romance, which subordinates all characterization to the development of the white hero and his love affair, their Native American characters still need to be variations of the Noble Red Man or Savage images associated with this formula. Such is not the case with the Canadian movie, *Black Robe*

(1991), which focuses on Eastern tribes in a way very different from Hollywood films like *The Last of the Mohicans*.

Black Robe establishes the profound differences between the culture of the whites and that of the Algonquin, Iroquois, and Huron tribes. Terence Rafferty notes that "the movie's portrayal of the Indians' mysticism is straightforward, unromanticized; it has an anthropological detachment" (Rafferty 1991, 120). In fact, the portrayal of the religious beliefs is just part of a generally detached view of both cultures as radically different. From the beginning, the Australian director of the film crosscuts between the cultures with matching shots of a Native American Medicine Man and a white clergyman dressing themselves to the sounds of their contrasting music. Then he juxtaposes similar high-angle shots of a wigwam and a European church. Played against this Old World versus New World visual background are the central conflicts of the Jesuit missionaries and the tribes, and the struggle among the tribes themselves for supremacy. The action begins when the missionary, Laforgue, and his young friend, Daniel, accompany their guides, a small group of Algonquin led by Chomina (August Schellenberg), to find the Huron. When the rigid Laforgue refuses to give the Algonquians any of the goods he is bringing to trade with the Huron, and Daniel falls in love with Chomina's daughter, Annuka (Sandrine Holt), the differences between the cultures and the uniqueness of Annuka emerge.

From her first appearance in the movie, the camera singles out Annuka with a series of close-ups that establish her as a significant presence, and, indeed, her character is very different from the traditional noble or savage female image. She has a completely unromantic and honest view of the physical and spiritual realities of life in the wilderness. When she notices that Daniel is watching her (many shots of her are from his perspective) and realizes her attraction to him, she accepts his furtive kiss, kisses him back, and makes love with him. The naturalness of their act is punctuated by the reaction of Laforgue, who sees them and then flogs himself to drive away his feelings of lust. In fact, Annuka sees the chastity of the missionaries as unnatural and evil; she says, "Black Robes are demons; they never have sex." Not only does she accept the physical realities of life, but she also lives by the spiritual realities of her tribal beliefs, which include an afterlife very different from that of the missionaries. She shows the power of her beliefs in the last moments she spends with her father as he prepares to die. Because she knows that he will die in the place he dreamed of earlier and thus enter the afterlife, she accepts his death quietly. Throughout the film, Annuka is a unique, unpredictable character that reveals a very different outlook from that of the white men her father has pledged to guide to the Huron tribe. Chomina, however, as a leader of his tribe and an ally of the French, has more difficult decisions than his daughter. After having a dream that he will die at the end of his journey, he decides to consult the holy man, Mestigoit (Yvan Labelle), who tells him to leave the company of the demon missionary. This advice, plus his disapproval of his daughter's romance and the anger of his people at Laforgue, convince him to leave the missionary. Not long afterward, however, Chomina's sense of honor and his political alliance to the French move him to return with his family to find Laforgue. This decision turns out to be a tragic one because, upon his return, the fierce Iroquois ambush his family, killing his wife (Tantoo Cardinal) and capturing him, his children, and the two white men. After the captives suffer a cruel beating as the Iroquois make them run the gauntlet, Chomina must also watch the murder of his son.

Like his daughter, Chomina is a strong character, who sees life in a very different way. During the night before the Iroquois will torture and kill their captives, Annuka again displays her practical strength of character by offering herself to the Iroquois guard and then knocking him out after he mounts her. Though this courageous act of his daughter enables them to escape from the Iroquois, Chomina, weakened by the ordeal, contracts pneumonia and dies as predicted in his dream of a Raven (death) and a snow-covered island. Thus, though Chomina's decision to return to Laforgue is honorable on one level, it does lead to the death of everyone in his family except Annuka. After the death of her father, she and Daniel know they must escape the influence of the missionary so that they can have a chance to make a new life in the wilderness.

The destructive influence of the missionary on the Algonquin family is recapitulated for a whole tribe when Laforgue finally reaches the Huron village. These people, who are decimated by the fever, are willing to go against their religion and be baptized in order to drive away the evil spirits of their disease. Though the tormented Laforgue knows that baptism will not help them, he goes through with the ceremony. On that ironic note, the movie ends with an epilogue, which explains that, after the Jesuits left, the Christianized Huron were eventually conquered by the fierce Iroquois.

Another Canadian movie, *Clearcut* (1991), takes an equally hard look at a similar conflict between white and First Nation people. This movie, *Black Robe*, and another Canadian movie, *Cold Journey* (1985) reveal a grim, unromantic attitude toward the conflicts between white and Native cultures quite unlike that of American films. Of all these Canadian films, *Clearcut* (1991) pushes audiences farthest into the real and potential violence of such conflicts. The central character of the film is an avenging spirit named Arthur (Graham Greene), who represents the other dangerously excessive side of traditional trickster spirits. Though Arthur has the same verbal sense of humor as the trickster-type characters of Philbert Bono in *Powwow Highway* (1988) or Harold Sinseer in *Harold of Orange* (1984), he has come for revenge and blood, not to trick and befuddle the white man. Wilf (Floyd Red Crow Westerman), the elder of the Ojibwa tribe whose land is being destroyed by the clear-cutting, tells a story to the tribe's white lawyer that explains the origin and danger of Arthur. In the old days an avenging spirit "stained the ground with the blood" of the tribe's enemies until he had to be stopped. Wilf tells the story to the lawyer because he realizes that Arthur is not only the ancient spirit but also the personification of the lawyer's own frustration and anger, which only he can ultimately stop.

The movie begins with the lawyer witnessing the police beating up members of the tribe at the site of the clear-cutting. A classic liberal who has failed in all his lawsuits against the lumber company, the lawyer can only seethe with ineffectual anger as he watches the violence. Wilf senses his problem and invites him to participate in a traditional sweat ceremony, to "purify yourself and to find out what you really want." After having a vision of blood and seeing the face of Arthur during the sweat, the lawyer realizes that "someone has to pay" for what is happening to the tribal land. Shortly thereafter, he meets the mysterious Arthur and suggests, tongue-in-cheek, that they could solve the problem of the clear-cutting by blowing up the lumber mill and skinning the manager alive. The lawyer can only joke about his outrage and desire for revenge because at his core he abhors violence and believes in the sanctity of the law. Arthur, however, has come to act out the feelings of the lawyer. For example, at his apartment, the lawyer is burning with frustration because he cannot stop the people next door from making noise. Then Arthur arrives and solves the problem by threatening them with a large commando knife and then wrapping duct tape around their arms and mouths. When he's finished, Arthur, who, unlike his namesake, believes not in chivalry but in vengeance, smiles at the shocked lawyer and says, "Now let's do some real work."

The "real work" is vengeance on the owner of the lumber mill. After Arthur kidnaps the lumberman and takes him into the wilderness, the lawyer, who is now also his prisoner, becomes horrified when he realizes that Arthur is going to take his earlier joke seriously and torture and kill the man. Arthur, whose dialogue takes on a crazy humor that plays on the movie stereotypes, says, "I could scalp him and be a real Indian. I should be a real Indian." Later, when the lawyer confronts him as he skins the lumberman's leg, Arthur says, "I am your friendly neighborhood cruel Indian," and then reminds the lawyer of white cruelty toward his people such as that of soldiers who cut off the breasts of Navajo women and played catch with them. When two policemen come and Arthur kills one and wounds the other, he says to the wounded man, "It's the Indian guy that's supposed to be dead, that's what you think," before he kills him with a wooden war club. As Arthur's actions become and more violent, Wilf must remind the lawyer that his anger is real and "someone must pay." He must also warn the lawyer that, like the ancient avenging spirit, Arthur has to be stopped.

After the three men arrive at a sacred place with ancient pictographs, Arthur, who is becoming more and more troubled, forces the men to do a sweat ceremony, "to purify ourselves for what is coming next," and then finally provokes the lawyer into a violent fight. During the fight the lawyer loses his glasses (the last emblem of his civilized self) and shoots Arthur. Last seen in an extreme close-up before he sinks into the water from which he came, Arthur gives the lawyer a look that says, "Now you understand that I am the dark part of your own anger." After the disappearance of Arthur, the lawyer finally understands the identity of an Ojibwa girl, Polly (Tia Smith), whom he saw at the beginning smoking a cigarette and now sees, upon his return to the village, wearing the medallion of Arthur. He knows the ancient spirit can change shapes and be an innocent child or come back as a bloody adversary whenever his tribe or Mother Earth is threatened.

The violence in *Clearcut* is excessive in parts, but it is only a small part of the film's passionate and somewhat heavy-handed commitment to expressing the uniqueness of the tribe's ceremonies and its feeling for the land. Like the lawyer, the audience learns a new mythology of the environment, a new sense of the evil forces released by violence to Mother Earth. This environmental theme, in fact, is somewhat common in recent films dealing with native people such as *Emerald Forest* (1985), *Journey to Spirit Island* (1988), *Powwow Highway* (1988), and *Medicine Man* (1992). The next representative film, *Thunderheart* (1992) continues this environmental theme.

Though a more glossy Hollywood production than *Clearcut*, *Thunderheart* also focuses on the struggle of a tribe to preserve both its traditional values and the resources of its land. The film is directed by an Englishman, Michael Apted, who a year before had made the documentary, *Incident at Oglala* (1991), an in-depth exploration of AIM, the killing of two FBI agents at Pine Ridge Sioux Reservation, and the trial of Leonard Peltier. This experience obviously heightened his awareness not only of the conflicts between traditional and modern values on contemporary reservations, but also of the beauties and mysteries of the South Dakota landscape. A *Variety* critic comments that *Thunderheart* "takes a poignant, witty and often deeply moving journey into the Indian community to reveal the secrets of the Badland landscapes, the messages carried by animals and the magic of the ancient beliefs and ceremonies, all against the backdrop of historical oppression" (Mar. 30, 1992). The audience makes this "journey" into Lakota culture with Ray Lavoi, an FBI agent of mixed-blood Sioux-Lakota heritage, as he finds his native identity through interaction with tribal policeman Walter Crow Horse (Graham Greene), traditional elder, Grandpa Sam Reaches (Chief Ted Thin Elk), and radical leaders Maggie Eagle Bear (Sheila Tousey) and Jimmy Looks Twice (John Trudell).

When Ray Lavoi first meets Walter Crow Horse they are almost a complete study in opposites. Ray is dressed in the classic FBI uniform, a dark suit, white shirt, striped tie, and expensive dark glasses, while Crow Horse, the tribal policeman, wears faded jeans, denim jacket, cowboy hat, and cheap sunglasses. Ray Lavoi responds with the trained intensity of the FBI agent as he fails to recognize Crow Horse as a law officer and subdues him violently. As he is being held to the ground, Crow Horse, on the other hand, reacts with his typical laid-back humor when he says, "You guys got off on the wrong exit. You looking for Mount Rushmore?" He also tells Ray that he has to "make the journey." The differences between these characters start to disappear, however, when Ray Lavoi begins to take the same "journey" toward his Lakota identity that Crow Horse took earlier.

Later, when Crow Horse meets Ray at a powwow, they are still at odds, even though they are beginning to respect each other as investigators. Crow Horse tells Ray about his childhood, during which he, like Ray, was ashamed of his Native American heritage: "When we played cowboys and Indians, I was always Gary Cooper." He then explains that the ARM (Aboriginal Rights Movement—a fictional AIM) radical warriors and their spiritual leader, Grandpa Sam, helped him to take pride in his Lakota heritage. After this exchange, the two men go to Grandpa Sam's trailer and have one more fight before the old man comes out and berates them for "acting like a couple of old women," and then invites them in to watch TV. This breaks the tension, cements their friendship, and marks the beginning of their fight against the evil forces of the FBI and the goons of the tribal council chairman. A sign of their connection to Grandpa Sam is the fact that Crow Horse now wears the Ray Ban sunglasses, which Ray traded to Grandpa Sam, who then traded them to Crow Horse.

As with Crow Horse, Ray and Jimmy Looks Twice (played by former AIM spokesman John Trudell) are at first antagonists who meet when the FBI agents interrupt the sweat ceremony to apprehend Jimmy. Again, after Ray accepts Grandpa Sam as his elder, he begins to understand that Jimmy is a new kind of warrior who uses the old beliefs to protect the environment and heritage of their people. Later, when Ray sees Jimmy at Grandpa Sam's trailer, Jimmy explains his fight against the evil government forces: "They have to kill us because they can't break our spirit. . . . It's in our DNA, you have to do what the old man (Grandpa) says. . . . There is a way to live with the earth and a way not to live with the earth; we choose the way of earth—it's about power, Ray!" Just before this scene, Ray receives the same message from the other ARM leader, Maggie Little Bear, a character to whom he is also drawn as he accepts his Lakota identity.

As with Crow Horse and Jimmy Looks Twice, Ray has several angry exchanges with Maggie before he gains her respect. Their relationship changes when Ray, who is visiting Maggie's grandmother during an attack on Maggie's house by reservation goons, risks his life to take her wounded son to the hospital. Later, when they meet for the last time, they share an intimate conversation in which Ray admits he knew his Native American father and says, "I was ashamed of him so I buried him, but my own people dug him up, my own people." Later in their conversation, she explains to him that the real power of her people lies in the natural resources of the reservation, and especially the river, which she knows is being poisoned. As she and Ray part, with the hint of romantic feelings, she calmly tells him she is going to "the source" and that he will have to do the same. The "source" turns out to be Red Rock Table where the forces of evil are preparing to mine uranium. In that lonely place, Ray and Crow Horse find her body. (The mystery of her murder parallels that of AIM member Anna Mae Aquash, and is only one of numerous parallels between the characters of the film and historical figures.)

With the death of Maggie and the imprisonment of Jimmy, the responsibility to carry on their fight falls on Ray and Crow Horse. By this time, Ray has been prepared by several dream visions of his ancestors, one of whom Grandpa Sam tells him is Thunderheart, a warrior who fought at the Wounded Knee Battle. With this realization of his warrior spirit, Ray joins his friend, Crow Horse, to take on the FBI and the reservation goons, whom they lead on a wild chase until cornered at an area called "the stronghold." However, just as they are about to be killed, Grandpa Sam and other traditional people, seen holding rifles on the bluff behind the heroes in sweeping low-angle shots, rescue them and stop the government's evil plan to destroy the reservation with the uranium mines. Though quite stirring, this rescue is pure Hollywood (with hints of earlier scenes in westerns) and quite a contrast to the more ambiguous and realistic ending of *Clearcut*.

Despite this ending, *Thunderheart* is certainly the strongest of the Hollywood films at giving an empathetic view of the sense of humor and respect for tribal rituals and traditions that help Native Americans survive on contemporary reservations. Grandpa Sam, wonderfully acted by Ted Thin Elk in the tradition of Chief Dan George, has a trickster sense of humor in his appreciation of Mr. Magoo on TV and in his trading of objects with Ray, which is humorous at first and then significant at the end when Ray gives him his Rolex and, with a laugh, he gives Ray the sacred pipe, a symbol of his new warrior identity. The other character who has a distinctive sense of humor throughout the film is Walter Crow Horse. For example, when Ray tells him about his dream, Crow Horse teases his new friend: "You had yourself a vision. Most people wait a lifetime, but along comes an instant Indian, with a fucking Rolex and new pair of shoes, and a goddamned FBI man to top it all off, and he has a vision!" Even Ray, after he sheds his FBI demeanor, shows some humor when he calls the stray dog he acquires Jimmy, as a joke on that character's reputation as a shape changer. In addition to the humor, the valuing of tribal tradition can be seen in Ray's learning of his new identity through an acceptance of visions and the rituals of the warrior.

The final representative movie, *Smoke Signals* (1998), also has stirring scenes, but focuses on more universal human themes like the relationship between fathers and sons. Based on two stories from Sherman Alexie's collection of stories, *The Lone Ranger and Tonto Fistfight in Heaven*, the movie essentially deals with the relationship of Arnold Joseph (Gary Farmer) and his son, Victor (Adam Beach), which turns on Arnold's accidental starting of a tragic fire, his descent into alcoholism, and Victor's deep resentment of his father's actions. Though Arnold truly loves his family, he leaves the reservation because of guilt for his drinking, which led to the fire, and abusive treatment of his wife and son. When news of Arnold's death in his self-exile comes to the reservation, Victor and his friend, Thomas (Adam Evans), whose parents were killed in the fire, take a bus trip to collect the remains of Arnold. On this trip, which Thomas pays for and Victor very reluctantly takes, flashbacks establish the characters of the two travelers and Arnold.

During the trip, the filmmakers use the characters to make fun of the traditional Hollywood images of Native Americans. One of the famous statements of the typical stoical, noble Red Man is "It's a good day to die." Taken from Thomas Berger's novel, *Little Big Man*, and voiced by the Cheyenne leader, Old Lodge Skins, in the film version, the saying has little or no historical veracity, and yet has become well known. At one point on the trip, Thomas is talking about the kindness of Arnold and says that they decided it was "a good day to have breakfast." Earlier, at the beginning of the film the news announcer notes that "it is a good day to be indigenous." This wry humor continues in a scene in which Victor teaches

Thomas how to be a typical "Indian." After criticizing Thomas for seeing *Dances with Wolves* (in which Native American characters smile), Victor explains that real warriors have to look into the distance with a slight scowl on their face and look like they just came back from a buffalo hunt. And Thomas replies, "but our tribe were fishermen." Later Victor tries the look with the hostile bus driver and it completely fails. Toward the end of the trip, after the mild mannered Thomas comes out of a building with long hair and a "Fry Bread Power" T-shirt, the two young men have some fun with an iconic western hero noted for his grim tight-lipped look with their song "John Wayne's Teeth."

The humor on the bus balances the sad flashbacks to the deterioration of Arnold due to guilt about the fire and his resulting drunkenness and abuse of his family, even though he still loves them dearly. When the two young men arrive at the place Arnold lived after he left his family and stopped drinking, they meet Suzy Song (Irene Bedard), the young Native American who took care of Arnold and loved him her own way. She gives Victor a new and more positive view of his father, who lived in a trailer by himself before he died. Finally Victor goes into the trailer, which still has the smell of death, and finds personal items that show his father always loved him. As a token of respect, Victor cuts off his long hair, just as Arnold had done earlier as a sign of respect for Thomas's parents. After this, Victor and Thomas decide to bring the ashes of Arnold back to his reservation, though Victor still feels alienated from his father. After a harrowing trip in Arnold's old pickup back to the reservation, Victor and Thomas each take half of the ashes.

Thomas, who really is at the center of the movie's meaning because he knows the truth about Arnold and the ways of his tribe, decides to go up to the bridge where he and Arnold had met and throw the ashes into the boiling water of the river because he sees Arnold as one of the "Salmon people." Though Victor finally reconciles with his father and also throws the ashes in the river, Thomas is the one to give the moving tribute to the struggles of fathers and sons. As a voice-over, with high-angle-shot images of the wild river and moving music in the background, he says, "How do we forgive our fathers? Maybe in a dream. Do we forgive our fathers for leaving us too often, or forever, when we were little? Maybe for scaring us with unexpected rage, or making us nervous because there never seemed to be any rage there at all? Do we forgive our fathers for marrying, or not marrying, our mothers? Or divorcing, or not divorcing, our mothers? And shall we forgive them for their excesses of warmth or coldness? Shall we forgive them for pushing, or leaning? For shutting doors or speaking through walls? For never speaking, or never being silent? Do we forgive our fathers in our age, or in theirs? Or in their deaths, saying it to them or not saying it. If we forgive our fathers, what is left?"

How can anyone not be moved by these words and maybe forget for a moment that this is a film dealing with contemporary Native Americans? Thomas is aware of such gripping struggles, but also never loses his sense of humor. This can be seen in another comment he makes about Arnold, "Arnold got arrested, you know. But he got lucky. They charged him with attempted murder. Then they plea-bargained that down to assault with a deadly weapon. Then they plea-bargained that down to being an Indian in the twentieth century. Then he got two years in Walla Walla." These words of Thomas are good examples of how the film blends serious human issues with wry Native American humor. This technique allows the film to make serious points about Native American life without beating the viewer over the head. In other words, the film tells its story in its own way. This is what is new about Native American film, and what we will see in most of the films of the 2000s.

Films of the 2000s

At the beginning of *Christmas in the Clouds* (2005), the wise and humorous elder narrator of this film produced by a Native American tribe, says, "You've probably heard lots of stories about Indians riding the plains, wearing next to nothing, and shooting off arrows, but this is a story of now-a-day Indians." New films telling the stories of contemporary Native Americans will be represented by *Atanarjuat: The Fast Runner* (2001), *Skins* (2002), *The Business of Fancy Dancing* (2002), and *Barking Water* (2009). In these films, Native Americans control much of the plots, filming, and acting and establish a thematic pattern and empathy for these cultures. We will also look at two recent big-budget Hollywood films that reinterpret two recurring stories about stereotypical Native Americans. *The New World* (2006) significantly revises the recurring story of Pocahontas, and *The Lone Ranger* (2013) almost completely reinterprets the well-known story of Tonto and the Lone Ranger.

The first of the representative movies, *Atanarjuat: The Fast Runner* (2001) is an Inuit movie financed by that First Nation and the National Film Board of Canada. It is an almost perfect example of native people telling their own story because it was directed by and acted by Inuit people in their language, Inukitit, and is based on a traditional Inuit folk story. This might suggest that the movie not only would only be appealing to a small audience, but also that it would be amateurish in its use of film techniques. Neither is true. The movie played to quite large audiences and is now considered a true classic in the history of the movies. It shows that native people can tell their stories in a universal and artistic fashion by merging an epic tale with the wealth of detail one expects in a documentary.

Using high-definition TV cameras rather than film cameras, which are adversely affected by the frigid temperatures, the filmmakers begin with shots of the vastness and brilliant color of the arctic setting. Then they cut to a close-up of boots in the snow, to the head of the Inuit character, and to a medium shot of the dogs pulling the sled. This editing technique, which continues throughout the film, brings the viewer into the picture and involves them directly in the epic story. (See the book by Michael Evans [2010] for a detailed explanation of how this film was made.)

The story begins with the curse of an evil shaman, which poisons the camp of Atanarjuat's parents. A voice-over explains the effect of the curse: "We never knew what he was or why it happened. Evil came to us like Death. It just happened and we had to live with it." Then the story flashes forward to a time when Atanarjuat

(Natar Ungalaaq) and his brother are young men and the same age as the evil Oki (Peter Henry Arnatsiaq), the son of the leader of the camp, Suari (Eugene Ipkanak), who was involved in the original curse. Oki and Atanarjuat both want to marry Atuat (Sylvia Ivalu), who loves Atanarjuat, but was betrothed to Oki. To settle the issue, they have a head-punching duel in which the first man knocked to the floor of the warmly and dimly lit igloo wins. After each man endured the punch of his opponent, Oki is downed by the second punch and Atanarjuat claims Atuat as his wife. This, in turn, sets up the story of Oki's attempt at revenge.

Atanarjuat eventually also takes Puja (Lucy Tulugarjuk), the sister of Oki, as a wife and later exiles her from his camp when he discovers her and his brother having sexual intercourse. She returns to her brother's camp and accuses Atanarjuat of beating her. This lie intensifies Oki's desire for revenge and motivates him, and several other friends, to seek out the camp of Atanarjuat. The crosscutting between the attackers and Atanarjuat and his brother sleeping in their tent intensifies the attack, which results in the murder of the brother and the beginning of Atanarjuat's naked run across the ice. The cuts between the pursuers and Atanarjuat heighten the seemingly hopeless running escape. However, after he has collapsed on the ice, an old man who turns out to be Oki's great uncle rescues him. After the old man and his family hide Atanarjuat from Oki and his men, and then nurse him back to health, Atanarjuat and his rescuer's family return to the camp of Sauri, where Atanarjuat is joyfully reunited with his wife, Atuat, who has also returned. In the meantime, Oki, who is angry that his father won't let him have Atuat as a wife, rapes her and kills the old man. Then Atanarjuat plans his own bloodless revenge on Oki by preparing an igloo that has a slick, icy floor. When Oki and his henchmen come to visit and kill Atanarjuat, he puts on caribou spike shoes and easily subdues the men who slide and fall on the icy floor. However, he does not kill Oki with his club and lets it be known that the killing will stop. In the final scene, the old man who had rescued Atanarjuat uses the magic of the walrus to subdue and destroy the evil shaman from the beginning of the story. A female elder then forgives Oki, Puja, and their men, but makes them leave and never return. So, at the end of this epic story, the family has rid itself of the evil of the shaman's curse and now lives joyously.

The audience of this movie is so drawn into this story by the skill of the filmmakers that they may see it as a documentary, rather than a well-crafted narrative film. Maybe to jog the audience into thinking about the meaning of the movie, the end credits show the cast in modern dress, complete with contemporary sunglasses.

The second representative movie, *Skins* (2002), is based on the novel by Adrian Louis and directed by Chris Eyre. In this movie, which is a sad and realistic depiction of life on Pine Ridge Reservation in South Dakota, the director of *Smoke Signals* looks at another side of Native American life on reservations. The movie begins with long shots of the ramshackle houses of the reservation and a voice-over detailing the pathetic economic state of the people. Then the director cuts to a long shot of the placid faces on Mount Rushmore, a very popular attraction for tourists, who then bypass the reservation. The documentary-type beginning sets the context for the very human story of two Native American brothers, Mogie Yellow Lodge (Graham Greene) and Rudy Yellow Lodge (Eric Schweig).

To develop the story Chris Eyre uses flashbacks from the present to the time when the brothers were younger. As Rudy is standing over a bathroom sink while looking in a mirror and rubbing off black coloring on his face, he sees a spider on the sink. This is followed by a flashback to when they were boys and Mogie was carrying Rudy because a spider had bitten him in the "balls." This connects the brothers with the spider, which is one of the shapes the traditional Lakota trickster takes. The spider appears two more times, one of which is near the end of the movie when Rudy is carrying out his brother's wishes at Mount Rushmore. This spider motif suggests that Mogie and Rudy, in their own misguided and sad ways, may represent the spirit of the trickster returning to vanquish the evil spirits of lawlessness and alcoholism on the reservation.

A little later, the audience finds out that Mogie and his friend, Verdell Weasel Tail (Gary Farmer), are alcoholics. However, they also see that Mogie is addicted to alcohol in large part because he is angry about his past and present life on the reservation. In a flashback, his alcoholic father becomes violent with him, his brother, and mother. Mogie's drinking helps him escape temporarily the anger provoked by these bad memories of his youth, his own drunken behavior with his family, and his fighting in Vietnam, where he received three Purple Hearts. When he returned to the reservation where he, like many other Vietnam vets, received no hero's welcome, he once again had to face the grim life on the reservation referred to at the beginning of the movie. Although he is angry and remorseful, he also has a sense of humor and an awareness of his tribal traditions. In a football game, while Rudy is being flashy in his running past his opponents, Mogie tackles him and reminds Rudy that "showing off is not a Lakota virtue." Later, after he has been terribly burned, he can still make a joke about the hunting skills of the Crow tribe, who were traditional enemies of the Lakota.

The audience also finds out that Mogie is not alone in his anger and remorse. Rudy turns out to be a vigilante, who disguises himself with the black facial coloring and a pullover mask to punish members of his tribe, some of whom used a baseball bat to beat to death a young Lakota man. After this, we again see him wiping off his vigilante black color as he again looks at a spider on the sink. His vigilante anger returns when he sees a TV report on a liquor store that sells to tribal members. Again in his disguise, he douses the store with gasoline and sets it on fire, only to find out that Mogie was on the liquor store roof and was terribly burned. Rudy is devastated by his brother's injuries and the fact that he, a law officer, has taken the law into his own hands and caused this tragedy.

The key to the power of these scenes is the acting of Graham Greene as Mogie and Eric Schweig as Rudy. For example, when Mogie, scarred from his burns and suffering from cirrhosis of the liver, is watching a western on TV with his son and Rudy, his expression intensifies his words. As the movie typically glorifies the soldier at the expense of the Native Americans, Mogie tells the historical story of the Wounded Knee massacre of 1890, the last of the "battles" between the U.S. soldiers and the Lakota. He gives details of the vicious killing of starving warriors and women and children on that winter day. Ending his account of the massacre by mentioning the fact that the union soldiers received medals of honor for their part in the massacre, his face mirrors his anger and frustration. Then in the next moment, Rudy tells Mogie that he is a vigilante and Mogie's expression instantaneously changes to a sly mocking look, and he responds with typical humor, "Like Rambo?" After this quip, Rudy's face, which had a look of anger and horror, immediately takes on a smile of appreciation for his brother's ability to find humor in a grim confession.

As the plot moves on, the contrast between the brothers becomes clearer. When Rudy tells Mogie that a reservation family has let his friend, Verdell, die an agonizing death, Mogie vows revenge. However, when Mogie dons his Vietnam uniform, sneaks up to the house of the family, and gets the guilty man in his sights, he decides not to take the law into his own hands and he removes his finger from the trigger. He will not become a vigilante like Rudy.

Not long after this, Mogie's cirrhosis leads to his death, and the tribe gives him a hero's funeral. After the funeral, Rudy decides that he must honor a promise he made to his brother to desecrate the faces on Mount Rushmore for him. He buys a five-gallon can of red paint and laboriously climbs to the top of the monument, where he again sees the spider or trickster. That spider helps him to feel that his trickster brother is there with him, and he throws the open can of paint onto the face of George Washington. The red paint dripping down the nose of the founder of the United States is rich in the symbolism of the blood the "Redmen" shed at the hands of the whites.

Though the ending of the movie is upbeat in the sense that Rudy has achieved catharsis and a connection to his brother, it also reminds the audience that Pine Ridge is a place of bloodshed and sadness for its inhabitants. Roger Ebert offers a fitting conclusion: "*Skins* is a portrait of a community almost without resources to save itself. We know from 'Smoke Signals' that Eyre also sees another side to his people, but the anger and stark reality he uses here are potent weapons. The movie is not about a crime plot, not about whether Rudy gets caught, not about how things work out. It is about regret. Graham Greene achieves the difficult task of giving a touching performance even though his character is usually drunk, and it is the regret he expresses, to his son and to his brother, that carries the movie's burden of sadness. To see this movie is to understand why the faces on Mount Rushmore are so painful and galling to the first Americans. The movie's final image is haunting" (Ebert 2002). This image also repeats the image of Mount Rushmore at the beginning, except this time we see the connection to the people of Pine Ridge.

Like *Skins*, the next representative movie also deals with life on a contemporary reservation. Adapted from Sherman Alexie's book of stories and poems, *The Business of Fancydancing* (1992), directed by Alexie, tells the stories of three contemporary Native Americans: Seymour Polatkin (Evan Adams), a gay poet, who has a big following among white audiences; Aristotle Joseph (Gene Tagaban), a young radical who lives on the reservation; and Agnes Roth (Michelle St. John), a mixed blood who has returned to the Spokane reservation to teach and who was or is connected romantically to the two male characters. All three interact on the reservation when Seymour returns for the funeral of their friend, Mouse (Swil Kanim), the most openly self-destructive character of the group. Though the main purpose of the movie seems to be a narrative of a complicated autobiographical book, Alexie, as a neophyte director, uses techniques such as silent movie title cards, a mysterious interviewer, flashbacks, and odd crosscutting to distance and sometimes confuse the audience. As he does with the book, Alexie creates many questions, but few answers, about the nature of a contemporary Native American artist like himself.

Seymour Polatkin, the poet who speaks to white audiences, is probably Alexie's most autobiographical character because he is a noted author. A mysterious interviewer and members of his white audiences ask Seymour questions about the nature of Native American artists. For example, when the black female interviewer pushes Seymour on the "real" meaning of his Russian name, he replies, "Well, I'd bet you don't want to get into a long and detailed discussion about colonialism and the missionary position." He uses this sly evasion and another in which he tells a white audience that is curious about his sexual orientation a story his grandmother told about a chicken that was gay. The punch line comes when he notes that she finally decides to eat him because she realizes that a gay chicken is just a chicken. Such comments leave the interviewer and the somewhat confused audience with the feeling that he is a clever artist who steadfastly refuses to talk directly about himself or his art. Later, when he is not in front of an audience, he says something straightforward about his life as a revered poet in the city, "The Reservation just won't let me go." He then decides he must return to the reservation for the funeral of his friend, Mouse, who was never evasive in his expression of the painful truth and ended his tortured life with suicide.

Seymour's arrival at the reservation brings him in contact with his friend since boyhood, Aristotle, who is almost a polar contrast and probably another side of Sherman Alexie's personality. Aristotle is the macho, angry Native American who can't really function off the reservation. He mocks Seymour after he returns for the funeral, "Man, you like it out here don't you? Playing Indian, putting on the beads and feathers for all these white people. Out here you're their little public relations warrior. You're a super Indian. You're the expert and the authority. But at home man, you're just little Indian who cries too much." In addition to giving a sense of Aristotle's angry character, this statement is similar to the ones that appear throughout the movie on silent film title cards on which appear comments about what his tribe thinks of Seymour. These title cards break up the flow of the movie and distance the audience from the narrative. Their purpose seems to be another somewhat obvious cinematic way of getting at what the tribe thinks of Seymour or Alexie without having them appear in the movie.

As the character of Aristotle becomes more and more angry (and maybe one-dimensional), he finally goes over the edge and beats up a white tourist who is lost on the reservation. Aristotle's wild and angry energy appeals to Agnes Roth, who is part Jewish and part Spokane, and stands between the two extremes of Seymour and Aristotle. She is smart and practical and comes back to teach the youth of the reservation. She doesn't believe in the evasion or anger of the other two characters and may represent the middle ground of Alexie's personality. Though it angers Aristotle, she welcomes Seymour, her former boyfriend in college, back to the reservation, and encourages him to readopt some of the traditional tribal ideas, especially those that relate to the funeral of his friend, Mouse. She shows her practical side when she responds to Aristotle, who says, "God, how did we make fry bread so sacred? This stuff is so bad for us. Indians are too fat, you know." And Agnes replies, "Yeah, but it's so good." Later she says to Seymour about his desire to be a noted writer, "It's your ambition that made the rez a prison." She understands that Seymour must pay the price, especially with his white audiences, for being a well-known writer. He can't have both the approval and traditions of the reservation and the adulation of the city people at the same time. Possibly Alexie himself might accept this middle-ground view of the Native American artist, but the audience can't be sure because of the way he complicates the excesses of the two central male characters.

Throughout the movie, Alexie uses flashbacks and crosscutting, to emphasize differences between the two men in Agnes's life. Near the end of the movie the differences intensify when Seymour says to Aristotle, "I deserved a better life than I was born into. But I made it better with nobody's help, including shit from you. And I got no help from any of these goddamn Indians here. I had to do it myself." And Aristotle replies, "You write about these goddamn Indians! Telling me you did it yourself! These Indians that you write about, they're helping you every day, each and every one of them; every house, every story, every poem. They're helping you. Telling me you had nobody. We've been helping you since you were born." This exchange epitomizes the ambition and anger of Seymour and the resentment and anger of Aristotle, which has destroyed their friendship and their balance as contemporary Native Americans. Agnes has achieved a kind of balance, but she can only watch as excess and self-pity diminish her friends.

Sherman Alexie has taken on a big challenge in this movie by focusing on contemporary young Native American characters whose lives become grim on and off the reservation because of their self-centered excesses. Unlike the script he wrote for *Smoke Signals*, which had humor and appeal for a broad audience, the script for this movie has only flashes of ironic humor. However, as Elvis Mitchell notes, "The director's dry sincerity leavens the sentiment of this quasi-autobiographical film, a tale about the burden of constantly being asked who you are and where you come from, a question that artists of color constantly hear, either from others or themselves. Mr. Alexie is smart enough to know it's never satisfactorily answered" (Mitchell 2002). Though the somewhat self-indulgent technique of this movie may confuse the audience at times, it allows a distance for the audience to evaluate the dilemmas of contemporary Native American activists, artists, and reservations.

The next representative movie, *Barking Water*, directed by Sterlin Harjo, also deals with a painful return to a reservation. However, it also explores the major human themes of friendship, love, and the process of dying, with techniques much more straightforward than that of *The Business of Fancydancing*. The recurring close-ups of the two main characters and their resulting film presence are what carry the power in the simple story line of this movie. Frankie (Richard Ray Whitman), an older Seminole who has terminal cancer, and Irene (Casey Camp-Horinek), a Native American woman who is his only real friend and former lover, travel in a well-used station wagon across the back roads of Oklahoma to see his daughter and granddaughter in Wevoka, Oklahoma, the city of Barking Water, the adopted home of the Seminole Nation. Irene promises to get him home to Wevoka, but their trip becomes a kind of emotional homecoming for the two of them.

As they travel across Oklahoma, the director often flashes back to gold-tinted scenes that show various stages of their earlier time as lovers. After one scene, Irene expresses her hurt because Frankie has left her. Although she says that she will never be able to love him again, her affection for him grows as the trip goes on. After another more happy flashback scene, Frankie says, "I still love you. Always have and always will." On the road trip itself, they experience visits to relatives, a stop at a farm field for Irene to give the weakening Frankie a sage smudging ceremony, which is misinterpreted as voodoo by the farmer who owns it, before they become friends. As their trip continues, the basic goodness and appreciation of the characters for each other grows. Close-ups of the worn but proud faces of the two Native American actors Ray Whitman and Casey Camp-Horinek express the characters' affection and sadness in a powerfully simple way. Each new stop, such as the picking up of a couple whose car has stalled, or going to a church meeting, brings them closer together and Frankie closer to death before they reach Wevoka. Near the end, Frankie says, "Seems so strange, you know, I won't be feeling this rain anymore or feeling this wind. Always thought I'd go out in . . . go to sleep and never wake up. This going slow shit, slowly losing control. Yeah. I still got my mind. So weird, you know, I finally feel like I am figuring it out and damn I'm out the door." After this, we see Frankie and Irene in close-ups looking at each other.

Stephen Holden comments on such scenes, "During those silences the camera studies Frankie's and Irene's handsome, haggard faces, which convey, more than words, the dignity of two people who have lived intensely and carry many regrets. Frankie's deep, rumbling voice, even when weakened, lends his remarks a weighty finality" (Holden 2010, 28).

Before Frankie's death, Irene wraps his shivering body in a blanket as a preparation for his death, and he sees horses, which have a special meaning for him because they remind him of his earlier life. These are the same horses that appear in one of the first shots of the movie—a black-and-white close-up of him stroking their heads. His life has taken a circle toward death. Shortly thereafter Frankie dies, and

Irene cries and holds his hand in silence, before she brings his body to what could have been home—his daughter's house. During this final sequence, a female voice sings a song in a voice-over, just as the film began with a female voice singing a jaunty song while Frankie escapes from the hospital. Throughout the film, music with a country feeling helps set the atmosphere of the Oklahoma landscape. In this backcountry setting, the overwhelming feeling of this movie is the dignity of these simple but powerful characters.

Though other movies from the 2000s such as *Christmas in the Clouds* (2001), *Run, Broken Yet Proud* (2009), *Imprint* (2007), or *Winter in the Blood* (2013) give an intimate look at contemporary Native American life in movies made by Native American filmmakers, we will now look at the more controversial other side of the 2000s: big-budget films in which white directors reinterpret the stories of Pocahontas and the Lone Ranger.

The next representative movie, *The New World* (2005), directed by Terence Malik, tells the familiar quasi-historical story or legend of Pocahontas, Captain John Smith, John Rolfe, and the founding of the Jamestown colony in Virginia. The "New World" for the pilgrims is North America and the tribe of Powhatan, whereas for the tribe the "New World' is the European religious pilgrims, their ships, and eventually the manicured gardens of England. Like *Black Robe* and, in some ways, *Amistad*, the film reveals some of the similarities of the cultures and opportunities lost because of characters belonging to different races that had too rigid an adherence to their traditional ways of living, languages, and values. The pilgrims come from a European monarchy and the tribe of Powhatan (August Schellenberg) is also a sophisticated North American monarchy, as is illustrated in the first scene of him in the longhouse. Pocahontas (Q'orianka Kircher) and Captain John Smith (Colin Farrell) are examples of what could have happened between the two cultures. In this early part of the movie, the symphonic and operatic background music emphasizes the seriousness of this cultural meeting, which later becomes a place of cultural clash.

After Pocahontas (who is never called this in the movie) saves the life of Captain John Smith, he stays with the tribe and comes to appreciate their way of life not as a dream for the future but as a real possibility, as he notes in a voice-over, "They are gentle, loving, faithful, lacking in all guile and trickery. The words denoting lying, deceit, greed, envy, slander, and forgiveness have never been heard. They have no jealousy, no sense of possession. Real, what I thought a dream." He also realizes what the New World could mean for his people: "Here the blessings of the earth are bestowed upon all. None need grow poor. Here there is good ground for all, and no cost but one's labor. We shall build a true common wealth, hard work and self-reliance our virtues. We shall have no landlords to rack us with high rents or extort the fruit of our labor." However, because he was originally considered a traitor, and again will be seen as a traitor when he returns to his people, he never has a chance to communicate what he has learned because he is exiled.

For a short time before hostility takes over, John Smith and Pocahontas are also the only two people from their cultures who try to learn each other's languages. In some tender scenes dominated by soft medium and close-up shots, they share Algonquin and English words as their affection for each other grows. Their time together and their sharing of languages are, however, stopped by bad feelings between the two cultures. The English pilgrims and the tribe of Powhatan become enemies, partially because a member of the tribe took something that he considered communal property, an action that the English considered stealing. He was severely punished for his "crime." This caused Powhatan not only to send John Smith back to his people but also to disown his beloved daughter.

After this cultural misunderstanding, the tone of the movie changes. Powhatan's tribe attacks the fort and a brutal battle ensues, with numerous quick cuts to hand-to-hand fighting and longer shots from cannons and muzzleloaders of the pilgrims. Any hope for merging the cultures is obviously gone. After the battle, John Smith is again considered a traitor and is sent away, and Pocahontas is branded a traitor by her tribe, which moves away, deeper into the forest.

At this point the English pilgrims feel that God has favored them and given them the New World. Pocahontas is now seen in a white dress and has been baptized and given the name, Rebecca. After a long and heartfelt courting, Pocahontas marries John Rolfe (Christian Bale), who is portrayed as a kind and sensitive man, and they have a baby. Shortly thereafter, they go to England where Pocahontas, accompanied by a member of her tribe, Opechancanough (Wes Studi), is treated like royalty and finally does meet the King and Queen of England. She also sees John Smith again, but the turn her life has taken leaves little between them. What does impress Pocahontas are the massive, manicured English gardens and elegantly trimmed trees, which the camera lingers on as the contrast to the wild beauty of the New World. In a number of the shots, Pocahontas is with her little boy, who is almost always seen from behind. Again in the background is the symphonic and elegiac music as Pocahontas raises her arms near a pool in a gesture she made near the beginning of the film when she experienced ecstasy in her own culture. Her awe for this new setting is brief, however, because she is soon seen in a bed where she dies of either pneumonia or tuberculosis.

At the end of this movie there is a sadness and sense of loss for this young woman and her culture. She is quite different from the long line of media portrayals of this character; as Manohla Dargis writes, "Like those Indian princesses who have long been a favorite of Hollywood, the pop Pocahontas who later emerged in song and cartoons is a comfortable fiction, at least for a country eager to tell its story in the best possible light. In that telling, Pocahontas is the noble savage exalted by an impulse to self-sacrifice for a white man. In Mr. Malick's telling, Pocahontas is a woman whose story has the reach of myth and the tragic dimension of life" (Dargis 2005). As the critic suggests, the interpretation of Pocahontas in this movie invites new thinking about her story. Her character is far from the traditional image of the Native American woman even though her historical marriage and death fit the general pattern for this character type.

The last of the representative big-budget movies is *The Lone Ranger* (2013), which has a tone that is far different from the elegiac one of *The New World*. Whether the film is a shoot-from-the-hip spoof or a more serious satire of westerns is a question much debated by film critics. Some see satire and a wacky tone that constantly call to attention the inconsistencies and contradictions in the story. They feel that these elements and the patchwork of allusions to other classic westerns may well deconstruct the Lone Ranger legend forever. Other mainly Native American critics pan the film as racist because of the clopped movie "Indian" film language of Tonto, and the fact that he is played by a white actor. They also argue that westerns always portray a white supremacist point of view and the story of the Lone Ranger is essentially irredeemable and never should have been portrayed again in a movie (*Indian Country Today Media Network* Staff, July 8, 2013). Both approaches provide valid ways to analyze the movie.

The film does have many allusions to classic westerns, such as Monument Valley, the setting for most of John Ford's westerns. The movie also alludes to Ford in the parallel it draws between the portrayals of the Comanche attack on the ranch house in John Ford's *The Searchers* and the attack on Rebecca Reid's (Ruth Wilson) hideout. In another parallel, the close-up of scorpions in *The Lone Ranger* clearly suggests a motif used at the beginning of many Sam Peckinpah westerns. These and other somewhat more subtle allusions to the films of Arthur Penn and Clint Eastwood make *The Lone Ranger* a kind of crazy quilt of the westerns. These allusions and the strange way in which the ancient Tonto retells the stories of the two heroes in his deadpan satiric tone may well not only twist up the genre of the western but also the long-established legend of the Lone Ranger.

At the beginning of the movie, the audience, along with a boy dressed like the Lone Ranger, meets Tonto (Johnny Depp) in a carnival Wild West sideshow diorama entitled "The Noble Savage in his Native Habitat." When the ancient Tonto moves the boy draws his cap gun and shoots, but Tonto just wants to trade a dead mouse for the boy's peanuts. He then starts the "real" story of the Lone Ranger in a way that is reminiscent of the ancient Jack Crabb's story in Arthur Penn's *Little Big Man*. With the William Tell Overture in the background, the music used as the theme of the old *Lone Ranger* TV series, old Tonto moves us back in time and places us in Monument Valley, a place far removed from Texas, where the traditional story is set. Then, in another twist, we see Tonto and the Lone Ranger (Armie Hammer) robbing a bank. It soon becomes clear that Tonto is neither Noble Red Man nor Savage.

Tonto tells the story using the movie "Indian" language for his character and "plain English" for that of John Reid (the Lone Ranger). He is quite serious when he tells how the white men tricked him as a boy and gave him a pocket watch reward. This deception, white villains taking advantage of Native Americans to further their own evil ends, is a motif in the westerns. And in this film, the deception resulted in the death of Tonto's family and his beloved pet crow. Thus he, not the Lone Ranger, has the motivation to seek revenge or justice on the Cavendish gang, and thus is really the "hero" of the movie. This is what leads to him becoming a kind of shaman with the white and black paint on his face and the strange crow headdress. However, he also can become a comedian. He displays a wry sense of humor in his retelling of the legend, especially in his description of the spirit horse, Silver. Shortly thereafter, the director cuts back to the carnival sideshow with the boy in his costume and old Tonto, who tries to feed the dead crow the boy's peanuts. These cuts to the sideshow continue throughout the film and remind the audience that what they are seeing is just a story told by an ancient man who has been trapped in an image, and a story that is probably trying to make the boy in the Lone Ranger outfit question his reverence for the wild west and cowboy heroes.

As Tonto's story continues, when he and the Lone Ranger are fighting the evil Cavendish gang, we have another example of Tonto's deadpan humor. The Lone Ranger shoots and breaks a rope that drops a beam on two of the villains. Tonto says, "Nice shot." The Lone Ranger replies, "That was supposed to be a warning shot." And Tonto replies, "In that case, not so good." Another example occurs close to the end when the Lone Ranger, with the William Tell Overture rolling in the background, gets Silver to rear up the way Clayton Moore did in the TV series, and Tonto says, "Never do that again." The new and somewhat nerdy Lone Ranger responds, "Sorry." In addition to the humor, the film once again turns around the visual tradition of Silver rearing up associated with the original story.

In the thrilling, yet unbelievable action of the final sequence, with the William Tell Overture at a high volume in the background, the Lone Ranger first rides Silver along the top of a fast moving train and then through the train while Tonto swings on a ladder attached to one of the train cars in the best tradition of the Buster Keaton silent films. Given that this sequence happens after the realistic slaughter of Chief Big Bear's (Saginaw Grant) Comanche warriors by soldiers using repeating rifles and Gatling guns, the audience can soon realize that the ending action, with its wild crosscutting, is really a parody of such scenes in the westerns. It is also an example of Tonto's wild changes of tone in his story.

After the extended action resolution, the film again cuts to the Wild West sideshow, the ancient Tonto, and the boy in the Lone Ranger outfit. The confused look of the boy as he puts his Lone Ranger mask on again is testimony to the contradictions and excesses of Tonto's story in which his character, part shaman and part comedian, has some depth, unlike that of the Lone Ranger who is a one-dimensional, and surprisingly bland character. As the credits roll, Tonto leaves the diorama and slowly walks into the real Monument Valley—or is it the fictional land of John Ford, where we, like the boy in the sideshow, can never be sure about what is real and what is unreal? The legend of the Lone Ranger may live on for a while in reruns of the older versions, but this movie tries hard to deconstruct the legend.

Although *The Lone Ranger* (2013) was a flop at the box office, it was a kind of critical success and may be more appreciated in the future unless the legend and the traditional western have already died. Although this movie had a wider audience than the movies of the Native American filmmakers discussed above, these latter films, and *Christmas in the Clouds*, alluded to briefly in the introductory paragraph, mark the real advance in the portrayal of Native Americans in film during the 2000s. Finally some Native American filmmakers had the chance to tell their own stories. In the next section, we will look at other independent, contemporary films that paved the way for the accomplishments of this new era.

Images of Contemporary Native Americans

THE MORE REALISTIC AND EMPATHETIC DEPICTIONS of Native American characters in the movies are, of course, built on the realization that the traditional images of the Savage and Noble Red Man are empty stereotypes. For example, a member of the Stockbridge Munsee Tribe in Wisconsin, the descendants of the Mohicans, reminded his audience that the Native American characters in Cooper's novel and the 1992 *The Last of the Mohicans* had nothing to do with his tribe, which, he noted with a sly smile, seems to be still among us. We all know that in the fictions of literature and narrative films, any correspondence to real life is "purely coincidental." However, we must keep reminding ourselves that seeing Native American characters in a film is not seeing real Native American people of the past or present. Even for those of us who know Native American people and their history, this is not easy, because we have witnessed the images of the Noble Red Man and Savage so many times that they simply feel comfortable. For example, in *The Last of the Mohicans* (1992), the savage and treacherous Magua (Wes Studi with a "Mohawk" and bare chest), who brutally kills Uncas, is such a grand contrast to the noble and loyal Chingachgook (a well-dressed Russell Means with nice long hair), who is like a father to the hero, Hawkeye. Or in *Dances with Wolves* (1990), the fierce leader of the Pawnee (again Wes Studi with a "Mohawk" and bare chest), who riddles a mule skinner with arrows and mutilates him, balances so nicely against the noble and handsome Lakota holy man, Kicking Bird (Graham Greene with pretty hair and fancy dress), who befriends the hero, John Dunbar. And the violent death of the Savage that occurs in these films, especially the killing of Magua by Chingachgook, seems so right. On the other hand, we resonate (we males, at least) to the deep, enduring feelings shared by the white heroes and their noble Native American friends. And, in spite of our knowledge that the characters are designed to please white audiences, we may respond to the Hollywood formula and feel a tender sympathy for these honorable Native Americans and their friends Hawkeye or John Dunbar as they face a sad and threatening future at the ends of the movies.

However, starting in the 1970s, and intensifying in the 1990s and 2000s, independent movies broke from these comfortable images of the hostile Savage and the friendly Noble Red Man and portrayed contemporary Native Americans as fictional characters significant in and of themselves, not only as contrasts to the white heroes, as is always the case in the westerns. In *House Made of Dawn* (1972), *Three Warriors* (1977), *Harold of Orange* (1984), *Powwow Highway* (1988), and *Imprint* (2007), principal Native American characters, played by Native American actors, find strength and identity in a return to traditional tribal values and rituals. Although these characters are fictional and sometimes sanitized versions of their counterparts in the novels, they allow the films to explore contemporary themes of life on reservations and in the cities. Native American grandfathers and grandmothers serve their communities as elders who teach youths in extended Native American families. Thereby young Native Americans witness the power of dreams, trickster stories, and traditional tribal codes. Such themes drawn from the real world of past and present Native Americans build an understanding of Native American tribal traditions as distinct and worthy of respect. This understanding is a step away from the comfortable images of the western, and a step toward the less comfortable knowledge that can lead to empathy for Native American cultures.

The first of the representative movies, *House Made of Dawn* (1972), with a screenplay written by N. Scott Momaday from his novel, is probably the most complicated and disturbing story. Like the novel, the movie has a circular structure in that it starts and finishes with the main character, Abel (Larry Littlebird), running a ceremonial course, which his grandfather (Mesa Bird) had run many years before. The remainder of the film is a fabric of flashbacks and voice-overs that tell the story of Abel's growing up with his grandfather, his fighting in Vietnam, his killing of an evil albino and serving a prison term, and his attempt to survive in Los Angeles. This central part of the film dramatizes Abel's struggle before he returns to his reservation for the ceremonial run. His two choices are the traditional ways of his grandfather or life in the city as represented by his Navajo friend, Ben Benally (Jay Varela); Millie, a white social worker; and John Tosomah (John Saxon), a priest of an urban Native American church.

At the beginning of the film, Abel is with his dying grandfather, who had been his teacher and his only family. After the old man's death, Abel, seen from a high-angle perspective, prepares for the ritual of the run by taking off his shirt, removing the bandages from his hands (the result of a severe beating by a city policeman), and rubbing himself with ashes. This perspective, which emphasizes his vulnerability at the beginning of the ceremony, will be reversed at the end of the movie when he completes the run. As Abel takes his first steps, a voice-over translation of his grandfather's Pueblo language describes how the old man had run the race many years ago and concludes with, "Those who run are the life that flows in our people." While Abel runs ever more vigorously, the audience finds out through flashbacks why Abel decided to return to his grandfather's land for this healing run.

In the main flashback to his life in Los Angeles, Abel encounters Tosomah, Millie, and Ben. Tosomah, because of his intensely verbal, intellectual, and cynical approach to life, has little effect on Abel: in a peyote ceremony led by the priest, Abel is the only one who cannot express his feelings in words. This suggests that, unlike the rituals of his grandfather, the nontraditional ceremonies of Tosomah have no power for him. Millie, the white social worker, has a stronger effect because she and Abel fall in love. However, this romance is very low-key and when Millie sees that the city has literally and figuratively beaten up Abel, she advises him to go home. He accepts separation from her with little emotional strain. Abel's main struggle is the decision to separate from the only true friend he's ever had, Ben Benally.

Ben Benally has learned how to survive in the city by accepting the new ways of Tosomah and giving in to the dominance of his foreman and an evil policeman. After a meeting with the policeman during which Ben's hands shake with fear and Abel's remain still, Abel asks Ben, "What happened? Don't you ever want to go home?" Ben answers, "Ain't nothing back there. Just old people dying." In addition to cutting himself off from his relatives and compromising his self-respect, Ben has lost contact with his basic Navajo traditions. When he tries to sing one of his tribal songs, he cannot remember it and needs Abel to sing it for him. Later, after Abel stands up to the evil policeman and takes a terrible beating, he finally realizes that he is too different from his friend to survive in the city. With Ben's encouragement, he decides to go home. At a bus depot, Abel and Ben say goodbye in a scene that brings the contrasts between them to a touching climax. Seen in two shots and individual close-ups, the two characters, skillfully underplayed by the actors, barely hold back their tears as they speak to each other slowly and quietly. Abel asks, "What's it going to be like?" Ben replies, "Sometime we'll meet out there and get drunk. We'll go out real early; we'll just see how it is out on the mesa. We'll sing the old songs and we'll get drunk and it will be the last time and it will be beautiful, the way it used to be, the way it always was." The scene ends with a close up of Abel, whose eyes show the realization that he will never see his friend again.

The film transitions from this somber farewell back to the frame of the ceremonial run. At this point Abel, who has run a long way, falls and lies on the ground, panting with exhaustion until he again hears the words, "Those who run are the life that flows in the people." This reminder of the run's spiritual and symbolic meaning gives him the courage to get up and run on. Soon Abel finds his wind and, seen from a low angle, which emphasizes his new strength, he runs up the ridges and changes into the traditional runner with long hair and a breechclout. Then, bathed in golden light, he runs freely toward the sun and a new identity based on the old values, an ending more unequivocally positive than that of the novel.

Native American actors infuse the same quality into *Three Warriors* (1977), another movie in which a young Native American finds a new identity by a return to his reservation and the values of his grandfather (Charles White Eagle). Sensing that his grandson, Michael (McKee Redwing), a teenager who is ashamed to be a Native American, needs help, the old man summons his daughter-in-law (Lois Red Elk) and her family to the reservation. Michael, of course, doesn't want to be there and not only does a lot of sulking, but also is rude to his grandfather. However, the old man has the patience of one who knows how to teach by example. Seen in a low-angle shot (the camera establishes his significance with a pattern of low-angle and close-up shots), he assures his daughter-in-law that "Michael will find peace." However, before the Grandfather teaches Michael the pride of the traditional warrior, he decides to educate a young U.S. Ranger newly assigned to protecting the wild horses on federal land near the reservation.

As the ranger berates the people of the village for not helping to protect the mustangs (with Michael watching), grandfather reminds him that "they're your horses," and then teaches him a lesson in politeness. When the ranger asks him why he had cooperated with the previous ranger, grandfather replies that the other ranger had learned how to be polite in the Native American way by always saying when he met him, "Hey, Uncle, how's your bones?" Then Grandfather, displaying the shrewdness of the trickster, manipulates the ranger into giving him and Michael a ride to a rodeo, where he buys, for a very low price, a fine Palomino. Though the horse appears to be broken down, the old man, a very knowledgeable horseman, can see that it is just temporarily lame. Later, he cons the ranger into taking them and the horse back to the reservation. When the ranger drops them off, he says to the old man, "Hey, Uncle, how's your bones," and Grandfather acknowledges his politeness by inviting him to supper.

Though Michael has witnessed all of this, he still doesn't understand the cleverness and wisdom of the old man; in fact he still thinks his grandfather is "a stupid old man." However, he soon learns his lesson when he is forced to accompany his grandfather into the mountains. With all the whining of a typical teenager, Michael still resists his grandfather. For example, when he fails to secure their food in a tree as he had been told to do, a bear takes it and he and his grandfather have a very sparse supper. Holding the only can left behind by the bear, Grandfather, with a sly smile, says to the boy, "Tomorrow I will tell you what our people did—before chicken gumbo soup." The next day he makes a bow and arrows for Michael, teaches him how to fish, and tells him about the strength the eagle feather gives to the warrior. Then he sends Michael and his horse to the secret springs of the warriors for their healing ritual. When the boy returns, he asks about his father, a man who had been a source of shame for him. His grandfather explains that Michael's father was a warrior, a good man who sometimes drank because he couldn't take the pain of his times. After this painful revelation, the grandfather teaches Michael how to catch the eagle and pull a feather from its tail. After Michael succeeds, he gives the feather to his grandfather in recognition of his new love for him and his father. As a final indication of his pride, he names his horse "Three Warriors" after his grandfather, father, and himself.

In the last part of the film, he shows his strength as a warrior by rescuing his horse from evil rustlers who are slaughtering mustangs for their meat. Though this part has a certain "kids' show" quality, it does lead to a strong, emotional ending. Michael and his grandfather are seen in an intimate close-up of their heads as the old man shows his understanding of the challenges the young man will face: "You have learned the old ways, Michael, but they are not the only ways. Yours is a new song, the song of a proud warrior. This song will stay in your heart as you learn the new ways. You will come back."

Though each of the above movies has some nice touches of humor, they all focus on serious, and sometimes wrenching, changes in the central characters. Like these films, *Harold of Orange* (1984) deals with the power of tribal traditions, but in the humorous fashion of trickster stories. In fact, this short movie (about thirty minutes), with a screenplay by noted Native American author Gerald Vizenor, is a contemporary trickster tale in which Harold Sinseer (Charlie Hill) and his merry band survive by conning grant foundations. At the beginning, Harold speaks to the audience in a monologue: "We are the warriors of Orange, tricksters in the new school of social acupuncture where a little pressure fills the pocket book. We keep a clean coffee house, tend to our miniature oranges and speak about mythic revolutions on the reservation. What more is there to tell?" He then joins his fellow warriors and hands out old ties, which they put on as amulets before they board their orange bus and head for the city and a meeting with the grant foundation. Having already received a grant for growing miniature orange trees on a remote part of the reservation, they are now out for a new grant to fund the building of coffee houses on the reservation, where they will serve a unique new pinch bean brew. After arriving in the city, Harold, seen from a low angle that suggests his power over the grant foundation, gives a bogus presentation to foundation members. Then he invites them to join his warriors on the orange bus for a trip to a park where they will play an Anglos-vs.-"Indians" softball game, one the warriors will intentionally lose to butter up the members before they vote on the grant.

On this trip, a rather twitty little man, known to be very skeptical about the new grant request, finally gets the attention of the warrior of Orange sitting next to him and listening to tribal songs on his headphones. The little man tells him that he had just read an article in *National Geographic* about the population of Indians at the time of Columbus. The warrior responds, "Who?" and the white man asks again, "How many Indians were here then?" The warrior answers, "None. Not one. Columbus never discovered anything and when he never did, he invented us as Indians because we never heard the term before he dropped it by accident." Then the man says, "Let me rephrase the question. How many tribal people were here when Columbus invented Indians?" The warrior replies, "49,732,000,196 . . ." and the man, with a sheepish look, says, "Well, I see—that many." This is just one of numerous examples in which the warriors of Orange use the methods of the trickster to tease and manipulate the white characters.

After the softball game, in which Harold wears layers of red "Indian" T-shirts and white "Anglo" T-shirts so he can change sides at will (like the trickster), everyone goes back to the foundation's building for the vote on the grant. Ironically, at the meeting the little man who is opposed to the grant asks a racist question, a mistake that motivates the rest of the politically correct group to award the grant. After his latest success, Harold plays one more trick by getting the head of the foundation to donate $1,000 for what will be his grandmother's second $1,000 traditional funeral. At the end, then, Harold and his warriors have survived and even prospered by understanding that the traditional spirit of the trickster will enable them to befuddle and ultimately control those who are in power.

In *Powwow Highway* (1988), the traditions of the warrior and the trickster are also the key to the survival and identity of the two central characters, Buddy Red Bow (A Martinez) and Philbert Bono (Gary Farmer). Based on the zany novel by David Seals, the movie makes the two main characters more noble than their counterparts in the novel and both cleans up and diminishes the main female character, Bonnie Red Bow (Joanelle Nadine). In the film, the pivotal character is Philbert, a hulking Cheyenne who, like the trickster, is always hungry for food and adventure. His transformation into a warrior progresses as he gathers power by drawing on the Cheyenne traditions of the warhorse, the medicine bundle, and the stories of the trickster, Wihio. Like the trickster, Philbert moves in strange and seemingly misguided ways to the warrior identity, but in the process he makes a believer of the cynical Buddy.

Philbert's decision to acquire a war pony, one that turns out to be a dilapidated old car, is his first step toward becoming a warrior. He gets the idea from a TV ad in which a car salesman, wearing a war bonnet, sits on the hood of a car and says, "Come off the 'res' and pick up your war pony today." Like the vigilant trickster, Philbert finds the right course of action from a most unlikely electronic source, just as he does later when he watches a scene from a W. S. Hart western and gets the idea of pulling the bars off Bonnie Red Bow's jail cell. At the used car lot, when he looks out the window at an old brown Buick, he has a vision (enhanced with electronic music and golden lighting) of a pinto running in slow motion. Knowing that this car, a castoff of white society, will become a magic pony if infused with the warrior spirit, he trades a lid of marijuana for it and names it Protector. His willingness to give up the marijuana for his war pony is significant because it marks his rejection of a nontraditional way to gain the power of the traditional warrior.

Now that Philbert has found his war pony, he is ready to continue his quest to become a warrior, a quest that takes shape when Buddy asks him for a ride to Santa Fe, where his sister, Bonnie, has been framed by the local police, and put in jail. Philbert agrees and shares Buddy's joint (an action he never repeats after he becomes a warrior). As they drive away from the reservation, Buddy asks him if he can count on him, and Philbert, already showing his warrior pride, answers in their native tongue, "We are Cheyenne!" However, Philbert's growth as a warrior is not complete and another electronic device, this time a CD radio Buddy had installed in the car, speaks to the potential trickster and warrior in him. After being asked by a Native American truck driver for his warrior name, he tells him that he knows part of it is "Whirlwind." The man tells him to visit Bear Butte, the most sacred place in South Dakota, and he turns the car directly away from their destination.

While Buddy sleeps through the whole event, Philbert arrives at Bear Butte, the place the legendary Cheyenne holy man Sweet Medicine performed the sacred ceremonies of the tribe (the film uses different names for the place and holy man). After he makes it halfway to the top, he finds a frame of a sweat lodge and in it he sleeps and has a vision of Sweet Medicine, who offers him the sacred pipe. At the top, just as he is about to bite into his Hershey candy bar, he sees gifts for the spirits left in the trees by other Native Americans, and he leaves his candy bar, a tremendous sacrifice for him. Then he has a vision of being an eagle that sees for miles in every direction. His elation at finding his ancestral past and the rest of his warrior name, "Dreamer," is so great that on his return he rolls down the last part of the butte. At the bottom, he meets Buddy, who has just found out that they are in South Dakota rather than Colorado. Buddy yells at him, but backs off when Philbert, now aware of his own strength, lifts him off the ground and lets him know he will never be pushed around again.

After they are on the road again, Philbert's new awareness that religious power is essential to the warrior prompts him to stop the car at a river so he can sing a song to the setting sun. Despite Buddy's complaints, he walks into the river and sings until Buddy joins him and haltingly starts to sing with him. After a touching silhouette shot of the two friends singing vigorously together, the two men return to the car, where Philbert finds a pebble in his boot that becomes the first token for his warrior's medicine bundle. He finds the second token after stopping in a snowstorm in Nebraska to look at the historical marker for Fort Robinson. After he has a vision of Dull Knife and his Cheyenne people escaping from the fort, he finds a white stone of the ancestors for his bundle. At the end of the film, after his car has crashed down a steep hill and burst into flames, he miraculously escapes and walks up the hill holding the door handle, which will then protect him after the loss of his war pony, Protector. The traditional bundle, however, has four tokens, as Philbert tells Bonnie's son. So even after Philbert has completed his quest to rescue Bonnie (and thus after the end of the film), he still must be looking for a new token to continue his growth as a Cheyenne warrior.

In addition to the medicine bundle and war pony, Philbert also has the knowledge of the warrior because he has been taught the traditional stories of his people. With the large smoke stacks of a plant in the background, he tells a trickster story to Buddy and his friends Wolf Tooth (Wayne Waterman) and Imogene (Margo Kane). Seen from a low angle, which emphasizes the authority of his words, he says, "Wihio the trickster is sometimes a man and sometimes an animal, but he mostly likes pulling antics and telling dirty jokes. One day he saw some plums floating down the creek. Now, Wihio loves to eat so he reached for the plums, but they disappeared and he fell into the creek. He crawled out all soaking wet and saw the plums again shimmering in the water and he kept diving and they kept disappearing." Philbert then explains that three days later Wihio's wife found him and, after he told her what had happened, she says, "Stupid dog of a dog! The plums are still on the tree." Then she tells him that he is like those people "chasing shadows while the true thing is hanging right over their heads." After Philbert finishes his story by noting that Wihio's wife hit him over the head with a pan, Wolf Tooth and Imogene praise him for his knowledge, but Buddy sees the story as a fairy tale that has no relevance to modern reservations where white men are stealing natural resources. Philbert responds that the "trickster won't let this happen. Wihio is the creator of the universe. He will play a little trick on the white man. Wait, you will see."

Philbert's trickster story dramatizes the difference between Buddy and himself. Philbert has gained the power of the warrior by looking in the right places, inside himself and at the traditional values of his tribe. Buddy, on the other hand, like Wihio, is looking in the wrong places, outside of his tradition and only at the evils of white society. Filled with anger and righteousness, he thinks like the white liberal he hates, always considering the big issues and blaming others rather than himself. As these two unlikely buddies approach Santa Fe, another incident underscores the differences between them. While Buddy is reaching for his pistol under the dashboard, he finds a tarantula and is about to smash it when Philbert swerves the car to save the spider. When Buddy falls out of the car and sees that his gun is broken, he yells at his friend, who calmly reminds him "the trickster takes many forms. We must keep our medicine good." Now Buddy, the Vietnam veteran and member of AIM, will not be able to solve his problems with the violence of the gun. On the other hand, Philbert recognizes that the spider is sacred to his people and may even be a trickster who will help them accomplish their quest. Also, Philbert is now so infused with the warrior spirit that he realizes he no longer needs marijuana and refuses the joint Buddy offers him.

In fact, Buddy never does rescue his sister, Bonnie. That feat belongs to Philbert, who has earned his warrior name, Whirlwind Dreamer, and has found his medicine bundle. With the help of his Buick war pony, only Philbert has the magic to pull away the bars and part of the wall. He rescues Bonnie and Buddy, but also eludes the police and government agents, escapes a seemingly fatal car accident, and finally walks off with his friends to a new and better life on the reservation. Though this ending may seem like a fairy tale to some viewers, it can also be seen as the conclusion to a trickster story in which Philbert mixes the tricks of the cowboy hero (or even the knight in shining armor) with his newfound power as a Cheyenne warrior and triumphs over all who would thwart him. As he said earlier in the movie, "the trickster will play a little trick on the white man." This is probably not the last "little trick" Philbert will play on the white man as he grows into a modern Cheyenne warrior.

Like the other films, *Powwow Highway* reveals the power of traditional values for contemporary Native Americans. This theme is also central to the last and most contemporary of the representative movies, *Imprint* (2007), which was produced by Chris Eyre. The central character of this film, Shayla Stonefeather (Tonantzin Carmelo), is a successful lawyer who lives in Denver and has a white boyfriend who works with her in a large law firm. After she convinces a jury to convict a young Lakota man for a murder and comes home because her father is fatally ill, the struggle between her work as a lawyer and her responsibilities as a tribal person begin. When she sees her mother, Rebecca (Carla Rae) at their reservation home, their conversation suggests a big part of her problem: Her mother says, "I remember a little girl who used to save all of her change in a jar because she wanted something to hand the man outside the supermarket. You've changed so much." Shayla replies, "Yes, I've changed. I grew up! You know, maybe white government would like to see us disappear off the face of the earth but that doesn't change the fact that our biggest problems are self-inflicted." Her mother replies, "You're right. Our biggest problems are self-inflicted by people like you. Who have the wisdom and spirit to bring about change but instead choose to turn your back on your people." Throughout the rest of the movie, Shayla learns how to find and use her "wisdom and spirit" as she slowly accepts that her traditional Lakota values will unlock her powers.

To suggest the supernatural and spiritual nature of the change Shayla must undergo, and possibly to make this film more popular with young audiences, some techniques from the horror film genre are used throughout. When Shayla goes to her old room on the second floor of her reservation home, near the room of her missing brother, she hears thumping footsteps and other eerie sounds and music of the sort associated with horror films. When she goes to the barn, similar sounds and weird images and visions confront her. What helps her through these psychological traumas are the words of an elder medicine man (David Bald Eagle). He tells her, "You have closed many doors in your life. You can't really listen and what you face will frighten you." Afterward Shayla experiences even more eerie sounds and visions in the darkness of her house and tries to escape by riding her horse into the countryside where she has a recurring vision of a wolf and eventually meets the medicine man again. This time he teaches her about listening to the land. He says, "I listen to the screams of the wounded and dying carried on the wind across the prairie. It was about this time when the white men attacked, they slaughtered them. They slaughtered defenseless men, women and children. Their blood spilled here on this ground. We forget about these things, but the trees—they remember. The rocks and the earth . . . they remember when we forget. The story forever imprinted, imprinted on this land. If we listen they will guide us, give us visions, tell us stories. Past, present and future all touch one another. Time doesn't exist. For spirits, time doesn't exist. Can you hear the cries?" Shayla replies, "No. I'm sorry, I don't hear anything." He replies, "But you have heard voices and you have seen visions?" She replies, "Are you saying something happened at my house?" And he replies, "I do not know the message. The message is for you."

After more scary experiences, she finds out that her missing brother who she thought was killed by her father, Sam Stonefeather (Charles White Buffalo) is alive.

She makes peace with her father and actually smiles for once. She also finally accepts the ways of her tribe, as is partially evidenced by her giving a drunken member of the tribe a sandwich as she leaves the store. She also gets rid of her rather nasty white lawyer boyfriend and leaves the door open for a romance with Tom Greyhorse (Michael Spears), a Pine Ridge tribal policeman. At the end, as she is driving, she sees the mysterious wolf for the last time, as maybe a sign that she is now listening to the spirits and living the good values of her Pine Ridge Lakota tribe.

On the levels of content and theme, all these above independent films promote empathy by depicting the details of tribal cultures fully enough for white audiences to see that they are different from their own, but worthy of respect. To a much greater degree, then, as the most enlightened westerns, they also reveal the flavor of Native American life in various parts of the country. Woven into their plots are simple realities of life such as preparing meals, joking and arguing at the dinner table, washing clothes, struggling to get up in the morning, or hugging and kissing. Such details like these, and others in new films like *Broken, Yet Brave* (2009) humanize the Native American characters in a way largely nonexistent in Hollywood films.

On the level of film or movie technique, these movies enhance their portrayals by the use of Native American or First Nation actors whose movie presence and acting ability give a strong impression of the characters as unique human beings. In fact it is hard to imagine the grandfather in *Three Warriors* not being played by Charles White Eagle; or Harold in *Harold of Orange* without Charley Hill; or Earl, the vegetarian chef in *Christmas in the Clouds*, without Graham Greene; or Abel in *House Made of Dawn* without Larry Littlebird; or Shayla Stonefeather in *Imprint* without Tonantzin Carmela. The patterns of low-angle and close-up shots of these actors enhance their movie presence and add to their impact in the overall plots. Another little-recognized technique that augments the emotion and themes of these movies is the background music, which is often written and performed by Native Americans musicians.

Though the film or movie techniques may not quite match the glossy production standards of Hollywood movies, all are of high enough quality to entertain and move general film audiences in positive ways. However, what has given these films the freedom to avoid the formulas of Hollywood, has also limited them to rather small audiences. Our challenge is to find larger audiences by using these movies in high school and college classes and by including them in university and public library programs. Now that cable television and the Internet are available to many people, we can also advocate for their showing on these more universal media. Also, many of these movies have been transferred to DVD, and a few to Blu-ray, and are available for purchase at Amazon.com. For a modest rental fee, they can also be streamed from Amazon, Netflix, and other sites.

Way back in 1967, a Native American writer considered the effect of Hollywood "Indians" on his children. "I think they wonder when we are going to win?

I remember seeing such a movie when one of my boys was a kid. We came out of the movies and he pulled my hand and said, 'Daddy, we pretty near won that one'" (Armstrong 1971, 155).

If enough people can see this new generation of movies maybe the traditional images of the Savage and Noble Red Man will fade into the sunset and be replaced by films in which Native American filmmakers can tell their own stories, stories that seldom, if ever, end with a lost battle.

Entries A–Z

THE ENTRIES IN THIS SECTION PROVIDE a new canon of most sound films and a solid representation of silent films (and the rare animated short) in which Native American and First Nation characters play a significant role. Although the canon of such films will, of course, always be growing, this compendium will offer some new starting points for interpretation.

The alphabetical entries will provide basic information about individual films. Each entry contains details about the distributors or production team, year of release, directors, screenwriters, literary source (when applicable), cast members (with character names in parentheses, and specs (such as running time, whether the film is in black and white or color, or if it's a silent work).

The availability of the film on DVD, Blu-ray, VHS (if not available on DVD), or streaming sources such as Amazon Instant Video will be indicated. Films go out of print without notice, but once a title has been produced on DVD or VHS, it may be obtained through some means, whether purchased directly through a vendor, accessed from a library, or rented from some other resource. Amazon has many titles available on Instant Video and they are likely to continue adding rarer titles that might not make it to a DVD. Most, if not all, titles listed as VHS are only available through vendors selling used copies. On the other hand, many companies (Warner Archive Collection, MGM Limited Edition Collection, Universal Archives, for example) are now producing DVDs on demand, making many more titles available than they might have otherwise. I have indicated the most common—and in most cases, only—manufacturer of each title in parentheses after the format. If "Availability" is indicated by "NA" (not available), it is still possible that title may be released in the future.

Finally, the nation or tribe featured in the film will be identified, followed by categories of image portrayals, a brief plot summary, and quotes from critics when available or appropriate. When information is not available or wasn't found, "NA" is indicated. Because the plot summaries are brief, they will, of course, never catch the nuances of the film and are always meant to be just a preface to a careful viewing and interpretation of selected films. This book emphasizes similarities among the films, whereas a careful viewing of individual films will almost always reveal a fascinating series of variations.

The categories of image portrayals in individual films are somewhat arbitrary and sometimes overlapping; however, they do stem from and expand the meanings of the two major fictional images, the Savage and the Noble Red Man characters.

A staple of the western is, of course, the excitement and cruelty of an attack by Native American warriors on the homes of settlers, wagon trains, groups of soldiers, stagecoaches, and so on. Often a minor part of the plot, the attack is central to the portrayal of the Savage, and the theme of the Native American as threat to progress or western expansion as promulgated by the Monroe Doctrine. During their attacks, Native Americans sometimes take whites, especially females, as prisoners. Such kidnapping, and also torture and the use of fire, are typical evil deeds of this character type. Other categories of these evil deeds are motivated by drunkenness and vengeance. In the entries, we will see these negative traits of fictional Native Americans not only in westerns but also in the portrayals of contemporary characters in a few more recent films.

The other extreme in the portrayal of Native Americans in the movies is the image of the sometimes doomed Noble Red Man character. In the noble Native American, the emotions of vengeance and revenge are tempered by a strong sense of justice. Though the line between justice and vengeance is sometimes a thin one, the noble characters are always on the side of justice and peace. They also value honor and courage among themselves and in the white heroes, who are often their friends. In fact, friendship with whites is often one of the key traits of this character, with two of many examples being the Lone Ranger and Tonto and Hawkeye, Chingachgook, and Uncas. Such friendship is often marked by strong loyalty, generosity, and gratitude to the white characters. However, because of their noble, and sometimes childlike, emotions, such Native American characters sometime misjudge whites who are really villains and want to take advantage of them. This leads to them becoming victims of the villains. Often the Native Americans can only be rescued by their white friends who intervene and treat them in an overtly paternalistic way.

Many of the positive traits of the noble Native American male and female, especially loyalty, are revealed in romances between Native Americans and whites. In the standard pattern for mixed-romance plots, the Native American characters, especially if female, finally are rejected or die. The story of Sonseeahray, the dark and beautiful Apache wife of Tom Jeffords in *Broken Arrow* who is killed at the end of the film, is a prime example of this pattern, which rather obviously suggests that white audiences, especially those of westerns, had a strong distaste for miscegenation. However, audiences seem to be less concerned about romances between peaceful Native Americans, who live with their tribes in remote camps.

In the 1950s, the highpoint of the western genre, the films often feature a peace-loving chief. These noble characters, such as Cochise of *Broken Arrow*, often contrast with hostile members of their tribe (Geronimo) and become friends with the white heroes because they realize that they have no chance to overcome the ever-growing numbers of whites. For them, peace, not warfare, is the way to a better future. Such peace-loving chiefs who accept the inevitability of white dominance are often far from historical reality, but they obviously appeal to the audiences in this era of the western.

Because of the dominance of the western, with its basically white supremacist subtext, few of the films in the early periods deal with Native American characters in contemporary settings. This type of film becomes more prominent in the later periods of film history. Because the fictional characters in these later films, especially those of Native American filmmakers, are more fully realized as human beings, this category is harder to pin down. Some of these characters are Native social activists, victims of white society, or athletic and military heroes. Another common contemporary character type is the young Native American who must face the challenges of living in a white society and find a new, healthier identity through his or her extended family and wise elders who impart traditional tribal skills and values.

The above categories, and other related ones, will appear in the entries, and offer motifs that will encourage the study of comparisons. Much of the other information about individual films comes from the World Wide Web or Internet, especially the huge film databases, *IMDb* and *Wikipedia* and *Overview-TCM*. All or most of these resources will appear when the title of the film is entered into one of the major search engines, with *Google* probably being the best. The search engines will also provide numerous references to film reviews, especially in sites such as *Rotten Tomatoes* and the *New York Times*. The most volatile of the categories is availability because films are constantly being added, while a few are subtracted. Probably the best site for determining the availability of a film is *Amazon.com*, which sells and rents film for instant view. *Netflix* and numerous video renting and streaming companies are also good possibilities.

Though there are contemporary reviews for the following films, only quotes from reviews that deal with the portrayal of Native American characters will be included in the entries. These critical perspectives, along with the plot summaries, are meant to provide enough information to encourage the selection of movies for further research and interpretation.

A

ACROSS THE PLAINS (Monogram, 1939)
DIRECTOR: Spencer Gordon Bennet
SCREENPLAY: Robert Emmett Tansey
CAST: Jack Randall (Cherokee), Dennis Moore (Kansas Kid)
SPECS: 59 minutes; Black & White
AVAILABILITY: DVD (Alpha Home Entertainment); Amazon Instant Video
NATION: Cherokee

IMAGE PORTRAYAL: Friendship; loyalty

SUMMARY: Cherokee (Jack Randall), a good white man raised by a friendly tribe, rescues his bad brother from the gang of villains who raised him. The tribe that adopted Cherokee also helps him foil an attack by the villains.

ACROSS THE WIDE MISSOURI (MGM, 1951)

DIRECTOR: William Wellman

SCREENPLAY: Talbot Jennings, Frank Cavett, based on the book by Bernard Devoto

CAST: Clark Gable (Flint Mitchell), Ricardo Montalban (Iron Shirt), J. Carrol Naish (Looking Glass, Nez Perce chief), Maria Elena Marques (Kamiah)

SPECS: 78 minutes; Color

AVAILABILITY: DVD (Warner Archive Collection); Amazon Instant Video

NATION: Blackfeet; Nez Perce

IMAGE PORTRAYAL: Hostile warrior; romance between a Native American woman and a white man

SUMMARY: Flint marries a Blackfeet, Kamiah, and tries to live on land controlled by the hostile young Ironshirt. When Chief Looking Glass is killed, the hostiles attack and Ironshirt and Kamiah die during the fighting. After the death of his wife, Flint takes their son to the mountains and lives with friends from the tribe.

The narrator in the film (Howard Keel) comments, "My father told me that for the first time, he saw these Indians as he had never seen them before—as people with homes and traditions and ways of their own. Suddenly they were no longer savages. They were people who laughed and loved and dreamed."

AFRICA TEXAS STYLE (Paramount, 1967)

DIRECTOR: Andrew Marton

SCREENPLAY: Andy White

CAST: Hugh O'Brian (Jim Sinclair), Tom Nardini (John Henry)

SPECS: 109 minutes; Color

AVAILABILITY: VHS (Republic Entertainment); Amazon Instant Video

NATION: Navajo

IMAGE PORTRAYAL: Friendship

SUMMARY: John Henry is the Navajo companion of Jim Sinclair, who helps him round up wild animals in an African reserve.

AGAINST A CROOKED SKY (Doty-Dayton, 1975)

DIRECTOR: Earl Bellamy

SCREENPLAY: Douglas Stewart and Eleanor Lamb

CAST: Richard Boone (Russian Hablakuk), Geoffery Land (Temkai), Henry Wilcoxon (Cut Tongue), Stewart Petersen (Sam Sutter), Brenda Venus (Ashkea), Vince St. Cyr (Cheyenne Chief, Shokobob), Gordon Hanson (Chief Shumeki)

SPECS: 89 minutes; Color

AVAILABILITY: DVD (Echo Bridge Entertainment); Amazon Instant Video

NATION: Cheyenne

IMAGE PORTRAYAL: Kidnapping

SUMMARY: In the remake of *The Searchers*, Sam Sutter and an old Russian search for his sister after hostile warriors from the tribe of Temkai kidnap her. When they find her, Cutter must take the "crooked sky" test of shielding the woman from an arrow. Finally, the Russian helps him rescue her from the tribe.

CRITICS: A *Variety* critic notes that the film "harks back to the not-so-good old days when Indians were depicted as lascivious villains bent on kidnapping white girls and murdering pet dogs. . . . It's amazing that this film was made in 1975" (December 24, 1975).

ALIEN THUNDER (Onyx Films, 1973)

DIRECTOR: Claude Fournier

SCREENPLAY: George Malko

CAST: Donald Sutherland (Sgt. Dan Candy), Gordon Tootoosis (Almighty Voice), Chief Dan George (Sounding Sky), Lenny George (Rolling Grass), Ernestine Gamble (Small Face), Vincent Daniels (Many Birds)

SPECS: 93 minutes; Color

AVAILABILITY: DVD (Scorpion Entertainment); Amazon Instant Video

NATION: Cree

IMAGE PORTRAYAL: Attacks on settlers; First Nation people as victims

SUMMARY: In the wilds of Saskatchewan, a Mountie pursues a cunning and victimized Cree, Almighty Voice, who lays traps for him before the policeman finally kills him.

ALL HANDS ON DECK (20th Century Fox, 1961)

DIRECTOR: Norman Taurog

SCREENPLAY: Donald R. Morris, Jay Sommers, based on the novel by Morris

CAST: Pat Boone (Lt. Victor Donald), Buddy Hackett (Shrieking Eagle Garfield)

SPECS: 100 minutes; Color

AVAILABILITY: DVD (20th Century Fox Cinema Archives)

NATION: Chickasaw

IMAGE PORTRAYAL: Contemporary Native American; Native American as butt of humor

SUMMARY: In this comedy, Shrieking Eagle Garfield is a Chickasaw who wears a feather in his sailor hat. After seeing a cowboy and Indian movie, he tears apart the theatre and threatens to scalp the admirals.

ALL THE YOUNG MEN (Columbia, 1960)

DIRECTOR: Hall Bartlett

SCREENPLAY: Hall Bartlett

CAST: Alan Ladd (Sgt. Kincaid), Sidney Poitier (Sgt. Eddie Towler), Mario Alcade (Hunter)
SPECS: 90 minutes; Color
AVAILABILITY: VHS (Good Times Home Video); Amazon Instant Video
NATION: NA
IMAGE PORTRAYAL: Contemporary Native American; friendship; Native American soldier
SUMMARY: In this film about the Korean War, a Native American soldier sides with a black sergeant, because he also has experienced prejudice.

ALLEGHENY UPRISING (RKO, 1939)
DIRECTOR: William A. Seiter
SCREENPLAY: P. J. Wolfson, based on the book, *The First Rebel*, by Neil H. Swanson
CAST: Claire Trevor (Janie MacDougal), John Wayne (Jim Smith)
SPECS: 81 minutes; Black & White
AVAILABILITY: DVD (Warner Home Video)
NATION: NA
IMAGE PORTRAYAL: Attack on settlers
SUMMARY: Jim Smith and his men, with the help of Janie MacDougal, pose as Native Americans to stop the selling of liquor and guns to a hostile tribe who use the guns against the settlers.

ALONG THE OREGON TRAIL (Republic, 1947)
DIRECTOR: R. G. Springsteen
SCREENPLAY: Earle Snell
CAST: Monte Hale (Monte Hale), Clayton Moore (Greg Thurston)
SPECS: 61 minutes; Color
AVAILABILITY: NA
NATION: NA
IMAGE PORTRAYAL: Attack on settlers
SUMMARY: Greg Thurston and his men steal rifles to arm hostile warriors for an uprising that will benefit their evil purposes. Monte Hale tries to stop this villainy.

AMBUSH (MGM, 1950)
DIRECTOR: Sam Wood
SCREENPLAY: Marguerite Roberts, Luke Short
CAST: Robert Taylor (Ward Kinsman), Arlene Dahl (Ann Duverall), Charles Stevens (Diablito), Chief Thundercloud (Tana)
SPECS: 90 minutes; Black & White
AVAILABILITY: DVD (Warner Archive Collection)
NATION: Apache
IMAGE PORTRAYAL: Attack on settlers; kidnapping

SUMMARY: Ward Kinsman and Ann Duverall, whose sister was captured by the hostile Apaches of Diablito, search for her. Eventually, Ward kills Tana, an Apache captive, and rescues the woman with the help of the cavalry, who kill Diablito and many of his tribe.

AMBUSH AT CIMARRON PASS (20th Century Fox, 1958)
DIRECTOR: Jodie Copelan
SCREENPLAY: Richard G. Taylor, John K. Butler, Robert A. Reeds, Robert E. Wood
CAST: Scott Brady (Sgt. Matt Blake), Clint Eastwood (Keith Williams)
SPECS: 73 minutes; Black & White
AVAILABILITY: DVD (Olive Films); Amazon Instant Video
NATION: Apache
IMAGE PORTRAYAL: Attack on soldiers
SUMMARY: Sgt. Blake and his Union troops join Confederate Keith Williams and are attacked by Apaches who are after guns.

AMBUSH AT TOMAHAWK GAP (Columbia, 1953)
DIRECTOR: Fred Sears
SCREENPLAY: David Lang
CAST: John Hodiak (McCord), Maria Elena Marques (Navajo Girl)
SPECS: 73 minutes; Color
AVAILABILITY: DVD (Sony Pictures Choice Collection)
NATION: Apache
IMAGE PORTRAYAL: Attack on settlers
SUMMARY: McCord and fellow ex-convicts are hunting when Apaches attack them with flaming arrows.

AMERICA (United Artists, 1924)
DIRECTOR: D. W. Griffith
SCREENPLAY: Robert W. Chambers, based on his novel *The Reckoning*
CAST: Neil Hamilton (Nathan Holden), Lionel Barrymore (Capt. Walter Butler), Riley Hatch (Chief Joseph Brant)
SPECS: 141 minutes; Black & White; Silent
AVAILABILITY: DVD (Image Entertainment); Amazon Instant Video
NATION: Iroquois; Mohawk; Six Nations
IMAGE PORTRAYAL: Attack on soldiers
SUMMARY: In this film about the revolutionary period, Mohawks led by Chief Joseph Brant and other tribes of the Six Nations join Capt. Butler to fight with the British against the American colonists. In some of the battles British soldiers disguise themselves as Mohawks. In the final climactic battle, the hostile tribes attack a fort and, as they break the gates and are about to kill the women inside, Nathan Holden and his group of Native Americans come to the rescue.

AMERICAN INDIAN GRAFFITI: THIS THING LIFE (Restless Native Productions, 2003)
DIRECTORS: Tvli Jacob, Steven Judd
SCREENPLAY: Tvli Jacob, Steven Judd
CAST: Terri Poahway (Stephanie), Randi LeClair (Rachel), Steven Judd (Steve), Richard Ray Whitman (Barry), Raven Lockwood (A'an)
SPECS: NA; Color
AVAILABILITY: NA
NATION: NA
IMAGE PORTRAYAL: Contemporary Native Americans; troubled Native Americans
SUMMARY: Four Native Americans interact in one summer. Stephanie is a recent high school graduate who deals with guilt and rejection. Rachel, Stephanie's best friend is agonizing over the death of her mother and brother. Steve is a well-known artist who has lost his sense of creativity and goals. And Barry is a heavy-drinking mechanic who feels guilt over causing two deaths and seeks isolation until young A'an helps him find peace.

THE ANIMALS (Levitt–Pickman, 1971)
DIRECTOR: Ron Joy
SCREENPLAY: Richard Bakalyan
CAST: Michele Carey (Alice McAndrew), Henry Silva (Chatto), Keenan Wynn (Pudge Elliot)
SPECS: 86 minutes; Color
AVAILABILITY: DVD (Geneon Video) as *Five Savage Men*
NATION: NA
IMAGE PORTRAYAL: Friendship; loyalty
SUMMARY: Chatto rescues Alice McAndrew, who has been raped, and he helps her track down the guilty men and kills them. At the end, however, a posse mistakes him for the villain and kills him.

ANNIE GET YOUR GUN (MGM, 1950)
DIRECTOR: George Sidney
SCREENPLAY: Sidney Sheldon, based on the Broadway musical (book by Dorothy and Herbert Fields)
CAST: Betty Hutton (Annie Oakley), Howard Keel (Frank Butler), J. Carrol Naish (Chief Sitting Bull), Chief Yowlachie (Little Horse), John War Eagle (Indian Brave)
SPECS: 107 minutes; Color
AVAILABILITY: DVD (Warner Home Video)
NATION: Sioux
IMAGE PORTRAYAL: Friendship; loyalty

SUMMARY: In this musical, Sitting Bull is the friend of Annie and helps her win the man she loves, Frank Butler. He and Little Horse adopt her into their Sioux tribe, which also acts during the attacks staged in Buffalo Bill's Wild West Show.

ANNIE OAKLEY (RKO, 1935)
DIRECTOR: George Stevens
SCREENPLAY: Joel Sayre, John Twist
CAST: Barbara Stanwyck (Annie Oakley), Preston Foster (Toby Walker), Chief Thunderbird (Chief Sitting Bull)
SPECS: 90 minutes; Black & White
AVAILABILITY: DVD (Warner Home Video)
NATION: Sioux
IMAGE PORTRAYAL: Friendship; loyalty
SUMMARY: The heroine performs in Buffalo Bill's Wild West Show with her friend Sitting Bull and his Sioux tribe. Sitting Bull shows his friendship by helping her to win Toby Walker, the man she loves. His character also adds humor when he has trouble dealing with some of the modern conveniences of civilized life.

APACHE (United Artists, 1954)
DIRECTOR: Robert Aldrich
SCREENPLAY: James R. Webb, based on the novel by Paul Wellman
CAST: Burt Lancaster (Massai), Jean Peters (Nalinle), Monte Blue (Geronimo)
SPECS: 94 minutes; Color
AVAILABILITY: DVD (MGM-UA Video)
NATION: Apache
IMAGE PORTRAYAL: Attack on soldiers; justice; romance between Native Americans
SUMMARY: This film tells the story of Massai, one of Geronimo's band, who escapes while being taken to prison and wages a harsh one-man war against the army. When Massai finally stops fighting, the government doesn't punish him because it decides that his resistance was part of a declared war. At the end, he and his beloved Nalinle will live together in peace.
CRITICS: A *Variety* critic comments on the acting: "Lancaster and Miss Peters play their Indian roles understandingly without usual screen stereotyping. As played, these two top characters are humans, surprisingly loquacious in contrast to the usual clipped redskin portrayals" (June 30, 1954).

APACHE AMBUSH (Columbia, 1955)
DIRECTOR: Fred F. Sears
SCREENPLAY: David Lang
CAST: Bill Williams (James Kingston), Richard Jaeckel (Lee Parker)
SPECS: 68 minutes; Black & White

AVAILABILITY: DVD (Sony Picture Choice Collection)
NATION: Apache
IMAGE PORTRAYAL: Attack on soldiers
SUMMARY: Apaches and Mexican bandits raid settlers and have a large battle with an army of post–Civil War soldiers in order to get their hands on new repeating rifles.
CRITICS: A *Variety* critic comments: "One thing about this pic; it won't make the distributor very popular in Mexico or with Indians. Both are shown up in the worst possible light" (August 10, 1954).

APACHE CHIEF (Lippert, 1949)
DIRECTOR: Frank McDonald
SCREENPLAY: George D. Green, Leonard S. Picker
CAST: Alan Curtis (Young Eagle), Russell Hayden (Black Wolf), Carol Thurston (Watona), Trevor Bardette (Chief Big Crow), Francis McDonald (Mohaska), Ted Hecht (Pani), Alan Wells (Lame Bull), Billy Wilkerson (Grey Cloud), Rodd Redwing (Tewa)
SPECS: 60 minutes; Black & White
AVAILABILITY: NA
NATION: Apache
IMAGE PORTRAYAL: Attack on wagon train; peace-loving chief; romance between Native Americans
SUMMARY: Grey Cloud leads an attack on a wagon train and is killed. After Big Crow and Black Wolf continue his evil ways, the peace-loving Young Eagle kills Black Wolf and rescues his beloved Watona.

APACHE COUNTRY (Columbia, 1952)
DIRECTOR: George Archainbaud
SCREENPLAY: Norman S. Hall
CAST: Gene Autry (Gene Autry), Tony Whitecloud's Jemez Indians (Indian Dancers)
SPECS: 63 minutes; Black & White
AVAILABILITY: NA
NATION: Apache
IMAGE PORTRAYAL: Attack on settlers
SUMMARY: When villains provide guns and whiskey to the Apache and incite them to attack innocent settlers, Gene Autry and his sidekick come to the rescue.

APACHE DRUMS (Universal, 1951)
DIRECTOR: Hugo Fregonese
SCREENPLAY: David Chandler, based on "Stand at Spanish Boot" by Harry Brown
CAST: Stephen McNally (Sam Leeds), Chinto Gusman (Chache)

SPECS: 75 minutes; Color
AVAILABILITY: NA
NATION: Apache
IMAGE PORTRAYAL: Attack on a town; drunkenness
SUMMARY: The Apaches of Chache attack a town called Spanish Boot. One of the characters says about the Apache: "You see, they don't drink to get drunk. Their drinking is like praying. And then they kill."

APACHE GOLD (WINNETOU I) (Columbia, 1965)
DIRECTORS: Harold Reinl, Stipe Delic
SCREENPLAY: Harald G. Petersson, based on the novel by Karl May
CAST: Lex Barker (Old Shatterhand), Pierre Brice (Winnetou)
SPECS: 101 minutes; Color; dubbed for U.S. audience
AVAILABILITY: NA
NATION: Apache
IMAGE PORTRAYAL: Friendship; loyalty
SUMMARY: This film and its sequels, *Last of the Renegades—Winnetou II* (1966), *The Desperado Trail—Winnetou III* (1967), and *Shatterhand* (1964) are based on novels by Karl May, a German writer very popular in Europe but little known in the United States. Old Shatterhand and Winnetou, the Apache chief, become friends and thwart the efforts of the villain who is after gold on the tribe's land. The sequels use the same writers, cast, and crew. They deal with the two heroes against the railroad and a villain and renegade warriors who kill Winnetou.

APACHE RIFLES (20th Century Fox, 1964)
DIRECTOR: William Witney
SCREENPLAY: Charles B. Smith, Kenneth Gamet, Richard Schayer
CAST: Audie Murphy (Capt. Jeff Stanton), Michael Dante (Red Hawk), Linda Lawson (Dawn Gillis)
SPECS: 92 minutes; Color
AVAILABILITY: DVD (VCI Entertainment)
NATION: Apache
IMAGE PORTRAYAL: Attack on settlers; mixed-blood Native American; romance between a Native American woman and a white man
SUMMARY: When villains after gold incite the Apaches of Red Hawk to war, Capt. Stanton, who has been ordered to stop the Apache raids, falls in love with a mixed-blood, Dawn Gillis, and comes to the rescue.

APACHE TERRITORY (Columbia, 1958)
DIRECTOR: Ray Nazarro
SCREENPLAY: Charles Marion, George W. George, based on the novel *Last Stand at Papago Wells* by Louis L'Amour

CAST: Rory Calhoun (Logan Cates), Barbara Bates (Jennifer Fair)
SPECS: 77 minutes; Color
AVAILABILITY: DVD (Warner Archive Collection)
NATION: Apache
IMAGE PORTRAYAL: Attack on soldiers
SUMMARY: Apaches pin down a group of soldiers and start killing them one by one. Logan Cates, who has rescued a white woman from them, uses gunpowder for bombs and the survivors escape in a dust storm.

APACHE TRAIL (MGM, 1943)
DIRECTOR: Richard Thorpe
SCREENPLAY: Ernest Haycox, Maurice Geraghty
CAST: Lloyd Nolan (Trigger Bill), Donna Reed (Rosalia Martinez)
SPECS: 66 minutes; Black & White
AVAILABILITY: NA
NATION: Apache
IMAGE PORTRAYAL: Attack on settlers
SUMMARY: Apaches attack a stagecoach station and demand the others give up the villain, Trigger Bill.
CRITICS: A *Variety* reviewer comments that "the film's major detail, the uprising of the Apaches against the whites, is something that's long since seen its best picture days" (January 14, 1943).

APACHE UPRISING (Paramount, 1966)
DIRECTOR: R. G. Springsteen
SCREENPLAY: Max Lamb, Harry Sanford, based on their book *Way Station*
CAST: Rory Calhoun (Jim Walker), Corinne Calvet (Janice MacKenzie), Abel Fernandez (Apache Warrior)
SPECS: 90 minutes; Color
AVAILABILITY: VHS (Paramount Home Video); Amazon Instant Video
NATION: Apache
IMAGE PORTRAYAL: Attack on stagecoach
SUMMARY: Apaches release white captives in exchange for one of theirs. Then more attacks occur.

APACHE WAR SMOKE (MGM, 1952)
DIRECTOR: Harold Kress
SCREENPLAY: Jerry Davis, Ernest Haycox
CAST: Gilbert Roland (Peso Herrera), Robert Horton (Tom Herrera), Glenda Farrell (Fanny Webson)
SPECS: 67 minutes; Black & White
AVAILABILITY: NA
NATION: Apache

IMAGE PORTRAYAL: Attack on stagecoach

SUMMARY: When Tom Herrera refuses to hand over to the Apache his brother, Peso, who robbed and killed several members of their tribe, Apaches attack.

APACHE WARRIOR (20th Century Fox, 1957)

DIRECTOR: Elmo Williams

SCREENPLAY: Carroll Young, Kurt Neumann, Eric Norden

CAST: Keith Larson (Katawan/The Apache Kid), Jim Davis (Ben Ziegler), George Keymas (Chato), Rodolfo Acosta (Marteen), John Miljan (Chief Nantan), Michael Carr (Apache Brave), Eugenia Paul (Liwana)

SPECS: 74 minutes; Black & White

AVAILABILITY: NA

NATION: Apache

IMAGE PORTRAYAL: Friendship; justice; loyalty; romance between Native Americans

SUMMARY: Keith Larsen ("Apache Kid"), a scout who helps the hero hunt down hostile Apaches, goes to jail after he avenges his brother's murder by killing Chato. With the help of the rebel Apache, Marteen, he escapes and marries Liwana. Eventually, Ben Ziegler becomes his friend again and forgives his crime because he realizes the Kid was practicing Apache justice.

APACHE WOMAN (American International Pictures, 1955)

DIRECTOR: Roger Corman

SCREENPLAY: Lou Rusoff

CAST: Lloyd Bridges (Rex Moffett), Joan Taylor (Anne LeBeau), Lance Fuller (Armand)

SPECS: 69 minutes; Color

AVAILABILITY: VHS (Columbia Tristar)

NATION: Apache

IMAGE PORTRAYAL: Evil mixed-bloods; mixed-blood Native American

SUMMARY: Rex Moffett finds out that murders thought to be committed by reservation Apaches were actually done by the mixed-blood femme fatale Anne and her college-educated brother, Armand.

APOCALYPTO (Buena Vista, 2006)

DIRECTOR: Mel Gibson

SCREENPLAY: Mel Gibson, Fahad Sabina

CAST: Rudy Youngblood (Jaguar Paw), Raoul Trujillo (Zero Wolf), Gerardo Taracena (Middle Eye)

SPECS: 139 minutes; Color

AVAILABILITY: DVD and Blu-Ray (Buena Vista / Touchstone Home Entertainment)

NATION: Mayan (sixteenth century)

IMAGE PORTRAYAL: Hostile warriors; peace-loving chief

SUMMARY: Warriors from the savage Zero Wolf's tribe of Mayans attack the peaceful tribe of Jaguar Paw in order to sacrifice him. He escapes and, after a very long chase, hides in the jungle until he returns to save his family from the evil Mayans.

CRITICS: Mick LaSalle in the *San Francisco Chronicle* wrote: "The mission seems to have been to show cruelty, and then a justification was found for it. And so at the beginning we get a quote from Will Durant: 'A great civilization is not conquered from without until it has destroyed itself from within.' Aha! So that's Gibson's purpose in showing one Mayan tribe attacking, raping, enslaving, torturing, bludgeoning, stabbing, spearing, impaling, eviscerating, dissecting and decapitating the other! It's a cautionary tale" (December 8, 2006).

ARCTIC MANHUNT (Universal, 1949)

DIRECTOR: Ewing Scott

SCREENPLAY: Oscar Brodney, Joel Malone, based on the novel *Narana of the North* by Ewing Scott

CAST: Mikel Conrad (Mike Jarvis), Carol Thurston (Narana), Wally Cassell (Tooyuk)

SPECS: 60 minutes; Black & White

AVAILABILITY: NA

NATION: Eskimo

IMAGE PORTRAYAL: Romance between a Native American woman and a white man

SUMMARY: An Eskimo woman, Narana, loses the white man she loves, Mike Jarvis, when he dies in the wilderness. She is then reunited with her Eskimo lover, Tooyuk.

ARIZONA (Columbia, 1940)

DIRECTOR: Wesley Ruggles

SCREENPLAY: Claude Binyon, Clarence Budington Kelland

CAST: Jean Arthur (Phoebe Titus), William Holden (Peter Muncie), Porter Hall (Lazarus Ward), Frank Hill (Apache Chief, Mano)

SPECS: 125 minutes; Black & White

AVAILABILITY: DVD (Sony Pictures)

NATION: Apache

IMAGE PORTRAYAL: Attack on covered wagons

SUMMARY: Incited by the evil Lazarus Ward, Apaches of Chief Mano attack a wagon train, but the cavalry and Peter Muncie, who drives a herd of cattle into the charging Indians, save the day.

ARIZONA BUSHWHACKERS (Paramount, 1968)

DIRECTOR: Lesley Selander

SCREENPLAY: Steve Fisher, Andrew Craddock
CAST: Howard Keel (Lee Travis), Yvonne De Carlo (Jill Wyler), Scott Brady (Tom Rile)
SPECS: 87 minutes; Color
AVAILABILITY: VHS (Paramount; Out of Print); Amazon Instant Video
NATION: Apache
IMAGE PORTRAYAL: Attack on town
SUMMARY: Supplied with rifles by Tom Rile, Apaches attack a town and are defeated by the townspeople.

ARIZONA RAIDERS (Columbia, 1965)
DIRECTOR: William Witney
SCREENPLAY: Alex Gottlieb, Mary Willingham, Willard Willingham, Frank Gruber, Richard Schayer
CAST: Audie Murphy (Clint), Gloria Talbott (Martina)
SPECS: 85 minutes; Color
AVAILABILITY: DVD (Sony Pictures Home Entertainment); Amazon Instant Video
NATION: Yaqui
IMAGE PORTRAYAL: Friendship; loyalty
SUMMARY: Clint rescues Martina, the daughter of the Yaqui chief, from outlaws, and her tribe helps him bring a gang of outlaws to justice.

AROUND THE WORLD IN 80 DAYS (United Artists, 1956)
DIRECTOR: Michael Anderson
SCREENPLAY: James Poe, John Farrell, S. J. Perelman, based on the novel by Jules Verne
CAST: David Niven (Phileas Fogg), Cantinflas (Passepartout)
SPECS: 183 minutes; Color
AVAILABILITY: DVD (Warner Home Video)
NATION: Sioux
IMAGE PORTRAYAL: Attack on railroads
SUMMARY: After the travelers arrive in the Wild West, they meet a peaceful tribe who smoke the pipe with the engineer and do an orderly circle dance in an idyllic village. Then they encounter hostile Sioux who attack their train and capture Fogg's friend, Passepartout, whom they are about to burn at the stake when the cavalry come to the rescue.

ARROW IN THE DUST (Allied Artists, 1954)
DIRECTOR: Lesley Selander
SCREENPLAY: L. L. Foreman, Don Martin
CAST: Sterling Hayden (Bart Laish), Tom Tully (Crowshaw)
SPECS: 79 minutes; Color

AVAILABILITY: NA
NATION: Apache; Pawnee
IMAGE PORTRAYAL: Attack on wagon train
SUMMARY: Bart Laish stops deadly attacks by the Pawnee and Apaches when he destroys the wagon, which held the guns, and ammunition they were after.
CRITICS: A *New York Times* critic notes that the film dramatizes "the threat of murderous red savages intent on wiping out settlers and troopers" (May 1, 1954).

ARROWHEAD (Paramount, 1953)
DIRECTOR: Charles Marquis Warren
SCREENPLAY: Charles M. Warren, based on the novel by W. R. Burnett
CAST: Charlton Heston (Ed Bannon), Jack Palance (Toriano), Katy Jurado (Nita), Frank Dekova (Chief Chattez)
SPECS: 105 minutes; Color
AVAILABILITY: DVD (Paramount Home Video); Amazon Instant Video
NATION: Apache
IMAGE PORTRAYAL: Attacks on settlers
SUMMARY: Raised by the Apache of Chief Chattez and loved by Apache woman, Nita, Ed Bannon becomes a true hater of his adopted tribe. Finally, he defeats the warlike leader, Toriano, who returns to the Apache and leads them against the whites. Bannon is a notable example in the line of hate-filled characters who suggest the idea that to know Native Americans is to hate them.
CRITICS: *New York Times* critic Bosley Crowther comments on this attitude in the film: "Whatever feelings of friendship for the American Indian may have been shown in a few open-minded Westerns lately, it is plain that producer Nate Holt is having no truck with any such ideas. To him an Indian is still a treacherous dog" (September 16, 1953).

AT OLD FORT DEARBORN (Bison, 1912)
DIRECTOR: Frank Monty
SCREENPLAY: NA
CAST: Mona Darkfeather (Singing Bird)
SPECS: Black & White; Silent
AVAILABILITY: NA
NATION: NA (Historically, the Potawatomi)
IMAGE PORTRAYAL: Romance between a Native American woman and a white man
SUMMARY: Singing Bird loves a soldier who is captured by her tribe. When she tries to rescue him, her own people kill her.
CRITICS: G. F. Blaisdell in *Moving Picture World* notes that "Little Mona Darkfeather . . . has a role that will prove to be popular—that of a friend of the soldiers" (September 28, 1912).

ATANARJUAT: THE FAST RUNNER (Igloolik Isama Productions, NFBC, 2001)
DIRECTOR: Zacharias Kunuk
SCREENPLAY: Paul Apak Angilirq and Norman Cohn
CAST: Natar Ungalaaq (Atanarjuat), Sylvia Ivalu (Atuat), Peter Henry Arnatsiaq (Oki), Lucy Tulugarjuk (Puja), Eugene Ipkarnak (Sauri, the chief), Pauloosie Qulitalik (Quilitalik)
SPECS: 142 minutes; Color
AVAILABILITY: DVD (Columbia Tristar Home Entertainment)
NATION: Inuit
IMAGE PORTRAYAL: Vengeance
SUMMARY: Discussed on page 69, this film tells the story of how, after winning a violent contest with Oki, Atanarjuat takes Atuat, who had been promised to Oki, as his wife. After Atanarjuat also marries Oki's sister, Puja, Oki and his friends kill Atanarjuat's brother and chase him across the ice. An Inuit family rescues him and eventually returns him to his small extended family, where he is reunited to Atuat and brings Oki to justice by having him banished from the group. This is an Inuit folk story that happens in ancient times.
CRITICS: *New York Times* critic A. O. Scott comments: "'The Fast Runner' includes some unforgettable sequences, shot in the smoky interiors of igloos, out on the ice and in fields of yellow grass and purple clover during the brief spring thaw. The most astonishing scene—during which Oki and his minions, after a brutal assault on their enemy's tent, pursue the naked, barefoot Atanarjuat across a vast expanse of ice—has already become something of a classic, a word that will quickly be bestowed on the film as a whole" (March 30, 2002).

AT PLAY IN THE FIELDS OF THE LORD (Universal, 1992)
DIRECTOR: Hector Babenco
SCREENPLAY: Jean Claude Carriere, Hector Babenco, based on the novel by Peter Matthiessen
CAST: Tom Berenger (Lewis Moon)
SPECS: 189 minutes; Color
AVAILABILITY: VHS (Universal Pictures; Out of Print); Amazon Instant Video
NATION: Niaruna of the Amazon Basin
IMAGE PORTRAYAL: Contemporary Native Americans; endangered South American natives; mixed-blood Native American
SUMMARY: A mixed-blood Cheyenne pilot leaves the group of missionaries he is guiding and joins an Amazonian tribe, the Niaruna, who at first thinks he is Kisu, an evil sky god. After learning their language (the native tongue with subtitles) and being adopted by the tribe, he infects them with a deadly flu. At the end those who are left in the tribe reject him as a god.

B

BAD BASCOMB (MGM, 1946)
DIRECTOR: S. Sylvan Simon
SCREENPLAY: William R. Lipton, Grant Garett, D. A. Loxley
CAST: Wallace Beery (Zeb Bascomb), Margaret O'Brien (Emmy), J. Carrol Naish (Bart Yancy)
SPECS: 120 minutes; Black & White
AVAILABILITY: NA
NATION: NA
IMAGE PORTRAYAL: Attack on wagon train
SUMMARY: Incited by the villain, Bart Yancy, warriors attack a Mormon wagon train, and, in what may be the ultimate put-down of their fighting ability, Emmy fends them off with a peashooter.

BAD LANDS (RKO, 1939)
DIRECTOR: Lew Landers
SCREENPLAY: Clarence Upson Young
CAST: Robert Barrat (Sheriff Bill Cummings), Noah Beery Jr. (Chick Lyman), Jack Payne (Apache Jack), Billy Wilkerson (Apache Warrior)
SPECS: 70 minutes; Black & White
AVAILABILITY: NA
NATION: Apache
IMAGE PORTRAYAL: Attack on settlers
SUMMARY: Apaches pick off a posse led into a trap by Apache Jack one by one until soldiers save the last survivor, Bill Cummings.

BADLANDS OF DAKOTA (Universal, 1941)
DIRECTOR: Alfred E. Green
SCREENPLAY: Gerald Geraghty, Harold Schumate
CAST: Robert Stack (Jim Holliday), Ann Rutherford (Anne Grayson), Addison Richards (General Custer)
SPECS: 74 minutes; Black & White
AVAILABILITY: NA
NATION: Sioux
IMAGE PORTRAYAL: Attack on town
SUMMARY: Angered by the gold rush to the Black Hills and the presence of Custer's soldiers, Sioux attack a white town. The cavalry, led by Custer, drives off the warriors.

BARKING WATER (Lorber Films, 2009)
DIRECTOR: Sterlin Harjo
SCREENPLAY: Sterlin Harjo

CAST: Casey-Camp Horinek (Irene), Richard Ray Whitman (Frankie), Bebe Harjo (Bebe)
SPECS: 85 minutes; Color
AVAILABILITY: DVD (Lorber Films); Amazon Instant Video
NATION: Oklahoma tribes; Seminole
IMAGE PORTRAYAL: Contemporary Native American; old Native American; noble Native American
SUMMARY: Discussed on page 75, this film tells the story of two elderly Native Americans, Frankie, who is dying from cancer, and Irene his former lover, who travel to try to make it to his home before he dies. On the trip they forgive each other and reaffirm their love.
CRITICS: *New York Times* critic Stephen Holden comments: "The Oklahoma flatlands enhance the film's cosmic perspective, as do the silences in a screenplay whose rhythms and dialogue often feel self-consciously stagy. During those silences the camera studies Frankie's and Irene's handsome, haggard faces, which convey, more than words, the dignity of two people who have lived intensely and carry many regrets. Frankie's deep, rumbling voice, even when weakened, lends his remarks a weighty finality" (May 11, 2010).

BATTLE AT APACHE PASS (Universal, 1952)
DIRECTOR: George Sherman
SCREENPLAY: Gerald Drayson Adams
CAST: John Lund (Maj. Jim Colton), Jeff Chandler (Chief Cochise), Susan Cabot (Nono), Jay Silverheels (Geronimo)
SPECS: 85 minutes; Color
AVAILABILITY: NA
NATION: Apache
IMAGE PORTRAYAL: Friendship; hostile warrior; peace-loving chief
SUMMARY: Discussed on page 28, this film tells the story of peace-loving Cochise who prevails over the hostile Geronimo and finally makes a treaty with the government. This is a prequel to *Broken Arrow*. At the end, Cochise fights Geronimo hand to hand and defeats him, but decides to make him an outcast rather than killing him. Nona, the wife of Cochise, has their baby and all ends well.

BATTLE OF ROGUE RIVER (Columbia, 1954)
DIRECTOR: William Castle
SCREENPLAY: Douglas Heyes
CAST: George Montgomery (Frank Archer), Michael Granger (Chief Mike), Richard Denning (Stacey Wyatt)
SPECS: 71 minutes; Color
AVAILABILITY: DVD (Sony Pictures Home Entertainment)
NATION: NA
IMAGE PORTRAYAL: Peace-loving chief

SUMMARY: The tribe of Chief Mike, a leader who wants peace, makes a treaty with Archer. Stacy Wyatt lies about the intentions of the tribe and provokes an attack on the Native American village. The tribe defeats the attackers, and, finally, peace is achieved.

THE BATTLES OF CHIEF PONTIAC (Realart, 1952)
DIRECTOR: Felix Feist
SCREENPLAY: Jack DeWitt
CAST: Lex Barker (Kent McIntire), Helen Westcott (Winifred Lancaster), Lon Chaney Jr. (Chief Pontiac), Larry Chance (Hawkbill)
SPECS: 72 minutes; Black & White
AVAILABILITY: DVD (Alpha Video)
NATION: Ottawa
IMAGE PORTRAYAL: Attack on settlers; friendship; hostile warrior; peace-loving chief
SUMMARY: The evil leader of some Hessians tries to wipe out the Ottawa of Chief Pontiac by sending them blankets infested with smallpox. However, Lt. Kent McIntire, a friend of the chief, warns the tribe, and they get revenge by wrapping up their attackers in infected blankets. Kent also rescues Winifred from the hostile Hawkbill.

BEFORE TOMORROW (LE JOUR AVANT LE LENDEMAIN) (Arnot Video Production 2008)
DIRECTORS: Marie-Hélène Cousineau, Madeline Ivalu
SCREENPLAY: Susan Avingaq, Marie-Hélène Cousineau, Madeline Ivalu, based on a novel by Jørn Riel
CAST: Madeline Ivalu (Ninioq), Paul-Dylan Ivalu (Maniq), Mary Qulitalik (Kuutujuk)
SPECS: 93 minutes; Color
AVAILABILITY: DVD (Arnait Video Productions)
NATION: Inuit
IMAGE PORTRAYAL: Contemporary First Nation people; troubled First Nation people
SUMMARY: In this third film in the *Fast Runner* trilogy, Ninioq, her friend Kuutujuk, and grandson Maniq are dropped off on a remote island to catch fish and dry them. When the other people fail to pick them up, they take their canoe and return to the village where they find everyone dead because of a smallpox epidemic started by whites. They return to the small island where Kuutujuk dies and Ninioq faces death.
CRITICS: Greg Quill of the *Toronto Star* comments, "*Before Tomorrow* is endowed with a rich humanity and an almost heroic stoicism" (March 27, 2009).

BEHOLD MY WIFE (Paramount, 1920)
DIRECTOR: George Melford

SCREENPLAY: Frank Condon, based on the novel *Translation of a Savage* by Gilbert Parker

CAST: Mabel Julienne Scott (Lali), Milton Sills (Frank Armour), Fred Huntley (Chief Eye-of-the-Moon)

SPECS: 70 minutes; Black & White; Silent

AVAILABILITY: NA

NATION: NA

IMAGE PORTRAYAL: Romance between Native American woman and white man

SUMMARY: This film tells the story of Lali from the tribe of Chief Eye-of-the-Moon, whom an Englishman marries as revenge on his very proper family. He sends her to England to embarrass his family, but she learns their manners and gains their respect and that of her husband, who reunites with her.

BEHOLD MY WIFE (Paramount, 1934)

DIRECTOR: Mitchell Leisen

SCREENPLAY: Grover Jones, Vincent Lawrence, based on the novel *The Translation of a Savage* by Gilbert Parker

CAST: Sylvia Sidney (Tonita Storm Cloud), Gene Raymond (Michael Carter), Charles Middleton (Juan Storm Cloud), Jim Thorpe (Indian Chief), Greg Whitespear (Medicine Man)

SPECS: 79 minutes; Black & White

AVAILABILITY: NA

NATION: NA

IMAGE PORTRAYAL: Romance between Native American woman and white man

SUMMARY: This film tells the story of Tonita Storm Cloud, the daughter of a chief. When Michael Carter marries her to get back at his family, she finally realizes his motives and tries to avenge herself.

BEND OF THE RIVER (Universal, 1952)

DIRECTOR: Anthony Mann

SCREENPLAY: Bordon Chase, based on the novel *Bend of the Snake* by William Gulick

CAST: James Stewart (Glyn McLyntock), Arthur Kennedy (Emerson Cole)

SPECS: 91 minutes; Color

AVAILABILITY: DVD (Universal Studios Home Video)

NATION: Shoshone

IMAGE PORTRAYAL: Attack on wagon train

SUMMARY: Glyn McLyntock and Emerson Cole kill a small band of hostile Shoshone who attack a wagon train on its way to Oregon.

BIG EDEN (Jour de Fete Films, 2000)

DIRECTOR: Thomas Bezucha

SCREENPLAY: Thomas Bezucha
CAST: Arye Gross (Henry Hart), Eric Schweig (Pike Dexter)
SPECS: 118 minutes; Color
AVAILABILITY: DVD (Wolfe Video)
NATION: NA
IMAGE PORTRAYAL: Contemporary Native American; homosexuality; romance between Native American man and white man
SUMMARY: Henry Hart, a successful New York artist, comes to a small Montana town dreaming of a former male lover who lived there, but he falls in love with Pike Dexter, a Native American man who owns the general store there. The town approves and encourages their love.

THE BIG SKY (RKO, 1952)
DIRECTOR: Howard Hawks
SCREENPLAY: Dudley Nichols, based on the novel by A. B. Guthrie Jr.
CAST: Kirk Douglas (Jim Deakins), Elizabeth Threatt (Teal Eye), Dewey Martin (Boone Caudill), Hank Worden (Poordevil)
SPECS: 140 minutes; Black & White
AVAILABILITY: VHS (Warner Home Video; Out of Print)
NATION: Blackfoot; Crow
IMAGE PORTRAYAL: Attack on settlers; romance between a Native American woman and a white man
SUMMARY: On a river journey, Jim Deakins falls in love with Teal Eye, a Blackfoot whom the leader has taken along so he will be able to trade with her people. Along with Poordevil, the group fights hostile Crow and French traders. At the end, Boone Caudill and Teal Eye declare their love and decide to live with her tribe.

THE BIG TRAIL (Fox, 1930)
DIRECTOR: Raoul Walsh
SCREENPLAY: Hal G. Everts
CAST: John Wayne (Breck Colman), Chief John Big Tree, Nino Cochise, and Iron Eyes Cody play Native Americans in unaccredited roles.
SPECS: 125 minutes; Black & White
AVAILABILITY: DVD and Blu-Ray (Fox Searchlight)
NATION: NA
IMAGE PORTRAYAL: Attack on wagon train
SUMMARY: Once again, a hostile tribe attacks a wagon train.
CRITICS: A *Variety* reviewer comments that "the silly melodrama commences to weary, for it's the same thing over and over again, including the Indian attack on the wagon trains made corral" (October 29, 1930).

BILLY JACK (Warner Bros., 1971)
DIRECTOR: T. C. Frank (Tom Laughlin)

SCREENPLAY: Tom Laughlin, Delores Taylor

CAST: Tom Laughlin (Billy Jack), Delores Taylor (Jean Roberts), Stan Rice (Martin)

SPECS: 114 minutes; Color

AVAILABILITY: DVD and Blu-Ray (Image Entertainment); Amazon Instant Video

NATION: NA

IMAGE PORTRAYAL: Contemporary Native American; mixed-blood Native American; Native American activist

SUMMARY: Billy Jack, a mixed-blood Vietnam Green-Beret who does tribal rattlesnake dances and rides a Triumph cycle, defends Native American children and their teacher from villains in the nearby town. When the villains kill a boy from the reservation school and rape the teacher, Billy Jack uses his judo skills to punish them and then gives himself up to avoid more violence.

CRITICS: A *New York Times* critic comments that in Billy Jack there is "something of both Tonto and the Lone Ranger. . . . He is a comic strip character with delusions of grandeur" (March 11, 1973).

BILLY JACK GOES TO WASHINGTON (Taylor-Laughlin, 1977)

DIRECTOR: Tom Laughlin

SCREENPLAY: Tom Laughlin, Delores Taylor

CAST: Tom Laughlin (Billy Jack), Delores Taylor (Jean Roberts)

SPECS: 155 minutes; Color

AVAILABILITY: DVD (Image Entertainment); Amazon Instant Video

NATION: NA

IMAGE PORTRAYAL: Contemporary Native American; mixed-blood Native American; Native American activist

SUMMARY: In this remake of *Mr. Smith Goes to Washington*, appointed senator Billy Jack takes on the whole U.S. government in his fight for justice for his people and everyone else.

BILLY TWO HATS (United Artists, 1973)

DIRECTOR: Ted Kotcheff

SCREENPLAY: Alan Sharp

CAST: Desi Arnaz Jr. (Billy Two Hats), Gregory Peck (Arch Deans), Sian Barbara Allen (Esther Spencer), Henry Medicine Hat (Indian), Anthony Scott (Indian)

SPECS: 99 minutes; Color

AVAILABILITY: DVD (MGM Limited Edition Collection)

NATION: Kiowa

IMAGE PORTRAYAL: Attack on wagon; mixed-blood Native American; romance between Native American man and white woman

SUMMARY: Billy Two Hats, a mixed-blood Kiowa, protects his wounded outlaw white friend and falls in love with Esther Spencer. At the end, he gives his friend a Kiowa burial and leaves with Esther.

BLACK CLOUD (Old Post Films, 2004)
DIRECTOR: Ricky Schroder
SCREENPLAY: Ricky Schroder
CAST: Eddie Spears (Black Cloud), Russell Means (Bud), Julia Jones (Sammi), Joannelle Romero (Victoria Nez)
SPECS: 97 minutes; Color
AVAILABILITY: DVD (New Line Home Video); Amazon Instant Video
NATION: Navajo
IMAGE PORTRAYAL: Contemporary Native American; Native American athlete; romance between Native American man and white woman; troubled Native American
SUMMARY: A talented Navajo boxer struggles with his ancestry and white prejudice. He overcomes his anger; reconciles with his girlfriend, Sammi; and becomes an Olympic contender.

BLACK DAKOTAS (Columbia, 1954)
DIRECTOR: Ray Nazarro
SCREENPLAY: DeVallon Scott, Ray Buffum
CAST: John Bromfield (Mike Daugherty), John War Eagle (Chief War Cloud), Jay Silverheels (Black Buffalo)
SPECS: 65 minutes; Color
AVAILABILITY: DVD (Sony Pictures Home Entertainment)
NATION: Sioux
IMAGE PORTRAYAL: Hostile warrior; peace-loving chief
SUMMARY: War Cloud, the chief of the Sioux who wants peace, and the hostile, ambitious Black Buffalo are confronted with a fake treaty that promises gold to the tribe. At the end, Mike Daugherty saves the day, and War Cloud agrees to peace when he gets the real treaty from President Lincoln and the gold.
CRITICS: A *New York Times* critic notes that the film "remains a far cry from history" (October 2, 1954).

BLACK GOLD (Monogram, 1947)
DIRECTOR: Phil Karlson
SCREENPLAY: Agnes Christine Johnston, Caryl Coleman
CAST: Anthony Quinn (Charley Eagle), Katherine De Mille (Sarah Eagle), Ducky Louie (Davey)
SPECS: 90 minutes; Color
AVAILABILITY: NA
NATION: NA
IMAGE PORTRAYAL: Romance between Native Americans
SUMMARY: Charley Eagle and his wife, Sarah, become millionaires when oil is discovered on their land. They adopt a Chinese boy, Davey, and buy a race-horse named Black Gold. After much trouble with the horse, Davey rides him to a win in a big race.

CRITICS: A *Variety* critic notes that the film "is commendable for there is not a single Indian-uttered 'ugh' in the dialogue" (October 15, 1947).

BLACK ROBE (Alliance Entertainment, 1991)
DIRECTOR: Bruce Beresford
SCREENPLAY: Brian Moore, based on his novel which drew from the *Jesuit Relations*
CAST: Lothaire Bluteau (Father LaForgue), Aden Young (Daniel), Sandrine Holt (Annuka), August Schellenberg (Chomina), Tantoo Cardinal (Chomina's Wife), and many other First Nation actors in supporting roles.
SPECS: 101 minutes; Color
AVAILABILITY: DVD (MGM Home Entertainment)
NATIONS: Algonquin; Huron; Iroquois (Mohawk); Montagnais
IMAGE PORTRAYAL: Attacks on Native Americans; romance between a Native American woman and a white man
SUMMARY: Discussed on page 62, this film takes place in seventeenth-century Canada. The missionary, Father LaForgue, who strives to convert the native peoples ultimately sets up the destruction of the friendly Algonquin Chomina, and later the Huron tribe, who are conquered by the fierce Iroquois. LaForgue's young friend Daniel and Annuka, the daughter of Chomina, fall in love.
CRITICS: In his book, *From a Native Son*, Ward Churchill comments: "The only Indians exempted from what is plainly meant to be seen as the disgusting quality of indigenous existence are the Hurons, at least those who have converted to Christianity" (1996, 432).

BLAZING ACROSS THE PECOS (Columbia, 1948)
DIRECTOR: Ray Nazarro
SCREENPLAY: Norman S. Hall
CAST: Charles Starrett (Durango Kid), Charles Wilson (Ace Brockway), Chief Thundercloud (Chief Bear Claw)
SPECS: 55 minutes; Black & White
AVAILABILITY: DVD (Sony Pictures Home Entertainment)
NATION: NA
IMAGE PORTRAYAL: Friendship; peace-loving chief
SUMMARY: The Durango Kid, who is a friend of Chief Bear Claw, deals with Ace Brockway who is running guns to Bear Claw's tribe and later establishes peace.

BLAZING ARROWS (Western Pictures, 1922)
DIRECTOR: Henry McCarty
SCREENPLAY: Henry McCarty, Lew Meehan
CAST: Lester Cuneo (Sky Fire), Francelia Billington (Martha Randolf), Clark Comstock (Gray Eagle), Laura Howard (Mocking Bird)
SPECS: Black & White; Silent

AVAILABILITY: DVD (Grapevine Video)
NATION: NA
IMAGE PORTRAYAL: Romance between a Native American man and a white
  woman; white man adopted by Native Americans
SUMMARY: Sky Fire, a student at Columbia, falls in love with Martha Randolf,
  who rejects him because of his race. Later he returns to the West and rescues
  the same woman from the evil Gray Eagle. At the end, he marries Martha after
  he finds out that he is really a white man who had been adopted by a Native
  American.

BLOOD ARROW (20th Century Fox, 1958)
DIRECTOR: Charles Marquis Warren
SCREENPLAY: Fred Freiberger
CAST: Scott Brady (Dan Kree) Phyllis Coates (Bess Johnson), Richard Gilden
  (Little Otter), Rocky Shahan (Taslatch)
SPECS: 76 minutes; Black & White
AVAILABILITY: NA
NATION: Blackfoot
IMAGE PORTRAYAL: Attack on settlers; friendship
SUMMARY: When hostile Blackfeet led by Little Otter attack a Mormon woman,
  Bess Johnson, bringing serum to sick families, some whites and Taslatch come
  to her rescue.

BLOOD ON THE ARROW (Allied Artists, 1964)
DIRECTOR: Sidney Salkow
SCREENPLAY: Robert E. Kent, Mark Hanna
CAST: Dale Robertson (Wade Cooper), Robert Carricart (Kai La)
SPECS: 91 minutes; Color
AVAILABILITY: NA
NATION: Apache
IMAGE PORTRAYAL: Attack on settlers; friendship; kidnapping
SUMMARY: The Apache tribe of Kai La attacks a trading post, and kills everyone
  except the outlaw Wade Cooper, who becomes the hero. They also kidnap a
  boy. Eventually the hero leads the warriors into a trap and rescues the child.

BLUE GAP BOY'Z (Better World, 2008)
DIRECTOR: Travis Holt Hamilton
SCREENPLAY: Travis Holt Hamilton
CAST: Ernest David Tsossie III (James Nez), Vincent Craig (Jessie), James Bila-
  gody (Jodie)
SPECS: 90 minutes; Color
AVAILABILITY: NA
NATION: Navajo

IMAGE PORTRAYAL: Contemporary Native Americans

SUMMARY: When a German music producer arrives, James, Jessie, and Jody, a Navajo band, try to be chosen for a trip to Europe. This is a zany comedy with lots of music.

BORN LOSERS (American International, 1966)

DIRECTOR: T. C. Frank (Tom Laughlin)

SCREENPLAY: Elizabeth James

CAST: Tom Laughlin (Billy Jack), Elizabeth James (Vicky Barrington)

SPECS: 113 minutes; Color

AVAILABILITY: DVD (Image Entertainment)

NATION: NA

IMAGE PORTRAYAL: Contemporary Native American; mixed-blood Native American; Native American activist

SUMMARY: Billy Jack, a mixed-blood, rescues a woman from a motorcycle gang. He dies at the end; however, the character was resurrected in the popular Billy Jack films of the 1970s.

BRAVE WARRIOR (Columbia, 1952)

DIRECTOR: Spencer G. Bennet

SCREENPLAY: Robert E. Kent

CAST: Jon Hall (Steve Ruddell), Jay Silverheels (Tecumseh), Harry Cording (Shayne MacGregor) Michael Ansara (The Prophet), Billy Wilkerson (Chief Little Cloud)

SPECS: 72 minutes; Color

AVAILABILITY: DVD (Sony Pictures Choice Collection)

NATION: Shawnee

IMAGE PORTRAYAL: Hostile warriors; peace-loving chief

SUMMARY: Aided by Tecumseh, chief of the Shawnee, Steve Randall deals with Shayne MacGegor who is inciting hostile members of the tribe, led by the Prophet and Chief Little Cloud, to make war against the settlers.

BRAVEHEART (Producers Dist. Corp., 1925)

DIRECTOR: Alan Hale

SCREENPLAY: Mary O'Hara, based on the play by William C. deMille

CAST: Rod La Rocque (Braveheart), Lillian Rich (Dorothy Nelson), Frank Hagney (Ki-Yote), Tyrone Power Sr. (Chief Standing Rock), Jean Acker (Sky Arrow)

SPECS: 71 minutes; Black & White; Silent

AVAILABILITY: DVD (Alpha Video; Grapevine Video)

NATION: NA

IMAGE PORTRAYAL: Hostile warrior; peace-loving chief; romance between Native American man and white woman; romance between Native Americans

SUMMARY: Braveheart, a scholar and All-American football player at an Eastern college, lies to protect a white friend. When he is found out, he has to return in disgrace to his homeland. Later he vindicates himself by winning fishing rights for his tribe. After Ki-Yote incites his tribe to kidnap Dorothy Nelson, Braveheart comes to her rescue and realizes she is the person he loved in college. However, at the end he decides to marry a woman from his tribe, Sky Arrow.

BREAKHEART PASS (United Artists, 1976)
DIRECTOR: Tom Gries
SCREENPLAY: Alistair MacLean, based on his novel
CAST: Charles Bronson (Deakin), Eddie Little Sky (White Hand)
SPECS: 95 minutes; Color
AVAILABILITY: DVD (MGM); Blu-ray (Kino Lorber)
NATION: Paiute
IMAGE PORTRAYAL: Attack on railroads
SUMMARY: The Paiutes of White Hand conspire with the villains and attack people on a train.

BROKEN ARROW (20th Century Fox, 1950)
DIRECTOR: Delmer Daves
SCREENPLAY: Albert Maltz, based on the novel *Blood Brother* by Elliot Arnold
CAST: James Stewart (Tom Jeffords), Jeff Chandler (Cochise), Debra Paget (Sonseeahray), Jay Silverheels (Gokia-Geronimo), Chris Yellow Bird (Nochale), J. W. Cody (Pionsenay), John War Eagle (Nahilzay), Iron Eyes Cody (Teese)
SPECS: 93 minutes; Color
AVAILABILITY: DVD (20th Century Fox Home Entertainment)
NATION: Apache
IMAGE PORTRAYAL: Peace-loving chief; romance between Native American woman and white man
SUMMARY: Discussed on page 26, this film tells the story of Cochise, the friend of Tom Jeffords, who chooses the difficult way of peace for his tribe. Tom Jeffords marries Sonseeahray, who is killed by outlaws at the end.

THE BROKEN DOLL (Biograph, 1910)
DIRECTOR: D. W. Griffith
SCREENPLAY: Belle Taylor
CAST: Gladys Egan (Little Indian Girl), Kate Bruce (Indian), Dark Cloud (Indian Chief), Francis J. Grandon (Indian), Guy Hedlund (Indian), Dell Henderson (Indian)
SPECS: 17 minutes; Black & White; Silent
AVAILABILITY: NA
NATION: NA
IMAGE PORTRAYAL: Friendship; loyalty

SUMMARY: In this film, subtitled "A Tragedy of the Indian Reservation," a white man brutally kills a Native American. When the chief of his tribe prepares to take revenge, a little girl from the tribe who had been given a doll by a white child shows her gratitude by warning the whites, only to be killed in the fighting.

BROKEN LANCE (20th Century Fox, 1954)
DIRECTOR: Edward Dmytryk
SCREENPLAY: Richard Murphy, Phillip Yordan
CAST: Spencer Tracy (Joe Devereaux), Katy Jurado (the Senora, Joe's mixed-blood wife), Robert Wagner (Joe Jr.), Eduard Franz (Two Moons)
SPECS: 96 minutes; Color
AVAILABILITY: DVD (20th Century Fox Home Entertainment)
NATION: Comanche
IMAGE PORTRAYAL: Mixed-blood Native American; romance between a mixed-blood Native American man and a white woman; romance between a Native American woman and a white man
SUMMARY: A white man married to a "Comanche princess" and his family struggle against white society's contempt and prejudice. After her husband dies, the wife and her mixed-blood son, Joe, keep the peace. At the end, Joe breaks the lance of war. Like *Flaming Star* (1960), the film is a strong indictment of racism.

BUCK AND THE PREACHER (Columbia, 1972)
DIRECTOR: Sidney Poitier
SCREENPLAY: Ernest Kinoy, Drake Walker
CAST: Sidney Poitier (Buck), Harry Belafonte (the Preacher), Enrique Lucero (Indian Chief), Julie Robinson (Sinsie)
SPECS: 102 minutes; Color
AVAILABILITY: DVD (Sony Pictures Home Entertainment)
NATION: NA
IMAGE PORTRAYAL: Friendship; loyalty
SUMMARY: With his sister Sinsie as interpreter, the chief of a beleaguered tribe, who turns out to be a shrewd bargainer, gives Buck five days to bring his wagon train through their land. Later the tribe helps Buck and the Preacher to escape from the villains and a few warriors rescue them during the final shootout.

BUFFALO BILL (20th Century Fox, 1944)
DIRECTOR: William Wellman
SCREENPLAY: Aeneas MacKensie, Clements Ripley, Cecil Kramer, Frank Winch
CAST: Joel McCrea (Buffalo Bill Cody), Linda Darnell (Dawn Starlight), Anthony Quinn (Chief Yellow Hand)
SPECS: 90 minutes; Color

AVAILABILITY: DVD (20th Century Fox Home Entertainment)
NATION: Cheyenne
IMAGE PORTRAYAL: Attack on soldiers; romance between a Native American
  woman and a white man
SUMMARY: In one part of the film, Buffalo Bill, who respects and defends Native Americans, finally kills his former friend, Yellow Hand, in a hand-to-hand
  fight, and thus allows the cavalry to come to the rescue in a large battle in which
  many Cheyenne are killed. Dawn Starlight, a Native American schoolteacher
  who loves Buffalo Bill, dies during this battle. Once again the love of a Native
  American woman for a white man makes it necessary for her to die before the
  film ends.

BUFFALO BILL AND THE INDIANS, OR SITTING BULL'S HIS-TORY LESSON (United Artists, 1976)

DIRECTOR: Robert Altman
SCREENPLAY: Alan Rudolph, Robert Altman, based on the Arthur Kopit play,
  The Indians
CAST: Paul Newman (Buffalo Bill), Frank Kaquitts (Sitting Bull), Will Sampson
  (William Halsey, the interpreter)
SPECS: 123 Minutes; Color
AVAILABILITY: DVD (MGM Home Entertainment)
NATION: Sioux
IMAGE PORTRAYAL: Wise elder
SUMMARY: In this film, Buffalo Bill Cody hires Sitting Bull and his interpreter,
  William Halsey, to be in his Wild West Show. Sitting Bull, who communicates
  with Buffalo Bill only through his interpreter, remains impervious to the crazy
  outbursts of Buffalo Bill, who can only symbolically triumph over him in a fake
  battle at the end of the show.
CRITICS: Vincent Canby in the *New York Times* comments, "There's a rueful
  exchange between Bill and Sitting Bull's aide when the chief announces that
  the scene he wants to play will dramatize white men murdering Indian women
  and children. Bill is appalled. Says Annie Oakley (played with a mixture of great
  charm and fierce determination by Geraldine Chaplin), 'He just wants to show
  the truth to the people.' Answers Bill, 'I have a better sense of history.' And of
  show business" (June 25, 1976).

BUFFALO BILL IN TOMAHAWK TERRITORY (United Artists, 1952)

DIRECTOR: Bernard B. Ray
SCREENPLAY: Sam Neuman, Nat Tanchuck
CAST: Clayton Moore (Buffalo Bill), Rodd Redwing (Running Deer), Chief
  Yowlachie (Chief White Cloud), Chief Thundercloud (Black Hawk), Charlie
  Hughes (Pinfeathers)

SPECS: 66 minutes; Black & White
AVAILABILITY: DVD (Alpha Video)
NATION: Sioux
IMAGE PORTRAYAL: Hostile warrior; peace-loving chief
SUMMARY: By disguising themselves as warriors and attacking wagon trains, villains who are after gold try to turn the soldiers against the Sioux tribe of Chief White Cloud. Buffalo Bill, who survives an attack by Running Deer, the son of White Cloud, discovers the plot and offers the tribe a herd of cattle as payment from the government. White Cloud accepts and peace is established.

BUFFALO BILL ON THE U.P. TRAIL (Aywon Films, 1926)
DIRECTOR: Frank Mattison
SCREENPLAY: NA
CAST: Roy Stewart (Buffalo Bill), Felix Whitefeather (White Spear)
SPECS: 6 reels; Black & White; Silent
AVAILABILITY: NA
NATION: NA
IMAGE PORTRAYAL: Attack on railroads; attack on settlers
SUMMARY: When the chief's hostile son, White Spear, starts a buffalo stampede to cover his attack, Buffalo Bill comes to the rescue.

BUFFALO BILL RIDES AGAIN (Screen Guild, 1947)
DIRECTOR: Bernard B. Ray
SCREENPLAY: Frank Gilbert, Barney A. Sarecky
CAST: Richard Arlen (Buffalo Bill), Gil Patric (Simpson), Chief Many Treaties (Chief Brave Eagle), Charles Stevens (White Mountain), Shooting Star (Yellow Bird)
SPECS: 69 minutes; Black & White
AVAILABILITY: DVD (Sinister Cinema); Amazon Instant Video
NATION: NA
IMAGE PORTRAYAL: Friendship; loyalty; peace-loving chief
SUMMARY: Buffalo Bill thwarts the efforts of oil-hungry villains, led by Simpson, who are inciting the tribe of Chief Brave Eagle to attack the settlers. White Mountain and Young Bird help Buffalo Bill escape from an attack by the villains. At the end the evil plot of Simpson is exposed and peace is established with the tribe.

THE BUGLE CALL (Triangle, 1916)
DIRECTOR: Reginald Barker
SCREENPLAY: C. Gardiner Kaufman
CAST: William Collier Jr. (Billy), Joe Goodboy (Lame Bear)
SPECS: 5 reels; Black & White; Silent
AVAILABILITY: NA

NATION: NA
IMAGE PORTRAYAL: Attack on a fort
SUMMARY: By a clever deception, warriors divert the main body of troops and
    then attack the undermanned fort. However, a boy named Billy plays the bugle
    call and in turn tricks them into thinking the troops are returning.

BUGLES IN THE AFTERNOON (Warner Bros., 1952)
DIRECTOR: Roy Rowland
SCREENPLAY: Daniel Mainwaring, Harry Brown, based on the novel by Ernest
    Haycox
CAST: Ray Milland (Kern Shafer), John War Eagle (Red Owl)
SPECS: 85 minutes; Color
AVAILABILITY: VHS (Lions Gate)
NATION: Sioux
IMAGE PORTRAYAL: Attack on a fort
SUMMARY: The hostile Sioux of Red Owl attack Fort Lincoln and later defeat
    Custer at the Battle of Little Big Horn.
CRITICS: A *New York Times* critic comments: the "already time-worn tale, has
    been poked along with such leaden pretentiousness by Director Roy Rowland
    that this film should be given back to the Indians. And judging by the expres-
    sions of the contributing Sioux, they want no part of it" (March 5, 1952).

BULLWHIP (Allied Artists, 1958)
DIRECTOR: Harmon Jones
SCREENPLAY: Arlen Buffington
CAST: Guy Madison (Steve Daley), Rhonda Fleming (Julie Cheyenne O'Malley),
    Burt Nelson (Pine Hawk)
SPECS: 80 minutes; Color
AVAILABILITY: VHS (Republic Pictures)
NATION: Cheyenne
IMAGE PORTRAYAL: Mixed-blood Native American; romance between a Na-
    tive American woman and a white man
SUMMARY: A convicted man, Steve Dailey, agrees to marry an unknown
    woman who turns out to be Cheyenne O'Malley, a strong-willed mixed-blood
    woman. After many struggles and twists of fate, they accept each other. Pine
    Hawk is a friend of Cheyenne O'Malley.

THE BUSINESS OF FANCYDANCING (Outrider Pictures, 2002)
DIRECTOR: Sherman Alexie
SCREENPLAY: Sherman Alexie
CAST: Evan Adams (Seymour Polatkin), Michelle St. John (Agnes Roth), Gene
    Tagaban (Aristotle Joseph), Swil Kanim (Mouse)
SPECS: 103 minutes; Color
AVAILABILITY: DVD (Fox Lorber)

NATION: Spokane

IMAGE PORTRAYAL: Contemporary Native Americans; mixed-blood Native American; troubled Native Americans

SUMMARY: Discussed on page 72, this complicated film tells the story of three contrasting Native Americans: Seymour Polatkin, a gay poet who has left the reservation and is lionized by white readers, Aristotle Joseph, a fierce young man who does not leave the reservation, and Agnes Roth, a mixed-blood who returns to the reservation as a teacher. Seymour returns to the reservation for the funeral of his friend, Mouse, and the drama intensifies.

CRITICS: In *Film Threat*, the reviewer, Doug Brunell, comments: "This film makes it abundantly clear what happens to those who leave whatever culture they are part of, whether it be an ethnic group, a sexual group or an educational sphere. Their self-imposed (and sometimes forced) exile produces guilt, rage and self-loathing" (December 8, 2002).

C

CAHILL, U.S. MARSHALL (Warner Bros., 1973)

DIRECTOR: Andrew V. McLaglen

SCREENPLAY: Harry Julian Fink, Rita Fink, Barney Slater

CAST: John Wayne (J. D. Cahill), Neville Brand (Lightfoot)

SPECS: 103 minutes; Color

AVAILABILITY: DVD (Warner Home Video)

NATION: Comanche

IMAGE PORTRAYAL: Friendship; loyalty; mixed-blood Native American

SUMMARY: Lightfoot (Neville Brand), a mixed-blood Comanche, is the wise and loyal friend of Cahill, who dies while trying to save his friend.

CRITICS: Vincent Canby in the *New York Times* notes that Lightfoot is "an excellent tracker who talks like a social worker" (July 12, 1973).

CALL HER SAVAGE (Fox, 1932)

DIRECTOR: John F. Dillon

SCREENPLAY: Edwin J. Burke, based on the novel by Tiffany Thayer

CAST: Clara Bow (Nasa Springer), Gilbert Roland (Moonglow), Weldon Heyburn (Ronasa, Nasa's biological father)

SPECS: 88 minutes; Black & White

AVAILABILITY: NA

NATION: NA

IMAGE PORTRAYAL: Attack on wagon train; friendship; mixed-blood Native American; white man adopted by Native Americans

SUMMARY: After some wild and rebellious behavior, Nasa Springer, the daughter of a white woman and Native American man, finds out about her Indian heritage and reconnects with her mixed-blood friend, Moonglow.

CRITICS: Josh Bell, in a review on *Not Coming to a Theater Near You*, comments that Nasa's mother "turns out to be a hell-raiser with a thing for Native Americans, which provides a simplistic and fairly racist explanation for Nasa's untamable nature" (April 23, 2012).

THE CALL OF THE WILD (Biograph, 1908)
DIRECTOR: D. W. Griffith
SCREENPLAY: D. W. Griffith, loosely based on the novel by Jack London
CAST: Charles Inslee (Redfeather), Florence Lawrence (Gladys Penrose)
SPECS: 16 minutes; Black & White; Silent
AVAILABILITY: NA
NATION: NA
IMAGE PORTRAYAL: Romance between a Native American man and a white woman
SUMMARY: In this film, subtitled "The Sad Plight of the Civilized Redman," George Redfeather, from the Carlisle Indian School, proposes to Gladys Penrose. When she refuses to marry him, he angrily returns to the land of his tribe. Later, when the woman ends up in his area, he captures her and is about to take revenge when she uses a religious argument to persuade him to have mercy on her.

CANADIAN PACIFIC (20th Century Fox, 1949)
DIRECTOR: Edwin Marin
SCREENPLAY: Jack Dewitt, Kenneth Gamet
CAST: Randolph Scott (Tom Andrews), Jane Wyatt (Dr. Edith Cabot), Chief Yowlachie (Indian Chief)
SPECS: 95 minutes; Color
AVAILABILITY: NA
NATION: NA
IMAGE PORTRAYAL: Attack on railroads; peace-loving chief
SUMMARY: An evil fur trader incites a tribe to attack the railroad workers. After the attack is finally stopped, the Indian chief asks for peace.

THE CANADIANS (20th Century Fox, 1961)
DIRECTOR: Burt Kennedy
SCREENPLAY: Burt Kennedy
CAST: Robert Ryan (William Gannon) Teresa Stratas (the White Squaw), Michael Pate (Chief Four Horns)
SPECS: 85 minutes; Color
AVAILABILITY: NA
NATION: Sioux
IMAGE PORTRAYAL: Vengeance
SUMMARY: After villains kidnap the White Squaw, a Sioux war party led by Chief Four Horns take their revenge by using stampeding horses to drive them off a cliff.

CANCEL MY RESERVATION (Warner Bros., 1972)
DIRECTOR: Paul Bogart
SCREENPLAY: Bob Fisher, Arthur Marx, based on the novel *The Broken Gun* by Louis L'Amour
CAST: Bob Hope (Dan Bartlett), Henry Darrow (Joe Little Cloud), Chief Dan George (Old Bear), Betty Ann Carr (Mary Little Cloud)
SPECS: 99 minutes; Color
AVAILABILITY: DVD (Shout! Factory)
NATION: NA
IMAGE PORTRAYAL: Native Americans as victims
SUMMARY: Dan Bartlett tries to solve the murder of Mary Little Cloud with the help of her father, Joe Little Cloud, and Old Bear, a mystic. At the end, he finds out that a rancher killed the young woman.

CAPTAIN APACHE (AKA DEATHWORK) (Scotia International, 1971)
DIRECTOR: Alexander Singer
SCREENPLAY: Philip Yordan, Milton Sperling, based on the novel by S. E. Whitman
CAST: Lee Van Cleef (Captain Apache)
SPECS: 89 minutes; Color
AVAILABILITY: DVD (Geneon)
NATION: Apache
IMAGE PORTRAYAL: Friendship
SUMMARY: Captain Apache, an Apache Union officer, investigates the murder of an Indian agent and stops a conflict with his tribe by discovering that the villain had incited them to war to get at gold and oil on tribal land.

CAPTAIN JOHN SMITH AND POCAHONTAS (United Artists, 1953)
DIRECTOR: Lew Landers
SCREENPLAY: Aubrey Wisberg, Jack Pollexfen
CAST: Anthony Dexter (Captain John Smith), Jody Lawrance (Pocahontas), Stuart Randall (Opechanco), Douglas Dumbrille (Chief Powatan), Shepard Menken (Nantaquas), Franchesca De Scaffa (Mawhis), Joan Dixon (Lacuma)
SPECS: 75 minutes; Color
AVAILABILITY: DVD (MGM Home Entertainment)
NATION: Powatan
IMAGE PORTRAYAL: Romance between Native American woman and a white man
SUMMARY: Pocahontas saves the life of John Smith and marries him to keep the peace with the settlers. Her father, the wise old Chief Powatan, reluctantly approves of the match but the hostile Opechanco rebels and joins the villains. At the end, John Smith sails for England, and Pocahontas stays behind to remarry and keep the peace.

CAPTAIN OF GRAY HORSE TROOP (Vitagraph, 1917)

DIRECTOR: William Wobert

SCREENPLAY: NA

CAST: Antonio Moreno (Captain George Curtis), Otto Lederer (Crawling Elk), Al Jennings (Cut Finger), Neola May (Cut Finger's wife)

SPECS: 5 reels; Black & White; Silent

AVAILABILITY: NA

NATION: NA

IMAGE PORTRAYAL: Native Americans as victims

SUMMARY: Ranchers use their influence in the U.S. Government to steal land from the tribe of Crawling Elk, Cut Finger, and his wife. The hero, Captain Curtis, intervenes and establishes peace with the tribe.

CRITICS: A *Variety* critic comments: "Instead of making all 'Injuns' merely firewater drinkers, it places them in the attitude of being the abused nation" (May 18, 1917).

THE CAPTIVE GOD (Triangle, 1916)

DIRECTOR: Charles Swickard

SCREENPLAY: Monte M. Katterjohn

CAST: William S. Hart (Chiapa), Enid Markey (Lolomi), Robert McKim (Montezuma), Dorothy Dalton (Tecolote), P. Dempsey Tabler (Mexitli)

SPECS: 50 minutes; Black & White; Silent

AVAILABILITY: NA

NATION: Aztec

IMAGE PORTRAYAL: Romance between a Native American woman and a white man

SUMMARY: After Chiapa, a Spaniard, grows up with the Tehuan tribe, who consider him a god, the Aztecs of Montezuma and the warrior Mexitli capture Chiapa. As he is about to be killed, his lover, Lolomi, the daughter of Montezuma, comes to his rescue, and he is reunited with his Tehuan tribe.

CRITICS: A *Variety* critic notes that the story "is at once thrilling and carries an air of mystic romance that is compelling" (July 7, 1916).

CARDIGAN (American, 1922)

DIRECTOR: John Noble

SCREENPLAY: Based on the novel by Robert W. Chambers

CAST: William Collier Jr. (Michael Cardigan), Betty Carpenter (Silver Heels), Frank Montgomery (Chief Logan)

SPECS: 70 minutes; Black & White; Silent

AVAILABILITY: NA

NATION: Cayuga

IMAGE PORTRAYAL: Romance between a Native American woman and a white man

SUMMARY: The Cayuga tribe of Chief Logan starts a war and captures Cardigan, who loves Silver Heels. At the last moment he is saved from being burned at the stake.

CRITICS: A *Variety* critic notes that the tribe is "costumed as the old Biograph company presented their Indians" (February 24, 1922).

THE CARIBOU TRAIL (20th Century Fox, 1950)
DIRECTOR: Edwin Marin
SCREENPLAY: Frank Guber, John Rhodes Sturdy
CAST: Randolph Scott (Jim Redfern), Fred Libby (Chief White Buffalo)
SPECS: 81 minutes; Color
AVAILABILITY: VHS (Delta Library)
NATION: Blackfoot
IMAGE PORTRAYAL: Attack on cowboys
SUMMARY: The warlike Blackfoot tribe of Chief White Buffalo attack a cattle drive.

CASINO JACK (ATO Pictures, 2010)
DIRECTOR: George Hickenlooper
SCREENPLAY: Norman Snider
CAST: Kevin Spacey (Jack Abramoff), Graham Greene (Bernie Sprague), Eric Schweig (Chief Poncho)
SPECS: 108 minutes; Color
AVAILABILITY: DVD (20th Century Fox Home Entertainment)
NATION: NA
IMAGE PORTRAYAL: Contemporary Native Americans
SUMMARY: In this film about Jack Abramoff, the notorious lobbyist, Bernie Sprague and Chief Poncho represent some of the six tribes he fleeced. These tribes play a rather small part in the movie.

CAT BALLOU (Columbia, 1965)
DIRECTOR: Elliot Silverstein
SCREENPLAY: Walter Newman, Frank Pierson, based on the novel *The Ballad of Cat Ballou* by Roy Chanslor
CAST: Jane Fonda (Cat Ballou), Lee Marvin (Kid Shelleen/Tim Strawn), Tom Nardini (Jackson Two Bears)
SPECS: 97 minutes; Color
AVAILABILITY: DVD (Sony Pictures Home Entertainment)
NATION: NA
IMAGE PORTRAYAL: Friendship
SUMMARY: In this comic western, Jackson Two Bears is the best-educated member of the gang. At one point, when he gets into a fight, he says, "Well, everyone else was doing it. I got the right to share in the fun without regard to race, creed, or color according to the Fourteenth Amendment."

CATTLE QUEEN OF MONTANA (RKO, 1954)
DIRECTOR: Allan Dwan
SCREENPLAY: Robert Blees, Howard Estabrook, Thomas Blackburn

CAST: Barbara Stanwyck (Sierra Nevada Jones), Lance Fuller (Colorados), Anthony Caruso (Natchakoa), Yvette Duguay (Starfire), Rodd Redwing (Powhani)
SPECS: 88 minutes; Color
AVAILABILITY: DVD (VCI Entertainment)
NATION: Blackfoot
IMAGE PORTRAYAL: Attack on settlers; drunkenness; hostile warrior; peace-loving chief
SUMMARY: Coloradas, a college-educated chief of the Blackfeet, helps Sierra Jones fight the villain and hostile, whiskey-drinking warriors from his tribe led by Natchakoa.
CRITICS: A *Variety* reviewer writes: "In the picture's favor is an attempt to depict the problems of the Redmen in fighting the encroachment of their land by the white settlers. The Indians are not all evil, scalp-hunting devils" (December 31, 1953).

THE CHARGE AT FEATHER RIVER (Warner, 1953)
DIRECTOR: Gordon Douglas
SCREENPLAY: James R. Webb
CAST: Guy Madison (Miles Archer), Vera Miles (Jenny McKeever), Helen Westcott (Anne McKeever), Fred Carson (Chief Thunder Hawk)
SPECS: 95 minutes; Color
AVAILABILITY: NA
NATION: Cheyenne
IMAGE PORTRAYAL: Attack on soldiers; romance between a Native American man and a white woman
SUMMARY: In this 3D film, Miles Archer rescues two women from the Cheyenne. One of them, Jenny McKeever, is in love with their chief, Thunder Hawk. His warriors give chase and attack the hero's party at the river and not only are they defeated but also Thunder Hawk is killed.

CHARLEY ONE EYE (Paramount, 1973)
DIRECTOR: Don Chaffey
SCREENPLAY: Keith Leonard
CAST: Richard Roundtree (Black Man), Roy Thinnes (Indian), Nigel Davenport (Bounty Hunter)
SPECS: 96 minutes; Color
AVAILABILITY: Odeon Entertainment
NATION: NA
IMAGE PORTRAYAL: Native American as victim
SUMMARY: A Black Man and a stoic, crippled Native American become friends as they try to escape from a bounty hunter. When he catches them, violence follows.

CHATO'S LAND (United Artists, 1972)
DIRECTOR: Michael Winner
SCREENPLAY: Gerald Wilson
CAST: Charles Bronson (Pardon Chato), Sonia Rangan (Chato's Woman)
SPECS: 110 minutes; Color
AVAILABILITY: DVD (MGM Home Entertainment)
NATION: Apache
IMAGE PORTRAYAL: Vengeance
SUMMARY: A posse pursues Chato, an Apache leader who killed in self-defense a sheriff who raped and killed his wife. He hunts them down and takes his revenge.

CHEROKEE UPRISING (Monogram, 1950)
DIRECTOR: Lewis D. Collins
SCREENPLAY: Daniel B. Ullman
CAST: Whip Wilson (Bob Foster), Forrest Taylor (Indian Agent William Welch), Iron Eyes Cody (Longknife), Chief Yowlachie (Gray Eagle)
SPECS: 57 minutes; Color
AVAILABILITY: NA
NATION: NA
IMAGE PORTRAYAL: Attack on settlers; drunkenness
SUMMARY: An evil Indian agent, William Welch, uses whiskey to incite the tribe of Long Knife to attack wagon trains. Gray Eagle is a ranch hand who is killed. Bob Foster stops the attacks by exposing the evil designs of the agent.

THE CHEROKEE WORD FOR WATER (Toy Gun Films, 2013)
DIRECTORS: Tim Kelly, Charlie Soap
SCREENPLAY: Louise Rubacky, Tim Kelly, Gary Miranda
CAST: Kimberly Guerrero (Wilma Mankiller), Moses Brings Plenty (Charlie Soap), Steve Reevis (Johnson Soap), Darryl Tonemah (Chief Ross Swimmer)
SPECS: 92 minutes; Color
AVAILABILITY: NA
NATION: Cherokee
IMAGE PORTRAYAL: Contemporary Native American; Native American activist; inspirational leaders
SUMMARY: Told from the perspective of Cherokee leaders Wilma Mankiller and her husband, Charlie Soap, this film tells about how water was finally brought to rural Oklahoma houses, a project that inspired other self-help work in Native American communities.

CHEYENNE AUTUMN (Warner Bros., 1964)
DIRECTOR: John Ford
SCREENPLAY: James R. Webb, based on the novel by Mari Sandoz

CAST: Richard Widmark (Capt. Thomas Archer), Sal Mineo (Red Shirt), Ricardo Montalban (Little Wolf), Gilbert Roland (Dull Knife), Delores Del Rio (Spanish Woman)
SPECS: 154 minutes; Color
AVAILABILITY: DVD (Warner Home Video)
NATION: Cheyenne
IMAGE PORTRAYAL: Peace-loving chief
SUMMARY: Discussed on page 36, this film deals with the trek of Dull Knife and Little Wolf and their bands of Cheyenne to their homeland in Montana. At the end, after the two bands have signed a treaty, Little Wolf kills Red Shirt and goes into exile. Dull Knife and his band go to their reservation after peace is restored.
CRITICS: Bosley Crowther in the *New York Times* comments: "It is a stark and eye-opening symbolization of a shameful tendency that has prevailed in our national life—the tendency to be unjust and heartless to weaker peoples who get in the way of manifest destiny" (December 24, 1964).

A CHEYENNE BRAVE (Pathe, 1910)
DIRECTOR: James Young Deer
SCREENPLAY: NA
CAST: George Larkin, James Young Deer
SPECS: Black & White; Silent
AVAILABILITY: NA
NATION: Cheyenne
IMAGE PORTRAYAL: Romance between Native Americans
SUMMARY: Warriors from two different tribes fight for the hand of a maiden. Her Cheyenne lover wins and takes her to the land of his people.
CRITICS: A *Moving Picture World* reviewer calls the film "one of most, if not the most, remarkable Indian pictures ever produced. . . . All the actors taking part in this picture are real Indians or sufficiently well made up to pass as such" (August 6, 1910, 299).

CHIEF CRAZY HORSE (Universal, 1955)
DIRECTOR: George Sherman
SCREENPLAY: Franklin Coen, Gerald Drayson Adams
CAST: Victor Mature (Crazy Horse), Suzan Ball (Black Shawl), Ray Danton (Little Big Man), Keith Larson (Flying Hawk), Paul Guilfoyle (Worm), Robert Warwick (Spotted Tail), Morris Ankrum (Red Cloud), Stuart Randall (Old Man Afraid), Pat Hogan (Dull Knife), Henry Wills (He Dog)
SPECS: 86 minutes; Color
AVAILABILITY: NA
NATION: Sioux-Lakota
IMAGE PORTRAYAL: Peace-loving chief

SUMMARY: Crazy Horse is the prophesied leader of the Sioux of Flying Hawk, Worm, Spotted Tail, Red Cloud, Old Man Afraid, and He Dog. After winning battles, he is convinced by a white friend and his wife, Black Shawl, to make peace with the whites. At the end, Little Big Man kills him.

CRITICS: A *Time* critic notes that the film "pays a Technicolor installment on Hollywood's debt to the American Indian: after years of getting clobbered, the redskins this time win three battles in a row over the U.S. Cavalry" (May 30, 1955, 86).

CHIEF WHITE EAGLE (Lubin, 1912)

DIRECTOR: Romaine Fielding

SCREENPLAY: Romaine Fielding

CAST: Romaine Fielding (Chief White Eagle), Mary E. Ryan (Estrella), Richard Wangermann (The Major)

SPECS: Black & White; Silent

AVAILABILITY: NA

NATION: NA

IMAGE PORTRAYAL: Romance between a Native American man and a white woman

SUMMARY: White Eagle, educated in an Eastern school, murders a white woman who cruelly rejected his love. After he goes home to become chief of his tribe, a reluctant white man hunts him down and kills him. At the end both the man and the tribe pray for White Eagle.

CHRISTMAS IN THE CLOUDS (Majestic Films, 2001)

DIRECTOR: Kate Montgomery

SCREENPLAY: Kate Montgomery

CAST: Timothy Vahle (Ray Clouds on Fire), Sam Vlahos (Joe Clouds on Fire), Mariana Tosca (Tina Littlehawk), Graham Greene (Earl—the chef), Sheila Tousey (Mary), Rosalind Ayres (Mabel), Rita Coolidge (Ramona). Numerous other Native American actors play minor roles in this Native American production.

SPECS: 96 minutes; Color

AVAILABILITY: DVD (Hannover House)

NATION: NA

IMAGE PORTRAYAL: Contemporary Native Americans; romance between a Native American man and white woman; romance between Native Americans

SUMMARY: This romantic comedy is narrated by old Joe Clouds on Fire. At the end, Ray Clouds on Fire and Tina Littlecloud finally overcome mistaken identity and declare their love. Joe Clouds on Fire ends up with Mabel. There are also the running gags of Earl, the vegetarian chef.

CRITICS: In the *Chicago Sun Times,* critic Roger Ebert comments: "The history is made because the movie is about affluent Native American yuppies. So many movies about American Indians deal in negative stereotypes that it's nice to find one that takes place at an upscale Indian-owned ski resort. The only alcoholic in the cast is a white undercover investigator for a guidebook" (December 1, 2005).

CHUKA (Paramount, 1967)
DIRECTOR: Gordon Douglas
SCREENPLAY: Richard Jessup, based on his novel
CAST: Rod Taylor (Chuka), Victoria Vetri (Helena Chavez), Marco Lopez (Hanu, Chief of the Arapaho)
SPECS: 95 minutes; Color
AVAILABILITY: DVD (Warner Archive Collection)
NATION: Arapaho
IMAGE PORTRAYAL: Attack on a fort; friendship
SUMMARY: Chuka aids Hanu, Chief of the Arapaho, by giving food to his starving tribe. Later Hanu's warriors kill everyone in the fort except Chuka and his woman, whom Hanu lets live because of Chuka's earlier help.

CLEARCUT (Northern Arts, 1992)
DIRECTOR: Ryszard Bugajski
SCREENPLAY: Robert Forsyth, based on the novel by M. T. Kelly
CAST: Graham Greene (Arthur), Tom Jackson (Tom Starblanket), Raoul Trujillo (Eugene), Floyd "Red Crow" Westerman (Wilf), Ron Lea (Peter Maguire), Rebecca Jenkins (Louise)
SPECS: 100 minutes; Color
AVAILABILITY: NA
NATION: NA
IMAGE PORTRAYAL: Contemporary Native Americans; evil spirit
SUMMARY: Discussed on page 63, this film tells the story of Arthur, the personification of an ancient Ojibwa avenging spirit and the dark side of a liberal white lawyer named Peter Maguire. While lumbermen destroy the forests of the Ojibwa, Arthur takes his revenge on the owner of the lumber mill by skinning him as the owner has done to the trees.
CRITICS: Stephen Holden of the *New York Times* notes: "The deepest character is the tribe's chief, a man of few words whom Mr. Westerman imbues with an anguished benignity. All-knowing yet powerless to change the course of events, this elder is the film's grieving spiritual guide" (August 21, 1992).

COLD JOURNEY (National Film Board of Canada, 1976)
DIRECTOR: Martin Defalco
SCREENPLAY: Martin Defalco, David Jones
CAST: Buckley Petawabano (Buckley), John Yesno (Johnny Yesno), Chief Dan George (Old John)

SPECS: 75 minutes; Color
AVAILABILITY: NA
NATION: Cree; Ojibwa
IMAGE PORTRAYAL: Contemporary First Nation people; troubled First Nation people
SUMMARY: This film tells the sad story of Buckley, a Canadian Cree teenager who doesn't fit in with his family or at a boarding school. An Ojibwa, young Johnny Yesno, befriends him and the elder, old John, gives him advice, but in the end he can't find an identity that he can live with, and he freezes to death, alone.

COLORADO TERRITORY (Warner Bros., 1949)
DIRECTOR: Raoul Walsh
SCREENPLAY: John Twist, Edmund H. North
CAST: Joel McCrea (Wes McQueen), Virginia Mayo (Colorado Carson)
SPECS: 94 minutes; Color
AVAILABILITY: DVD (Warner Archive Collection)
NATION: NA
IMAGE PORTRAYAL: Mixed-blood Native American; romance between Native American woman and a white man
SUMMARY: Colorado Carson is a mixed-blood lover of the outlaw Wes McQueen, and dies with him at the end.

COLT .45 (Warner Bros., 1950)
DIRECTOR: Edwin Marin
SCREENPLAY: Thomas W. Blackburn
CAST: Randolph Scott (Steve Farrell), Chief Thundercloud (Walking Bear)
SPECS: 74 minutes; Color
AVAILABILITY: DVD (Warner Home Video)
NATION: NA
IMAGE PORTRAYAL: Friendship; loyalty
SUMMARY: Steve Farrell and the friendly tribe of Walking Bear (Chief Thunder Cloud), whose life Steve has saved, help him overcome a gang of outlaws.
CRITICS: A New York Times reviewer comments: "Chief Thundercloud simply slays 'em with his dead pan and his magnetic arrows. As a matter of fact—and incidentally—more damage seems to be done by the swift, silent shafts of the Indians than by the bullets from the celebrated guns" (May 6, 1950).

COLUMN SOUTH (Universal, 1953)
DIRECTOR: Frederick De Cordova
SCREENPLAY: William Sackheim
CAST: Audie Murphy (Lt. Jed Sayre), Robert Sterling (Capt. Lee Whitlock), Dennis Weaver (Menguito)

SPECS: 92 minutes; Color
AVAILABILITY: NA
NATION: Navajo
IMAGE PORTRAYAL: Attack on a fort; friendship
SUMMARY: Lee Whitlock incites Navajo led by Menguito to make war, but the hero, Jed Sayre, a friend of Menguito, foils his plans. Later the Navajo warriors attack the fort but are defeated.

COMANCHE (United Artists, 1956)
DIRECTOR: George Sherman
SCREENPLAY: Carl Krueger
CAST: Dana Andrews (Jim Read), Kent Smith (Quanah Parker), Henry Brandon (Black Cloud), Mike Mazurki (Flat Mouth), Tony Carbajal (Little Snake)
SPECS: 87 minutes; Color
AVAILABILITY: NA
NATION: Comanche
IMAGE PORTRAYAL: Hostile warriors; peace-loving chief
SUMMARY: Despite the opposition of Black Cloud and his hostile warriors, Flat Mouth and Little Snake, Chief Quanah Parker of the Comanche agrees to peace. Because of the efforts of Jim Reed, who kills Black Cloud in hand-to-hand combat, Quanah Parker accepts a treaty.

COMANCHE STATION (Columbia, 1960)
DIRECTOR: Budd Boetticher
SCREENPLAY: Burt Kennedy
CAST: Randolph Scott (Jefferson Cody), Foster Hood (Comanche Lance Bearer), Joe Molina (Comanche Chief), Vince St. Cyr (Comanche Warrior)
SPECS: 74 minutes; Color
AVAILABILITY: DVD (Sony Pictures Home Entertainment)
NATION: Comanche
IMAGE PORTRAYAL: Attack on settlers
SUMMARY: After the Comanche capture a white woman, Jefferson Cody trades with them to secure her release. When Comanche warriors later attack the station, they are driven off.

COMANCHE TERRITORY (Universal, 1950)
DIRECTOR: George Sherman
SCREENPLAY: Lewis Meltzer, Oscar Brodney
CAST: Maureen O'Hara (Katie Howard), Macdonald Carey (Jim Bowie), Pedro de Cordoba (Quisima), Rick Vallin (Pakanah)
SPECS: 76 minutes; Color
AVAILABILITY: NA
NATION: Comanche

IMAGE PORTRAYAL: Friendship; loyalty; peace-loving chief
SUMMARY: Chief Quisima of the Comanche controls his hostile warriors and makes friends with the hero, Jim Bowie, who saves the tribe by finding a treaty stolen by villains and by bringing them guns so they can defend themselves.
CRITICS: A *Variety* critic notes: "This is one of the few recent screen vehicles in which the Indians are never cast as villains" (April 5, 1950).

THE COMANCHEROS (20th Century Fox, 1961)
DIRECTOR: Michael Curtiz
SCREENPLAY: James Edward Grant, Clair Huffaker, based on the novel by Paul Wellman
CAST: John Wayne (Captain Jake Cutter), Stuart Whitman (Paul Regret), Ina Balin (Pilar Graile), Nehemiah Persoff (Graile), Lee Marvin (Tully Crow), George Lewis (Iron Shirt)
SPECS: 107 minutes; Color
AVAILABILITY: DVD (20th Century Fox Home Entertainment)
NATION: Comanche
IMAGE PORTRAYAL: Attack on settlers
SUMMARY: Captain Cutter and Paul Regret fight the evil Comancheros and the hostile Comanches led by Iron Shirt.
CRITICS: A *New Yorker* critic notes that in "Hollywood the only good Comanches are dead Comanches" and then observes, "Have you ever noticed in Westerns that the white men can be shot and wounded not once but many times, while Indians who get shot almost always die instantly?" (December 9, 1961, 235).

COMATA, THE SIOUX (Biograph, 1909)
DIRECTOR: D. W. Griffith
SCREENPLAY: Stanner E. V. Taylor
CAST: James Kirkwood (Comata), Marion Leonard (Clear Eyes), Verner Clarges (Indian Chief), Arthur Johnson (Bud Watkins)
SPECS: 10 minutes; Black & White; Silent
AVAILABILITY: NA
NATION: Sioux
IMAGE PORTRAYAL: Romance between Native Americans; romance between Native American woman and a white man
SUMMARY: Clear Eyes leaves her tribe to live with Bud Watkins and they have a child. After he abandons her for a white woman, she goes off toward the Black Hills with Comata, who has loved and watched over her from the beginning.

THE COMMAND (Warner Bros., 1954)
DIRECTOR: David Butler
SCREENPLAY: Samuel Fuller, Russell S. Hughes, based on the novel, *Rear Guard*, by James Warner Bellah

CAST: Guy Madison (Capt. Robert MacClaw), Joan Weldon (Martha Cutting), Larry Chance (Indian Brave), Billy Wilkerson (Indian Chief)
SPECS: 94 minutes; Color
Availability: DVD and BLU-RAY (Warner Archive Collection)
NATION: NA
IMAGE PORTRAYAL: Attack on wagon train; Native Americans as victims
SUMMARY: Captain MacClaw leads a wagon train that is attacked by hostile warriors. Martha Cutting leaves colored clothing infected with chicken-pox to be picked up by the tribe.

THE CONQUERING HORDE (Paramount, 1931)
DIRECTOR: Edward Sloman
SCREENPLAY: Grover Jones, William Slavens McNutt, based on the novel by Emerson Hough
CAST: Richard Arlen (Dan McMasters), Chief Standing Bear (Chief White Cloud), Ian Maclaren (Marvin Fletcher)
SPECS: 75 minutes; Black & White
AVAILABILITY: NA
NATION: NA
IMAGE PORTRAYAL: Peace-loving chief
SUMMARY: By killing a woman from the tribe of White Cloud (Chief Standing Bear), the villain, Marvin Fletcher, incites them to attack a group of cattlemen. At the end the hero, Dan McMasters, turns Fletcher over to the tribe and peace is restored.

CONQUEST OF COCHISE (Columbia, 1953)
DIRECTOR: William Castle
SCREENPLAY: Arthur Lewis, DeVallon Scott
CAST: John Hodiak (Cochise), Robert Stack (Maj. Tom Burke), Steven Ritch (Tukiwah), Carol Thurston (Terua), Rodd Redwing (Red Knife), Joy Page (Consuelo de Cordova), Joseph Waring (Running Cougar)
SPECS: 70 minutes; Color
AVAILABILITY: DVD (Sony Pictures Home Entertainment)
NATION: Apache; Comanche
IMAGE PORTRAYAL: Peace-loving chief; romance between a Native American woman and a white man
SUMMARY: Discussed on page 29, this film tells the story of how Cochise, who falls in love with Consuelo de Cordova after the death of his wife, Terua, keeps the peace despite the efforts of hostile warriors from his tribe and from his former allies, the Comanches of Red Knife and Running Cougar.

COTTER (Reel Media International, 1973)
DIRECTOR: Paul Stanley
SCREENPLAY: William D. Gordon

CAST: Don Murray (Cotter), Carol Lynley (Leah), Rip Torn (Roy), Sherry Jackson (Shasta)
SPECS: 94 minutes; Color
AVAILABILITY: DVD (Miracle Pictures)
NATION: Sioux
IMAGE PORTRAYAL: Drunkenness
SUMMARY: Cotter, a Sioux rodeo clown with a drinking problem, returns to his homeland, only to be wrongly blamed for the murder of a rancher because of his reputation as a drinker.

THE COVERED WAGON (Paramount, 1923)
DIRECTOR: James Cruze
SCREENPLAY: Jack Cunningham, based on the novel by Emerson Hough
CAST: J. Warren Kerrigan (Will Banion), Lois Wilson (Molly Wingate), Tully Marshall (Jim Bridger), Guy Oliver (Kit Carson)
SPECS: 98 minutes; Black & White; Silent
AVAILABILITY: VHS (Paramount)
NATION: NA
IMAGE PORTRAYAL: Attack on wagon trains; romance between a Native American woman and a white man
SUMMARY: In this first big-budget western, hordes of hostile braves attack the wagon train, which has formed a circle as a defensive arrangement; this became a standard in the later westerns. Tim McCoy, the technical adviser for the film, used 750 members of various western tribes for the attack sequences. The hero, Jim Bridger (Tully Marshall), has two Indian wives, played by Native American actors.

THE COWBOY AND THE INDIANS (Columbia, 1949)
DIRECTOR: John English
SCREENPLAY: Dwight Cummins, Dorothy Yost
CAST: Gene Autry (Himself), Jay Silverheels (Chief Lakohna), Sheila Ryan (Dr. Nan), Claudia Drake (Lucy Broken Arm), Charles Stevens (Broken Arm), Frank Lackteen (Blue Eagle), Chief Yowlachie (Chief Long Arrow), Iron Eyes Cody (Indian Farmer)
SPECS: 68 minutes; Black & White
AVAILABILITY: Amazon Instant Video
NATION: NA
IMAGE PORTRAYAL: Mixed-blood Native American; Native Americans as victims; romance between Native Americans
SUMMARY: A crooked Indian agent reduces a tribe to starvation by confiscating their stock and selling their food for his own profit. Gene Autry, aided by a mixed-blood doctor, Nan Palmer, gets food for the tribe and brings the villain to justice. At the end, Nan and young Chief Lakohna fall in love. Other

members of the tribe are Lucky Broken Arm, Broken Arm, Blue Eagle, and Chief Long Arrow.

COWBOYS AND INDIANS (Screen Media Films, 2011)
DIRECTORS: Aaron Burk, Tyler Burk
SCREENPLAY: Aaron Burk, Tyler Burk
CAST: Alvin Cowan (Captain Bugle), Kate Maloney (Patricia), Dennis Ambriz (Falling Star), Andrew Pinon (Bad Face), Duane Minard (Golden Eagle), Jimmy James Jr. (Chief White Elk)
SPECS: 86 minutes; Color
AVAILABILITY: Screen Media Films
NATION: NA
IMAGE PORTRAYAL: Hostile warriors; kidnapping
SUMMARY: In this pathetic return to the western, Captain Bugle rescues a white woman, Patricia, from the hostile Black Claw tribe. Chief White Elk is a peace-loving man as is Golden Eagle. Falling Star is the evil medicine man that wants war. At the end peace is restored.

COWBOYS AND INDIANS (ABC Payroll and Production, 2013)
DIRECTOR: Ian McCrudden
SCREENPLAY: Ian McCrudden
CAST: Ian McCrudden (Twisty), Maria Johnson (Angel), Kyle Agnew (Gas)
SPECS: NA
AVAILABILITY: NA
NATION: Paiute
IMAGE PORTRAYAL: Contemporary Native Americans; Native Americans as victims
SUMMARY: Angel, a lovely Paiute woman is raped and has a son named Gas. The son and a cowboy, Twisty, become friends and eventually are reunited with Angel.

THE CREATOR'S GAME (KOAN, 1999)
DIRECTOR: Bruce Troxell
SCREENPLAY: Bruce Troxell
CAST: Dakota House (Daniel Cloud), Celeste Wilson (Delanna Cloud), Al Harrington (Old Snow)
SPECS: 102 minutes; Color
AVAILABILITY: DVD (Koan)
NATION: Iroquois
IMAGE PORTRAYAL: Contemporary Native American
SUMMARY: Daniel Cloud must find a good coaching job to save his family store. After arriving at a university, he learns that lacrosse is the only sport that needs

a coach. His sister, Delanna, and grandfather, Old Snow, help him to learn that the Great Spirit gave lacrosse to his tribe and he finally draws on his tribal traditions to create a winning team.

CROOKED ARROWS (20th Century Fox, 2012)
DIRECTOR: Steve Rash
SCREENPLAY: Brad Riddell, Todd Baird
CAST: Brandon Routh (Joe Logan), Gil Birmingham (Ben Logan), Chelsea Ricketts (Nadie Logan), Crystal Allen (Julie Gifford), Dennis Ambriz (Crooked Arrow), Kakaionstha Betty Deer (Grandma Logan), Tyler Hill (Jimmy Silverfoot) and numerous other Native American actors.
SPECS: 105 minutes; Color
AVAILABILITY: DVD (20th Century Fox); Amazon Instant Video
NATION: Sunaquot
IMAGE PORTRAYAL: Contemporary Native American; Native American athlete
SUMMARY: In this feel-good sports film, Joe Logan, a Native American business man and developer, finds his Sunaquot tribal roots with the help of his father, Ben; his elder, Crooked Arrow; and his grandmother. He then coaches a winless Native American lacrosse team, which are called the Crooked Arrows, to the state championship. He also falls in love with the white schoolteacher, Julie Gifford.

CRY BLOOD, APACHE (Golden Eagle, 1970)
DIRECTOR: Jack Starrett
SCREENPLAY: Sean MacGregor, Harold Roberts
CAST: Jody McCrea (Pitcalin), Marie Gahva (Jemme), Dan Kemp (Vittorio), Carolyn Stellar (Cochalla), Carroll Kemp (Old Indian), Andy Anza (Crippled Indian), Markus Rudnick (Indian)
SPECS: 82 minutes; Color
AVAILABILITY: DVD (Miaracle Pictures): Amazon Instant Video
NATION: Apache
IMAGE PORTRAYAL: Romance between a Native American woman and a white man; vengeance
SUMMARY: When Apaches refuse to reveal the location of a gold mine, a group of whites kill everyone in the band except Jemme and her brother, Vittorio. After Vittorio hunts down and gets his revenge on most of the whites, Jemme kills him before he takes the life of Pitcalin, whom she loves.

CURSE OF THE RED MAN (Selig, 1911)
DIRECTOR: Francis Boggs
SCREENPLAY: Lanier Bartlett
CAST: Tom Santschi (Terapai), Kathlyn Williams
SPECS: 1 reel; Black & White; Silent

AVAILABILITY: NA
NATION: Apache
IMAGE PORTRAYAL: Drunkenness
SUMMARY: A Native American who learns to drink while going to college struggles with alcoholism after he returns to live with his tribe and is rejected.

CUSTER OF THE WEST (Cinerama, 1967)

DIRECTOR: Robert Siodmak
SCREENPLAY: Bernard Gordon, Julian Zimet
CAST: Robert Shaw (Custer), Kieron Moore (Chief Dull Knife)
SPECS: 143 minutes; Color
AVAILABILITY: DVD (MGM-UA Home Entertainment)
NATION: Cheyenne; Sioux
IMAGE PORTRAYAL: Attack on soldiers
SUMMARY: Influenced by politicians, Custer and his soldiers massacre a band of the Cheyenne at Washita. Afterward, he becomes troubled, searches his soul, and decides to fight for the rights of Native Americans until his last battle with the Sioux and Cheyenne of Dull Knife (Kieron Moore) at Little Big Horn.

CUSTER'S LAST FIGHT (Bison, 1912)

DIRECTOR: Francis Ford
SCREENPLAY: Richard V. Spenser
CAST: Francis Ford (Custer), William Eagle Shirt (Sitting Bull)
SPECS: 30 minutes; Black & White; Silent
AVAILABILITY: NA
NATION: Cheyenne; Sioux
IMAGE PORTRAYAL: Attack on soldiers
SUMMARY: The film deals with the whole story: the arrival of white settlers, the discovery of gold in the Black Hills, the battle at Little Big Horn, and the aftermath, especially that of the Sioux and Sitting Bull.
CRITICS: This version of Custer's final battle with the Plains tribes provokes a racist comment from *Moving Picture World* critic Louis Reeves Harrison, who believes that filmmakers who created the "Noble Redman" should be made to live with real Indians, who are "merciless to the weak, inhuman in their outrages on white women and children . . . and incapable of gratitude" (June 22, 1912, 1118).

D

DAKOTA INCIDENT (Republic, 1956)

DIRECTOR: Lewis K. Foster
SCREENPLAY: Frederick Louis Fox

CAST: Linda Darnell (Amy Clarke), Dale Robertson (John Banner), Charles Horvath (Cheyenne Leader)
SPECS: 88 minutes; Color
AVAILABILITY: VHS (Lions Gate); Amazon Instant Video
NATION: Cheyenne
IMAGE PORTRAYAL: Attack on stagecoach; gratitude
SUMMARY: Hostile Cheyenne led by an unnamed leader pin down a group of whites in a gully and eventually kill most of them. At one point John Banner lets one warrior live and the warrior shows his gratitude.

THE DALTON GANG (Donald Barry Productions, 1949)
DIRECTOR: Ford Beebe
SCREENPLAY: Ford Beebe
CAST: Don Barry (Marshal Larry West), Robert Lowery (Blackie Dalton), George J. Lewis (Chief Irahu)
SPECS: 58 minutes; Black & White
AVAILABILITY: DVD (VCI Home Video)
NATION: NA
IMAGE PORTRAYAL: Friendship
SUMMARY: The friendly tribe of Chief Irahu helps Larry West track the Dalton gang.

DANCES WITH WOLVES (Tig Productions, 1990)
DIRECTOR: Kevin Costner
SCREENPLAY: Michael Blake, based on his novel
CAST: Kevin Costner (John Dunbar), Mary McDonnell (Stands with a Fist), Graham Greene (Kicking Bird), Rodney A. Grant (Wind in His Hair), Floyd Westerman (Ten Bears), Tantoo Cardinal (Black Shawl), Jimmy Herman (Stone Calf), Michael Spears (Otter), Jason R. Lone Hill (Worm), Wes Studi (Pawnee Warrior). Numerous other Native American actors appear in the film as minor characters.
SPECS: 181 minutes; Color
AVAILABILITY: DVD and Blu-ray (MGM Home Entertainment); Amazon Instant Video
NATION: Pawnee; Sioux
IMAGE PORTRAYAL: Friendship; hostile warrior; loyalty
SUMMARY: Discussed on page 58, this immensely popular film tells the story of the friendship between John Dunbar and the noble tribe of Ten Bears, Kicking Bird, and Wind-in-His Hair. Dunbar falls in love with Stands with a Fist, who turns out to be a white woman. The opposing savage tribe is led by a hostile Pawnee warrior.
CRITICS: Vincent Canby in the *New York Times* comments on the Camp of Ten Bears: "This Sioux camp not only looks as neat as a hausfrau's pin, but also

unlived-in. It's a theme-park evocation, without rude odors to offend the sensitive nostril" (November 9, 1990).

DANGEROUS VENTURE (United Artists, 1947)
DIRECTOR: George Archainbaud
SCREENPLAY: Doris Schroeder, Clarence E. Mulford
CAST: William Boyd (Hopalong Cassidy), Fritz Leiber (Xeoli), Patricia Tate (Talu)
SPECS: 59 minutes; Black & White
AVAILABILITY: DVD (Echo Bridge)
NATION: Aztec
IMAGE PORTRAYAL: Native Americans as victims
SUMMARY: When villains disguised as Native Americans and a scientist try to exploit the isolated Talnec tribe of Talu and Xeoli, descendants of the Aztecs, Hopalong Cassidy comes to the rescue and stops a human sacrifice.

DANIEL BOONE (Edison, 1907)
DIRECTORS: Wallace McCutcheon, Edwin S. Porter
SCREENPLAY: NA
CAST: William Craven (Daniel Boone), Florence Lawrence (Boone's Daughter)
SPECS: 1 reel; Black & White; Silent
AVAILABILITY: NA
NATION: NA
IMAGE PORTRAYAL: Kidnapping; torture
SUMMARY: A warlike tribe kidnaps Boone's daughter, who has befriended a young Native American woman from the tribe. When Boone tries to rescue her, he is captured and tortured. Finally he is rescued by his horse and gets his revenge by killing the chief of the tribe.

DANIEL BOONE (RKO, 1936)
DIRECTOR: David Howard
SCREENPLAY: Daniel Jarrett, Edgecumb Pinchon
CAST: George O'Brien (Daniel Boone), George Regas (Black Eagle), Chief John Big Tree (Wyandotte warrior), John Carradine (Simon Girty)
SPECS: 75 minutes; Black & White
AVAILABILITY: DVD (Alpha Video)
NATION: NA
IMAGE PORTRAYAL: Attack on settlers, friendship; loyalty
SUMMARY: Led by a gun-selling villain, Simon Girty, a hostile tribe attacks Daniel Boone's settlement and is about to break through when rain washes out their tunnels. Black Eagle is the friend of Daniel Boone who saves his life.
CRITICS: A *Variety* critic notes that the film uses "a lot of phony histrionics and make-believe hysterical Indian fighting. . . . It's an Indian opera a la mode" (October 28, 1936).

DANIEL BOONE, TRAILBLAZER (Republic, 1956)
DIRECTORS: Albert Gannaway, Ishmael Rodriguez
SCREENPLAY: Tom Hubbard, John Patrick
CAST: Bruce Bennett (Daniel Boone), Lon Chaney Jr. (Black Fish)
SPECS: 76 minutes; Color
AVAILABILITY: DVD (Alpha Video); Amazon Instant Video
NATION: Shawnee
IMAGE PORTRAYAL: Attack on a wagon train; peace-loving chief
SUMMARY: Incited by villains, Shawnee warriors attack a wagon train led by
    Daniel Boone. Eventually, he convinces Chief Blackfish to make peace, even
    though the chief has lost two sons.

THE DARK WIND (Seven Arts Pictures, 1999)
DIRECTOR: Errol Morris
SCREENPLAY: Neal Jimenez, Eric Bergren, based on the novel by Tony Hillerman
CAST: Lou Diamond Phillips (Officer Jim Chee), Fred Ward (Lieutenant Joe
    Leaphorn), Gary Farmer (Cowboy Albert Dashee), and numerous other Native
    American actors playing minor parts.
SPECS: 111 Minutes; Color
AVAILABILITY: DVD (Artisan Home Entertainment); Amazon Instant Video
NATION: Hopi; Navajo
IMAGE PORTRAYAL: Contemporary Native Americans
SUMMARY: Jim Chee and Joe Leaphorn, Navajo policemen, investigate a rob-
    bery, plane crash, and apparent murder discovered by Cowboy Albert Dashee,
    a Hopi policeman, before they solve the crimes that are disrupting the relation-
    ship between the Navajo and Hopi tribes.

DAUGHTER OF THE WEST (Film Classics, 1949)
DIRECTOR: Harold Daniels
SCREENPLAY: Irwin Franklyn, Raymond L. Schrock, Robert E. Callahan
CAST: Martha Vickers (Lolita Moreno), Phillip Reed (Navo White Eagle), Pedro
    de Cordoba (Chief Wykomas), Marion Carney (Okeeman), Luz Alba (Wa-
    teeka), Tommy Cook (Ponca), and Willow Bird (A Medicine Man)
SPECS: 77 minutes; Color
AVAILABILITY: NA
NATION: Navajo
IMAGE PORTRAYAL: Romance between Native Americans
SUMMARY: An educated Navajo, Navo White Eagle is in love with Lolita
    Moreno, a mixed-blood teacher, and he eventually marries her after she finds
    out the she is the daughter of the famous Ramona. Navo brings to justice an
    Indian agent who gives liquor to the tribe so he can steal their mineral rights.

DAVY CROCKETT, INDIAN SCOUT (United Artists, 1950)
DIRECTOR: Lew Landers

SCREENPLAY: Richard Schayer, Ford Beebe
CAST: George Montgomery (Davy Crockett), Phillip Reed (Red Hawk), Robert Barrat (James Lone Eagle), Billy Wilkerson (High Tree), Chief Thundercloud (Sleeping Fox), Ellen Drew (Frances Oatman)
SPECS: 71 minutes; Black & White
AVAILABILITY: DVD (MGM Limited Edition Collection); Amazon Instant Video
NATION: NA
IMAGE PORTRAYAL: Mixed-blood Native American; romance between Native Americans
SUMMARY: Aided by his loyal friend, Red Hawk, Davy Crockett rescues army troops from the hostile tribe of Chief Lone Eagle, High Tree, and Sleeping Fox. Later, the noble Red Hawk falls in love with Frances, a mixed-blood who had been a spy for the hostile tribe.
CRITICS: A *Variety* critic writes that the film "hews to the formula ingredients of howling Indians, ambushed wagon trains, disloyal mixed-bloods and a slight touch of romance" (January 11, 1950).

THE DAWN MAKER (Triangle, 1916)
DIRECTOR: William S. Hart
SCREENPLAY: C. Gardner Sullivan
CAST: W. S. Hart (Joe Elk), Blanche White (Alice McRae), Joe Goodboy (Chief Troubled Thunder)
SPECS: 50 minutes; Black & White; Silent
AVAILABILITY: NA
NATION: NA
IMAGE PORTRAYAL: Mixed-blood Native American; romance between a mixed-blood Native American man and a white woman
SUMMARY: Joe Elk, a mixed-blood, falls in love with a white woman and struggles over whether to be loyal to his white or his Native American values. When Chief Trouble Thunder's tribe captures the woman and her white lover, he decides to rescue them. At the end, badly wounded from the rescue, he accepts the Native American way by doing the dance of The Dawn Maker before he dies.

DAY OF THE EVIL GUN (MGM, 1968)
DIRECTOR: Jerry Thorpe
SCREENPLAY: Charles Marquis Warren, Eric Bercovici
CAST: Glenn Ford (Lorn Warfield)
SPECS: 95 minutes; Color
AVAILABILITY: DVD (Warner Home Video)
NATION: Apache
IMAGE PORTRAYAL: Attack on a town; kidnapping

SUMMARY: Apaches kidnap Lorn Warfield's family and capture him when he attempts a rescue. Later the Apache attack a town.

DEAD MAN (Miramax, 1995)
DIRECTOR: Jim Jarmusch
SCREENPLAY: Jim Jarmusch
CAST: Johnny Depp (William Blake), Gary Farmer (Nobody)
SPECS: 121 Minutes; Black & White
AVAILABILITY: DVD (Miramax Home Entertainment)
NATION: NA
IMAGE PORTRAYAL: Friendship; loyalty
SUMMARY: In this film, which Jarmusch calls "a psychological Western" the mysterious Native American outcast, Nobody, rescues William Blake, whom he thinks is the English poet. Nobody leads him into a western world of crime and murder until he puts him out to sea to find a better world.

DEADWOOD '76 (Fairway, 1965)
DIRECTOR: James Landis
SCREENPLAY: Arch Hall Sr., John Landis
CAST: Arch Hall Jr. (Billy May), La Donna Cottier (Little Bird), Gordon Schwenk (Spotted Snake)
SPECS: 97 minutes; Color
AVAILABILITY: DVD (Alpha Video); Amazon Instant Video
NATION: NA
IMAGE PORTRAYAL: Kidnapping; romance between a Native American woman and a white man
SUMMARY: The tribe of Spotted Snake captures Billy, who falls in love with Little Bird. Later, when two cowboys rape her, Billy kills them, only to be lynched by a mob.

DEATH CURSE OF TARTU (Thunderbird, 1967)
DIRECTOR: William Grefe
SCREENPLAY: William Grefe
CAST: Fred Pinero (Ed Tison), Babette Sherrill (Julie Tison), Douglas Hobardt (Tartu)
SPECS: 87 minutes; Color
AVAILABILITY: DVD (Image Entertainment)
NATION: Seminole
IMAGE PORTRAYAL: Vengeance
SUMMARY: Tartu, a Seminole witch doctor who had been dead for four hundred years, takes revenge on students who tamper with his grave by changing into deadly animals like an alligator. Two survivors, the Tisons, finally kill Tartu.

THE DEERSLAYER (Republic, 1943)
DIRECTOR: Lew Landers
SCREENPLAY: John W. Krafft, P. S. Harrison, E. B. Derr, based on the novel by James Fenimore Cooper
CAST: Bruce Kellogg (Deerslayer), Larry Parks (Jingo-Good), Yvonne De Carlo (Princess Wah-Tah), Trevor Bardette (Chief Rivanoak), Robert Warwick (Chief Uncas), Chief Many Treaties (Chief Brave Eagle), Princess Whynemank (Indian Girl), William Edmund (Huron Sub-chief)
SPECS: 67 minutes; Black & White
AVAILABILITY: NA
NATION: Huron
IMAGE PORTRAYAL: Attack on a fort
SUMMARY: Deerslayer helps his friend, Jingo-Good, rescue his beloved Princess Wah-Tah from the Hurons. After several captures and escapes, the hero and his friends defeat hostile Hurons.
CRITICS: A *Variety* reviewer comments on the title character: "Deerslayer is a super-hero who continually eludes the Indians, and, when he's captured, easily escapes in the most convenient spots for script purposes" (November 10, 1943).

THE DEERSLAYER (20th Century Fox, 1957)
DIRECTOR: Kurt Neumann
SCREENPLAY: Carroll Young, Kurt Neumann, Dalton Trumbo, based on the novel by James Fenimore Cooper
CAST: Lex Barker (Deerslayer), Rita Moreno (Hetty), Carlos Rivas (Chingachgook), Joseph Vitale (Huron Chief), John Halloran (Old Warrior)
SPECS: 78 minutes; Color
AVAILABILITY: NA
NATION: Huron; Mohican
IMAGE PORTRAYAL: Attacks on soldiers; friendship
SUMMARY: Deerslayer, who is raised by Mohicans, joins his blood brother, Chingachgook, to save a villain who, unknown to them has been taking Huron scalps from the Hurons. When the tribe goes on the warpath to get back the scalps, the heroes find out that the man is a villain and that his daughter, Hetty is really a Mohican he stole from the tribe. They stop the war and take Hetty back to her home.

DESERT GOLD (Paramount, 1936)
DIRECTOR: James P. Hogan
SCREENPLAY: Stuart Anthony, Robert Yost, based on the novel by Zane Grey
CAST: Buster Crabbe (Chief Moya), Monte Blue (Chet Kasedon), Tom Keene (Randolph Gale), Marsha Hunt (Judith Belding)
SPECS: 58 minutes; Black & White
AVAILABILITY: DVD (Lions Gate)

NATION: NA

IMAGE PORTRAYAL: Romance between a Native American man and a white woman

SUMMARY: With the help of Randolph Gale, Chief Moya and his tribe prevail over Chet Kasedon, who is after their gold. Chief Moya falls in love with Judith but eventually falls off a cliff at the end.

DESERT PURSUIT (Monogram, 1952)
DIRECTOR: George Blair

SCREENPLAY: Scott Darling, based on the novel by Kenneth Perkins

CAST: Billy Wilkerson (Ceremony Leader), Robert Bice (Tomaso), Frank Lackteen (Indian Bodyguard), Gloria Talbott (Indian Girl)

SPECS: 71 minutes; Black & White

AVAILABILITY: NA

NATION: California Mission

IMAGE PORTRAYAL: Attack on outlaws

SUMMARY: The Mission tribe of the Ceremony Leader, Tomaso, and an Indian Bodyguard, who have been converted to Christianity at first think that outlaw Arabs riding camels and pursuing a white couple are the Three Kings. Finally, they see the truth and provide a bodyguard to lead the couple to safety.

THE DESERT RAVEN (Allied Artists, 1965)
DIRECTOR: Alan S. Lee

SCREENPLAY: Alan S. Lee, Rachel Romen

CAST: Rachel Romen (Raven), Bea Silvern (Rena), Robert Terry (Bert)

SPECS: 90 minutes; Black & White

AVAILABILITY: NA

NATION: NA

IMAGE PORTRAYAL: Romance between a Native American woman and a white man

SUMMARY: Though watched over closely by her mother, Rena, Raven falls in love with a white man whom she promises to marry when he gets out of prison. At the end Rena and Bert, the leader of the evil gang, are killed.

THE DESERTER (Paramount, 1971)
DIRECTORS: Niksa Fulgosi, Burt Kennedy

SCREENPLAY: Clair Huffaker, Stuart J. Byrne, William H. James

SPECS: 100 minutes; Color

AVAILABILITY: VHS (Paramount Home Video)

CAST: Ricardo Montalban (Natchai), Mimmo Palmara (Chief Mangus Durango), Bekim Fehmiu (Captain Victor Kaleb)

NATION: Apache

IMAGE PORTRAYAL: Attack on Native Americans

SUMMARY: After the Apaches of Chief Durango and Natchai kill his wife in an attack, Captain Kaleb follows the tribe into Mexico and kills all the Apache warriors in a bloody battle.

THE DEVIL HORSE (Pathe, 1926)
DIRECTOR: Fred Jackman
SCREENPLAY: Hal Roach, Stan Laurel
CAST: Rex, the Wonder Horse (Devil Horse), Yakima Canutt (Dave Carson), Bob Kortman (Prowling Wolf)
SPECS: 68 minutes; Black & White
AVAILABILITY: DVD (Grapevine Video)
NATION: NA
IMAGE PORTRAYAL: Attack on wagon train; kidnapping
SUMMARY: After the tribe of Prowling Wolf attacks a wagon train, the only survivors, Dave Carson and a colt named Devil Horse, pursue their adversaries. Later when Prowling Wolf incites his tribe to attack a fort, Dave Carson, riding Devil Horse (which can recognize Native Americans by their smell), comes to the rescue and gains revenge.

DEVIL'S DOORWAY (MGM, 1950)
DIRECTOR: Anthony Mann
SCREENPLAY: Guy Trosper
CAST: Robert Taylor (Lance Poole), Chief John Big Tree (Thundercloud)
SPECS: 84 minutes; Black & White
AVAILABILITY: DVD (Warner Archive Collection)
NATION: Shoshone
IMAGE PORTRAYAL: Native American as victim
SUMMARY: Discussed on page 33, this film tells the story of Lance Poole, a military hero who returns to his ranch and must fight to save it. At the end, a female lawyer fails to help him, and he dies defending his land. This film is one of the early attempts to build sympathy for Native Americans.
CRITICS: A *New York Times* critic comments: "Perhaps it is too late now to change the course of fiction which has established the American Indian as a ruthless savage, but our movie makers appear to be endeavoring to right some of the wrong they themselves have done the red man over the years" (November 10, 1950).

THE DEVIL'S MISTRESS (Holiday Pictures, 1966)
DIRECTOR: Orville Wanzer
SCREENPLAY: Orville Wanzer
CAST: Joan Stapleton (Athaliah)
SPECS: 66 minutes; Color
AVAILABILITY: NA

NATION: NA
IMAGE PORTRAYAL: Mixed-blood Native American; vengeance
SUMMARY: Athaliah, a mixed-blood, uses her magical powers to take revenge on cowboys who raped her and killed the man she lived with. Her favorite method is the kiss of death.

DIRTY DINGUS MAGEE (MGM, 1970)
DIRECTOR: Burt Kennedy
SCREENPLAY: Tom Waldman, Frank Waldman, Joseph Heller, based on the novel *The Ballad of Dingus Magee* by David Markson
CAST: Frank Sinatra (Dingus Billy Magee), Michele Cary (Anna Hot Water), Paul Fix (Crazy Blanket, Anna's father)
SPECS: 91 minutes; Color
AVAILABILITY: DVD (Warner Home Video)
NATION: NA
IMAGE PORTRAYAL: Romance between Native American woman and white man
SUMMARY: In this comedy, which satirizes the western, Dingus Billy Magee's lover is Anna Hot Water, a nymphomaniac Native American whom Chief Crazy Blanket wants for his woman. After escaping from a sheriff and the chief with Anna's help, Dingus Magee finally leaves her because he can't keep up with her sexual demands.

DISTANT DRUMS (Warner Bros., 1951)
DIRECTOR: Raoul Walsh
SCREENPLAY: Niven Busch, Martin Rackin
CAST: Gary Cooper (Capt. Quincy Wyatt), Larry Carper (Ocala)
SPECS: 101 minutes; Color
AVAILABILITY: DVD, Blu-ray (Olive Films)
NATION: Seminole
IMAGE PORTRAYAL: Attacks on soldiers
SUMMARY: Capt. Wyatt rescues prisoners of the Seminole by killing their Chief, Ocala, in a hand-to-hand duel under water. Finally, a troop of soldiers rescues the survivors as the Seminole hostiles mount their big attack.

A DISTANT TRUMPET (Warner Bros., 1964)
DIRECTOR: Raoul Walsh
SCREENPLAY: John Twist, Richard Fielder, Albert Beich, based on the novel by Paul Horgan
CAST: Troy Donahue (Matthew Hazard)
SPECS: 117 minutes; Color
AVAILABILITY: DVD (Warner Home Video)
NATION: Apache

IMAGE PORTRAYAL: Friendship; loyalty

SUMMARY: After the Apache tribe of Chief War Eagle has been driven into Mexico, Matt Hazard, whose life War Eagle saves, persuades the government to give the tribe a reservation in Arizona. Hazard will not accept his military awards unless the government gives the Apache a reservation.

CRITICS: A *Variety* critic comments on the depiction of the battles: "Hardly a white man bites the dust, yet the Redmen consistently get picked off like ducks at a shooting gallery. How one-sided can you get?" (May 27, 1964).

THE DOE BOY (Doe Boy Productions, 2001)

DIRECTOR: Randy Redroad

SCREENPLAY: Randy Redroad

CAST: James Duval (Hunter), Kevin Anderson (Hank, his father), Jeri Arredondo (Maggie, his mother), Gordon Tootoosis (Marvin Flying Fish)

SPECS: 86 minutes; Color

AVAILABILITY: DVD (Fox Lorber)

NATION: Cherokee

IMAGE PORTRAYAL: Contemporary Native American; mixed-blood Native American; troubled Native American; wise elder

SUMMARY: Hunter is a mixed-blood Cherokee who is a hemophiliac who is bitter about his white heritage. When Hunter goes hunting with his white father he mistakenly kills a doe, and after this humiliation he visits his Cherokee grandfather, Marvin Flying Fish, for advice.

DRAGOON WELLS MASSACRE (Allied Artists, 1957)

DIRECTOR: Harold D. Schuster

SCREENPLAY: Warren Douglas, Oliver Drake

CAST: Barry Sullivan (Link Ferris), John War Eagle (Apache Chief)

SPECS: 88 minutes; Color

AVAILABILITY: NA

NATION: Apache

IMAGE PORTRAYAL: Attack on a wagon train

SUMMARY: Apaches, led by a hostile chief, attack a wagon train passing through their country.

DRUM BEAT (Warner Bros., 1954)

DIRECTOR: Delmer Daves

SCREENPLAY: Delmer Daves

CAST: Alan Ladd (Johnny MacKay), Marisa Pavan (Toby), Rudolfo Acosta (Scarface Charlie), Charles Bronson (Kintpuash-Captain Jack), Anthony Caruso (Manok)

SPECS: 111 minutes; Color

AVAILABILITY: DVD (Warner Home Video)

NATION: Modoc

IMAGE PORTRAYAL: Hostile warrior; romance between a Native American woman and a white man

SUMMARY: As Johnny MacKay tries to establish a treaty with the Modoc tribe of the rebellious Captain Jack, two friendly members of the tribe, Manok and Toby help him. After Toby, who loves the hero, gives her life to save him, he finally kills Captain Jack in hand-to-hand combat.

DRUMS ACROSS THE RIVER (Universal, 1954)

DIRECTOR: Nathan Juran

SCREENPLAY: Lawrence Roman, John K. Butler

CAST: Audie Murphy (Gary Brannon), Jay Silverheels (Taos), Morris Ankrum (Chief Ouray), Ken Terrell (Red Knife)

SPECS: 78 minutes; Color

AVAILABILITY: DVD (Universal Studios)

NATION: Ute

IMAGE PORTRAYAL: Peace-loving chief

SUMMARY: To get at their gold, the villain starts trouble with the Ute tribe of Chief Ouray, Taos, and Red Knife. After the tribe kills the villains for violating their burial grounds, Gary Brannon, whose mother had been killed by hostile warriors, finally decides to help Chief Ouray keep the peace.

DRUMS ALONG THE MOHAWK (20th Century Fox, 1939)

DIRECTOR: John Ford

SCREENPLAY: Lamar Trotti, Sonya Levien, based on the novel by Walter D. Edmonds

CAST: Henry Fonda (Gil Martin), Chief John Big Tree (Blue Back)

SPECS: 104 minutes; Color

AVAILABILITY: DVD (20th Century Fox Home Entertainment)

NATION: Iroquois

IMAGE PORTRAYAL: Attacks on a fort; friendship; loyalty

SUMMARY: Discussed on page 21, this film tells the story of the colonists' struggles with the British loyalists and their allies, the savage Iroquois. The hero is Gil Martin and Blue Back is his taciturn Native American friend. At the end, Gil Martin brings reinforcements and they stop the vicious Iroquois attack on the fort at German Flats.

DRUMS OF THE DESERT (Paramount, 1927)

DIRECTOR: John Waters

SCREENPLAY: John Stone, based on the novel by Zane Grey

CAST: Bernard Segal (Chief Brave Bear)

SPECS: Black & White; Silent

AVAILABILITY: NA

NATION: Navajo

IMAGE PORTRAYAL: Native Americans as victims

SUMMARY: When Chief Brave Bear and his Navajo tribe try to resist the efforts of oil-hungry villains to force them off their land and desecrate their sacred altars, the cavalry comes to their aid.

DUEL AT DIABLO (United Artists, 1966)

DIRECTOR: Ralph Nelson

SCREENPLAY: Michael M. Grilikhes, Marvin H. Albert, based on Albert's novel *Apache Uprising*

CAST: James Garner (Jess Remsberg), John Hoyt (Chata), Eddie Little Sky (Alchise), Bibi Anderson (Ellen Grange), Dennis Weaver (Willard Grange)

SPECS: 103 minutes; Color

AVAILABILITY: DVD (MGM Home Entertainment); Blu-ray (Kino Lorber); Amazon Instant Video

NATION: Apache

IMAGE PORTRAYAL: Romance between a Native American man and a white woman; torture

SUMMARY: Apaches led by Chata and Alchise attack and torture Willard Grange, who has rejected his wife, Ellen, because she had a baby with the Apache chief's son. Willard had also killed the Comanche wife of Jess Remsberg, who stops the Apaches and lets Willard die.

CRITICS: A *Time* critic comments: "If anything, *Diablo* proves that it can be extremely difficult to promote racial harmony while playing cowboys and Indians" (July 1, 1966, 78).

DUEL IN THE SUN (Selznick, 1946)

DIRECTOR: King Vidor

SCREENPLAY: David O. Selznick, Oliver H. P. Garrett, based on the novel by Niven Busch

CAST: Jennifer Jones (Pearl Chavez), Joseph Cotton (Jesse McCanles), Gregory Peck (Lewt McCanles)

SPECS: 130 minutes; Color

AVAILABILITY: DVD (Anchor Bay Entertainment)

NATION: NA

IMAGE PORTRAYAL: Mixed-blood Native American; Native Americans as victims

SUMMARY: Discussed on page 24, this film tells the story of Pearl Chavez, a young mixed-blood desired by two brothers, one good, Jesse McCanles, and the other bad, Lewt McCanles. A victim of prejudice and her own passionate nature, she dies in the arms of her lover, Lewt, who refuses to marry her and tries to kill his brother.

E

EAGLE'S WING (Rank, 1979)
DIRECTOR: Anthony Harvey
SCREENPLAY: John Briley, Michael Syson
CAST: Martin Sheen (Pike), Sam Waterston (White Bull), Jorge Luke (Red Sky), Jose Carlos Ruiz (Lame Wolf)
SPECS: 111 minutes; Color
AVAILABILITY: DVD (VCI Entertainment)
NATION: Comanche
IMAGE PORTRAYAL: Honor
SUMMARY: A Comanche warrior, White Bull, struggles with a white man for the possession of a white horse called Eagle's Wing. At the end, he leaves the woman he had captured and rides off alone on Eagle's Wing.

THE EDUCATION OF LITTLE TREE (Paramount, 1997)
DIRECTOR: Richard Friedenberg
SCREENPLAY: Earl Hamner Jr., Don Sipes, Richard Friedenberg, based on the novel by Forrest Carter
CAST: James Cromwell (Granpa), Tantoo Cardinal (Granma, a Cherokee), John Ashton (Little Tree), Graham Greene (Willow John, a Cherokee)
SPECS: 112 minutes; Color
AVAILABILITY: DVD (Paramount Home Video)
NATION: Cherokee
IMAGE PORTRAYAL: Contemporary Native American; mixed-blood Native American; wise elder
SUMMARY: A young mixed-blood orphan goes to live with his grandparents. His Granma and Willow John teach him the wisdom and traditions of his Cherokee tribe. Later he is rescued from an evil Indian School and returns to those who love and teach him.

EL CONDOR (National General, 1970)
DIRECTOR: John Guillermin
SCREENPLAY: Larry Cohen, Steven W. Carabatsos
CAST: Jim Brown (Luke), Lee Van Cleef (Jaroo), Iron Eyes Cody (Santana)
SPECS: 102 minutes; Color
AVAILABILITY: DVD (Warner Archive Collection)
NATION: Apache
IMAGE PORTRAYAL: Attack on a fort
SUMMARY: Renegade Apaches led by Santana help Luke and Jaroo attack a Mexican fort. At the end, Santana dies.

THE EMERALD FOREST (Embassy, 1985)
DIRECTOR: John Boorman
SCREENPLAY: Rospo Pallenberg
CAST: Charley Boorman (Tomme), Dira Paes (Kachiri), Powers Boothe (Bill Markham), Ruy Polanah (Chief Wanadi)
SPECS: 114 minutes; Color
AVAILABILITY: DVD (MGM Home Entertainment)
NATION: Indigenous people of the Brazilian Rain forests
IMAGE PORTRAYAL: Contemporary endangered South American natives; kidnapping
SUMMARY: Discussed on page 53, this film tells the story of a white boy, Tomme, who is adopted by a peaceful Amazonian tribe called the Invisible People. After he becomes a member of the tribe by going through their manhood rites, he marries a young woman from the tribe. The other indigenous people in the area are the hostile Fierce People, who pursue and capture Bill Markham, who is looking for his son. After his son and his tribe rescue Bill, he comes to respect them and helps them defeat the Fierce People. At the end, Bill blows up a dam and lets his son, now the chief after the death of Chief Wanadi, live in peace for a while. Kachiri, the wife of Tomme, and he watch as his people enjoy their new but temporary freedom.

EMPIRE OF DIRT (Redcloud Studios, 2013)
DIRECTOR: Peter Stebbings
SCREENPLAY: Shannon Masters
CAST: Cara Gee (Lena), Shay Eyre (Peeka), Jennifer Podemski (Minerva), Sarah Podemski (Charmaine)
SPECS: 99 minutes; Color
AVAILABILITY: NA
NATION: Cree
IMAGE PORTRAYAL: Contemporary First Nation people; troubled First Nation people
SUMMARY: When Peeka, the teenage daughter of single mother Lena, overdoses in Toronto, Lena returns to her small town and reconnects with her mother, Minerva (Minnie). In this process, the family is reunited and they find new identities in their tribal ways.

THE EXILES (Pathe, 1966)
DIRECTORS: Kent MacKenzie, Richard Kaplan
SCREENPLAY: Kent MacKenzie
CAST: Yvonne Williams, Homer Nish, Tom Reynolds, and others play themselves
SPECS: 72 minutes; Black & White
AVAILABILITY: DVD (Oscilloscope Laboratories)

NATION: NA
IMAGE PORTRAYAL: Contemporary Native Americans; troubled Native Americans
SUMMARY: Three young Native Americans, Yvonne, who is pregnant, Homer and Tommy, who have serious drinking problems, leave their reservation and go to Los Angeles. At the beginning there are cuts to Curtis pictures and a voice-over: "Once the American Indian lived in the ordered freedom of his own culture. Then, in the nineteenth century, the white man confined him within the boundaries of the tribal reservation." After realizing they don't fit in the city, they go to a hilltop near the freeways and, in a futile gesture, try to sing and dance in the traditional ways.

EXPIRATION DATE (Silverline Entertainment, 2006)
DIRECTOR: Rick Stevenson
SCREENPLAY: Hamish Gunn, Rick Stevenson
CAST: Robert A. Guthrie (Charles Silvercloud III), Sascha Knopf (Bessie), Ned Romero (Old Native Man), Nakotah LaRance (Native Teen)
SPECS: 94 minutes; Color
AVAILABILITY: DVD (Rivercoast Films)
NATION: NA
IMAGE PORTRAYAL: Contemporary Native American; mixed-blood Native American; romance between a mixed-blood Native American man and a white woman; wise elder
SUMMARY: This film is a story told by a tribal elder to a young man who is going to stop dancing and leave the reservation. In it, Charles Silvercloud III is convinced that a milk truck will hit him because his immediate relative has been killed in this way. Then he meets Bessie and falls in love with her and his luck changes.
CRITICS: *Variety* critic Justin Chang comments: "Lessons about living life to the fullest, even in the face of adversity, are expressed as the desire to 'go down dancing'—a sentiment illustrated beautifully in a scene of Native American dance that becomes the film's centerpiece. References to Charlie's culture are otherwise subtle, and sometimes put across with affectionate humor" (September 14, 2006).

F

THE FAR HORIZONS (Paramount, 1955)
DIRECTOR: Rudolph Maté
SCREENPLAY: Winston Miller, Edmund H. North, based on the novel *Sacajawea of the Shoshones* by Della Gould Emmons
CAST: Fred MacMurray (Captain M. Lewis), Charlton Heston (Lt. William Clark), Donna Reed (Sacajawea), Larry Pennell (Wild Eagle), Julia Montoya (Crow Woman), Eduardo Noriega (Cameahwait, Sacajawea's brother)

SPECS: 108 minutes; Color
AVAILABILITY: DVD (Paramount Pictures)
NATION: Shoshone
IMAGE PORTRAYAL: Attack on settlers; romance between a Native American
    woman and a white man
SUMMARY: This film about the Lewis and Clark expedition focuses on the
    initially unrequited love of Sacajawea of the Shoshone for Lt. Clark. Wild
    Eagle, her intended from her tribe, also loves her. After helping the expedition
    reach its goal, by warning of attacks by hostile tribes and nursing the heroes,
    Sacajawea decides to leave Clark and return to her people, even though she
    still loves him.

A FIGHT FOR LOVE (Universal, 1919)

DIRECTOR: John Ford
SCREENPLAY: Eugene B. Lewis
CAST: Joe Harris (Black Michael), Neola May (Indian Girl), John Big Tree (Swift
    Deer), Harry Carey (Cheyenne Harry)
SPECS: 60 minutes; Black & White; Silent
AVAILABILITY: NA
NATION: NA
IMAGE PORTRAYAL: Evil mixed-blood; hostile warrior; mixed-blood Native
    American
SUMMARY: A treacherous mixed-blood, Black Michael, kills a Native American
    in a fight over a woman from his tribe. After Cheyenne Harry is blamed for the
    crime, he hunts down the mixed-blood and kills him.

FIGHTING CARAVANS (Paramount, 1931)

DIRECTORS: Otto Brower, David Burton
SCREENPLAY: Edward E. Paramore Jr., Keene Thompson, Agnes Brand Leahy,
    based on the novel *Wagon Wheels* by Zane Grey
CAST: Gary Cooper (Clint Belmet), Fred Kohler (Lee Murdock)
SPECS: 92 minutes; Black & White
AVAILABILITY: DVD (Lions Gate); Amazon Instant Video
NATION: Cheyenne; Kiowa
IMAGE PORTRAYAL: Attack on wagon train
SUMMARY: Stirred up by Lee Murdock, a hostile Kiowa and Cheyenne attack
    a wagon train. Clint Belmet diverts them with an explosion and the cavalry
    arrives just in time.
CRITICS: A *Variety* critic notes that "It's a long wait for the inevitable Indian at-
    tack" (April 1, 1931).

FIGHTING PIONEERS (Resolute, 1935)

DIRECTOR: Harry Fraser

SCREENPLAY: Harry Fraser, Charles E. Roberts
CAST: Rex Bell (Lt. Bentley), Ruth Mix (Wa-No-Na), Chief Thundercloud (Eagle Feathers), Chief Standing Bear (Chief Black Hawk), Guate Mozin (Crazy Horse)
SPECS: 54 minutes; Black & White
AVAILABILITY: DVD (Alpha Home Entertainment)
NATION: Crow
IMAGE PORTRAYAL: Hostile warrior; peace-loving chief
SUMMARY: Crow Chief Black Hawk chooses his daughter, Wa-No-Na, over Eagle Feathers, to lead the tribe when he dies. After his death, with the aid of Lt. Bentley, she foils the attack of Eagle Feather's hostile warriors. At the end, she establishes a peace treaty.

FINDING MARY MARCH (Malo Film Group, 1988)
DIRECTOR: Ken Pittman
SCREENPLAY: Ken Pittman
CAST: Rick Boland (Ted Buchans—Micmac guide), Jacinta Cormier (Mary March), Yvon Joe (Micmac Boy), Tara Manual (Bernadette Buchans), Andree Pelletier (Nancy George)
SPECS: 100 minutes; Color
AVAILABILITY: NA
NATION: Beothuk of Newfoundland
IMAGE PORTRAYAL: Native Americans as victims
SUMMARY: Micmac guide Ted Buchans searches for his wife, Bernadette, who lost her way looking for the last of the Beothuk tribe, Mary March, who was given a special burial by the few remaining tribe. Nancy George, a native photographer searching for her cultural roots, also is looking for the graves of the Beothuk. At the end, Nancy and Ted rebury the body of Mary March, a member of a tribe that Europeans hunted down for sport in the 1800s.

FISH HAWK (CFDC, 1979)
DIRECTOR: Donald Shebib
SCREENPLAY: Blanche Hanalis, based on the novel by Mitchell Jayne
CAST: Will Sampson (Fish Hawk), Charley Fields (Corby Boggs)
SPECS: 94 minutes; Color
AVAILABILITY: DVD (GT Media / GAIAM Americas)
NATION: Cherokee
IMAGE PORTRAYAL: Drunkenness; friendship
SUMMARY: After his family dies of smallpox, Fish Hawk drinks heavily until his drunkenness leads to the death of his dog and threatens his friendship with a young Corby Boggs. After saving Corby's life and teaching him important lessons, a now sober Fish Hawk leaves to find his own people and learn their ways before he dies.

FLAGS OF OUR FATHERS (Paramount, 2006)
DIRECTOR: Clint Eastwood
SCREENPLAY: William Broyles Jr., Paul Haggis, based on the book by James Bradley with Ron Powers
CAST: Adam Beach (Ira Hayes)
SPECS: 132 minutes; Color
AVAILABILITY: DVD (DreamWorks Video); Amazon Instant Video
NATION: Pima
IMAGE PORTRAYAL: Contemporary Native American; drunkenness; Native American soldier
SUMMARY: The U. S. government brings three war heroes associated with raising the flag on Iwo Jima to raise money for the war effort. One of the men is Ira Hayes of the Pima tribe. Troubled by his celebrity and image as a hero, he takes to drinking.
CRITICS: In the *Chicago Sun Times*, critic Roger Ebert comments on Ira Hayes: "But the most complex and tragic is the American Indian Hayes, who America wanted to be a hero, but not an American; he is routinely addressed as 'chief,' is refused service at a bar because he is not white, is condescended to by dignitaries. One fatuous public official memorizes some allegedly Pima words and addresses them to Hayes, who does not understand. 'What's-a matter, chief? Don't know your own lingo?' Hayes responds coolly, 'I guess I've been off the reservation for too long'" (November 29, 2007).

FLAMING FEATHER (Paramount, 1952)
DIRECTOR: Ray Enright
SCREENPLAY: Frank Gruber, Gerald Drayson Adams
CAST: Victor Jory (Lucky Lee aka Sidewinder), Carol Thurston (Turquoise)
SPECS: 77 minutes; Color
AVAILABILITY: Amazon Instant Video
NATION: Ute
IMAGE PORTRAYAL: Attacks on settlers; romance between a Native American woman and a white man
SUMMARY: The outlaw, Sidewinder, leads a group of hostile Utes who terrorize local ranchers. Turquoise, a Ute woman, loves Sidewinder but finally kills him.

FLAMING FRONTIER (20th Century Fox, 1958)
DIRECTOR: Sam Newfield
SCREENPLAY: Louis Stevens
CAST: Bruce Bennett (Capt. Jim Hewson), Larry Solway (Chief Little Crow), Shane Rimmer (Running Bear)
SPECS: 70 minutes; Black & White
AVAILABILITY: NA
NATION: Ojibwa; Sioux

IMAGE PORTRAYAL: Attack on soldiers; mixed-blood Native American; peace-loving chief

SUMMARY: Captain Jim Hewson, a mixed-blood Sioux, tries to make peace with his childhood friend, Sioux Chief Little Crow and Running Bear. After an attack by hostile Ojibwa and other plots to make Little Crow go to war, the responsible villains are killed and Capt. Hewson and Little Crow declare peace.

FLAMING STAR (20th Century Fox, 1960)

DIRECTOR: Don Siegel

SCREENPLAY: Clair Huffaker, Nunnally Johnson, based on Huffaker's novel *Flaming Lance*

CAST: Elvis Presley (Pacer Burton), Dolores del Rio (Neddy Burton), Rodolfo Acosta (Buffalo Horn), Miriam Goldina (Ph'sha Knay), Steve Forrest (Clint Burton)

SPECS: 101 minutes; Color

AVAILABILITY: DVD (20th Century Fox Home Entertainment)

NATION: Kiowa

IMAGE PORTRAYAL: Mixed-blood Native American; Native Americans as victims

SUMMARY: Discussed on page 41, this film tells the story of the prejudice toward mixed-blood, Pacer Burton and his Kiowa mother, Neddie. When his parents are killed he chooses the Kiowa, whereas his half brother chooses the whites.

CRITICS: A. H. Weiler in the *New York Times* notes that "the Indians are not simply presented as heavies but also as beleaguered men being ruthlessly deprived, in their view, of their lands" (December 17, 1960).

FLAP or THE LAST WARRIOR (Warner Bros., 1970)

DIRECTOR: Carol Reed

SCREENPLAY: Clair Huffaker, based on his novel *Nobody Loves a Drunken Indian*

CAST: Anthony Quinn (Flapping Eagle), Claude Akins (Lobo Jackson), Tony Bill (Eleven Snowflake), Shelley Winters (Dorothy Bluebell), Victor Jory (Wounded Bear Mr. Smith), Victor French (Sgt. Rafferty), Susana Miranda (Ann Looking Deer), Rudy Diaz (Larry Standing Elk), Pedro Regas (She'll-Be-Back-Pretty-Soon), Anthony Caruso (Silver Dollar), John War Eagle (Luke Wolf).

SPECS: 106 minutes; Color

AVAILABILITY: DVD (Warner Archive Collection)

NATION: NA

IMAGE PORTRAYAL: Contemporary Native Americans; mixed-blood Native American; romance between Native Americans; troubled Native Americans

SUMMARY: On an unknown reservation, Flapping Eagle is a hard-drinking war hero who, along with his friends Lobo Jackson and Eleven Snowflake, battles a construction company and steals a train for his tribe. Loved by Dorothy Bluebell and given dubious help by a self-styled lawyer, Wounded Bear Mr. Bear Smith, Flapping Eagle is finally killed by his enemy, Rafferty, a brutal mixed-blood policeman.

CRITICS: A *Variety* critic notes that the film makes "no attempt to show any Indian as a responsible person" (October 28, 1970). Howard Thompson in the *New York Times* provides another viewpoint: "The plight of the American Indian is no laughing matter. The laughter here makes it matter even more" (January 1, 1971).

FLESHBURN (Crown Inter., 1984)
DIRECTOR: George Gage
SCREENPLAY: George Gage, Beth Gage, based on the novel *Fear in a Handfull of Dust* by Brian Garfield
CAST: Sonny Landham (Calvin Duggai)
SPECS: 90 minutes; Color
AVAILABILITY: DVD (Rhino); Amazon Instant Video
NATION: Navajo
IMAGE PORTRAYAL: Vengeance
SUMMARY: Calvin Duggai, a Navajo who deserted because of his tribal beliefs is judged by psychiatrists as insane, escapes from a mental institution, and takes revenge on those who had him committed.

FOLLOW ME HOME (New Millennia Films, 1996)
DIRECTOR: Peter Bratt
SCREENPLAY: Peter Bratt
CAST: Steve Reevis (Freddy), Akima (Akima)
SPECS: 100 minutes; Color
AVAILABILITY: NA
NATION: NA
IMAGE PORTRAYAL: Contemporary Native American
SUMMARY: Three mural artists, one of whom is Freddy, a Native American who is a recovering alcoholic, start on a trip to Washington, D.C., to paint a mural on the White House, but encounter their demons and triumph over them in the middle of the country.

FOR THE LOVE OF MIKE (20th Century Fox, 1960)
DIRECTOR: George Sherman
SCREENPLAY: D. D. Beauchamp
CAST: Richard Basehart (Father Phelan), Danny Bravo (Michael Little Bear), Rex Allen (Rex Allen), Armando Silvestre (Tommy Eagle), Elsa Cardenas (Mrs. Eagle)
SPECS: 87 minutes; Color
AVAILABILITY: NA

NATION: NA

IMAGE PORTRAYAL: Friendship; gratitude

SUMMARY: Michael Little Bear, Native American teenager who lives at a rectory with Father Phalen and another priest enters his horse, Pueblo, in a horse race and wins. After telling Rex Allen the truth about the heritage of his horse, both he and the church are rewarded.

FOREST ROSE (Thanhouser, 1912)

DIRECTOR: Theodore Marston

SCREENPLAY: Theodore Marston, based on the novel by Emerson Bennett

CAST: Marguerite Snow (The Forest Rose), Harry Marks (Indian Chief)

SPECS: Black & White; Silent

AVAILABILITY: NA

NATION: NA

IMAGE PORTRAYAL: Attack on settlers

SUMMARY: A hostile tribe attacks a pioneer and kidnaps his daughter, Forest Rose.

CRITICS: This film provokes another racist comment from Louis Reeves Harrison, a *Moving Picture World* critic: "There is very little that can be truthfully represented as ideal in the character of a people gloating over the hideous torture of innocent women and children. They represent a hindering and utterly useless element in the civilization of mankind" (November 30, 1912, 861).

FORT APACHE (RKO, 1948)

DIRECTOR: John Ford

SCREENPLAY: Frank S. Nugent, based on the story "Massacre" by James Warner Bellah

CAST: John Wayne (Capt. Kirby York), Henry Fonda (Lt. Col. Owen Thursday), Miguel Inclan (Cochise)

SPECS: 125 minutes; Color

AVAILABILITY: DVD (Warner Home Video); Amazon Instant Video

NATION: Apache

IMAGE PORTRAYAL: Attack on soldiers, friendship

SUMMARY: Angered by a crooked Indian agent, Cochise and his Apaches massacre a troop of cavalry led by an inexperienced and arrogant officer, Lt. Col. Thursday, who attacks the Apache against the advice of Capt. York. At the end, Cochise brings the flag of the troop to York and spares his life because he knows York is an honorable man and friend to Native Americans.

FORT BOWIE (United Artists, 1958)

DIRECTOR: Howard W. Koch

SCREENPLAY: Maurice Tombragel

CAST: Ben Johnson (Capt. Thomas Thompson), Maureen Hingert (Chanzana), Larry Chance (Victorio)

SPECS: 80 minutes; Black & White
AVAILABILITY: DVD (20th Century Fox Home Entertainment)
NATION: Apache
IMAGE PORTRAYAL: Attack on a fort; romance between a Native American woman and a white man
SUMMARY: After soldiers kill a band of Apaches who were trying to surrender, the warriors of Victorio attack and occupy a fort. With help from Chanzana, a woman from the tribe who loves him, Capt. Thompson leads the soldiers as they retake the fort. At the end, Thompson and Chanzana declare their love.
CRITICS: A *Variety* critic comments: "A switch is made from usual films in this category by having the cavalry storm their own fort" (February 5, 1958).

FORT COURAGEOUS (20th Century Fox, 1965)
DIRECTOR: Lesley Selander
SCREENPLAY: Richard H. Landau
CAST: Fred Beir (Sgt. Lucas), Harry Lauter (Joe, a Native American scout), Michael Carr (Indian), George Sawaya (Indian)
SPECS: 72 minutes; Black & White
AVAILABILITY: DVD (20th Century Fox Home Entertainment)
NATION: NA
IMAGE PORTRAYAL: Attacks on soldiers
SUMMARY: A small group of soldiers led by Sgt. Lucas fight off many attacks by hostile warriors. Finally the warriors throw the lance of gallantry over the walls and leave the fort as a show of respect for their courage.

FORT DEFIANCE (United Artists, 1951)
DIRECTOR: John Rawlins
SCREENPLAY: Louis Lantz
CAST: Dane Clark (Johnny Tallon), Ben Johnson (Ben Shelby), Iron Eyes Cody (Brave Bear)
SPECS: 82 minutes; Color
AVAILABILITY: DVD (MGM Limited Edition Collection); Amazon Instant Video
NATION: Navajo
IMAGE PORTRAYAL: Attack on a stagecoach
SUMMARY: A group of Navajo, angered at the government's attempt to move them to Oklahoma, is led by Brave Bear on an attack of a stagecoach. The cavalry comes to the rescue.

FORT DOBBS (Warner Bros., 1958)
DIRECTOR: Gordon Douglas
SCREENPLAY: George W. George, Burt Kennedy
CAST: Clint Walker (Gar Davis)

SPECS: 93 minutes; Black & White
AVAILABILITY: DVD (Warner Archive Collection); Amazon Instant Video
NATION: Comanche
IMAGE PORTRAYAL: Attack on a fort
SUMMARY: Using a new repeating rifle, Gar Davis and his men defend settlers and the fort from a series of Comanche attacks.

FORT MASSACRE (United Artists, 1958)
DIRECTOR: Joseph N. Newman
SCREENPLAY: Martin Goldsmith
CAST: Joel McCrea (Sgt. Vinson), Susan Cabot (Piute Girl), Anthony Caruso (Pawnee, Indian scout), Larry Chance (Moving Cloud), Francis McDonald (Old Piute)
SPECS: 80 minutes; Color
AVAILABILITY: DVD (MGM Limited Edition Collection); Amazon Instant Video
NATION: Apache; Paiute
IMAGE PORTRAYAL: Attack on soldiers
SUMMARY: Moving Cloud, a young Apache warrior kills Pawnee and attacks a hateful Sgt. Vinson and his troop. At the end, the old Paiute refuses to turn against the Apaches.
CRITICS: The film provokes a snide comment from a *Variety* reviewer about the acting: "Susan Cabot, as an Indian girl is a beaut but no Paiute" (April 30, 1958).

FORT OSAGE (Monogram, 1952)
DIRECTOR: Lesley Selander
SCREENPLAY: Daniel B. Ullman
CAST: Rod Cameron (Tom Clay), Morris Ankrum (Arthur Pickett), Douglas Kennedy (George Keane), Iron Eyes Cody (Osage Brave–Blue Shirt), Francis McDonald (Osage Chief)
SPECS: 72 minutes; Color
AVAILABILITY: DVD (Warner Home Video)
NATION: Osage
IMAGE PORTRAYAL: Attack on settlers; friendship; peace-loving chief; vengeance
SUMMARY: After Pickett and Keane break a treaty, and Keane attacks and massacres an Osage village led by Blue Shirt, the Osage tribe threatens an attack on the fort. However, Tom Clay, a friend of the Osage chief, convinces the tribe to punish the villain and make peace.

FORT TI (Columbia, 1953)
DIRECTOR: William Castle

SCREENPLAY: Robert E. Kent
CAST: George Montgomery (Capt. Jed Horn), Joan Vohs (Fortune Mallory), Phyllis Fowler (Running Otter)
SPECS: 73 minutes; Color
AVAILABILITY: NA
NATION: NA
IMAGE PORTRAYAL: Attack on a fort; attack on settlers; romance between a Native American woman and a white man
SUMMARY: In this 3D film, hostile braves attack the fort. Capt. Jed Horn, who helps save the fort, chooses Fortune Mallory even though Running Otter loves him.

FORT UTAH (Paramount, 1967)
DIRECTOR: Lesley Selander
SCREENPLAY: Steve Fisher, Andrew Craddock
CAST: John Ireland (Tom Horn), Scott Brady (Dajin)
SPECS: 83 minutes; Color
AVAILABILITY: Amazon Instant Video
NATION: NA
IMAGE PORTRAYAL: Attacks on a wagon train
SUMMARY: After Dajin, a mutinous soldier and his gang kill women and children from their tribe, warriors attack a fort and stagecoach. When the body of Dajin is handed over to the warriors, they stop the attack on the fort.

FORT VENGEANCE (Allied Artists, 1953)
DIRECTOR: Lesley Selander
SCREENPLAY: Daniel B. Ullman
CAST: James Craig (Dick Ross), Morris Ankrum (Crowfoot), Michael Granger (Sitting Bull), Paul Marion (Eagle Heart), Peter Mamakos (Broken Lance)
SPECS: 75 minutes; Color
AVAILABILITY: DVD (Warner Archive Collection); Amazon Instant Video
NATION: Blackfeet; Sioux
IMAGE PORTRAYAL: Hostile warriors; peace-loving chief
SUMMARY: Despite the efforts of Sitting Bull and Broken Lance, the hostile Sioux, the peace-loving chief of the Canadian Blackfeet, Crowfoot, and Dick Ross avert a war. Ross exonerates the son of Crowfoot, Eagle Heart, from the charge of murder by finding the real murderer, and the tribe agrees to peace.

FORT YUMA (United Artists, 1955)
DIRECTOR: Lesley Selander
SCREENPLAY: Danny Arnold
CAST: Peter Graves (Lt. Ben Keegan), John Hudson (Sgt. Jonas), Joan Taylor (Francesca), Abel Fernandez (Mangas)

SPECS: 78 minutes; Color

AVAILABILITY: DVD (MGM Limited Edition Collection); Amazon Instant Video

NATION: Apache

IMAGE PORTRAYAL: Attacks on soldiers; romance between Native American woman and white man

SUMMARY: After soldiers kill his father at a peace parley, Mangas attacks the soldiers of Ben Keegan and his Apache scout, Jonas. His sister, Francesca, who loves Keegan, is killed while trying to warn him of the attack. Finally, Mangas leads his disguised Apache warriors on an attack on the fort.

40 GUNS TO APACHE PASS (Columbia, 1967)

DIRECTOR: William Witney

SCREENPLAY: Willard W. Willingham, Mary Willingham

CAST: Audie Murphy (Capt. Coburn), Michael Keep (Cochise), Kenneth Tobey (Corporal Bodine)

SPECS: 95 minutes; Color

AVAILABILITY: Amazon Instant Video

NATION: Apache

IMAGE PORTRAYAL: Attack on a fort

SUMMARY: After hostile Apaches led by Cochise attack his soldiers and settlers, Captain Coburn struggles to stop Corporal Bodine from selling repeating rifles to the Apaches. At the end, Cochise is defeated.

48 HOURS (Paramount, 1982)

DIRECTOR: Walter Hill

SCREENPLAY: Roger Spottiswoode, Walter Hill, Larry Gross, Steven E. de Souza

CAST: Eddie Murphy (Reggie Hammond), Nick Nolte (Jack Cates), James Remar (Albert Ganz), Sonny Landham (Billy Bear)

SPECS: 96 minutes; Color

AVAILABILITY: DVD (Paramount Home Video); Amazon Instant Video

NATION: NA

IMAGE PORTRAYAL: Contemporary Native American; troubled Native American

SUMMARY: Billy Bear, a large and mean Native American, and Albert Ganz, a psychopathic killer, are the antagonists of the heroes.

FOUR GUNS TO THE BORDER (Universal, 1954)

DIRECTOR: Richard Carlson

SCREENPLAY: George Van Marter, Franklin Coen, Louis L'Amour

CAST: Rory Calhoun (Ray Cully), Jay Silverheels (Yaqui)

SPECS: 83 minutes; Color

AVAILABILITY: NA
NATION: Apache
IMAGE PORTRAYAL: Attack on settlers, attack on Native Americans
SUMMARY: Renegade Apaches kill Yaqui, one of Ray Cully's outlaw gang.

FOUR SHEETS TO THE WIND (First Look International, 2007)
DIRECTOR: Sterlin Harjo
SCREENPLAY: Sterlin Harjo
CAST: Jeri Arrendondo (Cora Smallhill, the mother), Laura Bailey (Francie), Cody
    Lightning (Cufe Smallhill), Tamara Podemski (Miri Smallhill), Jon Proudstar
    (Jim), Richard Ray Whitman (Frankie Smallhill)
SPECS: 81 minutes; Color
AVAILABILITY: DVD (Millennium); Amazon Instant Video
NATION: Creek; Seminole
IMAGE PORTRAYAL: Contemporary Native Americans
SUMMARY: Cufe Smallhill puts his dad's body in a pool (as his dad had wanted)
    and visits his sister, Miri, in Tulsa and finds a friend in Francie who listens to
    him. In the meantime Miri, who is estranged from her mother, Cora, lets her
    life spin out of control.
CRITICS: In a *Moviefone* review, Kim Voynar comments, "I knew I was going
    to like *Four Sheets to the Wind* within the first ten minutes of the film, when in
    voice-over narration in the Muscogee native language with English subtitles,
    the storyteller wryly noted, 'Every now and then, good things happen in Okla-
    homa'—before leading the audience headlong into a story that begins with
    death. What follows is a lovely tale about communication, family, forgiveness,
    and 'something resembling love,' told through the story of a Native American
    family in small-town Oklahoma" (January 31, 2007).

FOXFIRE (Universal, 1955)
DIRECTOR: Joseph Pevney
SCREENPLAY: Ketti Frings, Anya Seton
CAST: Jane Russell (Amanda Lawrence), Jeff Chandler (Jonathan Dartland), Celia
    Lovsky (Princess Saba)
SPECS: 87 minutes; Color
AVAILABILITY: NA
NATION: Apache
IMAGE PORTRAYAL: Mixed-blood Native American; romance between
    mixed-blood Native American and a white woman; a wise elder
SUMMARY: Jonathan Dartland, a mixed-blood Apache mining engineer, has
    trouble living with his white wife, Amanda, as they search for an Apache trea-
    sure. However, his wise old mother, Princess Saba, helps the couple to appreci-
    ate each other by bridging their cultural gap.

FREE WILLY (Warner, 1993)
DIRECTOR: Simon Wincer
SCREENPLAY: Keith Walker, Cory Blechman
CAST: August Schellenberg (Randolph Johnson), Jason James Richter (Jesse)
SPECS: 112 minutes; Color
AVAILABILITY: DVD (Warner Home Video)
NATION: Haida
IMAGE PORTRAYAL: Contemporary Native American; Wise elder
SUMMARY: Randolph Johnson, a Haida who cares for Willy, the killer whale, befriends the rebellious young hero, Jesse. After teaching him the Haida myth of Orca, the killer whale, Randolph encourages the boy's affection for Willy and eventually helps him free the whale.

THE FRIENDLESS INDIAN (Pathe, 1913)
DIRECTOR: NA
SCREENPLAY: NA
CAST: NA
SPECS: 1 reel, Black & White; Silent
AVAILABILITY: NA
NATION: NA
IMAGE PORTRAYAL: Friendship
SUMMARY: A man rejected by his own tribe rescues a little white girl, but is then also rejected by the whites.
CRITICS: A *Moving Picture World* reviewer comments: "Condemned to walk alone, a Red Man saves a life and is given only a nod for thanks—after all, he is an Indian" (July 12, 1913, 232).

FROM OUT OF THE BIG SNOWS (Vitagraph, 1915)
DIRECTOR: Theodore Marston
SCREENPLAY: Bennett Cohen
CAST: George Cooper (Jean La Salle)
SPECS: 3 reels; Black & White; Silent
AVAILABILITY: NA
NATION: NA
IMAGE PORTRAYAL: Mixed-blood Native American; romance between a mixed-blood Native American and a white woman; vengeance
SUMMARY: When Jean La Salle, a mixed-blood, finds out his white lover has rejected him for a doctor, he seeks his revenge by tying the man to a tree so wolves can devour him.
CRITICS: A *Variety* reviewer notes the villain is a "half-breed, who with inborn cunning professes friendship for the white man so that he may later dispose of him" (August 13, 1915).

FRONTIER FURY (Columbia, 1943)
DIRECTOR: William Berke
SCREENPLAY: Betty Burbridge
CAST: Charles Starrett (Steve Langdon), Billy Wilkerson (Chief Eagle Feather), Stanley Brown (Gray Bear), Chief Yowlachie (Nuyaka)
SPECS: 55 minutes; Black & White
AVAILABILITY: NA
NATION: NA
IMAGE PORTRAYAL: Native Americans as victims
SUMMARY: The villains capture a good Indian agent, Steve Langdon, steal the tribe's money, and kill his friend, Gray Bear, the son of Chief Eagle Feather. Eventually Steve Langdon defeats the villains, retrieves the money, and is reinstated as Indian agent.

FRONTIER UPRISING (Zenith, 1961)
DIRECTOR: Edward L. Cahn
SCREENPLAY: Orville H. Hampton, George Bruce
CAST: Jim Davis (Jim Stockton), Herman Rudin (Chief Taztay)
SPECS: 68 minutes; Black & White
AVAILABILITY: DVD (Sinister Cinema); Amazon Instant Video
NATION: Modoc
IMAGE PORTRAYAL: Attack on soldiers; attack on wagon train
SUMMARY: When the Modoc tribe of Chief Taztay, who is supporting the Mexicans, attacks a wagon train and traps a troop of soldiers in a canyon, Jim Stockton comes to the rescue.

THE FRONTIERSMAN (MGM, 1927)
DIRECTOR: Reginald Barker
SCREENPLAY: Gordon Rigby, Tom Miranda, Madeleine Ruthven, Rose B. Wills
CAST: Tim McCoy (John Dale), Frank Hagney (White Snake), Chief John Big Tree (Grey Eagle)
SPECS: 5 reels; Black & White; Silent
AVAILABILITY: NA
NATION: Creek
IMAGE PORTRAYAL: Attack on a fort
SUMMARY: After the Creek tribe, led by White Snake and Grey Eagle, massacre an entire fort and captures a white woman, John Dale and his soldiers rescue her and stop the uprising.

FROZEN JUSTICE (Fox, 1929)
DIRECTOR: Allan Dwan
SCREENPLAY: Sonya Levien, Owen Davis, based on a novel by Ejnar Mikkelsen

CAST: Leonore Ulric (Talu), Robert Frazer (Lanak), Ullrich Haupt (Captain Jones)
SPECS: 73 minutes; Black & White
AVAILABILITY: NA
NATION: Eskimo
IMAGE PORTRAYAL: Mixed-blood Native American; romance between a Native American woman and a white man
SUMMARY: Talu, a mixed-blood Eskimo who leaves her husband, Lanak, to go off with a wicked captain of a ship, Captain Jones, suffers for her choice and returns to die in her husband's arms.

FROZEN RIVER (Sony Pictures Classics, 2008)
DIRECTOR: Courtney Hunt
SCREENPLAY: Courtney Hunt
CAST: Melissa Leo (Ray Eddy), Misty Upham (Lila Littlewolf), John Canoe (Bernie Littlewolf), Michael Skye (Billy Three Rivers)
SPECS: 97 minutes; Color
AVAILABILITY: DVD (Sony Pictures Home Entertainment); Amazon Instant Video
NATION: Mohawk
IMAGE PORTRAYAL: Contemporary First Nation people; troubled First Nation people
SUMMARY: Driven by their dire circumstances, a white woman, Ray Eddy, and a young Mohawk woman, Lila Littlewolf, smuggle aliens across the border of a reservation in the United States and Canada. When her tribal officials punish Lila, Ray decides to give herself up to help Lila and her children.
CRITICS: *New York Times* critic Stephen Holden comments: "Racism is a fact of life. The state police have a double standard for Indians and whites; a white driver is much less likely to be stopped and questioned. Lila makes no secret of her hatred of whites. Ray has her own ethnic qualms. What if the Pakistanis she is carrying across the border are terrorists?" (August 1, 2008).

FURY AT FURNACE CREEK (20 Century Fox, 1948)
DIRECTOR: H. Bruce Humberstone
SCREENPLAY: Charles G. Booth, Winston Miller, David Garth
CAST: Albert Dekker (Leverett), Jay Silverheels (Little Dog)
SPECS: 88 minutes; Black & White
AVAILABILITY: DVD (20th Century Fox Home Entertainment)
NATION: Apache
IMAGE PORTRAYAL: Attack on a fort; Native Americans as victims
SUMMARY: Spurred on by whites that want control of silver resources on Apache land, the tribe of Little Dog attacks and massacres a cavalry troop at Fort Furnace, which they burn down. Finally all of the Apaches are killed except Little Dog who finally kills the villain, Leverett.

G

GENERAL CUSTER AT LITTLE BIG HORN (Sunset, 1926)
DIRECTOR: Harry L. Fraser
SCREENPLAY: Carrie E. Rawles
CAST: John Beck (General Custer)
SPECS: 76 minutes; Black & White; Silent
AVAILABILITY: NA
NATION: Cheyenne; Sioux
IMAGE PORTRAYAL: Attack on soldiers
SUMMARY: Once again Custer fights the Sioux of Gall and Sitting Bull and Cheyenne of Little Horse in the most famous battle of the Indian wars. These Native American leaders decide to go to war to preserve their freedom on the plains. At the end, Sitting Bull is taken prisoner.
CRITICS: A *Variety* reviewer comments: "Aside from showing in as much detail as possible how the Indians got together for the clash that killed Custer, it has no moral lesson; mainly historical, a stark tragedy of the plains, showing bodies strewn all over 40 acres or so of land" (November 2, 1927).

GERONIMO (Paramount, 1939)
DIRECTOR: Paul Sloane
SCREENPLAY: Paul Sloane
CAST: Preston Foster (Captain Starrett), Chief Thundercloud (Geronimo), Gene Lockhart (Gillespie)
SPECS: 89 Minutes; Black & White
AVAILABILITY: NA
NATION: Apache
IMAGE PORTRAYAL: Attacks on settlers; attacks on soldiers
SUMMARY: Geronimo and his band of hostile Apaches, provided with guns and ammunition by Gillespie, kill women and children and wipe out almost an entire troop of soldiers before Captain Starrett captures him.
CRITICS: Frank Nugent in the *New York Times* comments on the title character: "All this is not intended as a reflection on Geronimo himself, who is a remarkably genuine redskin with a vocabulary of one grunt and a histrionic repertoire of two expressions: grim, and very grim. Whether or not Geronimo's role is even a 'speaking role' within the narrow limits laid down by the Screen Actors' Guild contract is something which would have to be determined by the delicate legal machinery of that organization. Our own vote would be in the negative—not because we wish to deprive Chief Thunder Cloud of the additional union wage, but simply because we doubt that there is even an Indian language in which so much hard service is demanded of a single monosyllable" (February 8, 1940).

GERONIMO (United Artists, 1962)
DIRECTOR: Arnold Laven
SCREENPLAY: Pat Fielder, Arnold Laven
CAST: Geronimo (Chuck Connors), Kamala Devi (Teela), Amando Silvestre (Natchez), Ross Martin (Mangas), Enid Jaynes (Huera), Denver Pyle (Senator Conrad)
SPECS: 101 minutes; Color
AVAILABILITY: DVD (MGM Limited Edition Collection)
NATION: Apache
IMAGE PORTRAYAL: Attacks on settlers; peace-loving chief
SUMMARY: Discussed on page 35, Geronimo, Mangas, and Huera surrender only to find that their tribe has to live on a reservation. When a villain tries to take over part of the reservation for raising cattle, Geronimo goes to Mexico, and from there he raids the whites. Eventually, Washington sends Senator Conrad, who offers Geronimo and his wife, Teela, a more just treaty and peace is restored.
CRITICS: A *Variety* critic writes, "In fact, the Indians of Fielder's scenario are unbelievably henpecked, domesticated and generally wishy-washy— proud and arrogant in their war-making but meek enough to be bossed about by a frail, lone white woman in more intimate business" (December 31, 1961).

GERONIMO JONES (Learning Corp., 1970)
DIRECTOR: Bert Salzman
SCREENPLAY: Bert Salzman
CAST: Martin Soto (Geronimo Jones), Chief Geronimo Kuth Le (Grandfather)
SPECS: 21 minutes; Color
AVAILABILITY: NA
NATION: Apache
IMAGE PORTRAYAL: Contemporary Native American; troubled Native American
SUMMARY: In this short film, a young Apache boy gets caught between the values of the past and present when he trades an old medallion for a TV. When he gives the TV to his grandfather they are struck by their relationship with contemporary society.

GERONIMO: AN AMERICAN LEGEND (Columbia, 1993)
DIRECTOR: Walter Hill
SCREENPLAY: John Milius, Larry Gross
CAST: Jason Patric (Charles Gatewood), Gene Hackman (General Crook), Kevin Tighe (General Miles), Rodney Grant (Mangas), Steve Reevis (Chato), Victor Aaron (Ulzana), Rino Thunder (Old Nana)
SPECS: 115 minutes; Color

AVAILABILITY: DVD (Sony Home Pictures Entertainment); Amazon Instant Video

NATION: Apache

IMAGE PORTRAYAL: Peace-loving chief

SUMMARY: In this film narrated by a sympathetic young soldier, Geronimo is a fierce but dignified warrior. After some of the older Apaches opt for peace, Geronimo decides to fight and eludes the soldiers of Generals Crook and Miles. Accompanied by Apache scout, Chato, the young voice-over narrator, and an honorable lieutenant pursue Geronimo, Mangas, and his small band into Mexico. Finally the lieutenant finds them and Geronimo decides on surrender as a way of saving his people from more suffering.

CRITICS: Roger Ebert in the *Chicago Sun Times* comments on the title character: "Geronimo himself, played by Wes Studi, is seen as a man of considerable insight, able to live off the land and launch deadly raids, yet contemplative about his role. He was responsible for the deaths of many white settlers, including women and children, but he points out to Crook with perfect logic that the 'white eyes' had also killed many Indians, including women and children, and that these deaths must not be described as murder, but as war" (December 10, 1993).

GERONIMO'S LAST RAID (American, 1912)

DIRECTOR: John Emerson

SCREENPLAY: John Emerson

CAST: J. Warren Kerrigan (Lt. Parker), Pauline Bush (Pauline Wilkins)

SPECS: 2 reels; Black & White; Silent

AVAILABILITY: NA

NATION: Apache

IMAGE PORTRAYAL: Attack on settlers; capture

SUMMARY: The Apaches of Geronimo capture Pauline Wilkins and then Lt. Parker, and they are about to burn him at the stake when the cavalry comes to the rescue.

CRITICS: A *Moving Picture World* reviewer notes that the film has "action and lots of it, for those who like clashes between Indians and settlers and who are stirred by dashing attacks of the U.S. Cavalry and cowboys on the redskins" (September 14, 1912, 1054).

THE GHOST DANCE (Ahremess, 1980)

DIRECTOR: Peter F. Buffa

SCREENPLAY: Robert M. Sutton, Peter F. Buffa

CAST: Julie Amato (Dr. Kay Foster), Victor Mohica (Tom Eagle), Henry Bal (Nahalla/Aranjo), Frank Salsedo (Ocacio), Felicia Leon (Rea), Frank Soto (Basowaya)

SPECS: 96 minutes; Color

AVAILABILITY: VHS (TWE Video)
NATION: NA
IMAGE PORTRAYAL: Contemporary Native American; romance between Native American man and a white woman
SUMMARY: In this horror movie, archeologists find the mummified body of Nahalla, a revengeful Ghost Dance leader, who takes over the body of Aranjo and starts killing people. Despite the efforts of Ocacio to do away with the evil spirit, Nahalla takes over the psyche of Dr. Foster.

GHOST TOWN (United Artists, 1956)
DIRECTOR: Allen H. Miner
SCREENPLAY: Jameson Brewer
CAST: Kent Taylor (Anse Conroy), John Smith (Duff), Serena Sande (Maureen), Edmund Hashim (Dull Knife), Chief Ted Nez (Fire Knife)
SPECS: 77 minutes; Black & White
AVAILABILITY: DVD (MGM Limited Edition Collection)
NATION: Cheyenne
IMAGE PORTRAYAL: Attack on a stagecoach; mixed-blood Native American; romance between mixed-blood Native American woman and a white man
SUMMARY: The Cheyenne tribe of Dull Knife attacks a stagecoach until Fire Knife brokers a peace. Duff and Maureen, a mixed-blood, fall in love at the end.

THE GLORIOUS TRAIL (First National Pictures, 1928)
DIRECTORS: Albert S. Rogell, Harry Joe Brown
SCREENPLAY: Marion Jackson, Don Ryan
CAST: Ken Maynard (Pat O'Leary), Chief Yowlachie (High Wolf)
SPECS: 65 Minutes; Black & White; Silent
AVAILABILITY: NA
NATION: NA
IMAGE PORTRAYAL: Attacks on settlers; attack on wagon trains
SUMMARY: Stirred up by a villain, the tribe of Chief High Wolf attacks settlers, work crews, and wagon trains.

THE GLORY GUYS (United Artists, 1965)
DIRECTOR: Arnold Laven
SCREENPLAY: Sam Peckinpah, based on the novel by Hoffman Birney
CAST: Tom Tryon (Captain Demas Harrod)
SPECS: 112 minutes; Color
AVAILABILITY: NA
NATION: Cheyenne; Sioux
IMAGE PORTRAYAL: Attack on soldiers

SUMMARY: Though the Native American actors are not in the credits and the setting is changed, this film is based on the Battle of Little Big Horn and has some spectacular battle sequences.

THE GODDESS OF LOST LAKE (Paralta, 1918)
DIRECTOR: Wallace Worsley
SCREENPLAY: Jack Cunningham, M. Van de Water
CAST: Louise Glaum (Mary Thorne), Frank Lanning (Eagle)
SPECS: 5 reels; Black & White; Silent
AVAILABILITY: NA
NATION: NA
IMAGE PORTRAYAL: Mixed-blood Native American; romance between a mixed-blood Native American woman and a white man
SUMMARY: A Native American legend tells that whoever sacrifices his life for that of a brave killed at the lake long ago will inherit the gold at the bottom of the lake. The father of the mixed-blood heroine, Mary Thorne, fulfills the legend when he allows himself to be killed by Eagle, one of the many who have waited at the lake since the original killing. His daughter takes the gold and then marries an Englishman.

THE GOLD HUNTERS (Davis Dist., 1925)
DIRECTOR: Paul Hurst
SCREENPLAY: NA
CAST: David Butler (Roderick Drew), Hedda Nova (Minnetake), Al Hallett (Mukoki), Noble Johnson (Wabigoon)
SPECS: 70 minutes; Black & White; Silent
AVAILABILITY: NA
NATION: NA
IMAGE PORTRAYAL: Romance between Native American woman and a white man
SUMMARY: The hero, Roderick Drew, who rescues Minnetake from a gang of villains after gold, eventually finds the gold and falls in love with the young woman. Other Native American characters are Mukoki and Wabigoon.

GRAYEAGLE (Howco International, 1977)
DIRECTOR: Charles B. Pierce
SCREENPLAY: Charles B. Pierce, Brad White, Michael Sajbel
CAST: Ben Johnson (John Colter), Lana Wood (Beth Colter), Iron Eyes Cody (Standing Bear), Alex Cord (Grayeagle), Paul Fix (Running Wolf), Jacob Daniels (Scar), Blackie Wetzell (Medicine Man), Cheyenne Rivera (Shoshone Brave), Wayne Wells (Shoshone Brave), Bill Lafromboise (Indian at Fort), Don Wright (Indian at Fort)
SPECS: 104 minutes; Color

AVAILABILITY: DVD (MGM Limited Edition Collection)
NATION: Cheyenne; Shoshone
IMAGE PORTRAYAL: Romance between Native Americans
SUMMARY: John Colter and his friend, Standing Bear, pursue Grayeagle, a noble
   Cheyenne warrior, who kidnaps Beth, the supposed daughter of Colter. How-
   ever, Running Wolf is the real father of Beth. Eventually, Grayeagle and Beth
   fall in love. After he fights off the hostile Shoshone braves, he returns to her. At
   the end, they are ready to live happily together in the wilderness.

THE GREAT SCOUT AND CATHOUSE THURSDAY (American
   International, 1976)
DIRECTOR: Don Taylor
SCREENPLAY: Richard Alan Shapiro
CAST: Lee Marvin (Sam Longwood), Oliver Reed (Joe Knox)
SPECS: 102 minutes; Color
AVAILABILITY: DVD (MGM Limited Edition Collection); Amazon Instant Video
NATION: NA
IMAGE PORTRAYAL: Friendship; mixed-blood Native American; vengeance
SUMMARY: Joe Knox, the educated mixed-blood Native American friend of the
   hero, Sam Longwood, helps him to get revenge on a crooked partner. He also
   goes for personal revenge by trying to infect whites with syphilis.

THE GREAT SIOUX MASSACRE (Columbia, 1965)
DIRECTOR: Sidney Salkow
SCREENPLAY: Marvin A. Gluck, Sidney Salkow
CAST: Philip Carey (Colonel Custer), Michael Pate (Sitting Bull), Iron Eyes Cody
   (Crazy Horse)
SPECS: 91 minutes; Color
AVAILABILITY: Amazon Instant Video
NATION: Sioux
IMAGE PORTRAYAL: Attack on soldiers
SUMMARY: Custer, who initially is a friend to the plains tribes and an enemy of
   crooked politicians and greedy Indian agents, finally agrees to take on the tribes
   because of his own political ambitions. Sitting Bull and Crazy Horse lead the
   Sioux in the defeat of Custer at the Battle of Little Big Horn. This film is far
   from historical reality.

THE GREAT SIOUX UPRISING (Universal, 1953)
DIRECTOR: Lloyd Bacon
SCREENPLAY: Melvin Levy, J. Robert Bren, Gladys Atwater, Frank Gill Jr.
CAST: Jeff Chandler (Jonathan Westgate), John War Eagle (Chief Red Cloud),
   Glenn Strange (Gen. Stand Watie), Julia Montoya (Heyoka), Dewey Drapeau
   (Teo-Ka-Ha), Lyle Bettger (Stephen Cook)

SPECS: 80 minutes; Color
AVAILABILITY: NA
NATION: Sioux
IMAGE PORTRAYAL: Peace-loving chief
SUMMARY: When Stephen Cook steals horses from the Sioux of Red Cloud, the hero, Jonathan Westgate, averts a war by working out a plan for the tribe to sell horses to ranchers. In the meantime, Stand Watie, a Cherokee, is trying to make the Union look bad to the Sioux.

GREY OWL (20th Century Fox, 1999)
DIRECTOR: Richard Attenborough
SCREENPLAY: William Nicholson
CAST: Pierce Brosnan (Grey Owl), Annie Galipeau (Pony), Nathaniel Arcand (Ned White Bear), Graham Greene (Jim Bernard). A large number of other Native American and First Nation actors and dancers appear in a powwow sequence.
SPECS: 120 minutes; Color
AVAILABILITY: DVD (Lions Gate); Amazon Instant Video
NATION: Ojibwa
IMAGE PORTRAYAL: Romance between a Native American woman and a white man
SUMMARY: A real-life trapper, Archie Grey Owl, poses as a Native American and has learned the ways of the Ojibwa tribe. Eventually he marries an Iroquois woman, Pony-Anahareo. After becoming an environmentalist, writing a book, and achieving fame, he reveals that he is a white man.
CRITICS: *Variety* critic Brendan Kelly comments: "The core problem is the script, which combines static dialogue with lack of psychological depth. There is some talk of a kid obsessed with 'Red Indians,' but that's about as far as the insight goes" (October 4, 1999).

GUARDIAN OF THE WILDERNESS (Sunn Classics, 1976)
DIRECTOR: David O'Malley
SCREENPLAY: Casey Conlon, David O'Malley, Charles E. Sellier Jr.
CAST: Denver Pyle (Galen Clark), Don Shanks (Teneiya)
SPECS: 112 minutes; Color
AVAILABILITY: NA
NATION: NA
IMAGE PORTRAYAL: Friendship; loyalty
SUMMARY: Teneiya is the Native American friend of Galen Clark, who helps him build a cabin in the wilderness, which eventually becomes Yosemite Park.

GUN BROTHERS (United Artists, 1956)
DIRECTOR: Sidney Salkow

SCREENPLAY: Gerald Drayson Adams, Richard Schayer
CAST: Buster Crabbe (Chad Santee), Lita Milan (Meeteetse), Ann Robinson (Rose)
SPECS: 94 minutes; Color
Availability: DVD (MGM Limited Edition Collection); Amazon Instant Video
NATION: Cheyenne
IMAGE PORTRAYAL: Romance between a Native American woman and a white man
SUMMARY: Meeteetse is the companion of Chad, who finally falls in love with Rose

THE GUN THAT WON THE WEST (Columbia, 1955)
DIRECTOR: William Castle
SCREENPLAY: Robert E. Kent
CAST: Richard Denning (Dakota Jack Gaines), Dennis Morgan (Jim Bridger), Robert Bice (Chief Red Cloud), Michael Morgan (Afraid of Horses)
SPECS: 71 minutes; Color
AVAILABILITY: DVD (Sony Pictures Home Entertainment)
NATION: Sioux
IMAGE PORTRAYAL: Attack on soldiers; hostile warrior; peace-loving chief
SUMMARY: After several attempts at peace with the Sioux of the wise Chief Red Cloud and hostile Afraid of Horses, the sympathetic heroes, Dakota Jack Gaines and Jim Bridger and a troop of soldiers, using the new Springfield rifle, fight and defeat the tribe of Red Cloud after the killing of several warriors finally provokes them to go to war.

GUNMAN'S WALK (Columbia, 1958)
DIRECTOR: Phil Karlson
SCREENPLAY: Frank S. Nugent, Ric Hardman
CAST: Kathryn Grant (Clee Chouard), Chief Blue Eagle (Black Horse), James Darren (Davy Hackett), Bert Convy (Paul Chouard)
SPECS: 97 minutes; Color
AVAILABILITY: VHS (Columbia Pictures Home Video)
NATION: Sioux
IMAGE PORTRAYAL: Friendship; loyalty; mixed-blood Native American; romance between a mixed-blood Native American woman and a white man
SUMMARY: Davy Hackett falls in love with Clee Chouard, a mixed-blood, and hires Black Horse and Paul Chouard to work on the ranch. This provokes his brother, who also loves Clee, to become an evil gunman.

GUNMEN FROM LAREDO (Columbia, 1959)
DIRECTOR: Wallace MacDonald
SCREENPLAY: Clarke Reynolds

CAST: Robert Knapp (Gil Reardon), Maureen Hingert (Rosita), Charles Horvath (Coloradas), X Brands (Delgados)
SPECS: 67 minutes; Color
AVAILABILITY: NA
NATION: Apache
IMAGE PORTRAYAL: Vengeance
SUMMARY: Gil Reardon kills Delgados, the son of Coloradas, and Coloradas pursues Reardon and a young Mexican woman, Rosita, whom he rescued. At the end, Gil Reardon kills Coloradas in hand-to-hand combat.

GUNS OF FORT PETTICOAT (Columbia, 1957)
DIRECTOR: George Marshall
SCREENPLAY: Walter Doniger, C. William Harrison
CAST: Audie Murphy (Lt. Frank Hewitt), Charles Horvath (Indian Leader), Geronimo Kuth Le (Indian Leader)
SPECS: 82 minutes; Color
AVAILABILITY: VHS (Good Times Video)
NATION: Cheyenne
IMAGE PORTRAYAL: Attack on fort
SUMMARY: Frank Hewitt and a group of women work together to defeat the Cheyenne warriors of the two leaders, who are angry about the Sand Creek massacre.

H

THE HALF BREED (Triangle, 1916)
DIRECTOR: Allan Dawn
SCREENPLAY: Anita Loos, Bret Harte
CAST: Douglas Fairbanks (Lo Dorman), Alma Rubens (Teresa), Jewel Carmen (Nellie)
SPECS: 50 minutes; Black & White; Silent
AVAILABILITY: DVD (Classic Video Streams: in "The Actors: Rare Films of Douglas Fairbanks Sr. Vol. 2")
NATION: NA
IMAGE PORTRAYAL: Mixed-blood Native American; romance between a mixed-blood Native American man and a white woman
SUMMARY: Lo Dorman, or Sleeping Water, is the son of a Native American woman who had been seduced by a white settler. He spends his early life alone in the forest because the whites drive him from the town. Later he is rejected by Nellie and then finds happiness with Teresa.

THE HALF-BREED (Assoc. First National Pictures, 1922)
DIRECTOR: Charles Taylor

SCREENPLAY: Charles Taylor, based on the play, *Half Breed: a Tale of Indian Country*
CAST: Wheeler Oakman (Delmar Spavinaw), Ann May (Doll Pardeau)
SPECS: 6 reels; Black & White; Silent
AVAILABILITY: NA
NATION: NA
IMAGE PORTRAYAL: Mixed-blood Native American; romance between a Native American man and a white woman; vengeance
SUMMARY: This film tells the story of Delmar Spavinaw. An educated man, he finds various ways to take his revenge on a judge who evicted his Native American mother from her land. At the end he leaves with Doll Pardeau.

THE HALF-BREED (RKO, 1952)
DIRECTORS: Stuart Gilmore, Edward Ludwig
SCREENPLAY: Harold Shumate, Richard Wormser, Charles Hoffman, Robert Hardy Andrews
CAST: Jack Buetel (Charlie Wolf), Robert Young (Dan Craig), Judy Walsh (Nah-Lin), Jay Silverheels (Apache), Chief Thundercloud (Apache)
SPECS: 81 minutes; Color
AVAILABILITY: DVD (Warner Archive Collection)
NATION: Apache
IMAGE PORTRAYAL: Friendship; loyalty; mixed-blood Native American
SUMMARY: Charlie Wolf, an Apache mixed-blood whose sister, Nah-Lin, has been murdered, joins Dan Craig in bringing to justice villains who are trying to start a war so they can get at gold on the reservation. At the end Charlie Wolf returns to his reservation.
CRITICS: A *New York Times* reviewer notes that the film "does profess concern for Indians of 1867, which is commendable but hardly timely. Perhaps it will give somebody an idea for a motion picture about the plight of the contemporary Indian, the Navajos of the Southwest, for instance" (July 5, 1952).

THE HALLELUJAH TRAIL (United Artists, 1965)
DIRECTOR: John Sturges
SCREENPLAY: John Gay, based on the novel by William Gulick
CAST: Martin Landau (Chief Walks Stooped Over), Robert J. Wilke (Chief Five Barrels), Jim Burk (Elks-Runner)
SPECS: 165 minutes; Color
AVAILABILITY: DVD (MGM/UA Home Entertainment); Amazon Instant Video
NATION: Sioux
IMAGE PORTRAYAL: Attack on a wagon train; drunkenness
SUMMARY: In this spoof of westerns, the whiskey-loving Sioux warriors of Chief Walks Stooped Over, Elks Runner, and Chief Five Barrels kidnap ladies from the Temperance League and attack a circled wagon train and later circle the wagons themselves as the cavalry attacks them.

HANBLECEYA (Tribal Alliance Productions, 2005)
DIRECTOR: Steven Edell
SCREENPLAY: Steven Edell
CAST: Saginaw Grant (Grandfather), Cody Lighting (Teenage Boy), Zahn Mc-
    Clamon (Father)
SPECS: 11 minutes; Color
AVAILABILITY: NA
NATION: Lakota
IMAGE PORTRAYAL: Contemporary Native American
SUMMARY: A teenage Lakota boy struggles with a father who accepts the white
    man's ways and a Grandfather who only believes in the traditions of the tribe.
    To resolve this he experiences a *hanbleceya*, or vision quest.

HANG YOUR HAT ON THE WIND (Buena Vista, 1969)
DIRECTOR: Larry Landsburgh
SCREENPLAY: Paul West, Larry Landsburgh
CAST: Rick Natoli (Goyo, Indian Boy) Angel Tompkins (Fran Harper)
SPECS: 48 minutes; Color
AVAILABILITY: NA
NATION: NA
IMAGE PORTRAYAL: Gratitude; honor
SUMMARY: In this Disney film, a Navajo boy named Goyo finds a valuable
    escaped racehorse and adopts him. Later, however, he gives the horse back to
    Fran Harper and then rescues it from Mexican bandits. As a reward he gets his
    own saddle and pony from Fran Harper.

HANK WILLIAMS FIRST NATION (Extra Butter Pictures, 2005)
DIRECTOR: Aaron James Sorensen
SCREENPLAY: Aaron James Sorensen
CAST: Gordon Tootoosis (Adelard Fox), Jimmy Herman (Uncle Martin), Stacy
    Da Silva (Sarah Fox), Colin Van Loon (Jacob Fox), Bernard Starlight (Huey
    Bigstone), Edna Rain (Grandma), Raymond Carafelle (Chief Chicken-Wings)
SPECS: 92 minutes; Color
AVAILABILITY: DVD (Alliance Films)
NATION: Cree
IMAGE PORTRAYAL: Contemporary First Nations people
SUMMARY: Uncle Martin, with his nephew, Jacob Fox, leaves a remote reserve
    in Canada on a Greyhound bus to visit the grave of Hank Williams in the
    United States to see if he is really dead. As the American news picks up on the
    story, turmoil ensues at the reserve, especially for Chief Chicken-Wing and
    Huey and Sarah, who are being raised by Adelard Fox.

HAROLD OF ORANGE (Film in the Cities, 1984)
DIRECTOR: Richard Weise

SCREENPLAY: Gerald Vizenor
CAST: Charlie Hall (Harold Sinseer), Michael Anthony Hall (Plumero), numerous
    other Native Americans play other minor roles
SPECS: 30 minutes; Color
AVAILABILITY: Amazon Instant Video
NATION: NA
IMAGE PORTRAYAL: Contemporary Native Americans
SUMMARY: Discussed on page 85, this satiric comedy tells the story of Harold
    Sinseer and his merry trickster warriors who con grants from institutions for
    bizarre schemes such as growing miniature oranges or pinch beans for a reserva-
    tion coffee house.

HARRY AND TONTO (20th Century Fox, 1974)
DIRECTOR: Paul Mazursky
SCREENPLAY: Paul Mazursky, Josh Greenfeld
CAST: Art Carney (Harry Coombes), Chief Dan George (Sam Two Feathers)
SPECS: 115 minutes; Color
AVAILABILITY: DVD (20th Century Fox Home Entertainment)
NATION: NA
IMAGE PORTRAYAL: Contemporary Native American; friendship
SUMMARY: After meeting in jail, Harry and humorous old Sam Two Feathers
    become friends.
CRITICS: In the *Chicago Sun Times* Roger Ebert notes: "This leads to the
    film's most hilarious scene. Harry is tossed into a cell already occupied by
    an ancient Indian (Chief Dan George) who has been arrested for practicing
    medicine without a license. The two old men gravely discuss recent televi-
    sion shows and the problem of bursitis, and the chief cures Harry's aching
    shoulder in return for an electric blender. Chief Dan George is so solemn, so
    understated, with Mazursky's dialogue that the result is a great comic scene"
    (January 1, 1974).

HAWKEN'S BREED (MLG Properties, 1987)
DIRECTOR: Charles B. Pierce
SCREENPLAY: Charles B. Pierce
CAST: Peter Fonda (Hawken), Serene Hedin (Spirit)
SPECS: 89 minutes; Color
AVAILABILITY: VHS (Anchor Bay)
NATION: Shawnee
IMAGE PORTRAYAL: Romance between a Native American woman and a
    white man
SUMMARY: Hawken falls in love with a Shawnee woman, Spirit, and they fight
    hostile Shawnee warriors. After they are separated, Hawken rescues her, and
    they live a long and happy life together.

THE HEART OF A SIOUX (Lubin, 1910)
DIRECTOR: NA
SCREENPLAY: NA
CAST: NA
SPECS: Black & White; Silent
AVAILABILITY: NA
NATION: NA
IMAGE PORTRAYAL: Romance between a Native American woman and a white man
SUMMARY: A Sioux girl falls in love with her white teacher, and, though her love is unrequited, she saves the man's life twice.
CRITICS: A reviewer for *Moving Picture World* argues that such movies are showing that the Indians, contrary to the stereotype of them as "stolid, unemotional people," experience strong emotions. He believes that this film will "go far to remove the stigma which this oft-repeated assertion, that Indians lack heart, has placed upon the race" (August 20, 1910, 407).

HEART OF AN INDIAN (Bison, 1912)
DIRECTOR: Thomas Ince
SCREENPLAY: Thomas Ince
CAST: Francis Ford (Indian Chief), Ann Little (Indian Mother)
SPECS: 20 minutes; Black & White; Silent
AVAILABILITY: NA
NATION: NA
IMAGE PORTRAYAL: Attack on settlers; friendship
SUMMARY: The Indian Chief of a tribe steals a baby from a white woman to replace the dead child of his wife, the Indian Mother. The white mother comes to the camp of the Chief and is captured by the tribe, which is then wiped out by the settlers. When the Indian Mother sees how much the white woman loves her baby, she gives it back.
CRITICS: In his memoir, Iron Eyes Cody notes that the film showed "some tender exchanges between a white woman and an Indian maiden on the theme of motherhood" (Cody 1982, 32).

THE HEART OF WETONA (Select, 1919)
DIRECTOR: Sidney Franklin
SCREENPLAY: Mary Murillo, George Scarborough
CAST: Norma Talmadge (Wetona), Fred Huntly (Chief Quannah), Princess Uwane Yea (Nauma), Chief White Eagle (Nipo), Black Lizard (Eagle)
SPECS: 72 minutes; Black & White; Silent
AVAILABILITY: NA
NATION: Comanche
IMAGE PORTRAYAL: Mixed-blood Native American; romance between a mixed-blood Native American woman and a white man; vengeance

SUMMARY: This film tells the story of Wetona, a mixed-blood, educated by the whites, who is seduced by a cowardly white engineer, who then leaves her. Her father, Chief Quannah, gains revenge by killing the man, and later Wetona marries a good Indian agent.

HEAVEN WITH A GUN (MGM, 1969)
DIRECTOR: Lee H. Katzin
SCREENPLAY: Richard Carr
CAST: Glenn Ford (Jim Killian), Barbara Hershey (Leloopa)
SPECS: 101 minutes; Color
AVAILABILITY: DVD (Warner Archive Collection); Amazon Instant Video
NATION: NA
IMAGE PORTRAYAL: Native Americans as victims
SUMMARY: Jim Killian protects a young Native American, Leloopa, and punishes the man who assaulted her.

THE HERITAGE OF THE DESERT (Paramount, 1924)
DIRECTOR: Irvin Willat
SCREENPLAY: Albert Shelby Le Vino, based on the novel by Zane Grey
CAST: Bebe Daniels (Mescal), Lloyd Hughes (Jack Hare), Ernest Torrence (August Naab)
SPECS: 6 reels; Black & White; Silent
AVAILABILITY: NA
NATION: NA
IMAGE PORTRAYAL: Friendship; mixed-blood Native American; romance between a Native American woman and a white man; romance between a mixed-blood woman and a white man
SUMMARY: With the help of a friendly tribe, August Naab rescues Mescal, a mixed-blood, who marries Jack Hare

HIAWATHA (Independent Moving Pictures Co. of America, 1909)
DIRECTOR: William V. Ranous
SCREENPLAY: Based on the poem by Henry Wadsworth Longfellow
CAST: Gladys Hulette (Hiawatha)
SPECS: 15 minutes; Black & White; Silent
AVAILABILITY: NA
NATION: Ojibwa; Sioux
IMAGE PORTRAYAL: Romance between Native Americans
SUMMARY: In this early adaptation of Longfellow's famous poem, Hiawatha, an Ojibwa, overcomes many obstacles before he can marry Minnehaha, a member of the hostile Sioux tribe.
CRITICS: A *Variety* critic reflects a common stereotype when he notes that "the actors, both men and women, seemingly cannot secure the natural abandon of the Indian" (October 30, 1909).

HIAWATHA (Colonial Motion Picture, 1913)
DIRECTOR: F. E. Moore
SCREENPLAY: Based on the poem by Henry Wadsworth Longfellow
CAST: Hilde Hadges (Hiawatha), Soon-goot (Minnehaha)
SPECS: 40 minutes; Black & White; Silent
AVAILABILITY: NA
NATION: Ojibwa; Sioux
IMAGE PORTRAYAL: Romance between Native Americans
SUMMARY: This adaptation of Longfellow's poem about the adventures of Hi-
    awatha, the Ojibwa, and his love for Minnehaha, the Sioux, uses all Native
    American actors.
CRITICS: *Moving Picture World* reviewer W. Stephen Bush comments on the
    acting and subject matter of the film: "We have had such a fearful surfeit of
    blood-thirsty Indians, scalping Indians, howling Indians, gambling Indians and
    murdering and burning Indians in the cheap films, that it was like a breath of
    fresh air to see real human Indians enacting before us an old Indian legend.
    . . . The Indians of these reels show all that stoic and impressive calm which
    the white man has never quite been able to understand" (March 8, 1913, 980).

HIAWATHA (Monogram, 1952)
DIRECTOR: Kurt Neumann
SCREENPLAY: Daniel Ullman, Arthur Strawn, based on the poem of Henry
    Wadsworth Longfellow
CAST: Vince Edwards (Hiawatha), Yvette Duguay (Minnehaha), Keith Larsen
    (Pau Puk Keewis), Morris Ankrum (Iagoo), Eugene Iglesias (Chibiabos)
SPECS: 80 minutes; Color
AVAILABILITY: DVD (Warner Archive Collection); Amazon Instant Video
NATION: Ojibwa; Sioux
IMAGE PORTRAYAL: Romance between Native Americans
SUMMARY: This film tells the story of the love between the Ojibwa man, Hi-
    awatha, and a Sioux woman, Minnehaha. When the hostile Pau Puk Keewis
    tries to start trouble with the Sioux, Hiawatha stops him and eventually kills
    him in hand-to-hand combat. After Hiawatha finds out that his father was really
    a Dakota Sioux, he gets permission from his tribe to marry Minnehaha.
CRITICS: A *New York Times* critic comments on the acting: "Vincent Edwards is
    wooden but handsome in the title role; Yvette Duguay is a pretty but improb-
    able Minnehaha; Keith Larsen is a standard heavy as the scheming and blood-
    thirsty Pau Puk Keewis. The setting is adequately primeval even if it is closer to
    Hollywood than the shores of Gitche Gumme" (December 26, 1952).

HIAWATHA'S RABBIT HUNT (Warner Bros., 1941)
DIRECTOR: Fritz Freleng
SCREENPLAY: Michael Maltese

CAST: Elmer Fudd, Bugs Bunny
SPECS: 8 minutes; Color
AVAILABILITY: DVD (Warner Home Video)
NATION: NA
IMAGE PORTRAYAL: Hiawatha story
SUMMARY: Bugs Bunny is reading the Song of Hiawatha when an Elmer Fudd–
like Hiawatha approaches in a canoe. Hiawatha lures Bugs into a cooking pot,
but Bugs sees the plot and torments Hiawatha until he escapes in his canoe.
At the end Bugs is again reading Longfellow when Hiawatha returns and gives
Bugs an insulting kiss. Bugs rubs it off as Hiawatha again departs.

HILLS OF OLD WYOMING (Paramount, 1937)
DIRECTOR: Nate Watt
SCREENPLAY: Maurice Geraghty, Clarence E. Mulford
CAST: William Boyd (Hopalong Cassidy) Steve Clemente (Lone Eagle), Chief Big
Tree (Chief Big Tree)
SPECS: 78 minutes; Black & White
AVAILABILITY: DVD (Paramount Pictures)
NATION: NA
IMAGE PORTRAYAL: Evil mixed blood; friendship; mixed-blood Native
American; peace-loving chief
SUMMARY: Rustlers on a reservation kill Lone Eagle, a mixed-blood who was
part of the gang to cause trouble between a tribe and the cattlemen. Hopalong
Cassidy saves the day by convincing Chief Big Tree to make peace by joining
the ranchers against the rustlers and outlaws.

HOMBRE (20th Century Fox, 1967)
DIRECTOR: Martin Ritt
SCREENPLAY: Irving Ravetch, Harriet Frank Jr., based on the novel by Elmore
Leonard
CAST: Paul Newman (John Russell/Hombre)
SPECS: 111 minutes; Color
AVAILABILITY: DVD (20th Century Fox Home Entertainment); Amazon In-
stant Video
NATION: Apache
IMAGE PORTRAYAL: Attack on settlers; white man adopted by Native Americans
SUMMARY: Discussed on page 38, this film tells the story of a white man who
embraces the Apache way of life and sacrifices himself for a group of people
who don't deserve it.
CRITICS: Bosley Crowther in the *New York Times* comments: "And, finally,
when Mr. Newman, heroically committed to do the Big Thing you feel certain
he is going to do from the start, comes forth and does it, it is mindful of the selfless sacrifices made by the Indian hero in 'Broken Arrow'" (March 22, 1967).

THE HOMECOMING OF JIMMY WHITECLOUD (Tricor Entertainment, 2001)
DIRECTOR: Paul Winters
SCREENPLAY: Paul Winters
CAST: David Midthunder (Jimmy Whitecloud), Lee Whitestar (John Spotted Bear), Victoria Regina (Sally Meets the Moon), Marcos Akiaten (Native Warrior), Akima (Lonnie), Mark S. Brien (Bloody Knife), Robert Diola (Little Hawk)
SPECS: 100 minutes; Color
AVAILABILITY: NA
NATION: NA
IMAGE PORTRAYAL: Romance between Native Americans; wise elder
SUMMARY: Ruthless New York mobsters chase Jimmy from the city to his reservation in Arizona, where he finds love and joins his grandfather and other members of the tribe to fight the mobsters. In this process, he forgets the big city ways and adopts his tribal values.

HONDO (Warner Bros., 1953)
DIRECTOR: John Farrow
SCREENPLAY: James Edward Grant, based on a novel by Louis L'Amour
CAST: John Wayne (Hondo Lane), Michael Pate (Chief Vittorio), Rodolfo Acosta (Silva), James Arness (Lennie-Army Indian Scout)
SPECS: 83 minutes; Color
AVAILABILITY: DVD (Paramount Home Entertainment); Amazon Instant video
NATION: Apache
IMAGE PORTRAYAL: Peace-loving chief
SUMMARY: Hondo, who grew up with the Apache and respects the honorable Chief Vittorio, fights against the hostile warriors of Silva.
CRITICS: A *Variety* critic comments that "Vittorio . . . is shown as a just leader concerned about the problems of his people and bewildered by the white man's violation of treaties" (November 25, 1953).

HOUSE MADE OF DAWN (Firebird, 1972)
DIRECTOR: Richardson Morse
SCREENPLAY: Richardson Morse, based on the novel by N. Scott Momaday
CAST: Larry Littlebird (Abel), Judith Doty (Milly), Jay Varela (Benally), Skeeter Vaughan (the Albino)
SPECS: 90 minutes; Color
AVAILABILITY: VHS (New Line Home Video)
NATION: Pueblo
IMAGE PORTRAYAL: Contemporary Native American; troubled Native American; wise elder
SUMMARY: Discussed on page 82, this film tells the story of Abel, who struggles with living in the city. His best friend is Benally and his antagonist is the Albino.

While in Los Angeles, he falls in love with a white social worker, Milly, who finally convinces him to return to his reservation.

THE HUNTRESS (Assoc. First National Pictures, 1923)
DIRECTORS: John Francis Dillon, Lynn Reynolds
SCREENPLAY: Percy Heath, based on the novel by Hulbert Footner
CAST: Colleen Moore (Bela), Snitz Edwards (Musq'oosis), Lalo Encinas (Beavertail), Chief Big Tree (Otebaya)
SPECS: 60 minutes; Black & White; Silent
AVAILABILITY: NA
NATION: NA
IMAGE PORTRAYAL: Romance between a Native American man and a white woman
SUMMARY: A white woman adopted by the tribe of Musq'oosis, Beavertail, and Otebaya finally leaves so she can avoid marrying a man from the tribe and give herself to the white man she loves.
CRITICS: A *Variety* reviewer comments: "The story deals with Indians and the old theme of the girl who thought she was a member of the redskins but who found out later that some careless parents had deserted her. And with the discovery that she isn't Indian comes a desire to capture a white husband" (October 11, 1923).

I

I KILLED GERONIMO (Eagle Lion, 1950)
DIRECTOR: John Hoffman
SCREENPLAY: Sam Neuman, Nat Tanchuck
CAST: James Ellison (Capt. Jeff Packard), Chief Thundercloud (Geronimo)
SPECS: 62 minutes; Black & White
AVAILABILITY: NA
NATION: Apache
IMAGE PORTRAYAL: Attack on a wagon train
SUMMARY: Captain Packard stops the smuggling of guns to the Apache and kills Geronimo while his warriors are attacking a wagon train.

IMPRINT (Linn Productions, 2007)
DIRECTOR: Michael Linn
SCREENPLAY: Michael Linn, Keith Davenport
CAST: Tonantzin Carmelo (Shayla Stonefeather), Carla-Rae (Rebecca Stonefeather), Michael Spears (Tom Greyhorse), Cory Brusseau (Jonathan Freeman), Charles White Buffalo (Sam Stonefeather), Joseph Medicine Blanket (Robbie Whiteshirt), Dave Bald Eagle (Medicine Man)
SPECS: 84 minutes; Color

AVAILABILITY: DVD (MTI Home Video)

NATION: Lakota

IMAGE PORTRAYAL: Contemporary Native American; troubled Native American; wise elder

SUMMARY: Discussed on page 89, this film tells the story of Shayla Stonefeather, a big city attorney, who has prosecuted Robbie White Shirt, a fellow Lakota, in a murder trial and returns to her reservation to see her dying father, Sam. After hearing loud sounds and seeing scary visions and riding to the countryside where she meets a Medicine man, she comes to appreciate her tribal values and rejects her white boyfriend, Cory.

CRITICS: *Variety* critic Joe Leydon comments: "Carmelo sustains sympathy and interest as she subtly shades a familiar stereotype—a disillusioned skeptic who re-embraces her ancestral culture—with enough specificity to resemble a flesh-and-blood human being. Linn's attractive lensing of the South Dakota locales also helps 'Imprint' make a generally favorable impression" (March 28, 2007).

IN THE DAYS OF THE THUNDERING HERD (Selig, 1914)

DIRECTORS: Colin Campbell, Francis J. Grandon

SCREENPLAY: Gilson Willets

CAST: Tom Mix (Tom Mingle), Bessie Eyton (Sally Madison), Wheeler Oakman (Chief Swift Wing), Red Wing (Starlight)

SPECS: 48 minutes; Black & White; Silent

AVAILABILITY: DVD (Alpha Home Entertainment)

NATION: NA

IMAGE PORTRAYAL: Attack on a wagon train; friendship; romance between a Native American man and white woman; romance between a Native American woman and a white man

SUMMARY: The tribe of Chief Swift Wing attacks a wagon train and captures Tom Mingle and Sally Madison. Then Chief Swift Wing falls in love with Sally. However, a young woman from the tribe, Starlight, is attracted to Tom and helps the captives escape.

CRITICS: A *Variety* critic bemoans the stock, disrespectful treatment of the Native Americans: "the former kings of the plains are also permitted to run into the range of the camera, fire occasionally and help lengthen out the feature" (August 16, 1915).

IN THE LONG AGO (Selig, 1913)

DIRECTOR: Colin Campbell

SCREENPLAY: Lanier Bartlett

CAST: Wheeler Oakman (Dreamer, the Indian lover/Modern Lover), Bessie Eyton (Starlight/the Modern Sweetheart), Frank Clark (Starlight's Father/the Modern Girl's Father) Tom Santschi (Indian Warrior), Henry Otto (the Medicine Man)

SPECS: 1 reel; Black & White; Silent
AVAILABILITY: NA
NATION: NA
IMAGE PORTRAYAL: Romance between a Native American man and woman
SUMMARY: In an ancient legendary era, by playing a windpipe made from the thighbone of a great chief, Dreamer revives his lover, Starlight, who has been under a spell. Then two modern lovers are compared to the legendary ones.

INDIAN AGENT (RKO, 1948)
DIRECTOR: Lesley Selander
SCREENPLAY: Norman Houston
CAST: Tim Holt (Dave Taylor), Noah Beery Jr. (Chief Red Fox), Claudia Drake (Torquoise), Iron Eyes Cody (Wovoka), Harry Woods (Carter)
SPECS: 65 minutes; Black & White
AVAILABILITY: DVD (Warner Archive Collection; in "Tim Holt Western Classics, Volume 2")
NATION: NA
IMAGE PORTRAYAL: Native Americans as victims
SUMMARY: When a crooked agent, Carter, diverts funds for the reservation and puts the tribe in danger of starvation, the tribe of Red Fox and Wavoka threatens war. However, Dave Taylor foils the villain and keeps the peace.

INDIAN BROTHERS (Biograph, 1911)
DIRECTOR: D. W. Griffith
SCREENPLAY: NA
CAST: Frank Opperman (Indian Chief), Wilfred Lucas (Indian Chief's Brother), Guy Hedlund (the Renegade)
SPECS: 18 minutes; Black & White; Silent
AVAILABILITY: NA
NATION: NA
IMAGE PORTRAYAL: Courage; honor; vengeance
SUMMARY: In this film subtitled "The Story of an Indian's Honor," a renegade brave kills the ailing chief of the tribe. When the man's brother finds out about the murder, he captures the man and punishes him.

THE INDIAN FIGHTER (United Artists, 1955)
DIRECTOR: Andre De Toth
SCREENPLAY: Frank Davis, Robert L. Richards
CAST: Kirk Douglas (Johnny Hawks), Elsa Martinelli (Onahti), Eduard Franz (Red Cloud), Harry Landers (Grey Wolf), Hank Worden (Crazy Bear), Walter Matthau (Wes Todd), Lon Chaney Jr. (Chivington)
SPECS: 88 minutes; Color
AVAILABILITY: DVD (MGM/UA Home Entertainment); Amazon Instant Video

NATION: Sioux

IMAGE PORTRAYAL: Peace-loving chief; romance between a Native American woman and a white man

SUMMARY: When Johnny Hawk falls in love with Onahti, the daughter of Chief Red Cloud, and neglects his duties as a wagon master, Todd and Chivington who are after gold incite Grey Wolf and other hostile braves to war. At the end, Grey Wolf is killed, and Hank turns over Todd to Red Cloud, who agrees to peace and allows Hawk to marry Onahti.

CRITICS: A *Newsweek* critic notes that Hollywood's "tribesmen have, of late, been getting nobler and nobler, and occasionally they even come out all right, always with the understanding white man passing the peace pipe" (January 9, 1956, 71).

THE INDIAN IN THE CUPBOARD (Columbia Tristar, 1995)

DIRECTOR: Frank Oz

SCREENPLAY: Melissa Mathison, based on the novel by Lynne Reid Bank

CAST: Hal Scardino (Omri), Lightfoot (Little Bear, the Indian), David Keith (Boone, the Cowboy)

SPECS: 96 minutes; Color

AVAILABILITY: DVD (Sony Pictures Home Entertainment)

NATION: Iroquois

IMAGE PORTRAYAL: Friendship; loyalty

SUMMARY: In this children's story, a boy named Omri finds a key that brings a plastic Indian named Little Bear to life. Omri goes back in time and learns about Little Bear's wife and his Iroquois tribe. Omrie also bring to life Boone, a cowboy from the past. Little Bear and Boone fight each other but then become friends. At the end Omri lets each of his little friends go back to their own eras.

CRITICS: Janet Maslin in the *New York Times* comments: "The film could use more playfulness, since Little Bear himself is also on the earnest side. (Hollywood seems in no mood to afford much playfulness to its sincere Indian characters these days.)" (July 14, 1999).

THE INDIAN LAND GRAB (Champion, 1910)

DIRECTOR: NA

SCREENPLAY: NA

CAST: NA

SPECS: Black & White; Silent

AVAILABILITY: NA

NATION: NA

IMAGE PORTRAYAL: Romance between a Native American man and a white woman

SUMMARY: A young man sent by his tribe to fight against land grabbing fails to secure the land rights of his tribe because he is tricked by the daughter of a crooked politician. After he returns home and is about to be punished for his failure, the daughter, who has repented and realizes she loves the young man, appears with a document protecting the tribe's land. Then he and the woman are married and live among his people.

INDIAN PAINT (Eagle American, 1965)

DIRECTOR: Norman Foster

SCREENPLAY: Norman Foster, based on the novel by Glen Balch

CAST: Johnny Crawford (Nishko), Jay Silverheels (Chief Hevatanu), Pat Hogan (Sutamakis), George Lewis (Nopawallo), Joan Hallmark (Amatula), Cinda Siler (Petala), Bill Blackwell (Satako), Al Doney (Latoso), Marshall Jones (Comanche Leader), Suzanne Goodman (Widow of Latoso), Warren L. Dodge (Second Comanche)

SPECS: 91 minutes; Color

AVAILABILITY: Amazon Instant Video

NATION: Arikara; Comanche; Snake

IMAGE PORTRAYAL: Friendship; honor

SUMMARY: Nishko, son of Hevatanu, the chief of the Arikara, rescues his white stallion from the Comanche. After many adventures, including being captured by the Comanche, Nishko allows his horse to go free, but the horse follows him when he returns to his people.

INDIAN ROMEO AND JULIET (Vitagraph, 1912)

DIRECTOR: Laurence Trimble

SCREENPLAY: Hal Reid, based on the play *Romeo and Juliet* by William Shakespeare

CAST: Wallace Reid (Oniatore/Romeo), Florence Turner (Ethona/Juliet), Henry T. Morey (Kowa/Paris), Hal Reid (Rohowaneh/Capulet), Adelaide Ober (Neok/Nurse), Hal Wilson (Oyenkwa/Friar)

SPECS: 1 reel; Black & White; Silent

AVAILABILITY: NA

NATION: Huron; Mohican

IMAGE PORTRAYAL: Romance between Native Americans

SUMMARY: Two lovers, one a Huron and the other a Mohican, die because of the hostility between the tribes.

INDIAN RUNNER'S ROMANCE (Biograph, 1909)

DIRECTOR: D. W. Griffith

SCREENPLAY: Stanner E. V. Taylor

CAST: Owen Moore (Blue Cloud), Mary Pickford (Blue Cloud's Wife), James Kirkwood, (the Cowboy), Mack Sennett (Indian)

SPECS: 11 minutes; Black & White; Silent

AVAILABILITY: NA

NATION: Sioux

IMAGE PORTRAYAL: Romance between Native Americans; vengeance

SUMMARY: A cowboy kidnaps the wife of Blue Cloud, a Sioux runner, and tortures her to make her tell the location of a hidden mine. Blue Cloud hunts him down, kills him, and brings his wife home.

CRITICS: A *Variety* critic comments on the acting: "Made-up Indians are usually a travesty, but in this case both in appearance and action the redskin is natural" (September 28, 1914).

THE INDIAN SERVANT (Great Northern, 1914)

DIRECTOR: D. W. Griffith

SCREENPLAY: NA

CAST: NA

SPECS: Black & White; Silent

AVAILABILITY: NA

NATION: NA

IMAGE PORTRAYAL: Native American as butt of humor

SUMMARY: This comedy makes fun of a Native American whose behavior is inappropriate in white society. Brought home to be a servant by a foreign diplomat, he takes bonnets from the heads of young women in a millinery shop, improperly flirts with them, and then almost wrecks the house of the diplomat when he paints himself and the children and does a war dance with them.

THE INDIAN SQUAW'S SACRIFICE (Motion Picture Distributors, 1910)

DIRECTOR: NA

SCREENPLAY: NA

CAST: NA

SPECS: 1 reel; Black & White; Silent

AVAILABILITY: NA

NATION: NA

IMAGE PORTRAYAL: Romance between a Native American woman and a white man

SUMMARY: The title character, Noweeta, nurses a white man back to health and then marries him. After they have a child, her husband meets a white woman he had loved before. When Noweeta realizes that her husband still loves the woman, she goes off to the woods and kills herself so that her husband will be free to marry the white woman.

INDIAN TERRITORY (Columbia, 1950)

DIRECTOR: John English

SCREENPLAY: Norman S. Hall

CAST: Gene Autry, James Griffith (the Apache Kid, a mixed-blood), Charles
    Stevens (Soma), Frank Lackteen (Indian), Chief Thundercloud (Indian), Chief
    Thundersky (Lookout), Chief Yowlachie (Indian)
SPECS: 70 minutes; Black & White
AVAILABILITY: DVD (Image Entertainment)
NATION: Apache
IMAGE PORTRAYAL: Attacks on a wagon train; friendship; mixed-blood Na-
    tive American; peace-loving chief
SUMMARY: Gene Autry brings to justice villains who have been selling guns to
    hostile warriors in the tribe of Gene's friend Soma. The young renegades make
    raids against the whites until Gene and the cavalry stop them. The Apache Kid
    starts out a villain but eventually saves Gene's life.

INDIAN UPRISING (Columbia, 1952)
DIRECTOR: Ray Nazarro
SCREENPLAY: Kenneth Gamet, Richard Schayer
CAST: George Montgomery (Captain McCloud), Miguel Inclan (Geronimo)
SPECS: 75 minutes; Color
AVAILABILITY: VHS (Good Time Home Video)
NATION: Apache
IMAGE PORTRAYAL: Native Americans as victims
SUMMARY: To get at gold on land, politicians and whites incite the Apache tribe
    to break a treaty brokered between Captain McCloud and Geronimo and to
    start a war. At the end, Geronimo is tricked and captured. McCloud apologizes
    and offers Geronimo his sword.
CRITICS: A *Variety* critic notes: "This basic good vs. evil motivation has been
    done before. As usual the hero is the peace keeper, the villains are the exploiters
    and the Indians are the losers" (December 26, 1952).

THE INDIAN WARS (Col. William F. Cody Historical Pictures, 1914)
DIRECTORS: Vernon Day, Theodore Wharton
SCREENPLAY: Charles King
CAST: William F. Cody (himself), Short Bull (Indian), Black Elk (Indian)
SPECS: 5 reels; Black & White; Silent
AVAILABILITY: NA
NATION: Plains tribes, including Cheyenne; Sioux
IMAGE PORTRAYAL: Attacks on soldiers
SUMMARY: This film chronicles the major battles, including Little Big Horn
    (Brownlow 1979, 224–35).
CRITICS: A *Moving Picture World* reviewer advises his readers to take children to
    the film "for an afternoon with the great leaders of our army, with great chiefs
    of our Indian tribes and two hours in the open world that has been made sacred
    by heroic blood of the nations fighting heroes" (September 12, 1914, 1500).

INJUN FENDER (Duke U. and Magic Tramp Midnight Opera Co., 1974)
DIRECTOR: Robert Cordier
SCREENPLAY: Robert Cordier
CAST: Dennis Campbell (Fender)
SPECS: 100 minutes; Color
AVAILABILITY: NA
NATION: NA
IMAGE PORTRAYAL: Contemporary Native American; troubled Native
    American
SUMMARY: Set in the late 1960s, this film tells the story of a Native American rock
    musician who takes out his frustrations in his songs and by killing white people.

THE INVADERS (Kay-Bee, 1912)
DIRECTORS: Francis Ford, Thomas H. Ince
SCREENPLAY: C. Gardiner Sullivan
CAST: William Eagle Shirt (Sioux Chief), Ann Little (Sky Star)
SPECS: 41 minutes; Black & White; Silent
AVAILABILITY: DVD (Alpha Home Entertainment; bonus on *The Sundown
    Trail*)
NATION: Sioux
IMAGE PORTRAYAL: Attack on a fort; romance between a Native American
    woman and a white man
SUMMARY: Sky Star, a young woman from the Chief's Sioux tribe, loves a sur-
    veyor who has come with other whites into her land and thus violates a treaty.
    In the following war and attack on a fort, she is killed.

IOLA'S PROMISE (Biograph, 1912)
DIRECTOR: D. W. Griffith
SCREENPLAY: Belle Taylor
CAST: Mary Pickford (Iola), Alfred Paget (Jack Harper)
SPECS: 18 minutes; Black & White; Silent
AVAILABILITY: NA
NATION: NA
IMAGE PORTRAYAL: Gratitude
SUMMARY: Discussed on page 14, this film, subtitled "How the Little Indian
    Maiden Paid Her Debt of Gratitude," tells the story of Iola, whom Alfred Paget,
    a prospector, rescues after she is captured. Later she repays his kindness by res-
    cuing his fiancée as her tribe is preparing to burn her at the stake. The white
    woman escapes, but Iola is fatally wounded after she tells Paget the location of
    a gold mine.

THE IRON HORSE (Fox, 1924)
DIRECTOR: John Ford

SCREENPLAY: Charles Kenyon, John Russell, Charles Darnton
CAST: Chief John Big Tree (Cheyenne Chief), Chief White Spear (Sioux Chief), Charles Stevens (Indian), Chief Eagle Wing (Indian)
SPECS: 150 minutes; Black & White; Silent
AVAILABILITY: DVD (20th Century Fox)
NATION: Cheyenne; Sioux
IMAGE PORTRAYAL: Attack on railroads; attack on settlers
SUMMARY: This film portrays the building of the western railroad lines. Hordes of warriors led by a Cheyenne chief (Chief Big Tree) and a Sioux chief (Chief White Spear) attack railroad workers and trains because they see the railroad lines as a threat to their way of life
CRITICS: A *Variety* reviewer notes that the film is a fine example of "the great theme of Indians and soldiers" (September 3, 1924).

THE IROQUOIS TRAIL (United Artists, 1950)
DIRECTOR: Phil Karlson
SCREENPLAY: Richard Schayer, based on the novels of James Fenimore Cooper
CAST: George Montgomery (Hawkeye), Monte Blue (Chief Sagamore), Sheldon Leonard (Chief Ogane), Iron Eyes Cody (Huron Indian), Troy Melton (Huron Brave), Chief Thundercloud (Ottawa Chief)
SPECS: 85 minutes; Black & White
AVAILABILITY: NA
NATION: Huron; Mohican; Ottawa
IMAGE PORTRAYAL: Attacks by hostile tribes; friendship; loyalty
SUMMARY: This film follows the exploits of Hawkeye and Sagamore, his faithful companion, as they fight warriors from the Huron and Ottawa tribes.

ISLAND OF THE BLUE DOLPHINS (Universal, 1964)
DIRECTOR: James B. Clark
SCREENPLAY: Jane Klove, Tedd Sherdeman, based on the novel by Scott O'Dell
CAST: Celia Millus (Karana), Larry Domasin (Ramo), Ann Daniel (Tutok), Carlos Romero (Chowig), Hal John Norman (Kimki)
SPECS: 93 minutes; Color
AVAILABILITY: DVD (Universal Studios)
NATION: Chumash
IMAGE PORTRAYAL: Native Americans as victims
SUMMARY: A Chumash girl, Karana, is abandoned for almost twenty years on an Aleutian island after villains kill her father, Chowig, and her brother, Ramo. She survives numerous hardships before missionaries rescue her.

IT STARTS WITH A WHISPER (Canada, 1993)
DIRECTORS: Ann Gronau, Shelley Niro
SCREENPLAY: Ann Gronau, Shelley Niro

CAST: Elijah Harper, Elizabeth Burning, Debra Doxater, Everly Miller, Elizabeth Doxater
SPECS: 27 minutes; Color
AVAILABILITY: DVD (Canada Filmmaker Distribution Center)
NATION: Iroquois; Six Nations
IMAGE PORTRAYAL: Contemporary First Nation people; troubled First Nation people
SUMMARY: A First Nation young woman, Shanna Sabbath, goes on a mythic journey to Niagara Falls guided by her aunts. She also encounters Elijah Harper, a much respected leader. Finally, her respect for her people past and present grows through this experience.
CRITICS: The Canada Filmmaker Distribution Center describes the film as "a celebration of the strength, wisdom, beauty and humor of Native women; of Native culture and people, surviving and thriving."

J

JACK MCCALL, DESPERADO (Columbia, 1953)
DIRECTOR: Sidney Salkow
SCREENPLAY: John O'Dea, David Chandler
CAST: George Montgomery (Jack McCall), Douglas Kennedy (Bill Hickok), Jay Silverheels (Red Cloud), Eugene Iglesias (Grey Eagle)
SPECS: 76 minutes; Color
AVAILABILITY: NA
NATION: Sioux
IMAGE PORTRAYAL: Friendship; loyalty; peace-loving chief
SUMMARY: Jack McCall rescues the son of Red Cloud, Grey Eagle, and becomes the friend of Red Cloud who does not want to wage war with those who want the gold on his land. Eventually, McCall kills the real villain, Bill Hickok.

JAMESTOWN (Pathe, 1923)
DIRECTOR: Edwin L. Hollywood
SCREENPLAY: Roswell Dague, Mary Johnston
CAST: Dolores Cassinelli (Pocahontas), Leslie Austin (John Rolfe)
SPECS: 40 minutes; Black & White; Silent
AVAILABILITY: NA
NATION: Algonquin
IMAGE PORTRAYAL: Romance between a Native American woman and a white man
SUMMARY: The colonists hold Pocahontas hostage to force her father, Powhatan, and his tribe to join them in fighting the Spanish. At the end, the mar-

riage of Pocahontas and John Rolfe brings peace between the tribe and the whites.

JEREMIAH JOHNSON (Warner Bros., 1972)
DIRECTOR: Sydney Pollack
SCREENPLAY: John Milius, Edward Anhalt, based on the novel *Mountain Man* by Vardis Fisher and the story "Crow Killer" by Raymond Thorp and Robert Bunker
CAST: Robert Redford (Jeremiah Johnson), Delie Bolton (Swan), Joaquin Martinez (Paint His Shirt Red), Richard Angarola (Chief Two-Tongues Lebeaux)
SPECS: 108 minutes; Color
AVAILABILITY: DVD (Warner Home Video)
NATION: Blackfoot; Crow
IMAGE PORTRAYAL: Romance between a Native American woman and a white man; vengeance
SUMMARY: Jeremiah Johnson; his wife, Swan, the daughter of Blackfeet chief, Two-Tongues Lebeaux; and his adopted son become a devoted and happy family. However, when he violates a Crow Burial ground by leading soldiers through it, the warriors of Paints His Shirt Red kill Swan and the boy. After Johnson takes revenge by killing many Crow, Paints His Shirt Red finally makes peace with him.
CRITICS: A *Variety* critic notes that the film provides "a newer look at Indian-white relations, without branding either as good or bad but of differing, yet clear-cut, cultures that could have existed side by side with some understanding" (May 10, 1972).

JIM THORPE, ALL AMERICAN (Warner Bros., 1951)
DIRECTOR: Michael Curtiz
SCREENPLAY: Douglas Morrow, Everett Freeman, Vincent X. Flaherty, based on the memoir by Jim Thorpe with Russell Birdwell
CAST: Burt Lancaster (Jim Thorpe), Charles Bickford (Pop Warner), Phyllis Thaxter (Margaret Miller), Jack Big Head (Little Boy), Dick Wesson (Ed Guyac), Nestor Paiva (Hiram Thorpe), Al Mejia (Louis Tewanema)
SPECS: 107 minutes; Black & White
AVAILABILITY: DVD (Warner Home Video)
NATION: Fox; Sauk
IMAGE PORTRAYAL: Romance between a Native American man and a white woman
SUMMARY: This film tells the story of Jim Thorpe, the Sauk and Fox athlete from Oklahoma who became a star in baseball, football, and Olympic field and track. After the loss of his 1912 Olympic medals, the decline of his professional football career, the death of his son, and divorce from his wife, Margaret Miller,

he is reduced to driving a dump truck. However, encouraged by his favorite coach, Pop Warner, he finally comes back to a productive life by teaching young athletes.

JIMMY P: PSYCHOTHERAPY OF A PLAINS INDIAN (Why Not Productions, 2013)

DIRECTOR: Arnaud Desplechin

SCREENPLAY: Arnaud Desplechin, Kent Jones, Julie Peyr, based on the poem "Tribal Ceremony" by Sherman Alexie and the book *Reality and Dreams* by George Devereux,

CAST: Benicio Del Toro (Jimmy Picard), Mathieu Amalric (Georges Devereux), A Martinez (Bear Willie Claw), Gary Farmer (Jack), Jennifer Podemski (Doll), Michael Greyeyes (Allan)

SPECS: 117 minutes; Color

AVAILABILITY: DVD (MPI Home Video); Amazon Instant Video

NATION: Blackfoot

IMAGE PORTRAYAL: Contemporary Native American; troubled Native American

SUMMARY: Jimmy P, a member of the Blackfoot tribe, struggles with psychological problems as a veteran of World War Two and works with a psychologist who has some knowledge of Native American culture. The issues Jimmy faced growing up as a Native American are only hinted at.

CRITICS: *Chicago Sun Times* critic Matt Zoller Seitz comments: "Although it would of course have been preferable for the character to have been played by a Native American (del Toro is Puerto Rican), the actor compensates by rejecting the noble savage and 'Big Chief' clichés handed down by American films, even comparatively sensitive ones. He creates a character who's just an ordinary American war veteran who happens to be Native American, and who's grappling to make sense of his present-tense troubles, his battlefield experience and his childhood pain as any white hero would" (February 14, 2014).

THE JINGLE DRESS (Lodge Pole Films, 2014)

DIRECTOR: William Eigen

SCREENPLAY: William Eigen

CAST: Chaske Spencer (John Red Elk), Stacey Thunder (Elsie Red Elk), Steve Reevis (Buff), Kimberly Guerrero (Janet Red Elk), S'Nya Sanchez-Hohenstein (Rose Red Elk)

SPECS: 98 minutes; Color

Availability: NA

NATION: Ojibwa

IMAGE PORTRAYAL: Contemporary Native Americans; troubled Native Americans

SUMMARY: After hearing that their uncle is dead, John Red Elk and his family move from their northern Minnesota reservation to the big city of Minneapolis where they struggle with city life. After the mother of the family makes a jingle dress for her daughter, Rose, and she dances in it, they come to a better understanding of their tribal traditions.

JOE PANTHER (Artist's Creation, 1976)
DIRECTOR: Paul Krasny
SCREENPLAY: Dale Eunson, based on the novel by Zachary Ball
CAST: Ray Tracey (Joe Panther), A Martinez (Billy Tiger), Ricardo Montalban (Turtle George), Gem Thorpe Osceola (Tommy Panther), Monika Ramirez (Jenny Rainbow), Lois Red Elk (Joe's mother)
SPECS: 110 minutes; Color
AVAILABILITY: VHS (Warner Home Video)
NATION: Seminole
IMAGE PORTRAYAL: Contemporary Native American; troubled Native American; wise elder
SUMMARY: Joe Panther, a Seminole who fights alligators, his friend, Billy Tiger, and Turtle George, a wise man who gives the two young men advice, try to find their place in society.
CRITICS: A *Variety* critic notes that "where the film fudges is in the simplistic treatment of Indians' struggles with white society. . . . The problem is much more complex than the film's rosy resolution makes it seem" (November 3, 1976).

JOHNNY RENO (Paramount, 1966)
DIRECTOR: R. G. Springsteen
SCREENPLAY: R. Steve Fisher, Andrew Craddock
CAST: Dana Andrews (Johnny Reno), Lyle Bettger (Jess Yates), Paul Daniel (Chief Little Bear), Rodd Redwing (Indian Brave)
SPECS: 83 minutes; Color
AVAILABILITY: DVD (Paramount Home Video); Amazon Instant Video
NATION: NA
IMAGE PORTRAYAL: Attack on a town; romance between a Native American man and a white woman; vengeance
SUMMARY: When Chief Little Bear finds out that his son was killed for loving a white woman, his warriors attack a town and take revenge on the killers, henchmen of Jess Yates. Johnny Reno who was falsely accused as the killer is innocent and is spared by the tribe.

JOHNNY TIGER (Universal, 1966)
DIRECTOR: Paul Wendkos
SCREENPLAY: Thomas Blackburn, Paul Crabtree, Philip Wylie, based on the story "Tiger on the Outside" by R. John Hugh

CAST: Chad Everett (Johnny Tiger), Ford Rainey (Sam Tiger), Pamela Melendez (Shalonee), Robert Taylor (George Dean), Brenda Scott (Barbara Dean)
SPECS: 102 minutes; Color
AVAILABILITY: VHS (Spotlite Video)
NATION: Seminole
IMAGE PORTRAYAL: Mixed-blood Native American; romance between a mixed-blood Native American man and a white woman
SUMMARY: Johnny Tiger, a mixed-blood Seminole and grandson of Chief Sam Tiger, is caught between a white teacher, George Dean, who wants him to educate himself so he can teach his people new ways, and his grandfather, who wants him to be a traditional Seminole. Johnny chooses education, marries the teacher's daughter, Barbara Dean, and promises his dying grandfather to use his knowledge to help his people as their new chief.

JOURNEY THROUGH ROSEBUD (GFS, 1972)
DIRECTOR: Tom Gries
SCREENPLAY: Albert Ruben
CAST: Robert Forster (Frank), Kristoffer Tabori (Danny), Victoria Racimo (Shirley)
SPECS: 93 minutes; Color
AVAILABILITY: NA
NATION: Sioux
IMAGE PORTRAYAL: Contemporary Native Americans; drunkenness; mixed-blood Native American; romance between a mixed-blood Native American woman and a white man; troubled Native Americans; vengeance
SUMMARY: A hip draft dodger, Danny, drifts onto the Rosebud Sioux Reservation and makes friends with Frank, an alcoholic and rebellious Vietnam vet. He also falls in love with Shirley, the activist ex-wife of Frank. After learning of the problems on the reservation and witnessing the suicide of Frank, he gives up and moves on.
CRITICS: A *Newsweek* critic notes that "these sentimentalized Indians seem no more real, arouse little more compassion than the ones who used to bite the dust in the B Westerns" (April 24, 1972, 89).

JOURNEY TO SPIRIT ISLAND (Seven Wonders Enter., 1988)
DIRECTOR: Laszlo Pal
SCREENPLAY: Laszlo Pal, Crane Webster
CAST: Bettina Bush (Maria), Maria Antoinette Rogers (Jimmy Jim), Tony Acierto (Hawk), Tarek McCarthy (Klim), Harry McCarthy (Tribal Chairman), Lester Greene (Tipskin)
SPECS: 93 minutes; Color
AVAILABILITY: VHS (United American Video)
NATION: Nahkut

IMAGE PORTRAYAL: Contemporary Native American; wise elder

SUMMARY: Discussed on page 55, this film tells the story of Maria, a teenage Native American who, along with her brother, Klim, and two white friends, stops the development of the sacred island into a resort, which is the idea of a greedy college-educated Native American, Hawk. With the special help of her grandmother, Jimmy Jim, Maria finds her true tribal identity.

JUSTICE OF THE FAR NORTH (Columbia, 1925)
DIRECTOR: Norman Dawn

SCREENPLAY: Norman Dawn

CAST: Arthur Jasmine (Umluk), Marcia Manon (Wamba), Winter Blossom (Nootka), Charles Reisner (Mike Burke)

SPECS: 57 minutes; Black & White; Silent

AVAILABILITY: NA

NATION: Eskimo

IMAGE PORTRAYAL: Romance between a Native American woman and a white man; romance between Native Americans

SUMMARY: Umluk, an Eskimo, returns to his igloo to find that the woman he is to marry, Wamba, has been enticed away by Mike Burke. Umluk follows them and struggles to get Wamba back, but ends up marrying Nootka, her faithful and loving sister, who has been kidnapped by Mike Burke.

K

THE KENTUCKIAN (Biograph, 1908)
DIRECTOR: Wallace McCutcheon

SCREENPLAY: Stanner E. V. Taylor, based on a play by Augustus Marvin

CAST: NA

SPECS: Black & White; Silent

AVAILABILITY: NA

NATION: NA

IMAGE PORTRAYAL: Romance between a Native American woman and a white man

SUMMARY: A rich young man goes west, is wounded, and is nursed back to health by a Native American woman. He marries her and they have a son. Later, she realizes her husband is struggling with the question of whether to return to the East with a socially unacceptable spouse and is ready to give up his inheritance. She understands his dilemma and solves his problem by committing suicide.

A KENTUCKY PIONEER (Selig, 1910)
DIRECTOR: NA

SCREENPLAY: NA

CAST: NA

SPECS: Black & White; Silent
AVAILABILITY: NA
NATION: NA
IMAGE PORTRAYAL: Friendship; loyalty
SUMMARY: Warlike braves kidnap a woman betrothed to a young pioneer, but she escapes with the help of a young Native American woman from their tribe. As the hostiles pursue both women into a town and attack, other settlers come to the rescue.
CRITICS: A *Variety* critic notes that the contrasting of a noble character to her savage tribe is "a theme displayed many times before" (October 8, 1910).

KID RODELO (Paramount, 1966)
DIRECTOR: Richard Carlson
SCREENPLAY: Jack Natteford, based on the novel by Louis L'Amour
CAST: Don Murray (Kid Rodelo), Jose Villasante (Cavalry Hat)
SPECS: 91 minutes; Black & White
AVAILABILITY: Amazon Instant Video
NATION: Yaqui
IMAGE PORTRAYAL: Attacks on settlers
SUMMARY: Cavalry Hat, a Yaqui chief, kills the villain and pursues Kid Rodelo, who finally kills Cavalry Hat.

KILIAN'S CHRONICLE: THE MAGIC STONE (Capstone Film, 1995)
DIRECTOR: Pamela Berger
SCREENPLAY: Pamela Berger
CAST: Christopher Johnson (Kilian), Amelia G. Bingham (Medicine Woman), Jonah Ming Lee (Kitchi), Gino Montesinos (Contacook), Jorge Cano Moreno (Indian), Eva Kim (Turtle)
SPECS: 95 minutes; Color
AVAILABILITY: DVD (Lara Classics)
NATION: NA (Ancient East Coast tribe)
IMAGE PORTRAYAL: Friendship; loyalty; romance between Native American woman and a white man
SUMMARY: Kilian lands on the east coast of pre-America and becomes friends with Contacook, a powerful young warrior; Kitchi, a young Native American who sees Kilian as his guardian; and Turtle, with whom he eventually falls in love. These members of a pre-Algonquin tribe, and the Medicine Woman, teach Kilian the ways of their tribe, to which he is much attracted. Later, they seek to protect him when a Viking lands and pursues him.

KING OF THE GRIZZLIES (Buena Vista, 1970)
DIRECTOR: Ron Kelly

SCREENPLAY: Jack Speirs, Rod Peterson, Norman Wright, based on the book *The Biography of a Grizzly* by Ernest Thompson

CAST: John Yesno (Moki), Chris Wiggins (the Colonel)

SPECS: 93 minutes; Color

AVAILABILITY: DVD (Walt Disney Studios Home Entertainment)

NATION: Cree

IMAGE PORTRAYAL: Wise elder

SUMMARY: Moki, a young Cree, who feels a connection to the grizzlie, Wahb, protects the Colonel from a now full-grown bear, which he had cared for as a cub.

KING OF THE STALLIONS (Monogram, 1942)

DIRECTOR: Edward Finney

SCREENPLAY: Sherman L. Lowe, Arthur St. Claire

CAST: Chief Thundercloud (Hahawi), Rick Vallin (Sina-Oga/Little Coyote), Barbara Felker (Princess Telenika), Chief Yowlachie (Chief Matapotan), J. W. Cody (Manka)

SPECS: 63 minutes; Black & White

AVAILABILITY: DVD (Alpha Home Entertainment—as *Code of the Red Man*); Amazon Instant Video

NATION: NA

IMAGE PORTRAYAL: Wise elder

SUMMARY: Two exiles from their tribe, old Hahawi and young Little Coyote meet in the forest and the old man teaches the youth how to communicate with animals. Eventually Little Coyote makes friends with the wild stallion (Nakoma) and realizes that the horse is not the evil stallion that has been helping the villains rustle wild horses. Nakoma defeats the evil stallion and Hahawi and Little Coyote return to their tribe.

KINGS OF THE SUN (United Artists, 1963)

DIRECTOR: J. Lee Thompson

SCREENPLAY: Elliot Arnold, James R. Webb

CAST: Yul Brynner (Chief Black Eagle), George Chakiris (Balam), Shirley Anne Field (Ixchel), Richard Basehart (Ah Min), Leo Gordon (Hunac Ceel)

SPECS: 108 minutes; Color

AVAILABILITY: DVD (20th Century Fox Home Entertainment); Blu-ray (Kino Lorber); Amazon Instant Video

NATION: Mayan

IMAGE PORTRAYAL: Romance between Native Americans

SUMMARY: After the evil Hunac Ceel attacks the Mayans led by Balam, they flee to the north where they are confronted by the tribe of Black Eagle. However, when Balam saves the life of Black Eagle even though he has fallen in love with Balam's woman, Ixchel, the tribes unite and defeat the warriors of Hunac Ceel.

During that battle, Black Eagle dies while saving the life of Balam, who is then reunited with Ixchel.

KISSED BY LIGHTNING (Independent, 2009)
DIRECTOR: Shelley Niro
SCREENPLAY: Ken Chubb
CAST: Kateri Walker (Mavis Dogblood), Rachelle White Wind Arbez (Kateri), Sean Baek (Sun-June), Eric Schweig (Bug), Michael Grey Eyes (Jessie Lightning). Monique Mojica (Grandmother)
SPECS: 89 minutes; Color
AVAILABILITY: NA
NATION: Mohawk
IMAGE PORTRAYAL: Romance between First Nation people
SUMMARY: Mavis Dogblood, a Mohawk artist, struggles to get over the death of her husband, Jessie Lightning. After a visit to her Grandmother, she marries her friend and lover, Bug.

KIT CARSON (Bison, 1910)
DIRECTOR: Fred J. Balshofer
SCREENPLAY: NA
CAST: NA
SPECS: 1 reel; Black & White; Silent
AVAILABILITY: NA
NATION: NA
IMAGE PORTRAYAL: Attack on settlers
SUMMARY: Kit Carson rescues settlers from an attack.
CRITICS: A *Moving Picture World* reviewer notes that the film has all the "features of the old time frontier story" including "a surrounding band of whooping redskins, showering arrows into the stockade" (September 10, 1910, 575).

KIT CARSON (Paramount, 1928)
DIRECTOR: Alfred L. Werker, Lloyd Ingraham
SCREENPLAY: Frederic Hatton, Francis Marion, Paul Powell
CAST: Fred Thomson (Kit Carson), Dorothy King (Sing-in the-Clouds)
SPECS: 8 reels; Black & White; Silent
AVAILABILITY: NA
NATION: NA
IMAGE PORTRAYAL: Friendship; vengeance
SUMMARY: When Kit Carson rescues Sing-in-the-Clouds, the daughter of a Blackfeet chief, the tribe declares their lasting friendship. Later, when a villain kills the young woman, Carson takes revenge by throwing him off a cliff into the Blackfeet circle of death.

KIT CARSON (United Artists, 1940)
DIRECTOR: George B. Seitz
SCREENPLAY: George Bruce, Evelyn Wells
CAST: Jon Hall (Kit Carson), Iron Eyes Cody (Indian), Al Kikume (Indian Chief), Chief Many Treaties (Indian Chief), Jay Silverheels (Indian), Charles Soldani (Indian)
SPECS: 97 minutes; Black & White
AVAILABILITY: DVD (Henstooth Video); Amazon Instant Video
NATION: Shoshone
IMAGE PORTRAYAL: Attack on wagon train; attack on soldiers
SUMMARY: Kit Carson, who leads soldiers and a wagon train to California, fights off an attack by the Shoshone tribe.

KIVALINA OF THE ICE LANDS (B.C.R. Productions, 1925)
DIRECTOR: Earl Rossman
SCREENPLAY: Earl Rossman, based on his story
CAST: Kivalina (Kivalina), Aguvaluk (Native Guide)
SPECS: 60 minutes; Black & White; Silent
AVAILABILITY: NA
NATION: Eskimo
IMAGE PORTRAYAL: Romance between Native Americans
SUMMARY: In this film with an all-Eskimo cast, Aguvaluk, who is told by the witch doctor that he must kill forty seals and a silver fox before he can marry Kivalina, accomplishes the feats and marries his beloved.
CRITICS: A *Variety* critic notes that in this film "all the various activities of the tribe are depicted" (July 1, 1925).

L

LAND RAIDERS (Columbia, 1970)
DIRECTOR: Nathan Juran
SCREENPLAY: Ken Pettus, Jesse Lasky Jr., Pat Silver
CAST: Telly Savalas (Vincente Cardenas)
SPECS: 101 minutes; Color
AVAILABILITY: DVD (Sony Pictures Home Entertainment); Amazon Instant Video
NATION: Apache
IMAGE PORTRAYAL: Attack on a town; attacks on wagon train; vengeance
SUMMARY: When Vince Cardenas incites Apaches to war to decrease the value of their land and then frames them for the killing of an Indian agent, they retaliate by attacking a stagecoach. In what becomes a cycle of revenge, the whites attack the Apache village and the Apaches attack the town.

LARAMIE (Columbia, 1949)

DIRECTOR: Ray Nazarro

SCREENPLAY: Barry Shipman

CAST: Charles Starrett (Steve Holden/Durango Kid), Shooting Star (Chief Eagle), Rodd Redwing (Indian Lookout), Jay Silverheels (Running Wolf), Robert J. Wilke (Cronin)

SPECS: 55 minutes; Black & White

AVAILABILITY: DVD (Sony Pictures Home Entertainment)

NATION: NA

IMAGE PORTRAYAL: Native Americans as victims

SUMMARY: Steve Holden saves the day after gun-runners, led by Cronin, try to start a war with the tribe of Chief Eagle and his son, Running Wolf by murdering Chief Eagle.

THE LAST FRONTIER (Columbia, 1955)

DIRECTOR: Anthony Mann

SCREENPLAY: Philip Yordan, Russell S. Hughes, based on the novel *The Gilded Rooster* by Richard Emery Roberts

CAST: Victor Mature (Jed Cooper), Manuel Donde (Red Cloud), Guillermo Calles (Spotted Elk), Pat Hogan (Mungo)

SPECS: 98 minutes; Color

AVAILABILITY: DVD (Sony Pictures Home Entertainment); Amazon Instant Video

NATION: NA

IMAGE PORTRAYAL: Attack on a fort; attack on soldiers

SUMMARY: After being provoked by an excessive officer, the tribes of Red Cloud and Spotted Elk attack the soldiers and drive them back to their fort. With the fire power of cannons and the help of Jed Cooper and his friend, Mungo, the soldiers survive the attack.

CRITICS: A *New York Times* critic notes that in the early films the soldiers were noble and the Native Americans were savage until "civilization" reversed the images, and in this film "civilization has got so far that everybody is ornery" (December 8, 1955).

THE LAST HUNT (MGM, 1956)

DIRECTOR: Richard Brooks

SCREENPLAY: Richard Brooks, based on the novel by Richard Lott

CAST: Robert Taylor (Charlie Gilson), Debra Paget (Indian Girl), Ed Lonehill (Spotted Hand), Russ Tamblyn (Jimmy O'Brien)

SPECS: 108 minutes; Color

AVAILABILITY: DVD (Warner Archive Collection); Amazon Instant Video

NATION: NA

IMAGE PORTRAYAL: Mixed-blood Native American; romance between a Native American woman and a white man

SUMMARY: A malicious buffalo hunter, Charlie Gilson, vies with his companion for the affections of a young Native American woman. After beating a mixed-blood, Jimmy O'Brien, and killing young Spotted Hand, the evil hunter finally freezes to death.

LAST OF THE COMANCHES (Columbia, 1953)
DIRECTOR: Andre De Toth
SCREENPLAY: Kenneth Gamet
CAST: John War Eagle (Black Cloud), Johnny Stewart (Little Knife), Broderick Crawford (Sgt. Matt Trainor)
SPECS: 85 minutes; Color
AVAILABILITY: VHS (Good Times Video)
NATION: Comanche
IMAGE PORTRAYAL: Attack on settlers; attack on soldiers; friendship; loyalty
SUMMARY: When the Comanches of Black Cloud attack a group of whites trapped in an abandoned mission, Little Knife, who had earlier been helped by whites, shows his gratitude and friendship by helping the Cavalry and Sgt. Trainor to rescue them.

LAST OF THE DOGMEN (Savoy Pictures, 1995)
DIRECTOR: Tab Murphy
SCREENPLAY: Tab Murphy
CAST: Tom Berenger (Lewis Gates), Barbara Hershey (Professor Sloan, a professor of Native American history), Steve Reevis (Yellow Wolf), Helen Calahasen (Wife of Yellow Wolf), Dawn Lavand (Indian Girl), Sidel Standing Elk (Lean Bear), Eugene Blackbear (Spotted Elk)
SPECS: 118 minutes; Color
AVAILABILITY: DVD (HBO Home Video)
NATION: Cheyenne
IMAGE PORTRAYAL: Friendship; loyalty
SUMMARY: A trapper, Lewis Gates leads Professor Sloan to a remote valley in the wilderness where surviving Cheyenne warriors live. After becoming friends of the tribe, they prevent another massacre of the tribe. In the film, Professor Sloan says, "Well, they (Native Americans) gave us romance, myths, legends. They gave us a history. The Indians shaped the character of our whole nation." Gates, referring to past massacres, replies, "We picked a hell of a way to say thank you, didn't we."

LAST OF THE LINE (Bison, 1914)
DIRECTOR: Jay Hunt
SCREENPLAY: Thomas H. Ince, C. Gardiner Sullivan
CAST: Joe Goodboy (Gray Otter), Sessue Hayakawa (Tiah)
SPECS: 20 minutes; Black & White; Silent
AVAILABILITY: NA

NATION: NA
IMAGE PORTRAYAL: Drunkenness
SUMMARY: Gray Otter, who returns from college a hopeless alcoholic, joins some renegades who break a treaty made by his father. Because of this he is forced to kill his son, Tiah, though he does it in a way that makes the young man look like a hero.

THE LAST OF THE MOHICANS (Associated Producers, 1920)

DIRECTORS: Clarence Brown, Maurice Tourneur
SCREENPLAY: Robert Dillon, based on the novel by James Fenimore Cooper
CAST: Wallace Beery (Magua), Alan Roscoe (Uncas), Harry Lorraine (Hawkeye), Theodore Lorch (Chingachgook)
SPECS: 73 minutes; Black & White; Silent
AVAILABILITY: DVD (Sling Shot Entertainment); Amazon Instant Video
NATION: Huron; Mohican
IMAGE PORTRAYAL: Attack on settlers; friendship; hostile warrior; loyalty
SUMMARY: Hawkeye and his friends, Chingachgook and Uncas, struggle with the evil Magua, who leads a vicious attack on the fort.
CRITICS: A *Variety* reviewer comments on the violence of the attack: "Someone gets firewater to the redskins and they take part in an orgy of blood and suggested rapine that was terrible enough in print, but unspeakable in a picture" (January 7, 1920).

THE LAST OF THE MOHICANS (United Artists, 1936)

DIRECTOR: George Seitz
SCREENPLAY: Philip Dunne, John L. Balderston, Paul Perez, Daniel Moore, based on the novel by James Fenimore Cooper
CAST: Randolph Scott (Hawkeye), Bruce Cabot (Magua), Robert Barrat (Chingachgook), Philip Reed (Uncas)
SPECS: 91 minutes; Black & White
AVAILABILITY: DVD (Henstooth Video); Amazon Instant Video
NATION: Huron; Mohican
IMAGE PORTRAYAL: Attack on a fort; attack on settlers; friendship; hostile warrior; loyalty
SUMMARY: Discussed on page 19, Hawkeye and his friends, Chingachgook and Uncas, rescue the daughters of Colonel Munro. After the Colonel agrees to surrender, Magua attacks the soldiers evacuating the fort. At the end, Magua kills Uncas, whose lover, Cora, jumps off the cliff to join him in death, and then Chingachgook kills Magua, after which Hawkeye and his lover, Alice, try to console Chingachgook.

THE LAST OF THE MOHICANS (Morgan Creek Productions, 1992)

DIRECTOR: Michael Mann

SCREENPLAY: John L Balderston, Paul Perez, Daniel Moore, Michael Mann, Christopher Crowe, based on the novel by James Fenimore Cooper

CAST: Daniel Day-Lewis (Hawkeye), Madeleine Stowe (Cora Munro), Jodhi May (Alice Munro), Russell Means (Chingachgook), Eric Schweig (Uncas), Wes Studi (Magua)

SPECS: 112 minutes; Color

AVAILABILITY: DVD (20th Century Fox Home Entertainment); Amazon Instant Video

NATION: Huron; Mohican

IMAGE PORTRAYAL: Friendship; loyalty; romance between a Native American man and a white woman

SUMMARY: Discussed on page 60, Hawkeye and his noble friends Chingachgook and Uncas protect the Munro sisters from the French and savage Magua. After Magua and hostile Hurons capture the sisters and a British soldier, Hawkeye shows his bravery under torture and mercifully shoots the soldier who is being tortured by the Huron. Then Magua kills Uncas and Chingachgook avenges his son by killing Magua.

LAST OF THE REDMEN (Columbia, 1947)

DIRECTOR: George Sherman

SCREENPLAY: Herbert Dalmas, George H. Plympton, based on the novel *The Last of the Mohicans* by James Fenimore Cooper

CAST: Michael O'Shea (Hawkeye), Buster Crabbe (Magua), Rick Vallin (Uncas), War Eagle (Indian), Chief Many Treaties (Iroquois Chief), Little Plant (Indian), Eagle Saenz (Indian), Chief Sky Eagle (Indian), Shooting Star (Indian)

SPECS: 79 minutes; Color

AVAILABILITY: VHS (Sony Pictures Home Entertainment)

NATION: Huron; Iroquois; Mohican

IMAGE PORTRAYAL: Attacks on settlers; friendship; hostile warrior; loyalty

SUMMARY: Hawkeye and Uncas escort children through the wilderness and are attacked by Magua and his hostile Huron.

THE LAST OUTPOST (Paramount, 1951)

DIRECTOR: Lewis R. Foster

SCREENPLAY: Daniel Mainwaring, Winston Miller, George Worthing Yates, David Lang

CAST: Ronald Reagan (Capt. Vance Britten), Charles Brunner (Apache-Victorio), Iron Eyes Cody (Mangas Coloradas), Charles Evans (Chief Grey Cloud), John War Eagle (Geronimo), Chief Yowlachie (Cochise)

SPECS: 89 minutes; Color

AVAILABILITY: DVD (Ivy Films); Amazon Instant Video

NATION: Apache

IMAGE PORTRAYAL: Native Americans as victims; vengeance

SUMMARY: When a white man kills Grey Cloud, the warriors of Geronimo, Victorio, Mangas Coloradas, and Cochise prepare an attack, but are defeated when the Cavalry attacks them.

THE LAST ROUND-UP (Columbia, 1947)

DIRECTOR: John English
SCREENPLAY: Jack Townley, Earle Snell
CAST: Gene Autry, Trevor Bardette (Indian Chief), Iron Eyes Cody (Indian), J. W. Cody (Indian), Art Dillard (Indian), Alex Montoya (Indian Charlie), Rodd Redwing (Louie), Jay Silverheels (Sam Luther), Billy Wilkerson (Indian Herder)
SPECS: 77 minutes; Black & White
AVAILABILITY: DVD (Image Entertainment)
NATION: NA
IMAGE PORTRAYAL: Native Americans as victims; paternalism
SUMMARY: To stop a possible uprising, Gene Autry gets new and fertile lands for a tribe led by a Chief played by Trevor Bardette whose valuable land and water had been appropriated by the townspeople.

LAUGHING BOY (MGM, 1934)

DIRECTOR: W. S. Van Dyke
SCREENPLAY: John Colton, John Lee Mahin, based on the novel by Oliver La Farge
CAST: Ramon Novarro (Laughing Boy), Lupe Velez (Slim Girl), Chief Thunderbird (Laughing Boy's Father), Catalina Rambula (Laughing Boy's Mother), Harlan Knight (Wounded Face), William B. Davidson (Hartshorne), Philip Armenta (Yellow Singer), Deer Spring (Jesting Squaw's Son), Pellicana (Red Man), Sidney Bracey (White Feather), and other Native American actors
SPECS: 79 minutes; Black & White
AVAILABILITY: NA
NATION: Navajo
IMAGE PORTRAYAL: Romance between a Native American woman and a white man; romance between Native Americans
SUMMARY: This film tells the tragic love story of Slim Girl and Laughing Boy, a young Navajo. After the two are married, Slim Girl, who had been raised by whites, takes a white lover, Hartshorne, and plays him against her husband. Finally Laughing Boy finds her in a house near the railroad tracks where she meets her lover, and he kills her with an arrow intended for the man she is with.

THE LAW RIDES AGAIN (Monogram, 1943)

DIRECTOR: Alan James
SCREENPLAY: Frances Kavanaugh

CAST: Ken Maynard (U.S. Marshall), Hoot Gibson (U.S. Marshall), Emmett Lynn (Eagle Eye, the Scout), Chief Thundercloud (Thundercloud), Chief Many Treaties (Chief Barking Fox), Kenneth Harlan (John Hampton)
SPECS: 58 minutes; Black & White
AVAILABILITY: DVD (Alpha Video); Amazon Instant Video
NATION: NA
IMAGE PORTRAYAL: Native Americans as victims
SUMMARY: Ken Maynard and Hoot Gibson bring to justice a crooked Indian agent, John Hampton, who is starting trouble with the tribe of Thundercloud and Barking Fox. Eagle Eye finds the evidence that shows the evil intent of Hampton.

LAWLESS PLAINSMEN (Columbia, 1942)
DIRECTOR: William Berke
SCREENPLAY: Luci Ward
CAST: Charles Starrett (Steve Rideen), Stanley Brown (Tascosa), Nick Thompson (Chief Ochella)
SPECS: 59 minutes; Black & White
AVAILABILITY: DVD (VCI Entertainment; on "Charles Starrett Western Double Feature Vol. 1")
NATION: Pima
IMAGE PORTRAYAL: Attack on wagon trains
SUMMARY: The Pima tribe of Ochella attacks a wagon train because the whites killed one of their people, Tascosa, son of Ochella. The hero, Steve Rideen, tries to make peace and is captured, but the cavalry comes to the rescue.
CRITICS: A *Variety* critic notes that "the story's a standard one of the unscrupulous white man making a deal with the Indians to attack a wagon train" (June 10, 1942).

THE LEGEND OF THE LONE RANGER (Universal, 1981)
DIRECTOR: William A. Fraker
SCREENPLAY: Ivan Goff, Ben Roberts, Michael Kane, William Roberts, Gerald B. Derloshon
CAST: Klinton Spilsbury (The Lone Ranger), Michael Horse (Tonto), Christopher Lloyd (Butch Cavendish)
SPECS: 98 minutes; Color
AVAILABILITY: DVD (Lion's Gate Home Entertainment); Amazon Instant Video
NATION: Comanche
IMAGE PORTRAYAL: Friendship; loyalty
SUMMARY: After villains kill his mother, John Reid, aka the Lone Ranger, grows up with Tonto's tribe, and the two young friends become blood brothers. Later

Tonto rescues the Lone Ranger, and they, in turn, rescue President Grant from the evil Butch Cavendish gang.

CRITICS: A *Variety* critic notes that the "Indians are presented in a more modernist, revisionist light" (May 20, 1981).

LEGEND OF WOLF MOUNTAIN (Majestic Entertainment, 1992)
DIRECTOR: Craig Clyde
SCREENPLAY: Craig Clyde, James Hennessy
CAST: Bo Hopkins (Ranger Steven Haynes), Don Shanks (Simcoe-the Wolf Spirit)
SPECS: 91 minutes; Color
AVAILABILITY: DVD (Halestone Distribution)
NATION: NA
IMAGE PORTRAYAL: Native American spirit
SUMMARY: In this family movie, the ancient spirit of the wolf that lives on the mountain takes the form of a Native American, Simcoe, and protects some children who are being pursued by escaped convicts. Near the end of the film, the Native American spirit man gives one of the kids a historical sketch of his people and their attitudes towards the environment.

LEGENDS OF THE FALL (Tristar, 1995)
DIRECTOR: Edward Zwick
SCREENPLAY: Susan Shilliday, William D. Wittliff, based on the novella by Jim Harrison
CAST: Brad Pitt (Tristan), Gordon Tootoosis (One Stab), Tantoo Cardinal (Pet), Karina Lombard (Isabel Two)
SPECS: 133 minutes; Color
AVAILABILITY: DVD (Sony Pictures Home Entertainment); Amazon Instant Video
NATION: Cree
IMAGE PORTRAYAL: Friendship; loyalty; romance between Native American women and white men
SUMMARY: After the family moves to Montana, One Stab, the patriarch's Cree friend, narrates their story. After he loses his true love, Tristan, the wild son who reveres Native American life, marries Isabel Two, the daughter of Pet, the Cree wife of a white man. The complicated story of the family works its way to a sad ending.

THE LESSER BLESSED (Entertainment One, 2012)
DIRECTOR: Anita Doron
SCREENPLAY: Anita Doron, based on the novel by Richard Van Camp
CAST: Joel Evans (Larry Sole), Benjamin Bratt (Jed), Kiowa Gordon (Johnny Beck), Chloe Rose (Juliet Hope), Tamara Podemski (Verna Sole)

SPECS: 86 minutes; Color
AVAILABILITY: DVD (Monterey Video); Amazon Instant Video
NATION: Tlicho
IMAGE PORTRAYAL: Contemporary First Nation people; troubled First Nation people
SUMMARY: This Canadian film tells the story of Larry Sole, a member of the Tlicho tribe, who lives in a remote community and struggles with alienation as a high school student. He searches for his identity as a tribal person and a citizen of the contemporary world.

THE LIGHT IN THE FOREST (Buena Vista, 1958)
DIRECTOR: Herschel Daugherty
SCREENPLAY: Lawrence Edward Watkin, based on the novel by Conrad Richter
CAST: James MacArthur (True Son/Johnny Butler), Joseph Calleia (Chief Cuyloga), Rafael Campos (Half Arrow), Dean Fredericks (Niskitoon)
SPECS: 83 minutes; Color
AVAILABILITY: VHS (Walt Disney Home Video)
NATION: NA
IMAGE PORTRAYAL: White man adopted by Native Americans
SUMMARY: The Delaware of Chief Cuyloga capture a white boy, whom they adopt as True Son. He lives happily with the tribe until a treaty forces them to return him to his natural parents. Unhappy with white society at first, he finally learns that there are good and bad people in both cultures.

LITTLE BIG HORN (Lippert, 1951)
DIRECTOR: Charles Marquis Warren
SCREENPLAY: Charles Marquis Warren, Harold Shumate
CAST: Lloyd Bridges (Capt. Phillip Donlin), Rodd Redwing (Cpl. Arika)
SPECS: 86 minutes; Black & White
AVAILABILITY: DVD (VCI Entertainment)
NATION: Crow; Sioux
IMAGE PORTRAYAL: Attack on soldiers
SUMMARY: As a cavalry squad that includes Cpl. Arika, a Crow scout, tries to get to Custer to warn him of the impending Sioux ambush, warriors kill all of them before they can complete their mission.

LITTLE BIG MAN (National General, 1970)
DIRECTOR: Arthur Penn
SCREENPLAY: Calder Willingham, based on the novel by Thomas Berger
CAST: Dustin Hoffman (Little Big Man/Jack Crabb), Chief Dan George (Old Lodge Skins), Aimee Eccles (Sunshine), Robert Little Star (Little Horse), Cal

Bellini (Younger Bear), Ruben Moreno (Shadow That Comes in Sight), Steve Shemayne (Burns Red in the Sun)

SPECS: 139 minutes; Color

AVAILABILITY: DVD (Paramount Home Video)

NATION: Cheyenne; Sioux

IMAGE PORTRAYAL: Attack on soldiers; peace-loving chief; romance between a Native American woman and a white man

SUMMARY: Discussed on page 43, this film deals with the relationship between a white man, Little Big Man, and his surrogate father, Old Lodge Skins, the peace-loving chief of the Cheyenne who finally joins the Sioux for the Battle of Little Big Horn.

CRITICS: *Chicago Sun Times* critic Roger Ebert comments: "Penn has allowed the Indians in the film to speak ordinary, idiomatic English. Most movie Indians have had to express themselves with an 'um' at the end of every other word: 'Swap-um wampum plenty soon,' etc. The Indians in 'Little Big Man' have dialogue reflecting the idiomatic richness of Indian tongues; when Old Lodge Skins simply refers to Cheyennes as 'the Human Beings,' the phrase is literal and meaningful and we don't laugh" (January 1, 1970).

LITTLE DOVE (Indieflix, 2008)

DIRECTOR: Brandy Rainey Amstel

SCREENPLAY: Brandy Rainey Amstel, Steve Barcik

CAST: Indiana Adams (Little Dove), Joseph David (Running Bear), Mark A. Hernandez (Big Wolf), John O'Dell (Talks Alot)

SPECS: 12 minutes; Color

AVAILABILITY: DVD (Set It Off! Productions)

NATION: Apache; Comanche

IMAGE PORTRAYAL: Romance between Native Americans

SUMMARY: An Apache girl, Little Dove, who is married, falls in love with a Comanche warrior. Their love goes against their tribal beliefs. All the dialogue is in the Apache and Comanche languages.

LITTLE DOVE'S ROMANCE (Bison, 1911)

DIRECTOR: Fred J. Balshofer

SCREENPLAY: NA

CAST: Red Wing (Little Dove), Charles Inslee (Burns), James Young Deer (Native American)

SPECS: 1 reel; Black & White; Silent

AVAILABILITY: NA

NATION: NA

IMAGE PORTRAYAL: Romance between a Native American woman and a white man; romance between Native Americans

SUMMARY: Little Dove falls in love with a white man, but after he explains that he cannot marry her, she agrees to marry the Native American who loves her.

CRITICS: A *Moving Picture World* critic comments that the film shows "something of Indian manners and customs . . . in a way that shows a sympathetic understanding of the Indian mind" (September 9, 1911, 692).

LITTLE HIAWATHA (United Artists, 1937)
DIRECTOR: David Hand
SCREENPLAY: NA
CAST: NA
SPECS: 9 minutes; Color
AVAILABILITY: NA
NATION: NA
IMAGE PORTRAYAL: Hiawatha story
SUMMARY: Little Hiawatha arrives in a canoe and all the animals watching laugh when he falls into a water hole. He chases them with his wet pants falling down and a grasshopper spits in his face. After more animal laughter, Hiawatha decides to shoot a rabbit, but can't bring himself to do it and breaks his bow and arrows. This pleases the animals and they protect him when a mother bear chases him. Finally Hiawatha paddles away as the animals wave farewell.

THE LITTLE INDIAN MARTYR (Selig, 1912)
DIRECTOR: Colin Campbell
SCREENPLAY: Lanier Bartlett
CAST: Roy Clark (Chiquito), Tom Santschi (Padre Juan)
SPECS: 1 reel; Black & White; Silent
AVAILABILITY: NA
NATION: NA
IMAGE PORTRAYAL: Friendship; loyalty
SUMMARY: A rebellious mission tribe tries to make Chiquito, a boy from the tribe, promise to kill Padre Juan, a kindly priest for whom the boy works. However, Chiquito remains loyal, warns the priest, and then is killed by his own people.

LO, THE POOR INDIAN (Kalem, 1910)
DIRECTOR: NA
SCREENPLAY: NA
CAST: NA
SPECS: Black & White; Silent
AVAILABILITY: NA
NATION: NA
IMAGE PORTRAYAL: Native American as victim

SUMMARY: A man who doesn't know or understand the laws of the white man is put in jail for stealing a horse to save the lives of his wife and child.

CRITICS: A *Moving Picture World* reviewer notes that the film "should arouse a sense of the injustice which has been meted out to unfortunate Indians on the supposed intention of following the white man's ideas of justice" (April 9, 1910, 553).

THE LONE RANGER (Warner Bros., 1956)

DIRECTOR: Stuart Heisler

SCREENPLAY: Herb Meadow

CAST: Clayton Moore (Lone Ranger), Jay Silverheels (Tonto), Michael Ansara (Angry Horse), Frank DeKova (Chief Red Hawk), Lyle Bettger (Reece Kilgore)

SPECS: 86 minutes; Color

AVAILABILITY: DVD (VCI Entertainment); Amazon Instant Video

NATION: NA

IMAGE PORTRAYAL: Friendship; loyalty

SUMMARY: In this first of two feature films based on the popular TV series, the Lone Ranger and Tonto bring to justice an evil rancher, Kilgore, who is fomenting trouble between the whites and Chief Red Hawk so that he can take silver from the tribe's land. Warriors kidnap the villain's daughter but the Lone Ranger fights Angry Horse and rescues her.

THE LONE RANGER (Walt Disney Pictures, 2013)

DIRECTOR: Gore Verbinski

SCREENPLAY: Justin Haythe, Ted Elliott, Terry Rossio

CAST: Johnny Depp (Tonto), Armie Hammer (John Reid/Lone Ranger), William Fichtner (Butch Cavendish), Saginaw Grant (Chief Big Bear)

SPECS: 149 minutes; Color

AVAILABILITY: DVD and Blu-ray (Walt Disney Home Entertainment); Amazon Instant Video

NATION: Comanche

IMAGE PORTRAYAL: Attack on railroads; friendship; justice; loyalty; vengeance

SUMMARY: This film is discussed on page 78. Tonto narrates this film that turns the Lone Ranger story upside down. Tonto is the hero who wants justice because the Butch Cavendish gang hoodwinked him in his youth. Chief Big Bear is the Chief of the Comanche who are defeated near the end.

THE LONE RANGER AND THE LOST CITY OF GOLD (United Artists, 1958)

DIRECTOR: Lesley Selander

SCREENPLAY: Eric Freiwald, Robert Schaefer, George W. Trendle

CAST: Clayton Moore (The Lone Ranger), Jay Silverheels (Tonto), John Miljan (Chief Tomache), Maurice Jara (Redbird), Belle Mitchell (Caulama), Lisa Montell (Paviva), Dean Fredericks (Dr. James Rolfe)
SPECS: 81 minutes; Color
AVAILABILITY: DVD (VCI Entertainment)
NATION: NA
IMAGE PORTRAYAL: Friendship; loyalty; romance between Native Americans
SUMMARY: When villains try to gain control of a tribal mine, the Lost City of Gold, the Lone Ranger and Tonto thwart the plot and return the mine to the tribe of Chief Tomache, Redbird, and Caulama. The beautiful Paviva and Dr. James Rolfe, whom she loves and who is really a Native American, also benefit from the Lone Ranger and Tonto's help.

LONE STAR (American Film Co., 1916)
DIRECTOR: Edward Sloman
SCREENPLAY: Kenneth B. Clarke
CAST: William Russell (Lone Star)
SPECS: 5 reels; Black & White; Silent
AVAILABILITY: NA
NATION: NA
IMAGE PORTRAYAL: Native American as victim
SUMMARY: On a Nebraskan reservation, Lone Star, who gains fame as a surgeon is scorned by his tribe for following white ways and rejected by the whites because he is a Native American.

LONELY HEART (Affiliated Dist., 1921)
DIRECTOR: John O'Brien
SCREENPLAY: NA
CAST: Kay Laurel (Lonely Heart), Escamilio Fernandez (Peter Blue Fox)
SPECS: 50 minutes; Black & White; Silent
AVAILABILITY: NA
NATION: NA
IMAGE PORTRAYAL: Romance between a Native American woman and a white man
SUMMARY: In the setting of the Oklahoma oil fields, Lonely Heart, who is betrothed to Peter Blue Fox, falls in love with a white man. When Blue Fox is murdered, she is accused, but is then exonerated when another member of her tribe confesses. At the end, she marries the white man.

THE LONELY TRAIL (Primex Pictures, 1922)
DIRECTOR: NA
SCREENPLAY: NA
CAST: Fred Beauvais (Pierre Benoit)

SPECS: Black & White; Silent
AVAILABILITY: NA
NATION: NA
IMAGE PORTRAYAL: Vengeance
SUMMARY: Pierre, a Native American guide, rescues a white woman from the villain. When Pierre realizes that the villain is also the one who had seduced and deserted his sister, he takes his revenge.

THE LONERS (Fanfare, 1972)
DIRECTOR: Sutton Roley
SCREENPLAY: John Lawrence, Barry Sandler
CAST: Dean Stockwell (Stein), Hal John Norman (Stein's Father)
SPECS: 79 minutes; Color
AVAILABILITY: NA
NATION: Navajo
IMAGE PORTRAYAL: Contemporary Native Americans; mixed-blood Native American; troubled Native Americans
SUMMARY: Stein, a mixed-blood Navajo, joins two other motorcyclists, gets in trouble, and escapes with them to the reservation, where his father is saddened by his son's rejection of the Navajo ways. When the young men leave the reservation, they are killed.

LOVE IN A TEPEE (Imperial, 1911)
DIRECTOR: NA
SCREENPLAY: NA
CAST: NA
SPECS: 150 mm (split reel); Black & White; Silent
AVAILABILITY: NA
NATION: NA
IMAGE PORTRAYAL: Drunkenness; romance between a Native American woman and a white man
SUMMARY: Bad Eye wants his daughter, Hyacinth, to marry a Mexican whom she detests. He is done in by his drinking when the Mexican thinks that Bad Eye, who is lying under a blanket in a drunken stupor, is the daughter and carries him away. This allows his daughter to go away with the cowboy she really loves.

M

MA AND PA KETTLE (Universal, 1949)
DIRECTOR: Charles Lamont
SCREENPLAY: Al Lewis, Herbert Margolis, Lou Morheim

CAST: Marjorie Main (Ma Kettle), Percy Kilbride (Pa Kettle), Lester Allen (Geo-duck), Chief Yowlachie (Crowbar)
SPECS: 76 minutes; Black & White
AVAILABILITY: DVD (Universal Studios Home Entertainment)
NATION: NA
IMAGE PORTRAYAL: Native Americans as butts of humor
SUMMARY: Crowbar and Geoduck are the humorous stoic Native American friends of Pa. These characters, portrayed by various actors, appear in most of the Ma and Pa Kettle movies.

MACKENNA'S GOLD (Columbia, 1969)
DIRECTOR: J. Lee Thompson
SCREENPLAY: Carl Foreman, based on the novel by Heck Allen
CAST: Gregory Peck (MacKenna), Omar Sharif (Colorado), Julie Newmar (Hesh-Ke), Ted Cassidy (Hachita), Camilla Sparv (Inga)
SPECS: 128 minutes; Color
AVAILABILITY: DVD (Sony Pictures Home Entertainment); Amazon Instant Video
NATION: Apache
IMAGE PORTRAYAL: Attack on settlers; romance between a Native American woman and a white man
SUMMARY: As MacKenna searches for gold in a valley sacred to the Apache, a woman from the tribe, Hesh-Ke, falls in love with him and competes with a white woman, Inga, for his affection. When Apache warriors attack and cause a rock slide, Hesh-Ke, her companion, Hachita, and everyone but the hero and his woman die in the valley.

THE MAID OF NIAGARA (Pathe, 1910)
DIRECTOR: Theodore Wharton
SCREENPLAY: Pierce Kingsley
CAST: NA
SPECS: 195 minutes; Black & White; Silent
AVAILABILITY: NA
NATION: NA
IMAGE PORTRAYAL: Romance between Native Americans
SUMMARY: When his beloved Red Doe is sacrificed to the Spirit of the Falls, Esoomet, a young Iroquois, drowns himself so he can be with her in the afterworld.

THE MAIDEN OF THE PIE-FACED INDIANS (Edison, 1911)
DIRECTOR: NA
SCREENPLAY: NA

CAST: John R. Cumpson (Little Fauntleroy—a Cowboy Hero), Rolinda Bainbridge (Ha-Ha Minnie—the Indian Maiden), Robert Brower (Indian Chief)
SPECS: 150 minutes (split reel); Black & White; Silent
AVAILABILITY: NA
NATION: NA
IMAGE PORTRAYAL: Kidnapping; torture
SUMMARY: A savage tribe captures the Cowboy Hero and tortures him before Ha-Ha Minnie rescues him.

MAJOR DUNDEE (Columbia, 1965)
DIRECTOR: Sam Peckinpah
SCREENPLAY: Harry Julian Fink, Oscar Saul, Sam Peckinpah
CAST: Charlton Heston (Major Dundee), Michael Pate (Sierra Charriba)
SPECS: 123 minutes; Color
AVAILABILITY: DVD (Sony Pictures Home Entertainment); Amazon Instant Video
NATION: Apache
IMAGE PORTRAYAL: Attacks on settlers
SUMMARY: The hero and his soldiers pursue into Mexico the Apache band of Sierra Charriba, who have kidnapped children and massacred settlers.
CRITICS: Eugene Archer in the *New York Times* comments: "This particular West is an ugly place, and the director's camera searches intractably for its grimmest aspects" (April 8, 1965).

A MAN CALLED HORSE (National General, 1970)
DIRECTOR: Elliot Silverstein
SCREENPLAY: Jack DeWitt, Dorothy M. Johnson
CAST: Richard Harris (John Morgan/A Man Called Horse), Judith Anderson (Buffalo Cow Head), Manu Tupou (Yellow Hand), Corrina Tsopel (Running Deer), Eddie Little Sky (Black Eagle), Lina Marin (Thorn Rose), Tamara Garina (Elk Woman), Terry Leonard (Striking Bear), Iron Eyes Cody (Medicine Man), Tom Tyon (Medicine Man)
SPECS: 114 minutes; Color
AVAILABILITY: DVD (Paramount Home Video)
NATION: Shoshone; Sioux
IMAGE PORTRAYAL: Romance between a Native American woman and a white man
SUMMARY: Discussed on page 44, this film tells the story of John Morgan, an Englishman captured by the Sioux tribe of Yellow Hand. Finally, he is adopted by the tribe, becomes a warrior, and falls in love with Running Deer, who is killed in the final battle with the Shoshone.

MAN IN THE WILDERNESS (Warner Bros., 1971)
DIRECTOR: Richard Sarafian
SCREENPLAY: Jack DeWitt

CAST: Richard Harris (Zachary Bass)
SPECS: 104 minutes; Color
AVAILABILITY: DVD (Warner Home Video); Amazon Instant Video
NATION: NA
IMAGE PORTRAYAL: Friendship; loyalty
SUMMARY: A friendly Native American Chief helps Zachary Bass, after he survives a vicious bear attack. They deal with the villains who had left Bass to die.

THE MAN WHO PAID (Producer's Security Corp., 1922)
DIRECTOR: Oscar Apfel
SCREENPLAY: Marion Brooks
CAST: Frank Montgomery (Songo)
SPECS: 5 reels; Black & White; Silent
AVAILABILITY: NA
NATION: NA
IMAGE PORTRAYAL: Vengeance
SUMMARY: The tribe of Songo helps an evil trapper kidnap a white woman. However, when they find out he has double-crossed them, they kill him.

THE MANITOU (Avco Embassy, 1978)
DIRECTOR: William Girdler
SCREENPLAY: William Girdler, Jon Cedar, Thomas Pope, based on the novel by Graham Masterson
CAST: Michael Ansara (John Singing Rock), Susan Strasberg (Karen Tandy), Burgess Meredith (Dr. Snow)
SPECS: 104 minutes; Color
AVAILABILITY: DVD (Anchor Bay Entertainment)
NATION: Sioux
IMAGE PORTRAYAL: Wise elder
SUMMARY: John Singing Rock, a contemporary Sioux medicine man, works with Dr. Snow and exorcises a four-hundred-year-old demon spirit that has attached itself to a tumor on the back of Karen Tandy.

MANY RIVERS TO CROSS (MGM, 1955)
DIRECTOR: Roy Rowland
SCREENPLAY: Harry Brown, Guy Trosper, Steve Frazee
CAST: Robert Taylor (Bushrod Gentry), Eleanor Parker (Mary Stuart Cheme), Ralph Moody (Sandak), Abel Fernandez (Slangoh)
SPECS: 94 minutes; Color
AVAILABILITY: DVD (Warner Home Video), Amazon Instant Video
NATION: Shawnee
IMAGE PORTRAYAL: Attack on settlers
SUMMARY: Bushrod rescues Mary, who is about to be killed by the Shawnee tribe of Sandak and Slangoh.

MAP OF THE HUMAN HEART (Miramax Films, 1993)
DIRECTOR: Vincent Ward
SCREENPLAY: Louis Nowra, Vincent Ward
CAST: Jason Scott Lee (Avik), Anne Parillaud (Albertine), Clotilde Courau (Rainee), Jayco Pitseolak (Avik's Grandmother), Rebecca Vevee (Inuit Cook), Josape Kopalee (Inuit Elder)
SPECS: 109 minutes; Color
AVAILABILITY: DVD (Echo Bridge Home Entertainment); Amazon Instant Video
NATION: Inuit; Metis
IMAGE PORTRAYAL: Mixed-blood Native American; romance between First Nation people
SUMMARY: In a film concerned with the suffering and displacement of native Canadian peoples, a mixed-blood Inuit named Avik falls in love with a Metis, Albertine. After an intense relationship as teenagers, they are separated for years. Finally, they meet again during World War II and have a child together, only to be separated again forever. Their whole story is seen in a flashback from the perspective of an aged and sick Avik.
CRITICS: Janet Maslin in the *New York Times* notes that "The film lingers a while in the Eskimos' world, observing such sights as a wizened old woman with dotted lines tattooed into the folds of her face, who plays a primitive accordion to celebrate the killing of a seal. (One of the film's undeniable strengths is the eerie authenticity of its Eskimo episodes)" (April 23, 1993).

MARIE ANNE (Canadian Film Production, 1978)
DIRECTOR: Martin Walters
SCREENPLAY: George Salverson, Marjorie Morgan
CAST: Andree Pelletier (Marie-Ann Lagimodiere) Tantoo Cardinal (Tantou), Gordon Tootoosis (Chief Many Horses), Bill Dowson (Factor Bird), John Juliani (Jean-Baptiste Lagiomodiere)
SPECS: 88 minutes; Color
AVAILABILITY: NA
NATION: NA
IMAGE PORTRAYAL: Romance between a Native American woman and a white man
SUMMARY: Marie-Anne appeases her husband, John-Baptiste, and his hot-blooded native common-law wife, Tantou, by allowing herself to be adopted by Chief Many Horses. Both women have babies, but her adoption keeps Tantou at bay.

THE MASSACRE (Biograph, 1914)
DIRECTOR: D. W. Griffith
SCREENPLAY: D. W. Griffith

CAST: Wilfred Lewis (Stephen), Alfred Paget (Indian Chief)
SPECS: 20 minutes; Black & White; Silent
AVAILABILITY: NA
NATION: NA
IMAGE PORTRAYAL: Attack on a wagon train; vengeance
SUMMARY: Warriors who are avenging an attack on their village circle a wagon train and kill everyone but a woman and her child before the cavalry comes to the rescue.

MASSACRE (First National, 1934)
DIRECTOR: Alan Crosland
SCREENPLAY: Ralph Block, Sheridan Gibney, Robert Gessner
CAST: Richard Barthelmess (Chief Joe Thunderhorse), Ann Dvorak (Lydia), James Eagles (Adam Thunderhorse), Chief John Big Tree (Indian Judge), Iron Eyes Cody (Indian), Noble Johnson (Indian Leader), George Reed (Chief Black Star), Chief Standing Bear (Indian), Chief Thunderbird (Indian)
SPECS: 70 minutes; Black & White
AVAILABILITY: NA
NATION: Sioux
IMAGE PORTRAYAL: Native Americans as victims; romance between Native Americans
SUMMARY: Joe Thunderhorse, a college-educated Sioux, rides in a Wild West show and flirts with white women. However, he finds a new sense of responsibility when his father asks him to help his tribe fight villains who are exploiting them on their reservation. Joe Thunderhorse goes to Washington, wins back his tribe's rights, and marries an educated Native American woman, Lydia.
CRITICS: A *Variety* critic comments on the presence of the lead white actor, Richard Barthelmess: "Worst of all, when surrounded by other big chiefs who are Indians on the up and up, he doesn't look like an Indian any more than Jimmy Durante looks like a Chinaman" (January 23, 1934).

MASSACRE (20th Century Fox, 1956)
DIRECTOR: Louis King
SCREENPLAY: D. D. Beauchamp, Fred Freiberger, William Tunberg
CAST: Dane Clark (Ramon), Jaimie Fernandez (Juan Pedro)
SPECS: 76 minutes; Color
AVAILABILITY: NA
NATION: Yaqui
IMAGE PORTRAYAL: Attack on outlaws
SUMMARY: Supplied with guns by treacherous smugglers, Yaqui warriors attack and kill the smugglers and a group of Mexican soldiers who are pursuing the smugglers.

MASSACRE CANYON (Columbia, 1954)
DIRECTOR: Fred F. Sears
SCREENPLAY: David Lang
CAST: Philip Carey (Lt. Richard Faraday), Steve Ritch (Black Eagle), Chris Alcaide (Running Horse)
SPECS: 66 minutes; Black & White
AVAILABILITY: NA
NATION: Apache
IMAGE PORTRAYAL: Attack on a wagon train
SUMMARY: Led by Black Eagle and Running Horse, Apache warriors attack a wagon train carrying rifles.

MASSACRE RIVER (Monogram, 1949)
DIRECTOR: John Rawlins
SCREENPLAY: Louis Stevens
CAST: Guy Madison (Larry Knight), Iron Eyes Cody (Chief Yellowstone)
SPECS: 78 minutes; Black & White
AVAILABILITY: DVD (Warner Archive Collection)
NATION: NA
IMAGE PORTRAYAL: Attack on soldiers (provoked)
SUMMARY: A tribe led by Chief Yellowstone, who believes in peace but is provoked to war, fights several battles with soldiers from an army post.

MASTERSON OF KANSAS (Columbia, 1954)
DIRECTOR: William Castle
SCREENPLAY: Douglas Heyes
CAST: George Montgomery (Bat Masterson), Jay Silverheels (Yellow Hawk)
SPECS: 73 minutes; Color
AVAILABILITY: DVD (Sony Pictures Choice Collection)
NATION: Kiowa
IMAGE PORTRAYAL: Friendship; loyalty; peace-loving chief
SUMMARY: Bat Masterson helps his peace-loving friend, Yellow Hawk, who wants peace even after villains try to steal the Kiowas' rich grasslands.

MAVERICK (Warner Bros., 1994)
DIRECTOR: Richard Donner
SCREENPLAY: William Goldman
CAST: Mel Gibson (Bret Maverick), Graham Greene (Joseph)
SPECS: 127 minutes; Color
AVAILABILITY: DVD (Warner Home Video); Amazon Instant Video
NATION: NA
IMAGE PORTRAYAL: Friendship
SUMMARY: Joseph, who leads a rambling band of warriors, is a friend of the hero. A con man (or trickster) himself, Joseph helps Maverick to hoodwink

his adversaries by having his men pretend to be hostile warriors. In the process of this trick, and another one in which he lets a Russian nobleman shoot at an "Indian," he manages to outdo his friend in the business of conning. Joseph also offers some snide comments about the film-inspired stereotypes of his people.

CRITICS: Caryn James in the *New York Times* comments, "Among the most elaborate and entertaining is a sequence in which Graham Greene plays Joseph, a smooth-operating Indian who masquerades as a me-want-wampum type of guy. When Joseph and his tribe, in full war paint, surround Maverick, Annabelle and Coop, it's a good thing Maverick can speak Joseph's Indian dialect" (May 20, 1994).

MCLINTOCK! (United Artists, 1963)
DIRECTOR: Andrew V. McLaglen
SCREENPLAY: James Edward Grant
CAST: John Wayne (George W. McLintock), Perry Lopez (Davey Elk), Michael Pate (Puma)
SPECS: 127 minutes; Color
AVAILABILITY: DVD and Blu-ray (Paramount Home Video); Amazon Instant Video
NATION: Comanche
IMAGE PORTRAYAL: Attack on settlers; friendship; Native Americans as victims
SUMMARY: McLintock takes up the cause of Davey Elk and Puma, Comanches just released from prison, and eventually keeps the peace between the tribe and the ranchers.

THE MCMASTERS (Chevron, 1970)
DIRECTOR: Alf Kjellin
SCREENPLAY: Harold Jacob Smith
CAST: Brock Peters (Benjie), David Carradine (White Feather), Nancy Kwan (Robin)
SPECS: 90 minutes; Color
AVAILABILITY: DVD (Reel Enterprises); Amazon Instant Video
NATION: NA
IMAGE PORTRAYAL: Endangered South American natives; friendship; loyalty; romance between a Native American woman and a black man
SUMMARY: White Feather gives his sister, Robin, to Benjie, who had helped him and his tribe. After some troubled times, Robin and Benjie are married. At the end, her brother's tribe rescues the couple in a time of distress.

MEDICINE MAN (Hollywood Pictures, 1992)
DIRECTOR: John McTiernan
SCREENPLAY: Tom Schulman, Sally Robinson

CAST: Sean Connery (Dr. Robert Campbell), Lorraine Bracco (Dr. Rae Crane), Rodolfo De Alexandre (Tanaki), Francisco Tsiren Tsere Rereme (Jahausa), Angelo Barra Moreira (Medicine Man)
SPECS: 106 minutes; Color
AVAILABILITY: DVD (Hollywood Pictures Home Entertainment); Amazon Instant Video
NATION: NA
IMAGE PORTRAYAL: Contemporary Native Americans; friendship; loyalty; Native Americans as victims
SUMMARY: Dr. Campbell, who is living with the noble Amazonian tribe of Tanaki and Jahausa, whose language he knows and with whom he has a good-natured friendship, finds a flower and insects that promise a cure for cancer. Near the end, however, road builders burn the village and destroy his research. After this, the doctor follows the tribal Medicine Man deeper into the jungle to continue his research and enjoy the company of his female colleague, Dr. Crane.

MEEK'S CUTOFF (Oscilloscope Pictures, 2010)
DIRECTOR: Kelly Reichardt
SCREENPLAY: Jonathan Raymond
CAST: Michelle Williams (Emily Tetherow), Bruce Greenwood (Stephen Meeks), Rod Rondeaux (The Indian)
SPECS: 104 minutes; Color
AVAILABILITY: DVD (Oscilloscope Laboratories); Amazon Instant Video
NATION: NA
IMAGE PORTRAYAL: Friendship; loyalty
SUMMARY: In this very realistic film, a wagon train, which includes Emily Tetherow loses faith in their white guide, Stephen Meek, and reluctantly follows a Native American guide whom they have captured.
CRITICS: *Chicago Sun Times* critic Roger Ebert comments on the Native American guide: "The Indian, first seen alone on a high ledge watching them, is portrayed in a particular way. Unlike the fierce closeups of Indian warriors we've been trained on in many Westerns, he is an enigmatic man, self-contained, observing, mostly held in the film's usual long and medium shots. We don't know what he's thinking. Why should we? In circa 1845, the two cultures were alien to each other" (May 11, 2011).

THE MENDED LUTE (Biograph, 1909)
DIRECTOR: D. W. Griffith
SCREENPLAY: Stanner E. V. Taylor
CAST: Florence Lawrence (Rising Moon), Frank Powell (Chief Great Elk Horn), Owen Moore (Little Bear), James Kirkwood (Standing Rock), Red Wing (Indian), James Young Deer (Indian)

SPECS: 11 minutes; Black & White; Silent
AVAILABILITY: NA
NATION: Sioux
IMAGE PORTRAYAL: Romance between Native Americans
SUMMARY: Sioux warriors, Little Bear and Standing Rock are vying for Chief
  Great Elk Horn's daughter, Rising Moon, and her father gives her to the high-
  est bidder, Standing Rock, the one she doesn't love. After she leaves her new
  husband for Little Bear, the two are captured and are about to be burned at the
  stake when Standing Rock, impressed by their love and bravery, sets them free.

MESQUITE'S GRATITUDE (Kalem, 1911)
DIRECTOR: NA
SCREENPLAY: NA
CAST: Marin Sais (Mesquite), Vincente Howard (Slim), Harry Haskins (The In-
  dian Chief)
SPECS: 1 reel; Black & White; Silent
AVAILABILITY: NA
NATION: NA
IMAGE PORTRAYAL: Romance between a Native American woman and a
  white man
SUMMARY: A cowboy, Slim, stops other ranch hands from taunting Mesquite.
  Later she helps him in a time of need, and he falls in love with her. At the end,
  he goes to her village and asks her to marry him.

THE MINE WITHIN THE IRON DOOR (Principal Pictures, 1924)
DIRECTOR: Sam Wood
SCREENPLAY: Hope Loring, Louis D. Lighton, Mary Alice Scully, Arthur F.
  Statter, based on the novel by Harold Bell Wright
CAST: Pat O'Malley (Hugh Edwards), Robert Frazer (Natachee)
SPECS: 80 minutes; Black & White; Silent
AVAILABILITY: NA
NATION: NA
IMAGE PORTRAYAL: Friendship; gratitude
SUMMARY: Hugh Edwards rescues Natachee, an educated man who has grown
  to hate whites because of their prejudice toward him. Natachee repays the man
  by showing him the location of a gold mine and by killing the villain.

MIRACLE AT SAGE CREEK (American World Pictures, 2005)
DIRECTOR: James Intveld
SCREENPLAY: Thadd Turner
CAST: David Carradine (Ike), Wes Studi (Chief Thomas), Marsam Holden (Sam-
  uel Red Eagle)
SPECS: 90 minutes; Color

AVAILABILITY: DVD (Screen Media); Amazon Instant Video
NATION: NA
IMAGE PORTRAYAL: Friendship
SUMMARY: In this Christmas movie, the Franklin and Red Eagle families strug-
gle to accept each other, but are brought together by a miracle.

THE MISSING (Sony Pictures Entertainment, 2003)
DIRECTOR: Ron Howard
SCREENPLAY: Ken Kaufman, based on the novel *The Last Ride* by Thomas
Eidson
CAST: Cate Blanchett (Magdalena Gilkeson), Tommy Lee Jones (Samuel Jones/
Chaa-duu-ba-its-iidan), Eric Schweig (Pesh-Chidin/El Brujo), Jay Tavare
(Kayitah), Steve Reevis (Two Stone), Simon R. Baker (Honesco), Deryle J.
Lujan (Naazhaao)
SPECS: 137 minutes; Color
AVAILABILITY: DVD (Sony Pictures Home Entertainment); Amazon Instant
Video
NATION: Apache
IMAGE PORTRAYAL: Attack on settlers; friendship; hostile warrior
SUMMARY: When Magdalena's husband is killed and her daughter kidnapped
by the renegade Apache, Pesh-Chidin, she and her father, Samuel Jones, join
Kayitah and his son, Honesco, to rescue the daughter. They finally catch the
vicious renegade and Samuel, Kayitah, Honesco, Pesh-Chidin, and Naazhaao
all die at the end. The character of Pesh-Chidin is a throwback to the vicious
savages of the earlier westerns.

THE MISSION (Warner Bros., 1986)
DIRECTOR: Roland Joffe
SCREENPLAY: Robert Bolt
CAST: Robert De Niro (Roderigo Mendoza), Jeremy Irons (Father Gabriel),
Bercelio Moya (Indian Boy), Sigifredo Ismare (Witch Doctor), Asuncion On-
tiveros (Indian Chief)
SPECS: 125 minutes; Color
AVAILABILITY: DVD (Warner Home Video); Amazon Instant Video
NATION: Guarani
IMAGE PORTRAYAL: Noble Native South Americans
SUMMARY: A Spanish Catholic priest, Father Gabriel, and a slave trader, Men-
doza who is converted and joins the religious order grow to respect and love the
local Guarani tribe led by a kind and peaceful chief. At the end, evil Portuguese
and Spanish forces provoke the tribe and the two heroes die in the fighting.

MOHAWK (20th Century Fox, 1956)
DIRECTOR: Kurt Neumann

SCREENPLAY: Maurice Geraghty, Milton Krims

CAST: Scott Brady (Jonathan Adams), Rita Gam (Onida), Neville Brand (Rokhawah), Mae Clarke (Minikah), Tommy Cook (Keoga), Ted de Corsia (Chief Kowanen), Michael Granger (Mohawk Priest)

SPECS: 80 minutes; Color

AVAILABILITY: DVD (Synergy Entertainment); Amazon Instant Video

NATION: Iroquois; Mohawk; Tuscarora

IMAGE PORTRAYAL: Attack on a fort; peace-loving chief; romance between a Native American woman and a white man

SUMMARY: Joined by a villain, Rokhawah and his hostile Mohawk warriors start a war by killing Keoga, the son of the wise, peace-loving Chief Kowanen and his wife, Miniah. Jonathan stops the hostility by killing Rokhawah in an attack on the fort. After the beautiful Onida falls in love with Jonathan, he goes to live with her.

A MOHAWK'S WAY (Biograph, 1910)

DIRECTOR: D. W. Griffith

SCREENPLAY: Stanner E. V. Taylor

CAST: Claire Mc Dowell (Indian Mother), Edith Haldeman (Indian Child), Dorothy Davenport (Indian), Francis J. Grandon (Medicine Man), Guy Hedlund (Indian), Jeanie Macpherson (Indian), Charles Hill Mailes (Indian)

SPECS: 17 minutes; Black & White; Silent

AVAILABILITY: NA

NATION: Mohawk

IMAGE PORTRAYAL: Gratitude; loyalty

SUMMARY: Mohawks wronged by a white woman's evil husband are about to kill the woman. At the last moment, a woman from the tribe, whose baby had earlier been saved by the white woman, comes to her rescue.

CRITICS: A contemporary author comments on the noble character in this film: "Here is the noble red man of James Fenimore Cooper. . . the Indian of romance who, as some people claim, never existed, but who is nevertheless the ideal type for story telling" (Friar and Friar 1972, 117).

THE MOHICAN'S DAUGHTER (American, 1922)

DIRECTORS: Sam Taylor, Stanner E. V. Taylor

SCREENPLAY: Stanner E. V. Taylor, based on the story "The Story of Jees Uck" by Jack London

CAST: Nancy Deaver (Jees Uck), Nick Thompson (Chatanna), Mortimer Snow (Nashinta)

SPECS: 5 reels; Black & White; Silent

AVAILABILITY: NA

NATION: Mohican

IMAGE PORTRAYAL: Mixed-blood Native American; romance between a Native American woman and a white man

SUMMARY: This film deals with the romantic struggles of Jees Uck, a mixed-blood whom Chatanna, the chief of her tribe, wants to marry. Though she loves a white man, she surrenders herself to the evil Chatanna. However, when the white man proves that the chief is guilty of killing Nashinta, she is able to marry him.

THE MOUNTAIN MEN (Columbia, 1980)
DIRECTOR: Richard Lang
SCREENPLAY: Fraser Clarke Heston
CAST: Charlton Heston (Bill Tyler), Brian Keith (Henry Frapp), Victoria Racimo (Running Moon), Stephen Macht (Heavy Eagle), David Ackroyd (Medicine Wolf), Cal Bellini (Cross Otter), Victor Jory (Iron Belly), Danny Zapien (Blackfoot Chief)
SPECS: 102 minutes; Color
AVAILABILITY: DVD (Sony Pictures Home Entertainment); Amazon Instant Video
NATION: Blackfoot
IMAGE PORTRAYAL: Hostile warrior; romance between a Native American woman and a white man
SUMMARY: Discussed on page 52, this film portrays a Blackfoot tribe led by Heavy Eagle, their diabolical chief, as vicious adversaries of Bill Tyler and the Blackfoot woman, Running Moon, whom he loves.

MUSTANG COUNTRY (Universal, 1976)
DIRECTOR: John C. Champion
SCREENPLAY: John C. Champion
CAST: Joel McCrea (Dan), Nika Mina (Nika)
SPECS: 79 minutes; Color
AVAILABILITY: DVD (Universal Studios)
NATION: NA
IMAGE PORTRAYAL: Friendship; loyalty
SUMMARY: A former rodeo star, Dan, helps a young runaway Native American, Nika, capture a mustang stallion.

MY LITTLE CHICKADEE (Universal, 1940)
DIRECTOR: Edward Cline
SCREENPLAY: Mae West, W. C. Fields
CAST: Mae West (Flower Belle Lee), W. C. Fields (Cuthbert J. Twillie), George Moran (Milton)
SPECS: 83 minutes; Black & White
AVAILABILITY: DVD (Universal Cinema Classics); Amazon Instant Video
NATION: NA
IMAGE PORTRAYAL: Attack on railroad; friendship

SUMMARY: In this comedy, Flower Belle Lee skillfully picks off warriors attacking the train she's on, and Cuthbert J. Twillie has an educated Native American friend named Milton who only speaks lines like "Big chief gottum new Squaw?" Or he just speaks in grunts.

N

NAKED IN THE SUN (Allied Artists, 1957)
DIRECTOR: R. John Hugh
SCREENPLAY: John Cresswell
CAST: James Craig (Osceola), Lita Milan (Chechotah), Dennis Cross (Coacoochee), Tony Morris (Micanopah), Barton MacLane (Wilson)
SPECS: 78 minutes; Color
AVAILABILITY: VHS (Republic Entertainment)
NATION: Seminole
IMAGE PORTRAYAL: Peace-loving chief; romance between Native Americans
SUMMARY: This film deals with the struggles between Seminoles led by Osceola and slave traders during the colonial period. An evil slave trader, Wilson, pursues Chechotah who marries Osceola. Eventually, Osceola, realizing that there never can be peace if he is free, sends his wife with his friend, Coacoochee, to a new location for the Seminole tribe while he remains in prison.

NATURALLY NATIVE (Red Horse Native Productions, 1998)
DIRECTORS: Jennifer Wynne Farmer, Valerie Red-Horse
SCREENPLAY: Valerie Red-Horse
CAST: Valerie Red-Horse (Vickie Lewis Bighawk), Yvonne Russo (Joanne Chapa), Irene Bedard (Tanya Lewis), Kimberly Guerrero (Karen Lewis), Pato Hoffmann (Steve Bighawk)
SPECS: 107 minutes; Color
AVAILABILITY: NA
NATION: NA
IMAGE PORTRAYAL: Contemporary Native Americans
SUMMARY: In this film financed by the Mashantucket Tribe, three sisters—Vickie Lewis Redhawk, Tanya Lewis, and Karen Lewis—create a line of cosmetics that they call "Naturally Native, "which are based on tribal remedies. Given that they were brought up in white society, they must struggle to reclaim their Native American roots and make their business a success.

NAVAJO (Lippert, 1952)
DIRECTOR: Norman Foster
SCREENPLAY: Norman Foster
CAST: Francis Kee Teller (Son of the Hunter), John Mitchell (Grey Singer), Mrs. Kee Teller (Good Weaver), Billy Draper (Billy-Ute guide)

SPECS: 70 minutes; Black & White
AVAILABILITY: NA
NATION: Navajo; Ute
IMAGE PORTRAYAL: Friendship; Native American as victim
SUMMARY: In this film story told by a narrator, Little Son of the Hunter, a Navajo boy forced to go to a white school, escapes to a canyon, tricks his pursuers, and then rescues them.

NAVAJO BLUES (Sullivan Entertainment, 1996)

DIRECTOR: Joey Travolta
SCREENPLAY: Richard Dillon
CAST: Steven Bauer (Nick Epps), Irene Bedard (Audrey Wyako), Charlotte Lewis (Elizabeth Wyako), Ed O'Ross (Not Lightning Struck), Michael Horse (Begay), Billy Daydoge (Grandfather Wyako)
SPECS: 90 minutes; Color
AVAILABILITY: DVD (Allumination)
NATION: Navajo
IMAGE PORTRAYAL: Contemporary Native American; mixed-blood Native American; romance between a mixed-blood Native American woman and a white man
SUMMARY: Nick Epps goes to the Navajo reservation on a witness protection plan and works with Audrey Wyako, a skilled tribal policewoman. They pursue and bring to justice Not Lightning Struck, a practitioner of witchcraft and killer of Audrey's Grandfather. Eventually, Nick falls in love with Audrey's half-sister, Elizabeth. At the end, Nick and Audrey kill an evil mobster.

NAVAJO JOE (United Artists, 1966)

DIRECTOR: Sergio Corbucci
SCREENPLAY: Piero Regnoli, Fernando Di Leo, Ugo Pirro
CAST: Burt Reynolds (Navajo Joe), Maria Cristina Sani (Joe's Wife), Nicoletta Machiavelli (Estella)
SPECS: 93 minutes; Color
AVAILABILITY: DVD (MGM)
NATION: Navajo
IMAGE PORTRAYAL: Vengeance
SUMMARY: Navajo Joe takes harsh revenge on villains who kill his wife and everyone else in his village. As he kills them one by one, he rescues Estella, a Native American, and saves the entire town even though the people are prejudiced against him.

NAVAJO RUN (American, 1964)

DIRECTOR: Johnny Seven
SCREENPLAY: Jo Heims
CAST: Johnny Seven (Mathew Whitehawk), Warren Kemmerling (Luke Grog), Virginia Vincent (Sarah Grog)

SPECS: 75 minutes; Black & White
AVAILABILITY: NA
NATION: Navajo
IMAGE PORTRAYAL: Vengeance
SUMMARY: Luke Grog tricks Mathew Whitehawk by having his wife, Sarah, nurse him back to health from a rattlesnake bite to get him into the woods so he can hunt him down as he has done before with other Navajos. Mathew, however, survives and takes his revenge by killing the villain with a rattlesnake.

THE NEBRASKAN (Columbia, 1953)
DIRECTOR: Fred Sears
SCREENPLAY: David Lang, Martin Berkeley
CAST: Philip Carey (Wade Harper), Maurice Jara (Wingfoot), Jay Silverheels (Spotted Bear), Pat Hogan (Yellow Knife), Nick Thompson (Medicine Man)
SPECS: 68 minutes; Color
AVAILABILITY: DVD (Sony Pictures Choice Collection)
NATION: Comanche; Sioux
IMAGE PORTRAYAL: Friendship; loyalty; vengeance
SUMMARY: Wingfoot, the friend of Wade Harper, is unjustly accused of killing a friendly chief, Thundercloud. Chief Spotted Bear, the real murderer who wants to kill Wingfoot, starts a war because Harper will not hand over his friend. At the end, Yellow Knife, the son of Spotted Bear, who has been rescued by Harper, rescues him from burning at the stake, kills Spotted Bear, and promises that he and Wingfoot will make peace.

NEOLA, THE SIOUX (Exposition Players Corp. and 101 Ranch, 1915)
DIRECTOR: E. E. Blackwell
SCREENPLAY: NA
CAST: Chief Eagle Eye (Chief Eagle Eye), Pedro Leone (Red Deer), Neola Mae (Neola)
SPECS: Black & White; Silent
AVAILABILITY: NA
NATION: Sioux
IMAGE PORTRAYAL: Romance between Native Americans
SUMMARY: A white man who raped Neola is forced to marry her and later abandons her. Red Deer, who had originally forced Neola's marriage, but has since reformed, finds her and asks her to join him as a performer in the 101 Ranch Western Show. Later, Red Deer kills Neola's evil husband, is exonerated, and then pledges his love and promises that he and Neola will soon get married.

NEVADA SMITH (Paramount, 1966)
DIRECTOR: Henry Hathaway
SCREENPLAY: John Michael Hayes, based on the novel, The Carpetbaggers by Harold Robbins
CAST: Steve McQueen (Nevada Smith), Janet Margolin (Neesa)

SPECS: 128 minutes; Color
AVAILABILITY: DVD (Warner Home Video); Amazon Instant Video
NATION: Kiowa
IMAGE PORTRAYAL: Mixed-blood Native American; romance between Native Americans; vengeance
SUMMARY: The mixed-blood hero, Nevada Smith, is driven to avenge the killing of his white father and Native American mother. When he is hurt during his quest, Neesa, a Kiowa prostitute, brings him to the camp of her people to recover. Though they fall in love, he leaves her to pursue his revenge.

NEVER CRY WOLF (Buena Vista, 1983)
DIRECTOR: Carroll Ballard
SCREENPLAY: Curtis Hanson, Sam Hamm, Richard Kletter, based on the book by Farley Mowat
CAST: Charles Martin Smith (Farley Mowat/Tyler Smith), Zachary Ittimangnaq (Ootek), Samson Jorah (Mike)
SPECS: 105 minutes; Color
AVAILABILITY: DVD (Buena Vista Home Entertainment); Amazon Instant Video
NATION: Inuit
IMAGE PORTRAYAL: Friendship
SUMMARY: In this film, a voice-over narrator plays a big part. The Inuit wise man, Ootek, befriends Farley Mowat/Tyler Smith and teaches him the wolf myths. Another Inuit character is Mike, who is meant to be a companion and translator for Tyler, but is really a man who hunts wolves for a living.

NEW MEXICO (United Artists, 1951)
DIRECTOR: Irving Reis
SCREENPLAY: Max Trell
CAST: Lew Ayres (Capt. Hunt), Ted de Corsia (Chief Acoma), Jeff Corey (Coyote)
SPECS: 76 minutes; Color
AVAILABILITY: DVD (Alpha Video)
NATION: Acoma
IMAGE PORTRAYAL: Attack on soldiers; friendship; peace-loving chief
SUMMARY: Although Captain Hunt tries to stop his friend, Chief Acoma, from fighting the villains after they break a treaty, some of his tribe, armed with weapons supplied by a crooked politician, finally make war. At the end, Acoma dies to save his son.

THE NEW WORLD (New Line Cinema, 2005)
DIRECTOR: Terrence Malick
SCREENPLAY: Terrence Malick
CAST: Colin Farrell (Captain John Smith), Q'orianka Kilcher (Pocahontas-Matooka), August Schellenberg (Powhatan), Michael Greyeyes (Rupwew), Wes

Studi (Opechancanough), Kalani Queypo (Parahunt), Irene Bedard (Pocahontas's mother), Thomas Clair (Patawomeck), Alex Rice (Patawomeck's wife), Billy Merasty (Kiskiak)

SPECS: 135 minutes; Color

AVAILABILITY: DVD (New Line Home Entertainment); Amazon Instant Video

NATION: Powhatan (Algonquin)

IMAGE PORTRAYAL: Attacks on a town; friendship; romance between a Native American woman and white men

SUMMARY: Discussed on page 76, this version of the Pocahontas story tells how the tribe of Powhatan captures Captain John Smith, and, after being saved by Pocahontas, he falls in love with her and learns to appreciate the ways of her tribe. After he returns to the fort both the whites and Native Americans consider the lovers traitors. John Smith is forced to leave, and Pocahontas is banished from her tribe and eventually marries John Rolfe. She and her husband and child, accompanied by Opechancanough, travel to England. There she and John Smith meet one last time before she dies.

CRITICS: *Chicago Sun Times* critic Roger Ebert comments: "We are surprised to see how makeshift and vulnerable the English forts are, how evolved the Indian culture is, how these two civilizations could have built something new together—but could not, because what both societies knew at that time did not permit it. Pocahontas could have brought them together. In a small way, she did. She was given the gift of sensing the whole picture, and that is what Malick founds his film on, not tawdry stories of love and adventure. He is a visionary, and this story requires one" (January 19, 2006).

NIGHTWING (Columbia, 1979)

DIRECTOR: Arthur Hiller

SCREENPLAY: Steve Shagan, Bud Shrake, and Martin Cruz Smith, based on Smith's novel

CAST: Nick Mancuso (Youngman Duran), Stephen Macht (Walker Chee), George Clutesi (Abner Tasupi), Virginia P. Maney (Old Squaw)

SPECS: 105 minutes; Color

AVAILABILITY: DVD (Sony Pictures Home Entertainment)

NATION: NA

IMAGE PORTRAYAL: Contemporary Native Americans; friendship; romance between a Native American man and a white woman

SUMMARY: Youngman Duran, a tribal policeman in love with a white woman, and Walker Chee try to eradicate vampire bats turned deadly by tribal magic. Abner Tasupi, a seer from the tribe, helps them deal with this threat to the whole area.

NORTH OF NEVADA (Monogram, 1924)

DIRECTOR: Albert Rogell

SCREENPLAY: Marion Jackson

CAST: Fred Thomson (Tom Tyler), George Magrill (Joe Deerfoot)

SPECS: Black & White; Silent

AVAILABILITY: NA
NATION: NA
IMAGE PORTRAYAL: Kidnapping
SUMMARY: Tom Tyler brings to justice Joe Deerfoot, an unscrupulous, college-educated Native American who deceives a boy and kidnaps a white woman in order to get his hands on a ranch.

NORTH OF THE GREAT DIVIDE (Republic, 1950)
DIRECTOR: William Witney
SCREENPLAY: Eric Taylor
CAST: Roy Rogers (Roy Rogers), Keith Richards (Tacona), Noble Johnson (Oseka Chief Nagura), Roy Barcroft (Banning)
SPECS: 67 minutes; Color
AVAILABILITY: DVD (Good Times Home Video)
NATION: Oseka tribe of Canada
IMAGE PORTRAYAL: Friendship; loyalty; Native Americans as victims
SUMMARY: Roy Rogers, an Indian agent and blood brother of the Oseka tribe of Chief Nagura, helps his friends by exposing the villain, Banning, who is tampering with the tribe's salmon fishing rights and causing starvation in the reservation.

NORTH STAR (Warner, 1996)
DIRECTOR: Nils Gaup
SCREENPLAY: Sergio Donati, Lorenzo Donati, Paul Ohl, Gilles Behat, Philippe Schwartz, based on the novel *The North Star* by Heck Allen
CAST: James Caan (Sean McLennon), Christopher Lambert (Hudson Saanteek), Mary Walker (Haina), Renny Hoalona Loren (Cheelik), Frank Salsedo (Nikki), Norman Charles (Tonga)
SPECS: 90 minutes; Color
AVAILABILITY: DVD (Warner Home Video); Amazon Instant Video
NATION: Eskimo
IMAGE PORTRAYAL: Justice
SUMMARY: The hero, Hudson Saanteek, tries to help the tribe he lives with after the villain, Sean McLennon, tries to steal their property rights. Hudson survives an attempted murder charge because of his tribal survival skills and kills the villain at the end.

NORTH WEST MOUNTED POLICE (Paramount, 1940)
DIRECTOR: Cecil B. De Mille
SCREENPLAY: Alan Le May, Jesse Lasky Jr., C. Gardiner Sullivan, based on the novel *The Royal Canadian Police* by R. C. Fetherstonhaugh
CAST: Gary Cooper (Dusty Rivers), Paulette Goddard (Louvette Corbeau), Walter Hampden (Big Bear), Robert Preston (Ronnie Logan)

SPECS: 126 minutes; Color
AVAILABILITY: NA
NATION: Cree; Metis
IMAGE PORTRAYAL: Attack on soldiers; mixed-blood Native American
SUMMARY: Louis Riel, the leader of mixed-bloods, called Metis, revolts against the Canadian government and, with his Cree allies, fights the Mounties. A beautiful Metis woman, Louvette Corbeau, entices Ronnie Logan to leave his post so the tribes allied with the Metis can attack. At the end, the Mounties makes peace with the wise Cree Chief, Big Bear.

NORTHWEST PASSAGE (MGM, 1940)
DIRECTOR: King Vidor
SCREENPLAY: Laurence Stallings, Talbot Jennings, based on the novel by Kenneth Roberts
CAST: Spencer Tracy (Maj. Robert Rogers), Robert Young (Langdon Towne), Andrew Pena (Konkapot), Chief Sky Eagle (Indian Man)
SPECS: 126 minutes; Color
AVAILABILITY: DVD (Warner Archive Collection)
NATION: Abenaki
IMAGE PORTRAYAL: Attack on soldiers; drunkenness
SUMMARY: Discussed on page 21, this film tells the story of Robert Rogers, who leads his Rangers on an arduous trek to take revenge on the Abenaki tribe at St. Francis for their earlier attack on the settlers.

O

OGALLAH (Powers, 1911)
DIRECTOR: NA
SCREENPLAY: NA
CAST: NA
SPECS: Black & White; Silent
AVAILABILITY: NA
NATION: Sioux
IMAGE PORTRAYAL: Vengeance
SUMMARY: A Sioux pursues a kidnapper of one of his people and finally takes his vengeance by killing him.
CRITICS: A *Moving Picture World* reviewer notes that the film "is an Indian picture which seems to illustrate the Indian characteristics as they are commonly understood. . . . There is no mawkish sentimentality. . . . It is savage and cruel, as Indians are by nature" (April 18, 1911, 782).

OH! SUSANNA (Republic, 1951)
DIRECTOR: Joseph Kane

SCREENPLAY: Charles Marquis Warren
CAST: Rod Cameron (Captain Webb Calhoun), Pedro de Cordoba (Pactola)
SPECS: 84 minutes; Color
AVAILABILITY: DVD (Sinister Cinema); Amazon Instant Video
NATION: Sioux
IMAGE PORTRAYAL: Attack on a fort; attack on soldiers; friendship
SUMMARY: In the Black Hills, warlike Sioux attack soldiers who are breaking a treaty. Finally, Captain Webb Calhoun meets with the Sioux Chief, Pactola, who recognizes him as a man who upholds the treaty and agrees to let the soldiers leave the fort.

OKLAHOMA JIM (Monogram, 1931)
DIRECTOR: Harry Fraser
SCREENPLAY: George Arthur Durlam, Harry Fraser
CAST: Oklahoma Bill Cody (Oklahoma Jim Kirby), Andy Shuford (Spotted Face), Iron Eyes Cody (War Eagle), J. W. Cody (Indian), Chief Many Treaties (Black Hawk), Artie Ortega (Big Bear), Ann Ross (Natoma), Chief White Eagle (Indian)
SPECS: 53 minutes; Black & White
AVAILABILITY: NA
NATION: NA
IMAGE PORTRAYAL: Native Americans as victims; romance between Native Americans
SUMMARY: Natoma, who is about to be married to War Eagle, has her forced marriage to a white man revealed, and she kills herself out of shame. Jim Kirby and Spotted Face stop her people from taking revenge on the whites by bringing two white men to the tribe so they can determine the guilty man and punish him.

OKLAHOMA TERRITORY (United Artists, 1960)
DIRECTOR: Edward L. Cahn
SCREENPLAY: Orville H. Hampton
CAST: Bill Williams (Temple Houston), Gloria Talbot (Ruth Red Hawk), Ted de Corsia (Chief Buffalo Horn), Grant Richards (Bigelow), X Brands (Running Cloud), Eddie Little Sky (Cherokee)
SPECS: 67 minutes; Black & White
AVAILABILITY: DVD (MGM Limited Edition Collection); Amazon Instant Video
NATION: Cherokee
IMAGE PORTRAYAL: Friendship; loyalty
SUMMARY: Bigelow commits a murder and then blames it on Buffalo Horn to start a war so he can get the tribe's land for a railroad. Temple Houston, who is a friend of Buffalo Horn, Running Cloud, and Ruth Red Hawk, is forced

to prosecute, and even has to break his friend out of jail, but finally wins the acquittal of Buffalo Horn.

CRITICS: A *Variety* critic, commenting on the white actors, notes that "Gloria Talbott looks about as much like an Injun as Ted de Corsia, who doesn't" (February 10, 1960).

THE OKLAHOMAN (Allied Artists, 1957)
DIRECTOR: Francis D. Lyon
SCREENPLAY: Daniel B. Ullman
CAST: Joel McCrea (John Brighton), Gloria Talbott (Maria Smith), Michael Pate (Charlie Smith), Anthony Caruso (Jim Hawk), Peter J. Votrian (Little Charlie Smith)
SPECS: 80 minutes; Color
AVAILABILITY: DVD (Warner Home Video)
NATION: NA
IMAGE PORTRAYAL: Native Americans as victims; romance between a Native American woman and a white man
SUMMARY: Greedy ranchers after his land try to frame Charlie Smith, a Native American rancher. John Brighton, whom Maria Smith loves, comes to the rescue. At the end, after Maria realizes that John loves a white woman, she leaves and returns to her father, Charlie.
CRITICS: A *New York Times* critic praises the film for portraying "A hero who is man enough to make a skin-conscious community ashamed of itself" (May 15, 1957).

OLD OVERLAND TRAIL (Republic, 1953)
DIRECTOR: William Witney
SCREENPLAY: Milton Raison
CAST: Rex Allen (Rex Allen), Leonard Nimoy (Chief Black Hawk), Roy Barcroft (John Anchor)
SPECS: 60 minutes; Black & White
AVAILABILITY: Amazon Instant Video
NATION: NA
IMAGE PORTRAYAL: Friendship; loyalty
SUMMARY: When John Anchor sells whiskey and rifles to Apache so they will attack a wagon train of workers and thus let him swindle the settlers, a good Indian agent, Rex Allen, who had saved the life of Chief Black Hawk earlier, helps the chief to stop the hostility. Finally, Black Hawk kills Anchor before he dies, and peace is restored.

OLDER THAN AMERICA (IFC Films, 2008)
DIRECTOR: Georgina Lightning
SCREENPLAY: Georgina Lightning, Christine K. Walker

CAST: Adam Beach (Johnny), Tantoo Cardinal (Auntie Apple), Dan Harrison (Walter Many Lightnings), Georgina Lightning (Rain), Wes Studi (Richard Two Rivers), Jeri Arredondo (Young Adult Irene), Noah Kol Balfour (Little Many Lightnings), Dennis Banks (Pete Goodfeather), Glen Gould (Steve Klamath), Rose Berens (Irene Many Lightnings), Crystle Lightning (Diane)
SPECS: 102 minutes; Color
AVAILABILITY: DVD (MPI Video)
NATION: Cree; Ojibwa
IMAGE PORTRAYAL: Contemporary Native Americans; Native Americans as victims; romance between Native Americans; troubled Native Americans
SUMMARY: In this film about Native American boarding schools, Rain, who is engaged to Johnny, has visions about the terrible way her mother, Irene, was treated in her boarding schools days because a priest categorized her as insane and really practiced ethnic genocide on her, her later husband, and the other inhabitants of the school. The film also deals with a good Native American politician, Steve Klamath, running against an evil white man.

ON DEADLY GROUND (Warner Bros., 1994)
DIRECTOR: Steven Seagal
SCREENPLAY: Ed Horowitz, Robin U. Russin
CAST: Steven Seagal (Forrest Taft), Joan Chen (Masu), Chief Irvin Brink (Silook), Apanguluk Charlie Kairaiuak (Tunrak), Elsie Pistolhead (Takanapsaluk), John Trudell (Johnny Redfeather)
SPECS: 101 minutes; Color
AVAILABILITY: DVD (Warner Home Video); Amazon Instant Video
NATION: Eskimo
IMAGE PORTRAYAL: Friendship; loyalty; Native Americans as victims
SUMMARY: Masu and her Eskimo father, Silook, who is later killed by a villain, rescue an injured Forrest Taft. After Silook's tribe cares for Taft, he takes on the villains with the help of Masu. There is some use of the Inuktitut language with subtitles.

ON THE WARPATH (Bison, 1912)
DIRECTOR: Reginald Barker
SCREENPLAY: NA
CAST: Art Acord (Young Arrow Head), Ann Little (Red Feather), William Clifford (Old Arrow Head), Sky Eagle (Old Yuma Chief)
SPECS: 20 minutes; Black & White; Silent
AVAILABILITY: NA
NATION: Apache; Yuma
IMAGE PORTRAYAL: Hostile warriors; peace-loving chief
SUMMARY: An old man, Arrow Head, dreams of ancient battles between fierce Apaches and a peace-loving Yuma tribe and of a romance between a man of one tribe and a woman, Red Feather, of the other.

ONE FLEW OVER THE CUCKOO'S NEST (United Artists, 1975)
DIRECTOR: Milos Forman
SCREENPLAY: Lawrence Hauben, Bo Goldman, based on the novel by Ken
    Kesey
CAST: Jack Nicholson (Randal P. McMurphy), Louise Fletcher (Nurse Ratched),
    Will Sampson (Chief Bromden)
SPECS: 133 minutes; Color
AVAILABILITY: DVD and Blu-ray (Warner Home Video); Amazon Instant
    Video
NATION: NA
IMAGE PORTRAYAL: Friendship; loyalty
SUMMARY: Chief Bromden befriends Randal McMurphy and sticks with him
    during his final agony caused by Nurse Ratched.
CRITICS: Pauling Kael in *The New Yorker* comments: "The film has its climactic
    Indian-white love-death, and at the end Kesey's reversal of the American leg-
    end (now the white man is sacrificed for the Indian) is satisfying on the deepest
    pop-myth level" (December 1, 1975, 134).

100 RIFLES (20th Century Fox, 1969)
DIRECTOR: Tom Gries
SCREENPLAY: Clair Huffaker, Tom Gries, based on the novel by Robert
    MacLeod
CAST: Burt Reynolds (Yaqui Joe Herrera), Raquel Welch (Sarita), Jim Brown
    (Lyedecker)
SPECS: 110 minutes; Color
AVAILABILITY: DVD (20th Century Fox Home Entertainment)
NATION: Yaqui
IMAGE PORTRAYAL: Friendship; loyalty; mixed-blood Native American; ro-
    mance between Native Americans
SUMMARY: Yaqui Joe is a mixed-blood Yaqui who tries to get rifles for his re-
    pressed tribe. He loves Sarita, a leader of rebel warriors, who wins Lyedecker
    over to the side of the tribe. At the end, after Sarita dies in the fight, Lyedecker,
    who has been leading the Yaqui, hands over the leadership to Yaqui Joe, who
    decides to live with his tribe.

ON THE ICE (On the Ice Productions, 2011)
DIRECTOR: Andrew Okpeaha MacClean
SCREENPLAY: Andrew Okpeaha MacClean
CAST: Josiah Patkotak (Qualli), Frank Qutuq Irelan (Aivaaq), John Miller (James),
    Teddy Kyle Smith (Egasak). As was the case with the Inuit in *The Fast Runner*,
    all the actors and the filmmakers are Inupiaq-Eskimo in this unique Inupiaq
    story.
SPECS: 96 minutes; Color
AVAILABILITY: DVD (Millennium Media); Amazon Instant Video

NATION: Eskimo-Inupiat
IMAGE PORTRAYAL: Contemporary Eskimo culture
SUMMARY: In Barrow, Alaska, two young Eskimo men, Qualli and Aivaaq, are involved in the accidental death of a friend, James. They lie about what happens, and, as the people in the town become more suspicious, they go on a hunting trip with Egasak, the father of Qualli, and Qualli finally tells the truth about the accident when his father shows them the body of James. At the end, Qualli walks alone on the vast ice field as he deals with finally making the right decision.

ONE LITTLE INDIAN (Buena Vista, 1973)
DIRECTOR: Bernard McEveety
SCREENPLAY: Harry Spaulding
CAST: James Garner (Keyes), Jay Silverheels (Jimmy Wolf), Rudy Diaz (The Apache), Clay O'Brien (Mark), Lois Red Elk (Blue Feather)
SPECS: 90 minutes; Color
AVAILABILITY: DVD (Buena Vista Home Entertainment); Amazon Instant Video
NATION: NA
IMAGE PORTRAYAL: Friendship; loyalty
SUMMARY: In this Disney film, Keyes gets in trouble for rescuing Native American women and children during a cavalry raid. He befriends a white boy named Mark living with the tribe of Jim Wolfe and Blue Feather, Mark's surrogate mother. Mark joins Keyes as they try to escape on a camel, and finally helps him prove his innocence

THE ONLY GOOD INDIAN (TLC Films, 2009)
DIRECTOR: Kevin Willmott
SCREENPLAY: Thomas L. Carmody
CAST: Wes Studi (Sam), Winter Fox Frank (Charlie), Delanna Studi (Aquene), David Midthunder (Nawkaw)
SPECS: 114 minutes; Color
AVAILABILITY: NA
NATION: Cherokee; Kickapoo
IMAGE PORTRAYAL: Contemporary Native American; troubled Native American
SUMMARY: Charlie is a young man who has escaped from a Native American training school in Kansas that he had been forced to attend. Sam, who has captured the young man, reevaluates the values that have allowed him to succeed in the white world and finally accepts his traditional Cherokee beliefs.

ONLY THE VALIANT (Warner Bros., 1951)
DIRECTOR: Gordon Douglas

SCREENPLAY: Edmund H. North, Harry Brown, based on a novel by Charles
    Marquis Warren
CAST: Gregory Peck (Capt. Richard Lance), Michael Ansara (Tucsos)
SPECS: 105 minutes; Black & White
AVAILABILITY: DVD (Olive Films)
NATION: Apache
IMAGE PORTRAYAL: Attack on soldiers
SUMMARY: Apaches led by Tucsos stage a series of attacks on soldiers who are
    trying to hold a strategic pass. In the final attack, more soldiers arrive and sub-
    due the Apaches with a Gatling gun. At the end, Richard Lance kills Tucsos.

OPEN RANGE (Paramount, 1927)
DIRECTOR: Clifford Smith
SCREENPLAY: Roy Briant, J. Walter Ruben, John Stone, based on the novel,
    Valley of Wild Horses by Zane Grey
CAST: Bernard Siegel (Brave Bear), Fred Kohler (Sam Hardman)
SPECS: 60 minutes; Black & White; Silent
AVAILABILITY: NA
NATION: NA
IMAGE PORTRAYAL: Attack on a town; vengeance
SUMMARY: Brave Bear, a chief bitter about white encroachment on his lands,
    seeks revenge by joining Sam Hardman in a plot to steal cattle from the ranch-
    ers. At the end, he attacks the town but is stopped by a cattle stampede, during
    which Hardman dies.

ORCA (Paramount, 1977)
DIRECTOR: Michael Anderson
SCREENPLAY: Luciano Vincenzoni, Sergio Donati
CAST: Richard Harris (Captain Nolan), Will Sampson (Jacob Umilak)
SPECS: 92 minutes; Color
AVAILABILITY: DVD (Paramount Home Entertainment)
NATION: NA
IMAGE PORTRAYAL: Contemporary Native American; wise elder
SUMMARY: Jacob Umilak joins the crew chasing Orca, the killer whale.

OREGON PASSAGE (Allied Artists, 1957)
DIRECTOR: Paul Landres
SCREENPLAY: Jack DeWitt, based on the novel by Gordon D. Shirreffs
CAST: John Ericson (Lt. Niles Ord), Toni Gerry (Little Deer), H. M. Wynant
    (Black Eagle), Paul Fierro (Nato)
SPECS: 80 minutes; Color
AVAILABILITY: DVD (Warner Archive Collection)
NATION: Shoshone

IMAGE PORTRAYAL: Attack on settlers; romance between a Native American woman and a white man

SUMMARY: The Shoshone of Chief Black Eagle attack and kill some settlers. Niles Ord, who has fallen in love with Little Deer, and has been helped by Nato, finally kills Black Eagle in hand-to-hand combat. As the warriors of Black Eagle prepare to attack the fort, the soldiers, who have been hiding in a cemetery outside the fort, surprise the warriors and subdue them.

OREGON TRAIL SCOUTS (Republic, 1947)

DIRECTOR: R. G. Springsteen

SCREENPLAY: Earle Snell

CAST: Allea Lane (Red Ryder), Robert Blake (Little Beaver), Frank Lackteen (Chief Running Fox), Billy Cummings (Barking Squirrel), Roy Barcroft (Bill Hunter)

SPECS: 58 minutes; Black & White

AVAILABILITY: DVD (VCI Home Video)

NATION: NA

IMAGE PORTRAYAL: Friendship; loyalty; mixed-blood Native American

SUMMARY: By kidnapping the grandson of Chief Running Fox, Little Beaver, Hunter tries to gain trapping rights and to break an agreement Red Ryder made with the tribe. However, the boy escapes and lets Running Squirrel be the next chief of his tribe so that he can be the companion of Red Ryder and join him on his quest to establish law and order in the West. This character, known for his response "You bet-ch-em," also appears in two other 1947 Republic films directed by R. G. Springsteen, *Marshall of Cripple Creek* and *Rustlers of Devil's Canyon.*

CRITICS: A *Variety* critic comments on the character of Little Beaver in the latter film: "Young Bobby Blake as an Indian kid will appeal to the juves" (July 9, 1947).

THE OREGON TRAIL (20th Century Fox, 1959)

DIRECTOR: Gene Fowler

SCREENPLAY: Gene Fowler Jr., Louis Vittes

CAST: Fred MacMurray (Neal Harris), Gloria Talbott (Shona Hastings)

SPECS: 86 minutes; Color

AVAILABILITY: DVD (20th Century Fox Cinema Archives)

NATION: NA

IMAGE PORTRAYAL: Attacks on soldiers; romance between a mixed-blood Native American woman and a white man

SUMMARY: During an attack on a wagon train, hostile warriors capture Neal Harris, who, unknown to them, supports the rights of the tribe. Harris is eventually rescued by a mixed-blood Native American woman, Shona Hastings. After helping the soldiers control the hostiles, he decides to live with his beloved Shona.

THE ORPHAN (Fox, 1920)
DIRECTOR: J. Gordon Edwards
SCREENPLAY: Roy Somerville, based on the novel by Clarence E. Mulford
CAST: William Farnum (The Orphan), Louise Lovely (Helen Shields)
SPECS: 60 minutes; Black & White; Silent
AVAILABILITY: NA
NATION: NA
IMAGE PORTRAYAL: Attack on a stagecoach
SUMMARY: The Orphan, originally an outlaw, fights off a hostile tribe as they
   attack a stagecoach, and he rescues a white woman.
CRITICS: A *Variety* critic notes that such westerns "hand out film food to a
   grown-up audience, consisting of a fast riding horseman picking off Indian
   braves after 'white squaws' in a stagecoach, or else on the warpath, picking
   them off as an expert would demolish clay pipes at a shooting gallery" (April
   30, 1920).

OUT OF THE SNOWS (Selznick, 1920)
DIRECTOR: Ralph Ince
SCREENPLAY: Irvin J. Martin, E. Lord Corbett
CAST: Zena Keefe (Anitah), Red Eagle (Lone Deer)
SPECS: 6 reels; Black & White; Silent
AVAILABILITY: NA
NATION: NA
IMAGE PORTRAYAL: Vengeance
SUMMARY: In the Canadian Northwest, Anitah, a Native American woman,
   kills a white man who slanders her. When whites kill her in retaliation, a man
   from her tribe, Lone Deer, takes harsh revenge on them.

THE OUTLAW JOSEY WALES (Warner Bros., 1976)
DIRECTOR: Clint Eastwood
SCREENPLAY: Philip Kaufman, Sonia Chernus, based on the novel, *Gone to
   Texas* by Forrest Carter
CAST: Clint Eastwood (Josey Wales), Chief Dan George (Lone Watie), Geraldine
   Keams (Little Moonlight), Will Sampson (Ten Bears)
SPECS: 135 minutes; Color
AVAILABILITY: DVD (Warner Home Video); Amazon Instant Video
NATION: Cherokee; Comanche
IMAGE PORTRAYAL: Friendship; loyalty
SUMMARY: Discussed on page 46, this film about the aftermath of the Civil War
   deals with the friendships between Josey Wales and Lone Watie, Little Moon-
   light, and Ten Bears as he pursues the murderers of his wife and son.
CRITICS: Film critic Roger Ebert in the *Chicago Sun Times* comments on the per-
   formance of Chief Dan George: "George achieves the same magical effect here

that he did in '*Harry and Tonto*,' trading Mixmasters for Indian medicine in a jail cell: He's funny and dignified at once. He joins up with the outlaw Eastwood, and their relationship is a reminder of all those great second bananas from the Westerns of the 1940s—the grizzled old characters played by Gabby Hayes and Smiley Burnette. But Chief Dan George brings an aura to his role that audiences seem to respond to viscerally. He has his problems (he's humiliated, as an Indian, that he's grown so old he can no longer sneak up behind people), but he has a humanity that's just there, glowing. He's as open with his personality as Josey Wales is closed; it's a nice match" (January 1, 1976).

OUTLAW TRAIL (Monogram, 1944)
DIRECTOR: Robert Tansey
SCREENPLAY: Frances Kavanaugh, Alan James
CAST: Hoot Gibson (Hoot Gibson), Bob Steele (Bob Steele), Chief Thundercloud (Chief), Jim Thorpe (Henchman Spike)
SPECS: 54 minutes; Black & White
AVAILABILITY: DVD (MGM Limited Edition Collection); Amazon Instant Video
NATION: NA
IMAGE PORTRAYAL: Friendship; loyalty
SUMMARY: Chief (Thundercloud) becomes one of the three Trail Blazers and shares in their heroic exploits. This character also appears in *Sonora Stagecoach*, another 1944 Trail Blazers film.

THE OUTSIDER (Universal, 1961)
DIRECTOR: Delbert Mann
SCREENPLAY: William Bradford Huie and Stewert Stern
CAST: Tony Curtis (Ira Hayes), James Franciscus (James B. Sorenson), Vivian Nathan (Nancy Hayes), Edmund Hashim (Jay Morago)
SPECS: 108 minutes; Black & White
AVAILABILITY: NA
NATION: Pima
IMAGE PORTRAYAL: Drunkenness; Native American as butt of humor; Native American as victim
SUMMARY: This film tells the sad story of Ira Hayes, one of the soldiers who raised the American flag on Iwo Jima, from the time he leaves his Pima reservation to become a soldier to his death from alcoholism ten years later. The story chronicles the treatment of his fellow soldiers, who called him "Chief"; his inability to handle his fame; the death of his white friend, James Sorenson; and his tribe's rejection, all of which lead him to a life of isolation and alcoholism. Though befriended by Jay Morago, the chief of the Pima, and helped by his mother, Nancy Hayes, he dies a broken man.

P

THE PALE FACE (First National, 1922)
DIRECTOR: Buster Keaton
SCREENPLAY: Buster Keaton
CAST: Buster Keaton (Little Chief Paleface), Virginia Fox (Indian Maiden), Joe
    Roberts (Indian Chief)
SPECS: 20 minutes; Black & White; Silent
AVAILABILITY: DVD (FilmRise)
NATION: NA
IMAGE PORTRAYAL: Native Americans as a butt of humor; torture
SUMMARY: In this comedy, a tribe captures the hero, Paleface, and tries to burn
    him at the stake, but his asbestos clothing saves him. Because he doesn't burn,
    they think he is a god and adopt him into the tribe as Little Chief Paleface. Later
    he saves the tribe from being cheated by crooked oilmen. A version of this film
    was remade in 1948 as a vehicle for a Bob Hope comedy.

PALE FACE'S WOOING (Kalem, 1909)
DIRECTOR: NA
SCREENPLAY: NA
CAST: NA
SPECS: Black & White; Silent
AVAILABILITY: NA
NATION: NA
IMAGE PORTRAYAL: Kidnapping; romance between a Native American
    woman and a white man
SUMMARY: Little Red Heart loves a cowboy, but her father wants her to marry
    a man from their tribe whom he has chosen for her. To stop the romance, her
    father and the man he intends for his daughter's husband capture the cowboy
    and are about to kill him. However, Little Red Heart rescues the cowboy, who
    kills his rival and threatens to kill her father. When Little Red Heart intercedes,
    he relents. Then her father forgives them and agrees to their marriage.
CRITICS: A *Variety* reviewer notes that such "Indian subjects are always interest-
    ing. They have the freshness of the wild" (November 27, 1909).

PATH OF SOULS (American United Entertainment, 2012)
DIRECTOR: Jeremy Torrie
SCREENPLAY: Jeremy Torrie
CAST: Nathaniel Arcand (Leroy Littlebear), Russell Badger (Tobasonakwut),
    Adam Beach (Joe Beardsley), Laura Harris (Grace Hudson), Blake Taylor (Fred
    Alan Wolf), Corey Sevier (Brandon Eckhardt)

SPECS: 137 minutes; Color
AVAILABILITY: NA
NATION: NA
IMAGE PORTRAYAL: Contemporary First Nation people
SUMMARY: In this Canadian film, Grace Hudson, the grieving wife of Joe, tries to finish Joe's thesis by traveling to sacred places in Native North America with her friend, Brandon. In the process of this increasingly spiritual journey they meet Native elders who teach them about dark matter, worm holes, parallel universes, and shape-shifting spirits.

PATHFINDER (20th Century Fox, 2007)
DIRECTOR: Marcus Nispel
SCREENPLAY: Laeta Kalogridis, Nils Gaup
CAST: Moon Bloodgood (Starfire), Russell Means (Pathfinder), Jay Tavare (Blackwing), Nathaniel Arcand (Wind in Tree), Wayne Charles Baker (Indian Father), Michelle Thrush (Indian Mother), Ray G. Thunderchild (Elder), Duane Howard (Elder), Brandon Oakes (Elder), Karl Urban (Ghost)
SPECS: 99 minutes; Color
AVAILABILITY: DVD (20th Century Fox Home Entertainment); Amazon Instant Video
NATION: NA
IMAGE PORTRAYAL: Native Americans as victims; romance between a Native American woman and white man
SUMMARY: The Vikings rape and pillage the Native American tribe of Pathfinder, Blackwing, and Wind in the Tree, and leave behind a sword and a boy the tribe calls Ghost. When the Vikings return years later, Ghost, who has become a member of the tribe and loves Starfire, uses the sword to rout the Vikings and save the tribe.

THE PATHFINDER (Columbia, 1953)
DIRECTOR: Sidney Salkow
SCREENPLAY: Robert E. Kent, based on the novel by James Fenimore Cooper
CAST: George Montgomery (Pathfinder), Jay Silverheels (Chingachgook), Rodd Redwing (Mingo Chief Arrowhead), Elena Verdugo (Lokawa), Chief Yowlachie (Eagle Feather), Ed Coch Jr. (Uncas), Rus Conklin (Togamak), Vi Engraham (Ka-letan)
SPECS: 78 minutes; Color
AVAILABILITY: NA
NATION: Mingoe; Mohican; Tuscarora
IMAGE PORTRAYAL: Attack on soldiers
SUMMARY: Pathfinder and his friends Chingachgook and Uncas spy for the British on the French and hostile Mingoes of Chief Arrowhead, who had devastated a Mohican village. At the end, the British rescue Pathfinder.

PAWNEE (Republic, 1957)
DIRECTOR: George Waggner
SCREENPLAY: George Waggner, Louis Vittes, Endre Bohem
CAST: George Montgomery (Paul Fletcher), Charlotte Austin (Dancing Fawn), Ralph Moody (Chief Wise Eagle), Charles Horvath (Crazy Fox)
SPECS: 80 minutes; Color
AVAILABILITY: Amazon Instant Video
NATION: Pawnee
IMAGE PORTRAYAL: Hostile warrior; peace-loving chief; romance between a Native American woman and a white man
SUMMARY: Crazy Fox, a hostile brave who has taken control of the peace-loving Wise Eagle's tribe, leads an attack on a wagon train. Finally Paul Fletcher (Pale Arrow), who grew up with the tribe and is contemplating a return to his adopted people, stops the hostiles by killing Crazy Fox in hand-to-hand combat. At the end he chooses white society and decides to marry a white woman rather than Dancing Fawn, a Pawnee woman who loves him.

PEARL (Freestyle Entertainment, 2010)
DIRECTOR: King Hollis
SCREENPLAY: Thomas Bailey, Donna Carlton, Margaret Reynolds
CAST: Elijah De Jesus (Pearl Carter), Robert S. Ball (Will Rogers), Andrew Sensenig (George Carter Sr.), Angela Gair (Lucy Carter), Isabel Archuleta (Opaletta Carter), Tom Huston (Wiley Post)
SPECS: 106 minutes; Color
AVAILABILITY: DVD (Chickasaw Nation and Media 13)
NATION: Chickasaw
IMAGE PORTRAYAL: Contemporary Native American
SUMMARY: Taught by Wiley Post and strongly encouraged by her father, George, Pearl becomes a daredevil pilot. Though her mother, Lucy, and sister, Opaletta, disapprove in different ways, Pearl becomes well known.

POCAHONTAS (Disney Pictures, 1995)
DIRECTORS: Mike Gabriel, Eric Goldberg
SCREENPLAY: Carl Binder, Susannah Grant, Philip LaZebnik
CAST: Irene Bedard (voice of Pocahontas)
SPECS: 81 minutes; Color
AVAILABILITY: DVD (Walt Disney Home Video); Amazon Instant Video
NATION: Algonquin
IMAGE PORTRAYAL: Romance between Native American woman and white man
SUMMARY: The film tells the well-known story with numerous historical inaccuracies such as the dream of the spinning arrow.

CRITICS: Rita Kempley in the *Washington Post* writes, "All Disney has really done in its 33rd animated feature is revive the stereotype of the Noble Savage" (June 23, 1995).

POCAHONTAS II: JOURNEY TO THE NEW WORLD (Disney Pictures, 1998)
DIRECTORS: Tom Ellery, Bradley Raymond
SCREENPLAY: Allen Estrin, Cindy Marcus, Flip Kobler
CAST: Irene Bedard (voice of Pocahontas)
SPECS: 72 minutes; Color
AVAILABILITY: DVD (Walt Disney Home Video); Amazon Instant Video
NATION: Algonquin
IMAGE PORTRAYAL: Romance between a Native American woman and a white man
SUMMARY: Pocahontas travels to England and tries to stop the wars between the British and Native Americans

POCAHONTAS: THE LEGEND (PFA Films, 1999)
DIRECTOR: Daniele J. Suissa
SCREENPLAY: Donald Martin, Daniele Suissa
CAST: Sandrine Holt (Pocahontas), Miles O'Keeffe (John Smith), Gordon Tootoosis (Powhatan), Billy Merasty (Kocoum). Other First Nation actors play members of Powhatan's tribe.
SPECS: 102 minutes; Color
AVAILABILITY: DVD (Gaiam Entertainment); Amazon Instant Video
NATION: Algonquin
IMAGE PORTRAYAL: Peace-loving chief; romance between Native American woman and a white man
SUMMARY: John Smith is captured by the tribe of Powhatan and falls in love with Pocahontas, and the ways of her people. After numerous complications, Powhatan offers peace to the settlers if John Smith will leave the new world. Pocahontas watches sadly as he leaves. John Rolfe does not appear in the film.

PONY EXPRESS (Paramount, 1953)
DIRECTOR: Jerry Hopper
SCREENPLAY: Charles Marquis Warren, Frank Gruber
CAST: Charlton Heston (Buffalo Bill Cody), Pat Hogan (Chief Yellow Hand), Forrest Tucker (Wild Bill Hickok)
SPECS: 101 minutes; Color
AVAILABILITY: DVD (Olive Films); Amazon Instant Video
NATION: Sioux
IMAGE PORTRAYAL: Attack on soldiers

SUMMARY: After the Sioux have captured Buffalo Bill Cody, he has a hand-to-hand fight with their Chief Yellow Hand and defeats him. Later Cody and Wild Bill Hickok come to the rescue in a climactic battle with the Sioux.

THE PONY EXPRESS (Paramount, 1925)

DIRECTOR: James Cruze
SCREENPLAY: Henry James Forman, Walter Woods
CAST: Al Hart (Senator Glen), Frank Lackteen (Charlie Bent)
SPECS: 110 minutes; Black & White; Silent
AVAILABILITY: DVD (Grapevine Video)
NATION: Sioux
IMAGE PORTRAYAL: Attack on a town; mixed-blood Native American
SUMMARY: A mixed-blood, Charlie Bent, who works for the villain, Senator Glen, leads a band of Sioux on an attack of Julesburg.

PONY SOLDIER (20th Century Fox, 1952)

DIRECTOR: Joseph Newman
SCREENPLAY: John C. Higgins, Garnett Weston
CAST: Tyrone Power (Duncan MacDonald), Thomas Gomez (Natayo Smith), Cameron Mitchell (Konah), Anthony Numkena (Comes Running), Adeline De Walt Reynolds (White Moon), Stuart Randall (Standing Bear), Muriel Landers (Small Face, Smith's wife), Nipo T. Strongheart (Medicine Man), Grady Galloway (Shemawgun), Richard Thunder-Sky (Indian), John War Eagle (Indian), Penny Edwards (Emerald Neeley)
SPECS: 82 minutes; Color
AVAILABILITY: Blu-ray (Twilight Time)
NATION: Cree
IMAGE PORTRAYAL: Hostile warrior; peace-loving chief
SUMMARY: Constable Duncan MacDonald and his mixed-blood companion, Natayo, make friends with the Northern Cree of Chief Standing Bear, young Comes Running, Konah, White Moon, Small Face, Shemawgun, and a Medicine Man. This happens after the tribe has crossed the border to hunt and then attacks American cavalrymen who have killed some of their braves. Aided by the friendly Chief Standing Bear and Comes Running, who kill the hostile sub-chief Konah, the heroes stop a war and lead the tribe back to Canada.
CRITICS: Bosley Crowther in the *New York Times* comments: "Anything but the old-time movie redskins, full of festering resentments and booze, these are fine and upstanding representatives of a racial minority" (December 20, 1952).

POWWOW HIGHWAY (Hand Made Films, 1988)

DIRECTOR: Jonathan Wacks
SCREENPLAY: Janet Heaney, Jean Stawarz, based on the novel by David Seals

CAST: A Martinez (Buddy Red Bow), Gary Farmer (Philbert Bono), Joannelle Nadine Romero (Bonnie Red Bow), Sam Vlahos (Chief Joseph), Wayne Waterman (Wolf Tooth), Margot Kane (Imogene), Geoffrey Rivas (Sandy Youngblood), John Trudell (Louis Short Hair), Wes Studi (Buff), Chrissie McDonald (Jane Red Bow), Maria Antoinette Rogers (Aunt Harriet), Rodney Grant (Brave on Horse), Graham Greene (Vietnam Vet), and other Native American actors in minor roles.

SPECS: 88 minutes; Color

AVAILABILITY: DVD (Image Entertainment); Amazon Instant Video

NATION: Cheyenne

IMAGE PORTRAYAL: Contemporary Native American; Native American activist

SUMMARY: Discussed on page 86, this film, one of the first to be based on a Native American novel with primarily Native American actors, tells the story of Philbert Bono and Buddy Red Bow as they ride in an old Buick to rescue Buddy's sister. In the process of the road trip, they have many adventures and gain a new awareness of their Cheyenne traditional values.

CRITICS: Janet Maslin in the *New York Times* comments on the central character of Philbert Bono: "The scene-stealing figure in '*Powwow Highway*,' a road movie populated by Cheyenne Indian characters in the vicinity of Lame Deer, Mont., is a sweetly mystical giant named Philbert Bono (Gary Farmer). Philbert is notable for his tremendous appetite, his unflappably even keel, and his determination to find some kind of spiritual core in contemporary American Indian life. When Philbert sees a salesman on television wearing a headdress to hawk used cars (offering 'heap big savings'), he is too serene to take offense. Instead, he buys a car from this man and decides to think of it as a war pony" (March 24, 1989).

THE PRAIRIE (Screen Guild, 1948)

DIRECTOR: Frank Wisbar

SCREENPLAY: Arthur St. Claire, based on the novel by James Fenimore Cooper

CAST: Charles Evans (Ishmael Bush), Alan Baxter (Paul Hover), Chief Thundercloud (Eagle Feather), Chief Yowlachie (Matoreeh), Jay Silverheels (Running Deer)

SPECS: 66 minutes; Black & White

AVAILABILITY: NA

NATION: Pawnee; Sioux

IMAGE PORTRAYAL: Friendship; kidnapping; loyalty

SUMMARY: The Sioux tribe of Matoreeh and Running Deer kidnaps a pioneer family. One of the heroes, Paul Hover, is a friend of Eagle Feather, a Pawnee brave.

PRAIRIE SCHOONERS (Columbia, 1940)

DIRECTOR: Sam Nelson

SCREENPLAY: Robert Lee Johnson, Fred Myton, based on the story, "Into the Crimson West" by George Cory Franklin

CAST: Bill Elliott (Wild Bill Hickok), Jim Thorpe (Chief Sanche), Lucien Maxell (Pawnee Boy)

SPECS: 58 minutes; Black & White

AVAILABILITY: NA

NATION: Pawnee; Sioux

IMAGE PORTRAYAL: Peace-loving chief

SUMMARY: Wild Bill Hickok, a guide for the wagon train, deals with the tribe of Chief Sanche who are struggling to protect their land. The chief finally lets the wagon train pass through his land.

CRITICS: A *Variety* critic comments: "The plot does the redskins dirt, maybe Indians encamped in Colorado at that time were that dumb but it hardly is conceivable. . . . Another quaint twist is the failure of the Indians to come out victorious although outnumbering the white settlers about two to one" (November 13, 1940).

PRAIRIE THUNDER (Warner Bros., 1937)

DIRECTOR: B. Reeves Eason

SCREENPLAY: Ed Earl Repp

CAST: Albert J. Smith (Lynch), Yakima Canutt (High Wolf)

SPECS: 55 minutes; Black & White

AVAILABILITY: NA

NATION: Kiowa

IMAGE PORTRAYAL: Attack on railroads

SUMMARY: Supplied with guns by the villain, Lynch, the Kiowa tribe of High Wolf attacks a construction camp and town of railroad and telegraph workers.

CRITICS: A *Variety* critic comments that "the plot is reminiscent of past Indian epics and carries stock shots of war dances, etc. from them" (December 1, 1937).

A PRISONER OF THE MOHICANS (Pathe, 1911)

DIRECTOR: Joseph A. Golden

SCREENPLAY: Anthony Coldeway

CAST: Pearl White (The White Girl)

SPECS: 1 reel; Black & White; Silent

AVAILABILITY: NA

NATION: Mohican

IMAGE PORTRAYAL: Gratitude

SUMMARY: Mohicans capture a white girl who had earlier helped a poor, starving Native American. This Native American man shows his gratitude by rescuing her from the Mohican camp and returning her to her parents.

THE PROPHECY (Paramount, 1979)
DIRECTOR: John Frankenheimer
SCREENPLAY: David Seltzer
CAST: Robert Foxworth (Rob), Armand Assante (John Hawks), George Clutesi
    (M'Rai), Victoria Racimo (Ramona)
SPECS: 102 minutes; Color
AVAILABILITY: DVD (Paramount Home Video)
NATION: Opies
IMAGE PORTRAYAL: Contemporary Native Americans; Native Americans as
    victims
SUMMARY: The hero, Rob, helps the Opie tribe of John Hawks when pollution
    from a paper mill threatens their existence. M'Rai is a seer who finds out that
    animals have been turned into monsters because of mercury poisoning. The
    main monster is Katadin, which resembles a bear, and kills whites and Native
    Americans.

A PUEBLO LEGEND (Biograph, 1912)
DIRECTOR: D. W. Griffith
SCREENPLAY: D. W. Griffith
CAST: Mary Pickford (The Indian Girl), Wilfred Lucas (The Indian Girl's Great
    Brother), Robert Harron (The Great Brother's Friend), J. Jiquel Lanoe (The
    Sun Priest), Charles Hill Mailes (The Old Man, a Pueblo), Jack Pickford
    (Young Brave)
SPECS: 1 reel; Black & White; Silent
AVAILABILITY: NA
NATION: Apache; Pueblo
IMAGE PORTRAYAL: Romance between Native Americans
SUMMARY: The high priest tells the tribe about a turquoise stone that fell from
    the heavens, a stone that would bring great happiness and wealth. Then the
    tribe chooses one of its leaders to go and find the stone.

Q

QUANTEZ (Universal, 1957)
DIRECTOR: Harry Keller
SCREENPLAY: R. Wright Campbell, Ann Edwards
CAST: Fred MacMurray (Gentry), Michael Ansara (Delgadito)
SPECS: 80 minutes; Color
AVAILABILITY: DVD (Universal Vault Series)
NATION: Apache
IMAGE PORTRAYAL: Attack on outlaws
SUMMARY: Apaches led by Delgadito attack a gang of outlaws heading for the
    Mexican border.

QUINCANNON, FRONTIER SCOUT (United Artists, 1956)

DIRECTOR: Lesley Selander

SCREENPLAY: John C. Higgins and Don Martin, based on the novel, *Frontier Feud*, by Will Cook

CAST: Tony Martin (Linus Quincannon), Ron Randell (Capt. Bell), Ed Hashim (Iron Wolf)

SPECS: 83 minutes; Color

AVAILABILITY: DVD (MGM Limited Edition Collection); Amazon Instant Video

NATION: Arapaho

IMAGE PORTRAYAL: Attack on a fort; drunkenness

SUMMARY: A villain, Capt. Bell, who has smuggled guns to the tribe of Iron Wolf and incited them to attack a fort is brought to justice at the end, and Quincannon is vindicated.

R

RACHEL AND THE STRANGER (RKO, 1948)

DIRECTOR: Norman Foster

SCREENPLAY: Waldo Salt, Howard Fast

CAST: Loretta Young (Rachel)

SPECS: 80 minutes; Black & White

AVAILABILITY: VHS (Warner Home Video)

NATION: Shawnee

IMAGE PORTRAYAL: Attack on settlers; Native Americans as victims

SUMMARY: Hostile Shawnee braves attack homesteaders in a cabin but are finally driven off.

CRITICS: A *Variety* critic comments: "A socko Indian raid . . . flaming arrows and war whoops pinpoint pioneer danger" (August 4, 1948).

RAIDERS OF TOMAHAWK CREEK (Columbia, 1950)

DIRECTOR: Fred Sears

SCREENPLAY: Barry Shipman, Eric Freiwald, Robert Schaefer

CAST: Charles Starrett (Steve Blake/the Durango Kid), Paul Marion (Flying Arrow)

SPECS: 55 minutes; Black & White

AVAILABILITY: NA

NATION: NA

IMAGE PORTRAYAL: Native Americans as victims

SUMMARY: Steve Blake—the Durango Kid, a new and good Indian agent—deals with an evil Indian agent who is exploiting the tribe of chief Flying Arrow by accusing them of murder. At the end, the Durango Kid brings the villain to justice.

RAIN IN THE MOUNTAINS (Foxhall Films, 2007)
DIRECTORS: Joel Metlen, Christine Sullivan
SCREENPLAY: Joel Metlen
CAST: Steve Pierre (Eric Smallhouse), Nick Erb (Todd Smallhouse), Audrey Seymour (Lindsay Smallhouse), Michael Treetop Jr. (Wapati)
SPECS: 90 minutes; Color
AVAILABILITY: DVD (Anderson Digital); Amazon Instant Video
NATION: NA
IMAGE PORTRAYAL: Contemporary Native Americans; Native Americans as butt of humor
SUMMARY: In this comedy-spoof, Eric Smallhouse tries to teach his son, Todd, the traditional ways of his tribe even though he doesn't really know what they are. His quest fails and he get into trouble with the law. The viewer may be torn on how to interpret the tone of this film.

THE RAINBOW TRAIL (Fox, 1925)
DIRECTOR: Lynn Reynolds
SCREENPLAY: Lynn Reynolds, based on a novel by Zane Grey
CAST: Tom Mix (John Shefford), Steve Clemente (Nas-Ta-Bega)
SPECS: 6 reels; Black & White
AVAILABILITY: NA
NATION: NA
IMAGE PORTRAYAL: Attack on wagon train
SUMMARY: The hero, John Shefford, comes to the rescue of a lone covered wagon under attack by the tribe of Nas-Ta-Bega.
CRITICS: A *Variety* reviewer points out a typical pattern: "The picture starts with an Indian attack . . . with Mix (the hero) riding to the rescue and the routing of the redskins" (June 3, 1925).

THE RAINBOW TRAIL (Fox, 1932)
DIRECTOR: David Howard
SCREENPLAY: Barry Connors, Philip Klein, based on a novel by Zane Grey
CAST: George O'Brien (Shefford), Robert Frazer (Lone Eagle), Winter Blossom (Singing Cloud), Iron Eyes Cody (John Tom)
SPECS: 65 minutes; Black & White
AVAILABILITY: NA
NATION: Navajo
IMAGE PORTRAYAL: Gratitude
SUMMARY: After Shefford rescues Singing Cloud, the sister of Lone Eagle, a member of the Navajo tribe, Lone Eagle shows his gratitude at the end of the film.
CRITICS: A *Variety* critic, commenting on the threat of a Navajo attack, notes that this adds "some Indian menace stuff" (February 2, 1932).

RAMONA (Biograph, 1910)
DIRECTOR: D. W. Griffith
SCREENPLAY: D. W. Griffith, Stanner E. V. Taylor, based on the novel by
    Helen Hunt Jackson
CAST: Mary Pickford (Ramona), Henry B. Walthall (Chief Alessandro)
SPECS: 17 minutes; Black & White; Silent
AVAILABILITY: DVD (Image Entertainment)
NATION: NA
IMAGE PORTRAYAL: Mixed-blood Native American; romance between Na-
    tive Americans
SUMMARY: In this film, subtitled "A Story of the Whiteman's Injustice to the
    Indian," Ramona, a mixed-blood, is the target of prejudice because of her mar-
    riage to Chief Alessandro.

RAMONA (Clune, 1916)
DIRECTOR: Donald Crisp
SCREENPLAY: Based on the novel by Helen Hunt Jackson
CAST: Adda Gleason (Ramona), Monroe Salisbury (Alessandro), Alice Morton
    Otten (Starlight)
SPECS: 14 reels; Black & White; Silent
AVAILABILITY: NA
NATION: NA
IMAGE PORTRAYAL: Mixed-blood Native American; romance between Na-
    tive Americans
SUMMARY: This is the second adaptation of Helen Hunt Jackson's novel about
    the tragic love of the mixed-blood Ramona and Chief Alessandro.
CRITICS: A *Variety* critic sees the film as "a plea for justice for the red man who
    has been robbed of his land by the constant encroachment of the American on
    his vested domain" (April 7, 1916).

RAMONA (United Artists, 1928)
DIRECTOR: Edwin Carewe
SCREENPLAY: Finis Fox, based on the novel by Helen Hunt Jackson
CAST: Dolores Del Rio (Ramona), Warner Baxter (Alessandro), Dorothy Teters
    (Indian)
SPECS: 80 minutes; Black & White
AVAILABILITY: NA
NATION: NA
IMAGE PORTRAYAL: Mixed-blood Native American; romance between Na-
    tive Americans
SUMMARY: In this third adaptation of the famous novel, Ramona, a mixed-
    blood raised by a cruel white man, defies her guardian and marries Chief
    Alessandro. Eventually she loses both her husband and child and wanders in

a state of amnesia until friends finally rescue her. (The film's director, Edwin Carewe—born James Fox—was of Chickasaw descent.)

RAMONA (20th Century Fox, 1936)
DIRECTOR: Henry King
SCREENPLAY: Lamar Trotti, based on the novel by Helen Hunt Jackson
CAST: Loretta Young (Ramona), Don Ameche (Alessandro), Chief Thundercloud (Pablo), and various other actors playing minor Native American roles
SPECS: 84 minutes; Color
AVAILABILITY: DVD (20th Century Fox Cinema Archives)
NATION: NA
IMAGE PORTRAYAL: Mixed-blood Native American; romance between Native Americans
SUMMARY: In this version, Ramona rejects the son of the family she works for and marries Alessandro. This leads to suffering at the hands of prejudiced whites because Alessandro is sent away and then killed. At the end, Ramona has only their baby and the man she rejected to console her.

THE RAMRODDER (Entertainment Ventures, 1969)
DIRECTOR: Van Guylder
SCREENPLAY: Van Guylder
CAST: Roger Gentry (The Ramrodder), Kathy Williams (Tuwana), Robert Aiken (Brave Eagle), Kedric Wolfe (Minowa), Catherine Share (Cochina), Marsha Jordan (Motula)
SPECS: 92 minutes; Color
AVAILABILITY: DVD (Something Weird Video)
NATION: NA
IMAGE PORTRAYAL: Vengeance
SUMMARY: A white man rapes a Native American woman and her tribe retaliates by raping a settler's daughter. The Ramrodder averts a war by handing over the man to the tribe, which punishes him with castration. Finally, the Ramrodder marries Princess Tuwana.

RANGER OF CHEROKEE STRIP (Republic, 1949)
DIRECTOR: Philip Ford
SCREENPLAY: Robert Creighton Williams, Earle Snell
CAST: Monte Hall (Steve Howard), Douglas Kennedy (Joe Bearclaws), Monte Blue (Chief Charles Hunter), Neyle Morrow (Tokata), Alix Talton (Mary Bluebird)
SPECS: 60 minutes; Black & White
AVAILABILITY: Amazon Instant Video
NATION: Cherokee
IMAGE PORTRAYAL: Native Americans as victims

SUMMARY: Steve Howard comes to the rescue of Joe Bearclaws, a Cherokee who has been framed by cattlemen intent on pushing the tribe from their territory. Joe is married to Mary Bluebird.

RED CLAY (Universal, 1927)
DIRECTOR: Ernest Laemmle
SCREENPLAY: Charles Logue, Richard Thorpe, Ruth Todd, Sarah Saddoris
CAST: William Desmond (Chief John Nisheto), Noble Johnson (Chief Bear Paw), Felix White Feather (Indian Chief), Ynez Seabury (Minnie Bear Paw)
SPECS: 50 minutes; Black & White; Silent
AVAILABILITY: NA
NATION: NA
IMAGE PORTRAYAL: Romance between a Native American man and a white woman
SUMMARY: Though Chief John Nisheto, a scholar and star college football player, saves the life of Jack Burr in wartime, the man objects to a romance between Chief Nisheto and his sister, Agnes Burr. After Chief Nisheto is fatally shot, Jack repents for his prejudiced attitude.
CRITICS: A *Variety* critic notes that the film "runs to the realistic, showing the probable results of an attempt by an Indian to mix with a white girl" (April 20, 1927).

RED LOVE (Davis Dist., 1925)
DIRECTOR: Edgar Lewis
SCREENPLAY: Lillian Case Russell
CAST: John Lowell (Thunder Cloud), Evangeline Russell (Starlight), F. Serrano Keating (James Logan/Little Antelope), Frank Montgomery (Two Crows), Dexter McReynolds (Scar Face)
SPECS: 6 reels; Black & White; Silent
AVAILABILITY: NA
NATION: Sioux
IMAGE PORTRAYAL: Mixed-blood Native American; romance between Native Americans
SUMMARY: Thunder Cloud, a Sioux and graduate of Carlisle, goes away with Starlight, the mixed-blood daughter of the sheriff. Consequently, his brother, Little Antelope, a tribal policeman, arrests him for kidnapping. However, at the end Thunder Cloud is exonerated and marries Starlight.

THE RED MAN AND THE CHILD (Biograph, 1908)
DIRECTOR: D. W. Griffith
SCREENPLAY: D. W. Griffith, based on the novel by Bret Harte
CAST: Charles Inslee (The Sioux), John Tansey (The Child)
SPECS: 14 minutes; Black & White; Silent

AVAILABILITY: NA
NATION: Sioux
IMAGE PORTRAYAL: Vengeance
SUMMARY: In this film, subtitled "The Story of an Indian's Vengeance," outlaws kill an old miner and kidnap his grandchild while their Native American friend, the Sioux, is away. When he returns, he rescues the child and avenges the killing of his old friend by killing all the outlaws.

THE RED MAN'S HONOR (Eclipse, 1912)
DIRECTOR: Gaston Roudes
SCREENPLAY: Joe Hamman
CAST: Joe Hamman (Red Hawk), Vesta Harold (June Dew)
SPECS: 2 reels; Black & White; Silent
AVAILABILITY: NA
NATION: NA
IMAGE PORTRAYAL: Honor
SUMMARY: Though really innocent, Red Hawk is accused of killing Seated Bear, his rival for the love of June Dew. The chief of the tribe rules that he must be executed one year later, and Red Hawk shows his honor by returning at the appointed time and dying with his beloved June Dew.

THE RED MAN'S PENALTY (Bison, 1911)
DIRECTOR: NA
SCREENPLAY: NA
CAST: NA
SPECS: 1 reel; Black & White; Silent
AVAILABILITY: NA
NATION: NA
IMAGE PORTRAYAL: Native Americans as victims; vengeance
SUMMARY: A mean and crooked Indian agent gives a tribe rotten meat. When the tribe retaliates because of this injustice, the cavalry attacks them and many are killed.

THE RED MOUNTAIN (Paramount, 1951)
DIRECTOR: William Dieterle
SCREENPLAY: George W. George, John Meredyth Lucas, George F. Slavin
CAST: Alan Ladd (Capt. Brett Sherwood), John Ireland (Gen. William Quantrill), Jay Silverheels (Little Crow), Herbert Belles (Indian Guard), Iron Eyes Cody (Ute Indian)
SPECS: 84 minutes; Color
AVAILABILITY: Amazon Instant Video
NATION: Ute
IMAGE PORTRAYAL: Attack on soldiers

SUMMARY: Incited by General Quantrill, Utes attack soldiers.
CRITICS: A *Variety* reviewer comments on the ending: "An all-out, shoot'em-up, waving flags-charging cavalry, red-skins-bite-the-dust finale that uses every cliche in the book" (November 14, 1951).

THE RED RAIDERS (Charles R. Rogers Productions, 1927)
DIRECTOR: Albert Rogell
SCREENPLAY: Marion Jackson, Don Ryan
CAST: Ken Maynard (Lieutenant John Scott), Chief Yowlachie (Lone Wolf)
SPECS: 70 minutes; Black & White; Silent
AVAILABILITY: DVD (Grapevine Video)
NATION: Sioux
IMAGE PORTRAYAL: Attack on fort; peace-loving chief
SUMMARY: Scar Face Charlie, an evil spy who goes against the advice of his Sioux elders, incites the Sioux tribe to attack a fort, but John Scott comes to the rescue. At the end, the death of the hostile Scar Face Charlie leads to peace.

THE RED, RED HEART (Bluebird, 1918)
DIRECTOR: Wilfred Lucas
SCREENPLAY: Bess Meredyth, based on the novel by Honore Morrow
CAST: Monroe Salisbury (Kut-le), Ruth Clifford (Rhoda Tuttle), Neola May (Molly)
SPECS: 5 reels; Black & White; Silent
AVAILABILITY: NA
NATION: NA
IMAGE PORTRAYAL: Kidnapping; romance between a Native American man and a white woman
SUMMARY: Kut-le, a young man educated at Yale, falls in love with Rhoda Tuttle after he cures her of a tarantula bite. When she rejects him, he kidnaps her and goes to the mountains of the West. Eventually she returns his love, and they decide to be married.

THE RED RIDER (Universal, 1925)
DIRECTOR: Clifford Smith
SCREENPLAY: Isadore Bernstein
CAST: Jack Hoxie (White Elk), Jack Pratt (Chief Black Panther), Natalie Warfield (Natauka), Marin Sais (Silver Waters), Francis Ford (Brown Bear), Frank Lanning (Medicine Man)
SPECS: 50 minutes; Black & White; Silent
AVAILABILITY: NA
NATION: NA
IMAGE PORTRAYAL: Romance between a Native American woman and a white man

SUMMARY: When White Elk rejects a Native American woman he is betrothed to because he loves a white woman, Chief Black Panther condemns him to death. However, after White Elk and the white woman escape, he finds out he is really a white man and they plan to be married. The Native American woman to whom he was betrothed agrees to commit suicide.

RED RIVER (United Artists, 1948)
DIRECTOR: Howard Hawks
SCREENPLAY: Borden Chase, Charles Schnee, based on the story by Chase
CAST: John Wayne (Thomas Dunson), Chief Yowlachie (Quo), Chief Sky Eagle (Indian Chief)
SPECS: 133 minutes; Color
AVAILABILITY: DVD and Blu-ray (Criterion); Amazon Instant Video
NATION: Comanche
IMAGE PORTRAYAL: Attack on cowboys; friendship
SUMMARY: Attacks by Comanches are just one of the obstacles that the hero and his cowboys overcome as they establish the Chisholm Trail. Quo is a friendly Native American who accompanies Thomas Dunson on the cattle drive.
CRITICS: A *Variety* critic notes that the film accurately depicts "the marauding Indians that bore down on the pioneers" (July 14, 1948).

RED SNOW (All American Film, 1952)
DIRECTORS: Harry Franklin, Boris Petroff
SCREENPLAY: Tom Hubbard, Orville H. Hampton, Robert Peters
CAST: Ray Mala (Sgt. Koovuk), Gloria Saunders (Alak—Sgt. Koovuk's wife), Philip Ahn (Taglu, the Spy), Robert Bice (Chief Nanu), Guy Madison (Lt. Phil Johnson)
SPECS: 75 minutes; Black & White
AVAILABILITY: NA
NATION: Eskimo
IMAGE PORTRAYAL: Contemporary Native American; friendship; loyalty; Native American activist
SUMMARY: An Eskimo soldier, Sgt. Koovuk, finds that the Russians are developing a new weapon in his area and he, along with other Eskimos, helps Lt. Johnson stop the Russians.

RED TOMAHAWK (A.C. Lyles Productions, 1967)
DIRECTOR: R. G. Springsteen
SCREENPLAY: Andrew Craddock, Steve Fisher
CAST: Howard Keel (Capt. Tom York)
SPECS: 82 minutes; Color
AVAILABILITY: NA
NATION: Sioux

IMAGE PORTRAYAL: Attacks on a town; attack on soldiers

SUMMARY: After the Battle of Little Big Horn, Tom York saves a town and a group of soldiers from a Sioux attack by securing Gatling guns. At the end, York and his guns defeat the Sioux warriors.

RED WING'S GRATITUDE (Vitagraph, 1909)

DIRECTOR: James Young Deer

SCREENPLAY: NA

CAST: Red Wing (Red Wing)

SPECS: Split reel; Black & White; Silent

AVAILABILITY: NA

NATION: NA

IMAGE PORTRAYAL: Gratitude

SUMMARY: White settlers save Red Wing from a beating by her own people. Later Red Wing shows her gratitude by helping a white girl captured by her tribe escape. As the two young women flee, the settlers come to their rescue, but Red Wing is wounded and dies in the arms of the white girl's father.

RED WING'S LOYALTY (Bison, 1910)

DIRECTOR: Fred J. Balshofer

SCREENPLAY: NA

CAST: Red Wing (Red Wing)

SPECS: 1 reel; Black & White; Silent

AVAILABILITY: NA

NATION: NA

IMAGE PORTRAYAL: Evil mixed-blood; friendship; loyalty; mixed-blood Native American

SUMMARY: A cavalry lieutenant who helps the maiden Red Wing after she had been hurt by an evil mixed-blood, later unknowingly kills her father in a battle. Despite this, she remains loyal and comes to his rescue after her tribe has captured him and is about to burn him at the stake. She brings soldiers who save the man's life and then reward Red Wing for her loyalty to the lieutenant.

THE RED WOMAN (World, 1917)

DIRECTOR: E. Mason Hopper

SCREENPLAY: Harry R. Durant

CAST: Mahlon Hamilton (Morton Deal), Gail Kane (Maria Temosach)

SPECS: 5 reels; Black & White; Silent

AVAILABILITY: NA

NATION: NA

IMAGE PORTRAYAL: Romance between a Native American woman and a white man

SUMMARY: The daughter of an Indian chief, Maria Temosach, gains high honors in an eastern college but returns to her tribe in New Mexico because she never was accepted by white society. Later she saves the life of Morton Deal, the son of a rich man, falls in love with him, and bears him a child. He abandons her for a while, but then returns, marries her, and lives with her in the West.

RED, WHITE AND BLACK (Hirschman-Northern, 1970)
DIRECTOR: John Cardos
SCREENPLAY: Marlene Weed
CAST: Robert Dix (Chief Walking Horse), Bobby Clark (Kayitah)
SPECS: 77 minutes; Color
AVAILABILITY: NA
NATION: NA
IMAGE PORTRAYAL: Attack on soldiers; friendship
SUMMARY: Soldiers kill a warrior from the tribe of Chief Walking Horse and Kayitah, who have been stealing horses. Though a black leader of the soldiers and Walking Horse are friends, they are forced to fight against each other.

REDSKIN (Paramount, 1929)
DIRECTOR: Victor Schertzinger
SCREENPLAY: Elizabeth Pickett, Julian Johnson
CAST: Richard Dix (Wing Foot), Julie Carter (Corn Blossom), Tully Marshall (Navajo Jim), George Regas (Notani), Noble Johnson (Pueblo Jim), Augustina Lopez (Grandma Yina), Bernard Siegel (Chahi)
SPECS: 82 minutes; Color and Black & White
AVAILABILITY: DVD (National Film Preservation Foundation; in "Treasures III: Social Issues in American Film, 1900–1934")
NATION: Navajo; Pueblo
IMAGE PORTRAYAL: Romance between Native Americans
SUMMARY: In this film, which is generally sympathetic toward Native Americans, Wing Foot, a Navajo educated in the East and an outcast from his tribe, falls in love with a classmate, Corn Blossom, a member of a rival Pueblo tribe. When he returns to his home, he discovers oil in the desert and uses an offer of oil rights to stop a war between the Pueblo tribe and his people. At the end, he marries Corn Blossom.

RENEGADES (Universal, 1989)
DIRECTOR: Jack Sholder
SCREENPLAY: Dave Rich
CAST: Keifer Sutherland (Buster McHenry), Lou Diamond Phillips (Hank Storm), Floyd Westerman (Red Crow)
SPECS: 106 minutes; Color
AVAILABILITY: DVD (Universal Studios Home Entertainment)

NATION: Lakota-Sioux

IMAGE PORTRAYAL: Contemporary Native American; friendship; loyalty

SUMMARY: Buster, an undercover cop, is wounded in a robbery in which Hank Storm's brother is killed and an ancient Lakota spear is stolen. Hank's father, medicine man Red Cloud, cures Buster. Then Buster and Hank, who are both outsiders, become friends and bring the villains to justice.

CRITICS: *New York Times* critic Caryn James comments: "The strong, smart Indians are positive stereotypes, but they're stereotypes nonetheless" (June 2, 1989).

REPRISAL! (Columbia, 1956)

DIRECTOR: George Sherman

SCREENPLAY: David P. Harmon, Raphael Hayes, David Dortort, based on the novel by Arthur Gordon

CAST: Guy Madison (Frank Madden/Neola), Felicia Farr (Catherine Cantrell), Kathryn Grant (Taini), Ralph Moody (Matara, grandfather of Frank Madden), Philip Breedlove (Takola), Victor Zamudio (Keleni)

SPECS: 74 minutes; Color

AVAILABILITY: NA

NATION: NA

IMAGE PORTRAYAL: Romance between a Native American man and a white woman

SUMMARY: Two people from the tribe of Takola and Keleni are unjustly hanged. At the urging of Taini and Catherine Cantrell, the hero, Frank Madden, a Native American posing as a white man, takes on the villains and brings them to justice. At the end, after his liaison with Taini is revealed as a lie to save his life, he falls in love with Catherine Cantrell.

CRITICS: A *Newsweek* critic notes: "The Indians, in line with current Hollywood practice, look pretty good. In fact, if this new morality continues, moviegoers may never see a bad Indian again" (November 19, 1956, 135–36).

RESERVATION WARPARTIES (Midthunder Productions, 2004)

DIRECTOR: Angelique Midthunder

SCREENPLAY: Jonathan Garfield, Angelique Midthunder

CAST: Steve De Doyer III (The Boy), David Midthunder (The Uncle), Tokala Clifford (JR), Steven Judd (Jim), Amber Midthunder (Little Sister)

SPECS: 13 minutes; Color

AVAILABILITY: NA

NATION: Lakota

IMAGE PORTRAYAL: Contemporary Native Americans; troubled Native Americans

SUMMARY: This short film, which takes place on a Lakota reservation, involves a question directed by a boy to his uncle, which leads to a discussion of alcoholism and hopes for a return to past values.

THE RETURN OF A MAN CALLED HORSE (Sandy Howard Productions, 1976)
DIRECTOR: Irvin Kershner
SCREENPLAY: Jack DeWitt, Dorothy M. Johnson
CAST: Richard Harris (John Morgan), Gale Sondergaard (Elk Woman), Jorge Luke (Running Bull), Enrique Lucero (Raven), Regino Herrera (Chief Lame Wolf), Pedro Damian (Standing Bear), Humberto Lopez (Thin Dog), Alberto Mariscal (Red Cloud), Eugenia Dolores (Brown Dove), Patricia Reyes Spindola (Gray Thorn), Ann De Sade (Moon Star)
SPECS: 129 minutes; Color
AVAILABILITY: DVD (MGM Video); Amazon Instant Video
NATIONS: Arikara; Yellow Hand
IMAGE PORTRAYAL: Friendship; loyalty; Native Americans as victims
SUMMARY: John Morgan returns from England to rescue his adopted Yellow Hand tribe of Chief Lame Wolf, his son, Standing Bear, Elk Woman, Raven, Moon Star, Thin Dog, and Gray Thorn. The Arikara of Running Bull, who work for evil French traders, have decimated the Yellow Hand tribe and taken their women to the fort of the French. After going through sweat and Sun Dance ceremonies, Morgan inspires the tribe to defeat the Arikara and the French. At the end, Morgan decides to spend the rest of his life with the Yellow Hand tribe.
CRITICS: A *Newsweek* reviewer comments: "The movie is too glib about Indian spirituality to be good, too self-conscious about being on the Indians' side to be wholly convincing" (August 16, 1976, 87).

THE RETURN OF JOSEY WALES (Reel Movies Inter., 1987)
DIRECTOR: Michael Parks
SCREENPLAY: Forrest Carter, based on his novel, *The Vengeance of Josey Wales*
CAST: Michael Parks (Josey Wales), Rafael Campos (Chato)
SPECS: 90 minutes; Color
AVAILABILITY: NA
NATION: Apache
IMAGE PORTRAYAL: Friendship; loyalty
SUMMARY: When Mexican villains kill the friend of Josey Wales, Chato, he goes to Mexico, takes revenge, and rescues an Apache girl who is about to be raped and hanged by an evil Mexican policeman.

REVOLT AT FORT LARAMIE (United Artists, 1957)
DIRECTOR: Lesley Selander
SCREENPLAY: Robert C. Dennis
CAST: Eddie Little Sky (Red Cloud)
SPECS: 73 minutes; Color
AVAILABILITY: NA

NATION: Sioux

IMAGE PORTRAYAL: Attack on a fort

SUMMARY: Red Cloud and his Sioux warriors demand money before they agree to a treaty. Finally, they attack the fort, but are defeated by Union soldiers aided by Confederates.

REVOLUTION (Warner Bros., 1985)

DIRECTOR: Hugh Hudson

SCREENPLAY: Robert Dillon

CAST: Al Pacino (Tom Dobbs), Skeeter Vaughan (Tonti), Larry Sellers (Honch-wah), Denis Lacroix (Iroquois Indian), Joseph Runningfox (Iroquois Indian), Harold Pacheco (Iroquois Indian), Graham Greene (Ongwata)

SPECS: 126 minutes; Color

AVAILABILITY: DVD (Warner Home Video); Amazon Instant Video

NATION: Huron; Iroquois

IMAGE PORTRAYAL: Friendship; gratitude; loyalty

SUMMARY: When Tom Dobbs kills two Iroquois, the Huron tribe of Tosti, Honchwah, and Ongwata make friends with him because the Iroquois are their enemies. They take Dobbs and his son to their camp and save the boy's life by cauterizing his wounded feet.

REZ BOMB (Roaring Fire Films, 2008)

DIRECTOR: Steven Lewis Simpson

SCREENPLAY: Steven Lewis Simpson

CAST: Tamara Feldman (Harmony), Trent Ford (Scott), Chris Robinson (Jaws—the Loan Shark), Russell Means (Dodds), Arlette Loud Hawk (Mrs. Phelps), Tokala Clifford (Chilik), Mo Brings Plenty (Johnny)

SPECS: 95 minutes; Color

AVAILABILITY: DVD (InYo Entertainment)

NATION: Lakota

IMAGE PORTRAYAL: Romance between a Native American woman and a white man

SUMMARY: In this film, which takes place on the Pine Ridge Lakota Reservation, Harmony, a Lakota woman and her white lover, Scott, get in trouble with an evil loan shark. Harmony, who is pregnant, goes undercover and Scott searches for her and a guitar in which money is hidden.

RIDE OUT FOR REVENGE (United Artists, 1957)

DIRECTOR: Bernard Girard

SCREENPLAY: Norman Retchin, based on the novel by Burt Arthur

CAST: Rory Calhoun (Tate), Joanne Gilbert (Pretty Willow), Lloyd Bridges (Capt. George), Frank DeKova (Chief Yellow Wolf), Vince Edwards (Chief Little Wolf, son of Yellow Wolf)

SPECS: 78 minutes; Black & White

AVAILABILITY: DVD (Shout! Factory; in "Movies 4 You: Western Classics")
NATION: Cheyenne
IMAGE PORTRAYAL: Peace-loving chief; romance between a Native American woman and a white man
SUMMARY: Cheyenne Chief Yellow Wolf is killed by order of Capt. George after he tries to use gold to make a treaty. Marshal Tate, who loves Pretty Willow, the daughter of Yellow Wolf, works against the villains to secure a place for the Cheyenne. At the end Pretty Willow is reunited with Tate, who has killed Capt. George.

RIDE, RANGER, RIDE (Republic, 1936)
DIRECTOR: Joseph Kane
SCREENPLAY: Dorell McGowan, Stuart E. McGowan, Bernard McConville, Karen DeWolf
CAST: Gene Autry, (Texas Ranger Gene Autry), Monte Blue (Chief Tavibo), Chief Thundercloud (Chief Little Wolf), Sonny Chorre (Comanche Warrior), Iron Eyes Cody (Comanche War Party Leader), Shooting Star (Comanche Warrior), Greg Whitespear (Crazy Crow)
SPECS: 63 minutes; Black & White
AVAILABILITY: DVD (BFS Entertainment; in "Famous Western Gunfighters"); Amazin Instant Video
NATION: Comanche
IMAGE PORTRAYAL: Attack on a wagon train
SUMMARY: The Comanches of Chief Little Wolf, aided by Chief Tavibo, a Native American interpreter for the army, attack a wagon train. Texas Ranger Gene Autry and the cavalry come to the rescue.

RIDERS OF VENGEANCE (Universal, 1919)
DIRECTOR: John Ford
SCREENPLAY: John Ford, Eugene B. Lewis, Harry Carey
CAST: Harry Carey (Cheyenne Harry), Seena Own (The Girl)
SPECS: 60 minutes; Black & White; Silent
AVAILABILITY: NA
NATION: Apache
IMAGE PORTRAYAL: Attack on a stagecoach
SUMMARY: Cheyenne Harry rescues a schoolteacher from a stagecoach being attacked by Apaches, and later saves a wounded man during another Apache attack.

RIO CONCHOS (20th Century Fox, 1964)
DIRECTOR: Gordon Douglas
SCREENPLAY: Joseph Landon, Clair Huffaker, based on Huffaker's novel
CAST: Stuart Whitman (Capt. Haven), Wende Wagner (Sally), Rudolfo Acosta (Bloodshirt)

SPECS: 107 minutes; Color
AVAILABILITY: DVD and Blu-ray (Shout! Factory); Amazon Instant Video
NATION: Apache
IMAGE PORTRAYAL: Romance between a Native American woman and a white man; torture
SUMMARY: The Apaches of Bloodshirt capture Capt. Haven, who is trying to stop villains from running guns to the tribe. When the Apaches torture him, a Native American woman, Sally, takes pity and helps him escape. After everyone has been killed except Haven and Sally, they leave together.

RIO GRANDE (Republic, 1950)
DIRECTOR: John Ford
SCREENPLAY: James Kevin McGuinness, James Warner Beliah
CAST: John Wayne (Lt. Col. Kirby Yorke), Barlow Simpson (Indian Chief)
SPECS: 105 minutes; Black & White
AVAILABILITY: DVD and Blu-ray (Olive Films); Amazon Instant Video
NATION: Apache
IMAGE PORTRAYAL: Attack on soldiers; drunkenness
SUMMARY: Apaches raid a cavalry outpost, and later the soldiers, led by Kirby Yorke, follow them into Mexico and rescue a group of children from the hostile and drunken warriors.
CRITICS: A *New York Times* critic notes that "John Ford's continuing war with the Red Man and his romance with the U.S. Cavalry . . . show a few signs of wear and tear" (November 20, 1950).

RIVER OF NO RETURN (20th Century Fox, 1954)
DIRECTOR: Otto Preminger
SCREENPLAY: Frank Fenton, Louis Lantz
CAST: Robert Mitchum (Matt Calder), Marilyn Monroe (Kay Weston)
SPECS: 91 minutes; Color
AVAILABILITY: DVD (20th Century Fox Home Entertainment); Amazon Instant Video
NATION: NA
IMAGE PORTRAYAL: Attack on settlers
SUMMARY: A hostile tribe burns down Matt Calder's cabin and pursues him, Kay Weston, and his son, who try to escape on a raft, down a powerful river. On a bluff, the warriors hurl rocks and shoot arrows at the raft, and then swim out to it and tear the blouse off Kay before the people on the raft escape.

ROCKY MOUNTAIN (Warner Bros., 1950)
DIRECTOR: William Keighley
SCREENPLAY: Winston Miller, Alan Le May, based on Le May's story "Ghost Mountain."
CAST: Errol Flynn (Capt. Lafe Barstow), Nakai Snez (Chief Man Dog)

SPECS: 83 minutes; Black & White
AVAILABILITY: DVD (Warner Home Video)
NATION: NA
IMAGE PORTRAYAL: Attack on soldiers
SUMMARY: Capt. Lafe Barstow and his Confederate soldiers stop an attack on a stagecoach by luring the hostile braves of Chief Man Dog away. Later they are all killed during an attack by a great number of warriors.

ROLL, THUNDER, ROLL! (Equity Pictures, 1949)
DIRECTOR: Lewis Collins
SCREENPLAY: Paul Franklin, Fred Harman
CAST: Jim Bannon (Red Ryder), Don Reynolds (Little Beaver)
SPECS: 60 minutes; Color
AVAILABILITY: NA
NATION: NA
IMAGE PORTRAYAL: Friendship
SUMMARY: Red Ryder and his young Native American companion, Little Beaver, stop a gang of bandits. These characters appear in three other 1949 films, *Cowboy and the Prizefighter*, *The Fighting Redhead*, and *Ride, Ryder, Ride*.
CRITICS: A *Variety* critic notes that Little Beaver "is given some sharp lines which will garner laughs, and his role as Red Ryder's junior detective should give juves some vicarious participation in the wild and woolly adventures" (May 11, 1949).

ROMANCE OF THE WEST (PRC, 1946)
DIRECTOR: Robert Emmett Tansey
SCREENPLAY: Frances Kavanaugh
CAST: Eddie Dean (Eddie Dean), Forrest Taylor (Father Sullivan), Chief Thundercloud (Chief Eagle Feather)
SPECS: 58 minutes; Color
AVAILABILITY: DVD (Mr. FAT-W Video)
NATION: NA
IMAGE PORTRAYAL: Native Americans as victims
SUMMARY: Villains intent on getting land rich with silver try to provoke the tribe of Chief Eagle Feather, but Eddie Dean and Father Sullivan believe in the tribe, stop the villains, and finally establish a new peace.

A ROMANCE OF THE WESTERN HILLS (Biograph, 1910)
DIRECTOR: D. W. Griffith
SCREENPLAY: Stanner E. V. Taylor
CAST: Mary Pickford (Indian), Alfred Paget (Indian), Arthur V. Johnson (Indian)
SPECS: 16 minutes; Black & White; Silent
AVAILABILITY: DVD (Classic Video Streams; as part of "The Actors: Rare Films of Mary Pickford, Vol. 2") Collection

NATION: NA

IMAGE PORTRAYAL: Romance between a Native American woman and a white man; romance between Native Americans; vengeance

SUMMARY: A young Native American woman, adopted by a white family, falls in love with a white man who cruelly rejects her. Later, she falls in love with a man from her tribe. Before returning to their native land, they take revenge on the man who rejected her.

CRITICS: The *Biograph Bulletin* describes the film as "a powerful illustration of one of the many indignities the redskins suffered" (Bowser 1973, 185).

ROOSTER COGBURN (Universal, 1975)

DIRECTOR: Stuart Millar

SCREENPLAY: Charles Portis

CAST: John Wayne (Rooster Cogburn), Katharine Hepburn (Eula Goodnight), Anthony Zerbe (Breed), Richard Romancito (Wolf)

SPECS: 108 minutes; Color

AVAILABILITY: DVD (Universal Studios Home Entertainment); Amazon Instant Video

NATION: NA

IMAGE PORTRAYAL: Native Americans as victims

SUMMARY: After villains, led by Breed, kill a minister and some of his young Native American wards, Wolf and the minister's daughter, Eula Goodnight, help Rooster Cogburn bring the villains to justice.

ROSE MARIE (MGM, 1954)

DIRECTOR: Mervyn LeRoy

SCREENPLAY: Ronald Millar, George Froeschel, based on the operetta by Otto A. Harbach and Oscar Hammerstein II

CAST: Fernando Lamas (James Duval), Joan Taylor (Wanda), Chief Yowlachie (Black Eagle)

SPECS: 104 minutes; Color

AVAILABILITY: DVD (Warner Archive Collection)

NATION: NA

IMAGE PORTRAYAL: Romance between a Native American woman and a white man

SUMMARY: In this remake of the 1936 musical, Wanda, the daughter of Chief Black Eagle, who is eventually murdered, falls in love with a trapper, James Duval, who finally jilts her. At the end, she confesses that she set up James to be burned at the stake.

RUN, BROKEN YET BRAVE (Five Stones Films, 2009)

DIRECTOR: Tom Simes

SCREENPLAY: Chris Funk, Tom Simes

CAST: Ariel Yurach (Ashley Littletent), Joseph Naytowhow (Joseph Littletent), Julie Janzen (Anna Littletent), Krystle Pederson (Jenny Littletent), Jennifer Dawn Bishop (Beverly Littletent)
SPECS: 93 minutes; Color
AVAILABILITY: DVD (MoMo Bay / Gaiam)
NATION: Cree
IMAGE PORTRAYAL: Contemporary First Nation people; troubled First Nation people
SUMMARY: A reluctant Ashley is sent to the home of her Grandfather, Joseph, who teaches her the traditions of the Cree Nation such as beading, and the virtues of respect and forgiveness. Ashley, who also serves as a voice-over narrator, shows these virtues after a family tragedy.

RUN APPALOOSA RUN (Walt Disney Productions, 1966)
DIRECTOR: Larry Lansburgh
SCREENPLAY: Janet Lansburgh, Larry Lansburgh
CAST: Walter Cloud (Tribal Chief), Jerry Gatlin (Gilly Trask), Adele Palacios (Mary Blackfeather)
SPECS: 47 minutes; Color
AVAILABILITY: Amazon Instant Video
NATION: Nez Perce
IMAGE PORTRAYAL: Contemporary Native American; Native American athlete
SUMMARY: In this Disney film, Mary Blackfeather, the finest rider of her Nez Perce tribe, wins a big race on her horse, Holy Smoke.

RUN OF THE ARROW (RKO Radio Pictures, 1957)
DIRECTOR: Samuel Fuller
SCREENPLAY: Samuel Fuller
CAST: Rod Steiger (O'Meara), Sara Montiel (Yellow Moccasin), Jay C. Flippen (Walking Coyote), Charles Bronson (Blue Buffalo), H. M. Wynant (Crazy Wolf), Frank DeKova (Red Cloud), Billy Miller (Silent Tongue)
SPECS: 86 minutes; Color
AVAILABILITY: Amazon Instant Video
NATION: Sioux
IMAGE PORTRAYAL: Attack on soldiers; hostile warrior; peace loving chief; romance between a Native American woman and a white man
SUMMARY: Discussed on page 33, this film tells the story of a Confederate soldier, O'Meara, who rejects white society and is taught the ways of the Sioux by his friend, Walking Coyote. After Yellow Moccasin helps O'Meara survive the "run of the arrow" ordeal, he marries her and they adopt Silent Tongue. Crazy Wolf, the chief of the Sioux and Blue Buffalo go against a truce negotiated by

Red Cloud and attack the soldiers. At the end, Yellow Moccasin and O'Meara leave her Sioux people.

CRITICS: *New York Times* critic Bosley Crowther comments on a common pattern in westerns: "Then along comes a renegade Indian—there's always one in every decent, respectable tribe—and starts shooting arrows at the soldiers. As usual, this means war! The cavalry goes after the Indians, the Indians retaliate. The first thing you know, tents are burning and everybody is having a high old time" (August 3, 1957).

RUNNING BRAVE (Walt Disney Pictures, 1983)

DIRECTOR: D. S. Everett (Donald Shebib)

SCREENPLAY: Henry Bean and Shiri Hendryx

CAST: Robby Benson (Billy Mills), Claudia Cron (Pat Mills). August Schellenberg (Billy's Father), Denis Lacroix (Frank Mills), Graham Greene (Eddie Mills), Maurice Wolfe (Uncle Chester), Carmen Wolfe (Joe American Horse)

SPECS: 106 minutes; Color

AVAILABILITY: DVD (Trinity Home Entertainment)

NATION: Ogalala Lakota

IMAGE PORTRAYAL: Contemporary Native American; mixed-blood Native American; Native American athlete; romance between a Native American man and a white woman

SUMMARY: Discussed on page 57, this film tells the story of Billy Mills, the mixed-blood Sioux who became an Olympic champion distance runner. His life on the reservation and the struggles of his family and friends play a rather small part. While at the University of Kansas, Billy falls in love with a white woman, Pat, but the affair is at first opposed by both families. After a period of separation, Billy and Pat marry before he wins the Olympic medal. The race itself becomes the high point of the film.

S

SACRED GROUND (Pacific Inter., 1984)

DIRECTOR: Charles B. Pierce

SCREENPLAY: Charles B. Pierce

CAST: Tim McIntire (Matt Colter), Jack Elam (Lum Witcher), Serene Hedin (Little Doe), Ty Randolph (Wannetta), Eloy Casados (Prairie Fox), Vernon Foster (Wounded Leg), Lefty Wild Eagle (Medicine Man), Larry Kenoras (Brave Beaver), Danny Wilson (Lone Brave)

SPECS: 100 minutes; Color

AVAILABILITY: DVD (Sterling Entertainment)

NATION: Paiute

IMAGE PORTRAYAL: Attack on settlers; romance between a Native American woman and a white man

SUMMARY: When Matt Colter and his family accidentally build their cabin on sacred burial grounds, the Paiute tribe burial party attacks, kills Little Doe, and kidnaps her baby. Colter takes a Paiute woman who has lost a baby to care for the son he has rescued. He then fights the Paiute tribe in a battle for survival.

SADDLEMATES (Republic, 1941)

DIRECTOR: Lester Orlebeck

SCREENPLAY: Albert DeMond, Herbert Dalmas, Bernard McConville, Karen DeWolf

CAST: Robert Livingston (Stoney Brooke), Bob Steele (Tucson Smith), and Rufe Davis (Lullaby Joslin) are the Three Mesquiteers, Peter George Lynn (Le Roque/Wanechee), Marty Faust (Chief Thunder Bird), Glenn Strange (Little Bear), Iron Eyes Cody (Black Eagle)

SPECS: 56 minutes; Black & White

AVAILABILITY: Amazon Instant Video

NATION: NA

IMAGE PORTRAYAL: Hostile warrior; peace-loving chief

SUMMARY: The Mesquiteers save a wagon train from an attack by the tribe of Chief Wanechee. After they stop another attack on a stagecoach, they make a peace treaty with Chief Thunder Bird.

SAGINAW TRAIL (Columbia, 1953)

DIRECTOR: George Archainbaud

SCREENPLAY: Dorothy Yost, Dwight Cummins

CAST: Gene Autry (Gene Autry), Myron Healey (Miller Webb), Rodd Redwing (Huron Chief), Charles Soldani (Indian), John War Eagle (Chief Red Bird), Billy Wilkerson (Fox Chief)

SPECS: 56 minutes; Black & White

AVAILABILITY: DVD (Shout! Factory!; in "Gene Autry Movie Collection 8")

NATION: NA

IMAGE PORTRAYAL: Native Americans as victims

SUMMARY: A villain, Miller Webb, disguises himself as a warrior and hires the renegade tribe of Red Bird and the hostile tribes of the Huron chief and the Fox chief to attack settlers in the Michigan woods. Gene Autry comes to the rescue of the settlers.

SALMONBERRIES (Pelemele Film, 1991)

DIRECTOR: Percy Adlon

SCREENPLAY: Percy Adlon, Felix O. Adlon

CAST: k. d. lang (Kotzebue), Rosel Zech (Roswitha), Angayuqaq Oscar Kawagley (Butch), Eugene Omiak (Ovy), Jane Lind (Noayak)

SPECS: 95 minutes; Color
AVAILABILITY: DVD (Wolfe Video); Amazon Instant Video
NATION: Eskimo
IMAGE PORTRAYAL: Contemporary Native American; mixed-blood Native American; romance between a mixed-blood Native American woman and a white woman
SUMMARY: In a remote Eskimo village, Kotzebue, a troubled mixed-blood Eskimo woman, who is thought to be a man at first, searches for her identity. In the process, she falls in love with a female German librarian, Roswitha, who lives in the village, and together they travel to Germany to find the truth of their pasts.

SANTE FE PASSAGE (Republic, 1955)
DIRECTOR: William Witney
SCREENPLAY: Lillie Hayward, Heck Allen
CAST: John Payne (Kirby Randolph), Faith Domergue (Aurelie St. Clair), Irene Tedrow (Ptewaquin), George Keymas (Chief Satank)
SPECS: 91 minutes; Color
AVAILABILITY: Amazon Instant Video
NATION: Kiowa
IMAGE PORTRAYAL: Mixed-blood Native American; romance between a mixed-blood Native American woman and a white man
SUMMARY: Chief Satank and his hostile Kiowa warriors attack a group that includes Kirby Randolph; his beloved, Aurelie, a mixed-blood; and her mother, Ptewaquin, a Kiowa. At the end, Ptewaquin kills Chief Satank and then is killed. Kirby and Aurelie are finally set to be married.

SANTEE (Crown Inter., 1973)
DIRECTOR: Gary Nelson
SCREENPLAY: Brand Bell
CAST: Glenn Ford (Santee), Jay Silverheels (John Crow)
SPECS: 93 minutes; Color
AVAILABILITY: DVD (Rhino Home Video)
NATION: NA
IMAGE PORTRAYAL: Friendship; loyalty
SUMMARY: John Crow, the loyal friend of Santee, helps him deal with a gang of outlaws.

SASKATCHEWAN (Universal, 1954)
DIRECTOR: Raoul Walsh
SCREENPLAY: Gil Doud
CAST: Alan Ladd (Thomas O'Rourke), Jay Silverheels (Cajou), Antonio Moreno (Chief Dark Cloud), Anthony Caruso (Spotted Eagle)

SPECS: 87 minutes; Color
AVAILABILITY: DVD (Universal)
NATION: Cree; Sioux
IMAGE PORTRAYAL: Friendship; loyalty
SUMMARY: Thomas O'Rourke, who was raised by the Cree and is blood brother of Cajou, tries to stop the hostile Sioux of Sitting Bull from inciting the Cree to war. Just as he and his men are about to be overrun by the Sioux, Cajou and his warriors come to the rescue.

THE SAVAGE (Bluebird, 1917)
DIRECTOR: Rupert Julian
SCREENPLAY: Elliott J. Clawson
CAST: Monroe Salisbury (Julio Sandoval), Ruth Clifford (Marie Louise), Allan Sears (Capt. McKeever)
SPECS: 5 reels; Black & White; Silent
AVAILABILITY: NA
NATION: NA
IMAGE PORTRAYAL: Honor; kidnapping; mixed-blood Native American
SUMMARY: The title character is Julio Sandoval, a mixed-blood who falls in love with Marie Louise and captures her. However, he finally decides to bring her home, and further shows his honor by giving up his life while rescuing her lover, Capt. McKeever.

THE SAVAGE (Paramount, 1952)
DIRECTOR: George Marshall
SCREENPLAY: Sydney Boehm, based on the novel by J. L. Foreman
CAST: Charlton Heston (War Bonnet), Joan Taylor (Luta), Don Porter (Running Dog), Ted de Corsia (Iron Breast), Ian McDonald (Chief Yellow Eagle), Angela Clarke (Pehangi), Michael Tolan (Long Mane)
SPECS: 95 minutes; Color
AVAILABILITY: Amazon Instant Video
NATION: Crow; Sioux
IMAGE PORTRAYAL: Hostile warriors; peace-loving chief; romance between a Native American woman and a white man
SUMMARY: War Bonnet, a white man raised by the Sioux of Yellow Eagle and his wife Pehangi, falls in love with Luta. After Luta dies in an attack by hostile Crow, War Bonnet refuses to lead his warriors against the soldiers. At the end, after he punishes Running Dog and Long Mane, he almost sacrifices his life in order to convince his tribe not to attack the fort, and he finally carries out Yellow Eagle's desire to make a peace treaty.

THE SAVAGE INNOCENTS (Paramount, 1960)
DIRECTOR: Nicholas Ray

SCREENPLAY: Nicholas Ray, Hans Ruesch, Franco Solinas, Baccio Bandini, based on Ruesch's novel *Top of the World*

CAST: Anthony Quinn (Inuk), Yoko Tani (Asiak), Marie Yang (Powtee), Kaida Horiuchi (Imina), Marco Guglielmi (Missionary)

SPECS: 110 minutes; Color

AVAILABILITY: Amazon Instant Video

NATION: Eskimo

IMAGE PORTRAYAL: Friendship; loyalty; romance between Native Americans (Eskimos)

SUMMARY: Inuk, a good-natured Eskimo, marries Asiak and provides for his wife's family. Their happiness is shattered, however, when a missionary, who is ignorant of Eskimo customs, refuses Inuk's offer of his wife for the night, and Inuk kills him. Two Mounties hunt Inuk down, but one of them, who accepts the differences of Eskimo culture and whom Inuk calls the "Man," finally lets Inuk and Asiak return to his people.

SAVAGE LAND (Savage Land Productions, 1994)

DIRECTOR: Dean Hamilton

SCREENPLAY: Dean Hamilton, Mike Snyder, Eric Parkinson

CAST: Graham Greene (Skyano), Corbin Bernsen (Quint), Brion James (Cyrus), Sonny Landham (Lassiter), Vincent Rain (Leatherfoot), Helen Calahasen (Medicine Woman)

SPECS: 98 minutes; Color

AVAILABILITY: DVD (Hannover House)

NATION: Cherokee

IMAGE PORTRAYAL: Friendship; loyalty

SUMMARY: In this children's film, a small group of Cherokee, led by Skyano, protect two youngsters from Quint, Cyrus, and Lassiter, who are bandits posing as Native Americans. Skyano befriends a boy and tells him about Cherokee history and culture. At the end, the friendly and good-natured Cherokee return the children to their father.

SAVAGE SAM (Buena Vista, 1963)

DIRECTOR: Norman Tokar

SCREENPLAY: Fred Gipson, William Tunberg, based on Gipson's novel

CAST: Brian Keith (Uncle Beck Coates), Rafael Campos (Young Warrior), Rodolfo Acosta (Bandy Legs), Par Hogan (Broken Nose), Dean Fredericks (Comanche Chief)

SPECS: 103 minutes; Color

AVAILABILITY: DVD (Walt Disney Video); Amazon Instant Video

NATION: Apache; Comanche

IMAGE PORTRAYAL: Kidnapping

SUMMARY: The faithful dog, Savage Sam (Son of Old Yeller), leads Uncle Coates to the harsh and hostile Apaches of Broken Nose and Bandy Legs, who have captured two children. At the end, the children are rescued.

THE SAVAGE SEVEN (American International, 1968)
DIRECTOR: Richard Rush
SCREENPLAY: Michael Fisher, Rosalind Ross
CAST: Adam Roarke (Kisum), Joanna Frank (Marcia Little Hawk), Robert Walker Jr. (Johnnie Little Hawk), Max Julien (Grey Wolf), John Cardos (Running Buck)
SPECS: 94 minutes; Color
AVAILABILITY: VHS (MGM/UA Video)
NATION: NA
IMAGE PORTRAYAL: Contemporary Native Americans; Native Americans as victims; romance between a Native American woman and a white man
SUMMARY: A biker gang, led by Kisum, who loves Marcia Little Hawk, harasses a reservation. Johnnie Little Hawk, Grey Wolf, and Running Buck fight the bikers and try to protect their women. However, when one of the bikers rapes one of the tribal women, the killing begins.

THE SCALPHUNTERS (United Artists, 1968)
DIRECTOR: Sydney Pollack
SCREENPLAY: William W. Norton
CAST: Burt Lancaster (Bass), Shelley Winters (Kate), Ossie Davis (Joseph Lee), Armando Silvestre (Chief Two Crows), Telly Savalas (Jim Howie)
SPECS: 102 minutes; Color
AVAILABILITY: DVD and Blu-ray (Kino Lorber Films); Amazon Instant Video
NATION: NA
IMAGE PORTRAYAL: Friendship; vengeance
SUMMARY: The clever Kiowa Chief Two Crows takes the furs of Bass and gives him a slave, Joseph Lee, whom his tribe had captured. Then the scalphunters, led by Jim Howie, attack the warriors of Two Crows and kill everyone but the chief. At the end, the Kiowa of Two Crows get their revenge on the scalphunters and spare only Bass, Lee, and a white woman of dubious virtue, Kate, who offers herself to Chief Two Crows.

SCALPS (Beatrice Film, 1987)
DIRECTORS: Claudio Fragasso, Bruno Mattei
SCREENPLAY: Bruno Mattei, Roberto Di Girolamo, Italo Gasperini, Richard Harrison
CAST: Vassili Karis (Matt), Mapi Galan (Yarin), Charly Bravo (Comanche Chief), Alberto Farnese (Colonel Connor)
SPECS: NA; Color
AVAILABILITY: NA
NATION: Comanche

IMAGE PORTRAYAL: Romance between a Native American woman and a white man; vengeance

SUMMARY: A troop led by Col. Conner kills all members of a Comanche tribe except a Comanche woman, Yarin. She escapes and finds a place to hide with a rancher named Matt, with whom she falls in love. Together they take revenge on Conner and his men and then return to the ranch.

SCARLET AND GOLD (Davis Dist., 1925)

DIRECTOR: Francis J. Grandon

SCREENPLAY: NA

CAST: Al Ferguson (Mounted Policeman McGee), Marie Pavis (Haida, Indian Maid), Lucille Du Bois (Ruth MacLean)

SPECS: 5 reels; Black & White; Silent

AVAILABILITY: NA

NATION: NA

IMAGE PORTRAYAL: Romance between a Native American woman and a white man

SUMMARY: A loyal Mountie marries an Indian maiden because she is carrying the child of another Mountie. When she discovers that he loves a white woman, Ruth MacLean, she kills herself so he can be free to marry the woman.

THE SCARLET WEST (First National, 1925)

DIRECTOR: John G. Adolfi

SCREENPLAY: Anthony Paul Kelly, Arch Heath

CAST: Robert Frazer (Cardelanche), Helen Ferguson (Nestina), Clara Bow (Miriam)

SPECS: 90 minutes; Black & White; Silent

AVAILABILITY: NA

NATION: NA

IMAGE PORTRAYAL: Romance between a Native American man and a white woman; Romance between Native Americans

SUMMARY: Cardelanche, an educated man rejected by his tribe, rescues the cavalry from hostile warriors and becomes an officer. He falls in love with a white woman, Miriam, but after learning of Custer's death he gives up his commission, and returns to his tribe and marries Nestina.

THE SEALED VALLEY (Metro, 1915)

DIRECTOR: Lawrence B. McGill

SCREENPLAY: Based on Hulbert Footner's novel

CAST: Dorothy Donnelly (Nahnya Crossfox), Jack W. Johnston (Dr. Cowdray), Rene Ditline (Kitty Sholto)

SPECS: 5 reels; Black & White; Silent

AVAILABILITY: NA

NATION: NA

IMAGE PORTRAYAL: Romance between a Native American woman and a white man

SUMMARY: Nahnya Crossfox lives with her parents in a valley full of gold called Indian's Paradise. Later, Nahnya seals herself in the valley to live the rest of her life alone, after deciding that the white man she loves, Dr. Cowdray, should be free to live with a white woman, Kitty Sholto.

THE SEARCHERS (Warner Bros., 1956)

DIRECTOR: John Ford

SCREENPLAY: Frank S. Nugent, based on the novel by Alan Le May

CAST: John Wayne (Ethan Edwards), Jeffrey Hunter (Martin Pawley), Natalie Wood (Debbie Edwards), Henry Brandon (Chief Cicatriz/Scar), Beulah Archuletta (Look)

SPECS: 119 minutes; Color

AVAILABILITY: DVD and Blu-ray (Warner Home Video); Amazon Instant Video

NATION: Comanche

IMAGE PORTRAYAL: Kidnapping; vengeance

SUMMARY: In this classic film, discussed on page 32, Chief Scar of the Comanche kidnaps two girls and kills their parents in revenge for the killing of his sons. Scar's warriors rape and kill one of the girls and he takes the other, Debbie, for his wife. After years of searching, Ethan Edwards and Martin Pawley find the Comanche, kill Scar, and rescue Debbie.

CRITICS: In the *Chicago Sun Times* Roger Ebert comments on the Western genre: "'*The Searchers*' was made in the dying days of the classic Western, which faltered when Indians ceased to be typecast as savages. Revisionist Westerns, including Ford's own '*Cheyenne Autumn*' in 1964, took a more enlightened view of Native Americans, but the Western audience didn't want moral complexity; like the audience for today's violent thrillers and urban warfare pictures, it wanted action with clear-cut bad guys" (November 25, 2001).

SECRET OF TREASURE MOUNTAIN (Columbia, 1956)

DIRECTOR: Seymour Friedman

SCREENPLAY: David Lang

CAST: Lance Fuller (Juan Avalrado), Susan Cummings (Tawana), Pat Hogan (Vahoe)

SPECS: 68 minutes; Black & White

AVAILABILITY: NA

NATION: Apache

IMAGE PORTRAYAL: Native Americans as victims

SUMMARY: Juan Alvarado who is after gold threatens the Apache tribe of Vahoe and Tawana. However, after Juan kills Vahoe and Tawana, he is trapped forever in the Apache valley of gold in Treasure Mountain.

SEMINOLE (Universal, 1953)
DIRECTOR: Budd Boetticher
SCREENPLAY: Charles K. Peck Jr.
CAST: Rock Hudson (Lance Caldwell), Anthony Quinn (Osceola), Hugh
    O'Brian (Kajeck), Ralph Moody (Kulak), Richard Carlson (Maj. Harlan De-
    gan), Barbara Hale (Revere)
SPECS: 87 minutes; Color
AVAILABILITY: DVD (Universal Vault Series)
NATION: Seminole
IMAGE PORTRAYAL: Mixed-blood Native American; Native Americans as
    victims; peace-loving chief; romance between a Native American man and a
    white woman
SUMMARY: Discussed on page 30, this film tells the story of Chief Osceola, a
    mixed-blood who is in love with a white woman, Revere, and who dies after
    being captured by an evil military leader, Major Degan. However, at the end,
    his tribe, led by the once hostile Kajeck, makes peace.

SEMINOLE UPRISING (Columbia, 1955)
DIRECTOR: Earl Bellamy
SCREENPLAY: Robert E. Kent, based on the novel by Curt Brandon
CAST: George Montgomery (Lt. Cam Elliott), Karin Booth (Susan Hannah),
    Steven Ritch (Black Cat), Rus Conklin (High Cloud), Jonni Paris (Malawa)
SPECS: 74 minutes; Color
AVAILABILITY: NA
NATION: Seminole
IMAGE PORTRAYAL: Attacks on settlers; kidnapping; mixed-blood Native
    American
SUMMARY: The Seminoles of mixed-blood Black Cat escape from their Florida
    reservation and go on raids in Texas, during which they capture a white
    woman, Susan Hannah. At the end Black Cat helps the hero, Cam Elliott and
    reveals that he is a white man.

SERGEANT RUTLEDGE (Warner Bros., 1960)
DIRECTOR: John Ford
SCREENPLAY: Willis Goldbeck, James Warner Bellah, based on his novel
CAST: Constance Towers (Mary Beecher), Woody Strode (Sgt. Braxton Rut-
    ledge), Jack Lewis (Indian)
SPECS: 111 minutes; Color
AVAILABILITY: DVD (Warner Home Video)
NATION: Apache
IMAGE PORTRAYAL: Attacks on settlers; attacks on soldiers
SUMMARY: In a series of flashbacks during the trial of Sgt. Braxton Rutledge, a
    black cavalryman, he is seen protecting Mary Beecher from hostile Apaches and
    stopping the cavalry from riding into an Apache ambush.

SERGEANTS 3 (United Artists, 1962)
DIRECTOR: John Sturges
SCREENPLAY: W. R. Burnett, based on the poem "Gunga Din" by Rudyard
   Kipling
CAST: Frank Sinatra (Sgt. Mike Merry), Dean Martin (Sgt. Chip Deal), Peter
   Lawford (Sgt. Larry Barrett), Michael Pate (Watanka), Richard Hale (White
   Eagle), Eddie Little Sky (Ghost Dancer), Henry Silva (Mountain Hawk)
SPECS: 112 minutes; Color
AVAILABILITY: DVD (MGM)
NATION: NA
IMAGE PORTRAYAL: Attack on soldiers
SUMMARY: In this comedy, the hostile tribe of Mountain Hawk, Watanka,
   White Eagle, and Ghost Dancer capture the three sergeants, who later manage
   to save the cavalry from an ambush.

SEVEN CITIES OF GOLD (20th Century Fox, 1955)
DIRECTOR: Robert D. Webb
SCREENPLAY: Richard L. Breen, John C. Higgins, Joseph Petracca, based on
   the novel *The Nine Days of Father Serra by* Isabelle Gibson Ziegler
CAST: Anthony Quinn (Capt. Gaspar de Portola), Michael Rennie (Father Juni-
   pero Serra), Jeffrey Hunter (Chief Matuwir), Rita Moreno (Ula)
SPECS: 103 minutes; Color
AVAILABILITY: VHS (Fox Home Entertainment); Amazon Instant Video
NATION: NA
IMAGE PORTRAYAL: Native Americans as victims; torture; vengeance
SUMMARY: In this story of the Spanish exploration of what would become Cali-
   fornia, soldiers led by Capt. Gaspar de Portola and his adversary, the missionary,
   Father Junipero Serra, deal with the tribe of Chief Matuwir. When Jose Men-
   dosa seduces Ula, a member of the tribe, she commits suicide because of shame,
   and the tribe threatens war until he gives himself up for punishment by torture.
CRITICS: Bosley Crowther in the *New York Times* comments: "We have seldom
   seen such acrobatic Indians as the painted and feathered demons who pop up
   here to harass and battle the Spaniards, until Father Serra passes a few small
   'miracles.' Fortunately, they speak English almost as well as the Spaniards, so he
   is able to communicate" (October 8, 1955).

7TH CAVALRY (Columbia, 1956)
DIRECTOR: Joseph H. Lewis
SCREENPLAY: Peter Packer, Glendon Swartout
CAST: Randolph Scott (Capt. Tom Benson), Barbara Hale (Martha Kellogg), Pat
   Hogan (Yellow Hawk)
SPECS: 75 minutes; Color
AVAILABILITY: Amazon Instant Video

NATION: Sioux

IMAGE PORTRAYAL: Attack on soldiers

SUMMARY: The tribe of Yellow Hawk surrounds soldiers who are at the Little Big Horn to bring the bodies of Custer and his men to a proper burial, even though the battleground has been designated a sacred place by Sitting Bull. Through the efforts of Tom Benson, the hostile warriors do not attack, and, when Custer's horse appears, they let the soldiers ride away.

SHADOW HAWK ON SACRED GROUND (Tapeworm Studio, 2005)

DIRECTOR: NA

SCREENPLAY: NA

CAST: Blackhawk Walters (Shadow Hawk)

SPECS: 93 minutes; Color

AVAILABILITY: DVD (Tomahawk Productions)

NATION: NA

IMAGE PORTRAYAL: Contemporary Native American; Native American athlete

SUMMARY: Shadow Hawk, who is training as a fireman, is torn between his Native American beliefs and the values of the white world.

SHADOW OF THE HAWK (Columbia, 1976)

DIRECTOR: George McCowan

SCREENPLAY: Norman Thaddeus Vane, Herbert Wright, Peter Jensen, Lynette Cahill

CAST: Jan-Michael Vincent (Mike), Chief Dan George (Old Man Hawk), Marianne Jones (Dsonoqua), Jacques Hubert (Andak)

SPECS: 92 minutes; Color

AVAILABILITY: DVD (Sony Pictures Entertainment)

NATION: NA

IMAGE PORTRAYAL: Contemporary Native American; evil spirit

SUMMARY: Old Man Hawk, who is fighting Dsonoqua, an evil spirit out for revenge, goes to the city to ask for help from his grandson, Mike. He agrees, but Dsonoqua works her evil magic on them as they return to the reserve.

SHADOW OF THE WOLF (Transfilm, 1992)

DIRECTORS: Jacques Dorfmann, Pierre Magny

SCREENPLAY: Jacques Dorfmann, Evan Jones, David Milhaud, Rudy Wurlitzer, based on the novel *Agaguk* by Yves Theriault

CAST: Lou Diamond Phillips (Agaguk), Toshiro Mifune (Kroomak), Jennifer Tilly (Igiyook)

SPECS: 112 minutes; Color

AVAILABILITY: DVD (Columbia Tristar Home Video)

NATION: Inuit

IMAGE PORTRAYAL: Romance between Native Americans; Native American spirit

SUMMARY: In this story of conflict between whites and the Inuit tribe, a Canadian policeman searches for Agaguk, an angry young Inuit who has murdered an evil trader, rebelled against his father, Kroomak, and escaped into the frozen wilderness with his beloved Igiyook. After his father kills the policeman, Agaguk returns to his village. At the end, Kroomak gives himself up to the Mounties to save his son. Then, as Agaguk flies away with the authorities in a plane, he turns into a hawk and escapes.

CRITICS: Roger Ebert of the *Chicago Sun Times* comments: "The notion of making a movie about Eskimo life is a good one, but why did the filmmakers feel obligated to connect it to a lame and unconvincing story about a murder investigation?" (March 5, 1993).

SHALAKO (Palomar Pictures International, 1968)
DIRECTOR: Edward Dmytryk
SCREENPLAY: James Griffith, Hal Hopper, Scott Finch, and Clarke Reynolds, based on the novel by Louis L'Amour
CAST: Sean Connery (Shalako), Brigitte Bardot (Countess Irina)
SPECS: 113 minutes; Color
AVAILABILITY: DVD (MGM Home Entertainment)
NATION: Apache
IMAGE PORTRAYAL: Attack on a stage coach; friendship
SUMMARY: The Apaches of Chato attack Europeans who are hunting on their land and brutally kill a white woman on a stage coach. At the end, Shalako rescues Countess Irina and beats Chato in a hand-to-hand fight, though he spares Chato's life when his father, the Apache chief, asks Shalako to do so.

SHE WORE A YELLOW RIBBON (RKO, 1949)
DIRECTOR: John Ford
SCREENPLAY: Frank S. Nugent, Laurence Stallings
CAST: John Wayne (Capt. Nathan Cutting Brittles), Chief John Big Tree (Chief Pony That Walks), Chief Sky Eagle (Chief Sky Eagle), Noble Johnson (Chief Red Shirt)
SPECS: 103 minutes; Color
AVAILABILITY: DVD (Warner Home Video); Amazon Instant Video
NATION: Arapaho
IMAGE PORTRAYAL: Attack on settlers
SUMMARY: The hostile warriors of Red Shirt, who belong to the tribe of wise old chief, Pony That Walks, attack a stage depot. However, Capt. Nathan Brittles stops an all-out war by attacking the hostiles in their camp at night and scattering their horses.

THE SHERIFF OF FRACTURED JAW (20th Century Fox, 1958)

DIRECTOR: Raoul Walsh

SCREENPLAY: Howard Dimsdale, Jacob Hay

CAST: Kenneth More (Jonathan Tibbs), Jayne Mansfield (Kate), Jonas Applegarth (Running Deer), Joe Buffalo (Red Wolf)

SPECS: 103 minutes; Color

AVAILABILITY: DVD (20th Century Fox Home Entertainment); Amazon Instant Video

NATION: NA

IMAGE PORTRAYAL: Friendship; loyalty

SUMMARY: In this spoof of westerns, an Englishman, Jonathan Tibbs, who rescues a stage coach from an attack by hostile warriors, becomes a sheriff, the blood brother of Running Deer, and the adopted son of Red Wolf.

SHOTGUN (Allied Artists, 1955)

DIRECTOR: Lesley Selander

SCREENPLAY: Clark Reynolds, Rory Calhoun, John C. Champion

CAST: Sterling Hayden (Clay Hardin), Guy Prescott (Ben Thompson), Paul Marion (Delgadito), Peter Coe (Apache), Yvonne De Carlo (Abby)

SPECS: 80 minutes; Color

AVAILABILITY: DVD (VCI Video)

NATION: Apache

IMAGE PORTRAYAL: Kidnapping; peace-loving chief

SUMMARY: Clay Hardin rescues a white woman, Abby, captured by the Apaches of Delgadito. After he is also captured, he shows his courage in a duel, and Delgadito lets him and Abby go.

SHOUTING SECRETS (Joker Film Productions, 2011)

DIRECTOR: Korrina Sehringer

SCREENPLAY: Mickey Blaine, Tvli Jacob, Steven Judd

CAST: Chaske Spencer (Wesley), Q'orianka Kilcher (Pinti), Tyler Christopher (Tushka), Gil Birmingham (Cal), Tantoo Cardinal (June), Tonantzin Carmelo (Caitlyn), Rodney A. Grant (Street Chief)

SPECS: 88 minutes; Color

AVAILABILITY: Amazon Instant Video

NATION: NA

IMAGE PORTRAYAL: Contemporary Native Americans

SUMMARY: Wesley is a Native American writer who travels to Arizona to see his mother, June, who has suffered a stroke. There he struggles with his brother, Tushka; June's husband, Cal; and his sister, Pinti as they try to take care of their mother and come together as a family.

SHOWDOWN AT WILLIAMS CREEK (NFB of Canada 1991)
DIRECTOR: Allan Kroeker
SCREENPLAY: John Gray, Gary Payne
CAST: Tom Burlinson (Kootenai Brown), Michelle Thrush (Olivia D'Lonais)
SPECS: 96 minutes; Color
AVAILABILITY: DVD (Synergy Entertainment); Amazon Instant Video
NATION: Metis
IMAGE PORTRAYAL: Attack on settlers; friendship; hostile warriors; loyalty; mixed-blood Native American; romance between a Native woman and a white man
SUMMARY: The Metis, Canadian mixed-bloods, nurse Kootenai Brown back to health after he is left to die in the wilderness. He then falls in love with Olivia D'Lonais and marries her. Meanwhile, villains sell liquor to more hostile tribes who then massacre white settlers.

THE SIEGE AT RED RIVER (20th Century Fox, 1954)
DIRECTOR: Rudolph Maté
SCREENPLAY: Sydney Boehm, J. Robert Bren, Gladys Atwater
CAST: Van Johnson (Jim Farraday), Richard Boone (Brett Manning), Rico Alaniz (Chief Yellow Hawk), Pilar Del Rey (Lukoa)
SPECS: 86 minutes; Color
AVAILABILITY: DVD (20th Century Fox Cinema Archives)
NATION: Shawnee
IMAGE PORTRAYAL: Attack on a fort
SUMMARY: Brett Manning sells a Gatling gun to hostile Shawnee led by Chief Yellow Hawk and helps them attack a Union fort. The hero, Jim Farraday, gets control of the gun after the warriors attack the fort and uses it to force the tribe to retreat. Lukoa, also a member of the tribe, has a baby before the attack.

THE SIGN INVISIBLE (First National, 1918)
DIRECTOR: Edgar Lewis
SCREENPLAY: Anthony Paul Kelly
CAST: Mitchell Lewis (Lone Deer), Hedda Nova (Winona), Joseph Heron (Bad Nose), Roy Midland (Towanah)
SPECS: 6 reels; Black & White; Silent
AVAILABILITY: NA
NATION: NA
IMAGE PORTRAYAL: Friendship; mixed-blood Native American; romance between Native Americans
SUMMARY: Lone Deer, a mixed-blood separated from his beloved Winona, is wounded in a fight to save a white woman and loses his sight. At the end, he is reunited with Winona, who is happy to devote the rest of her life to caring for him.

THE SILENT ENEMY (Paramount, 1930)
DIRECTOR: H. P. Carver
SCREENPLAY: Richard Carver, W. Douglas Burden, Chief Yellow Robe, Julian Johnson
CAST: Chief Yellow Robe (Chetoga), Chief Buffalo Child Long Lance (Baluk), Chief Akawanush (Dagwan), Mary Alice Nelson Archambaud (Neewa), Cheeka (Cheeka, Chetoga's son)
SPECS: 84 minutes; Black & White; Silent
AVAILABILITY: DVD (Image Entertainment)
NATION: Ojibwa
IMAGE PORTRAYAL: Romance between Native Americans
SUMMARY: Discussed on page 16, this film tells the story of an Ojibwa tribe that struggles to survive unending hunger (the silent enemy) in the far North. Bulak becomes chief after the death of Chetoga and though he loves Neewa, the daughter of Chetoga, he cannot marry her until he survives the treachery of Dagwan, who also wants Neewa for his wife. At the end, Baluk, the mighty hunter, saves the tribe and marries Neewa.

SILENT TEARS (National Film Board of Canada, 1998)
DIRECTOR: Shirley Cheechoo
SCREENPLAY: Shirley Cheechoo
CAST: Deldon Amos, Jack Burning, Shirley Cheechoo, Matthew Melting Tallow, Heather Rae, Elizabeth Trudeau
SPECS: 28 minutes; Color
AVAILABILITY: NA
NATION: Cree
IMAGE PORTRAYAL: Contemporary First Nation people
SUMMARY: Based on the story of the filmmaker, Shirley Cheechoo, growing up in the back country of Ontario. Her father is seriously ill and her mother must cure him without the help of modern medicine.

SILENT TONGUE (Belbo Films, 1993)
DIRECTOR: Sam Shepard
SCREENPLAY: Sam Shepard
CAST: Alan Bates (Eamon McCree), Richard Harris (Prescott Roe), Sheila Tousey (Awbonnie), Jeri Arredondo (Velada), Tantoo Cardinal (Silent Tongue), River Phoenix (Talbot Roe)
SPECS: 102 minutes; Color
AVAILABILITY: DVD (Lions Gate); Amazon Instant Video
NATION: Kiowa
IMAGE PORTRAYAL: Romance between a Native American woman and a white man; vengeance

SUMMARY: In this twisted tale of exploitation and revenge, a white man, Eamon McCree rapes a Kiowa woman named Silent Tongue and they eventually have two daughters. The greedy, drunken McCree trades his oldest daughter, Awbonnie, to Prescott Roe, who gives her to his son, Talbot. She dies while giving birth to Talbot's child. When Talbot ties his dead wife's body in a tree and refuses to set her free by burning her, the ghost of Awbonnie haunts all her tormentors, including her younger sister, Velada, whom the father of Talbot tries to buy. At the end, Talbot burns her body and her agonized spirit is freed. Finally, Silent Tongue gains her revenge when her tribe captures the man who raped her.

SIOUX BLOOD (MGM, 1929)
DIRECTOR: John Waters
SCREENPLAY: George C. Hull, Houston Branch, Harry Sinclair Drago, Lucille Newmark
CAST: Tim McCoy (Flood), Robert Frazer (Lone Eagle), Chief John Big Tree (Crazy Wolf)
SPECS: 60 minutes; Black & White; Silent
AVAILABILITY: NA
NATION: Sioux
IMAGE PORTRAYAL: Attack on settlers; kidnapping
SUMMARY: Two brothers are separated during a Sioux uprising. One is reared by whites and the other is captured by the Sioux. The former, Flood, becomes a scout who hates Native Americans and the latter, who takes the name Lone Eagle, becomes a hostile brave taught to hate whites by a medicine man, Crazy Wolf. Eventually, the brothers meet and Lone Eagle leaves the tribe to join his brother in white society. In the process, both learn some tolerance for the other culture.

SIOUX CITY (IRS Media, 1994)
DIRECTOR: Lou Diamond Phillips
SCREENPLAY: L. Virginia Browne
CAST: Lou Diamond Phillips (Jesse Rainfeather Goldman), Apesanahkwat (Clifford Rainfeather), Gary Farmer (Russell White), Tantoo Cardinal (Dawn Rainfeather), Jim Great Elk Waters (Redbow), Salli Richardson-Whitfield (Jolene Buckley)
SPECS: 102 minutes, Color
AVAILABILITY: DVD (Platinum Disc)
NATION: Sioux (Lakota)
IMAGE PORTRAYAL: Contemporary Native American; wise elder
SUMMARY: Jesse Rainfeather Goldman, who had been adopted by a Jewish family, returns to his reservation after he receives an amulet from his birth mother, Dawn. His grandfather, a Lakota medicine man, teaches him the tribal ways and Jesse uses his new knowledge to solve the murder of his mother.

SITTING BULL (United Artists, 1954)
DIRECTOR: Sidney Salkow
SCREENPLAY: Jack DeWitt, Sidney Salkow
CAST: Dale Robertson (Major Robert Parrish), J. Carrol Naish (Sitting Bull), Iron Eyes Cody (Crazy Horse), Douglas Kennedy (Col. Custer), Ana Robinson Calles (White Cloud), Felix Gonzales (Young Buffalo)
SPECS: 105 minutes; Color
AVAILABILITY: DVD (FilmRise)
NATION: Sioux
IMAGE PORTRAYAL: Peace-loving chief
SUMMARY: Discussed on page 31, this film tells the story of Sitting Bull, who is driven to war by Custer, but finally tries to defend a white friend, Robert Parrish, and makes peace.
CRITICS: *New York Times* Bosley Crowther comments on the totally fictional meeting of President Grant and Sitting Bull at the end of the film: "There is no need to waste much time noting that no such meeting ever occurred and that Sitting Bull beat it for Canada shortly after the Little Big Horn massacre. This outrageously phony climax is a convenience that merely justifies the prior activities and eleventh-hour deliverance of the soldier-hero of the story, who is pro-Indian throughout" (November 26, 1954).

SKINS (First Look International, 2002)
DIRECTOR: Chris Eyre
SCREENPLAY: Jennifer D. Lyne, based on the novel by Adrian C. Louis
CAST: Eric Schweig (Rudy Yellow Lodge), Graham Greene (Mogie Yellow Lodge), Gary Farmer (Verdell Weasel Tail), Noah Watts (Herbie Yellow Lodge, Mogie's son), Lois Red Elk (Aunt Helen), Michelle Thrush (Stella), Gil Birmingham (Sonny Yellow Lodge)
SPECS: 84 minutes; Color
AVAILABILITY: DVD (Millennium); Amazon Instant Video
NATION: Lakota
IMAGE PORTRAYAL: Contemporary troubled Native American; troubled Native American
SUMMARY: Discussed on page 70, this film deals with Rudy Yellow Lodge, a tribal policeman who is so disgusted about the alcoholism and violence on his reservation that he becomes a vigilante. His main struggle and contrast is his brother, Mogie, who is a rather hopeless alcoholic. At the end, Mogie dies and Rudy carries out his last wish in his own way.

SKIPPED PARTS (Trimark Pictures, 2000)
DIRECTOR: Tamra Davis
SCREENPLAY: Tim Sandlin, based on his novel
CAST: Jennifer Jason Leigh (Lydia Callahan), Michael Greyeyes (Hank Elkrunner)

SPECS: 100 minutes; Color

AVAILABILITY: DVD (Lions Gate); Amazon Instant Video

NATION: Blackfoot

IMAGE PORTRAYAL: Romance between a Native American man and a white woman

SUMMARY: Hank Elkrunner falls in love with a white woman, Lydia Callahan, much to the displeasure of her father. Lydia returns his love and they move in together.

SLAUGHTER TRAIL (RKO, 1951)

DIRECTOR: Irving Allen

SCREENPLAY: Sid Kuller

CAST: Brian Donlevy (Capt. Dempster), Ric Roman (Chief Paako)

SPECS: 78 minutes; Color

AVAILABILITY: VHS (Turner Home Entertainment)

NATION: Navajo

IMAGE PORTRAYAL: Attack on fort

SUMMARY: When a cavalry captain, Dempster, refuses to hand over to Chief Paako bandits who have killed several of his Navajo people, the tribe attacks the fort but kills only the bandits.

SMITH! (Buena Vista, 1969)

DIRECTOR: Michael O'Herlihy

SCREENPLAY: Louis Pelletier, based on the book by Paul St. Pierre

CAST: Glenn Ford (Smith), Chief Dan George (Ol'Antoine), Frank Ramirez (Gabriel Jimmyboy), Warren Oates (Walter Charlie), Jay Silverheels (McDonald Lasheway)

SPECS: 112 minutes; Color

AVAILABILITY: Amazon Instant Video

NATION: Nez Perce

IMAGE PORTRAYAL: Contemporary Native Americans; friendship; loyalty

SUMMARY: In this Disney film, Smith tries to hide and help Gabriel Jimmyboy, a Nez Perce who is wrongly accused of murder. When the young man goes to trial, Ol' Antoine replaces the evil interpreter, Walter Charlie, and helps Jimmyboy prove his innocence.

CRITICS: A *Variety* critic notes that the Native American actors from "Hollywood's Indian Actors Workshop of Jay Silverheels (who has a small but winning role in the courtroom) supplements the regional feeling of the film" (March 26, 1969).

SMOKE SIGNAL (Universal, 1955)

DIRECTOR: Jerry Hopper

SCREENPLAY: George F. Slavin, George W. George

CAST: Dana Andrews (Brett Halliday), Pat Hogan (Delche), William Talman (Capt. Harper)
SPECS: 88 minutes; Color
AVAILABILITY: NA
NATION: Ute
IMAGE PORTRAYAL: Attack on soldiers; vengeance
SUMMARY: In the Grand Canyon, Capt. Harper escapes from hostile Ute warriors led by Delche, who have been mistreated by Brett Halliday.

SMOKE SIGNALS (ShadowCatcher Entertainment, 1998)
DIRECTOR: Chris Eyre
SCREENPLAY: Sherman Alexie, based on two stories from his collection called *The Lone Ranger and Tonto Fistfight in Heaven.*
CAST: Adam Beach (the older Victor Joseph), Evan Adams (the older Thomas), Irene Bedard (Suzy Song), Gary Farmer (Arnold Joseph), Tantoo Cardinal (Arlene Joseph), Cody Lightning (the young Victor). Numerous other First Nation and Native Americans play supporting roles.
SPECS: 89 minutes; Color
AVAILABILITY: DVD (Echo Bridge Home Entertainment); Amazon Instant Video
NATION: Coeur d'Alene
IMAGE PORTRAYAL: Contemporary Native Americans; drunkenness; friendship; troubled Native Americans
SUMMARY: Discussed on page 67 this truly Native American film tells the story of the Joseph family, which involves a tragic fire, drunkenness, and apparent rejection when Arnold departs from his family. Victor and Thomas journey a long way to bring the ashes of Arnold back to the reservation. In the process, Victor reconciles with the memory of his father.
CRITICS: Roger Ebert in the *Chicago Sun Times* writes, "*Smoke Signals* is free of the oppressive weight of victim culture; these characters don't live in the past and define themselves by the crimes committed against their people. They are the next generation; I would assign them to Generation X if that didn't limit them too much" (July 3, 1998).

SNAKE RIVER DESPERADOES (Columbia, 1951)
DIRECTOR: Fred Sears
SCREENPLAY: Barry Shipman
CAST: Charles Starrett (The Durango Kid), Don Reynolds (Little Hawk), Monte Blue (Jim Haverly), Charles Horvath (Chief Black Eagle)
SPECS: 54 minutes; Black & White
AVAILABILITY: DVD (Sony Pictures Entertainment)
NATION: NA
IMAGE PORTRAYAL: Friendship; peace-loving chief

SUMMARY: The Durango Kid, with the help of his young companion, Little Hawk, brings to justice villains led by Jim Haverly, who sell rifles to the tribe and disguise themselves as Native Americans on raids against settlers to incite a war between the local tribe of Chief Black Eagle, the father of Little Hawk, and the ranchers.

THE SNOW WALKER (Infinity Media, 2003)

DIRECTOR: Charles Martin Smith
SCREENPLAY: Charles Martin Smith, based on the story "Walk Well My Brother" by Farley Mowat
CAST: Barry Pepper (Charlie Halliday), Annabella Piugattuk (Kanaalaq), Mariano Aupilardjuk (Elder Inuk), Peter Henry Arnatsiaq (Young Inuk)
SPECS: 103 minutes; Color
AVAILABILITY: DVD (Millenium); Amazon Instant Video
NATION: Inuit
IMAGE PORTRAYAL: Contemporary Native Americans
SUMMARY: On an arctic flight, Charlie and Kanaalaq, who is ill, are on the way to a hospital, when they crash land and must try to help each other survive. In the process, when Kanaalaq teaches some of her tribal techniques for survival, they come to a greater understanding of their very different cultures.

SOLDIER BLUE (Avco-Embassy, 1970)

DIRECTOR: Ralph Nelson
SCREENPLAY: John Gay, based on the novel *Arrow in the Sun* by Theodore Olson
CAST: Candice Bergen (Kathy "Cresta" Lee), Peter Strauss (Honus Gent), Jorge Rivero (Spotted Wolf), Jorge Russek (Running Fox), Aurora Clavel (Indian Woman)
SPECS: 112 minutes; Color
AVAILABILITY: DVD (Lionsgate); Amazon Instant Video
NATION: Cheyenne
IMAGE PORTRAYAL: Attack on Native Americans; Native Americans as victims
SUMMARY: Just as *Little Big Man* establishes a parallel between the killing in Vietnam and the Battle of Washita, this film finds Vietnam in the Sand Creek Massacre. After the Cheyenne of Spotted Wolf and Running Fox kill a party of soldiers, a cavalry unit attacks the tribe despite efforts of Honus Gent and Cresta, a white woman who had lived with the Cheyenne. During the attack, the soldiers commit graphically filmed atrocities such as raping and mutilating the children.
CRITICS: In the *Chicago Sun Times* critic Roger Ebert comments: "It is supposed to be a pro-Indian movie, and at the end the camera tells us the story was true, more or less, and that the Army chief of staff himself called the massacre shown in the film one of the most shameful moments in American history. So it was,

and of course we're supposed to make the connection with My Lai and take '*Soldier Blue*' as an allegory for Vietnam. But that just won't do. The film is too mixed up to qualify as a serious allegory about anything. And although it is pro-Indian, it is also white chauvinist. Like '*A Man Called Horse*,' another so-called pro-Indian film, it doesn't have the courage to be about real Indians. The hero in these films somehow has a way of turning out to be white" (January 1, 1970).

THE SON OF THE WOLF (R. C. Pictures, 1922)

DIRECTOR: Norman Dawn

SCREENPLAY: W. L. Heywood, based on a Jack London story

CAST: Wheeler Oakman (Scruff Mackensie), Edith Roberts (Chook-Ra), Thomas Jefferson (Chief Thling), Fred Stanton (The Bear), Arthur Jasmine (The Fox), Eagle Eye (Shaman)

SPECS: 5 reels; Black & White; Silent

AVAILABILITY: NA

NATION: NA

IMAGE PORTRAYAL: Romance between a Native American woman and a white man

SUMMARY: Scruff Mackensie falls in love with Chook-Ra, the daughter of Chief Thling Tinner, but then abandons her for a dance-hall girl. When Chook-Ra's father makes her return to the tribe, Mackensie sees the error of his ways and wins her back by killing her suitor, the Bear. At the end, they head back to civilization.

THE SONG OF HIAWATHA (Hallmark Entertainment, 1997)

DIRECTOR: Jeffrey Shore

SCREENPLAY: Earl W. Wallace, based on the poem by Henry Wadsworth Longfellow

CAST: Graham Greene (O Kagh), Litefoot (Hiawatha), Irene Bedard (Minnehaha), Russell Means (Mudjekeewis), Sheila Tousey (Nokomis), Adam Beach (Chibiabos), Gordon Tootoosis (Iagoo). Numerous other Native American actors in supporting roles.

SPECS: 120 minutes; Color

AVAILABILITY: DVD (Hallmark Home Entertainment)

NATION: Ojibwa; Sioux

IMAGE PORTRAYAL: Hiawatha story; romance between Native Americans

SUMMARY: In this well-known story, Hiawatha, an Ojibwa brave, must overcome various challenges as he pursues the love of Minnehaha, a Sioux woman, who dies at the end. In this film, the story of Hiawatha is told within a story of white traders meeting the tribe.

SONG OF THE LOON (Hollywood Cinema Assoc., 1970)

DIRECTOR: Andrew Herbert

SCREENPLAY: Richard Amory

CAST: Jon Iverson (Cyrus Wheelright), Lancer Ward (John), Morgan Royce (Ephraim MacIver), John Kalfas (Singing Heron), Martin Valez (Acomas), Michael Traxton (Tiasholah), Lucky Manning (Bear-Who-Dreams), Brad Della Valle (Tsi-Nokha), Robert Vilardi (Plum of the Night)
SPECS: 79 minutes; Color
AVAILABILITY: VHS (Something Weird Video)
NATION: NA
IMAGE PORTRAYAL: Romance between Native American men
SUMMARY: The tribe of Singing Heron, Acomas, Tsi-Nokha, Tiasholah, Plum of the Night, and Bear-Who-Dreams teach their customs to Ephraim MacIver, who comes to realize that gay men can have more than one relationship.

SONG OF THE WILDWOOD FLUTE (Biograph, 1910)
DIRECTOR: D. W. Griffith
SCREENPLAY: Mrs. James H. Ryan
CAST: Dark Cloud (Gray Cloud), Mary Pickford (Dove Eyes), Kate Bruce (Indian), Francis J. Grandon (Dove Eyes' Father), Deli Henderson (A Suitor), J. Jiquel Lanoe (Indian), Alfred Paget (Indian)
SPECS: 17 minutes; Black & White; Silent
AVAILABILITY: NA
NATION: NA
IMAGE PORTRAYAL: Romance between Native Americans
SUMMARY: After hearing Gray Cloud play the flute, Dove Eyes decides to marry him rather than another suitor. When Gray Cloud falls into a bear pit, his rival for the affection of Dove Eyes sees how she is suffering and shows his honor by rescuing her beloved.
CRITICS: A *Variety* critic notes that the "poor attempt by the principal characters to act as Indians is pitiable" (December 3, 1910).

SOUTHWEST PASSAGE (United Artists, 1954)
DIRECTOR: Ray Nazarro
SCREENPLAY: Harry Essex, Daniel Mainwaring
CAST: Rod Cameron (Edward Beale)
SPECS: 75 minutes; Color
AVAILABILITY: DVD (MGM Limited Edition Collection)
NATION: Apache
IMAGE PORTRAYAL: Attack on soldiers; attack on stagecoach
SUMMARY: Apache warriors at first think camels are a kind of god but later attack the whites traveling on the animals after they find a dead camel. Finally, Edward Beale, riding a camel, leads the warriors into a trap.

SPIRIT OF THE EAGLE (Queens Cross Productions, 1991)
DIRECTOR: Boon Collins

SCREENPLAY: Boon Collins, Joseph G. Tidwell

CAST: Dan Haggerty (Big Eli McDonaugh), William Smith (Hatchett), Trever Yarrish (Little Eli), Jeri Arredondo (Watawna), Don Shanks (Running Wolf), Pricilla Bettles (Medicine Woman), Reed David (Medicine Man)

SPECS: 93 minutes; Color

AVAILABILITY: DVD (Echo Bridge Entertainment)

NATION: NA

IMAGE PORTRAYAL: Friendship; loyalty

SUMMARY: In this children's film, Hatchett captures the young son of Big Eli and sells him to the tribe of Running Wolf and Watawna. Aided by his pet eagle, Big Eli finds his son and is wounded in his attempt to rescue him. Then Watawna comes to his rescue, and nurses him back to health. Finally, Big Eli, his boy, Little Eli, Watawna, and the eagle (who also had been wounded) live happily ever after.

SPIRIT OF THE WIND (Doyon Ltd., 1979)

DIRECTOR: Ralph Liddle

SCREENPLAY: Ralph Liddle, John Logue

CAST: Pius Savage (George Attla), George Clutesi (George's Father), Chief Dan George (Moses), Rose Attla Ambrose (Mother)

SPECS: 98 minutes; Color

AVAILABILITY: NA

NATION: Athabaskan

IMAGE PORTRAYAL: Contemporary Native American; troubled Native American; wise elder

SUMMARY: Discussed on page 47, this film tells the story of George Attla Jr., the Athabaskan dog sled racer who overcame tuberculosis and the frustrations of city life. When he returns to his home he gets a dog from Moses and instruction in racing from his father and learns how to be a champion.

SPIRIT: STALLION OF THE CIMARRON (Dreamworks, 2002)

DIRECTORS: Ken Asbury, Lorna Cook

SCREENPLAY: John Fusco

CAST: Matt Damon (voice of Spirit), Daniel Studi (voice of Little Creek), Meredith Wells (voice of Little Indian girl)

SPECS: 83 minutes; Color

AVAILABILITY: DVD and Blu-ray (Dreamworks Home Entertainment); Amazon Instant Video

NATION: Lakota

IMAGE PORTRAYAL: Friendship; loyalty

SUMMARY: In this animated film, a young Lakota man, Little Creek, rescues Spirit, who has earlier saved his life. At the end, Spirit returns to Little Creek's village and finds the mare he loves.

THE SQUAW MAN (Paramount, 1914)
DIRECTORS: Oscar Apfel, Cecil B. DeMille
SCREENPLAY: Cecil B. DeMille, Oscar Apfel, based on the play by Edwin Milton Royle
CAST: Dustin Farnum (Captain Wynnegate), Princess Red Wing (Nat-U-Ritch), Joseph Singleton (Chief Tabywana), Winifred Kingston (Lady Diana)
SPECS: 74 minutes; Black & White; Silent
AVAILABILITY: DVD (Warner Archive Collection)
NATION: Ute
IMAGE PORTRAYAL: Romance between a Native American woman and a white man
SUMMARY: This film deals with an Englishman, Captain Wynnegate, who marries Nat-U-Ritch, the daughter of the Ute Chief Tabywana. After she rescues her husband twice and has a child with him, she finds out that he loves Lady Diana and wants to return to his homeland. At the end, when her husband accidentally shoots her, she tells him that she is happy that she will not hold him back from marring Lady Diana, and then she dies. Given the popularity of this story, the film was remade with different actors by Cecil B. DeMille in 1918 and 1931.

THE SQUAW MAN'S SON (Lasky, 1917)
DIRECTOR: Edward J. LeSaint
SCREENPLAY: Charles Maigne, based on the novel *The Silent Call* by Edwin Milton Royle
CAST: Wallace Reid (Lord Effington), Anita King (Wah-na-gi)
SPECS: 50 minutes; Black & White; Silent
AVAILABILITY: NA
NATION: Ute
IMAGE PORTRAYAL: Mixed-blood Native American; romance between Native Americans
SUMMARY: An English mixed-blood, Lord Effington, the son of Wynnegate and Nat-U-Ritch, leaves his wife in England, comes to America to live with his tribe, and falls in love with Wah-na-gi, a Carlisle graduate who is teaching at the Indian agency. When she finds out her beloved is married, she is about to commit suicide. However, after she learns that his English wife has died, she marries her mixed-blood lover.

THE SQUAW'S LOVE (Biograph, 1911)
DIRECTOR: D. W. Griffith
SCREENPLAY: Stanner E. V. Taylor
CAST: Mable Normand (Wild Flower), Alfred Paget (Gray Fox), Dark Cloud (White Eagle), Claire McDowell (Silver Fawn)
SPECS: 17 minutes; Black & White; Silent
AVAILABILITY: NA

NATION: NA

IMAGE PORTRAYAL: Romance between Native Americans; vengeance

SUMMARY: White Eagle, betrothed to Silver Fawn, helps his exiled friend, Gray Fox, to leave the village of Silver Fawn and join Wild Flower, who is betrothed to Gray Fox, in the forest. When Silver Fawn sees Wild Flower leave, she mistakenly thinks White Eagle has fallen in love with her. After she takes revenge by throwing Wild Flower into the river, Gray Fox rescues his beloved Wild Flower. When the mistake is cleared up, all four lovers escape from the hostile tribe that is pursuing them.

STAGECOACH (United Artists, 1939)

DIRECTOR: John Ford

SCREENPLAY: Dudley Nichols, Ernest Haycox

CAST: John Wayne (Ringo Kid), White Horse (Geronimo), Chief John Big Tree (Indian Scout)

SPECS: 96 minutes; Black & White

AVAILABILITY: DVD (Criterion); Amazon Instant Video

NATION: Apache

IMAGE PORTRAYAL: Attack on a stagecoach

SUMMARY: Geronimo and his Apaches attack the stagecoach and are driven off by the cavalry. The Ringo Kid is one of the passengers. This classic western is probably the best example of Native Americans as a hidden threat. Inferior versions of this film were made in 1966 and 1986.

CRITICS: In the *Chicago Sun Times*, critic Roger Ebert comments: "The film's attitudes toward Native Americans are unenlightened. The Apaches are seen simply as murderous savages; there is no suggestion the white men have invaded their land. Ford shared that simple view with countless other makers of Westerns, and if it was crude in 1939 it was even more so as late as '*The Searchers*' (1956), the greatest Ford/Wayne collaboration. Only in his final film, '*Cheyenne Autumn*' (1964) did he come around to more humane ideas" (August 1, 2011).

THE STALKING MOON (National, 1968)

DIRECTOR: Robert Mulligan

SCREENPLAY: Alvin Sargent, Wendell Mayes, based on the novel by Theodore V. Olsen

CAST: Gregory Peck (Sam Varner), Eva Marie Saint (Sarah Carver), Robert Forster (Nick Tana), Nathaniel Narcisco (Salvaje)

SPECS: 109 minutes; Color

AVAILABILITY: DVD (Warner Home Video)

NATION: Apache

IMAGE PORTRAYAL: Mixed-blood Native American; vengeance

SUMMARY: Discussed on page 39, this film deals with the vengeance of Salvaje, an Apache renegade who is trying to get back his son, who is being protected by Sam Varner. Salvaje traps Varner and Sarah Carver, the mother of his son who lived with him for years, in a cabin. Varner is helped by Nick Tana, a mixed blood scout, who warns him that Salvaje is coming. At the end, Varner kills Salvaje in a bloody fight.

CRITICS: In the *Chicago Sun Times*, critic Roger Ebert comments: "The three are stalked by the Apache. The woman was his wife for 10 years, and the boy is his son. Under the circumstances, the Apache has a point. But Peck, reflecting the subtle racism that underlies the plot, assumes the Indian deserves to die. To be sure, the Indian massacres half of Arizona on his way to the showdown—but since the movie makes no point of that, why should we?" (February 11, 1969).

STALLION CANYON (Astor, 1949)
DIRECTOR: Harry Fraser
SCREENPLAY: Hy Heath
CAST: Ken Curtis (Curt Benson), Bill Hammond (Little Bear), Forrest Taylor (Tom Lawson)
SPECS: 72 minutes; Color
AVAILABILITY: DVD (Alpha Home Entertainment)
NATION: NA
IMAGE PORTRAYAL: Friendship; loyalty
SUMMARY: When his companion, Little Bear, is falsely charged with a murder, Curt Benson clears his name by revealing the guilt of Tom Lawson. Lawson gives the stallion that proves Little Bear's innocence to the boy, and he releases the horse to the wild herd.
CRITICS: A *Variety* critic comments that the actor "rides well as Little Bear but overdoes the heap-big Injun Talk" (June 1, 1949).

THE STAND AT APACHE RIVER (Universal, 1953)
DIRECTOR: Lee Sholem
SCREENPLAY: Arthur A. Ross, based on the novel by Robert J. Hogan
CAST: Steven McNally (Lane Dakota), Hugh Marlowe (Colonel Morsey), Edgar Barrier (Cara Blanca)
SPECS: 77 minutes; Color
AVAILABILITY: NA
NATION: Apache
IMAGE PORTRAYAL: Attack on a stagecoach
SUMMARY: A band of Apaches led by Cara Blanca approach a group of whites at Apache River peacefully until they see an old enemy, Colonel Morsey. Then they attack the stagecoach station.

STAY AWAY JOE (MGM, 1968)
DIRECTOR: Peter Tewksbury
SCREENPLAY: Michael A. Hoey, based on the novel by Dan Cushman

CAST: Elvis Presley (Joe Lightcloud), Burgess Meredith (Charlie Lightcloud), Katy Jurado (Annie Lightcloud), Susan Trustman (Mary Lightcloud), Quentin Dean (Mamie Callahan)
SPECS: 102 minutes; Color
AVAILABILITY: DVD (Warner Home Video); Amazon Instant Video
NATION: Navajo
IMAGE PORTRAYAL: Mixed-blood Native American; Native Americans as the butt of humor; romance between a mixed-blood Native American and a white woman
SUMMARY: In this comedy, the son of Charlie Lightcloud, Joe Lightcloud, a mixed-blood Navajo rodeo champion, tries to help his tribe by selling a prize stud bull, which is mistakenly thought to be a cow and is barbecued. Joe's step-mother, Annie, contributes to the mix-up by selling Charlie Lightcloud's cattle. At the end, Joe wins a big prize and thus rescues his father and stepmother. Joe is also in love with a white woman, Mamie Callahan.
CRITICS: A *Variety* critic comments: "The basic story—contemporary American Indians who are portrayed as laughable incompetents—is out of touch with latter day appreciation of some basic dignity in all human beings" (March 13, 1968).

THE STONE CHILD (Triple Martini Productions, 2007)
DIRECTOR: Christopher Martini
SCREENPLAY: Christopher Martini
CAST: Lorrel Goings (Mathew Walker), Marvin Goings (Ray Walker)
SPECS: 15 minutes; Color
AVAILABILITY: NA
NATION: Lakota
IMAGE PORTRAYAL: Contemporary Native American; mixed-blood Native American; troubled Native American
SUMMARY: In this short film, a mixed-blood boy, Mathew, and his Lakota father, Ray, ride in a van, go to a restaurant where Ray refuses to pay, and then travel to the Badlands where Mathew finds his own inner strength.

THE STORY OF WILL ROGERS (Warner Bros., 1952)
DIRECTOR: Michael Curtiz
SCREENPLAY: Frank Davis, Stanley Roberts, based on an article by Betty Blake Rogers
CAST: Will Rogers Jr. (Will Rogers), Jane Wyman (Betty Rogers), Carl Benton Reid (Senator Clem Rogers), Noah Berry Jr. (Wiley Post)
SPECS: 109 minutes; Color
AVAILABILITY: DVD (Warner Archive Collection)
NATION: Cherokee

IMAGE PORTRAYAL: Contemporary Native American; mixed-blood Native American; romance between a mixed-blood Native American man and a white woman

SUMMARY: Will Rogers, the son of Cherokee Senator Clem Rogers, falls in love with Betty Blake, who inspires him to leave his drifting rodeo days and become an entertainer.

STRONGHEART (Biograph, 1914)
DIRECTOR: James Kirkwood
SCREENPLAY: Frank E. Woods, based on a play by William C. deMille
CAST: Henry B. Walthall (Strongheart)
SPECS: 30 minutes; Black & White; Silent
AVAILABILITY: NA
NATION: NA
IMAGE PORTRAYAL: Romance between a Native American man and a white woman
SUMMARY: This film tells the story of Strongheart, who leaves his tribe and goes to college in the East. He becomes a football star and falls in love with a white woman, but gets in trouble when he lies to help a white friend who has cheated. When he finds out that his father has died and his tribe needs him, he respects his duty and returns.

SUNCHASER (Warner Bros., 1996)
DIRECTOR: Michael Cimino
SCREENPLAY: Charles Leavitt
CAST: Woody Harrelson (Dr. Reynolds), Jon Seda (Brandon 'Blue' Monroe), Talisa Soto (Navajo Woman), Victor Aaron (Webster Skyhorse)
SPECS: 122 minutes; Color
AVAILABILITY: DVD (Warner Home Video); Amazon Instant Video
NATION: Navajo
IMAGE PORTRAYAL: Contemporary Native American
SUMMARY: Brandon Monroe kidnaps Dr. Reynolds and takes him to a Navajo healing place where they interact with a Navajo Woman.

SUSANNAH OF THE MOUNTIES (20th Century Fox, 1939)
DIRECTOR: William Seiter
SCREENPLAY: Robert Ellis, Helen Logan, Fidel LaBarba, Walter Ferris, based on book by Muriel Dennison
CAST: Shirley Temple (Susannah Sheldon), Maurice Moscovitch (Chief Big Eagle), Martin Good Rider (Little Chief), Victor Jory (Wolf Pelt), Randolph Scott (Monty). Other Native Americans play minor roles.
SPECS: 79 minutes; Black & White
AVAILABILITY: DVD (20th Century Fox); Amazon Instant Video

NATION: Blackfoot
IMAGE PORTRAYAL: Friendship; hostile warrior; peace-loving chief
SUMMARY: The Blackfoot tribe of Chief Big Eagle and his son, Little Chief, are friendly Native Americans. Wolf Pelt and his renegades raid a railroad construction camp and a post of the Mounties. After the tribe captures Monty, Susannah goes to their camp and persuades Chief Big Eagle to demand a ritual that shows Wolf Pelt is the villain. Big Eagle then frees Monty and makes peace.

T

TAGGART (Universal, 1964)
DIRECTOR: R. G. Springsteen
SCREENPLAY: Robert Creighton Williams, based on the novel by Louis L'Amour
CAST: Tony Young (Taggart)
SPECS: 85 minutes; Color
AVAILABILITY: NA
NATION: Apache
IMAGE PORTRAYAL: Attack on a wagon train
SUMMARY: Attack on a wagon train and fort.
CRITICS: A *Variety* critic notes that "the script is traditional in the attitude towards Indians: the only good ones are dead ones" (December 9, 1964).

THE TALL TEXAN (Lippert, 1953)
DIRECTOR: Elmo Williams
SCREENPLAY: Samuel Roeca, Elizabeth Reinhardt
CAST: Lloyd Bridges (Ben Trask), George Steele (Jaqui)
SPECS: 84 minutes; Black & White
AVAILABILITY: DVD (VCI Home Video)
NATION: Comanche
IMAGE PORTRAYAL: Attack on settlers
SUMMARY: After whites break a treaty and seek gold on the Comanche land of Jaqui, his tribe attacks and kills most of them.

THE TALL WOMEN (Allied Artists, 1967)
DIRECTORS: Gianfranco Parolini, Sidney W. Pink, Rudolf Zehetgruber
SCREENPLAY: Mike Ashley, Theo Werner
CAST: Anne Baxter (Mary Ann), Gustavo Rojo (Gus McIntosh), Luis Prendes (Pope), Fernando Hilbeck (Chief White Cloud), Alejandra Nilo (White Cloud's wife)
SPECS: 101 minutes; Color
AVAILABILITY: NA

NATION: Apache

IMAGE PORTRAYAL: Hostile warrior; peace-loving chief

SUMMARY: Apache warriors led by Pope attack a wagon train and kill all but seven women. Gus McIntosh finds them and prepares for another attack. However, Chief White Cloud of Pope's tribe acknowledges the courage of the women and orders Pope not to attack them again. Finally, McIntosh leads them to safety.

TAZA, SON OF COCHISE (Universal, 1954)

DIRECTOR: Douglas Sirk

SCREENPLAY: George Zuckerman, Gerald Drayson Adams

CAST: Rock Hudson (Taza), Barbara Rush (Oona), Rex Reason (Naiche), Morris Ankrum (Grey Eagle), Eugene Iglesias (Chato), Ian MacDonald (Geronimo), James Van Horn (Skinya), Charles Horvath (Kocha), Jeff Chandler (Cochise)

SPECS: 79 minutes; Color

AVAILABILITY: DVD (Universal Pictures)

NATION: Apache

IMAGE PORTRAYAL: Hostile warrior; peace-loving chief; romance between Native Americans

SUMMARY: Taza tries to keep the peace, but his rebellious brother, Naiche, convinces the tribe to join with the hostile Geronimo and Grey Eagle. When the hostile warriors attack the cavalry, Taza helps the soldiers defeat them so that peace can be reestablished. Other Apache characters are Oona, the daughter of Grey Eagle and beloved of Taza, Chato, Skinya, Cochise, and Kocha.

CRITICS: A *Newsweek* critic notes that the film "is another chapter in Hollywood's long and truculent argument with the American Indian. This one, like many others, pays a kind of lip service to the idea that the Indians may be men of merit, but as usual they take a numerical licking" (March 1, 1954, 80).

THE TELEGRAPH TRAIL (Vitagraph, 1933)

DIRECTOR: Tenny Wright

SCREENPLAY: Kurt Kempler

CAST: John Wayne (Gus Trent), Albert J. Smith (Gus Lynch), Yakima Canutt (High Wolf)

SPECS: 54 minutes; Black & White

AVAILABILITY: DVD (Warner Home Video); Amazon Instant Video

NATION: NA

IMAGE PORTRAYAL: Attack on soldiers

SUMMARY: Urged on by Gus Lynch, who wants to control the area, a warlike tribe attacks a camp of men working on the transcontinental telegraph line. Gus Trent gets soldiers from a fort and defeats the warriors of High Wolf. This allows the telegraph to be finished.

CRITICS: A *Variety* critic comments: "This outline has been used before: the white man uses his Indian allies to check the march of progress" (April 4, 1933).

TELL THEM WILLIE BOY IS HERE (Universal, 1969)

DIRECTOR: Abraham Polonsky

SCREENPLAY: Abraham Polonsky, based on *Willy Boy: A Desert Manhunt* by Harry Lawton

CAST: Robert Redford (Christopher Cooper), Robert Blake (Willie), Katherine Ross (Lola), Mikel Angel (Old Mike)

SPECS: 98 minutes; Color

AVAILABILITY: DVD (Universal Vault Series)

NATION: Paiute

IMAGE PORTRAYAL: Native Americans as victims; romance between Native Americans

SUMMARY: Discussed on page 40, this film, this film tells the story of the tragic love between Willie, a Paiute, and Lola, his lover and then wife. After Willie accidentally kills Lola's father, old Mike, they try to escape from sheriff Christopher Cooper in the desert. Eventually Lola dies and Cooper, who is sympathetic toward Native Americans, reluctantly shoots Willie, whose gun is empty.

TEXAS ACROSS THE RIVER (Universal, 1966)

DIRECTOR: Michael Gordon

SCREENPLAY: Wells Root, Harold Greene, Ben Starr

CAST: Dean Martin (Sam Hollis), Alain Delon (Don Andrea), Joey Bishop (Kronk), Tina Aumont (Lonetta), Michael Ansara (Iron Jacket), Linden Chiles (Yellow Knife), Richard Farnsworth (Medicine Man)

SPECS: 101 minutes; Color

AVAILABILITY: DVD (Universal Vault Series)

NATION: Comanche

IMAGE PORTRAYAL: Friendship; romance between a Native American woman and a white man

SUMMARY: In this spoof of westerns, Sam Hollis rescues, and eventually falls in love with Lonetta, from the Comanche tribe of the Medicine Man, Chief Iron Jacket and his bumbling son, Yellow Knife. Sam Hollis's wisecracking Native American friend is Kronk.

TEXAS PIONEERS (Monogram, 1932)

DIRECTOR: Harry L. Fraser

SCREENPLAY: Harry L. Fraser

CAST: Bill Cody (Captain Bill Clyde), Chief Standing Bear (Chief Standing Bear), Iron Eyes Cody (Little Eagle), Ann Ross (Indian Girl)

SPECS: 58 minutes; Black & White; Silent

AVAILABILITY: DVD (Alpha Video; in "Vintage Western Double Feature")

NATION: NA

IMAGE PORTRAYAL: Attacks on forts; attacks on stage coach

SUMMARY: Using guns sold to them by a gang, the hostile tribe of Chief Standing Bear and Lone Eagle attacks a fort. Bill Clyde tries to infiltrate the gang to stop the gun running.

THEY DIED WITH THEIR BOOTS ON (Warner Bros., 1942)

DIRECTOR: Raoul Walsh

SCREENPLAY: Wally Kline, Aeneas MacKenzie

CAST: Errol Flynn (George Armstrong Custer), Anthony Quinn (Crazy Horse), Cyril Archambault (Lakota Sioux Warrior), Moses Brave (Lakota Sioux Warrior), Leo Chasing Hawk (Chief of Indian Scouts), Francis Zahn (Sans Arc Chief), Joshua White Shield (Cheyenne Chief), William Village Center (Mniconjou Chief), Jim Thorpe (Indian), Robert Schoenhut Sr. (Sioux Warrior), Frank Shooter (Lakota Sioux Warrior), Jack Red Bear (Shosone Chief), Joseph Fast Horse Sr. (Sioux Chief), Amos Elk Nation (Blackfeet Chief), Alvin Elk Nation (Ogalala Chief)

SPECS: 140 minutes; Color

AVAILABILITY: DVD (Warner Home Video); Amazon Instant Video

NATION: Cheyenne; Lakota Sioux; other tribes

IMAGE PORTRAYAL: Attack on soldiers; attack on stage coaches

SUMMARY: Discussed on page 22, this film follows the career of George A. Custer from his days at West Point to his last battle at Little Big Horn. In the last part of the film, the Sioux warrior, Crazy Horse, is Custer's main antagonist. Many Native American actors appear before and in the final battle.

CRITICS: Alex von Tunzelmann in *Guardian.com* comments on one of the many historical inaccuracies of the film: "Custer is shown trying to make peace with the Lakota Sioux nation. He is thwarted by an evil businessman, Ned Sharp, who announces that there is gold in the Black Hills and provokes a war. Sharp is fictional: the person who really announced that he had found gold in the Black Hills, causing a rush which violated the Treaty of Fort Laramie and started the Great Sioux war, was George Armstrong Custer" (February 11, 2009).

THEY RODE WEST (Columbia, 1954)

DIRECTOR: Phil Karlson

SCREENPLAY: DeVallon Scott, Frank Nugent, Leo Katcher

CAST: Robert Francis (Dr. Allen Seward), May Wynn (Manyi-ten), Stuart Randall (Chief Satanta), Eugene Iglesias (Red Leaf), Frank DeKove (Isatai), John War Eagle (Chief Quanah Parker), Maurice Jara (Spotted Wolf)

SPECS: 84 minutes; Color

AVAILABILITY: NA

NATION: Comanche; Kiowa

IMAGE PORTRAYAL: Gratitude; romance between a Native American man and a white woman

SUMMARY: The Kiowa of Satanta join the hostile Comanches of Chief Quanah Parker and threaten war. However, Dr. Seward keeps the peace by saving the life of Satanta's son, Red Leaf, and respecting Isatai, the Medicine Man. Red Leaf is married to Manyi-ten, a white woman who was raised by the tribe.

At the end, the Kiowa, who are suffering from malaria, are moved to higher ground.

THE THIRD WOMAN (Robertson Cole, 1920)
DIRECTOR: Charles Swickard
SCREENPLAY: J. Grubb Alexander, Raymond L. Schrock
CAST: Carlyle Blackwell (Luke Halliday), Louise Lovely (Eleanor Steele), Frank Lanning (Tonnawanna), Myrtle Owen (Mo-Wa)
SPECS: 5 reels; Black & White; Silent
AVAILABILITY: NA
NATION: NA
IMAGE PORTRAYAL: Mixed-blood Native American; romance between a mixed-blood Native American man and a white woman
SUMMARY: This film tells the story of an educated mixed-blood, Luke Halliday, who is struggling to decide whether to help the people of his tribe and marry one of them or return to a white woman he loves, Eleanor Steele, who eventually rejects him. At the end, he chooses to work for his tribe.

A THOUSAND ROADS (Mandalay Entertainment, 2005)
DIRECTOR: Chris Eyre
SCREENPLAY: Scott Garen, Joy Harjo
CAST: Jeremiah Bitsui (Johnny Chee), Candice Costello (Johnny Chee's Girlfriend), Riana Malabed (Dawn), John Trudell (Narrator)
SPECS: 40 minutes; Color
AVAILABILITY: DVD (Seven Arrows Telenova Productions)
NATIONS: Inupiat; Mohawk; Navajo; Quechua (Peru)
IMAGE PORTRAYAL: Contemporary Native Americans; troubled Native Americans
SUMMARY: A Mohawk stockbroker in Manhattan, an Inupiat young woman in Alaska, a Navajo gang member in New Mexico, and a Quechua healer in Peru each learn how to relate to their communities.

THREE GUNS FOR TEXAS (Universal, 1968)
DIRECTORS: Earl Bellamy, David Lowell Rich, Paul Stanley
SCREENPLAY: John D. F. Black
CAST: William Smith (Constable Joe Riley), Cliff Osmond (Running Antelope), Ralph Manza (Blue Dog), Shelley Morrison (Linda Little Trees)
SPECS: 99 minutes; Color
AVAILABILITY: NA
NATION: NA
IMAGE PORTRAYAL: Romance between Native American woman and white man

SUMMARY: Linda Little Trees falls in love (or lust) with Constable Joe when she sees him with his shirt off. She captures him so she can marry him, but his fellow Rangers rescue him.

THREE WARRIORS (Fantasy Films, 1977)
DIRECTOR: Kieth Merrill
SCREENPLAY: Sy Gomberg
CAST: McKee Redwing (Michael), Charles White-Eagle (Grandfather), Lois Red Elk (Mother), Randy Quaid (Ranger Hammond), Raydine Spino (Michael's Older Sister), Stacey Leonard (Michael's Younger Sister), Byron Patt (Michael's Father)
SPECS: 100 minutes; Color
AVAILABILITY: NA
NATION: Sioux
IMAGE PORTRAYAL: Contemporary Native American; troubled Native American; wise elder
SUMMARY: Discussed on page 83, this film tells the story of Michael, a teenage Native American from the city who visits his grandfather on the reservation. After acquiring a horse named Three Warriors and becoming friends with Ranger Hammon, Michael uses the knowledge and strength of his heritage that his grandfather taught him when he rescues his horse from evil thieves.

THUNDER (European International Films, 1983)
DIRECTOR: Fabrizio De Angelis (Larry Ludman)
SCREENPLAY: Fabrizio De Angelis, Dardano Sacchetti
CAST: Mark Gregory (Thunder), Bo Svenson (Sheriff Cook), Michele Mirabella (Dancing Crow)
SPECS: 86 minutes; Color
AVAILABILITY: NA
NATION: Navajo
IMAGE PORTRAYAL: Contemporary Native American; Native American activist
SUMMARY: Thunder, a Navajo, fights lawmen and owners of a construction company to stop them from destroying a tribal burial ground protected by a treaty signed by his grandfather. However, he is thrown out of town and beaten. He turns to violence to accomplish his mission.

A THUNDER OF DRUMS (MGM, 1961)
DIRECTOR: Joseph M. Newman
SCREENPLAY: James Warner Bellah
CAST: Richard Boone (Captain Maddocks), George Hamilton (Lt. Curtis McQuade),
SPECS: 97 minutes; Color

AVAILABILITY: DVD (Warner Archive Collection)
NATION: Apache
IMAGE PORTRAYAL: Attack on soldiers
SUMMARY: Hostile Apaches attack a few soldiers, who are saved by Captain Maddocks and his soldiers, who kill many of the warriors.
CRITICS: A *Variety* critic notes that the "Apaches [are] of the old screen school of all-bad Injuns" (August 30, 1961).

THUNDER OVER THE PRAIRIE (Columbia, 1941)
DIRECTOR: Lambert Hillyer
SCREENPLAY: Betty Burbridge, based on the book by James Rubel
CAST: Charles Starrett (Dr. Steve Monroe), Eileen O'Hearn (Nora Mandan), Stanley Brown (Roy Mandan), David Sharpe (Clay Mandan)
SPECS: 60 minutes; Black & White
AVAILABILITY: NA
NATION: NA
IMAGE PORTRAYAL: Native Americans as victims
SUMMARY: When a Native American medic, Roy Mandan, gets in trouble for revealing that a construction company mistreats its Native American workers, Dr. Steve Monroe, Roy's friend from medical school, comes to his rescue and proves his innocence.

THUNDER WARRIOR 2 (Fulvia Films, 1987)
DIRECTOR: Fabrizio De Angelis (Larry Ludman)
SCREENPLAY: Fabrizio De Angelis, Dardano Sacchetti
CAST: Mark Gregory (Thunder), Karen Reel (Sheila)
SPECS: 88 minutes; Color
AVAILABILITY: VHS (Trans World Entertainment)
NATION: Navajo
IMAGE PORTRAYAL: Contemporary Native American; Native Americans as victims
SUMMARY: Thunder escapes from prison and returns to his Navajo homeland to investigate the murder of a local chief. He and his wife, Sheila, must fight the corrupt police. (A third version of this film appeared in 1988.)

THUNDERHEART (Tri Star, 1992)
DIRECTOR: Michael Apted
SCREENPLAY: John Fusco
CAST: Val Kilmer (Ray Levoi), Graham Greene (Walter Crow Horse), Sheila Tousey (Maggie Eagle Bear), Ted Thin Elk (Grandpa Sam Reaches), John Trudell (Jimmy Looks Twice), Julius Drum (Richard Yellow Hawk), Fred Ward (Jack Milton), Sarah Brave (Maisy Blue Legs), Allan R. J. Joseph (Leo Fast Elk)

SPECS: 119 minutes; Color

AVAILABILITY: DVD (Sony Pictures Home Entertainment); Amazon Instant Video

NATION: Lakota

IMAGE PORTRAYAL: Contemporary Native American; friendship; mixed-blood Native American; Native American activist; wise elder

SUMMARY: Discussed on page 65, this film tells the story of a mixed-blood Lakota FBI agent, Ray Levoi, who goes to a reservation in South Dakota to solve a murder. When he discovers the government is involved in the murder and a plot to mine uranium on the reservation, he joins tribal policeman, Walter Crow Horse, and traditional elder Grandpa Sam Reaches to stop the plot and preserve the environment of the reservation. In the process, he finds his Lakota identity and is attracted to activist, Maggie Eagle Bear, who is eventually killed.

CRITICS: *Chicago Sun Times* critic Roger Ebert comments on the portrayal of the setting: "In '*Thunderheart*' we get a real visual sense of the reservation, of the beauty of the rolling prairie and the way it is interrupted by deep gorges, but also of the omnipresent rusting automobiles and the subsistence level of some of the housing. We feel that we're really there, and that the people in the story really occupy land they stand on" (April 3, 1992).

THE THUNDERING HERD (Paramount, 1925)

DIRECTOR: William Howard

SCREENPLAY: Lucian Hubbard, based on the novel by Zane Grey

CAST: Jack Holt (Tom Doan), Lois Wilson (Milly Fayre), Noah Beery Sr. (Randall Jett)

SPECS: 70 minutes; Black & White; Silent

AVAILABILITY: NA

NATION: NA

IMAGE PORTRAYAL: Attack on wagon train

SUMMARY: Warriors, angered by the slaughter of many buffalo that was wrongly blamed on them, surround a wagon train and are finally routed.

CRITICS: A *Variety* reviewer notes that the film "finished with some of the best Indian battle stuff that has been shown in a long, long while" (February 25, 1925).

THE THUNDERING HERD (Paramount, 1933)

DIRECTOR: Henry Hathaway

SCREENPLAY: Jack Cunningham, based on the novel by Zane Grey

CAST: Randolph Scott (Tom Doan)

SPECS: 62 minutes; Black & White

AVAILABILITY: DVD (Pop Flix: "Randolph Scott Western Collection" as *Buffalo Stampede*)

NATION: NA

IMAGE PORTRAYAL: Attack on settlers

SUMMARY: Warriors attack white hunters who are slaughtering buffaloes.

A TICKET TO TOMAHAWK (20th Century Fox, 1950)
DIRECTOR: Richard Sale
SCREENPLAY: Mary Loos, Richard Sale,
CAST: Dan Dailey (Johnny Jameson), Anne Baxter (Kit Dodge Jr.), Chief Yow-lachie (Pawnee), Chief Thundercloud (Crooked Knife), Charles Soldani (Black Wolf), Charles Stevens (Trancos), John War Eagle (Lone Eagle), Shooting Star (Crazy Dog)
SPECS: 90 minutes; Color
AVAILABILITY: NA
NATION: Arapaho; Pawnee
IMAGE PORTRAYAL: Friendship; loyalty
SUMMARY: Pawnee, the taciturn friend of Kit Dodge Jr. helps her to overcome villains who are competing with her. Crooked Knife and his Arapaho warriors also help Kit when her beloved Johnny Jameson, who was a friend of Crooked Knife in a Wild West show, uses fireworks to win over the tribe.

TIGER EYES (Amber Entertainment, 2012)
DIRECTOR: Lawrence Blume
SCREENPLAY: Lawrence Blume, based on the novel by Judy Blume
CAST: Willa Holland (Davey), Tatanka Means (Wolf/Martin Ortiz), Russell Means (Willie Ortiz), Frank Adakai (Tribal Elder)
SPECS: 92 minutes; Color
Availability: DVD (Freestyle Digital Media); Amazon Instant Video
NATION: Pueblo
IMAGE PORTRAYAL: Contemporary Native American; friendship
SUMMARY: In a canyon Wolf meets Davey, a young woman emotionally devastated by the murder of her father. He befriends her and helps her find emotional health. Part of this process involves tribal ceremonies with Wolf's father, Willie, and a tribal elder.

TOMAHAWK (Universal International Pictures, 1951)
DIRECTOR: George Sherman
SCREENPLAY: Silvia Richards, Maurice Geraghty, Daniel Jarrett
CAST: Van Heflin (Jim Bridger), Yvonne DeCarlo (Julie Madden), John War Eagle (Red Cloud), Susan Cabot (Monahseetah)
SPECS: 82 minutes; Color
AVAILABILITY: DVD (Universal Vault Series)
NATION: Cheyenne; Sioux
IMAGE PORTRAYAL: Attack on soldiers; friendship
SUMMARY: Jim Bridger, who is the friend of Monahseetah, joins soldiers to overcome the Sioux of Red Cloud.

CRITICS: Bosley Crowther in the *New York Times* comments, "*Tomahawk* is nothing exceptional in the cavalry-and-Indians line, outside of its generous imitation of pro-Indian sentiment" (February 19, 1951).

TOM AND HUCK (Walt Disney Pictures, 1995)
DIRECTOR: Peter Hewitt
SCREENPLAY: Stephen Sommers, David Loughery, based on the novel *The Adventures of Tom Sawyer* by Mark Twain
CAST: Jonathan Taylor Thomas (Tom Sawyer), Brad Renfro (Huck Finn), Eric Schweig (Injun Joe)
SPECS: 97 minutes; Color
AVAILABILITY: DVD (Walt Disney Home Video); Amazon Instant Video
NATION: NA
IMAGE PORTRAYAL: Hostile warrior
SUMMARY: Tom and Huck try to find evidence to help the town drunk, who is accused of a murder committed by Injun Joe, which Tom secretly witnessed.

TONKA (Walt Disney Productions, 1958)
DIRECTOR: Lewis R. Foster
SCREENPLAY: Lewis R. Foster, Lillie Hayward, based on the book *Comanche* by David Appel
CAST: Sal Mineo (White Bull), H. M. Wynant (Yellow Bull), Joy Page (Prairie Flower), Rafael Campos (Strong Bear), John War Eagle (Chief Sitting Bull)
SPECS: 97 minutes; Color
AVAILABILITY: Amazon Instant Video
NATION: Sioux
IMAGE PORTRAYAL: Attack on soldiers
SUMMARY: White Bull, the son of Prairie Flower and Sitting Bull, is a Sioux boy who trains his horse, Tonka, only to have his cousin, Yellow Bull, take the horse and sell it to a cavalry officer. Tonka is the only survivor after an arrogant, fanatical Custer leads his soldiers into the Battle of Little Big Horn. Near the end of the battle, White Bull, who is saved by his friend, Strong Bear, is reunited with Tonka.

THE TOTEM MARK (Selig, 1911)
DIRECTOR: Otis Turner
SCREENPLAY: Hobart Bosworth, Otis Turner
CAST: J. Barney Sherry (Sachem), Jane Keckley (Sachem's Wife), Jack Conway (Ojibwa Warrior), Hobart Bosworth (Lotokah), Bessie Eyton (Zeetah), Donald MacDonald (A Young Warrior), Major J. A. McGuire (Ojibwa Chief)
SPECS: 1 reel; Black & White; Silent
AVAILABILITY: NA
NATION: NA

IMAGE PORTRAYAL: Kidnapping; torture

SUMMARY: A warlike tribe kidnaps a white woman, and a group of women in the tribe, envious of her beauty, denounce her as a witch and set her adrift in the rapids of a river.

TRAIN TO TOMBSTONE (Lippert, 1950)

DIRECTOR: William Berke

SCREENPLAY: Orville H. Hampton, Victor West, Don Barry

CAST: Don Barry (Len Howard), Robert Lowery (Marshal Staley)

SPECS: 56 minutes; Black & White

AVAILABILITY: DVD (VCI Entertainment; on "Darn Good Westerns, Vol. 1")

NATION: NA

IMAGE PORTRAYAL: Attacks on railroads; hostile warriors

SUMMARY: Hostile warriors help villains stage attacks on trains.

CRITICS: A *Variety* critic comments on the lack of reality, noting that the attacks, with the "same Injun repeatedly falling off his pony," are "just plain funny in their ridiculousness" (September 6, 1950).

A TRAPPER AND THE REDSKINS (Kalem, 1910)

DIRECTOR: NA

SCREENPLAY: NA

CAST: NA

SPECS: Split reel; Black & White; Silent

AVAILABILITY: NA

NATION: NA

IMAGE PORTRAYAL: Kidnapping

SUMMARY: After a hostile tribe kidnaps a girl, her father, mother, and some neighbors rescue her and take revenge on the tribe.

CRITICS: A *Variety* reviewer writes: "The band is killed off in fine stockyard order and everything ends happily except for the Indians" (February 26, 1910).

THE TRAVELING SALESWOMAN (Columbia, 1950)

DIRECTOR: Charles F. Reisner

SCREENPLAY: Howard Dimsdale

CAST: Joan Davis (Mabel King), Andy Devine (Waldo), Chief Thundercloud (Running Deer)

SPECS: 75 minutes; Black & White

AVAILABILITY: DVD (Sony Pictures Choice Collection)

NATION: NA

IMAGE PORTRAYAL: Friendship

SUMMARY: In this comedy, a traveling saleswoman wins over the tribe of Chief Running Deer.

TREACHERY RIDES THE RANGE (Warner Bros., 1936)
DIRECTOR: Frank McDonald
SCREENPLAY: William Jacobs
CAST: Dick Foran (Capt. Red Taylor), Craig Reynolds (Wade Carter), Carlyle
    Moore Jr. (Little Big Wolf), Jim Thorpe (Chief Red Smoke), Frank Bruno
    (Little Fox), Dick Botiller (Antelope), Iron Eyes Cody (Little Deer)
SPECS: 56 minutes; Black & White
AVAILABILITY: NA
NATION: Comanche
IMAGE PORTRAYAL: Vengeance
SUMMARY: The villain, Carter, incites the Cheyenne tribe of Chief Red Smoke
    to break a treaty by killing one son and wounding another, Little Big Wolf.
    The chief, along with warrior Little Big Fox start a war. However, Capt. Red
    Taylor captures the villain and convinces the tribe to make peace.

THE TRIAL OF BILLY JACK (Taylor-Laughlin, 1974)
DIRECTOR: Tom Laughlin
SCREENPLAY: Tom Laughlin, Delores Taylor
CAST: Tom Laughlin (Billy Jack), Delores Taylor (Jean Roberts), Gus Grey-
    mountain (Blue Elk), Sacheen Littlefeather (Patsy Littlejohn), Rolling Thunder
    (Thunder Mountain), Buffalo Horse (Little Bear), Susan Sosa (Sunshine), Os-
    hannah Fastwolf (Oshannah).
SPECS: 170 minutes; Color
AVAILABILITY: DVD (Image Entertainment); Amazon Instant Video
NATION: NA
IMAGE PORTRAYAL: Contemporary Native American; mixed-Blood Native
    American; Native American activist
SUMMARY: Billy Jack returns from prison to deal with whites who are mistreat-
    ing students from the reservation school by trying to stop their use of TV for
    political action. After having a vision, he saves the day.
CRITICS: *New York Times* reviewer Vincent Canby comments: "It's also shot
    through with Indian (American) mysticism and self-improvement suggestions
    that evoke shades of Moral Re-Armament, which was never a hotbed for radi-
    cal political thinkers" (November 14, 1974).

THE TRIBAL LAW (Bison, 1912)
DIRECTORS: Otis Turner, Wallace Reid
SCREENPLAY: Wallace Reid
CAST: Wallace Reid (Tall Pine), Margarita Fischer (Starlight), Charles Inslee
    (Crouching Panther)
SPECS: 2 reels; Black & White; Silent
AVAILABILITY: NA
NATION: Hopi; Apache

IMAGE PORTRAYAL: Gratitude; romance between Native Americans; vengeance

SUMMARY: A Hopi maiden, Starlight, and an Apache, Tall Pine, marry despite a Hopi law against such a match. Starlight's jilted lover, Gray Wolf, tries to have them killed, but a Hopi man whom Tall Pine had helped earlier rescues them.

CRITICS: *Moving Picture World* critic G. F. Blaisdell notes that the film about Indians is "not of the orthodox sort—burning, raiding, soldiers to the rescue, and all of the regular program. It is a story of Indians as Indians, and in it are shown the habitations, the mode of life, some of the customs" (November 9, 1912, 536).

TRIUMPHS OF A MAN CALLED HORSE (Hesperia Films, 1983)

DIRECTOR: John Hough

SCREENPLAY: Ken Blackwell, Carlos Aured

CAST: Richard Harris (A Man Called Horse), Michael Beck (Koda), Ana De Sade (Redwing), Anne Seymour (Elk Woman), Miguel Angel Fuentes (Big Bear), Regino Herrera (Eye of the Bull), Patricia Paramo (Sioux Woman), Vicki Perez (Sioux Woman)

SPECS: 86 minutes; Color

AVAILABILITY: NA

NATION: Crow; Sioux

IMAGE PORTRAYAL: Attack on outlaws; mixed-blood Native American; Native American as victims

SUMMARY: After John Morgan/A Man Called Horse is invited to peace talks and then assassinated by a villain, his educated, mixed-blood Sioux son, Koda, returns to his tribe to try to keep the peace. Shortly thereafter, he falls in love with a Crow woman, Redwing, and together they fight villains who are after gold in the Black Hills and finally drive them from Sioux land.

TROOPER HOOK (United Artists, 1957)

DIRECTOR: Charles Marquis Warren

SCREENPLAY: David Victor, Martin Berkeley, Herbert Little Jr., Jack Schaefer

CAST: Joel McCrea (Sgt. Clovis Hook), Barbara Stanwyck (Cora Sutliff), Rodolfo Acosta (Nanchez)

SPECS: 81 minutes; Black & White

AVAILABILITY: DVD (MGM Limited Edition Collection)

NATION: Apache

IMAGE PORTRAYAL: Kidnapping; romance between a Native American man and a white woman

SUMMARY: A white woman, Cora Sutiff, captured by the Apache chief, Nanchez, has a son, Quito, by him. After Clovis Hook rescues Cora, her white husband rejects her and the boy. At the end, both Nanchez and her husband die, and Cora and Quito end up with Clovis Hook.

TRUE HEART (Orion, 1997)
DIRECTOR: Catherine Cyran
SCREENPLAY: Catherine Cyran
CAST: Kirsten Dunst (Bonnie), Zachary Ty Bryan (Sam), August Schellenberg (Khonanesta)
SPECS: 92 minutes; Color
AVAILABILITY: DVD (MGM); Amazon Instant Video
NATION: NA
IMAGE PORTRAYAL: Contemporary Native American; friendship; loyalty
SUMMARY: Bonnie and Sam, victims of a plane crash in the wilderness, meet Khonanesta and his large bear, Grandfather. The Native American teaches them how to survive, and they help him stop some villains who are illegally hunting bears.

A TRUE INDIAN BRAVE (Bison, 1910)
DIRECTOR: Fred J. Balshofer
SCREENPLAY: NA
CAST: James Young Deer
SPECS: 1 reel; Black & White; Silent
AVAILABILITY: NA
NATION: NA
IMAGE PORTRAYAL: Native Americans as victims; romance between Native Americans
SUMMARY: When settlers insult a young Native American woman, the man from her tribe who loves her comes to her defense. Then the whites try to lynch both of them.
CRITICS: A *Moving Picture World* critic comments that the filmmaker gave "a truer picture than he intended. He may have shown why some of the difficulties between whites and Indians began . . . and the conclusions will not be wholly flattering to the white men" (September 22, 1910, 689).

TULSA (Eagle Lion, 1949)
DIRECTOR: Stuart Heisler
SCREENPLAY: Frank S. Nugent, Curtis Kenyon, Richard Wormser
CAST: Susan Hayward (Cherokee Lansing), Pedro Armendariz (Jim Redbird), Iron Eyes Cody (Osage Indian), Billy Wilkerson (Lazy Mouse), Chief Yowlachie (Charlie Lightfoot),
SPECS: 90 minutes; Color
AVAILABILITY: DVD (VCI Video)
NATION: Cherokee; Osage
IMAGE PORTRAYAL: Mixed-blood Native American; Native Americans as victims
SUMMARY: Jim Redbird, a rancher, is the friend of mixed-blood oil wildcatter Cherokee, or Cherry, whose father had been killed by men after oil. He and

another rancher, Charlie Lightfoot, have oil on their land, but want to save space for their cattle. After Cherry builds some wells on their land, several wells catch fire, and they all finally agree to have some wells and also land for the cattle.

TUMBLEWEED (Universal, 1953)
DIRECTOR: Nathan Juran
SCREENPLAY: John Meredyth Lucas, based on the novel by Kenneth Perkins
CAST: Audie Murphy (Jim Harvey), Ralph Moody (Aguila), Eugene Iglesias (Tigre), Belle Mitchell (Tigre's Mother), Tony Urchel (Indian)
SPECS: 79 minutes; Color
AVAILABILITY: NA
NATION: Yaqui
IMAGE PORTRAYAL: Attack on wagon train; friendship
SUMMARY: The Yaqui tribe of Aguila and Tigre attacks a wagon train led by the hero, Jim Harvey. Though Harvey is a friend of Aguila, he cannot persuade the warriors to stop. Eventually the tribe again attacks, but is defeated, and before Aguila dies, he identifies the villain who incited the first attack.

TURQUOISE ROSE (Better World Distribution, 2007)
DIRECTOR: Travis Holt Hamilton
SCREENPLAY: Travis Holt Hamilton, Marjorie Coltrin Detiege, Jacob Johnson, Cara Rose Brown
CAST: Deshava Apachee (Harry Bahe), Natasha Kaye Johnson (Turquoise "Rose" Roanhorse), Ethel Begay (Masani, Rose's grandmother), Rhona Ray (Lillian Roanhorse, Rose's mother), Bria Sherinian (Michelle), Ernest David Tsosie III (Alvin Bahe), Katie Yazzie (Aunt Mary)
SPECS: 94 minutes; Color
AVAILABILITY: DVD (Better World Distribution)
NATION: Navajo
IMAGE PORTRAYAL: Contemporary Native American; romance between Native Americans; troubled Native American
SUMMARY: Turquoise Rose Roanhorse, a Navajo who was raised in a suburb of Phoenix and is a college student, must give up a trip to Europe to care for her sick grandmother on the Navajo reservation, where she finds love with Harry Bahe and fulfillment in the traditional Navajo way of life.

TUSKHA (Barcid Productions, 1997)
DIRECTOR: Ian D. Skorodin
SCREENPLAY: Ian D. Skorodin
CAST: Robert Eades (Marcus Beams), Tim Johnson (FBI agent)
SPECS: 90 minutes; Color
AVAILABILITY: NA
NATION: Choctaw

IMAGE PORTRAYAL: Contemporary Native American; Native American activist

SUMMARY: A Native American activist goes to Washington, D.C., to protest the treatment of his people by government agents, who burn down his house and kill most of his family.

TWO FLAGS WEST (20th Century Fox, 1950)
DIRECTOR: Robert Wise
SCREENPLAY: Casey Robinson, Curtis Kenyon, Frank S. Nugent
CAST: Joseph Cotten (Col. Clay Tucker), Jeff Chandler (Maj. Henry Kenniston), Linda Darnell (Elena)
SPECS: 92 minutes; Black & White
AVAILABILITY: NA
NATION: Kiowa
IMAGE PORTRAYAL: Vengeance
SUMMARY: After the haughty commander of a fort, Maj. Henry Kenniston, deliberately kills the son of the Kiowa Chief Santak, the tribe prepares to attack. However, they first shoot an arrow into the fort and promise to retreat if the killer of the chief's son is handed over to them. This happens and they kill Kenniston.

TWO RODE TOGETHER (Columbia, 1961)
DIRECTOR: John Ford
SCREENPLAY: Frank Nugent, based on the novel by Will Cook
CAST: James Stewart (Marshal Guthrie McCabe), Richard Widmark (Lt. Jim Gary), Linda Cristal (Elena de la Madriaga), Henry Brandon (Chief Quanah Parker), David Kent (Running Wolf), Woody Strode (Stone Calf)
SPECS: 109 minutes; Color
AVAILABILITY: Blu-ray (Twilight Time); Amazon Instant Video
NATION: Comanche
IMAGE PORTRAYAL: Kidnapping
SUMMARY: Guthrie McCabe and Jim Gary bring back to white society a young man raised by the Comanche, Running Wolf, and a Mexican woman, Elena. For years they have been the captives of Comanches led by Quanah Parker. The whites, however, lynch Running Wolf and reject Elena who had been forced to marry Stone Calf, a black man and rival of Quanah Parker in the Comanche tribe.

U

ULZANA'S RAID (Universal, 1972)
DIRECTOR: Robert Aldrich
SCREENPLAY: Alan Sharp

CAST: Burt Lancaster (McIntosh), Bruce Davison (Lt. Garnett DeBuin), Jorge Luke (Ke-Ni-Tay), Joaquin Martinez (Ulzana), Aimee Eccles (McIntosh's Indian Woman)
SPECS: 103 minutes; Color
AVAILABILITY: DVD (Universal Vault Series)
NATION: Apache
IMAGE PORTRAYAL: Attack on settlers; hostile warrior
SUMMARY: Discussed on page 45, this grim film depicts a small Apache band, led by Ulzana, which escapes from a reservation and attacks soldiers and settlers in a desperate attempt to survive. Sent to find and bring in Ulzana are Lt. DeBuin, McIntosh, and his Apache guide, Ke-Ni-Tay. They find a trail of devastation and finally kill all of the Apaches. In this process, the once compassionate DeBuin becomes a prejudiced killer.

UNCONQUERED (Paramount, 1947)
DIRECTOR: Cecil B. De Mille
SCREENPLAY: Charles Bennett, Fredric M. Frank, Jessie Lasky Jr., based on the novel *The Judas Tree* by Neil H. Swanson
CAST: Gary Cooper (Capt. Christopher Holden), Paulette Goddard (Abby), Boris Karloff (Guyasuta, Chief of the Senecas), Katherine DeMille (Hannah, the Chief's Daughter), Marc Lawrence (Sioto)
SPECS: 146 minutes; Color
AVAILABILITY: DVD (Universal Studios Home Entertainment)
NATION: Seneca
IMAGE PORTRAYAL: Attack on a fort
SUMMARY: During the time of Chief Pontiac's war, the Seneca Chief Guyasuta's tribe tortures Abby, who is then rescued by Capt. Chris Holden, who persuades the Chief and his medicine man, Sioto, to stop the torture. At the last moment, he helps those in the fort fight off a bloody Seneca attack by bringing in wagons of dead soldiers.
CRITICS: A *New York Times* film critic comments, "It is also deplorably evident that *Unconquered*, in this year of grace, is as viciously anti-redskin as *Birth of a Nation* was anti-Negro long years back" (October 19, 1947).

THE UNDEFEATED (20th Century Fox, 1969)
DIRECTOR: Andrew V. McLaglen
SCREENPLAY: James Lee Barrett, Stanley Hough, based on the novel by Lewis B. Patten
CAST: John Wayne (Col. John Henry Thomas), Rock Hudson (Col. James Langdon), Roman Gabriel (Blue Boy), Melissa Newman (Charlotte Langdon)
SPECS: 119 minutes; Color
AVAILABILITY: DVD (20th Century Fox Home Entertainment)
NATION: Cheyenne

IMAGE PORTRAYAL: Romance between a Native American man and a white woman

SUMMARY: Cheyenne warriors help Col. John Henry Thomas, whose adopted son, Blue Boy, is from their tribe. Blue Boy falls in love with Charlotte Langdon and is eventually punished by the whites for this romance.

CRITICS: *Chicago Sun Times* critic Roger Ebert comments on the romance and characterization: "McLaglen gets bogged down in an ineptly handled love triangle involving Hudson's daughter, Wayne's adopted Indian son and a young Confederate. The love affair mostly consists of the girl exchanging wisecracks with the Reb and long sighs with the Indian. Any racial overtones are muted by the casting of Roman Gabriel as the Indian (whose name, so help me God, is 'Blue Boy'). Gabriel looks about as Indian as one of the Beach Boys" (December 2, 1969).

UNDER NEVADA SKIES (Republic, 1946)
DIRECTOR: Frank McDonald
SCREENPLAY: Paul Gangelin, J. Benton Cheney, M. Coates Webster
CAST: Roy Rogers (Roy Rogers), George J. Lewis (Chief Flying Eagle), Iron Eyes Cody (Indian)
SPECS: 69 minutes; Black & White
AVAILABILITY: DVD (Alpha Home Entertainment); Amazon Instant Video
NATION: NA
IMAGE PORTRAYAL: Friendship
SUMMARY: Roy Rogers leads the tribe of Flying Eagle to a victory over the villains.

UNDER THE STAR SPANGLED BANNER (Kalem, 1908)
DIRECTOR: NA
SCREENPLAY: NA
CAST: NA
SPECS: 205 mm; Black & White; Silent
AVAILABILITY: NA
NATION: Sioux
IMAGE PORTRAYAL: Attack on settlers
SUMMARY: A hostile Sioux tribe attacks an immigrant family in a covered wagon but is driven off by the U.S. cavalry carrying the American flag.

THE UNFORGIVEN (United Artists, 1960)
DIRECTOR: John Huston
SCREENPLAY: Ben Maddow, based on the novel by Alan LeMay
CAST: Burt Lancaster (Ben Zachary), Audrey Hepburn (Rachel Zachary, a Kiowa woman), Carlos Rivas (Lost Bird)
SPECS: 125 minutes; Color
AVAILABILITY: DVD and Blu-ray (Kino Lorber); Amazon Instant Video

NATION: Kiowa

IMAGE PORTRAYAL: Native Americans as victims; romance between a Native American woman and a white man

SUMMARY: This film tells the story of Rachel Zachary, a Kiowa raised by a white family. When her racial identity is revealed, she and her family suffer prejudice from the whites. When the Kiowa warriors decide to attack her family because one of their warriors is killed, the hero, Ben Zachary, and a friend kill many Kiowas and Rachel kills her brother, Lost Bird. At the end Ben and Rachel are in love.

UNSEEING EYES (Goldwyn Cosmopolitan, 1923)

DIRECTOR: E. H. Griffith

SCREENPLAY: Bayard Veiller, Arthur Stringer

CAST: Lionel Barrymore (Conrad Dean), Walter Miller (Dick Helston), Francis Red Eagle (Singing Pine), Louis Deer (Eagle Blanket), Paul Panzer (Halfbreed), Dan Red Eagle (Halfbreed)

SPECS: 90 minutes; Black & White; Silent

AVAILABILITY: NA

NATION: NA

IMAGE PORTRAYAL: Friendship; loyalty; mixed-blood Native American

SUMMARY: Singing Pine rescues the heroes, Conrad Dean and Dick Helston, and nurses one of them back to health. Then, with the help of Eagle Blanket, the heroes triumph over Laird and his treacherous mixed-blood companions.

V

VALLEY OF THE SUN (RKO, 1942)

DIRECTOR: George Marshall

SCREENPLAY: Horace McCoy, Clarence Budington Kelland

CAST: James Craig (Jonathan Ware), Lucille Ball (Christine Larson), Antonio Moreno (Chief Cochise), Tom Tyler (Geronimo), Dean Jagger (Jim Sawyer)

SPECS: 78 minutes; Black & White

AVAILABILITY: NA

NATION: Apache

IMAGE PORTRAYAL: Friendship; hostile warrior; Native Americans as victims; peace-loving chief

SUMMARY: Apaches led by Geronimo and Cochise are driven to the edge of war by the evil Jim Sawyer. However, Jonathan Ware wins a hand-to-hand fight with Geronimo and rescues his friend, Cochise, in time to stop the war and make peace.

THE VANISHING AMERICAN (Paramount, 1925)

DIRECTOR: George Seitz

SCREENPLAY: Ethel Doherty, Lucien Hubbard, based on the novel by Zane Grey

CAST: Richard Dix (Nophaie), Lois Wilson (Marion Warner), Nocki (Indian Boy), Shannon Day (Gekin Yashi), Charles Stevens (Shoie)

SPECS: 110 minutes; Black & White; Silent

AVAILABILITY: DVD (Image Entertainment)

NATION: Navajo

IMAGE PORTRAYAL: Romance between a Native American man and a white woman

SUMMARY: Discussed on page 15, this film begins with a history of aboriginal peoples in America, which, in turn, illustrates the idea of the survival of the fittest. The main film then tells the story of Nophaie, the Navajo warrior, who falls in love with Marion Warner, the teacher on his reservation. He also has to deal with an evil agent, Booker. At the end, he dies while trying to stop the fighting between his tribe and the whites. His death obviously relates to the concept of the vanishing race.

CRITICS: A *Variety* critic's comment on the film reveals a common contemporary stereotype of Native Americans living on reservations: "The story itself calls attention to the vanishing of the real American, the Indian, off the face of the North American continent. Nothing is said about the Indians who are living in Oklahoma at this time and drawing down a weekly royalty of $1,750 and riding around in sedans which they discard immediately after a tire blows, so as to get a new car" (October 21, 1925).

A comment by another *Variety* reviewer on a film roughly contemporary to *The Vanishing American* reflects a similar prejudice. In *The Big Show* (1926), an Indian chief sits in a "majestic pose" with "folded arms and impassive face" as he dictates a letter to his daughter which instructs "his bank in Oklahoma to credit him with oil royalties immediately to cover his checks drawn for a new runabout for his daughter" (July 14, 1926).

THE VANISHING AMERICAN (Republic, 1955)

DIRECTOR: Joseph Kane

SCREENPLAY: Alan Le May, based on the novel by Zane Grey

CAST: Scott Brady (Blandy), Audrey Totter (Marion Warner), Forrest Tucker (Morgan), Gene Lockhart (Blucher), Gloria Castillo (Yashi), Julian Rivero (Etenia), Jay Silverheels (Beeteia), George Keymas (Coshanta), Charles Stevens (Quah-Tan), Glenn Strange (Beleanth),

SPECS: 90 minutes; Black & White

AVAILABILITY: NA

NATION: Apache; Navajo

IMAGE PORTRAYAL: Attacks on Native Americans; romance between a Native American man and a white woman; romance between Native Americans

SUMMARY: In this second version, Blandy is a Navajo who loves Marion Warner, who lives on the reservation. After overcoming a crooked trader, Morgan;

an evil Indian agent, Blucher;, and hostile Apaches led by Coshanta and Quah-Tan, Blandy settles down with his beloved Marion. Another Native American, Yashi, a young woman threatened by the villain, eventually escapes with her lover, Beeteia. And the Apaches kill old Navajo Chief Etenia.

THE VANISHING RACE (American, 1912)

DIRECTOR: Allan Dwan

SCREENPLAY: NA

CAST: J. Warren Kerrigan (Hoppe Indian Brave), Jessalyn Van Trump (Indian Maiden), George Periolat (Indian Elder), Louise Lester (Indian Elder)

SPECS: 1 reel; Black & White; Silent

AVAILABILITY: NA

NATION: NA

IMAGE PORTRAYAL: Native Americans as victims

SUMMARY: A family, the last members of the "Hoppe" tribe, face extinction because a white man rejects the love of the young daughter, the Indian Maiden. More killing on both sides leaves only the disgraced daughter.

THE VILLAIN (Rastar Pictures, 1979)

DIRECTOR: Hal Needham

SCREENPLAY: Robert G. Kane

CAST: Kirk Douglas (Cactus Jack), Paul Lynde (Nervous Elk)

SPECS: 89 minutes; Color

AVAILABILITY: VHS (Columbia Home Video)

NATION: NA

IMAGE PORTRAYAL: Native Americans as butt of humor

SUMMARY: This spoof of B westerns is difficult to categorize. Nervous Elk is an effeminate chief of a tribe whose rituals, horsemanship, treatment of white women, and rights to their own land are all ridiculed.

THE VIRGINIAN (Lasky, 1914)

DIRECTOR: Cecil B. DeMille

SCREENPLAY: Kirk La Shelle, based on the novel by Owen Wister

CAST: Dustin Farnum (The Virginian), Jack W. Johnston (Steve), Winifred Kingston (Molly Wood)

SPECS: 55 minutes; Black & White; Silent

AVAILABILITY: NA

NATION: NA

IMAGE PORTRAYAL: Attack on settlers

SUMMARY: Hostile warriors stage bloody attacks on the colonists.

CRITICS: A *Variety* critic comments on the unbelievable ways in which Indians are killed during these attacks: "The hero, who is badly wounded, spies an Indian several hundred feet away and shoots left-handed from his hip with fatal effect" (September 11, 1914).

W

WAGON MASTER (Argosy Pictures, 1950)
DIRECTOR: John Ford
SCREENPLAY: Frank S. Nugent, Patrick Ford
CAST: Ben Johnson (Travis Blue), Harry Carey Jr. (Sandy), Jim Thorpe (Navajo Indian), Movita (Young Navajo Indian)
SPECS: 86 minutes; Black & White
AVAILABILITY: DVD (Warner Home Video); Amazon Instant Video
NATION: Navajo
IMAGE PORTRAYAL: Vengeance
SUMMARY: Travis Blue and Sandy, who are leading the wagon train, make friends with a band of Navajo and they have a joint celebration. However, when a Mormon molests a woman from the tribe, they threaten war until the man is punished.

WAGON TRACKS (William S. Hart Productions, 1919)
DIRECTOR: Lambert Hillyer
SCREENPLAY: C. Gardner Sullivan
CAST: William S. Hart (Buckskin Hamilton), Jane Novak (Jane Washburn), Robert McKim (Donald Washburn)
SPECS: 64 minutes; Black & White; Silent
AVAILABILITY: DVD (Unknown Video); Amazon Instant Video
NATION: NA
IMAGE PORTRAYAL: Vengeance
SUMMARY: Hostile warriors threaten a wagon train. Later they kill a white man, Donald Washburn, who had killed one of their warriors, and earlier killed Buckskin's brother.
CRITICS: A *Variety* reviewer comments on such a standard use of the hostile tribe: "to form a climax, the Indians are dragged in" (August 15, 1919).

WAGON TRACKS WEST (Republic, 1943)
DIRECTOR: Howard Bretherton
SCREENPLAY: William Lively
CAST: Bill Elliot (Wild Bill Elliot), Gabby Hayes (Gabby), Tom Tyler (Clawtooth), Anne Jeffreys (Moon Hush), Rick Vallin (Dr. John Fleetwing), Robert Frazer (Robert Warren), Charles Miller (Brown Bear)
SPECS: 55 minutes; Black & White
AVAILABILITY: NA
NATION: Pawnee
IMAGE PORTRAYAL: Friendship; hostile warrior; romance between Native Americans
SUMMARY: Wild Bill Elliot helps Fleetwing, a Native American doctor in love with Moon Hush, to handle a corrupt Indian agent, Robert Warren, and Claw-

tooth, an evil medicine man, who are trying to force Fleetwing's tribe to leave the area by allowing a serious infection to exist in the Pawnee village. Brown Bear is already infected and eventually killed by Clawtooth.

CRITICS: A *Variety* critic comments on the character of Moon Hush: "The Femme lead could have been handled by a totem pole wired for sound. Anne Jeffreys, as the Indian maid doesn't even get to smile [and] has very few lines" (October 27, 1943).

WAGONS WEST (Silvermine Productions, 1952)

DIRECTOR: Ford Beebe

SCREENPLAY: Daniel B. Ullman

CAST: Rod Cameron (Jeff Curtis), Noah Beery Jr. (Arch Lawrence), Henry Brandon (Clay Cook), Frank Ferguson (Cyrus Cook), John Parrish (Chief Black Kettle), Charles Stevens (Kaw Chief)

SPECS: 70 minutes; Color

AVAILABILITY: NA

NATION: Cheyenne

IMAGE PORTRAYAL: Attack on a wagon train; peace-loving chief

SUMMARY: Cheyenne warriors of Chief Black Kettle and Kaw Chief, who are armed with rifles supplied by the Cooks, attack a wagon train heading for California. At the end, Jeff works a peace deal with Black Kettle.

WALK TALL (API, 1960)

DIRECTOR: Maury Dexter

SCREENPLAY: Joseph Fritz

CAST: Willard Parker (Capt. Ed Trask), Kent Taylor (Frank Carter), Felix Locher (Chief Black Feather), Dave DePaul (Buffalo Horn)

SPECS: 61 minutes; Color

AVAILABILITY: NA

NATION: NA

IMAGE PORTRAYAL: Friendship; loyalty

SUMMARY: With the help of Shoshone warriors Chief Black Feather and Buffalo Horn, Capt. Ed Trask stops Frank Carter whose attacks on the tribe could start a war.

WALK THE PROUD LAND (Universal, 1956)

DIRECTOR: Jesse Hibbs

SCREENPLAY: Gil Doud, Jack Sher, based on the biography of John Clum by Woodworth Clum

CAST: Audie Murphy (John Clum), Anne Bancroft (Tianay), Jay Silverheels (Geronimo), Tommy Rall (Taglito), Robert Warwick (Chief Eskiminzin), Eugene Mazzola (Tono), Anthony Caruso (Disalin), Eugene Igelesias (Chato), Marty Carrizosa (Pica), Mauruce Jara (Alchise)

SPECS: 89 minutes; Color
AVAILABILITY: NA
NATION: Apache
IMAGE PORTRAYAL: Romance between a Native American woman and a
  white man
SUMMARY: Also titled *Apache Agent*, this film tells the story of John Clum,
  an agent at the San Carlos Reservation who takes care of the Apache tribe
  of Geronimo, Taglito, Eskiminzin, Tono, Alchise, and Pica. Though loved
  by Tianay, Clum remains faithful to his wife. Finally, he brings peace to the
  reservation when he convinces Geronimo to surrender and live a life of law
  and order.
CRITICS: A *Time* critic notes that the film is "a western with a difference: the
  Indians, or most of them, are the good guys" (September 24, 1956, 92).

WAR ARROW (Universal, 1953)
DIRECTOR: George Sherman
SCREENPLAY: John Michael Hayes
CAST: Jeff Chandler (Major Howell Brady), Maureen O'Hara (Elaine), Suzan
  Ball (Avis), Henry Brandon (Maygro), Dennis Weaver (Pino), Jay Silverheels
  (Satanta), James Bannon (Roger Corwin)
SPECS: 78 minutes; Color
AVAILABILITY: DVD (Universal Studios Home Entertainment)
NATION: Kiowa; Seminole
IMAGE PORTRAYAL: Friendship; hostile warrior; loyalty; peace-loving chief
SUMMARY: After promising better land for a reservation, Major Brady, with the
  help of friendly Seminoles led by Maygro, puts down a Kiowa uprising incited
  by Roger Corwin and led by Satanta. Brady eventually falls in love with Elaine,
  and Avis, the daughter of Maygro, is jealous.

WAR DRUMS (United Artists, 1957)
DIRECTOR: Reginald Le Borg
SCREENPLAY: Gerald Drayson Adams
CAST: Lex Barker (Mangas Coloradas), Joan Taylor (Riva), Ben Johnson (Luke
  Fargo), Larry Chance (Ponce), John Colicos (Chino), Jil Jarmyn (Nona), Jeanne
  Carmen (Yellow Moon), Ward Elks (Delgadito)
SPECS: 75 minutes; Color
AVAILABILITY: DVD (MGM Limited Edition Collection)
NATION: Apache
IMAGE PORTRAYAL: Friendship; loyalty; mixed-blood Native American;
  peace-loving chief; romance between Native Americans
SUMMARY: Evil gold miners invade Apache land and hurt the sister of Mangas,
  Nona, and her son. This pushes the peace-loving Mangas Coloradas and his
  mixed-blood Mexican Comanche wife, Riva, into breaking a treaty. However,

Luke Fargo helps them escape an unjust punishment and join other members of their Apache tribe, Chino, Yellow Moon, and Delgadito, in a mountain hideout.

WAR PAINT (MGM, 1926)
DIRECTOR: W. S. Van Dyke
SCREENPLAY: Joseph Farnham, Charles Maigne, based on the novel by Peter B. Kyne
CAST: Tim McCoy (Lt. Tim Marshall), Pauline Starke (Polly Hopkins), Chief Yowlachie (Iron Eyes), Whitehorse (Chief White Hawk)
SPECS: 6 reels; Black & White; Silent
AVAILABILITY: NA
NATION: Arapaho
IMAGE PORTRAYAL: Attack on soldiers; friendship; loyalty
SUMMARY: Whites capture Iron Eyes, an Arapaho chief and medicine man. When he escapes and attacks the fort in revenge, Chief White Hawk helps Tim Marshall come to the rescue.
CRITICS: A *Variety* critic comments on the motivation for the attack: "Back in the days of the Indian extermination all of their uprisings were not wholly the fault of the red man. Perhaps the moving pictures some day will tell all the truth about the American Indian and his decline" (October 20, 1926).

WAR PAINT (United Artists, 1953)
DIRECTOR: Lesley Selander
SCREENPLAY: Richard Alan Simmons, Martin Berkeley, Fred Freiberger, William Tunberg
CAST: Robert Stack (Lt. Billings), Joan Taylor (Wanima), Keith Larsen (Taslik)
SPECS: 89 minutes; Color
AVAILABILITY: DVD (MGM Limited Edition Collection)
NATION: NA
IMAGE PORTRAYAL: Attack on soldiers; romance between a Native American woman and a white man
SUMMARY: Lt. Billings struggles to get a treaty to the tribe of Chief Gray Cloud against the wishes of his hostile son, Taslik. Billings and Wanima finally avert a war by delivering the treaty and exposing the villains. At the end they leave together for the tribe's camp.

WAR PARTY (20th Century Fox, 1965)
DIRECTOR: Lesley Selander
SCREENPLAY: William Marks, George Williams
CAST: Michael T. Mikler (Johnny Hawk), Laurie Mock (Nicoma), Charles Horvath (Wolf Hound), Guy Wilkerson (Wooden Face), Fred Krone (Indian), Don "Red" Berry (Sgt. Chaney)

SPECS: 73 minutes; Black & White
AVAILABILITY: NA
NATION: Comanche
IMAGE PORTRAYAL: Attack on soldiers; friendship
SUMMARY: Comanche warriors, led by Wolf Hound, attack a patrol sent out to bring help for troops pinned down by other members of the tribe. Though most of the men in the patrol die, Sgt. Chaney, with the help of Nicoma, manages to blow up the tribe's ammunition, kill the chief, and rescue the troop. Nicoma dies in the process of assisting Chaney.

WAR PARTY (Hemdale Film, 1988)
DIRECTOR: Franc Roddam
SCREENPLAY: Spencer Eastman
CAST: Billy Wirth (Sonny Crowkiller), Kevin Dillon (Skitty Harris), Tim Sampson (Warren Cutfoot), Dennis Banks (Ben Crowkiller), Saginaw Grant (Freddie Man Wolf), Rodney A. Grant (The Crow), Tantoo Cardinal (Sonny's Mother)
SPECS: 97 minutes; Color
AVAILABILITY: VHS (Warner Home Video)
NATION: Blackfoot; Crow
IMAGE PORTRAYAL: Contemporary Native Americans; troubled Native Americans
SUMMARY: Discussed on page 54, this film tells the story of three Blackfoot teenagers, Sonny Crowkiller, Skitty Harris, and Warren Cutfoot, who get caught up in a deadly battle with the townspeople and the National Guard when a staged re-creation of a historical battle for a town festival turns into a bloody fight. At the end, the three young warriors are hunted down with the help of the Crow and killed.
CRITICS: In the *Chicago Sun Times*, critic Roger Ebert notes, "There was a time in American history when such an assumption of racism would have been so routine it was invisible; look at the countless cowboy and Indian movies that never questioned the premise that the primary function of cowboys and Indians was to hate one another on sight, and want to kill one another. This movie basically doesn't question that premise, either" (September 29, 1989).

THE WAR WAGON (Universal, 1967)
DIRECTOR: Burt Kennedy
SCREENPLAY: Clair Huffaker, based on his novel
CAST: John Wayne (Taw Jackson), Kirk Douglas (Lomax), Howard Keel (Levi Walking Bear), Marco Antonio (Chief Wild Horse)
SPECS: 96 minutes; Color
AVAILABILITY: DVD (Universal Studios Home Entertainment)
NATION: Kiowa
IMAGE PORTRAYAL: Attack on a wagon train; friendship; loyalty; Native Americans as victims

SUMMARY: Levi Walking Bear, a cynical renegade who has learned from the whites how to grab all he can, is the friend of Taw Jackson. A starving Kiowa tribe, led by Chief Wild Horse, helps Jackson rob the war wagon, an armored stagecoach used to transport gold, which is carrying gold Jackson has been cheated out of. They manage to get the gold and stash it in flour barrels, but the plan goes awry and the gold falls into the hands of the Kiowa who think it is all flour.

WARPATH (Paramount, 1951)
DIRECTOR: Byron Haskin
SCREENPLAY: Frank Gruber
CAST: Edmond O'Brien (John Vickers), Forrest Tucker (Sgt. O'Hara)
SPECS: 95 minutes; Color
AVAILABILITY: Amazon Instant Video
NATION: Sioux
IMAGE PORTRAYAL: Attack on soldiers
SUMMARY: Vickers and O'Hara defeat a band of Sioux and they decide that it is too late to warn Custer about the Little Big Horn battle.
CRITICS: A *Variety* critic notes that this situation has become typical: "Putting the cavalry against the Indians has become a rather common storybook" (June 6, 1951).

WARRIOR GAP (Vital, 1925)
DIRECTOR: Alan James
SCREENPLAY: George Pyper, Charles King
CAST: Ben Wilson (Capt. Deane), Len Hayes (Chief Red Cloud)
SPECS: 5 reels; Black & White; Silent
AVAILABILITY: NA
NATION: Sioux
IMAGE PORTRAYAL: Attack on soldiers
SUMMARY: This film tells the story of Sioux Chief Red Cloud's attacks on the U.S. cavalry.

A WARRIOR'S HEART (California Pictures, 2011)
DIRECTOR: Michael F. Sears
SCREENPLAY: Martin Dugard
CAST: Kellan Lutz (Conor Sullivan), Adam Beach (Sgt. Major Duke Wayne)
SPECS: 86 minutes; Color
AVAILABILITY: DVD (Xenon); Amazon Instant Video
NATION: Iroquois—Six Nations
IMAGE PORTRAYAL: Contemporary Native American athlete; friendship; Native American athlete
SUMMARY: In this sports and romance film, Conor, a talented but angry player because of his father's death, is taught how to be a lacrosse warrior in a Six

Nations camp by Sgt. Major Duke Wayne, a Native American military and lacrosse warrior.

THE WAY WEST (Harold Hecht Productions, 1967)
DIRECTOR: Andrew V. McLaglen
SCREENPLAY: Ben Maddow, Mitch Lindemann, based on the novel by A. B. Guthrie Jr.
CAST: Kirk Douglas (William J. Tadlock), Robert Mitchum (Dick Summers), Richard Widmark (Lije Evans), Michael Keep (Indian Brave), Mike Lane (Sioux Chief), Eddie Little Sky (Sioux Warrior), Gary Morris (Paw-Kee-Mah), Mitchell Schollars (Indian Boy)
SPECS: 122 minutes; Color
AVAILABILITY: DVD (MGM Home Entertainment); Amazon Instant Video
NATION: Sioux
IMAGE PORTRAYAL: Attack on wagon train
SUMMARY: After the son of the Sioux chief is accidentally killed, William Tadlock has to hang a man to stop the tribe from taking revenge on the wagon train.

WELLS FARGO (Paramount, 1937)
DIRECTOR: Frank Lloyd
SCREENPLAY: Paul Schofield, Gerald Geraghty, Frederick J. Jackson, based on a story by Stuart N. Lake
CAST: Joel McCrea (Ramsay MacKay), Bernard Siegel (Pawnee)
SPECS: 97 minutes; Black & White
AVAILABILITY: NA
NATION: NA
IMAGE PORTRAYAL: Attacks on stage coaches
SUMMARY: Ramsay MacKay and his friend, Pawnee, fight a hostile tribe who attacks the Wells Fargo stagecoaches.

WEST OF NEVADA (First Division, 1936)
DIRECTOR: Robert Hill
SCREENPLAY: Robert Hill, based on the novel by Charles Kyson
CAST: Rex Bell (Jim Carden), Joan Barclay (Helen Haldain), Dick Botiller (Bald Eagle), Frank McCarroll (Slade Sangree), Forrest Taylor (Steven Cutting)
SPECS: 57 minutes; Black & White
AVAILABILITY: DVD (Alpha Video)
NATION: Navajo
IMAGE PORTRAYAL: Native Americans as victims
SUMMARY: After Slade Sangree and Steven Cutting try to steal gold from the peaceful Navajo tribe of Bald Eagle, Jim Carden helps the tribe bring them to justice.

CRITICS: A *Variety* critic notes that "juvenile audiences will thrill to see that redskins are once again in favor with the Hollywood chiefs" (July 22, 1936).

WESTERN UNION (20th Century Fox, 1941)

DIRECTOR: Fritz Lang

SCREENPLAY: Robert Carson, Jack Andrews, George Bruce, Horace McCoy, based on the novel by Zane Grey

CAST: Robert Young (Richard Blake), Randolph Scott (Vance Shaw), Dean Jagger (Edward Creighton), Barton MacLane (Jack Slade), Chief John Big Tree (Chief Spotted Horse)

SPECS: 95 min; Color

AVAILABILITY: DVD (20th Century Fox Cinema Archives)

NATION: NA

IMAGE PORTRAYAL: Peace-loving chief

SUMMARY: The tribe of Chief Spotted Horse threatens to attack the builders of the telegraph line after villains, led by Slade, and disguised as Native Americans attack the workers. However, when Edward Creighton shows the power of electricity to the tribe, Spotted Horse lets the line be built.

WESTWARD HO, THE WAGONS! (Walt Disney Productions, 1957)

DIRECTOR: William Beaudine

SCREENPLAY: Thomas W. Blackburn, based on the novel by Mary Jane Carr

CAST: Fess Parker (John 'Doc' Grayson), John War Eagle (Wolf's Brother), Iron Eyes Cody (Many Stars), Anthony Numkena (Little Thunder)

SPECS: 90 minutes; Color

AVAILABILITY: VHS (Walt Disney Home Video); Amazon Instant Video

NATIONS: Pawnee; Sioux

IMAGE PORTRAYAL: Attack on wagon train; friendship; loyalty

SUMMARY: At one point, warlike Pawnee attack a wagon train. Later, the hostile Sioux accept the settlers as friends after John 'Doc' Grayson helps Many Stars, their medicine man, save the life of Chief Wolf's Brother's son, Little Thunder.

WHEELS OF DESTINY (Ken Maynard Productions, 1934)

DIRECTOR: Alan James

SCREENPLAY: Nate Gatzert

CAST: Ken Maynard (Ken Manning), Dorothy Dix (Mary Collins), Philo McCullough (Rocky), Chief John Big Tree (Chief War Eagle)

SPECS: 46 minutes; Black & White

AVAILABILITY: NA

NATION: NA

IMAGE PORTRAYAL: Attack on a wagon train

SUMMARY: Incited by the villains, led by Rocky, who start a buffalo stampede, the tribe of Chief War Eagle attacks wagon trains.

WHEN THE LEGENDS DIE (20th Century Fox, 1972)
DIRECTOR: Stuart Millar
SCREENPLAY: Robert Dozier, based on the novel by Hal Borland
CAST: Richard Widmark (Red Dillon), Frederic Forrest (Tom Black Bull), John War Eagle (Blue Elk)
SPECS: 107 minutes; Color
AVAILABILITY: VHS (Playhouse Home Video)
NATION: Ute
IMAGE PORTRAYAL: Contemporary Native American; troubled Native American
SUMMARY: Discussed on page 48, this film portrays the mistreatment of Thomas Black Bull, a Ute bronco rider, by his own people and white society. An old Ute, Blue Elk, forces Tom to go to a school for Native Americans, a place that marks the beginning of his downfall. His next mentor is Red Dillon, a drunk who exploits him to the point that Tom, a man who loves animals, becomes known as "Horse Killer." At the end, after Red dies, Tom returns to his reservation to find his identity.
CRITICS: *New York Times* critic Vincent Canby comments on the purpose of the film: "It's also about Indian pride and identity, but it doesn't slug you over the head with these things in the manner of a movie like '*Journey through Rosebud*'" (October 20, 1972).

WHEN THE REDSKINS RODE (Columbia, 1951)
DIRECTOR: Lew Landers
SCREENPLAY: Robert E. Kent
CAST: Jon Hall (Prince Hannoc), Mary Castle (Elizabeth Leeds), Sherry Moreland (Morna), Pedro de Cordoba (Chief Shingiss), James Seay (George Washington)
SPECS: 78 minutes; Color
AVAILABILITY: NA
NATION: Delaware; Miamis; Wayandot
IMAGE PORTRAYAL: Attack on settlers; romance between Native Americans
SUMMARY: Chief Singiss of the Delaware, the father of Prince Hannoc, is killed by French spies, one of whom is Elizabeth Leeds. After helping Washington win a battle, Hannoc and the Native American woman he loves, Morna, and his Delaware defeat the French.

WHERE THE RIVERS FLOW NORTH (Caledonia Pictures, 1993)
DIRECTOR: Jay Craven
SCREENPLAY: Don Bredes, Jay Craven, based on the novel by Howard Frank Mosher
CAST: Rip Torn (Noel Lord), Tantoo Cardinal (Bangor), Michael J. Fox (Clayton Farnsworth)
SPECS: 106 minutes; Color

AVAILABILITY: DVD (Allumination)
NATION: NA
IMAGE PORTRAYAL: Romance between a Native American woman and a
    white man
SUMMARY: In remote Vermont, a rugged, fiercely proud old lumberman, Noel
    Lord, and his female Native American companion, Bangor, fight developers who
    want to build a dam that will flood the area. Bangor wants to leave and start over,
    but Noel fights her all the way. Both of these characters are extremely well acted.

WHERE THE TRAIL DIVIDES (Lasky, 1914)
DIRECTOR: James Neill
SCREENPLAY: Based on the novel by William Otis Lillibridge
CAST: Robert Edeson ("How" Landor), Antrim Short (Little "How"), Winifred
    Kingston (Bess Lander), Jack W. Johnston (Clayton Craig)
SPECS: 5 reels; Black & White; Silent
AVAILABILITY: NA
NATION: NA
IMAGE PORTRAYAL: Romance between a Native American man and a white
    woman
SUMMARY: How marries a white woman, Bess, but later lets her go so she can
    live in comfort in the East with a rich white man, Clayton Craig. When this
    man, who turns out to be an unfaithful criminal, is rejected by Bess, How brings
    her back to the West and they renew their marriage.

THE WHITE BUFFALO (Dino De Laurentiis Company, 1977)
DIRECTOR: J. Lee Thompson
SCREENPLAY: Richard Sale, based on his novel
CAST: Charles Bronson (Wild Bill Hickok/James Otis), Will Sampson (Crazy
    Horse/Worm)
SPECS: 97 minutes; Color
AVAILABILITY: DVD (MGM Limited Edition Collection); Amazon Instant
    Video
NATION: Sioux-Lakota
IMAGE PORTRAYAL: Vengeance
SUMMARY: Crazy Horse, whose daughter has been killed by the white buffalo,
    struggles with Wild Bill Hickok to be the one who kills the mythical beast. At
    the end the two rivals become friends and team up to kill the buffalo.

WHITE COMANCHE (Producciones Cinematograficas, 1968)
DIRECTOR: Jose Briz Mendez
SCREENPLAY: Frank Gruber, Robert I. Holt
CAST: Joseph Cotton (Sheriff Logan), William Shatner (Johnny Moon, Notah),
    Perla Cristal (White Fawn), Luis Rivera (Kah To), Gene Reyes (Comanche)

SPECS: 93 Minutes; Color
AVAILABILITY: DVD (Warner Archive Collection)
NATION: Comanche
IMAGE PORTRAYAL: Attack on a stage coach
SUMMARY: Twin sons of a Comanche mother grow up as Johnny Moon, a peace-loving man, and Notah, a fierce, peyote-crazed warrior. After Notah and his warriors attack a stagecoach and beat up a white woman, Johnny fights him in a one-on-one battle and kills him.

THE WHITE DAWN (Paramount, 1974)

DIRECTOR: Philip Kaufman
SCREENPLAY: James Houston, Martin Ransohoff, Thomas Rickman, based on Houston's novel
CAST: Warren Oates (Billy), Timothy Bottoms (Daggett), Louis Gossett Jr. (Portagee), Pilitak (Neevee), Sagiaktok (The Shaman), Simonie Kopapik (Sarkak), Joanasie Salamonie (Kangiak)
SPECS: 110 minutes; Color
AVAILABILITY: DVD (Warner Archive Collection); Amazon Instant Video
NATION: Eskimo
IMAGE PORTRAYAL: Contemporary Eskimo culture; romance between a Native American woman and a white man
SUMMARY: The film depicts the behavior of three white whalers—Billy, Daggett, and Portagee—stranded among the Eskimos. Daggett accepts his host's ways but falls in love with Neevee, while the other two introduce gambling, violent sports, and liquor. This behavior leads to trouble as the Eskimos, especially the Shaman, lose patience with the whalers' lack of knowledge of their culture.

WHITE EAGLE (Columbia, 1932)

DIRECTOR: Lambert Hillyer
SCREENPLAY: Fred Myton
CAST: Buck Jones (White Eagle), Frank Campeau (Gray Wolf), Robert Ellis (Jim Gregory)
SPECS: 65 minutes; Black & White
AVAILABILITY: NA
NATION: NA
IMAGE PORTRAYAL: Native Americans as victims
SUMMARY: White Eagle, a pony express rider, joins his father, Gray Wolf, to bring to justice villains, led by Jim Gregory, who disguise themselves as Native Americans and cause hostility between their tribe and the whites. At the end, White Eagle finds out that he is really a white man.

WHITE FANG 2: MYTH OF THE WHITE WOLF (Walt Disney Pictures, 1994)

DIRECTOR: Ken Olin
SCREENPLAY: David Fallon

CAST: Scott Bairstow (Henry Casey), Charmaine Craig (Lily), Al Harrington (Moses Joseph), Victoria Racimo (Katrin), Anthony Michael Ruivivar (Peter)
SPECS: 106 minutes; Color
AVAILABILITY: DVD (Walt Disney Home Video); Amazon Instant Video
NATION: Haida
IMAGE PORTRAYAL: Romance between a Native American woman and a white man
SUMMARY: After being rescued by Lily Joseph, the daughter of the Haida chief, Moses Joseph, Henry Casey is seen by the tribe as the spirit of the White Wolf. With the help of Lily, he saves the tribe from starvation by overcoming villains who have blocked the migration of the caribou. By the end, Henry and Lily are deeply in love and will live together with the tribe.
CRITICS: In a comment that could apply to a number of 1990s films, *Variety* critic Joe Leydon notes that the film's "screenplay keeps the narrative simple and politically correct. The Haida are depicted as noble, compassionate and intelligent, while just about every white man . . . is a rotten, duplicitous exploiter" (April 18, 1994).

WHITE FEATHER (Panoramic Productions, 1955)
DIRECTOR: Robert Webb
SCREENPLAY: Delmer Daves, Leo Townsend, John Prebble
CAST: Robert Wagner (Josh Tanner), Eduard Franz (Chief Broken Hand), Debra Paget (Appearing Day), Jeffrey Hunter (Little Dog), Hugh O'Brian (American Horse), Iron Eyes Cody (Indian Chief)
SPECS: 102 minutes; Color
AVAILABILITY: DVD (20th Century Fox Home Entertainment)
NATION: Arapaho; Blackfoot; Cheyenne
IMAGE PORTRAYAL: Peace-loving chief; romance between a Native American woman and a white man
SUMMARY: The hero, Josh Tanner, who is in charge of moving the Cheyenne of the peace-loving Chief Broken Hand to a new reservation, causes trouble when he falls in love with Appearing Day, who is betrothed to the son of the chief, Little Dog. After the death of Little Dog and his hostile friend, American Horse, Chief Broken Hand makes peace, and the tribe moves off to the reservation. At the end, Josh and Appearing Day are married and have a son.
CRITICS: A *New York Times* critic comments that "the Red Man . . . is a truly brave warrior but somehow a sad figure, resigned, at last, to the truth that the White Man is strong enough to oust him from his hunting grounds and that he must move to new lands" (February 17, 1955).

WHITE OAK (Paramount, 1921)
DIRECTOR: Lambert Hillyer
SCREENPLAY: Bennet Musson, William S. Hart
CAST: W. S. Hart (Oak Miller), Vola Vale (Barbara), Alexander Gaden (Mark Granger), Chief Standing Bear (Chief Long Knife)

SPECS: 75 minutes; Black & White; Silent
AVAILABILITY: DVD (Alpha Home Entertainment)
NATION: NA
IMAGE PORTRAYAL: Attack on wagon train
SUMMARY: Villainous Mark Granger plots with Chief Long Knife, and his tribe attacks a circled wagon train. At the end, Oak Miller comes to the rescue of his beloved Barbara, and Chief Long Knife kills Granger, who had raped his daughter.

WHITE SQUAW (Columbia, 1956)

DIRECTOR: Ray Nazarro
SCREENPLAY: Les Savage Jr., based on the novel by Larabie Sutter
CAST: May Wynn (Eetay-O-Wahnee), William Bishop (Bob Garth), David Brian (Sigrod), Frank De Kova (Yellow Elk), Neyle Morrow (Swift Arrow), George Keymas (Yotah)
SPECS: 75 minutes; Black & White
AVAILABILITY: DVD (Sony Pictures Choice Collection)
NATION: Sioux
IMAGE PORTRAYAL: Mixed-blood Native American; romance between a mixed-blood Native American woman and a white man
SUMMARY: Sigrod, the villain, tries to drive from their reservation the Sioux tribe of Yellow Elk, Yotah, and Swift Arrow, who have adopted Eetay-O-Wahnee. The hero, Bob Garth, who loves Eetay-O-Wahnee, comes to the rescue, and finally Sigrod dies in a burning tepee. At the end, the good whites vow peace and the rebuilding of the tribe's village.

WILD AND WOOLLY (Douglas Fairbanks Pictures, 1917)

DIRECTOR: John Emerson
SCREENPLAY: John Emerson, Anita Loos, Horace B. Carpenter
CAST: Douglas Fairbanks (Jeff Hillington), Eileen Percy (Nell Larabee), Sam De Grass (Steve Shelby)
SPECS: 72 minutes; Black & White; Silent
AVAILABILITY: DVD (Televista)
NATION: NA
IMAGE PORTRAYAL: Attack on a town
SUMMARY: In this comedy, Jeff Hillington, a rich Easterner, comes to a town that pretends to be the Wild West and that really becomes so when Native Americans attack. Hillington fights hostile drunken warriors and rescues a woman from their camp.
CRITICS: A *Variety* critic comments, "You've got to laugh when the hero rides into the midst of a bunch of drunken Indians, swings the girl on the back of his horse and makes a getaway without being shot" (June 22, 1917).

THE WILD BULL'S LAIR (Robertson-Cole Pictures 1925)

DIRECTOR: Del Andrews
SCREENPLAY: Marion Jackson

CAST: Fred Thompson (Dan Allen), Frank Hagney (Eagle Eye)
SPECS: 6 reels; Black & White; Silent
AVAILABILITY: NA
NATION: NA
IMAGE PORTRAYAL: Vengeance
SUMMARY: The tribe of Eagle Eye, a well-educated man who resents the loss of tribal lands, trains a wild bull, which is half buffalo, to lead the cattle of whites to their own remaining land.
CRITICS: A *Variety* reviewer notes that the film "is inhabited by a tribe of Indians (not the nice wild old Injuns of former days, but a group of college trained redskins who want to reclaim their land from the palefaces)" (August 26, 1925).

THE WILD DAKOTAS (Assoc. Releasing, 1956)

DIRECTORS: Sigmund Neufeld, Sam Newfield
SCREENPLAY: Thomas W. Blackburn
CAST: Bill Williams (Jim Henry), Jim Davis (Aaron Baring), John Miljan (Chief Antelope), Iron Eyes Cody (Red Rock)
SPECS: 73 minutes; Black & White
AVAILABILITY: Amazon Instant Video
NATION: Arapaho
IMAGE PORTRAYAL: Peace-loving chief
SUMMARY: When a villain, Aaron Baring, tries to cheat the Arapaho tribe of Chief Antelope out of their land, the hero, Jim Henry, who is a friend of Chief Antelope, exposes Baring's evil scheme and prevents a war. At the end, Chief Antelope and Jim establish peace.

THE WILD NORTH (MGM, 1952)

DIRECTOR: Andrew Marton
SCREENPLAY: Frank Fenton
CAST: Stewart Granger (Jules Vincent), Cyd Charisse (Indian Girl), John War Eagle (Indian Chief)
SPECS: 97 minutes; Color
AVAILABILITY: DVD (Warner Home Video)
NATION: Ojibwa
IMAGE PORTRAYAL: Romance between a Native American woman and a white man
SUMMARY: An Ojibwa woman from a tribe whose chief is played by John War Eagle falls in love with Jules Vincent and they end up together.

THE WILD WESTERNERS (Four-Leaf Productions 1962)

DIRECTOR: Oscar Rudolph
SCREENPLAY: Gerald Drayson Adams
CAST: James Philbrook (Marshal Jim McDowell), Guy Mitchell (Johnny Silver), Lisa Burkett (Yellow Moon), Hans Wedemeyer (Wasna)
SPECS: 107 minutes; Color

AVAILABILITY: VHS (Hollywood Movie Greats)
NATION: Sioux
IMAGE PORTRAYAL: Attack on outlaws
SUMMARY: The Sioux warriors of Yellow Moon and Wasna foil the scheme of the villain, Johnny Silver, and attack lawmen transporting gold to Union troops.

WINCHESTER '73 (Universal, 1950)
DIRECTOR: Anthony Mann
SCREENPLAY: Robert L. Richards, Borden Chase, Stuart N. Lake
CAST: James Stewart (Lin McAdam), Shelley Winters (Lola Manners), Rock Hudson (Young Bull)
SPECS: 92 minutes; Color
AVAILABILITY: DVD (Universal Studios Home Entertainment)
NATION: NA
IMAGE PORTRAYAL: Attack on soldiers
SUMMARY: As the famous gun won by Lin McAdam, passes through various lives, one of the stories is of Young Bull who leads his warriors on a raid of a cavalry encampment and is killed in the battle.

WIND RIVER (Mad Dog Productions, 2000)
DIRECTOR: Tom Shell
SCREENPLAY: Elizabeth Hanson, based on the book by Nicholas Wilson
CAST: Blake Heron (Nick Wilson/Yagaichi), A Martinez (Morogonai), Russell Means (Chief Washakie), Wes Studi (Pocatello), Patricia Van Ingen (Anuba). Several other Native American actors play minor parts.
SPECS: 91 minutes; Color
AVAILABILITY: DVD (Lions Gate)
NATION: Crow; Shoshone
IMAGE PORTRAYAL: White man adopted by Native Americans
SUMMARY: Chief Washakie has warriors from his tribe, led by Morogonai find a white boy, Nick Wilson (later called "Yagaichi"), who is adopted by the tribe and taught their ways. Later he becomes a well-known pony express rider.

WINDIGO (Lux Films, 1994)
DIRECTOR: Robert Morin
SCREENPLAY: Robert Morin
CAST: Donald Morin (Eddy Laroche), Guy Nadon (Jean Fontaine)
SPECS: 97 minutes; Color
AVAILABILITY: NA
NATION: Historically, the Algonquin tribes believe in varieties of a demonic spirit who is a shape-shifter and cannibal, sometimes a gaunt man and other times a giant.
IMAGE PORTRAYAL: Contemporary First Nation people; troubled First Nation people

SUMMARY: In a remote area of Quebec, an obsessed Eddy Laroche, the leader of the Aki, uses the windigo to take on the government and declares the traditional land of his tribe an independent state.

WINDTALKERS (MGM, 2002)
DIRECTOR: John Woo
SCREENPLAY: John Rice, Joe Batteer
CAST: Nicolas Cage (Sgt. Joe Enders), Adam Beach (Private Ben Yahzee), Roger Willie (Private Charles Whitehorse)
SPECS: 134 minutes; Color
AVAILABILITY: DVD (MGM Home Entertainment); Amazon Instant Video
NATION: Navajo
IMAGE PORTRAYAL: Contemporary Native Americans; Native American soldiers
SUMMARY: The hero, Joe Enders, more and more appreciates the contributions of Navajo codetalkers Ben Yahzee and Charles Whitehorse toward triumphing over the Japanese in World War II.

WINDWALKER (Santa Fe International, 1980)
DIRECTOR: Kieth Merrill
SCREENPLAY: Ray Goldrup, based on the novel by Blaine Yorgason
CAST: Trevor Howard (Old Windwalker), James Remar (Young Windwalker), Serene Hedin (Tashina), Nick Ramus (Smiling Wolf), Dusty McCrea (Dancing Moon)
SPECS: 108 minutes; Color
AVAILABILITY: DVD (Sterling Entertainment); Amazon Instant Video
NATION: Cheyenne; Crow
IMAGE PORTRAYAL: Attack on Native Americans; romance between Native Americans; wise elder
SUMMARY: Discussed on page 51, this film tells the precontact love story of young Windwalker and Tashina, who are finally reunited in the cloud spirit world after the old Windwalker rescues the family of his son from hostile Crow warriors.

WINTER IN THE BLOOD (Kitefliers Studios, Ranchwater Films, 2013)
DIRECTORS: Alex Smith, Andrew J. Smith
SCREENPLAY: Alex Smith, Andrew J. Smith, Ken White, based on the novel by James Welch
CAST: Chaske Spencer (Virgil First Raise), Julia Jones (Agnes), David Morse (Airplane Man), Gary Farmer (Lame Bull), Dana Wheeler Nicholson (Malvina), Lily Gladstone (Marlene), Casey Camp-Horinek (Teresa First Raise), Richard Ray Whitman (John First Raise), Saginaw Grant (Yellow Calf), David Cale (Bad Suit), Ken White (Shiny Suit), Michael Spears (Raymond Long Knife), Yancy Hawley (Mose)

SPECS: 105 minutes; Color
AVAILABILITY: DVD (Alive Mind); Amazon Instant Video
NATION: Blackfeet
IMAGE PORTRAYAL: Contemporary Native American; troubled Native American; wise elder
SUMMARY: Virgil First Raise, the son of First Raise and Teresa First Raise, wakes up in a ditch beaten and hung over and then finds out that his wife, Agnes, has left with his rifle. In his attempt to find Agnes and his gun he has drunken and dangerous interactions with Airplane Man, Malvina, and the Men in Suits. Finally he seeks out Yellow Calf in the mountains and his elder teaches him how to stand his ground and accept his memories. This realization leads to his strength as a tribal member. The film is based on the novel by James Welch, himself of Blackfeet (father) and Gros Ventre (mother) tribes.

WINTERHAWK (Charles B. Pierce Film Productions, 1975)
DIRECTOR: Charles B. Pierce
SCREENPLAY: Charles B. Pierce, Earl Smith
CAST: Michael Dante (Winterhawk), Dawn Wells (Clayanna), Leif Erickson (Guthrie), Gilbert Lucero (Crow), Ace Powell (Red Calf), Sacheen Little-feather (Pale Flower)
SPECS: 98 minutes; Color
AVAILABILITY: VHS (Gaiam Americas, Inc.); Amazon Instant Video
NATION: Blackfoot
IMAGE PORTRAYAL: Kidnapping; peace-loving chief; romance between Native American man and a white woman
SUMMARY: Whites attack Winterhawk, a Blackfoot chief who is only trying to find serum for the smallpox that is wiping out his tribe. He gets his revenge by kidnapping Clayanna, with whom he falls in love. At the end peace prevails.
CRITICS: A *Variety* critic notes that, "Pierce can't get inside the Indians he is trying to ennoble. Title character Michael Dante is little more than a cigar store Indian, speaking pidgin English and gazing balefully at the horizon" (January 28, 1976).

WOLF CALL (Monogram, 1939)
DIRECTOR: George Waggner
SCREENPLAY: George Waggner, based on the novel by Jack London
CAST: John Carroll (Mike Vance), Movita (Towana)
SPECS: 62 minutes; Black & White
AVAILABILITY: DVD (Alpha Home Entertainment)
NATION: NA
IMAGE PORTRAYAL: Romance between a Native American woman and a white man
SUMMARY: Sent to a mine in Canada by his father, who is disgusted by his wild ways, Mike Vance falls in love with the beautiful Towana, and his dog, Smoky, joins a pack of wolves.

WOLFEN (Orion, 1981)
DIRECTOR: Michael Wadleigh
SCREENPLAY: David M. Eyre Jr., Eric Roth, Michael Wadleigh, based on the
    novel by Whitley Strieber
CAST: Albert Finney (Dewey Wilson), Edward James Olmos (Eddie Holt), Dehl
    Berti (Old Indian)
SPECS: 115 minutes; Color
AVAILABILITY: DVD (Warner Home Video); Amazon Instant Video
NATION: NA
IMAGE PORTRAYAL: Contemporary Native American; Native American activist
SUMMARY: In this thriller, wolf-like hunters or spirits of Native Americans
    inhabit the South Bronx and prey on humans. Native American characters are
    Eddie Holt, an activist, and an old Indian who knows that the wolfen kill to
    protect their hunting ground.
CRITICS: A *Newsweek* critic notes that "though the movie pretends to be cham-
    pioning the Indians, it defames them" (August 3, 1981, 51).

THE WOMAN GOD FORGOT (Aircraft Pictures, 1917)
DIRECTOR: Cecil B. DeMille
SCREENPLAY: Jeannie Macpherson, William C. deMille
CAST: Wallace Reid (Alvarado), Raymond Hatton (Montezuma), Geraldine Far-
    rar (Tecza), Julia Faye (Tecza's handmaiden), Walter Long (Taloc), Theodore
    Kosloff (Guatemoco)
SPECS: 60 minutes; Black & White; Silent
AVAILABILITY: NA
NATION: Aztec
IMAGE PORTRAYAL: Native Americans as victims; romance between a Native
    American woman and a white man
SUMMARY: Though the daughter of Montezuma, Tecza, loves Alvarado, a
    Spanish soldier, her father insists that she marry his nephew, Guatemoco. After
    her tribe has captured the soldier and is about to kill him, she rescues him by
    bringing other Spanish soldiers, who spare her but kill all the rest of her people.

WYOMING (MGM, 1928)
DIRECTOR: W. S. Van Dyke
SCREENPLAY: Ruth Cummings, Madeleine Ruthven, Ross B. Wills, W. S.
    Van Dyke
CAST: Tim McCoy (Lt. Jack Colton), Charles Bell (Chief Big Cloud), Goes in
    the Lodge (Chief Chapulti), Chief John Big Tree (Indian)
SPECS: 5 reels; Black & White; Silent
AVAILABILITY: NA
NATION: NA
IMAGE PORTRAYAL: Courage; honor; peace-loving chief
SUMMARY: Chief Big Cloud, the son of Chief Chapulti and childhood friend
    of Lt. Jack Cotton, breaks a treaty by attacking his wagon train. Old Chief

Chapulti kills his own son to uphold the honor of his tribe and stop the fighting.

Y

THE YAQUI (Blue Bird, 1916)
DIRECTOR: Lloyd B. Carleton
SCREENPLAY: Based on the novel by Dane Coolidge
CAST: Hobart Bosworth (Chief Tambor), Goldie Caldwell (Modesta), Jack Curtis (Martinez)
SPECS: 5 reels; Black & White; Silent
AVAILABILITY: NA
NATION: Yaqui
IMAGE PORTRAYAL: Vengeance
SUMMARY: After the villain, Martinez, enslaves the Yaqui tribe of Chief Tambor, and his wife, Modesta kills herself to avoid being raped, Tambor, who is presumed dead, returns, avenges the death of his wife, and rescues his tribe from slavery.

THE YAQUI CUR (Biograph, 1913)
DIRECTOR: D. W. Griffith
SCREENPLAY: Stanner E. V. Taylor
CAST: Robert Harron (Strongheart), Kate Bruce (Strongheart's Mother), Walter Miller (Ocallo), Charles Hill Mailes (Yaqui Chief), Victoria Forde (Yaqui Chief's Daughter)
SPECS: 33 minutes; Black & White; Silent
AVAILABILITY: NA
NATION: Yaqui
IMAGE PORTRAYAL: Romance between Native Americans
SUMMARY: Strongheart, who learns white customs like smoking cigarettes and reading the Bible, loves a woman from his Yaqui tribe who will have nothing to do with him. Later he refuses to fight with the tribe of the Yaqui chief when they attack the whites. Finally, he gives his life to save the woman he had loved and lost.

YAQUI DRUMS (Allied Artists, 1956)
DIRECTOR: Jean Yarbrough
SCREENPLAY: D. D. Beauchamp, Jo Pagano, Paul L. Peil
CAST: J. Carrol Naish (Yaqui Jack), Rod Cameron (Webb Dunham)
SPECS: 71 minutes; Black & White
AVAILABILITY: NA
NATION: Yaqui

IMAGE PORTRAYAL: Evil mixed-bloods; kidnapping; mixed-blood Native American

SUMMARY: A villain, Yaqui Jack, angers the Yaqui tribe and they kidnap some whites, including the hero, Webb Dunham, who finally persuades the Mexican Army to make peace with the Yaqui. At the end the villain is killed.

THE YAQUI GIRL (Pathe, 1910)

DIRECTOR: James Young Deer

SCREENPLAY: NA

CAST: Virginia Chester (Silver Love)

SPECS: 1 reel; Black & White; Silent

AVAILABILITY: NA

NATION: Yaqui

IMAGE PORTRAYAL: Romance between a Native American woman and a white man

SUMMARY: A young Yaqui woman named Silver Love falls in love with a Mexican singer. When she finds out he is a bandit and has another lover, she bitterly rejects him.

YELLOW ROCK (Screen Media Ventures, 2011)

DIRECTOR: Nick Vallelonga

SCREENPLAY: Lenore Andriel, Steve Doucette

CAST: Michael Biehn (Tom Hanner), Michael Spears (Broken Wing), Eddie Spears (Angry Wolf), Lenore Andriel (Dr. Sarah Taylor), Joseph Billingiere (Chief White Eagle Feather)

SPECS: 89 minutes; Color

AVAILABILITY: DVD (Screen Media Films); Amazon Instant Video

NATION: NA

IMAGE PORTRAYAL: Hostile warrior; peace-loving chief

SUMMARY: In this film, which begins and ends with a Native American narrator and a shot of warriors lined up on their horses, five white men get permission to enter the land of the fictional Black Paw tribe of Chief White Eagle Feather, Broken Wing, and Angry Wolf through the request of Dr. Sarah Taylor, who tends to the tribe. After the men enter a forbidden burial ground, violence erupts and they are wiped out. At the end, the narrator predicts that the tribes will eventually disappear.

YELLOWNECK (Republic, 1955)

DIRECTOR: R. John Hugh

SCREENPLAY: Nat S. Linden, John Hugh

CAST: Stephen Courtleigh (The Colonel), Al Tamez (Seminole), Roy Nash Osceola (Seminole)

SPECS: 83 minutes; Color
AVAILABILITY: DVD (Synergy Entertainment)
NATION: Seminole
IMAGE PORTRAYAL: Attack on soldiers
SUMMARY: In the great swamp of Florida, hostile Seminoles attack five Confederate deserters called "yellownecks."

YELLOWSTONE KELLY (Warner Bros., 1959)
DIRECTOR: Gordon Douglas
SCREENPLAY: Burt Kennedy, based on the book by Heck Allen
CAST: Clint Walker (Yellowstone Kelly), John Russell (Chief Gall), Ray Danton (Sayapi), Andra Martin (Wahleeah)
SPECS: 91 minutes; Color
AVAILABILITY: DVD (Warner Archive Collection)
NATION: Arapaho; Seven Nations; Sioux
IMAGE PORTRAYAL: Friendship; loyalty; peace-loving chief; romance between a Native American Woman and a white man
SUMMARY: Yellowstone Kelly, a friend of Gall, the just and honorable chief of the Sioux, rescues Wahleeah, a captive Arapaho woman who falls in love with him. After the hero kills the hostile Sayapi, Gall reluctantly makes peace and, even though he loves her, lets Wahleeah go away with Kelly.

THE YELLOW TOMAHAWK (United Artists, 1954)
DIRECTOR: Lesley Selander
SCREENPLAY: Richard Alan Simmons, Harold Jack Bloom
CAST: Rory Calhoun (Adam), Peggie Castle (Katherine), Noah Beery Jr. (Tonio), Lee Van Cleef (Fire Knife), Rita Moreno (Honey Bear)
SPECS: 82 minutes; Color
AVAILABILITY: NA
NATION: Cheyenne
IMAGE PORTRAYAL: Attack on soldiers; romance between Native Americans
SUMMARY: The Cheyenne tribe of Tonio, Honey Bear, and Fire Knife declares war after an evil officer kills some of their women and children and breaks a treaty by preparing to build a fort on their land. After many whites are killed, Adam, a friend of Fire Knife, rescues the survivors, although he has to kill his friend in the process. At the end, Tonio and Honey Bear fall in love.
CRITICS: A *Variety* critic comments: "The story takes the redskins' side to show provocation for their attacks on a cavalry encampment" (May 19, 1954).

YOUNG BUFFALO BILL (Republic, 1940)
DIRECTOR: Joseph Kane
SCREENPLAY: Harrison Jacobs, Robert Yost, Gerald Geraghty, Norman Houston
CAST: Roy Rogers (Bill Cody), Chief Thundercloud (Akuna)

SPECS: 59 minutes; Black & White
AVAILABILITY: DVD (Alpha Video)
NATION: Comanche
IMAGE PORTRAYAL: Attack on settlers
SUMMARY: Bill Cody helps the cavalry stop the Comanche tribe of Akuna as they attack a ranch.

YOUNG DANIEL BOONE (Monogram, 1950)

DIRECTOR: Reginald LeBorg
SCREENPLAY: Clint Johnston, Reginald Le Borg, based on Johnston's novel
CAST: David Bruce (Daniel Boone), William Roy (Little Hawk), Nipo T. Strongheart (Walking Eagle)
SPECS: 71 minutes; Color
AVAILABILITY: NA
NATION: Shawnee
IMAGE PORTRAYAL: Attacks on soldiers; kidnapping
SUMMARY: Daniel Boone rescues two white women kidnapped by the tribe of Little Hawk and Walking Eagle. He accomplishes this by appearing to have magical power, which scares the warriors away.

Films by Nation **A**

NOT ALL FILMS THAT FEATURED Native Americans identified the nation represented in the narrative. Below is a list of films in which the Native American nation was identified (some films featured more than one nation).

ABENAKI
Northwest Passage (MGM, 1940)

ACOMA
New Mexico (United Artists, 1951)

ALGONQUIN
Black Robe (Alliance Entertainment, 1991)
Jamestown (Pathe, 1923)
The New World (New Line Cinema, 2006)
Pocahontas (Disney Pictures, 1995)
Pocahontas II Journey to the New World (Disney Pictures, 1998)
Pocahontas: The Legend (PFA Films, 1999)

APACHE
Ambush (MGM, 1950)
Ambush at Cimarron Pass (20th Century Fox, 1958)
Ambush at Tomahawk Gap (Columbia, 1953)
Apache (United Artists, 1954)
Apache Ambush (Columbia, 1955)
Apache Chief (Lippert, 1949)
Apache Country (Columbia, 1952)

Apache Drums (Universal, 1951)

Apache Gold (or Winnetou I) (Columbia, 1965)

Apache Rifles (20th Century Fox, 1964)

Apache Territory (Columbia, 1958)

Apache Trail (Columbia, 1958)

Apache Uprising (Paramount, 1966)

Apache War Smoke (MGM, 1952)

Apache Warrior (20th Century Fox, 1957)

Apache Woman (American International Pictures, 1955)

Arizona (Columbia, 1940)

Arizona Bushwhackers (Paramount, 1968)

Around the World in 80 Days (United Artists, 1956)

Arrowhead (Paramount, 1953)

Bad Lands (RKO, 1939)

Battle at Apache Pass (Universal, 1951)

Blood on the Arrow (Allied Artists, 1964)

Broken Arrow (20th Century Fox, 1950)

Captain Apache or Deathwork (Scotia Inter., 1971)

Chato's Land (United Artists, 1972)

Conquest of Cochise (Columbia, 1953)

Cry Blood, Apache (Golden Eagle, 1970)

Curse of the Red Man (Selig, 1911)

Day of the Evil Gun (MGM, 1968)

The Deserter (Paramount, 1971)

Dragoon Wells Massacre (Allied Artists, 1957)

Duel at Diablo (United Artists, 1966)

El Condor (National General, 1970)

Fort Apache (RKO, 1948)

Fort Bowie (United Artists, 1958)

Fort Massacre (United Artists, 1958)

Fort Vengeance (Allied Artists, 1953)

40 Guns to Apache Pass (Columbia, 1967)

Four Guns to the Border (Universal, 1954)

Foxfire (Universal, 1955)

Fury at Furnace Creek (20th Century Fox, 1948)

Geronimo (Paramount, 1939)

Geronimo (United Artists, 1962)

Geronimo: An American Legend (Columbia, 1993)

Geronimo's Last Raid (American, 1912)

Gunman from Laredo (Columbia, 1959)

The Half-Breed (RKO, 1952)

Hombre (20th Century Fox, 1967)

Hondo (Warner Bros., 1953)

Indian Territory (Columbia, 1950)

Indian Uprising (Columbia, 1952)
Land Raiders (Columbia, 1970)
The Last Outpost (Paramount, 1951)
Little Dove (Indieflix, 2008)
MacKenna's Gold (Columbia, 1969)
Major Dundee (Columbia, 1965)
Massacre Canyon (Columbia, 1954)
The Missing (Sony Pictures Entertainment, 2003)
On the Warpath (Bison, 1912)
Only the Valiant (Warner Bros., 1951)
A Pueblo Legend (Biograph, 1912)
Quantez (Universal, 1957)
The Return of Josey Wales (Reel Movies Inter., 1987)
Riders of Vengeance (Universal, 1919)
Rio Conchos (20th Century Fox, 1964)
Rio Grande (Republic, 1950)
Savage Sam (Buena Vista, 1963)
Secret of Treasure Mountain (Columbia, 1956)
Sergeant Rutledge (Warner Bros., 1960)
Shalako (Palomar Pictures International, 1968)
Shotgun (Allied Artists, 1955)
Southwest Passage (United Artists, 1954)
Stagecoach (United Artists, 1939)
The Stalking Moon (National, 1968)
The Stand at Apache River (Universal, 1953)
Taggart (Universal, 1964)
The Tall Women (Allied Artists, 1967)
Taza, Son of Cochise (Universal, 1954)
A Thunder of Drums (MGM, 1961)
The Tribal Law (Bison, 1912)
Trooper Hook (United Artists, 1957)
Ulzana's Raid (Universal, 1972)
Valley of the Sun (RKO, 1942)
The Vanishing American (Republic, 1955)
Walk the Proud Land (Universal, 1956)
War Drums (United Artists, 1957)

ARAPAHO

Chuka (Paramount, 1967)
Quincannon, Frontier Scout (United Artists, 1956)
She Wore a Yellow Ribbon (RKO, 1949)
Ticket to Tomahawk (20th Century Fox, 1950)
War Paint (MGM, 1926)

White Feather (20th Century Fox, 1955)
Wild Dakotas (Assoc. Releasing, 1956)
Yellowstone Kelly (Warner Bros., 1959)

ARIKARA
Indian Paint (Eagle American, 1963)
The Return of a Man Called Horse (United Artists, 1976)

ATHABASKAN
Spirit of the Wind (Doyon Ltd., 1979)

AZTEC
Spirit of the Wind (Doyon Ltd., 1979)

BEOTHUK OF NEWFOUNDLAND
Finding Mary March (Malo Film Group, 1988)

BLACKFOOT
Across the Wide Missouri (MGM, 1951)
Blood Arrow (20th Century Fox, 1958)
The Caribou Trail (20th Century Fox, 1950)
Cattle Queen of Montana (RKO, 1954)
Fort Vengeance (Allied Artists, 1953)
Jeremiah Johnson (Warner Bros., 1972)
Jimmy P: Psychotherapy of a Plains Indian (Why Not Productions, 2013)
The Mountain Men (Columbia, 1980)
War Party (Helmdale-Tri Star, 1988)
White Feather (20th Century Fox, 1955)
Winter in the Blood (Kitefliers Studios, Ranchwater Films, 2013)
Winterhawk (Howco International, 1975)

CALIFORNIA MISSION
Desert Pursuit (Monogram, 1952)

CAYUGA
Cardigan (American, 1922)

CHEROKEE
Across the Plains (Monogram, 1939)
Cherokee Uprising (Monogram, 1950)
Cherokee Word for Water (Top Guns Films, 2013)

The Doe Boy (Doe Boy Productions, 2001)
The Education of Little Tree (Paramount, 1997)
Fish Hawk (CFDC, 1979)
The Only Good Indian (TLC Films, 2009)
Ranger of Cherokee Strip (Republic, 1949)
Savage Land (Savage Land Productions, 1994)
The Story of Will Rogers (Warner Bros., 1952)
Tulsa (Eagle Lion, 1949)

CHEYENNE

Against a Crooked Sky (Doty-Dayton, 1975)
Buffalo Bill (20th Century Fox, 1944)
Bullwhip (Allied Artists, 1958)
The Charge at Feather River (Warner Bros., 1953)
Cheyenne Autumn (Warner Bros., 1964)
Cheyenne Brave (Pathe, 1910)
Custer of the West (Cinerama, 1967)
Custer's Last Fight (Bison, 1912)
Dakota Incident (Republic, 1956)
Fighting Caravans (Paramount, 1931)
General Custer at Little Big Horn (Sunset, 1926)
Ghost Town (United Artists, 1956)
The Glory Guys (United Artists, 1965)
Guns of Fort Petticoat (Columbia, 1957)
The Indian Wars (Col. William F. Cody Historical Pictures, 1914)
Last of the Dogmen (Savoy Pictures, 1995)
Little Big Man (National General, 1970)
Powwow Highway (Hand Made Films, 1988)
Ride Out for Revenge (United Artists, 1957)
Soldier Blue (Avco-Embassy, 1970)
They Died with Their Boots On (Warner Bros., 1942)
The Undefeated (20th Century Fox, 1969)
Wagons West (Monogram, 1952)
White Feather (20th Century Fox, 1955)
Windwalker (Pacific Inter., 1980)
The YellowTomahawk (United Artists, 1954)

CHICKASAW

All Hands on Deck (20th Century Fox, 1961)
Pearl (Freestyle Entertainment, 2010)

CHOCTAW

Tuskha (Barcid Productions, 1997)

CHUMASH
Island of the Blue Dolphins (Universal, 1964)

COEUR D'ALENE
Smoke Signals (Universal, 1955)

COMANCHE
Broken Lance (20th Century Fox, 1954)
Comanche (United Artists, 1956)
Comanche Station (Columbia, 1960)
Comanche Territory (Universal, 1950)
The Comancheros (20th Century Fox, 1961)
Conquest of Cochise (Columbia, 1953)
Eagle's Wing (Rank, 1979)
Fort Dobbs (Warner Bros., 1958)
The Heart of Wetona (Select, 1919)
Indian Paint (Eagle American, 1963)
Last of the Comanches (Columbia, 1953)
The Legend of the Lone Ranger (Universal, 1981)
Little Dove (Indieflix, 2008)
The Lone Ranger (Walt Disney Pictures, 2013)
McLintock! (United Artists, 1963)
The Nebraskan (Columbia, 1953)
The Outlaw Josey Wales (Warner Bros., 1976)
Red River (United Artists, 1948)
Ride, Ranger, Ride (Republic, 1936)
Savage Sam (Buena Vista, 1963)
Scalps (Beatrice Film, 1987)
The Searchers (Warner Bros., 1956)
The Tall Texan (Lippert, 1953)
Texas across the River (Universal, 1966)
They Rode West (Columbia, 1954)
Treachery Rides the Range (Warner Bros., 1936)
Two Rode Together (Columbia, 1961)
War Party (20th Century Fox, 1965)
White Comanche (Producciones Cinematograficas, 1967)
Young Buffalo Bill (Republic, 1940)

CREE (OJIBLACK, WHITTEE)
Alien Thunder (Onyx Films, 1973)
Empire of Dirt (Redcloud Studios, 2013)
Hank Williams-First Nation (Extra Butter Pictures, 2005)

King of the Grizzlies (Buena Vista, 1970)
Legends of the Fall (Tristar, 1995)
Northwest Mounted Police (Paramount, 1940)
Older Than America (IFC Films, 2008)
Pony Soldier (20th Century Fox, 1952)
Run, Broken Yet Brave (Five Stones Films, 2009)
Saskatchewan (Universal, 1954)
Silent Tears (National Film Board of Canada, 1998)

CREEK

Four Sheets to the Wind (First Look International, 2007)
The Frontiersman (MGM, 1927)

CROW

The Big Sky (RKO, 1952)
Fighting Pioneers (Resolute, 1935)
Jeremiah Johnson (Warner Bros., 1972)
Little Big Horn (Lippert, 1951)
The Savage (Paramount, 1952)
Triumphs of a Man Called Horse (Hesperia Films, 1983)
War Party (Helmdale-Tri Star, 1988)
Wind River (Lions Gate Films, 2000)

DELAWARE

When the Redskins Rode (Columbia, 1951)

ESKIMO-INUPIAT

Arctic Manhunt (Universal, 1949)
Frozen Justice (Fox, 1929)
Justice of the Far North (Columbia, 1925)
Kivalina of the Ice Lands (B.C.R. Productions, 1925)
North Star (Warner Bros., 1996)
On Deadly Ground (Warner Bros., 1994)
On the Ice (On the Ice Productions, 2011)
Red Snow (Columbia, 1952)
Salmonberries (Pelemele Film, 1991)
The Savage Innocents (Paramount, 1960)
The White Dawn (Paramount, 1974)

FOX

Jim Thorpe, All American (Warner Bros., 1951)

GUARANI

The Mission (Warner Bros., 1986)

HAIDA

Free Willy (Warner Bros., 1993)
White Fang 2: Myth of the White Wolf (Walt Disney Pictures, 1994)

HOPI

The Dark Wind (Seven Arts Pictures, 1999)
The Tribal Law (Bison, 1912)

HURON

Black Robe (Alliance Entertainment, 1991)
The Deerslayer (Republic, 1943)
Indian Romeo and Juliet (Vitagraph, 1912)
The Iroquois Trail (United Artists, 1950)
The Last of the Mohicans (Associated Producers, 1920)
The Last of the Mohicans (United Artists, 1936)
The Last of the Mohicans (Morgan Creek Productions, 1992)
Last of the Redmen (Columbia, 1947)
Revolution (Warner Bros., 1985)

INUIT

Atanarjuat: The Fast Runner (Igloolik Isama Productions, NFBC, 2001)
Before Tomorrow [Le jour avant le lendermain] (Arnot Video Production, 2008)
Map of the Human Heart (Miramax Films, 1993)
Never Cry Wolf (Buena Vista, 1984)
Shadow of the Wolf (Transfilm, 1992)
The Snow Walker (First Look International, 2003)

INUPIAT

A Thousand Roads (Mandalay Entertainment, 2005)

IROQUOIS

America (United Artists, 1924)
Black Robe (Alliance Entertainment, 1991)
The Creator's Game (KOAN, 1999)
Drums along the Mohawk (20th Century Fox, 1939)
The Indian in the Cupboard (Columbia Tristar, 1995)

It Starts with a Whisper (Canada, 1993)
Last of the Redmen (Columbia, 1947)
Mohawk (20th Century Fox, 1956)
Revolution (Warner Bros., 1985)
A Warrior's Heart (California Pictures, 2011)

KICKAPOO

The Only Good Indian (TLC Films, 2009)

KIOWA

Billy Two Hats (United Artists, 1973)
Fighting Caravans (Paramount, 1931)
Masterson of Kansas (Columbia. 1955)
Nevada Smith (Paramount, 1966)
Prairie Thunder (Warner Bros., 1937)
Silent Tongue (Belbo Films, 1993)
They Rode West (Columbia, 1954)
Two Flags West (20th Century Fox, 1950)
The Unforgiven (United Artists, 1963)
War Arrow (Universal, 1954)
The War Wagon (Universal, 1967)

LAKOTA

Hanbleceya (Tribal Alliance Productions, 2005)
Imprint (Linn Productions, 2007)
Reservation Warparties (Midthunder Productions, 2004)
Rez Bomb (Roaring Fire Films, 2008)
Running Brave (Buena Vista, 1983)
Skins (First Look International, 2002)
Spirit: Stallion of the Cimmarron (Dreamworks, 2002)
The Stone Child (Triple Martini Productions, 2007)
Thunderheart (Tri Star, 1992)

MAYAN

Apocalypto (Buena Vista, 2006)
Kings of the Sun (United Artists, 1963)

METIS

Map of the Human Heart (Miramax Films, 1993)
Showdown at Williams Creek (Kootenai Productions, 1991)

MIAMIS
When the Redskins Rode (Columbia, 1951)

MINGOE
The Pathfinder (Columbia, 1953)

MODOC
Drum Beat (Warner Bros., 1954)
Frontier Uprising (Zenith, 1961)

MOHAWK
America (United Artists, 1924)
Black Robe (Alliance Entertainment, 1991)
Frozen River (Sony Pictures Classics, 2008)
Kissed by Lightning (Independent, 2009)
Mohawk (20th Century Fox, 1956)
A Mohawk's Way (Biograph, 1910)
A Thousand Roads (Mandalay Entertainment, 2005)

MOHICAN
The Deerslayer (20th Century Fox, 1957)
Indian Romeo and Juliet (Vitagraph, 1912)
The Iroquois Trail (United Artists, 1950)
The Last of the Mohicans (Associated Producers, 1920)
The Last of the Mohicans (United Artists, 1936)
The Last of the Mohicans (Morgan Creek Productions, 1992)
Last of the Redmen (Columbia, 1947)
The Mohican's Daughter (American, 1922)
The Pathfinder (Columbia, 1953)
A Prisoner of the Mohicans (Pathe, 1911)

MONTAGNAIS
Black Robe (Alliance Entertainment, 1991)

NAHKUT
Journey to Spirit Island (Seven Wonders Enter., 1988)

NAVAJO
Black Cloud (Old Post Films, 2004)
Column South (Universal, 1953)

The Dark Wind (Seven Arts Pictures, 1999)
Daughter of the West (Film Classics, 1949)
Drums of the Desert (Paramount, 1927)
Fleshburn (Crown Inter., 1984)
Fort Defiance (United Artists, 1951)
Laughing Boy (MGM, 1934)
The Loners (Fanfare, 1972)
Navajo (Lippert, 1952)
Navajo Blues (Sullivan Entertainment, 1996)
Navajo Joe (United Artists, 1967)
Navajo Run (American, 1964)
The Rainbow Trail (Fox, 1932)
Redskin (Paramount, 1929)
Slaughter Trail (RKO, 1951)
Stay Away Joe (MGM, 1968)
Sunchaser (Warner Bros., 1996)
A Thousand Roads (Mandalay Entertainment, 2005)
Thunder Warrior (European International Films, 1983)
Thunder Warrior 2 (Trans World Entertainment, 1987)
Turquoise Rose (Better World Distribution, 2007)
The Vanishing American (Paramount, 1925)
The Vanishing American (Republic, 1955)
Wagon Master (RKO, 1950)
West of Nevada (First Division, 1936)
Windtalkers (MGM, 2002)

NEZ PERCE

Across the Wide Missouri (MGM, 1951)
Run Appaloosa Run (Buena Vista, 1966)
Smith! (Buena Vista, 1969)

OJIBWA

Cold Journey (National Film Board of Canada, 1976)
Flaming Frontier (20th Century Fox, 1958)
Hiawatha (Independent Moving Pictures Co. of America, 1909)
Hiawatha (Colonial Motion Picture, 1913)
Hiawatha (Monogram, 1952)
The Jingle Dress (Lodge Pole Films, 2014)
Older Than America (IFC Films, 2008)
The Silent Enemy (Paramount, 1930)
The Song of Hiawatha (The (Hallmark Home Entertainment, 1997)
The Wild North (MGM, 1952)

OPIES
The Prophecy (Paramount, 1979)

OSAGE
Fort Osage (Monogram, 1952)
Tulsa (Eagle Lion, 1949)

OSEKA
North of the Great Divide (Republic, 1950)

OTTAWA
The Battles of Chief Pontiac (Realart, 1952)
The Iroquois Trail (United Artists, 1950)

PAIUTE
Breakheart Pass (United Artists, 1976)
Cowboys and Indians (ABC Payroll and Production, 2013)
Fort Massacre (United Artists, 1958)
Sacred Ground (Pacific Inter., 1984)
Tell Them Willie Boy Is Here (Universal, 1969)

PAWNEE
Around the World in 80 Days (United Artists, 1956)
Arrow in the Dust (Allied Artists, 1954)
Pawnee (Republic, 1957)
Prairie Schooners (Columbia, 1940)
The Prairie (Screen Guild, 1948)
A Ticket to Tomahawk (20th Century Fox, 1950)
Wagon Tracks West (Republic, 1943)
Westward Ho, the Wagons (Buena Vista, 1957)

PIMA
Flags of Our Fathers (Paramount, 2006)
Lawless Plainsmen (Columbia, 1942)
The Outsider (Universal, 1961)

POWHATAN
Captain John Smith and Pocahontas (United Artists, 1953)
The New World (New Line Cinema, 2006)

PUEBLO

House Made of Dawn (Firebird, 1972)
A Pueblo Legend (Biograph, 1912)
Redskin (Paramount, 1929)
Tiger Eyes (Amber Entertainment, 2012)

QUECHUA (PERU)

A Thousand Roads (Mandalay Entertainment, 2005)

SAUK

Jim Thorpe, All American (Warner Bros., 1951)

SEMINOLE

Barking Water (Lorber Films, 2009)
Death Curse of Tartu (Thunderbird, 1967)
Distant Drums (Warner Bros., 1951)
Four Sheets to the Wind (First Look International, 2007)
Joe Panther (Artist's Creation, 1976)
Johnny Tiger (Universal, 1966)
Naked in the Sun (Allied Artists, 1957)
Seminole (Universal, 1953)
Seminole Uprising (Columbia, 1955)
War Arrow (Universal, 1954)
Yellowneck (Republic, 1955)

SENECA

Unconquered (Paramount, 1947)

SHAWNEE

Brave Warrior (Columbia, 1952)
Daniel Boone, Trailblazer (Republic, 1956)
Hawken's Breed (MLG Properties, 1987)
Many Rivers to Cross (MGM, 1955)
Rachel and the Stranger (RKO, 1948)
The Siege at Red River (20th Century Fox, 1954)
Young Daniel Boone (Monogram, 1950)

SHOSHONE

Bend of the River (Universal, 1952)
Devil's Doorway (MGM, 1950)

The Far Horizons (Paramount, 1955)
Grayeagle (Howco International, 1977)
Kit Carson (United Artists, 1940)
A Man Called Horse (National General, 1970)
Oregon Passage (Allied Artists, 1958)
Wind River (Lions Gate Films, 2000)

SIOUX

Annie Get Your Gun (MGM, 1950)
Annie Oakley (RKO, 1935)
Around the World in 80 Days (United Artists, 1956)
Badlands of Dakota (Universal, 1941)
Black Dakotas (Columbia, 1954)
Buffalo Bill and the Indians, or Sitting Bull's History Lesson (United Artists, 1976)
Buffalo Bill in Tomahawk Territory (United Artists, 1952)
Bugles in the Afternoon (Warner Bros., 1952)
The Canadians (20th Century Fox, 1961)
Chief Crazy Horse (Universal, 1955)
Comata, the Sioux (Biograph, 1909)
Cotter (Reel Media International, 1973)
Custer of the West (Cinerama, 1967)
Custer's Last Fight (Bison, 1912)
Dances with Wolves (Orion, 1990)
Flaming Frontier (20th Century Fox, 1958)
Fort Vengeance (Allied Artists, 1953)
General Custer at Little Big Horn (Sunset, 1926)
The Glory Guys (United Artists, 1965)
The Great Sioux Massacre (Columbia, 1965)
The Great Sioux Uprising (Universal, 1953)
The Gun That Won the West (Columbia, 1955)
Gunman's Walk (Columbia, 1958)
The Hallelujah Trail (United Artists, 1965)
The Heart of a Sioux (Lubin, 1910)
Hiawatha (Independent Moving Pictures Co. of America, 1909)
Hiawatha (Colonial Motion Picture, 1913)
Hiawatha (Monogram, 1952)
The Indian Fighter (United Artists, 1955)
Indian Runner's Romance (Biograph, 1909)
The Indian Wars (Col. William F. Cody Historical Pictures, 1914)
The Invaders (Kay-Bee, 1912)
The Iron Horse (Fox, 1924)
Jack McCall, Desperado (Columbia, 1953)
Journey through Rosebud (GFS, 1972)

Little Big Horn (Lippert, 1951)
Little Big Man (National General, 1970)
A Man Called Horse (National General, 1970)
The Manitou (Avco Embassy, 1978)
Massacre (First National, 1934)
The Mended Lute (Biograph, 1909)
The Nebraskan (Columbia, 1953)
Neola, the Sioux (Exposition Players Corp. and 101 Ranch, 1915)
Ogallah (Powers, 1911)
Oh! Susanna (Republic, 1951)
Pony Express (Paramount, 1953)
Prairie Schooners (Columbia, 1940)
The Prairie (Screen Guild, 1948)
Red Love (Davis Dist., 1925)
The Red Man and the Child (Biograph, 1908)
The Red Raiders (First National Pics., 1927)
Red Tomahawk (Paramount, 1967)
Renegades (Universal, 1989)
Revolt at Fort Laramie (United Artists, 1957)
Run of the Arrow (Universal, 1957)
Saskatchewan (Universal, 1954)
The Savage (Paramount, 1952)
7th Cavalry (Columbia, 1956)
Sioux Blood (MGM, 1929)
Sioux City (IRS Media, 1994)
Sitting Bull (United Artists, 1954)
The Song of Hiawatha (Hallmark Home Entertainment, 1997)
They Died with Their Boots On (Warner Bros., 1942)
Three Warriors (Fantasy Films, 1977)
Tonka (Buena Vista, 1958)
Triumphs of a Man Called Horse (Hesperia Films, 1983)
Under the Star Spangled Banner (Kalem, 1908)
Warpath (Paramount, 1951)
Warrior Gap (Vital, 1925)
The Way West (United Artists, 1967)
Westward Ho, the Wagons (Buena Vista, 1957)
The White Buffalo (United Artists, 1977)
White Squaw (Columbia, 1956)
The Wild Westerners (Columbia, 1962)
Yellowstone Kelly (Warner Bros., 1959)

SNAKE

Indian Paint (Eagle American, 1963)

SPOKANE
The Business of Fancy Dancing (Outrider Pictures, 2002)

SUNAQUOT
Crooked Arrows (20th Century Fox, 2012)

TLICHO
The Lesser Blessed (Entertainment One, 2012)

TUSCARORA
Mohawk (20th Century Fox, 1956)
The Pathfinder (Columbia, 1953)

UTE
Drums across the River (Universal, 1954)
The Red Mountain (Paramount, 1951)
Smoke Signal (Universal, 1955)
The Squaw Man's Son (Lasky, 1917)
When the Legends Die (20th Century Fox, 1972)

WAYANDOT
When the Redskins Rode (Columbia, 1951)

YAQUI
Arizona Raiders (Columbia, 1965)
Kid Rodelo (Paramount, 1966)
Massacre (20th Century Fox, 1956)
100 Rifles (20th Century Fox, 1969)
Tumbleweed (Universal, 1953)
The Yaqui (Blue Bird, 1916)
The Yaqui Cur (Biograph, 1913)
Yaqui Drums (Allied Artists, 1956)
The Yaqui Girl (Pathe, 1910)

YELLOW HAND
The Return of a Man Called Horse (United Artists, 1976)

YUMA
On the Warpath (Bison, 1912)

Image Portrayals of Native Americans

B

THE FOLLOWING IS A LIST of Native American portrayals in film. Some films portrayed the Native Americans in more than one way, so the same film may be listed more than once below (and are reflected in the main entries). The same title may be used on more than one film, so I have identified such films by the year of production in parentheses.

ATTACK ON A FORT

The Bugle Call
Bugles in the Afternoon
Chuka
Column South
The Deerslayer (1943)
Drums along the Mohawk
El Condor
Fort Bowie
Fort Dobbs
Fort Ti
40 Guns to Apache Pass
The Frontiersman
Fury at Furnace Creek
Guns of Fort Petticoat
The Invaders
The Last Frontier
The Last of the Mohicans (1936)
Mohawk
Oh! Susanna
Quincannon, Frontier Scout
The Red Raiders

Revolt at Fort Laramie
The Siege at Red River
Slaughter Trail
Texas Pioneers
Unconquered

ATTACK ON A TOWN
Apache Drums
Arizona Bushwhackers
Badlands of Dakota
Day of the Evil Gun
Johnny Reno
Land Raiders
The New World
Open Range
The Pony Express (1925)
Red Tomahawk
Wild and Woolly

ATTACK ON COVERED WAGON
Arizona

ATTACK ON COWBOYS
The Cariboo Trail
Red River

ATTACK ON NATIVE AMERICANS
Black Robe
The Deserter
Four Guns to the Border
Soldier Blue
The Vanishing American (1955)
Windwalker

ATTACK ON OUTLAWS
Desert Pursuit
Massacre (20th Century Fox, 1956)
Quantez
Triumphs of a Man Called Horse
The Wild Westerners

ATTACK ON RAILROAD(S)

Around the World in 80 Days
Breakheart Pass
Buffalo Bill on the U.P. Trail
Canadian Pacific
The Iron Horse
My Little Chickadee
The Lone Ranger (2013)
Prairie Thunder
Train to Tombstone

ATTACK ON SETTLERS

Alien Thunder
Allegheny Uprising
Along the Oregon Trail
Ambush
Ambush at Tomahawk Gap
Apache Country
Apache Rifles
Apache Trail
Arrowhead
Bad Lands
The Battles of Chief Pontiac
Blood Arrow
Blood on the Arrow
Buffalo Bill on the U.P. Trail
Cattle Queen of Montana
Cherokee Uprising
Comanche Station
The Comancheros
Daniel Boone (1936)
Duel at Diablo
The Far Horizons
Flaming Feather
Forest Rose
Fort Osage
Fort Ti
Four Guns to the Border
The Glorious Trail
Geronimo (1939)
Geronimo (1962)
Geronimo's Last Raid

Heart of an Indian
Hombre
The Iron Horse
The Iroquois Trail
Kid Rodelo
Kit Carson (1910)
Last of the Comanches
The Last of the Mohicans (1920)
The Last of the Mohicans (1936)
Last of the Redmen
MacKenna's Gold
Major Dundee
Many Rivers to Cross
McLintock!
The Missing
Oregon Passage
Rachel and the Stranger
River of No Return
Sacred Ground
Seminole Uprising
Sergeant Rutledge
She Wore a Yellow Ribbon
Showdown at Williams Creek
Sioux Blood
The Tall Texan
The Thundering Herd (1933)
Ulzana's Raid
Under the Star Spangled Banner
The Virginian
When the Redskins Rode
Young Buffalo Bill

ATTACK ON SOLDIERS

Ambush at Cimarron Pass
America
Apache
Apache Ambush
Apache Territory
Buffalo Bill
The Charge at Feather River
Custer of the West
Custer's Last Fight

The Deerslayer (1957)
Distant Drums
Flaming Frontier
Fort Apache
Fort Courageous
Fort Massacre
Fort Yuma
Frontier Uprising
General Custer at Little Big Horn
Geronimo
The Glory Guys
The Great Sioux Massacre
The Gun That Won the West
The Indian Wars
Kit Carson (1940)
The Last Frontier
Last of the Comanches
Little Big Horn
Little Big Man
Massacre River
New Mexico
Northwest Mounted Police
Northwest Passage
Oh! Susanna
Only the Valiant
The Oregon Trail
The Pathfinder
Pony Express (1953)
The Red Mountain
Red Tomahawk
Red, White and Black
Rio Grande
Rocky Mountain
Run of the Arrow
Sergeant Rutledge
7th Cavalry
Smoke Signal
Southwest Passage
The Telegraph Trail
They Died with Their Boots On
A Thunder of Drums
Tonka
War Paint (1926)

War Paint (1953)
War Party (1965)
Warpath
Warrior Gap
Winchester '73
Yellowneck
The Yellow Tomahawk
Young Daniel Boone

ATTACK ON STAGE COACHES

Apache Uprising
Apache War Smoke
Dakota Incident
Fort Defiance
Ghost Town
The Orphan
Riders of Vengeance
Shalako
Southwest Passage
Stagecoach
The Stand at Apache River
Texas Pioneers
They Died with Their Boots On
Wells Fargo
White Comanche

ATTACK(S) ON WAGON TRAIN(S)

Apache Chief
Arrow in the Dust
Bad Bascomb
Bend of the River
The Big Sky
The Big Trail
Billy Two Hats
Call Her Savage
The Command
The Covered Wagon
Daniel Boone, Trailblazer
The Devil Horse
Dragoon Wells Massacre
Fighting Caravans
Fort Utah
Frontier Uprising

The Glorious Trail
The Hallelujah Trail
I Killed Geronimo
Indian Territory
In the Days of the Thundering Herd (1914)
Kit Carson (1940)
Land Raiders
Lawless Plainsmen
The Massacre (1914)
Massacre Canyon
The Rainbow Trail (1925)
Ride, Ranger, Ride
Taggart
The Thundering Herd (1925)
Tumbleweed
Wagons West
The War Wagon
The Way West
Westward Ho, the Wagons
Wheels of Destiny
White Oak

CAPTURE
Geronimo's Last Raid
Sergeants 3
Wild and Woolly

CONTEMPORARY ENDANGERED SOUTH AMERICAN NATIVES
At Play in the Fields of the Lord
The Emerald Forest
The McMasters
The Mission

CONTEMPORARY ESKIMO CULTURE
On the Ice
The White Dawn

CONTEMPORARY FIRST NATION PEOPLE
Before Tomorrow
Frozen River
Hank Williams-First Nation

It Starts with a Whisper
Path of Souls
Silent Tears
Windigo

CONTEMPORARY NATIVE AMERICAN(S)

All the Young Men
American Graffiti: This Thing Life
At Play in the Fields of the Lord
Barking Water
Big Eden
Billy Jack
Billy Jack Goes to Washington
Black Cloud
Blue Gap Boy Z
Born Losers
The Business of Fancy Dancing
Casino Jack
Cherokee Word for Water
Christmas in the Clouds
Clearcut
Cowboys and Indians (2013)
The Creator's Game
Crooked Arrows
The Dark Wind
The Doe Boy
The Education of Little Tree
The Exiles
Expiration Date
Flags of Our Fathers
Flap
Follow Me Home
48 Hours
Four Sheets to the Wind
Free Willy
Geronimo Jones
The Ghost Dance
Hanbleceya
Harold of Orange
Harry and Tonto
House Made of Dawn
Imprint
Injun Fender

Jimmy P: Psychotherapy of a Plains Indian
The Jingle Dress
Joe Panther
Journey through Rosebud
Journey to Spirit Island
The Loners
Medicine Man
Naturally Native
Navajo Blues
Nightwing
Older Than America
On Deadly Ground
The Only Good Indian
Orca
Pearl
Powwow Highway
The Prophecy
Rain in the Mountains
Red Snow
Renegades
Reservation Warparties
Run Appaloosa Run
Running Brave
Salmonberries
The Savage Seven
Shadow Hawk on Sacred Ground
Shadow of the Hawk
Shouting Secrets
Sioux City
Skins
Smith!
Smoke Signals
The Snow Walker
Spirit of the Wind
The Stone Child
The Story of Will Rogers
Sunchaser
A Thousand Roads
Three Warriors
Thunder Warrior
Thunder Warrior 2
Thunderheart
Tiger Eyes
The Trial of Billy Jack

True Heart
Turquoise Rose
Tuskha
War Party (1988)
A Warrior's Heart
When the Legends Die
Windtalkers
Winter in the Blood
Wolfen

CONTEMPORARY FIRST NATION PEOPLE; TROUBLED FIRST NATION PEOPLE

Before Tomorrow
Cold Journey
Empire of Dirt
Frozen River
It Starts with a Whisper
The Lesser Blessed
Run, Broken Yet Brave
Windigo

COURAGE

Indian Brothers
Wyoming

DRUNKENNESS

Apache Drums
Cattle Queen of Montana
Cherokee Uprising
Cotter
Curse of the Red Man
Fish Hawk
Flags of Our Fathers
The Hallelujah Trail
Last of the Line
Love in a Tepee
Northwest Passage
The Outsider
Quincannon, Frontier Scout
Rio Grande
Smoke Signals

EVIL MIXED-BLOODS
Apache Woman
A Fight for Love
Hills of Old Wyoming
Red Wing's Loyalty
Yaqui Drums

EVIL SPIRIT
Clearcut
Shadow of the Hawk

FIRST NATION PEOPLE AS VICTIMS
Alien Thunder

FRIENDSHIP
Across the Plains
Africa Texas Style
All the Young Men
The Animals
Annie Get Your Gun
Annie Oakley
Apache Gold (or Winnetou I)
Apache Warrior
Arizona Raiders
Battle at Apache Pass
The Battles of Chief Pontiac
Blazing across the Pecos
Blood Arrow
Blood on the Arrow
A Broken Doll
Buck and the Preacher
Buffalo Bill Rides Again
Cahill, U.S. Marshall
Call Her Savage
Captain Apache or Deathwork
Cat Ballou
Chuka
Colt 45
Column South
Comanche Territory
The Dalton Gang

Dances with Wolves

Daniel Boone (1936)

Dead Man

The Deerslayer (1957)

A Distant Trumpet

Drums along the Mohawk

Fish Hawk

For the Love of Mike

Fort Apache

Fort Osage

The Friendless Indian

The Great Scout and Cathouse Thursday

Guardian of the Wilderness

Gunman's Walk

The Half-Breed (1952)

Harry and Tonto

Heart of an Indian

The Heritage of the Desert

Hills of Old Wyoming

The Indian in the Cupboard

Indian Paint

Indian Territory

The Iroquois Trail

Jack McCall, Desperado

A Kentucky Pioneer

Kilian's Chronicle: The Magic Stone

Kit Carson (1928)

Last of the Comanches

Last of the Dogmen

The Last of the Mohicans (1920)

The Last of the Mohicans (1936)

The Last of the Mohicans (1992)

Last of the Redmen

The Legend of the Lone Ranger

Legends of the Fall

The Little Indian Martyr

The Lone Ranger (1956)

The Lone Ranger (2013)

The Lone Ranger and the Lost City of Gold

Man in the Wilderness

Masterson of Kansas

Maverick

McLintock!

The McMasters
Medicine Man
Meeks Cutoff
The Mine within the Iron Door
Miracle at Sage Creek
The Missing
Mustang County
My Little Chickadee
Navajo
The Nebraskan
Never Cry Wolf
New Mexico
The New World
Nightwing
North of the Great Divide
Oh! Susanna
Oklahoma Territory
Old Overland Trail
On Deadly Ground
One Flew Over the Cuckoo's Nest
100 Rifles
One Little Indian
The Only Good Indian
Oregon Trail Scouts
The Outlaw Josey Wales
Outlaw Trail
The Prairie
Red River
Red Snow
Red, White and Black
Red Wing's Loyalty
Renegades
The Return of a Man Called Horse
The Return of Josey Wales
Revolution
Roll, Thunder, Roll
Santee
Saskatchewan
The Savage Innocents
Savage Land
The Scalphunters
Shalako
The Sheriff of Fractured Jaw

Showdown at Williams Creek
The Sign Invisible
Smith!
Smoke Signals
Snake River Desperadoes
Spirit of the Eagle
Spirit: Stallion of the Cimmarron
Stallion Canyon
Susannah of the Mounties
Texas across the River
Thunderheart
The Thundering Herd
A Ticket to Tomahawk
Tiger Eyes
Tomahawk
The Traveling Saleswoman
True Heart
Tumbleweed
Under Nevada Skies
Unseeing Eyes
Valley of the Sun
Wagon Tracks West
Walk Tall
War Arrow
War Drums
War Paint (1926)
War Party (1965)
A Warrior's Heart
The War Wagon
Westward Ho, the Wagons
Yellowstone Kelly

GRATITUDE

Dakota Incident
For the Love of Mike
Hang Your Hat on the Wind
Iola's Promise
The Mine within the Iron Door
A Mohawk's Way
A Prisoner of the Mohicans
The Rainbow Trail (1932)
Red Wing's Gratitude
Revolution

They Rode West
The Tribal Law

HIAWATHA STORY
Hiawatha's Rabbit Hunt
Little Hiawatha
The Song of Hiawatha

HOMOSEXUALITY
Big Eden
Salmonberries
Song of the Loon

HONOR
Eagle's Wing
Hang Your Hat on the Wind
Indian Brothers
Indian Paint
The Red Man's Honor
The Savage (1917)
Wyoming

HOSTILE WARRIOR
Across the Wide Missouri
Apocalypto
Battle at Apache Pass
The Battles of Chief Pontiac
Black Dakotas
Braveheart
Brave Warrior
Buffalo Bill in Tomahawk Territory
Cattle Queen of Montana
Comanche
Cowboys and Indians
Dances with Wolves
Drum Beat
A Fight for Love
Fighting Pioneers
Fort Vengeance
The Gun That Won the West
The Last of the Mohicans (1920)

The Last of the Mohicans (1936)
Last of the Redmen
The Missing
The Mountain Men
On the Warpath
Pawnee
Pony Soldier
Run of the Arrow
Saddlemates
The Savage (1952)
Showdown at Williams Creek
Susannah of the Mounties
The Tall Women
Taza, Son of Cochise
Tom and Huck
Train to Tombstone
Ulzana's Raid
Valley of the Sun
Wagon Tracks West
War Arrow
Yellow Rock

JUSTICE
Apache
Apache Warrior
The Lone Ranger (2013)
North Star

KIDNAPPING
Against a Crooked Sky
Ambush
Blood on the Arrow
Cowboys and Indians (2011)
Daniel Boone (1907)
Day of the Evil Gun
Deadwood '76
The Devil Horse
The Emerald Forest
The Maiden of the Pie-Faced Indians
North of Nevada
Pale Face's Wooing
The Prairie
The Red, Red Heart

The Savage (1917)
Savage Sam
The Searchers
Seminole Uprising
Shotgun
Sioux Blood
The Totem Mark
A Trapper and the Redskins
Trooper Hook
Two Rode Together
Winterhawk
Yaqui Drums
Young Daniel Boone

LOYALTY
Across the Plains
The Animals
Annie Get Your Gun
Annie Oakley
Apache Gold (or Winnetou I)
Apache Warrior
Arizona Raiders
A Broken Doll
Buck and the Preacher
Buffalo Bill Rides Again
Cahill, U.S. Marshall
Colt 45
Comanche Territory
Dances with Wolves
Daniel Boone (1936)
Dead Man
A Distant Trumpet
Drums along the Mohawk
Guardian of the Wilderness
Gunman's Walk
The Half-Breed (1952)
The Indian in the Cupboard
The Iroquois Trail
Jack McCall, Desperado
A Kentucky Pioneer
Kilian's Chronicle: The Magic Stone
Last of the Comanches
Last of the Dogmen

The Last of the Mohicans (1920)
The Last of the Mohicans (1936)
The Last of the Mohicans (1992)
Last of the Redmen
The Legend of the Lone Ranger
Legends of the Fall
The Little Indian Martyr
The Lone Ranger (1956)
The Lone Ranger (2013)
The Lone Ranger and the Lost City of Gold
Man in the Wilderness
Masterson of Kansas
The McMasters
Medicine Man
Meek's Cutoff
A Mohawk's Way
Mustang County
The Nebraskan
North of the Great Divide
Oklahoma Territory
Old Overland Trail
On Deadly Ground
One Flew Over the Cuckoo's Nest
100 Rifles
One Little Indian
Oregon Trail Scouts
The Outlaw Josey Wales
Outlaw Trail
The Prairie
Red Snow
Red Wing's Loyalty
Renegades
The Return of a Man Called Horse
The Return of Josey Wales
Revolution
Santee
Saskatchewan
Savage Innocents
Savage Land
The Sheriff of Fractured Jaw
Showdown at Williams Creek
Smith!
Spirit of the Eagle

Spirit: Stallion of the Cimmarron
Stallion Canyon
Ticket to Tomahawk
True Heart
Unseeing Eyes
Walk Tall
War Arrow
War Drums
War Paint (1926)
The War Wagon
Westward Ho, the Wagons
Yellowstone Kelly

MIXED-BLOOD NATIVE AMERICAN

Apache Rifles
Apache Woman
At Play in the Fields of the Lord
Billy Jack
Billy Jack Goes to Washington
Billy Two Hats
Born Losers
Broken Lance
Bullwhip
The Business of Fancydancing
Cahill, U. S. Marshall
Call Her Savage
Colorado Territory
The Cowboy and the Indians
Davy Crockett, Indian Scout
The Dawn Maker
The Devil's Mistress
The Doe Boy
Duel in the Sun
The Education of Little Tree
Expiration Date
A Fight for Love
Flaming Frontier
Flaming Star
Flap or The Last Warrior
Foxfire
From Out of the Big Snows
Frozen Justice

Ghost Town
The Goddess of Lost Lake
The Great Scout and Cathouse Thursday
Gunman's Walk
The Half Breed (1916)
The Half Breed (1922)
The Half-Breed (1952)
The Heart of Wetona
The Heritage of the Desert
Hills of Old Wyoming
Indian Territory
Johnny Tiger
Journey through Rosebud
The Last Hunt
The Loners
Map of the Human Heart
The Mohican's Daughter
Navajo Blues
Nevada Smith
North West Mounted Police
100 Rifles
The Oregon Trail
The Pony Express
Ramona (1910)
Ramona (1916)
Ramona (1928)
Ramona (1936)
Red Love
Red Wing's Loyalty
Running Brave
Salmonberries
Sante Fe Passage
The Savage (1917)
Seminole
Seminole Uprising
Showdown at Williams Creek
The Sign Invisible
The Squaw Man's Son
The Stalking Moon
Stay Away Joe
The Stone Child
The Story of Will Rogers
The Third Woman

Thunderheart
The Trial of Billy Jack
Triumphs of a Man Called Horse
Tulsa
Unseeing Eyes
War Drums
White Squaw
Yaqui Drums

NATIVE AMERICAN ACTIVIST
Billy Jack
Billy Jack Goes to Washington
Born Losers
Cherokee Word for Water
Powwow Highway
Red Snow
Thunder Warrior
Thunderheart
The Trial of Billy Jack
Tuskha
Wolfen

NATIVE AMERICAN AS BUTT OF HUMOR
All Hands on Deck
The Indian Servant
Ma and Pa Kettle
The Outsider
The Pale Face
Rain in the Mountains
Stay Away Joe
The Villain

NATIVE AMERICAN SOLDIER(S)
All the Young Men
Flags of Our Fathers
Windtalkers

NATIVE AMERICANS AS VICTIMS
Cancel My Reservation
Captain of Gray Horse Troop
Charley One Eye

The Command
The Cowboy and the Indians
Cowboys and Indians (2013)
Dangerous Venture
Devil's Doorway
Drums of the Desert
Duel in the Sun
Finding Mary March
Flaming Star
Frontier Fury
Fury at Furnace Creek
Heaven with a Gun
Indian Agent
Indian Uprising
Island of the Blue Dolphins
Laramie
The Last Outpost
The Last Round-Up
The Law Rides Again
Lo, the Poor Indian
Lone Star
Massacre (1934)
McLintock!
Medicine Man
Navajo
North of the Great Divide
Oklahoma Jim
The Oklahoman
Older Than America
On Deadly Ground
The Outsider
Pathfinder
The Prophecy
Rachel and the Stranger
Raiders of Tomahawk Creek
Ranger of Cherokee Strip
The Red Man's Penalty
The Return of a Man Called Horse
Romance of the West
Rooster Cogburn
Saginaw Trail (Saganaw Trail)
The Savage Seven
Secret of Treasure Mountain

Seminole
Seven Cities of Gold
Soldier Blue
Tell Them Willie Boy Is Here
Thunder over the Prairie
Thunder Warrior 2
Triumphs of a Man Called Horse
A True Indian Brave
Tulsa
The Unforgiven
Valley of the Sun
The Vanishing Race
The War Wagon
West of Nevada
White Eagle
The Woman God Forgot

NATIVE AMERICAN ATHLETE
Crooked Arrows
Run Appaloosa Run
Running Brave
Shadow Hawk on Sacred Ground
A Warrior's Heart

NATIVE AMERICAN SPIRIT
Legend of Wolf Mountain
Shadow of the Wolf

PEACE-LOVING CHIEF
Apache Chief
Apocalypto
Battle at Apache Pass
Battle of Rogue River
The Battles of Chief Pontiac
Black Dakotas
Blazing across the Pecos
Brave Warrior
Braveheart
Broken Arrow
Buffalo Bill in Tomahawk Territory
Buffalo Bill Rides Again

Canadian Pacific
Cattle Queen of Montana
Cheyenne Autumn
Chief Crazy Horse
Comanche
Comanche Territory
The Conquering Horde
Conquest of Cochise
Daniel Boone, Trailblazer
Drums across the River
Fighting Pioneers
Flaming Frontier
Fort Osage
Fort Vengeance
Geronimo (1962)
Geronimo: An American Legend
The Great Sioux Uprising
The Gun That Won the West
Hills of Old Wyoming
Hondo
The Indian Fighter
Indian Territory
Jack McCall, Desperado
Little Big Man
Masterson of Kansas
Mohawk
Naked in the Sun
New Mexico
On the Warpath
Pawnee
Pocahontas: The Legend
Pony Soldier
Prairie Schooners
The Red Raiders
Ride Out for Revenge
Run of the Arrow
Saddlemates
The Savage (1952)
Seminole
Shotgun
Sitting Bull
Snake River Desperadoes
Susannah of the Mounties
The Tall Women

Taza, Son of Cochise
Valley of the Sun
Wagons West
War Arrow
War Drums
Western Union
White Feather
Wild Dakotas
Winterhawk
Wyoming
Yellow Rock
Yellowstone Kelly

ROMANCE BETWEEN A MIXED-BLOOD NATIVE AMERICAN MAN AND A WHITE WOMAN

Broken Lance
Dawn Maker
Expiration Date
Foxfire
From Out of the Big Snows
The Half Breed
Johnny Tiger
Stay Away Joe
The Story of Will Rogers
The Third Woman

ROMANCE BETWEEN A MIXED-BLOOD NATIVE AMERICAN WOMAN AND A WHITE MAN

Ghost Town
The Goddess of Lost Lake
Gunman's Walk
The Heart of Wetona
The Heritage of the Desert
Journey through Rosebud
Navajo Blues
The Oregon Trail
Sante Fe Passage
White Squaw

ROMANCE BETWEEN A MIXED-BLOOD NATIVE AMERICAN WOMAN AND A WHITE WOMAN

Salmonberries

ROMANCE BETWEEN A NATIVE AMERICAN MAN AND A WHITE MAN
Big Eden

ROMANCE BETWEEN A NATIVE AMERICAN MAN AND A WHITE WOMAN
Billy Two Hats
Black Cloud
Blazing Arrows
Braveheart
The Call of the Wild
The Charge at Feather River
Chief White Eagle
Christmas in the Clouds
Desert Gold
Duel at Diablo
The Ghost Dance
The Half-Breed (1922)
The Huntress
In the Long Ago
The Indian Land Grab
Jim Thorpe, All American
Johnny Reno
The Last of the Mohicans (1992)
Little Dove's Romance
Night Wing
Red Clay
The Red, Red Heart
Reprisal
Running Brave
The Scarlet West
Seminole
Skipped Parts
Strongheart
They Rode West
The Thundering Herd
Trooper Hook
The Undefeated
The Vanishing American (1925)
The Vanishing American (1955)
Where the Trail Divides
Winterhawk

ROMANCE BETWEEN A NATIVE AMERICAN WOMAN AND A BLACK MAN

The McMasters

ROMANCE BETWEEN A NATIVE AMERICAN WOMAN AND A WHITE MAN

Across the Wide Missouri
Apache Rifles
Arctic Manhunt
At Old Fort Dearborn
Behold My Wife (1920)
Behold My Wife (1935)
The Big Sky
Black Robe
Broken Arrow
Broken Lance
Buffalo Bill
Bullwhip
Captain John Smith and Pocahontas
The Captive God
Cardigan
Colorado Territory
Comata, the Sioux
Conquest of Cochise
The Covered Wagon
Cry Blood, Apache
Deadwood '76
The Desert Raven
Dirty Dingus Magee
Drum Beat
The Far Horizons
Flaming Feather
Fort Bowie
Fort Ti
Fort Yuma
Frozen Justice
The Gold Hunters
Grey Owl
Gun Brothers
Hawken's Breed
The Heart of a Sioux
The Heritage of the Desert

The Indian Fighter
The Indian Squaw's Sacrifice
The Invaders
Jamestown
Jeremiah Johnson
Justice of the Far North
The Kentuckian
Kilian's Chronicle: The Magic Stone
The Last Hunt
Laughing Boy
Legends of the Fall
Little Big Man
Little Dove's Romance
Lonely Heart
Love in a Tepee
MacKenna's Gold
A Man Called Horse
Marie-Anne
Mesquite's Gratitude
Mohawk
The Mohican's Daughter
The Mountain Men
The New World
The Oklahoman
Oregon Passage
Pale Face's Wooing
Pathfinder
Pawnee
Pocahontas
Pocahontas II Journey to the New World
Pocahontas: The Legend
The Red Rider
The Red Woman
Rez Bomb
Ride Out for Revenge
Rio Conchos
A Romance of the Western Hills
Rose Marie
Run of the Arrow
Sacred Ground
The Savage Seven
The Savage (1952)
Scalps

Scarlet and Gold
The Sealed Valley
Showdown at Williams Creek
Silent Tongue
The Snow Walker
The Son of the Wolf
The Squaw Man
Texas across the River
Three Guns for Texas
The Thundering Herd
The Unforgiven
Walk the Proud Land
War Paint (1953)
Where the Rivers Flow North
The White Dawn
White Fang 2: Myth of the White Wolf
White Feather
The Wild North
Wolf Call
The Woman God Forgot
The Yaqui Girl
Yellowstone Kelly

ROMANCE BETWEEN FIRST NATION PEOPLE

Kissed by Lightning
Map of the Human Heart
Pocahontas: The Legend

ROMANCE BETWEEN NATIVE AMERICANS

Apache
Apache Chief
Apache Warrior
Black Gold
Braveheart
Cheyenne Brave
Christmas in the Clouds
Comata, the Sioux
The Cowboy and the Indians
Daughter of the West
Davy Crockett, Indian Scout
Flap or The Last Warrior
Grayeagle

Hiawatha (1909)
Hiawatha (1913)
Hiawatha (1952)
The Homecoming of Jimmy Whitecloud
In the Long Ago
Indian Romeo and Juliet
Indian Runner's Romance
Justice of the Far North
Kings of the Sun
Kivalina of the Ice Lands
Laughing Boy
Little Dove
Little Dove's Romance
The Lone Ranger and the Lost City of Gold
The Maid of Niagara
Massacre (1934)
The Mended Lute
Naked in the Sun
Neola, the Sioux
Nevada Smith
Oklahoma Jim
Older Than America
100 Rifles
A Pueblo Legend
Ramona (1910)
Ramona (1916)
Ramona (1928)
Ramona (1936)
Red Love
Redskin
A Romance of the Western Hills
Savage Innocents
The Scarlet West
Shadow of the Wolf
The Sign Invisible
The Silent Enemy
The Song of Hiawatha
Song of the Wildwood Flute
The Squaw Man's Son
The Squaw's Love
Taza, Son of Cochise
Tell 'Em Willie Boy Is Here
The Tribal Law
A True Indian Brave

Turquoise Rose
The Vanishing American (1955)
Wagon Tracks West
War Drums
When the Redskins Rode
Windwalker
The Yaqui Cur
The Yellow Tomahawk

ROMANCE BETWEEN NATIVE AMERICAN MEN
Song of the Loon

TORTURE
Daniel Boone (1907)
Duel at Diablo
The Maiden of the Pie-Faced Indians
The Pale Face
Rio Conchos
Seven Cities of Gold
The Totem Mark

TROUBLED FIRST NATION PEOPLE
Before Tomorrow
Cold Journey
Empire of Dirt
Frozen River
It Starts with a Whisper
The Lesser Blessed
Run, Broken Yet Brave
Windigo

TROUBLED NATIVE AMERICAN(S)
American Indian Graffiti: This Thing Life
Black Cloud
The Business of Fancy Dancing
The Doe Boy
The Exiles
Flap or *The Last Warrior*
48 Hours
Geronimo Jones
House Made of Dawn

Imprint
Injun Fender
Jimmy P: Psychotherapy of a Plains Indian
The Jingle Dress
Joe Panther
Journey through Rosebud
The Loners
Older Than America
The Only Good Indian
Reservation Warparties
Skins
Smoke Signals
Spirit of the Wind
The Stone Child
A Thousand Roads
Three Warriors
Turquoise Rose
War Party (1988)
When the Legends Die
Winter in the Blood

VENGEANCE

Atanarjuat: The Fast Runner
The Canadians
Chato's Land
Cry Blood, Apache
Death Curse of Tartu
The Devil's Mistress
Fleshburn
Fort Osage
From Out of the Big Snows
The Great Scout and Cathouse Thursday
Gunmen from Laredo
The Half-Breed (1922)
The Heart of Wetona
Indian Brothers
Indian Runner's Romance
Jeremiah Johnson
Johnny Reno
Journey through Rosebud
Kit Carson (1928)
Land Raiders

The Last Outpost
The Lone Ranger (2013)
The Lonely Trail
The Man Who Paid
The Massacre (1914)
Navajo Joe
Navajo Run
The Nebraskan
Nevada Smith
Ogallah
Open Range
Out of the Snows
The Ramrodder
The Red Man and the Child
The Red Man's Penalty
A Romance of the Western Hills
The Scalphunters
Scalps
The Searchers
Seven Cities of Gold
Silent Tongue
Smoke Signal
The Squaw's Love
The Stalking Moon
Treachery Rides the Range
The Tribal Law
Two Flags West
Wagon Master
Wagon Tracks
The White Buffalo
The Wild Bull's Lair
The Yaqui

WHITE MAN ADOPTED BY NATIVE AMERICANS

Call Her Savage
Hombre
The Light in the Forest
Wind River

WISE ELDER

Buffalo Bill and the Indians, or Sitting Bull's History Lesson

The Doe Boy
The Education of Little Tree
Expiration Date
Foxfire
Free Willy
The Homecoming of Jimmy Whitecloud
House Made of Dawn
Imprint
Joe Panther
Journey to Spirit Island
King of the Grizzlies
The Manitou
Orca
Sioux City
Spirit of the Wind
Three Warriors
Thunderheart
Windwalker
Winter in the Blood

Television Films

Although this guide focuses on feature films, television movies are significant because they reach fairly large audiences and also encode the traditional images of Native Americans. They follow the pattern of the feature films in that they also start to project more realistic and empathetic portrayals in the more recent movies. Some of them make a unique contribution to the evaluation of recurring images. For example, *Dance Me Outside* (1994) directly challenges the traditional images by contrasting them with realistic events and coloring everything with cleverly twisted humor. In *Medicine River* (1993), another Canadian offering, the filmmakers again use humor to portray an unusual and unconventional romantic comedy between Native characters played by First Nation and Native American actors. And, finally, *Grand Avenue* (1996) represents one of the few and most intense portrayals of the challenges faced by urban Native Americans. Hence, television movies are also a valuable source for the study of Native Americans in the visual media.

THE BROKEN CHAIN (Turner Pictures, 1993)
DIRECTOR: Lamont Johnson
SCREENPLAY: Earl W. Wallace
CAST: Eric Schweig (Thayendanegea/Joseph Brandt), Pierce Brosnan (Sir William Johnson), J. C. Whiteshirt (Lohaheo), Buffy Sainte-Marie (Mother Goshina), Wes Studi (Chief), Floyd Red Crow (tribe elder).
SPECS: 93 minutes; Color
AVAILABILITY: VHS (Warner Home Video)
NATION: Iroquois; Mohawk
IMAGE PORTRAYAL: Hostile warrior; peace-loving Native American
SUMMARY: Second in the series of Turner Network movies about Native Americans, this film tells the story of the Iroquois Confederacy and focuses on the life of the Mohawk warrior Thayendanegea, or Joseph Brandt, who is the voice-over narrator throughout the film. The foil to Joseph Brandt is Lohaheo,

his more traditional brother, who has visions of the Peace Maker of the Iroquois (Graham Greene) and refuses to fight other tribes in the Confederacy. Offering guidance to these young warriors are the traditional Mohawk chiefs (played by Floyd Red Crow Westerman and Wes Studi) and the council of clan women led by Mother Goshina. As the young men mature and gain stature in the tribe, they both find devoted wives and become fathers. Then, after the death of Lohaheo at the hands of the American revolutionaries, Joseph joins the British and thus contributes to the disintegration of the Confederacy. At the end, an epilogue explains that the Iroquois Confederacy still exists in a new contemporary form.

CALL OF THE WILD (Kraft Premier TV, 1993)
DIRECTOR: "Alan Smithee"
SCREENPLAY: Christopher Lofton, based on the novel by Jack London
CAST: Rick Schroder (John Thornton), Gordon Tootoosis (Charlie)
SPECS: 97 minutes; Color
AVAILABILITY: DVD (RHI Entertainment)
NATION: Tlingit; Yeehat
IMAGE PORTRAYAL: Friendship; Wise elder
SUMMARY: Charlie, a Tlingit, makes friends with the young hero and teaches him the values of his tribe. Their strong friendship continues to the end when hostile Yeehat warriors attack them and kill the hero.

CHEYENNE WARRIOR (New Horizons, 1994)
DIRECTOR: Mark Griffiths
SCREENPLAY: Michael P. Druxman
CAST: Pato Hoffmann (Soars Like a Hawk), Frankie Avina (Crazy Buffalo).
SPECS: 90 minutes; Color
AVAILABILITY: DVD (New Horizons)
NATION: Cheyenne
IMAGE PORTRAYAL: Friendship; Hostile warriors; Romance between a Native American man and a white woman
SUMMARY: After villains kill a white woman's husband and wound Soars Like a Hawk, the woman finds Hawk and nurses him back to health. To show his gratitude, Hawk brings the tribal midwife, who helps the woman through a difficult delivery. He also protects her from hostile members of his tribe led by his brother, Crazy Buffalo. By the end, Hawk and the woman have fallen in love, but, finally, they decide to separate and live with their own people.

CLIMB AN ANGRY MOUNTAIN (Warner, 1972)
DIRECTOR: Leonard Horn
SCREENPLAY: Joseph Calvelli, Sam Rolfe
CAST: Fess Parker (Sheriff Elisha Cooper), Joe Kapp (Joey Chilko)

SPECS: 97 minutes; Color
AVAILABILITY: None
NATION: NA
IMAGE PORTRAYAL: Contemporary Native Americans
SUMMARY: Lawmen pursue a Native American, in the wilderness of Mount
   Shasta.

COOPERSTOWN (Turner Pictures, 1993)
DIRECTOR: Charles Haid
SCREENPLAY: Lee Blessing
CAST: Alan Arkin (Harry Willette), Graham Greene (Raymond Maracle)
SPECS: Color
AVAILABILITY: PAL [UK] (Out of Print)
NATION: Mohawk
IMAGE PORTRAYAL: Contemporary Native Americans; Friendship
SUMMARY: This movie tells the story of two professional baseball players, Harry,
   a white man, and Raymond Maracle, a Mohawk. Harry, now an old man, finds
   out that Raymond, who died many years ago, has been chosen for the Baseball
   Hall of Fame. Though he has resented Raymond for years, the two men relive
   and reaffirm their friendship when the ghost of Raymond appears and the two
   of them take the trip to Cooperstown.

DANCE ME OUTSIDE (Cineplex-Odeon Films, 1994)
DIRECTOR: Bruce McDonald
SCREENPLAY: John Frizzell, Bruce McDonald, Don McKellar, based on the
   stories by W. P. Kinsella
CAST: Ryan Ragendra (Silas Crow), Sandrine Holt (Poppy), Adam Beach (Frank
   Fencepost), Jennifer Podemski (Sadie)
SPECS: 84 minutes; Color
AVAILABILITY: DVD (Video Service Corp)
NATION: N/A
IMAGE PORTRAYAL: Contemporary First Nation
SUMMARY: This Canadian film, which may not be a TV movie, deals with the
   story of Silas Crow; his girlfriend, Poppy; and Frank Fencepost and his girl-
   friend, Sadie. The two young men want to go to a mechanics school in To-
   ronto, and a short narrative that Silas must write becomes the basis for a series
   of events at their reserve that break down the traditional film images of Native
   Americans. One sad event is the murder of a tribal member by the white husband of a woman from the tribe, which sets up revenge plots. A Canadian TV
   series, *The Rez* (1996–1997), stemmed from the characters in this film.

THE DEERSLAYER (Schick Sunn, 1978)
DIRECTOR: Dick Friedenberg

SCREENPLAY: S. S. Schweitzer, based on the novel by James Fenimore Cooper.
CAST: Steve Forest (Hawkeye), Ned Romero (Chingachgook), Victor Mohica (Chief Rivenoak), Betty Ann Carr (Wa-Wa-Ta).
SPECS: 74 minutes; Color
AVAILABILITY: None
NATION: Mohican; Huron
IMAGE PORTRAYAL: Friendship; hostile warriors
SUMMARY: In this movie, the hero and his friend, Chingachgook fight the war-like Hurons of Chief Rivenoak.

DREAMSPEAKER (CBC, 1979)
DIRECTOR: Claude Jutra
SCREENPLAY: Cam Hubert
CAST: Ian Tracy (Peter), George Clutesi (Shaman), Jacques Hubert (mute man)
SPECS: 75 minutes; Color
AVAILABILITY: None
NATION: NA
IMAGE PORTRAYAL: Contemporary First Nation
SUMMARY: An emotionally disturbed white boy escapes from an institution and is taken in by an old shaman and his companion, a mute Native American man. In contrast to the scientific methods of the whites, the shaman's ancient way of healing brings some joy and health to the boy. When the old man dies, the boy, who has been taken back to the institution, commits suicide and rejoins the shaman in the afterlife.

GERONIMO (Turner Pictures, 1993)
DIRECTOR: Roger Young
SCREENPLAY: J. T. Allen
CAST: Joseph Runningfox (Geronimo), Nick Ramus (Mangas), August Schellenberg (Cochise)
SPECS: 102 minutes; Color
AVAILABILITY: VHS (Turner Home Entertainment; Out of Print)
NATION: Apache
IMAGE PORTRAYAL: Noble Native American
SUMMARY: The first in the series of Turner Network movies about Native Americans, this film chronicles the life of Geronimo to show that his rebelliousness was fully justified. As an old man visiting Washington, Geronimo tells his story to a young Apache and becomes a voice-over narrator while the film fades back to his youth. After he wins the hand of the woman he loves, the Mexicans attack his village and kill his wife, child, and mother. Then his chief, Mangas, chooses him to convince Cochise to join his band and punish the Mexicans. Later Geronimo marries the daughter of Cochise, and, even though U.S. soldiers kill his new wife, he agrees to honor the treaty Cochise makes

with General Howard. After the death of Cochise, the Apaches are forced onto the San Carlos Reservation, and Geronimo finally escapes to the mountains.

GRAND AVENUE (HBO Productions, 1996)
DIRECTOR: Daniel Sackheim
SCREENPLAY: Greg Sarris, based on his novel
CAST: Sheila Tousey (Molly), Deeny Cruz (Justine), Diane Debassige (Alice), Cody Lightning (Sheldon), Tantoo Cardinal (Nellie), August Schellenberg (Sherman)
SPECS: 167 minutes; Color
AVAILABILITY: VHS (Warner Home Video)
NATION: Pomo
IMAGE PORTRAYAL: Contemporary Native Americans; drunkenness; romance between a Native American woman and a black man
SUMMARY: This film, which teeters on the edge of melodrama, deals with the struggles of urban Native Americans. Molly and her family, Justine, Alice, and Sheldon, are forced to leave the reservation and live in the city. Molly struggles with her pride, a past romance, and alcoholism, while her rebellious daughter Justine flirts with trouble and death in the tough neighborhood. Molly's other daughter, Alice, finds strength and identity through the teachings of Nellie, an elder who lives nearby. At the end, Molly finds help in a recovering alcoholic, and, after a family tragedy, the family becomes healthier.

I HEARD THE OWL CALL MY NAME (CBS, 1973)
DIRECTOR: Daryl Duke
SCREENPLAY: Gerald Di Pego, based on the book by Margaret Craven
CAST: Tom Courtenay (Mark Bryan), Dean Jagger (Bishop), Paul Stanley (Jim Wallace), George Clutesi (George Hudson), Keetah (Marianne Jones)
SPECS: 90 minutes; Color
AVAILABILITY: VHS (VCI Home Video)
NATION: Kwakiutl
IMAGE PORTRAYAL: Contemporary First Nation people; First Nation people; Wise elder
SUMMARY: This film tells the story of a dying priest who is befriended by a tribe in remote British Columbia and learns how to accept death from them. George Hudson teaches Mark about accepting and Keetah befriends him.

IKWE (National Film Board of Canada, 1986)
DIRECTOR: Norma Bailey
SCREENPLAY: Wendy Lill
CAST: Hazel King (Ikwe), Geraint Wynn Davies (Angus), Gladys Taylor (N'okom)
SPECS: 58 minutes; Color
AVAILABILITY: DVD (National Film Board of Canada)

NATION: Ojibwa

IMAGE PORTRAYAL: Romance between a First Nation woman and a white man; First Nation people as victims

SUMMARY: This film tells the story of Ikwe, an Ojibwa woman who marries a white man and eventually leaves him and brings smallpox back to her tribe.

THE INCREDIBLE ROCKY MOUNTAIN RACE (Schick Sunn, 1977)

DIRECTOR: James L. Conway

SCREENPLAY: Thomas C. Chapman, David O'Malley

CAST: Christopher Connelly (Mark Twain), Forrest Tucker (Mike Fink), Larry Storch (Eagle Feather) Mike Mazurki (Crazy Horse)

SPECS: 100 minutes; Color

AVAILABILITY: VHS (VCI Home Video)

NATION: NA

IMAGE PORTRAYAL: Friendship

SUMMARY: Eagle Feather helps the hero win the race. Eagle Feather and Crazy Horse are both rather wacky characters.

ISHI: THE LAST OF HIS TRIBE (NBC, 1978)

DIRECTOR: Robert Ellis Miller

SCREENPLAY: Dalton Trumbo, Christopher Trumbo, based on the book *Ishi in Two Worlds* by Theodora Kroeber Quinn

CAST: Eloy Casados (Ishi), Dennis Weaver (Professor Benjamin Fuller)

SPECS: 100 minutes; Color

AVAILABILITY: None

NATION: Yahi

IMAGE PORTRAYAL: Friendship; Native American as victim

SUMMARY: This film tells the story of Ishi, who was found by a rancher when he was almost dead from exposure. An anthropologist became his friend and discovered that he was the last member of the northern California Yahi tribe.

LAKOTA WOMAN: SIEGE AT WOUNDED KNEE (Turner Pictures, 1994)

DIRECTOR: Frank Pierson

SCREENPLAY: Bill Kerby, based on the memoir by Mary Crow Dog with Richard Erdoes

CAST: Irene Bedard (Mary Crow Dog), Floyd Red Crow Westerman (Fool Bull), Tantoo Cardinal (Emily Moore), Joseph Runningfox (Leonard Crow Dog), Lawrence Bayne (Russell Means), Michael Horse (Dennis Banks), Lois Red Elk (Gladys Bissonette), August Schellenberg (Dick Wilson)

SPECS: 112 minutes; Color

AVAILABILITY: VHS (Warner Home Video; Out of Print)

NATION: Lakota

IMAGE PORTRAYAL: Contemporary Native American; Female AIM activist

SUMMARY: This film tells the story of Mary Crow Dog from the early days of her Christian schooling to her activities as an AIM member. Torn between the traditional views of her grandfather, Fool Bull, and her assimilated mother, Emily Moore, she runs away from home, finally overcomes her drinking problems, and falls in love. After he leaves, the now pregnant Mary joins AIM activists Leonard Crow Dog, Russell Means, Dennis Banks, and Gladys Bissonette in the battle with evil tribal council leader, Dick Wilson, and the takeover of Wounded Knee. At the end, after giving birth to her child, the Lakota woman finds a new identity as woman and Native American.

THE LAST OF HIS TRIBE (HBO Pictures, 1992)

DIRECTOR: Harry Hook

SCREENPLAY: Stephen Harrigan

CAST: Graham Greene (Ishi), Jon Voight (Professor Alfred Kroeber), Anne Archer (Henriette Kroeber)

SPECS: 90 minutes; Color

AVAILABILITY: DVD (HBO)

NATION: Yahi

IMAGE PORTRAYAL: Friendship; Native American as victim

SUMMARY: Ishi, the last member of the Yahi tribe of California, is taken into the home of an anthropology professor who eventually wrote a well-known book about him. Though the professor learns Ishi's language and helps him adapt to white society, he acts as though he owns Ishi as an object for study and never appreciates him or the story of his tribe on a human level.

THE LAST OF THE MOHICANS (Schick Sunn, 1977)

DIRECTOR: James L. Conway

SCREENPLAY: Stephen Lord, based on the James Fenimore Cooper novel

CAST: Steve Forest (Hawkeye), Ned Romero (Chingachgook), Don Shanks (Uncas), Robert Tessier (Magua).

SPECS: 120 minutes; Color

AVAILABILITY: None

NATION: Mohican; Huron

IMAGE PORTRAYAL: Friendship; hostile warrior

SUMMARY: This movie retells Cooper's story of the conflict between Hawkeye and his friends Chingachgook and Uncas and the hostile Huron, Magua.

LEGEND OF WALKS FAR WOMAN (NBC, 1982)

DIRECTOR: Mel Adamski

SCREENPLAY: Evan Hunter, based on the novel by Colin Stuart

CAST: Raquel Welch (Walks Far Woman), Nick Ramus (Left Hand Bull), George Clutesi (Grandfather), Nick Mancuso (Horse's Ghost)

SPECS: 120 minutes; Color
AVAILABILITY: VHS (Interglobal Home Video)
NATION: Blackfoot; Sioux
IMAGE PORTRAYAL: Romance between Native Americans; attack on soldiers
SUMMARY: In this movie, Walks Far Woman, daughter of a Blackfoot father and Sioux mother, joins a band of Sioux led by Left Hand Bull. After being captured by Grandfather, she finally wins the respect of his family. Eventually, she marries Horse's Ghost, who loses his mental balance after being wounded in the Battle of Little Big Horn. Finally forced to kill him, Walks Far Woman leaves the Sioux and lives with a mixed-blood trader.

THE LIGHTNING INCIDENT (USA Movie, 1991)
DIRECTOR: Michael Switzer
SCREENPLAY: Michael J. Murray
CAST: Nancy McKeon (Martha), Tantoo Cardinal (Vivian)
SPECS: 86 minutes; Color
AVAILABILITY: VHS (Paramount)
NATION: NA
IMAGE PORTRAYAL: Contemporary Native American; Heroic mother
SUMMARY: Years after her mother and Native American father had conducted an experiment in South America, which left all the women of a local tribe barren, the remaining members of the tribe, who have become a voodoo cult, take the baby of the couple's daughter (Nancy McKeon). Aided by a Native American doctor (Tantoo Cardinal), the young mother interprets her voodoo-inspired dreams, goes to South America, and rescues her baby.

MEDICINE RIVER (Academy Entertainment, 1993)
DIRECTOR: Stuart Margolin
SCREENPLAY: Thomas King, Anne MacNaughton, based on King's novel
CAST: Graham Greene (Will), Tom Jackson (Harlen Big Bear), Sheila Tousey (Louise Heavyman) Byron Chief-Moon (Clyde Whiteman), Maggie Black Kettle (Martha Old Crow)
SPECS: 94 minutes; Color
AVAILABILITY: VHS (Academy Home)
NATION: NA
IMAGE PORTRAYAL: Romance between a First Nation man and a white woman and a First nation woman
SUMMARY: This movie tells the story of a well-known First Nation photographer, Will, who returns to his reserve and finds himself in his tribal community. He is reintroduced by Harlen Big Bear and slowly falls in love with Louise Heavyman. As he reluctantly takes pictures of tribal elders, such as Maggie Old Crow, and plays basketball with the reserve team, he figuratively and literally comes back into the picture of his tribe and refuses to return to his job and white lover in the city.

MIRACLE IN THE WILDERNESS (TNT, 1992)
DIRECTOR: Kevin James Dobson
SCREENPLAY: Michael Michaelian, Jim Byrnes, based on the novel by Paul
    Gallico
CAST: Sheldon Peters Wolf Child (Chief Many Horses), Kris Kristofferson (Jeri-
    cho Adams), Kim Cattrall (Dora Adams), Steve Reevis (Grey Eye)
SPECS: 88 minutes; Color
AVAILABILITY: DVD (Warner Archive Collection)
NATION: Blackfoot
IMAGE PORTRAYAL: Capture; peace-loving chief
SUMMARY: In this Christmas movie, the hostile Blackfeet of Chief Many Horses
    capture a white family living in the wilderness. After being taken to the Black-
    feet village, the young mother tells the Nativity story to the chief and his tribe,
    complete with cuts to visuals of a Native American family acting out the story.
    The Nativity story pacifies the chief to the point that he banishes his hostile
    son Grey Eye and decides not to fight the cavalry who are prepared to attack
    his tribe.

THE MYSTIC WARRIOR (Wolper, 1984)
DIRECTOR: Richard T. Heffron
SCREENPLAY: Jed Rosebrook, based on the novel by Ruth Beebe Hill
CAST: Robert Beltran (Ahbleza), Devon Erickson (Heyatawin)
SPECS: 300 minutes; Color
AVAILABILITY: NA
NATION: Sioux
IMAGE PORTRAYAL: Romance between Native Americans
SUMMARY: In this mini-series based on Ruth Beebe Hill's *Hanta Yo*, a young
    Sioux warrior, Ahbleza, falls in love with a beautiful woman from the tribe and
    becomes the leader of the Sioux.

SON OF THE MORNING STAR (Republic, 1991)
DIRECTOR: Mike Robe
SCREENPLAY: Melissa Matheson, based on the novel by Evan S. Connell
CAST: Gary Cole (George Custer), Rodney A. Grant (Crazy Horse), Buffy
    Sainte-Marie (Kate Big Head)
SPECS: 187 minutes; Color
AVAILABILITY: VHS (Republic Pictures; Out of Print)
NATION: Sioux; Cheyenne
IMAGE PORTRAYAL: Attacks on soldiers
SUMMARY: This movie, based on Evan S. Connell's historical study of the same
    name, tells the story of Custer and the Plains tribes he fought. Custer's story is
    narrated by his wife, Libby, while the story of Crazy Horse, the central Lakota
    character, is paralleled to that of Custer by a female Cheyenne voice-over nar-
    rator, Kate Big Head.

SPIRIT RIDER (Owl TV and Credo Group, 1992)

DIRECTOR: Michael Scott

SCREENPLAY: Jean Stawarz, David Young, based on the novel by Mary-Ellen Lang Collura

CAST: Herbie Barnes (Jesse Threebears), Gordon Tootoosis (Joe Moon), Michelle St. John (Camilla), Adam Beach (Paul), Tom Jackson (Albert), Tantoo Cardinal (Marilyn), Graham Greene (Vern)

SPECS: 95 minutes; Color

AVAILABILITY: DVD (Bonneville Entertainment)

NATION: Ojibwa

IMAGE PORTRAYAL: Contemporary First Nation person; troubled First Nation person

SUMMARY: In this Canadian film, a rebellious young Ojibwa, Jesse Threebears struggles with his identity after being forced to return to his Reserve and live with his grandfather, Joe Moon. After falling in love with Camilla, he takes up horseback riding and suffers the insults of Paul, his rival for Camilla's affection. In a climactic horse race, he and Paul become friends, and he finds strength in his tribal identity. Other people at the Reserve, Albert, Marilyn, and Vern, also support Jesse in his struggles.

Films in Chronological Order D

1907

Daniel Boone (Edison)

1908

The Call of the Wild (Biograph)
The Kentuckian (Biograph)
The Red Man and the Child (Biograph)
Under the Star Spangled Banner (Kalem)

1909

Comata, the Sioux (Biograph)
Hiawatha (Independent Moving Pictures Co. of America)
Indian Runner's Romance (Biograph)
The Mended Lute (Biograph)
Pale Face's Wooing (Kalem)
Red Wing's Gratitude (Vitagraph)

1910

The Broken Doll (Biograph)
A Cheyenne Brave (Pathe)
The Heart of a Sioux (Lubin)
The Indian Land Grab (Champion)
The Indian Squaw's Sacrifice (Motion Picture Distributors)
A Kentucky Pioneer (Selig)
Kit Carson (Bison)
Lo, the Poor Indian (Kalem)
The Maid of Niagara (Pathe)

A Mohawk's Way (Biograph)
Ramona (Biograph)
Red Wing's Loyalty (Bison)
A Romance of the Western Hills (Biograph)
Song of the Wildwood Flute (Biograph)
A Trapper and the Redskins (Kalem)
A True Indian Brave (Bison)
The Yaqui Girl (Pathe)

1911

Curse of the Red Man (Selig)
Indian Brothers (Biograph)
Little Dove's Romance (Bison)
Love in a Tepee (Imperial)
The Maiden of the Pie-Faced Indians (Edison)
Mesquite's Gratitude (Kalem)
Ogallah (Powers)
A Prisoner of the Mohicans (Pathe)
The Red Man's Penalty (Bison)
The Squaw's Love (Biograph)
The Totem Mark (Selig)

1912

At Old Fort Dearborn (Bison)
Chief White Eagle (Lubin)
Custer's Last Fight (Bison)
Forest Rose (Thanhouser)
Geronimo's Last Raid (American)
Heart of an Indian (Bison)
Indian Romeo and Juliet (Vitagraph)
The Invaders (Kay-Bee)
Iola's Promise (Biograph)
The Little Indian Martyr (Selig)
On the Warpath (Bison)
A Pueblo Legend (Biograph)
The Red Man's Honor (Eclipse)
The Tribal Law (Bison)
The Vanishing Race (American)

1913

The Friendless Indian (Pathe)
Hiawatha (Colonial Motion Picture)

In the Long Ago (Selig)
The Yaqui Cur (Biograph)

1914

The Indian Servant (Great Northern)
The Indian Wars (Col. William F. Cody Historical Pictures)
In the Days of the Thundering Herd (Selig)
Last of the Line (Bison)
The Massacre (Biograph)
The Squaw Man (Paramount)
Strongheart (Biograph)
The Virginian (Lasky)
Where the Trail Divides (Lasky)

1915

From Out of the Big Snows (Vitagraph)
Neola, the Sioux (Exposition Players Corp. and 101 Ranch)
The Sealed Valley (Metro)

1916

The Bugle Call (Triangle)
The Captive God (Triangle)
The Dawn Maker (Triangle)
The Half Breed (Triangle)
Lone Star (American Film Co.)
Ramona (Clune)
The Yaqui (Blue Bird)

1917

Captain of Gray Horse Troop (Vitagraph)
The Red Woman (World)
The Savage (Bluebird)
The Squaw Man's Son (Lasky)
Wild and Woolly (Douglas Fairbanks Pictures)
The Woman God Forgot (Aircraft Pictures)

1918

The Goddess of Lost Lake (Paralta)
The Red, Red Heart (Bluebird)
The Sign Invisible (First National)

1919

A Fight for Love (Universal)
The Heart of Wetona (Select)
Riders of Vengeance (Universal)
Wagon Tracks (William S. Hart Productions)

1920

Behold My Wife (Paramount)
The Last of the Mohicans (Associated Producers)
The Orphan (Fox)
Out of the Snows (Selznick)
The Third Woman (Robertson Cole)

1921

Lonely Heart (Affiliated Dist.)
White Oak (Paramount)

1922

Blazing Arrows (Western Pictures)
Cardigan (American)
The Half-Breed (Assoc. First National Pictures)
The Lonely Trail (Primex Pictures)
The Man Who Paid (Producer's Security Corp.)
The Mohican's Daughter (American)
The Pale Face (First National)
The Son of the Wolf (R. C. Pictures)

1923

The Covered Wagon (Paramount)
The Huntress (Assoc. First National Pictures)
Jamestown (Pathe)
Unseeing Eyes (Goldwyn Cosmopolitan)

1924

America (United Artists)
The Heritage of the Desert (Paramount)
The Iron Horse (Fox)
The Mine within the Iron Door (Principal Pictures)
North of Nevada (Monogram)

1925

Braveheart (Producers Dist. Corp.)
The Gold Hunters (Davis Dist.)
Justice of the Far North (Columbia)
Kivalina of the Ice Lands (B. R. C. Productions)
The Pony Express (Paramount)
The Rainbow Trail (Fox)
Red Love (Davis Dist.)
The Red Rider (Universal)
Scarlet and Gold (Davis Dist.)
The Scarlet West (First National)
The Thundering Herd (Paramount)
The Vanishing American (Paramount)
Warrior Gap (Vital)
The Wild Bull's Lair (Robertson-Cole Pictures)

1926

Buffalo Bill on the U.P. Trail (Aywon Films)
The Devil Horse (Pathe)
General Custer at Little Big Horn (Sunset)
War Paint (MGM)

1927

Drums of the Desert (Paramount)
The Frontiersman (MGM)
Open Range (Paramount)
Red Clay (Universal)
The Red Raiders (Charles R. Rogers Productions)

1928

The Glorious Trail (First National Pictures)
Kit Carson (Paramount)
Ramona (United Artists)
Wyoming (MGM)

1929

Frozen Justice (Fox)
Redskin (Paramount)
Sioux Blood (MGM)

1930

The Big Trail (Fox)
The Silent Enemy (Paramount)

1931

The Conquering Horde (Paramount)
Fighting Caravans (Paramount)
Oklahoma Jim (Monogram)

1932

Call Her Savage (Fox)
The Rainbow Trail (Fox)
Texas Pioneers (Monogram)
White Eagle (Columbia)

1933

The Telegraph Trail (Vitagraph)
The Thundering Herd (Paramount)

1934

Behold My Wife (Paramount)
Laughing Boy (MGM)
Massacre (First National)
Wheels of Destiny (Ken Maynard Productions)

1935

Fighting Pioneers (Resolute)

1936

Daniel Boone (RKO)
Desert Gold (Paramount)
The Last of the Mohicans (United Artists)
Ramona (20th Century Fox)
Ride, Ranger, Ride (Republic)
Treachery Rides the Range (Warner Bros.)
West of Nevada (First Division)

1937

Hills of Old Wyoming (Paramount)
Little Hiawatha (United Artists)

Prairie Thunder (Warner Bros.)
Wells Fargo (Paramount)

1939

Across the Plains (Monogram)
Allegheny Uprising (RKO)
Bad Lands (RKO)
Drums along the Mohawk (20th Century Fox)
Geronimo (Paramount)
Stagecoach (United Artists)
Susannah of the Mounties (20th Century Fox)
Wolf Call (Monogram)

1940

Arizona (Columbia)
Kit Carson (United Artists)
My Little Chickadee (Universal)
North West Mounted Police (Paramount)
Northwest Passage (MGM)
Prairie Schooners (Columbia)
Young Buffalo Bill (Republic)

1941

Badlands of Dakota (Universal)
Hiawatha's Rabbit Hunt (Warner Bros.)
Saddlemates (Republic)
Thunder over the Prairie (Columbia)
Western Union (20th Century Fox)

1942

King of the Stallions (Monogram)
Lawless Plainsmen (Columbia)
They Died with Their Boots On (Warner Bros.)
Valley of the Sun (RKO)

1943

Apache Trail (MGM)
The Deerslayer (Republic)
Frontier Fury (Columbia)
The Law Rides Again (Monogram)
Wagon Tracks West (Republic)

1944

Buffalo Bill (20th Century Fox)
Outlaw Trail (Monogram)

1946

Bad Bascomb (MGM)
Duel in the Sun (Selznick)
Romance of the West (PRC)
Under Nevada Skies (Republic)

1947

Along the Oregon Trail (Republic)
Black Gold (Monogram)
Buffalo Bill Rides Again (Screen Guild)
Dangerous Venture (United Artists)
Last of the Redmen (Columbia)
The Last Round-Up (Columbia)
Oregon Trail Scouts (Republic)
Unconquered (Paramount)

1948

Blazing across the Pecos (Columbia)
Fort Apache (RKO)
Fury at Furnace Creek (20 Century Fox)
Indian Agent (RKO)
The Prairie (Screen Guild)
Rachel and the Stranger (RKO)
Red River (United Artists)

1949

Apache Chief (Lippert)
Arctic Manhunt (Universal)
Canadian Pacific (20th Century Fox)
Colorado Territory (Warner Bros.)
The Cowboy and the Indians (Columbia)
The Dalton Gang (Donald Barry Productions)
Daughter of the West (Film Classics)
Laramie (Columbia)
Ma and Pa Kettle (Universal)
Massacre River (Monogram)
Ranger of Cherokee Strip (Republic)

Roll, Thunder, Roll! (Equity Pictures)
She Wore a Yellow Ribbon (RKO)
Stallion Canyon (Astor)
Tulsa (Eagle Lion)

1950

Ambush (MGM)
Annie Get Your Gun (MGM)
Broken Arrow (20th Century Fox)
The Cariboo Trail (20th Century Fox)
Cherokee Uprising (Monogram)
Colt .45 (Warner Bros.)
Comanche Territory (Universal)
Davy Crockett, Indian Scout (United Artists)
Devil's Doorway (MGM)
I Killed Geronimo (Eagle Lion)
Indian Territory (Columbia)
The Iroquois Trail (United Artists)
North of the Great Divide (Republic)
Raiders of Tomahawk Creek (Columbia)
Rio Grande (Republic)
Rocky Mountain (Warner Bros.)
A Ticket to Tomahawk (20th Century Fox)
Train to Tombstone (Lippert)
Traveling Saleswoman (Columbia)
Two Flags West (20th Century Fox)
Wagon Master (Argosy Pictures)
Winchester '73 (Universal)
Young Daniel Boone (Monogram)

1951

Across the Wide Missouri (MGM)
Apache Drums (Universal)
Distant Drums (Warner Bros.)
Fort Defiance (United Artists)
Jim Thorpe, All American (Warner Bros.)
The Last Outpost (Paramount)
Little Big Horn (Lippert)
New Mexico (United Artists)
Oh! Susanna (Republic)
Only the Valiant (Warner Bros.)
The Red Mountain (Paramount)

Slaughter Trail (RKO)
Snake River Desperadoes (Columbia)
Tomahawk (Universal International Pictures)
Warpath (Paramount)
When the Redskins Rode (Columbia)

1952

Apache Country (Columbia)
Apache War Smoke (MGM)
Battle at Apache Pass (Universal)
Battles of Chief Pontiac (Realart)
Bend of the River (Universal)
The Big Sky (RKO)
Brave Warrior (Columbia)
Buffalo Bill in Tomahawk Territory (United Artists)
Bugles in the Afternoon (Warner Bros.)
Desert Pursuit (Monogram)
Flaming Feather (Paramount)
Fort Osage (Monogram)
The Half-Breed (RKO)
Hiawatha (Monogram)
Indian Uprising (Columbia)
Navajo (Lippert)
Pony Soldier (20th Century Fox)
Red Snow (All American Film)
The Savage (Paramount)
The Story of Will Rogers (Warner Bros.)
Wagons West (Silvermine Productions)
The Wild North (MGM)

1953

Ambush at Tomahawk Gap (Columbia)
Arrowhead (Paramount)
Captain John Smith and Pocahontas (United Artists)
The Charge at Feather River (Warner Bros.)
Column South (Universal)
Conquest of Cochise (Columbia)
Fort Ti (Columbia)
Fort Vengeance (Allied Artists)
The Great Sioux Uprising (Universal)
Hondo (Warner Bros.)
Jack McCall, Desperado (Columbia)

Last of the Comanches (Columbia)
The Nebraskan (Columbia)
Old Overland Trail (Republic)
The Pathfinder (Columbia)
Pony Express (Paramount)
Saginaw Trail (Columbia)
Seminole (Universal)
The Stand at Apache River (Universal)
The Tall Texan (Lippert)
Tumbleweed (Universal)
War Arrow (Universal)
War Paint (Bel-Air Productions)

1954

Apache (United Artists)
Arrow in the Dust (Allied Artists)
Battle of Rogue River (Columbia)
Black Dakotas (Columbia)
Broken Lance (20th Century Fox)
Cattle Queen of Montana (RKO)
The Command (Warner Bros.)
Drum Beat (Warner Bros.)
Drums across the River (Universal)
Four Guns to the Border (Universal)
Massacre Canyon (Columbia)
Masterson of Kansas (Columbia. 1954)
River of No Return (20th Century Fox)
Rose Marie (MGM)
Saskatchewan (Universal)
The Siege at Red River (20th Century Fox)
Sitting Bull (United Artists)
Southwest Passage (United Artists)
Taza, Son of Cochise (Universal)
They Rode West (Columbia)
The Yellow Tomahawk (United Artists)

1955

Apache Ambush (Columbia)
Apache Woman (American International Pictures)
Chief Crazy Horse (Universal)
The Far Horizons (Paramount)
Fort Yuma (United Artists)

Foxfire (Universal)
The Gun That Won the West (Columbia)
The Indian Fighter (United Artists)
The Last Frontier (Columbia)
Many Rivers to Cross (MGM)
Sante Fe Passage (Republic)
Seminole Uprising (Columbia)
Seven Cities of Gold (20th Century Fox)
Shotgun (Allied Artists)
Smoke Signal (Universal)
The Vanishing American (Republic)
White Feather (20th Century Fox)
Yellowneck (Republic)

1956

Around the World in 80 Days (United Artists)
Comanche (United Artists)
Dakota Incident (Republic)
Daniel Boone, Trailblazer (Republic)
Ghost Town (United Artists)
Gun Brothers (United Artists)
The Last Hunt (MGM)
The Lone Ranger (Warner Bros.)
Massacre (20th Century Fox)
Mohawk (20th Century Fox)
Quincannon, Frontier Scout (United Artists)
Reprisal (Columbia)
The Searchers (Warner Bros.)
Secret of Treasure Mountain (Columbia)
7th Cavalry (Columbia)
Walk the Proud Land (Universal)
White Squaw (Columbia)
The Wild Dakotas (Assoc. Releasing)
Yaqui Drums (Allied Artists)

1957

Apache Warrior (20th Century Fox)
The Deerslayer (20th Century Fox)
Dragoon Wells Massacre (Allied Artists)
Guns of Fort Petticoat (Columbia)
Naked in the Sun (Allied Artists)

The Oklahoman (Allied Artists)
Oregon Passage (Allied Artists)
Pawnee (Republic)
Quantez (Universal)
Revolt at Fort Laramie (United Artists)
Ride Out for Revenge (United Artists)
Run of the Arrow (RKO Radio Pictures)
Trooper Hook (Filmaster Productions)
War Drums (United Artists)
Westward Ho, the Wagons (Walt Disney Productions)

1958

Ambush at Cimarron Pass (20th Century Fox)
Apache Territory (Columbia)
Blood Arrow (20th Century Fox)
Bullwhip (Allied Artists)
Flaming Frontier (20th Century Fox)
Fort Bowie (United Artists)
Fort Dobbs (Warner Bros.)
Fort Massacre (United Artists)
Gunman's Walk (Columbia)
The Light in the Forest (Buena Vista)
The Lone Ranger and the Lost City of Gold (United Artists)
The Sheriff of Fractured Jaw (20th Century Fox)
Tonka (Walt Disney Productions)

1959

Gunmen from Laredo (Columbia)
The Oregon Trail (20th Century Fox)
Yellowstone Kelly (Warner Bros.)

1960

All the Young Men (Columbia)
Comanche Station (Columbia)
Flaming Star (20th Century Fox)
For the Love of Mike (20th Century Fox)
Oklahoma Territory (United Artists)
The Savage Innocents (Paramount)
Sergeant Rutledge (Warner Bros.)
The Unforgiven (United Artists)
Walk Tall (API)

1961

All Hands on Deck (20th Century Fox)
The Canadians (20th Century Fox)
The Comancheros (20th Century Fox)
The Exiles (Pathe)
Frontier Uprising (Zenith)
The Outsider (Universal)
A Thunder of Drums (MGM)
Two Rode Together (Columbia)

1962

Geronimo (United Artists)
Sergeants 3 (United Artists)
The Wild Westerners (Four-Leaf Productions)

1963

Kings of the Sun (United Artists)
McLintock! (United Artists)
Savage Sam (Buena Vista)

1964

Apache Rifles (20th Century Fox)
Blood on the Arrow (Allied Artists)
Cheyenne Autumn (Warner Bros.)
A Distant Trumpet (Warner Bros.)
Island of the Blue Dolphins (Universal)
Navajo Run (American)
Rio Conchos (20th Century Fox)
Taggart (Universal)

1965

Apache Gold (or Winnetou I) (Columbia)
Arizona Raiders (Columbia)
Cat Ballou (Columbia)
Deadwood '76 (Fairway)
The Desert Raven (Allied Artists)
Fort Courageous (20th Century Fox)
The Glory Guys (United Artists)
The Great Sioux Massacre (Columbia)
The Hallelujah Trail (United Artists)
Indian Paint (Eagle American)
Major Dundee (Columbia)
War Party (Steve Productions)

1966

Apache Uprising (Paramount)
Born Losers (American International)
The Devil's Mistress (Holiday Pictures)
Duel at Diablo (United Artists)
Johnny Reno (Paramount)
Johnny Tiger (Universal)
Kid Rodelo (Paramount)
Navajo Joe (United Artists)
Nevada Smith (Paramount)
Run Appaloosa Run (Walt Disney Productions)
Texas across the River (Universal)

1967

Africa Texas Style (Paramount)
Chuka (Paramount)
Custer of the West (Cinerama)
Death Curse of Tartu (Thunderbird)
Fort Utah (Paramount)
40 Guns to Apache Pass (Columbia)
Hombre (20th Century Fox)
Red Tomahawk (A.C. Lyles Productions)
The Tall Women (Allied Artists)
The War Wagon (Universal)
The Way West (Harold Hecht Productions)

1968

Arizona Bushwhackers (Paramount)
Day of the Evil Gun (MGM)
The Savage Seven (American International)
The Scalphunters (United Artists)
Shalako (Palomar Pictures International)
The Stalking Moon (National)
Stay Away Joe (MGM)
Three Guns for Texas (Universal)
White Comanche (Producciones Cinematograficas)

1969

Hang Your Hat on the Wind (Buena Vista)
Heaven with a Gun (MGM)
MacKenna's Gold (Columbia)
100 Rifles (20th Century Fox)
The Ramrodder (Entertainment Ventures)

Smith! (Buena Vista)
Tell Them Willie Boy Is Here (Universal)
The Undefeated (20th Century Fox)

1970

Cry Blood, Apache (Golden Eagle)
Dirty Dingus Magee (MGM)
El Condor (National General)
Flap or The Last Warrior (Warner Bros.)
Geronimo Jones (Learning Corp.)
King of the Grizzlies (Buena Vista)
Land Raiders (Columbia)
Little Big Man (National General)
A Man Called Horse (National General)
The McMasters (Chevron)
Red, White and Black (Hirschman-Northern)
Soldier Blue (Avco-Embassy)
Song of the Loon (Hollywood Cinema Assoc.)

1971

The Animals (Levitt-Pickman)
Billy Jack (Warner Bros.)
Captain Apache (*aka Deathwork*) (Scotia Inter.)
The Deserter (Paramount)
Man in the Wilderness (Warner Bros.)

1972

Buck and the Preacher (Columbia)
Cancel My Reservation (Warner Bros.)
Chato's Land (United Artists)
House Made of Dawn (Firebird)
Jeremiah Johnson (Warner Bros.)
Journey through Rosebud (GFS)
The Loners (Fanfare)
Ulzana's Raid (Universal)
When the Legends Die (20th Century Fox)

1973

Alien Thunder (Onyx Films)
Billy Two Hats (United Artists)
Cahill, U. S. Marshall (Warner Bros.)

Charley One-Eye (Paramount)
Cotter (Reel Media International)
One Little Indian (Buena Vista)
Santee (Crown Inter.)

1974

Harry and Tonto (20th Century Fox)
Injun Fender (Duke U. and Magic Tramp Midnight Opera Co.)
The Trial of Billy Jack (Taylor–Laughlin)
The White Dawn (Paramount)

1975

Against a Crooked Sky (Doty-Dayton)
One Flew Over the Cuckoo's Nest (United Artists)
Rooster Cogburn (Universal)
Winterhawk (Charles B. Pierce Film Productions)

1976

Breakheart Pass (United Artists)
Buffalo Bill and the Indians, or Sitting Bull's History Lesson (United Artists)
Cold Journey (National Film Board of Canada)
The Great Scout and Cathouse Thursday (American International)
Guardian of the Wilderness (Sunn Classics)
Joe Panther (Artist's Creation)
Mustang Country (Universal)
The Outlaw Josey Wales (Warner Bros.)
The Return of a Man Called Horse (Sandy Howard Productions)
Shadow of the Hawk (Columbia)

1977

Billy Jack Goes to Washington (Taylor–Laughlin)
Grayeagle (Howco International)
Orca (Paramount)
Three Warriors (Fantasy Films)
The White Buffalo (Dino De Laurentiis Company)

1978

The Manitou (Avco Embassy)
Marie-Anne (Canadian Film Production)

1979

Eagle's Wing (Rank)
Fish Hawk (CFDC)
Nightwing (Columbia)
The Prophecy (Paramount)
Spirit of the Wind (Doyon Ltd.)
The Villain (Rastar Pictures)

1980

The Ghost Dance (Ahremess)
The Mountain Men (Columbia)
Windwalker (Santa Fe International)

1981

The Legend of the Lone Ranger (Universal)
Wolfen (Orion)

1982

48 Hours (Paramount)

1983

Never Cry Wolf (Buena Vista)
Running Brave (Walt Disney Pictures)
Thunder Warrior (European International Films)
Triumphs of a Man Called Horse (Hesperia Films)

1984

Fleshburn (Crown International Pictures)
Harold of Orange (Film in the Cities)
Sacred Ground (Pacific Inter.)

1985

The Emerald Forest (Embassy)
Revolution (Warner Bros.)

1986

The Mission (Warner Bros.)

1987

Hawken's Breed (MLG Properties)
The Return of Josey Wales (Reel Movies Inter.)

Scalps (Beatrice Film)
Thunder Warrior 2 (Fulvia Films)

1988

Finding Mary March (Malo Film Group)
Journey to Spirit Island (Seven Wonders Enter.)
Powwow Highway (Hand Made Films)
War Party (Hemdale Film)

1989

Renegades (Universal)

1990

Dances with Wolves (Tig Productions)

1991

Black Robe (Alliance Entertainment)
Salmonberries (Pelemele Film)
Showdown at Williams Creek (NFB of Canada)
Spirit of the Eagle (Queens Cross Productions)

1992

At Play in the Fields of the Lord (Universal)
Clearcut (Northern Arts)
The Last of the Mohicans (Morgan Creek Productions)
Legend of Wolf Mountain (Majestic Entertainment)
Medicine Man (Hollywood Pictures)
Shadow of the Wolf (Transfilm)
Thunderheart (Tri Star)

1993

Free Willy (Warner Bros.)
Geronimo: An American Legend (Columbia)
It Starts with a Whisper (Canada)
Map of the Human Heart (Miramax Films)
Silent Tongue (Belbo Films)
Where the Rivers Flow North (Caledonia Pictures)

1994

Maverick (Warner Bros.)
On Deadly Ground (Warner Bros.)
Savage Land (Savage Land Productions)

Sioux City (IRS Media)
White Fang 2: Myth of the White Wolf (Walt Disney Pictures)
Windigo (Lux Films)

1995

Dead Man (Miramax)
The Indian in the Cupboard (Columbia Tristar)
Kilian's Chronicle: The Magic Stone (Capstone Film)
Last of the Dogmen (Savoy Pictures)
Legends of the Fall (Tristar)
Pocahontas (Disney Pictures)
Tom and Huck (Walt Disney Pictures)

1996

Follow Me Home (New Millennia Films)
Navajo Blues (Sullivan Entertainment)
North Star (Warner Bros.)
Sunchaser (Warner Bros.)

1997

The Education of Little Tree (Paramount)
The Song of Hiawatha (Hallmark Entertainment)
True Heart (Orian)
Tuskha (Barcid Productions)

1998

Naturally Native (Red Horse Native Productions)
Pocahontas II Journey to the New World (Disney Pictures)
Silent Tears (National Film Board of Canada)
Smoke Signals (Shadow Catcher Entertainment)

1999

The Creator's Game (KOAN)
The Dark Wind (Seven Arts Pictures)
Grey Owl (20th Century Fox)
Pocahontas: The Legend (PFA Films)

2000

Big Eden (Jour de Fete Films)
Skipped Parts (Trimark Pictures)
Wind River (Mad Dog Productions)

2001

Atanarjuat: The Fast Runner (Igloolik Isama Productions, NFBC)
Christmas in the Clouds (Majestic Films)
The Doe Boy (Doe Boy Productions)
The Homecoming of Jimmy Whitecloud (Tricor Entertainment)

2002

The Business of Fancydancing (Outrider Pictures)
Skins (First Look International)
Spirit: Stallion of the Cimarron (Dreamworks)
Windtalkers (MGM)

2003

American Indian Graffiti: This Thing Life (Restless Native Productions)
The Missing (Sony Pictures Entertainment)
The Snow Walker (Infinity Media)

2004

Black Cloud (Old Post Films)
Reservation Warparties (Midthunder Productions)

2005

Hanbleceya (Tribal Alliance Productions)
Hank Williams First Nation (Extra Butter Pictures)
Miracle at Sage Creek (American World Pictures)
The New World (New Line Cinema)
Shadow Hawk on Sacred Ground (Tapeworm Studio)
A Thousand Roads (Mandalay Entertainment)

2006

Apocalypto (Buena Vista)
Expiration Date (Silverline Entertainment)
Flags of Our Fathers (Paramount)

2007

Four Sheets to the Wind (First Look International)
Imprint (Linn productions)
Pathfinder (20th Century Fox)
Rain in the Mountains (Foxhall Films)
The Stone Child (Triple Martini Productions)
Turquoise Rose (Better World Distribution)

2008

Before Tomorrow [Le jour avant le lendermain] (Arnot Video Production 2008)
Blue Gap Boy'z (Better World)
Frozen River (Sony Pictures Classics)
Little Dove (Indieflix)
Older Than America (IFC Films)
Rez Bomb (Roaring Fire Films)

2009

Barking Water (Lorber Films)
Kissed by Lightning (Independent)
The Only Good Indian (TLC Films)
Run, Broken Yet Brave (Five Stones Films)

2010

Casino Jack (ATO Pictures)
Meeks Cutoff (Oscilloscope Pictures)
Pearl (Freestyle Entertainment)

2011

Cowboys and Indians (Screen Media Films)
On the Ice (On the Ice Productions)
Shouting Secrets (Joker Film Productions)
A Warrior's Heart (California Pictures)
Yellow Rock (Screen Media Ventures)

2012

Crooked Arrows (20th Century Fox)
The Lesser Blessed (Entertainment One)
Path of Souls (American United Entertainment)
Tiger Eyes (Amber Entertainment)

2013

The Cherokee Word for Water (Toy Gun Films)
Cowboys and Indians (ABC Payroll and Production)
Empire of Dirt (Redcloud Studios)
Jimmy P: Psychotherapy of a Plains Indian (Why Not Productions)
The Lone Ranger (Walt Disney Pictures)
Winter in the Blood (Kitefliers Studios, Ranchwater Films)

2014

The Jingle Dress (Lodge Pole Films)

Bibliography

WORKS CITED

Armstrong, Virginia I., ed. *I Have Spoken: American History Through the Voices of Indians*. Athens, OH: Swallow, 1971.

Bell, Josh. Review of *Call Her Savage*. *Not Coming to a Theater Near You*, April 23, 2012. http://www.notcoming.com/reviews/callhersavage/

Biskind, Peter. *Seeing Is Believing: How Hollywood Taught Us to Stop Worrying and Love the Fifties*. New York: Pantheon, 1983.

Bogdanovich, Peter. *John Ford*. Berkeley: University of California Press, 1968.

Bowser, Eileen, comp. *Biograph Bulletins, 1908–1912*. New York: Farrar, Straus and Giroux, 1973.

Brownlow, Kevin. *The War, the West and the Wilderness*. New York: Knopf, 1979.

Brunell, Doug. "Review of *The Business of Fancydancing*." *Film Threat*, December 8, 2002.

Calder, Jenni. *There Must Be a Lone Ranger: The American West in Film and in Reality*. New York: McGraw-Hill, 1977.

Churchill, Ward. *From a Native Son: Selected Essays on Indigenism 1985–1995*. New York: South End Press, 1996.

Cody, Iron Eyes. *Iron Eyes: My Life as a Hollywood Indian* (as told to Collin Perry). New York: Everest House, 1982.

Cooper, James F. *Last of the Mohicans. Works of J. Fenimore Cooper*, Vol. II. New York: Collier, 1892.

Dargis, Manohla. "When Virginia Was Eden, and Other Tales of History." *New York Times*, December 23, 2005.

Ebert, Roger. Review of *Christmas in the Clouds*. *Chicago Sun Times*. December 1, 2005.

Ebert, Roger. Review of *Flags of Our Fathers*. *Chicago Sun Times*. November 29, 2007.

Ebert, Roger. Review of *Geronimo*. *Chicago Sun Times*. December 10, 1993.

Ebert, Roger. Review of *Harry and Tonto*. *Chicago Sun Times*. January 1, 1974.

Ebert, Roger. Review of *Little Big Man*. *Chicago Sun Times*. January 1, 1970.

Ebert, Roger. Review of *Meek's Cutoff*. *Chicago Sun Times*. May 11, 2011.

Ebert, Roger. Review of *The New World*. *Chicago Sun Times*. January 19, 2006.

Ebert, Roger. Review of *The Outlaw Josey Wales*. *Chicago Sun Times*. January 1, 1967.

Ebert, Roger. Review of *The Searchers*. *Chicago Sun Times*. November 25, 2001.

Ebert, Roger. Review of *Skins*. *Chicago Sun Times*. October 18, 2002.

Ebert, Roger. Review of *Shadow of the Wolf*. *Chicago Sun Times*. March 5, 1993.

Ebert, Roger. Review of *Smoke Signal*. *Chicago Sun Times*. July 3, 1998.

Ebert, Roger. Review of *Soldier Blue*. *Chicago Sun Times*. January 1, 1970.

Ebert, Roger. Review of *Stagecoach*. *Chicago Sun Times*. August 1, 2011.

Ebert, Roger. Review of *The Stalking Moon*. *Chicago Sun Times*. February 11, 1969.

Ebert, Roger. Review of *Thunderheart*. *Chicago Sun Times*. April 3, 1992.

Ebert, Roger. Review of *The Undefeated*. *Chicago Sun Times*. December 2, 1969.

Ebert, Roger. Review of *War Party*. *Chicago Sun Times*. September 29, 1989.

Evans, Michael Robert. *The Fast Runner: Filming the Legend of Atanarjuat*. Lincoln: University of Nebraska Press, 2010.

Friar, Ralph E., and Natasha A. Friar. *The Only Good Indian: The Hollywood Gospel*. New York: Drama Book Specialists, 1972.

Georgakas, Dan. "They Have Not Spoken: American Indians in Film." *Film Quarterly* 25, no. 3 (Spring 1972): 26–32.

Gilliatt, Penepole. "Review of *Return of a Man Called Horse*," *New Yorker*, August 16, 1976, 87.

Holden, Stephen. "A Road Trip to the End of the Road." *New York Times*, May 11, 2010.

Holden, Stephen. "Review/Film, *Frozen River*: Only a Few More Smuggling Days Left before Christmas? It's Not a Wonderful Life." *New York Times*, August 1, 2008.

Indian Country Today Media Network Staff, "Depp Trying to 'Right the Wrongs of the Past' with Tonto." *Indian Country Today Media Network*, June 10, 2013. http://indiancountrytodaymedianetwork.com/2013/06/10/depp-trying-right-wrongs-past-tonto-149814

Indian Country Today Media Network Staff, "The Real Problem with a Lone Ranger Movie? It's the Racism, Stupid." *Indian Country Today Media Network*, July 8, 2013. http://indiancountrytodaymedianetwork.com/2013/07/08/real-problem-lone-ranger-movie-its-racism-stupid-150323

Jameson, Fredric. *Signatures of the Visible*. New York: Routledge, 1992.

Kael, Pauline. Review of *One Flew over the Cuckoo's Nest*. *New Yorker*, December 1, 1975, 134.

Kempley, Rita. "*Pocahontas*: A Hit or Myth Proposition." *Washington Post*, June 23, 1995.

La Salle, Mick. "Rape, Murder, Mayhem—There Goes the Civilization." *San Francisco Chronicle*, December 8, 2006.

Mitchell, Elvis. "A Poet Finds His Past Is Just Where He Left It." *New York Times*, October 18, 2002.

Moving Picture World, 1907–1919. Media History Digital Library. mediahistoryproject.org.

The New York Times Film Reviews 1913–2000 (22 volumes). New York: New York Times, 1970–2000.

Quill, Greg. "Inuit Life and Death." *Toronto Star*, March 27, 2009.

Rafferty, Terence. "Review of *Black Robe*." *New Yorker*, November 18, 1991, 120.

Review of *The Comancheros*. *New Yorker*. December 9, 1961, 235.

Review of *The Indian Fighter*. *Newsweek*. January 9, 1956, 71.

Review of *Journey through Rosebud*. *Newsweek*. April 24, 1972, 89.

Review of *Reprisal! Newsweek*. November 19, 1956, 135–36.

Review of *Return of a Man Called Horse*. *Newsweek*. August 16, 1976, 87.

Review of *Taza, Son of Cochise*. *Newsweek*. March 1, 1964, 80.

Review of *Walk the Proud Land*. *Time*. September 24, 1956, 92.

Review of *The Wolfen*. *Newsweek*. August 3, 1981, 51.

Scott, A. O. "The Fast Runner Atanarjuat (2001): Film Festival Review; A Far-Off Inuit World, in a Dozen Shades of White." *New York Times*, March 30, 2002.

Seitz, Matt Zoller. Review of *Jimmy P. Chicago Sun Times*. February 14, 2014.

Spehr, Paul C. *The Movies Begin: Making Movies in New Jersey, 1887–1920*. Newark, NJ: Newark Museum, 1977.

Variety Film Reviews: 1907–1984. Plus Supplements. New York: Garland, 1983.

von Tunzelmann, Alex. *They Died with Their Boots On: Overdressed, Overblown and So Over*. *Gaurdian.com*, February 11, 2009. http://www.theguardian.com/film/2009/feb/11/reel-history-errol-flynn-little-bighorn-general-custer.

Voynar, Kim. "Sundance Review: *Four Sheets to the Wind*." *Moviefone*, January 31, 2007. http://news.moviefone.com/2007/01/31/sundance-review-four-sheets-to-the-wind/.

Wagamese, Richard. *Keeper 'n Me*. Toronto: Anchor Canada, a Division of Random House Canada Limited, 2006.

Weaver, John T. *Twenty Years of Silents*. Metuchen, NJ: Scarecrow, 1971.

WORKS CONSULTED

Adams, Les, and Buck Rainey. *Shoot-Em-Ups: A Complete Reference Guide to Westerns of the Sound Era*. Metuchen, NJ: Scarecrow, 1986.

Aleiss, Angela. *Making the White Man's Indian: Native Americans and Hollywood Indians*. Santa Barbara, CA: Praeger, 2005.

Balshofer, Fred J., and Arthur C. Miller. *One Reel a Week*. Berkeley: University of California Press, 1967.

Bataille, Gretchen M., and Charles L. P. Silet, eds. "Annotated Checklist of Articles and Books on the Popular Images of the Indian in American Film." In *The Pretend Indians*. Ames: Iowa State University Press, 1980.

Buscombe, Edward, ed. *The BFI Companion to the Western*. New York: Atheneum, 1988.

Buscombe, Edward. *"Injuns": Native Americans in the Movies*. London: Reaktion Books, 2006.

Cumming, Denise K., ed. *Visualities: Perspectives on Contemporary American Indian Film and Art*. East Lansing: Michigan State University Press, 2011.

Deloria, Philip. *Playing Indian*. New Haven, CT: Yale University Press, 1999.

Frayling, Christopher. *Spaghetti Westerns*. London: Routledge, 1981.

French, Philip. *Westerns: Aspects of a Movie Genre*. London: Seeker and Warburg, 1973.

Garfield, Brian. *Western Films*. New York: Rawson Assoc., 1982.

Henderson, Robert M. *D. W. Griffith: The Years at Biograph*. New York: Farrar Straus and Giroux, 1970.

Hilger, Michael. *From Savage to Nobleman*. Lanham, MD: Scarecrow Press, 1995.

Hoffman, Elizabeth Delany. *American Indians and Popular Culture*. Santa Barbara, CA: Praeger, 2012.

Kilpatrick, Jacquelyn. *Celluloid Indians*. Lincoln: University of Nebraska Press, 1999.

Krafsur, Richard P., ed. *The American Film Institute Catalogue: Feature Films, 1961–1970*. New York: Bowker, 1976.

Leonard, Harold, ed. *The Film Index: A Bibliography. Vol. 1. The Film as Art*. New York: Museum of Modern Art Film Library and H. W. Wilson, 1941.

Logsdon, Judith, "The Princess and the Squaw: Images of American Indian Women in Cinema Rouge." *Women's Studies Librarian* (Summer 1992) (University of Wisconsin System): 13–17.

Marsden, Michael, and Jack Nachbar. "Images of Native Americans in Popular Film," Course File, *AFI Education Newsletter*, September–October, 1980, 4–7.

Marubbia, Elise. *Killing the Indian Maiden: Images of Native American Women in Film*. Lexington: University Press of Kentucky, 2009.

Mihesuah, Devon A. *American Indians: Stereotypes and Realities*. Atlanta, GA: Clarity Press, 2009.

Miller, Randall M., ed. *The Kaleidoscopic Lens: How Hollywood Views the Ethnic Groups*. Englewood, NJ: Jerome S. Ozer, 1980.

Munden, Kenneth W. *The American Film Institute Catalogue: Feature Films 1921–1930*. New York: Bowker, 1971.

Nachbar, Jack, et al. *Western Films 2. An Annotated Critical Bibliography from 1974 to 1987*. New York: Garland, 1988.

Nash, Jay Robert, and Stanley Ralph Ross. *Motion Picture Guide, Vol 7, 3355*. Chicago: Cinebooks, 1985.

Niver, Kemp R., comp. *Biograph Bulletins, 1896–1908*. Los Angeles: Artisan Press, 1971.

O'Connor, John E., and Martin A. Jackson, eds. *American History/American Film: Interpreting the Hollywood Image*. New York: Ungar, 1971.

O'Connor, John E. *The Hollywood Indian Stereotypes of Native Americans in Films*. Trenton: New Jersey State Museum, 1980.

Parish, James R., and Michael R. Pitts. *The Great Western Pictures*. Metuchen, NJ: Scarecrow Press, 1976.

Pilkington, William T., and Don Crahan. *Western Movies*. Albuquerque: University of New Mexico Press, 1979.

Place, J. A. *The Western Films of John Ford*. New York: Citadel, 1974.

Price, John A. "The Stereotyping of North American Indians in Motion Pictures." In *The Pretend Indians*, ed. Gretchen M. Bataille and Charles L. Silet. Ames: Iowa State University Press, 1980.

Rader, Dean. *Engaged Resistance: American Indian Art, Literature and Film from Alcatraz to NMAI*. Austin: University of Texas Press, 2011.

Reheja, Michelle H. *Reservation Reelism: Redfacing, Visual Sovereignty, and Representation of Native Americans in Film*. Lincoln: University of Nebraska Press, 2011.

Rollins, Peter C., and John O'Connor, eds. *Hollywood's Indians: The Portrayal of Native Americans in Film*. Lexington: University Press of Kentucky, 2003.

Rothel, David. *Who Was That Masked Man? The Story of the Lone Ranger*. New York: Barnes, 1976.

Sandoux, Jean Jacques. *Racism in Western Film from D. W. Griffith to John Ford: Indians and Blacks*. New York: Revisionist Press, 1980.

Sarf, Wayne Michael. *God Bless You, Buffalo Bill: A Layman's Guide to History and the Western Film*. East Brunswick, NJ: Associated University Press, 1983.

Singer, Beverly R. *Wiping the War Paint Off the Lens: Native American Film and Video*. Minneapolis: University of Minnesota Press, 2001.

Solomon, Stanley J. *Beyond Formulas: American Film Genres*. New York: Harcourt, 1976.

Spears, Jack. "The Indian on the Screen." In *Hollywood: The Golden Era*. New York: Barnes, 1971.

Stedman, Raymond W. *Shadows of the Indian*. Norman: University of Oklahoma Press, 1982.

Tompkins, Jane. *West of Everything: The Inner Life of Westerns*. New York: Oxford University Press, 1992.
Tuska, Jon. *The American Western in Film*. Lincoln: University of Nebraska Press, 1988.
Tuska, Jon. *The Filming of the West*. New York: Doubleday, 1976.
Weiss, Ken, and Ed Goodgold. *To Be Continued . . .* New York: Crown, 1972.

OTHER SOURCES

The American Indian Film Festival is an annual San Francisco festival begun in 1975, led by Michael Smith, which features virtually all the new films and documentaries produced and directed by Native Americans.

Some notable documentaries about contemporary Native American films and filmmakers:

Images of Indians: How Hollywood Stereotyped the Native American. Directed by Chris O'Brien and Jason Wilmer. Starz Encore Entertainment, 2003. This ten-year-old documentary is still valuable because it contains commentary from scholars and contemporary Native American filmmakers.

Reel Injun: On the Trail of the Hollywood Indian. Written and directed by Neil Diamond, Catherine Bainbridge, and Jeremiah Hayes. NFBC, Rezolution Pictures, 2009. This documentary features commentary by noted Indian and non-Indian filmmakers and actors, along with many clips from films.

Rich Hall's Inventing the Indian. Written by Rich Hall. Directed by Chris Cottam. BBC, 2012. Near the end of this long documentary, Rich Hall, an American comedian, tries to endear himself to his audience by making fun of his commentary on the portrayal of Native Americans in film. This, however, does not make up for his irritating and occasionally inaccurate evaluations. On the other hand, the numerous clips from films and the thoughts of notable Native Americans he interviews, make this piece worthwhile.

General Index

Lightning, Georgina, 241, 242
Lillibridge, William Otis, 333
Lincoln, Abraham, 46
Little Big Horn, 23, 32, 124, 142, 176,
    177, 195, 216, 265, 285, 291, 306, 312,
    329
Little Big Man, 42–44; novel, 2, 5, 9–10
Little Sky, Eddie, 44, 120, 154, 222, 240,
    268, 284, 330
Littlebird, Larry, 82, 90, 188
London, Jack, 126, 231, 295
Lone Ranger, 4, 5, 6, 9, 67, 69, 76, 78,
    79, 94, 115, 213, 214, 218, 219, 293
Lone Ranger, 78–80
Lone Ranger and Tonto Fistfight in Heaven
    (stories), 293
long shot, 8, 15, 16, 55, 61, 70
Longfellow, Henry Wadsworth, 185, 186,
    295
Lott, Richard, 208
Louis, Adrian C., 70, 291
low angle, 15, 16, 21, 38, 83, 85, 87
loyalty, 3, 7, 41, 94, 96, 100, 101, 103,
    105, 107, 120, 121, 123, 125, 135, 137,
    143, 144, 147, 152, 153, 178, 179, 181,
    192, 197, 198, 204, 209, 210, 211, 213,
    214, 217, 218, 219, 223, 226, 227, 228,
    231, 232, 235, 238, 240, 241, 242, 243,
    244, 246, 247, 248, 255, 264, 265, 267,
    268, 269, 277, 278, 287, 288, 292, 297,
    300, 311, 316, 321, 325, 326, 327, 328,
    331, 344

Mackenna's Gold (novel), 221
MacLean, Alistair, 119
MacLeod, Robert, 243
Magua, 20, 21, 58, 60, 61, 81, 210, 211
A Man Called Horse, 44–45
Manitou (novel), 223
Markson, David, 151
Martinez, A., 86
Marvin, Augustus, 203
"Massacre" (story), 163
Masterson, Bat, 226
Masterson, Graham, 223
Matthiessen, Peter, 109
May, Karl, 103

Mayan, 105, 106, 205
Means, Russell, 60, 81, 116, 211, 250,
    269, 295, 338
Means, Tatanka, 311
medium shot, 8, 69
Metis, 224, 239, 288
Miamis, 332
Mikkelsen, Ejnar, 170
Mills, Billy, 51, 57, 275
Mine within the Iron Door (novel), 229
Mingoe, 250
mixed-blood Native American, 103, 105,
    109, 115, 121, 125, 146, 157, 161, 168,
    169, 175, 176, 177, 179, 180, 181, 184,
    185, 202, 234, 239, 243, 246, 253, 275,
    277, 279, 288, 301, 302, 307, 315, 321,
    336
Modoc, 153, 170
Mohawk, 19, 20, 21, 24, 25, 59, 61, 81,
    99, 117, 171, 206, 231, 307
Mohican, 20, 61, 148, 193, 197, 210, 211,
    231, 250, 255
Momaday, N. Scott, 82, 188
Montagnais, 117
Moore, Brian, 117
Morris, Donald R., 97
Morrow, Honore, 263
Mosher, Howard Frank, 332
The Mountain Men, 52–53
Moving Picture World, 14, 19, 108, 132,
    142, 163, 169, 184, 195, 206, 217, 239,
    315
Mowat, Farley, 236, 294
Mulford, Charles E., 247
music, 10, 18, 53, 62, 68, 76, 77, 78, 86,
    89, 90, 119

Nahkut, 55, 202
Narana of the North (novel), 106
National Film Board of Canada, 69, 134,
    289
Native American: activist, 115, 119, 264,
    310, 314, 318, 341; athlete, 116, 141,
    275, 329; as butt of humor, 97, 194;
    soldier, 98; spirit, 214, 286
Native Americans as victims, 13, 140, 154,
    161, 241, 250, 283, 309, 316, 321, 341

Title Index

About the Author

Michael Hilger (BA, College of Saint Thomas, St. Paul, Minnesota; MA, Creighton University, Omaha, Nebraska; PhD, University of Nebraska, Lincoln, Nebraska) is a professor emeritus of English and American Indian studies at the University of Wisconsin at Eau Claire. He has produced video documentaries on interviews with elders at the reservation of the Lac Courte Oreilles Chippewa Band of Wisconsin, which are housed in the library of UW-EC and the Lac Court Oreilles Community College in Reserve, Wisconsin. He has also produced documentaries of interviews with American Indian elders who are veterans of World War II from various tribes and reservations in Wisconsin. He has published a filmography entitled *The American Indian in Film* (Scarecrow Press, 1986) and a book entitled *From Savage to Nobleman: Images of Native Americans in Film* (Scarecrow Press, 1995).

www.ingramcontent.com/pod-product-compliance
Ingram Content Group UK Ltd.
Pitfield, Milton Keynes, MK11 3LW, UK
UKHW051827210125
454034UK00008B/54

9 781442 240018